C. BO...

LES MOTS ENTRE EUX

WORDS AND THEIR COLLOCATIONS

LETTRES – SCIENCES HUMAINES

VOCABULAIRE ANGLAIS

OPHRYS

ISBN : 2-7080-0890-0

La loi du 11 mars 1957 n'autorisant, aux termes des alinéas 2 et 3 de l'Article 41, d'une part, que les « copies ou reproduction strictement réservées à l'usage privé du copiste et non destinées à une utilisation collective » et, d'autre part, que les analyses et les courtes citations dans un but d'exemple et d'illustration, « toute représentation ou reproduction intégrale, ou partielle, faite dans le consentement de l'auteur ou de ses ayants-droits ou ayants-cause, est illicite » (alinéa 1er de l'article 40).
Cette représentation ou reproduction, par quelque procédé que ce soit, constituerait donc une contrefaçon sanctionnée par les Articles 425 et suivants du Code pénal.

© Éditions Ophrys, 1998

OPHRYS, 6, avenue Jean-Jaurès, 05003 GAP CEDEX
OPHRYS, 10, rue de Nesle, 75006 PARIS

Préface

Ce livre est constitué d'une **sélection** de chapitres ou de sections de chapitres du volume complet, paru en septembre 1998 chez le même éditeur, sous le même titre général : LES MOTS ENTRE EUX.

Ce livre s'adresse aux élèves des CLASSES PREPARATOIRES section LETTRES et à ceux des ECOLES NORMALES SUPÉRIEURES, ainsi qu'aux étudiants en LETTRES et SCIENCES HUMAINES et à ceux préparant le CAPES ou l'AGREGATION de LETTRES MODERNES.

Grâce aux **COLLOCATIONS**, c'est-à-dire aux combinaisons possibles des mots entre eux (quels verbes, quels adjectifs, quels noms s'associent entre eux ? Quels sont les contextes d'emploi ?), ce livre permet d'apprendre à **se servir des mots**.

L'anglais qu'écrivent et parlent les élèves et les étudiants s'affinera, s'enrichira et deviendra plus authentique, **grâce à la présence de ces collocations**.

Des **EXERCICES** variés (phrases de thème en grand nombre, phrases anglaises à associer entre elles, etc), permettent une mise en pratique immédiate, précisent le sens des mots proposés et facilitent la mémorisation, tant pour le thème que pour la version.

Les **CORRIGES**, en fin de volume, donnent à l'étudiant la possibilité de s'auto-évaluer et/ou de travailler seul.

Une **TABLE DES MATIERES** détaillée et un **INDEX**, en français, faciliteront la recherche d'un champ lexical, d'une notion ou d'un mot-clé.

La transcription **PHONETIQUE** ou le schéma accentuel d'un très grand nombre de mots a été indiqué (avec les variantes américaines) chaque fois que cela a paru nécessaire.

Ce livre est un **LIVRE DE REFERENCE** auquel l'étudiant se reportera avant de rédiger un compte-rendu, une contraction de texte, un essai sur un thème donné ou de traduire un thème ou une version. Il s'y reportera aussi avant d'entamer un exposé oral, afin de s'approprier le maximum d'éléments lexicaux liés au sujet à traiter et de disposer ainsi d'un vocabulaire riche et précis.

∴

Ce livre regroupe le vocabulaire ayant trait à la **culture**, à l'**appréciation** en général, à l'**analyse** et au **commentaire littéraires** ; il comporte aussi du **vocabulaire descriptif** qui sera d'un grand secours en thème ou en version : ce que perçoivent les cinq sens, plus spécialement le domaine des **sons** et **lumières**, de la ville et de la campagne, des **mouvements** du corps et des déplacements, des choses et des objets ; à cela s'ajoute le vocabulaire nécessaire à la description du **comportement** et des sentiments humains, à la **communication** et aux **relations sociales et humaines**. Enfin, on trouvera du vocabulaire permettant de traiter des **relations abstraites** (cause, effet, ressemblance) ou de phénomènes de société liés à la **religion** ou à la **violence**.

∴

Il existe trois autres volumes, portant le même titre général, s'adressant à des publics différents :

1. Tout d'abord, le volume **complet** (de près de 30 000 mots) destiné essentiellement aux étudiants préparant le **CAPES** et l'**AGREGATION** (internes et externes) d'anglais, aux élèves des CLASSES PREPARATOIRES ainsi qu'à ceux des GRANDES ECOLES.

2. Un deuxième volume est destiné aux étudiants de la filière **LEA** et aux élèves des classes préparatoires à **HEC** et aux autres grandes écoles de commerce et scientifiques, aux étudiants en DROIT, en ECONOMIE, en SCIENCES et en MEDECINE.

Ce deuxième volume porte la **mention** : ECONOMIE – DROIT.

3. Enfin, un troisième volume s'adresse aux étudiants de BTS, des filières de **SCIENCES POLITIQUES** et de **COMMUNICATION**, ainsi qu'aux élèves des écoles de **JOURNALISME**, des CLASSES PREPARATOIRES aux GRANDES ECOLES (Sciences-Po, ENA, etc.).

Ce troisième volume porte la **mention** : POLITIQUE – COMMUNICATION.

∴

ABRÉVIATIONS

ch.	chose	p.	personne
qch.	quelque chose	qqn.	quelqu'un
fam.	familier	lit.	littéraire
fig.	figuré	old use	emploi désuet, terme daté

i.	intransitif	t.	transitif
v.	verbe	pl.	pluriel
sg.	singulier	inv.	invariable
prep.	préposition	conj.	conjonction
adj.	adjectif	adv.	adverbe
n.	nom		

U	uncountable (indénombrable)	US	usage américain
		sth.	something
C	countable (dénombrable)	GB	usage britannique
		sb.	somebody

Conventions phonétiques

La transcription phonétique ou le schéma accentuel d'un grand nombre de mots a été indiqué sur la base de différents critères. En règle générale, le schéma accentuel est donné pour les mots de deux syllabes (et plus) qui ne posent pas de problèmes de prononciation particuliers. L'ensemble de la transcription phonétique est donnée pour ceux dont la prononciation est difficilement prévisible.

Nous renvoyons aux ouvrages de Lionel Guierre et d'Alain Deschamps pour un exposé détaillé des règles d'accentuation et de prononciation suivies ici.

Pour l'ensemble de l'ouvrage, c'est la prononciation britannique qui est donnée, les variantes américaines n'étant précisées que lorsque cela nous a paru pédagogiquement nécessaire.

Les transcriptions reprennent l'alphabet phonétique international (IPA) et sont basées sur le dictionnaire de prononciation de J.C. Wells (LONGMAN). Elles apparaissent soit à droite, soit sous le mot concerné. Les accents de mot (principal, ['], et secondaire, [ˌ]) sont indiqués **avant** la syllabe concernée. Dans les schémas accentuels, chaque syllabe est représentée par un tiret.

Les caractères phonétiques en exposant représentent les phonèmes pouvant être ajoutés. Le symbole [‿] indique la possibilité de compression de deux phonèmes successifs (lors d'une élocution rapide par exemple).

François Chambraud a assuré le travail de phonétisation de l'ensemble de l'ouvrage.

Les phonèmes de l'anglais

1. CONSONNES

[p]	pan	[t]	ten	[k]	kill	[tʃ]	church
[b]	bat	[d]	dog	[g]	good	[dʒ]	judge
[f]	fan	[θ]	thing	[s]	sad	[ʃ]	shock
[v]	vote	[ð]	this	[z]	zone	[ʒ]	vision
[m]	milk	[n]	not	[ŋ]	king		
[l]	leak	[r]	rate	[h]	home		
[j]	year	[w]	wing				

2. VOYELLES

[ɪ]	big	[ɑː]	large	[aɪ]	pie	[ʊə]	poor
[e]	ten	[ɔː]	cork	[eɪ]	train	[aʊə]	hour
[æ]	cat	[ɜː]	bird	[əʊ]	boat	[aɪə]	fire
[ɒ]	dog	[iː]	seek	[aʊ]	mouse	[ə]	about
[ʌ]	but	[uː]	fool	[eə]	dare		
[ʊ]	bull	[ɔɪ]	toy	[ɪə]	beer		

1 Action

1. Choice, decision, purpose, necessity

Collocations

■ *Noms*

act	acte, action	*to perform an act of bravery/charity*
ambition [-'--]	ambition	*to lack ambition* (manquer d'ambition) *- to have great ambitions - to fulfil / achieve / realize one's ambitions* (réaliser ses ambitions) *- to do sth out of* (par) *ambition*
aim [eɪm]	but, objectif	*it may be sb's aim to do sth - to achieve one's immediate / long-term aims*
choice	choix	*to give / be given a choice between - to do sth by choice - a wide choice* (un large choix) *- to take one's choice* (faire son choix) *- to make a choice* (faire un choix) *- to have no choice but to do sth* (ne pouvoir que...)
commitment [-'---]	engagement	*commitment to sth / to do sth*
consistency [-'----]	cohérence, logique	*to need consistency - sth / sb may show a lack of consistency*
decision [-'---]	décision	*a decision on / about / against sth / to do sth - to make / take / come to / reach / arrive at a decision*
design [dɪ'zaɪn]	intention, dessein	*sth may be done by accident or by design* (volontairement) *- to have evil / good designs*
drive	énergie, dynamisme désir, pulsion	*sb's energy and drive - to lack / have enough drive to do sth to have the drive to do sth*
duty	devoir	*it's sb's duty to do sth* (il est du devoir de qqn de...) *- to have a strong sense of duty*
	obligations	*sb's duties may include sth / doing sth*
energy ['---]	énergie, vigueur	*to have a lot of energy / to be full of energy - to waste one's energy - a person of energy and ambition*
freewill	libre-arbitre	*to do sth of one's own freewill* (faire qch de son plein gré)
go-getter	fonceur, battant	*to be a go-getter*
impetus ['---]	élan, impulsion	*sth may give / provide (an) impetus to sth*
impulse ['--]	élan spontané, envie	*to do sth on a sudden impulse* (spontanément, sur un coup de tête) *- to feel an irresistible impulse to do sth*
intent [-'-]	intention	*to do sth with good / evil / malicious* (malveillant) *intent - to do sth with intent to harm* (nuire) */ kill / ... - to declare one's intent to do sth*
motive ['--]	raison, motif	*to do sth from the best motives / from motives of kindness - to question sb's base / honourable / underlying motive(s) for doing sth*
need	besoin, nécessité	*there may be a growing / basic need of / for sth / to do sth - if need be* (si nécessaire) *- to satisfy / fill / meet sb's need(s) - to feel no need to do sth - to be in dire* (cruel) *need of sth*
pioneer [paɪ ə'nɪə]	pionnier, précurseur	*to be a pioneer of sth in a particular field*

prospect ['--]	perspective, chance		*there may be some / little / a reasonable prospect of sth / for sth / of doing sth / that ... - to find a job with excellent prospects - to be faced with poor / bleak* (sinistre) */ good / cheerful* (réjouissant) *prospects*
purpose ['pɜːpəs]	but, objectif		*sb's purpose in life may be to do sth - sth may fulfil / serve a purpose - sb may achieve their purpose - to be given money for a specific purpose - to go somewhere for / with the express purpose of doing sth - for all practical purposes* (à toutes fins utiles)
pursuit [pəˈsjuːt]	activités, occupations		*to enjoy / have little time for worthwhile / intellectual / leisure pursuits*
scheme [skiːm]	plan, projet		*a scheme of work - to devise / foil* (contrecarrer) *a nefarious* (infâme) *scheme to do sth / for doing sth*
target ['tɑːgɪt]	but, objectif		*to set oneself a target* (se fixer un objectif) *- to meet* (atteindre) */ fail to meet* (ne pas atteindre) *one's targets - sb / sth may be the target of / an easy target for criticism - sth may be on / off target* (conforme / pas conforme aux prévisions)
will	volonté, détermination		*to have a will of one's own* (n'en faire qu'à sa tête) *- to have a weak / strong will / the will to sth - to do sth against one's will* (faire qch contre son gré) *- to work with a will* (travailler avec ardeur)
willingness	désir		*to show / express the / (a) willingness to do sth* (manifester le désir de faire qch)
willpower ['---]	volonté		*to do sth by sheer willpower* (arriver à qch uniquement par volonté) *- to have / demonstrate the willpower to do sth*
workaholic [ˌwɜːkəˈhɒlɪk]	bourreau de travail		*to be a regular* (vrai) *workaholic*
zest	élan, goût, enthousiasme		*to have a zest for sth / for life* (amour de la vie) *- to be full of zest*

■ *Adjectifs*

ambitious [-'--]	ambitieux		*ambitious person / project - to be ambitious to do sth* (avoir l'ambition de ...)
committed [-'--]	engagé		*committed writer / artist - to be committed to do / to doing sth* (avoir pris l'engagement de ...)
	fervent		*committed Christian*
	dévoué		*committed teacher / nurse*
	convaincu		*committed Marxist*
conscientious [ˌkɒnʃiˈenʃəs]	consciencieux		*conscientious person / piece of work*
consistent [-'--]	cohérent		*consistent person / behaviour / views*
	constant, régulier		*consistent improvement / support / loyalty*
dedicated ['----]	dévoué		*dedicated person - to be dedicated to one's work - to be dedicated to do / to doing sth* (se consacrer entièrement à qch)
engrossed [ɪnˈgrəʊst]	absorbé, captivé		*to be engrossed in one's work / thoughts / a book*
intent [-'-]	absorbé		*be intent on / upon sth*
	décidé à		*be intent on / upon doing sth*
meant	conçu, destiné		*sth may be meant for sb / sth / to do sth*
motivated	motivé		*to be (highly) motivated for sth / to do sth*
necessary ['----]	nécessaire		*sth / sb may be absolutely necessary to / for sth - it is necessary (for sb) to do sth*
set	résolu, déterminé		*to be set on sth / on doing sth* (vouloir à tout prix) *- to be (dead) set against sth* (s'opposer à) *- to be all set to do sth* (être prêt)
single-minded	déterminé, obstiné		*to be single-minded about sth / in one's efforts to do sth - to work with single-minded determination*

Action

unnecessary	inutile, superflu	(voir : *necessary*)
untapped	inexploité	*untapped resources / reserves / market*
unwilling	réticent, peu désireux de	*to be unwilling to do sth - sb's unwilling participation in sth*
up-and-coming	qui a de l'avenir, plein de promesses	*up-and-coming person*
venturesome ['ventʃəsəm]	entreprenant, aventureux risqué, hasardeux	*venturesome person - to be of a venturesome spirit venturesome action*
wilful	entêté, obstiné délibéré, volontaire prémédité	*wilful person wilful action wilful murder*
willing	désireux de, prêt à plein de bonne volonté	*to be willing to do sth willing pupil*
would-be	désireux (de devenir) prétendu, soi-disant	*would-be writer / singer would-be criminal*

■ *Verbes*

act	agir, se comporter	*to act responsibly / out of* (par) *fear / as interpreter* (servir de) */ like an adult / on sb's advice*
aim [eɪm]	avoir pour but / objectif	*to aim at sth / at quick promotion / for a place - to aim to do sth / at doing sth*
call for sth	nécessiter, exiger	*the situation calls for prompt action / quick thinking - this calls for a celebration* (ça se fête!)
cater for	pourvoir à, satisfaire	*to cater for the needs / tastes of sb*
cater to	se plier à, satisfaire	*to cater to the needs / desires of sb*
choose	choisir	*to choose sth / to do sth*
consider [-'---]	songer à	*to consider sth / doing sth*
contemplate ['---]	envisager	*to contemplate sth / doing sth*
decide	décider se décider pour	*to decide sth / to do sth to decide on sth*
design	concevoir, créer	*to design sth - sth may be designed for a particular purpose*
dither ['dɪðə]	hésiter, ne pas arriver à se décider	*to dither about / over sth / about doing sth*
get one's own way	arriver à ses fins	*to get one's own way in everything*
go back on	revenir sur	*to go back on one's word*
go in for	pratiquer, se consacrer à, choisir s'intéresser à, aimer	*to go in for sports / teaching / law* (souvent négativement) *I don't much go in for opera*
hesitate ['---]	hésiter	*to hesitate over sth / to do sth*
intend	avoir l'intention de	*to intend to do / doing sth - to be intended for sth / sb* (être conçu pour, être destiné à)
it's up to you	c'est à vous de décider	*it's up to him to do it or not* (c'est à lui de décider s'il souhaite le faire ou non)
make a point of	tenir absolument à	*to make a point of doing sth*
mean	avoir l'intention de destiner	*to mean to do sth to mean sth for sb*
meet	satisfaire, répondre à	*to meet sb's / needs / demand / expectations*
motivate ['---]	motiver	*to highly motivate sb for sth / sb to do sth*
need	avoir besoin de	*to need sth / to do sth*
opt	choisir	*to opt for sth / to do sth*

opt out	se retirer, choisir de ne pas participer	*to opt out of sth / out of doing sth*
pick	choisir	*to pick sth from a group / from a list / sb from / among the people present*
propose [-'-]	proposer, suggérer se proposer de	*to propose sth to sb - to propose doing* (qu'on fasse) *to propose to do sth*
resolve [rɪ'zɒlv]	se décider à, se résoudre à décider que	*to resolve to do sth* *to resolve that ...*
screen	sélectionner, faire passer des tests	*to screen sb for cancer - to screen candidates / applicants*
spare	accorder, consacrer	*to spare a few minutes / a thought - to spare the time to do sth* (trouver le temps de)
	épargner, éviter	*to spare (sb / oneself) sth - to spare sb the trouble of* (éviter à qqn d'avoir à)
tap	exploiter, tirer profit de	*to tap resources / reserves*
target ['tɑːgɪt]	cibler, viser, s'adresser à	*to target sb / sth - sth may be targeted at / on sb / sth*
venture ['ventʃə]	oser, se permettre de	*to venture a guess* (avancer une hypothèse) - *I venture to say that...* (j'oserais dire que…)
waver ['weɪvə]	hésiter, faiblir	*to waver (in one's resolution) between this and that*

Exercices sur le chapitre 1 (1)

1. Testez vos connaissances en traduisant les mots ou expressions ci-dessous :

A / engagé - B / cohérence - C / libre-arbitre - D / bourreau de travail - E / exploiter - F / to waver G / single-minded - H / would-be - I / scheme

2. Quel verbe correspond à chacune des définitions proposées ci-dessous?

A / to provide what is needed or wanted by somebody
B / to do something because one considers it important or necessary
C / to choose not to take part in something
D / to aim at something
E / to dare to go somewhere dangerous or to do something dangerous

3. Donnez un synonyme pour les mots proposés :

A / energy - B / purpose - C / to choose - D / on purpose - E / to be intent on one's work

4. Traduisez en anglais :

A / C'est une jeune femme pleine d'avenir. B / Il est intelligent mais il ne réussira pas parce qu'il manque de dynamisme. C / Mesdames et messieurs! Faites votre choix! D / Il eut l'envie irrésistible d'abandonner mais décida d'attendre encore un peu. E / Elle a été choisie parce qu'elle était consciencieuse, dévouée, et toujours désireuse d'apprendre. F / "Ne gaspillez pas votre énergie, n'agissez pas sur un coup de tête, faites toujours plus qu'il n'est nécessaire, ne revenez pas sur l'engagement que vous avez pris de pourvoir aux besoins des plus démunis, n'hésitez pas sur vos choix". G / "Vous ne manquez pas d'ambition, je le sais et je sais aussi que vous êtes un homme engagé et que, quand vous vous proposez de faire quelque chose, vous le faites, mais …." H / "A qui sont destinés ces conseils? Vous me croyez peu désireux de participer aux projets ambitieux de votre organisation? Vous savez pourtant que lorsque j'ai l'intention de faire quelque chose, je m'y consacre corps et âme."

2. Attempt, planning, preparation

Collocations

Noms

ability [-'---]	capacité	to show exceptional / outstanding ability at / in sth / to do sth
asset ['--]	atout, avantage	sth may be / prove to be an asset to sb / to a firm
attempt [-'-]	tentative	to make an abortive (infructueux) / all-out (maximum) / deliberate / successful attempt at sth / at doing sth / to do sth - to thwart (faire échouer) an attempt - an attempt may succeed / fail
caution	prudence, circonspection	to proceed (agir) with great caution - to use / exercise extreme caution in sth / in doing sth
check	vérification, contrôle, enquête	to order / conduct / do / run (effectuer) a routine / police / security check on sth / sb
	frein	sth may act as a check on / upon sth / sb - to hold / keep sth (contenir, maîtriser) in check
crack	tentative, essai	to have a crack at sth - to give sth a crack
directions	instructions, indications	to give / issue / follow instructions for sth / to do sth / that ... - directions for use (mode d'emploi)
effort ['--]	effort	to make / foil (contrecarrer) sb's strenuous (acharné) / all-out (maximum) / desperate / unsuccessful efforts at sth / to do sth - to spare no effort
endeavour [ɪn'devə]	effort, tentative	to make every endeavour to do sth - despite sb's best endeavours
go	essai	to have a go at sth / at doing sth - to do sth at the first go
inability [,--'---]	incapacité	sb's inability to do sth
incentive [ɪn'sentɪv]	motivation, incitation	to have no / lose one's incentive to do sth - to offer sb a strong incentive to sth
knack	tour de main, coup	to have / get a / the knack of sth / of / for doing sth
move	initiative, mesure	to make a brilliant / decisive / the first move
neglect [-'-]	négligence, abandon manquement	to suffer from neglect - sth may happen through neglect neglect of duty / of safety rules
plan	plan, projet	to make / draw up (établir) / devise (concevoir) / carry out / turn down (rejeter) a brilliant / feasible / impractical plan - a plan may fall through (échouer)
preparation	préparation	sth may require careful preparation - in preparation for sth
preparations	préparatifs	to make preparations for sth / for doing sth
prerequisite [priː'rekwəzɪt]	préalable, condition préalable	sth may be a prerequisite for sth
project ['prɒdʒekt]	projet (d'envergure)	to conceive / draw up (établir) / work out (élaborer) / carry out / shelve (laisser en suspens) a well-thought-out project
range [reɪndʒ]	champ, domaine	sth may be outside / beyond sb's range of responsibility / activities
	gamme, éventail	a wide / broad range of temperature / opinions - a whole range of cars
requirement	exigence, besoin condition requise	to set / establish the requirements for sth to fulfil / meet the requirements for sth
requisite ['rekwɪzɪt]	exigence objet nécessaire	the requisites for sth / of technology toilet requisites (accessoires de toilette)
scheme	projet, plan	to cook up (inventer) / devise / think up a wild-eyed (extravagant) scheme for sth / for doing sth / to do sth - the (overall) scheme of things (l'ordre des choses)

scope	étendue, portée	to extend / confine the scope of sth - sth may fall within / be beyond the scope of sth
	possibilité, perspective	to give sb little / full scope to do sth - a job with more scope
sketch	esquisse, ébauche	a rough sketch of sth
	résumé	a brief historical / biographical sketch
trial	essai, à titre d'essai	to give sth a trial - sth may be on trial - to do sth by trial and error (par tâtonnements) - a trial of strength (épreuve de force)
try	essai, coup	to give sth a try - to have a try at sth / at doing sth

■ *Adjectifs*

able	capable, en mesure de	to be able to do sth - an able man (compétent)
deft	adroit, habile	deft movements / fingers - to be deft at sth / at doing sth
faced	confronté à	to be faced with sth / with having to do sth
far-seeing	prévoyant, réfléchi	far-seeing person / decision / action
far-sighted	clairvoyant, perspicace	far-sighted person / plan / action - it is far-sighted to do sth
inexperienced [,--'---]	inexpérimenté	to be inexperienced at / in sth / at / in doing sth
minute [maɪ'njuːt]	minutieux	to do sth with minute care / in the minutest detail (dans le plus grand détail)
powerless	impuissant	to be powerless to do sth
proficient [-'--]	expérimenté, de bon niveau	proficient worker / student / driver - to be (quite) proficient at / in sth
ready	prêt	to be / get ready for sth / to do sth
set	prêt	to be (all) set for sth / to do sth
	(bien) décidé	to be (dead) set on sth / on doing sth / against sth
	fixe, fixé, indiqué	to do sth at set times / in the set order - to read the set books (au programme)
	avoir des chances de	to be well set to do sth (être bien parti pour)
strenuous	difficile, ardu	strenuous task / life / climb
	considérable, acharné	strenuous efforts / campaigner for sth
tentative ['---]	provisoire, à titre d'essai	tentative offer / plan / step / conclusion
unable	incapable, pas en mesure de	to be unable to do sth

■ *Verbes*

attempt [-'-]	tenter	to attempt sth / to do sth
check	vérifier, contrôler	to check sth / sb / on sth / on sb / into sb's story / private life / through files (dossiers) / that ...
	enrayer, contenir	to check oneself / an urge to do sth / one's anger
contrive [-'-]	inventer, imaginer	to contrive a device (dispositif) / machine
	trouver le moyen de	to contrive to do sth
	agencer, manigancer	to contrive a match (arranger un mariage) / meeting
do one's (level) best	faire de son mieux	to do one's (level) best to do sth
double-check	revérifier	to double-check sth for safety
empower	autoriser, habiliter	sth may empower sb to do sth
enable	permettre, donner la possibilité	sth may enable sb to do sth
endeavour [ɪn'devə]	s'efforcer	to endeavour to do sth
exert	exercer	to exert an influence / pressure
exert oneself	se donner la peine	to exert onesef to do sth
face	faire face, accepter	to face the facts / a problem / doing / having to do sth
	se présenter	a problem may face sb
mastermind	diriger, organiser	to mastermind an attack / operation / take-over (OPA)
neglect [-'-]	négliger	to wilfully neglect sth / sb / oneself / to do sth

plan	projeter, prévoir	*to plan sth / on sth / to do sth / on doing sth (US) / how to do sth*
	élaborer, préparer, organiser	*to plan sth / one's time / a surprise / visit*
prepare	préparer	*to prepare sth / sb for sth / sb to do*
	se préparer	*to prepare for sth / for an exam / to do sth*
range	aller de... à..., varier	*sth / prices / age / cost / text may range from so much to so much / from easy to difficult*
require	exiger, nécessiter	*sth may require skill / experience / care*
	exiger, requérir	*to require sth of sb / sb to do sth / that ...*
resort [-'-]	avoir recours à	*to resort to sth / to doing sth*
scheme	avoir pour projet, comploter, intriguer	*to scheme against sb / to do sth*
strive	s'évertuer à, lutter	*to strive for sth / for effect* (s'efforcer de se faire remarquer) */ for success / after sth / to do sth*
subject [-'-]	soumettre à	*to subject sb to a test / sth to intense heat*
submit [-'-]	se soumettre	*to submit to one's fate / to sb's demands*
	donner à examiner	*to submit sth to sb*
take to	se mettre à	*to take to sth / drink / the bottle / to doing sth*
try	essayer	*to try sth / hard for sth / to do sth / doing sth*
work out	élaborer, établir	*to work out a solution / plan / when... / how...*

Exercices sur le chapitre 1 (2)

1. Testez vos connaissances en traduisant les mots ci-dessous:

A / asset - B / proficient - C / move (n.) - D / to resort to sth - E / to range - F / to strive

2. Choisissez la ou les solutions possibles pour chaque phrase :

A / He showed great requisite / ability / requirement / caution in choosing the good answer.
B / He decided to have a try / trial / scope / go at it.
C / He is the one who strove / drew up / exerted / worked out / ranged the project.
D / The money he was given endeavoured / enabled / required / schemed him to buy a car.
E / You'd better contrive / face / check / mastermind the figures *(chiffres)*.
F / Nobody had tried / empowered / attempted / sketched to climb Mount Everest until then.
G / There is no doubt that far-seeing / far-sighted / proficient / powerless action is required in this case.

3. Traduisez en anglais:

A / Malgré des efforts considérables, il n'a pas réussi à comprendre le mode d'emploi de la télécommande. B / Qui a bien pu inventer un dispositif aussi extravagant? C / Personne ne l'avait préparé à lire ce genre de texte à l'école. D / Maintenant qu'il est à l'université, il est bien décidé à lire, avec un soin minutieux tous les livres au programme dans l'ordre indiqué, si ardue que soit la tâche, ce qui lui permettra, espère-t-il, de comprendre les notices techniques!

3. Ways and means

Collocations

■ *Noms*

chance GB [ɑː] / US [æ]	possibilité, chance que occasion, chance(s)	*there is little / no chance of sth happening / of sb doing sth / that... to stand a good chance of sth / to do sth - to give sb a chance - to have a / the chance to do sth / that... - to let a chance slip by* (laisser passer)
	risque	*to take a chance - to take the chance / no chance of sth / of doing sth*
device [-'-]	appareil, dispositif	*a clever / labour-saving device for sth / for doing sth*
	procédé, ruse	*it's just a device to attract notice*
jack of all trades	homme à tout faire	*to be a jack of all trades and master of none* (propre à tout et bon à rien)
manner	manière	*to do sth in an offhand* (désinvolte) */ matter-of-fact / sloppy* (bâclé) *manner*
means	moyen(s)	*to have / find / use a / the fair / foul / effective means to do sth*
	moyens (argent)	*to live within / beyond one's means*
method	méthode	*to lack method - to apply / devise / use a(n) obsolete / sure / up-to-date / sound* (sain) *method of / for sth / of / for doing sth*
occasion	occasion (spéciale), possibilité	*to have an / no occasion to do sth - on one / this / many occasion(s) - to celebrate a(n) unforgettable / festive* (de fête) *occasion - an occasion (for sth / for doing sth) may arise*
opportunity	possibilité, occasion	*to have / seize / take / lose a(n) unexpected / golden opportunity for sth / for doing sth / to do sth*
plight [aɪ]	situation (peu enviable)	*to be in a sad / desperate plight*
practice	pratique, habitude	*to make a regular practice of sth / of doing sth - it is normal / common practice to do sth*
predicament [-'---]	situation (difficile)	*to be in / get into / help sb out of an awkward predicament*
propriety [prə'praɪ_əti]	justesse, caractère approprié	*to doubt the propriety of sth / of doing sth*
step	pas, mesure	*to take steps towards sth / to do sth - sth may be the first step / a step in the right direction*
supervision [ˌ--'---]	surveillance	*to exercise supervision / tighten / ease up on one's strict / slack* (relâchée) *supervision of / over sth*
way	moyen, méthode, façon, manière	*to find a way to do sth - to have one's own way of doing sth - that's one way to look at it - to do sth this / that way / in a charming / kindly way*
	façon de faire, habitude	*to get used to sb's ways*

■ *Adjectifs*

available [ə'veɪləbl]	disponible	*to try every available means - to be readily available for sth / to do sth - sth may be available to sb*
chance	accidentel, non prévu, de hasard	*chance witness / meeting*
convenient [-'--]	commode, pratique	*convenient date / moment*
equal to	à la hauteur de	*to be equal to the task / to doing sth*
hectic	agité, trépidant	*to have / spend a hectic day / week - to lead a hectic life*
impracticable [-'-----]	irréalisable	*impracticable plan / idea / policy - it is impracticable to do sth*
makeshift	de fortune	*makeshift shelter / accommodation*

Action

methodical [-'---]	méthodique	*methodical person / manner / way of doing sth*
practicable	faisable, possible	*as far as practicable* (autant que possible) - *it is practicable to do sth*
practical	pratique, commode	*practical clothes / equipement*
	à l'esprit pratique	*practical person*
	concret, d'ordre pratique	*practical difficulties / experience - sth may be of no practical use*
proper ['prɒpə]	approprié	*proper clothes / tools / thing to say*
	convenable, normal	*it is proper to do sth / that …*
	qui convient, qu'il faut	*proper answer / word - to do sth in the proper way*
	vrai, véritable	*proper doctor / meal / job*
	véritable, complet	*proper disaster / fool / mess / miser / telling-off* (engueulade)
right	(le) bon, (celui) qui convient	*right direction / place / word / person*
	complet, total	*right idiot / mess*
self-sufficient [,--'---]	autonome	*self-sufficient person / country*
single-handed	seul, sans aucune aide	*to do sth single-handed*
speedy	rapide, prompt	*speedy car / recovery / diagnosis / settlement of a strike*
stop-gap	bouche-trou, de remplacement	*stop-gap measure / secretary*
suitable	approprié	*suitable date / time / place - sb / sth may be suitable for sth / for doing sth*
	convenable	*suitable time / clothes / behaviour*
tidy	bien rangé	*tidy room / pile - to keep / make a house tidy*
	ordonné	*tidy person*
untidy	en désordre	*untidy room / house / pile of books*
	désordonné	*untidy person*
wrong	mauvais, pas celui qu'il faut	*wrong book / place / time / answer*

■ *Verbes*

devise	concevoir, inventer	*to devise a(n) scheme / system / instrument*
do with	se contenter de	*sb may have to do with very little*
do without	se passer de	*to do without food / money*
gear [gɪə]	adapter, orienter	*to gear sth to sb's needs - sth may be geared for sth / to do sth*
go ahead	aller de l'avant	*to go ahead with a plan*
instruct	donner pour instruction	*to instruct sb to do sth / that…*
make do with	se débrouiller (avec ce qu'on a)	*to make do with sth / with very little / with expedients*
make light of	traiter à la légère	*to make light of sb's difficulties / handicaps*
make up one's mind	se décider	*to make up one's mind about sth / to do sth / what to do / which thing to choose*
proceed [prə'siːd]	poursuivre	*to proceed with sth*
	se passer	*to ask how sth is proceeding*
	passer à, se mettre à (faire)	*to proceed to the main business on the agenda / to do sth*
	procéder, s'y prendre	*not to know how to proceed*
step up	accélérer, intensifier	*to step up the pace / the output / production / one's efforts*
suit	convenir	*sth may suit sb perfectly*
supervise ['---]	surveiller, diriger	*to supervise sth / sb / a job / an activity / games / children / sb's dieting*
team up (with)	faire équipe (avec), collaborer	*to team up (with sb)*

Exercices sur le chapitre 1 (3)

1. Testez vos connaissances en traduisant les mots ou expressions ci-dessous:
A / device - B / chance - C / predicament - D / proper - E / to do without

2. Vous trouverez ci-dessous des amorces de phrases (A / à H /). Vous trouverez aussi des phrases qui font suite aux amorces A / à H /. Ces phrases de complément sont numérotés de 1 à 15.
Indiquez quel(s) numéro(s) doit / doivent être utilisé(s) pour compléter les amorces. (Un point d'exclamation (!) indique la fin d'une phrase).
Exemple: A 1 9

A / It is common practice for famous scientists - B / It is time to - C / They were instructed - D / Don't make light - E / Make up your mind - F / Let's proceed - G / A tidy boy - H / A practical person

1 / to make do - 2 / to the next - 3 / step up - 4 / of her difficulties ! - 5 / may become a suitable - 6 / stopgap secretary! - 7 / to go ahead - 8 / what to do next! - 9 / with expedients! - 10 / item on the agenda! - 11 / but can't be expected - 12 / does not keep his room - 13 / with an impracticable plan! - 14 / production! - 15 / to do everything single-handed! - 16 / untidy!

3. Traduisez en anglais:
A / Il faut se servir de tous les moyens disponibles, de tous les dispositifs légaux, pour sortir ces gens de leur situation douloureuse. B / Il faut se montrer à la hauteur de la tâche. C / Ces pauvres gens ne sont plus autonomes économiquement. D / Ils ne peuvent, toute leur vie, se contenter d'abris ou de logements de fortune. E / Il faut prendre des mesures d'urgence et surveiller leur application. F / Il faut adapter les crédits alloués aux besoins de ceux qui sont à la rue. G / Je ne mets pas en doute la justesse des projets du gouvernement, mais ... H / Si vous ne savez pas comment procéder, consultez-moi.

4. Action and activity

Collocations

■ *Noms*

action	action	*to take decisive / hasty / prompt action - to spur* (inciter) *sb into action - killed in action* (au combat) *- sth may be out of action*
activity	activité	*to engage in / take part in feverish activity - to resume* (reprendre) *one's activities - sth may paralyse / curb* (freiner) *sb's activity*
burden	fardeau, charge, poids	*sb may be a burden to sb - sth may be a heavy burden to bear - to relieve* (alléger) *the tax burden*
care	soin	*to take care of sth / to do sth / that ... - to do sth with great / the utmost care- sth may need / require meticulous care - 'handle with care'* (fragile)
drudgery	travail pénible, corvée	*to avoid / free sb from domestic drudgery - sth may be sheer drudgery*
	caractère pénible	*to complain about the drudgery of sth*
grind [graɪnd]	corvée, routine	*the daily grind - what a grind!*
routine [ruːˈtiːn]	routine, habitude routinière	*sth may become a daily / regular / dull routine*

Action

supply [sə'plaɪ]	provision, réserve	*to provide / lay in / replenish (one's) abundant / fresh supply / supplies of sth - sth may be in short supply* (manquer)
	fourniture	*supply of sth (gas, water) to sb - the law of supply and demand* (la loi de l'offre et la demande)
task GB [tɑːsk] / US [tæsk]	tâche	*to carry out / do / fulfill a ticklish* (délicat) */ hopeless / irksome* (irritant) *task - to set sb a task - sth may be / turn out to be no easy task*
undertaking [ˌ--'--]	entreprise	*to engage in a(n) expensive / joint / risky undertaking*
	engagement	*to give (sb) a (written) undertaking to do sth*
work	travail	*to do a lot of paper / back-breaking / exhausting / slipshod* (bâclé) *work - to put a lot of work into sth - to never do a stroke (of work)* (ne jamais faire le moindre travail) *- sth may be a fine piece of work* (un beau travail)
	emploi, lieu de travail	*to look for / find well-paid work - to be at / go to / leave work*
work(s)	ouvrage(s), œuvres	*sb's life work / complete works - work of art / of fiction*

■ *Adjectifs*

accountable	responsable	*to be / hold sb accountable to sb* (envers qqn) *for sth / for doing sth*
active	actif	*a physically / mentally active person - to be active in sth / in doing sth - to take an active part in sth*
to be in charge	être responsable, avoir la charge de	*to be / put sb in charge of sth / of doing sth - to take charge of sth / of doing sth*
busy ['bɪzi]	occupé	*busy person / line - to be busy with sth / doing sth - sth may keep sb busy*
	chargé	*busy day / period / schedule*
careful	prudent	*careful person / estimate - to be careful about / with sth / in doing sth / to do* (prendre soin) */ that ...*
	consciencieux	*careful person / work / survey*
	sérieux, attentif	*careful examination of sth*
careless	négligent	*careless person - to be careless about / with sth / in doing sth - it is careless (of sb) to do sth*
	peu soigné	*careless work*
	irréfléchi	*careless remark / comment*
free	libre, non occupé	*free seat / line - not to have a free moment - to keep one evening free*
idle	inoccupé, oisif, arrêté, à l'arrêt	*idle person / good-for-nothing / moment a machine may lie / stand idle*
to be at a loose end [luːs]	ne rien avoir à faire (d'urgent)	*(US) to be at loose ends*
on / off duty	de / pas de service, de garde	*to be on night-duty*
under way	en cours, en train	*economic recovery / a meeting / plan may be (well) under way - to get sth underway* (mettre en route)

■ *Verbes*

act	agir, se comporter	*to act sensibly towards sb / like a fool - to act dumb* (faire l'innocent) */ as though... - to act as an interpreter / on sb's advice - to act for the best / on behalf of sb* (au nom de qqn)
attend to	prêter / apporter (son) attention à	*to attend closely to sb's instructions / advice*
	s'occuper de	*to attend to sth / to sb / to one's duties - 'Are you being attended to?'*
	soigner	*to attend to a sick person / a wound*
avoid	éviter	*to avoid sth / sb / doing sth*
dispense with	se passer de	*to dispense with formalities / with luxury*

give up	renoncer, abandonner	*to give up sth / one's seat to sb / sb for dead / hope / doing sth - to give up on sb / sth* (perdre espoir)
	démissionner, quitter	*to give up a business / a job*
go without	se passer de	*to go without sleep / sleeping / food / eating / money / spending money*
handle	traiter, faire face à	*to handle a subject / crisis / death*
	s'y prendre avec	*to know how to handle sb / a problem / a job*
provide	fournir	*to provide sth for sb / sb with sth - sth may provide jobs / some privacy*
provide for	subvenir aux besoins de	*to provide for a family / for sb's future*
	se préparer à, prévoir	*to provide for sth / every contingency* (éventualité) */ a change*
see about	s'occuper de	*to see about sth / about doing sth*
see to	s'occuper de, prévoir	*to see to dinner / to arrangements - to get the brakes seen to* (faire examiner)
see (to it) that	veiller à ce que	*to see (to it) that sth is done / that sb does sth*
set about	se mettre à	*to set about (doing) one's work*
	s'y prendre avec	*not to know how to set about sth / about doing sth*
set out	commencer	*to set out with a definite intention / on a new career*
	se proposer de	*to set out to do sth*
supply [-'-]	fournir	*to supply sb / sb with sth / sth to sb*
tackle	s'attaquer	*to tackle a problem / task / book*
	interroger, contacter	*to tackle sb on / about sth*
toil	travailler dur, peiner	*to toil over sth / over an essay*
undertake [,--'-]	entreprendre	*to undertake sth / a job / research on sth / a responsibility* (assumer)
	s'engager	*to undertake to do sth*
work	travailler	*to work hard on / at sth / (at) doing sth / to a deadline* (avec un délai à respecter) */ to a budget* (avec un budget limité) */ for a living*
	faire travailler	*to work sb hard / oneself to death*

Exercices sur le chapitre 1 (4)

1. Testez vos connaissances en traduisant les mots ou expressions ci-dessous:

A / to tackle - B / grind (n.) - C / to see about sth - D / task - E / undertaking - F / to handle
G / to avoid - H / drudgery

2. Traduisez en anglais :

A / Il est temps d'agir et de prendre part aux activités de vos amis. B / Ce ne sera pas pour vous un trop lourd fardeau à porter que de les aider dans leur entreprise, si risquée et coûteuse qu'elle puisse paraître au premier abord. C / Etes-vous prêt à y mettre beaucoup de travail et de temps? D / Si oui, vous allez pouvoir commencer une carrière nouvelle. E / Ne me dites pas que vous ne savez pas comment vous y prendre! F / Si vous le souhaitez, je vous fournirai les documents nécessaires, pour que vous puissiez vous atteler à la tâche. G / Il faudra peut-être que vous vous passiez de sommeil pendant quelque temps, que vous renonciez à certaines habitudes. H / Il vous faudra apporter toute votre attention au moindre détail des projets en cours. I / Vous qui êtes habitué à rester oisif des heures entières, qui ne faites jamais rien chez vous, et qui évitez, ainsi, la routine quotidienne et les corvées de tout genre, vous allez être très occupé à vous occuper des gens! J / Ça va vous changer!

Action

5. Difficulties, obstacles and solutions

Collocations

■ *Noms*

advantage GB [əd'vɑːntɪdʒ] / US [əd'væntɪdʒ]	avantage	to have a(n) clear / unfair advantage over sb - sth may be an advantage to sb - it is an obvious advantage to do sth - it may be to sb's advantage to do sth - to take advantage of sth / sb / that ... (profiter que)
backlash	contre-coup, vive réaction	sth may provoke / produce a backlash of anger against sth
control [-'-]	contrôle, maîtrise	to have / gain / lose / be in control of sth / of power / over sth / sb - sth / sb may get out of control - to bring / keep sth under control
difficulty ['----]	difficulté	to have / experience difficulty in sth / in doing sth - to overcome / resolve / face / come across a difficulty - sth may cause / present great / serious difficulties for sb - a difficulty may arise
disadvantage [ˌ--'--]	désavantage, inconvénient	it is to sb's disadvantage to do sth - sth may offset / outweigh a disadvantage / put sb at a disadvantage
drawback	inconvénient	there may be drawbacks to sth / to a plan - sb's only drawback may be that ...
ease	facilité, aisance	to lead a life of ease and luxury - to do sth with ease - to be concerned about the ease with which terrorists can strike anywhere - extrawide doors for ease of access
easiness	facilité (de qch)	to be astonished at the easiness of some of the crossword puzzles
efficiency [-'---]	efficacité	sth may improve / impair (entamer) / increase sb's efficiency in sth / in doing sth
hardship	épreuve(s)	to bear / suffer great hardship(s) - it is a hardship for sb to do sth - to go through a life of hardship
hindrance ['hɪndrəns]	obstacle, entrave	sb may be more of a hindrance than a help - to do sth without any hindrance from anybody - sth may be sth of a hindrance to sb / sth
impediment	obstacle défaut	sth may be an impediment to sth to suffer from a speech impediment
improvement	amélioration	sth may bring about a significant / decided / slight / substantial improvement in sth / on sth - there may still be room for improvement
issue	question, problème	to bring up / raise / confuse / face / address (s'attaquer à) / settle the / a sensitive / serious / main issue - to take issue (ne pas être d'accord) with sb over sth
obstacle ['---]	obstacle	to raise / overcome a formidable (redoutable) obstacle to sth
ordeal [-'-]	épreuve, calvaire	to find sth an ordeal - to go through / undergo a trying (éprouvant) ordeal
pitfall	piège, embûche	to avoid / fall into a pitfall
quandary	dilemme	to be in a dreadful / hopeless quandary over / about sth / over whether or not to do sth / over which to choose
result [-'-]	résultat	to achieve / produce / evaluate / obtain lasting results - sth may be the direct / unfortunate result of sth - to do sth with the result that...
snag	difficulté, problème, hic	to come across / run into / hit a major snag - the (only) snag with sth / sb is that ...

solution	solution	*to find / apply a(n) easy / ingenious / bad solution to sth / to a problem*
stumbling block	obstacle, pierre d'achoppement	*sth may be the main / major stumbling block to sth*
trial	épreuve	*sth / sb may be a great trial to sb - it may be a trial doing sth*

■ *Adjectifs*

adverse ['--]	défavorable	*adverse comment / criticism / reaction*
	contraire	*sth may be adverse to sth / to one's interests*
awkward ['ɔːkwəd]	délicat	*awkward situation / problem / time / question*
	peu pratique	*awkward shape - sth may be awkward*
chancy	risqué	*chancy business / solution - sth may be a chancy thing to do*
difficult	difficile	*difficult task / life / question - to make things difficult for sb - it is difficult (for sb) to do sth - sb may find it difficult to do sth*
easy	facile	*easy exam / victory / language - to make things easy for sb - it is easy (for sb) to do sth*
effective	efficace, qui marche	*effective argument / measure / treatment - sth may be / prove to be effective against sth / in doing sth*
	en vigueur, applicable	*sth may become effective as from Jan. 1st next*
efficient	efficace	*efficient person / staff - to make efficient use of sth - to be efficient in sth / in doing sth - it is (not) efficient to do sth*
	bien fait, qui fonctionne bien	*efficient piece of work / machine*
faulty	défectueux	*faulty reasoning / machine / device / work / wiring* (installation électrique)
be in a fix	être mal parti	*to be in a bit of a fix*
foolproof	infaillible	*foolproof scheme / system*
	indéréglable	*foolproof video-recorder / machine / watch*
handy	commode, pratique, utile	*sb may be a handy person to have around* (chez soi) *- a place may be handy* (bien situé) *for the shops / work - it is handy to do sth*
	adroit	*to be handy at sth / with tools*
hard	dur, difficile	*hard question / problem - sth may be hard (for sb) to do - to find it hard to do sth - to learn sth the hard way*
intricate ['---]	complexe, compliqué	*intricate argument / mechanism / patterns* (motifs, dessins)
involved	complexe, compliqué	*involved excuse / argument / plot / story*
	impliqué	*to be / become involved in sth / with sb - to get (emotionally) involved with sb* (avoir une liaison)
plain	simple, sans prétentions	*plain soldier / dress / cooking / food*
	uni, sans mélange ni décoration	*plain black dress / carpet / paper* (non réglé) */ chocolate* (noir)
	clair, évident	*it is plain (to sb) that ... - to make sth plain to sb - to make it plain (to sb) that ...* (bien faire comprendre)
simple	simple, facile à comprendre	*simple reason / operation / fact*
	simple, sans prétentions	*simple person / style / dress / tastes / behaviour - to remain simple*
stiff	dur, ardu, sévère	*stiff competition / match*
	difficile à manier, à ouvrir	*stiff door-handle / drawer*
stringent	rigoureux, sévère	*stringent rules / measures / conditions / laws / requirements*
thankless	ingrat	*thankless person / task / job*
touchy	susceptible	*touchy person - to be touchy about sth*
	délicat, épineux	*touchy matter / issue / point*
tough [tʌf]	dur, pénible	*tough life / problem - to make things / it tough for sb - sth may be tough* (être un coup dur) *on sb*

Action

be through	avoir fini	*to be through with sth / with smoking* (ne plus fumer) / *with reading a book* (avoir fini de lire)
tricky	difficile, délicat, épineux	*tricky job / task / situation / problem*
trying	éprouvant, pénible	*trying person / time / journey / job / experience*

■ *Verbes*

be at one's wit's end	ne plus savoir que faire	**cut both ways**		être à double tranchant

Collocations

call off	annuler	*to call off a meeting / strike*
cancel	cancel	*to cancel an order* (commande) / *a reservation / an appointment*
catch up	rattraper	*to catch up with sb / catch sb up (by running) - to catch up on one's work*
do over	refaire	*to do over a house / task*
	tabasser	*to do sb over*
found	fonder, créer	*to found a town / business / organisation*
get out of hand	échapper à tout contrôle	*a child / meeting / situation may get out of hand*
hamper	gêner	*sth may hamper sb / sb's work / efforts / movements*
	entraver	*sth may hamper sb's project*
hinder ['hɪndə]	gêner	*sth may hinder sb / sb in their work*
	empêcher	*sth / sb may hinder sb from doing sth*
impair [-'-]	affaiblir, diminuer, endommager	*sth may impair sb's sight / hearing / chances of winning*
implement ['---]	mettre en œuvre, exécuter	*to implement a(n) plan / idea / policy / order*
improve	(s')améliorer	*sth / sb's health may improve (with time) - to improve sth / one's English / in sth / in English - to improve on acquaintance* (gagner à être connu)
materialise [mə'tɪəri̯ əlaɪz]	se réaliser, se concrétiser	*a promise / an offer may materialise*
prevent [-'-]	prévenir	*to try and prevent crime*
	empêcher	*sth / sb may prevent sb (from) doing sth / sb('s) doing sth*
quit	quitter	*to quit the premises* (les lieux) / *work / school*
	arrêter	*to quit doing sth / smoking*
refrain [-'-]	s'abstenir	*to refrain from sth / from contact with sb / from doing sth*
respond	réagir	*sth may respond to sth / to treatment*
	répondre, réagir	*to respond to an attack / to sb's speech / flattery / to being told that ...*
result (from) [-'-]	provenir, résulter de	*sth may result from sth / from (sb) doing sth*
result (in) [-'-]	avoir pour résultat	*sth may result in sth / in failure / in a fight / in (sb) doing sth*
settle	régler	*to settle a strike / disputes / differences* (différends) *by doing sth*
	fixer, décider	*to settle a date / where to go*
simplify	simplifier	*to simplify sth to excess*
solve [sɒlv]	résoudre	*to solve equations / a problem / case* (affaire) / *riddle* (énigme)
thwart [θwɔːt]	contrecarrer, contrarier	*sth / sb may thwart sb / sb's ambitions / plans / efforts*

Exercices sur le chapitre 1 (5)

1. Testez vos connaissances en traduisant les mots ou expressions ci-dessous:
A / faulty - B / foolproof - C / hindrance - D / to quit - E / handy - F / impediment - G / ordeal - H / pitfall

2. Ci-dessous se trouvent deux séries de phrases:
Les premières (de A à D) constituent les amorces. Les secondes (de 1 à 22) sont les phrases qui complètent les amorces.
Indiquez, pour chaque amorce, le numéro des phrases que vous avez choisies pour la compléter.
(Les phrases qui sont les dernières des quatre séries à trouver se terminent par le signe !!!).

A / If the kids get out of control B / I'll try to make as plain as possible
C / The decided improvement D / What's hindering the government

1 / an awkward issue 2 / you'll have difficulty 3 / in Johnny's school results 4 / in preventing them 5 / which is so intricate and tricky 6 / and his increased efficiency 7 / from settling 8 / from breaking the furniture 9 / that anybody involved 10 / results from the boy ('s) 11 / and you as a parent will have 12 / the strike, in spite of 13 / the thankless task 14 / avoiding the usual snags and pitfalls 15 / in trying to solve it 16 / admittedly adverse 17 / is bound to 18 / that one encounters when one 19 / but not unsurmountable conditions? !!! 20 / of doing over all the rooms!!! 21 / go through something of an ordeal !!! 22 / has to catch up on a whole term's work!!!

3. Traduisez en anglais:
A / Qu'est-ce qui a contrarié vos projets d'alphabétisation? B / Qu'est-ce qui les a empêchés de se concrétiser? C / Quels sont les obstacles redoutables qui vous ont gêné dans votre travail? D / Le manque d'argent a-t-il été la seule entrave à vos projets? E / Peut-être ne devrais-je pas soulever, ici et maintenant, ce problème grave? F / Peut-être cela va-t-il vous placer dans une situation délicate? G / Mais, je crois que votre projet se serait révélé efficace dans la lutte contre l'analphabétisme. H / Vous avez bien fait comprendre, je trouve, au grand public que la compétition est sévère et que les gens qui ne savent pas lire sont désavantagés par rapport aux autres. I / Je me demande ce qui a entravé vos efforts?

6. Success and failure

Collocations

■ *Noms*

accomplishment [-'---]	talent, exploit	*a person of great / many accomplishment(s)*
	réalisation, accomplissement	*the accomplishment of a task*
ace	as	*to be an ace at sth / at doing sth*
achievement [-'--]	exploit, réussite	*sth may be quite a(n) memorable / outstanding achievement*
	accomplissement	*to feel a real sense of achievement*
deed	action, acte	*to do / perform a heroic / noble / wicked deed - in word and in deed* (en parole et en actes) - *to do one's daily good deed* (BA)
failure	échec	*sth may be a complete failure / may end in failure / may be doomed to failure*
	raté	*sb may be a failure as a leader / at sth / at doing sth*
	manquement, fait de ne pas, non accomplissement	*to regret sb's failure to do sth / to keep their word*

Action

feat	exploit, prouesse	*to accomplish / perform a heroic / noteworthy feat of courage / of strength / of arms* (fait d'armes) *- it may be no mean* (mince) *feat / quite a feat to do sth*
flop	fiasco, bide	*sth / sb may be a complete flop* (*as an actor / as Hamlet*)
fulfil(l)ment [-'---]	réalisation, exécution accomplissement	*sth may be the fulfilment of sb's dream / ambition / plan to get a sense of personal fulfilment from sth*
hit	succès	*sth may be a great / big hit - sb may be / make a great hit* (plaire, conquérir) *with sb*
inconvenience [ˌɪnkən'viːniəns]	gêne, dérangement, inconvénient	*sth may be / cause great / minor inconvenience to sb sb may have to put up with the inconvenience of sth / of doing sth*
progress ['--]	progrès	*to make considerable / little / slow / steady progress in sth / towards sth / in doing sth - sb may be making good progress* (aller mieux) *- sth may hinder sb's progress*
	déroulement	*sth may be in progress* (en cours)
punishment ['---]	punition	*to deserve / get / receive / administer / inflict / suffer / take / escape just / harsh / cruel / severe / light punishment for sth / for doing sth*
reward [-'-]	récompense	*to give / offer / pay sb a reward for sth / for doing sth - to claim / receive a well-deserved reward from sb*
setback	échec, revers, contretemps	*to have / suffer a(n) minor / unexpected setback*
stalemate	impasse	*sth may end in a stalemate - to break* (débloquer) *a stalemate*
success [-'-]	succès	*to meet with / achieve great success / score a success* (remporter) *- to have no success in sth / in doing sth - to make a success of sth*

■ *Adjectifs*

futile GB ['fjuːtaɪl] / US ['fjuːtl]	vain, inutile futile, creux	*futile action / effort / attempt - it is futile to do sth futile idea / question / remark*
be home and dry	se tirer d'affaire sans dommage	*(US) to be home and free*
ineffective [ˌ--'--]	inefficace, sans effet	*ineffective person / staff / drug / policy*
inefficient	inefficace	*inefficient person / machine / system / use of sth*
be overcome	être accablé, bouleversé	*to be overcome by the heat / by the news / with joy* (déborder de) */ with grief*
be overwhelmed [ˌ--'-]	être bouleversé submergé	*to be overwhelmed by sth / sb's generosity to be overwhelmed with work*
successful	compétent, qui réussit couronné de succès	*successful person successful attempt / negotiation / start / outcome* (heureuse issue) */ performance / talks*
be successful	réussir être un succès	*to be highly successful at / in sth / with business / in doing sth a play / film / party may be successful*
unsuccessful [ˌ--'--]	qui ne réussit pas infructueux	*unsuccessful person / businessman unsuccessful attempt*
be unsuccessful	ne pas réussir être un four, être un échec	*to be unsuccessful in sth / in doing sth a play / film / performance / talks may be unsuccessful*
well-known	connu	*well-known person / fact / face - sth / sb may be well-known to sb*

■ *Verbes*

achieve	accomplir, réussir réaliser obtenir, atteindre	*not to achieve much in life to achieve a(n) dream / ambition / desire / one's objectives to achieve success / fame / independence / the impossible*

carry out	effectuer, remplir	*to carry out an experiment / inquiry / one's duties*
	réaliser, mettre à exécution	*to carry out a plan / promise / threat*
cope	faire face, s'en sortir, se débrouiller	*to find it difficult to cope with children / with problems / with all the work*
do sb good	faire du bien	*sth may do sb good / a lot of good / no good at all - it may do sb good to do sth*
do the trick	suffire, faire l'affaire	*a small dose may do the trick*
do / work wonders	faire des merveilles	*sth / a medicine may work wonders for sb / on sth / on a headache*
fail	échouer, ne pas réussir	*to fail a(n) test / exam - to fail in one's efforts / in maths / to do sth*
	négliger, manquer	*(not) to fail to do sth*
	ne pas + verbe	*to fail to see / understand sth*
flop	rater, faire un bide	*a(n) attempt / idea / play / actor / recipe may flop*
fulfil [-'-]	réaliser	*to fulfil a(n) dream / ambition / plan / oneself as an actor*
	accomplir, remplir, satisfaire	*to fulfil a promise / task / sb's need / desires / a condition / one's duties*
get by	se débrouiller	*to get by as best one can on a low salary / without sth*
get over sth	surmonter qch	*to get over a difficulty / an obstacle / one's shyness*
go places	réussir, aller loin	*to be clearly going places*
go wrong	se tromper	*sb may go wrong about / with sth*
	se détraquer, mal marcher, aller de travers	*sth / the TV may go wrong - sth may go wrong with the TV - everything / things may go wrong*
have had it	être fichu	*sb / sth has had it*
make headway	avancer, progesser	*to make some / no headway - not to make much headway in one's plans / with sth*
make it	réussir	*to make it in life / as a businessman*
	arriver (à un endroit)	*to make it to the airport / for 5 o'clock*
manage ['mænɪdʒ]	arriver (à faire)	*to manage / manage it (y arriver) - to manage a lot of work / a ten-mile walk / a smile / to do sth*
master GB ['mɑːstə] / US ['mæstər]	maîtriser, contrôler	*to master a skill / language / problem / one's emotions*
overcome [ˌ--'-]	surmonter, vaincre	*to overcome a(n) obstacle / difficulty / fear*
	triompher	*to overcome opposition / an enemy*
overwhelm [ˌ--'-]	accabler, bouleverser	*grief / sb's generosity may overwhelm sb*
pass with flying colours	réussir haut la main	*to pass an exam with flying colours*
perform	exécuter, accomplir, effectuer	*to perform a task / one's duty / a movement / a vital function (remplir) / an operation*
	interpréter	*to perform a part / a piece of music / well / badly*
punish	punir	*to punish sb severely for sth / for doing sth / by imprisonment*
reward [-'-]	récompenser	*to reward sb for sth / sb for doing sth / sb with money / with a gift*
succeed	réussir (à faire)	*to succeed in sth / in doing sth*
work out	résoudre, régler	*to work out a problem / one's differences* (différends)
	élaborer	*to work out a(n) plan / agreement / the details / a solution*
	se passer, se dérouler	*sth may work out as planned*

Action

Exercices sur le chapitre 1 (6)

1. Testez vos connaissances en traduisant les mots ou expressions ci-dessous :

A / to achieve - B / achievement - C / failure - D / setback - E / futile

2. Choisissez la ou les solutions possibles :

A / He - managed / flopped / failed / performed - to punish / get over / fulfil / overcome - the difficulty and was rewarded - of / at / on / for - doing so.
B / You say that somebody - has had it / is making headway / is being worked out / is overwhelmed - when everything in his life has gone - well-known / wrong / unsuccessful / home and dry.
C / He passed a difficult exam with - flipping / flying / fleeing / flopping - colours which was no small - hit / flop / stalemate / feat.

3. En vous aidant des exemples et des collocations qui vous ont été données dans ce chapitre (colonne de droite du vocabulaire), traduisez en anglais les expressions ou phrases suivantes :

A / Echapper à une punition méritée. B / Réclamer à sa cheftaine une récompense pour avoir fait régulièrement sa BA quotidienne. C / Accomplir un acte héroïque. D / Une femme aux talents multiples. E / Se terminer par un échec. F / Causer une gêne peu importante. G / Faire des progrès réguliers. H / Etre accablé de chagrin. I / Déborder de joie. J / Subir un échec inattendu. K / Faire des merveilles. L / Elaborer un plan. M / Régler un différend. N / Ses progrès sont encore très lents.

2
The mind and abstract relations

1. The mind

1.1. Bright or dull

■ *Noms*

dope	crétin, débile	highbrow ['haɪbraʊ]	intellectuel
egghead	intello	nitwit	niais, imbécile
halfwit	faible d'esprit, simplet	simpleton	simplet

Collocations

cunning	habileté	to show (great) cunning
folly	sottise, folie	it is folly to do sth
fool	idiot	to be no fool (savoir ce qu'on fait)
freak [fri:k]	phénomène, monstre fana	by a freak of nature (par un caprice de …) / a jazz freak
genius ['dʒi:ni̯əs]	génie	a budding genius (en herbe) / a stroke (un trait) of genius
intelligence [-'---]	intelligence	to show great / keen / limited / low intelligence
mind	esprit	to cultivate / develop one's mind - nimble mind (esprit souple) quick / inquisitive (curieux) / sound (sain) / unsound (dérangé) mind
think tank	groupe de réflexion	to set up (mettre en place) a think tank
whizz kid	petit génie, jeune prodige	a six-year old whizz-kid

■ *Adjectifs*

bright	intelligent, brillant	bright boy / idea / writer
clever	intelligent, habile	clever boy / idea / device clever with one's hands / at doing sth
cunning	malin, astucieux	cunning person / idea / plan / device - it is cunning of sb to do sth
dim	peu doué	dim person - to take a dim view of sth (ne pas approuver qqch)
dull	peu intelligent, lent	terribly / deadly dull person
dumb	stupide, irritant	dumb idea - to act dumb (faire l'idiot)
foolish	stupide, irréfléchi, imprudent	to look foolish - a foolish thing to do it is foolish (of sb) to do sth
freakish	bizarre, insolite	freakish person / weather conditions
gifted	doué	to be gifted for music - gifted children
intelligent	intelligent	intelligent person / animal / suggestion
mixed-up	désorienté, perturbé	mixed-up child
quick	rapide	to be quick to do sth / to anger
sharp	malin, vif	sharp person / mind

shrewd [ʃruːd]	astucieux, rusé, perspicace, judicieux	*shrewd businessman / politician* *shrewd guess / decision / move* (initiative)	
simple-minded	simple d'esprit, simplet	*simple-minded person / view / opinion*	
slow	lent	*to be slow of speech - to be slow to anger - to be slow to do sth* (falloir longtemps à qqn pour faire qch) - *to be slow in doing sth* (prendre son temps) - *to be slow-witted - to be slow / quick on the uptake* (avoir l'esprit lent / vif)	
stupid	stupide	*it is stupid of sb to do sth*	
witty	spirituel, plein d'esprit	*witty person / remark / comment*	

Exercices sur le chapitre 2 (1.1)

1. Testez vos connaisssances en traduisant les mots ci-dessous :

A / whizz kid - B / nitwit - C / gifted - D / dumb - E / freakish - F / think tank - G / halfwit - H / dull
I / spirituel - J / astucieux - K / crétin, débile (n.) - L / intello (n.)

2. Traduisez en anglais :

A / Ce qu'il a fait a pu paraître irréfléchi, mais en réalité il a fait preuve d'une grande habileté.
B / Vous semblez ne pas approuver mon comportement et penser que toutes mes idées que, personnellement, je trouve brillantes, sont stupides. C / Vous pensez que je suis un imbécile ou seulement un simple d'esprit ?

3. A quel mot correspond chaque définition?

A / slow in understanding and learning   B / skilful and talented   C / clever and judicious

4. Complétez à l'aide d'un des mots ci-dessous :

genius - highbrow - freakish - witty - dumb

A / You tend to think you are a _____ , don't you? B / _____ weather conditions have spoilt our holiday. C / You a real _____ , you're only interested in intellectual pursuits. D / He always tries to be _____ in conversation. E / Don't be so _____ it's irritating!

1.2. Interested or bored

Collocations

■ *Noms*

accuracy ['----]	exactitude	*to praise the accuracy of sth / sb's accuracy in doing sth*	
attention	attention	*to pay great attention to sth*	
bore	raseur, casse-pieds corvée	*a frightful bore* *it is a bore to wash the dishes*	
boredom	ennui	*out of boredom* (par ennui) - *sheer boredom* (ennui à l'état pur)	
ground	raison, fondement	*to have grounds for suspecting / to suspect that ...*	
heed	attention	*to pay heed to sth / sb / to take heed of* (prêter attention à) *sth*	
interest	intérêt (qu'on éprouve)	*to arouse / revive* (faire renaître) */ show / lose interest in sth*	
point	intérêt (de qqch)	*what's the point of sth / of doing sth?* (à quoi ça rime?)	

The mind and abstract relations

regard	attention, prise en considération	*to have / show regard for sth* (tenir compte de qqch)
sense	bon sens	*to show sense - common sense - make sense* (avoir un sens)

■ *Adjectifs*

accurate ['---]	exact, précis	*to be accurate in doing sth*
bored	qui s'ennuie	*to be bored (stiff / to death) with sth / with doing sth*
boring	ennuyeux	*it is boring to do sth*
far-fetched	excessif	*far-fetched comparison / claim* (prétention)
groundless	sans fondement	*groundless fears - to prove* (se révéler être) *groundless*
inaccurate [-'---]	inexact, peu précis	*inaccurate statement / estimate / weapon*
interested ['----]	intéressé	*to be interested in sth / to do sth*
interesting ['----]	intéressant	*it is interesting to do sth*
irksome ['ɜːksəm]	ennuyeux, agaçant	*irksome noise / vibration / duties*
obsessed [-'-]	obsédé	*to be obsessed by the need for secrecy / with money*
pointless	sans intérêt	*pointless exercise - it is pointless to do sth*
rational ['---]	rationnel	*it is rational to do sth*
senseless	absurde, insensé	*senseless killing / violence / argument*
sensible	sensé	*sensible answer / choice person*
tedious ['tiːdi̯əs]	pénible, fastidieux	*tedious job / exercise / person*
unattended	non surveillé	*to leave one's luggage unattended*
uninterested	indifférent à	*to be totally uninterested in sth / to do*
uninteresting	inintéressant	*to find sb / sth most uninteresting*
wearisome ['wɪərisəm]	ennuyeux; fatigant	*wearisome task*
weary ['wɪəri]	las, fatigué	*to be / to grow weary of sth / of doing sth*

■ *Verbes*

attend (to)	s'occuper de	*are you being attended to?- to have lots of things to attend to*
examine [-'---]	examiner	*to examine sth thoroughly for sth* (à la recherche de)
flag	faiblir, se relacher	*attention / interest may flag*
go into	examiner en detail	*to go into a question / the details*
heed	bien prêter attention à	*to heed sb's advice / warnings*
mind	faire attention à	*to mind the step / what sb says*
observe	observer, faire remarquer	*to observe sth / sb / that …*
point out	attirer l'attention sur	*to point out that… / how difficult sth is*
probe	chercher à découvrir	*to probe for sth / into sth* (enquêter sur)
reason	raisonner	*to reason sb into / out of sth* (convaincre qqn d'accepter qch / de renoncer à qch)
review [-'-]	revoir, réviser	*to review arrangements / the situation / one's options*
scrutinize ['skruːtɪnaɪz]	examiner attentivement	*to scrutinize sth / sb closely*
survey	examiner, inspecter	*to survey a report / a book*

Exercices sur le chapitre 2 (1.2)

1. Testez vos connaissances en traduisant les mots ci-dessous :
A / ground - B / irksome - C / pointless - D / sensible - E / weary

2. Joignez une phrase de droite à une phrase de gauche :

A / Anybody's interest would flag
B / Somebody ought to point out to him
C / They are trying to revive interest
D / Nobody has yet managed to reason him
E / He found surveying that long uninteresting report
F / He gave up attending to the matter

1. that great accuracy is needed in probing into suspected murder.
2. out of sheer boredom, I should think.
3. out of reviewing long-standing arrangements every other week.
4. hearing such a bore going into such fastidious details.
5. in matters that nobody takes any heed of any more.
6. a senseless wearisome task.

3. Trouvez les lettres manquantes :
A / _BS_S_E_ (adj.) B / _RK__M_ (adj.) C / _E_I_U_ (adj.) D / E_AM_N_ (v.)
F / _EE_ (n.)

1.3. Conscious and curious

Collocations

■ *Noms*

consciousness	conscience	*to raise sb's political consciousness - to have consciousness of one's importance - consciousness that...*
curiosity	curiosity	*to do sth out of* (par) *curiosity - to arouse / excite / satisfy sb's curiosity*
guess	supposition	*to have / take a guess at sth* (essayer de deviner) *- to make a good / wild guess* (deviner juste / au pif) *- it is anybody's guess* (il est impossible de prévoir)
idea	idée	*not to have the faintest / slightest idea - to have a pretty good idea of sth - to have no idea* (ne pas savoir du tout)
notion	idée, opinion	*to get the notion that...* (s'imaginer que)
oversight ['---]	omission, erreur	*due to / by / through an oversight* (par erreur)
thought	pensée	*to give sth a lot of thought* (bien réfléchir) *- to be lost / deep in thought - the mere thought of it* (rien que d'y penser) *- to have no thought of doing sth* (n'avoir aucunement l'intention de)

■ *Adjectifs*

aware	conscient; au courant	*to be / become aware of sth / that... - not as far as I am aware* (pas que je sache)
conscious	conscient	*to be all too conscious of one's shortcomings* (être tout à fait conscient de ses faiblesses)
curious	curieux	*to be curious to know - to be curious about sth*
noticeable ['nəʊtɪsəbl]	visible	*noticeable improvement / it is noticeable that...*
unaware	inconscient	*to be unaware of sth / that ...*
unconscious	inconscient	*to be unconscious of noise around oneself*

The mind and abstract relations 25

understandable	compréhensible	*sth may be understandable to sb - it is understandable that ...*
unforeseeable	imprévisible	*unforeseeable events / effects / consequences*
unforeseen	imprévu	*unforeseen circumstances / problems*
unknown	inconnu	*fear of the unknown - to be unknown to sb*

■ *Verbes*

catch on	devenir populaire	*fashions / styles may catch on with sb* (auprès de)
change one's mind	changer d'avis	*to change one's mind about sth*
collect one's thoughts	reprendre ses esprits	*also: to collect oneself*
consider [-'--]	considérer	*to consider that... - consider oneself lucky - to consider sth / sb to be...*
	réfléchir à	*to consider the situation / suggestions / a proposal*
cross one's mind	traverser l'esprit	*it may cross sb's mind that ...*
dawn on sb	devenir clair pour qqn	*it may dawn on sb that ...*
disregard [,--'-]	ne tenir aucun compte de	*to disregard instructions / remarks / warnings*
find	constater	*to find that ... / how difficult sth is*
find out	découvrir	*to find out the truth / to find out about sth*
guess	deviner	*to guess right / wrong - to guess how old sb is / that ...*
know better than to do	avoir la sagesse de ne pas ...	*to know better than to do sth* (se garder de) *- he should have known better* (il a manqué de jugeotte)
not to be able to make head or tail of	ne rien comprendre à	*I can't make head or tail of what he says*
make out	comprendre, distinguer, déchiffrer	*not to be able to make out sb's address / what sb says*
muse	rêvasser, songer	*to muse on / upon sth*
notice	remarquer	*to notice sb / sth / that ...*
occur to sb [ə'kɜː]	venir à l'esprit	*it may occur to sb that...*
overlook [,--'-]	oublier, négliger	*to overlook sb / sth / details / the small print / a problem*
	ne pas tenir compte de	*to overlook sb's bad behaviour / mistakes*
ponder	méditer	*to ponder over sth*
	réfléchir	*to ponder on / upon sth*
pore over	étudier longuement	*to pore over a book / the details*
pry	fouiller, fouiner	*to pry into sb's affairs / life*
	se montrer indiscret	*to tend to pry*
rack one's brains	se creuser les méninges	*to rack one's brains for an answer / to find sth*
realise	se rendre compte	*to realise sth / how difficult sth is / that ...*
reflect	réfléchir	*to reflect on sth / on what to do / that...* (se dire que)
search	chercher, fouiller	*to search sb's face for signs of sth - to search one's mind / memory for details - to search for a cure - to search after inner peace*
seek	chercher à obtenir	*to seek sb's advice / approval -to seek refuge / asylum / reelection*
take into account	tenir compte de	*to take into account a fact / surroundings / that ...*
take no notice	ne pas tenir compte de	*to take no notice of sb's advice / of what sb says*
think	penser	*to think (that ...)- think to oneself* (se dire que)
think of	penser à	*to think of sb / sth - to think of doing sth* (envisager de)
think twice	y réfléchir à deux fois	*to think twice before making a decision*
think better of	se raviser	*to want to do sth, then to think better of it*
understand	comprendre	*to understand sth / sb / why / that ... - make oneself understood* (se faire comprendre)

Exercices sur le chapitre 2 (1.3)

1. Testez vos connaissances en traduisant les mots ci-dessous:

A / noticeable - B / to collect one's thoughts - C / to notice - E / to overlook (2 sens)
F / se creuser les méninges - G / se rendre compte que - H / chercher, fouiller

2. Traduisez les phrases suivantes:

A / Pourquoi ne pas essayer de deviner d'où vient l'erreur? B / Il est bien compréhensible que vous ayez besoin de temps pour étudier soigneusement un texte inconnu de vous. C / Il n'a nullement l'intention de changer d'avis. D / Ne vous est-t-il jamais venu à l'esprit que vous parlez si vite que les gens ne comprennent rien à ce que vous dites?

3. Remettez les mots dans l'ordre pour constituer une phrase cohérente:

A / at me it on last dawned - I that better had twice think - prying his life into private before
B / better ought you know to - to all muse long than day - unforeseeable upon events
C / point your in my advice seeking is there no - my disregard since always instructions you

1.4. Knowledge

Collocations

■ Noms

field	domaine, champ	*the field of history / science / law - sth may be outside sb's field (of research)*
inkling	(vague) idée	*to have some inkling that ... / of sth - not to have the slightest inkling*
knowledge ['nɒlɪdʒ]	connaissance(s)	*to have a good / an excellent / a thorough knowledge of sth - to (the best of) my knowledge - it's common knowledge that ...*
layman ['leɪmən]	non spécialiste, profane	*to be a layman in law matters*
scholar	chercheur, érudit	*not to be much of a scholar* (ne pas être très savant) - *a Greek scholar*
working knowledge	connaissances suffisantes, adéquates	*to have working knowledge of a language*

■ Adjectifs

be acquainted	connaître	*to be / become acquainted with sth / sb*
ignorant ['---]	ignorant	*to be ignorant (of / about sth)*
learned ['lɜːnɪd]	érudit	*learned professor / judge*
shallow	peu profond	*shallow play / book / explanation / knowledge / person*
superficial [,--'--]	superficiel	*superficial knowledge / analysis / questions / person*

■ Verbes

know	savoir, connaître	*to know sth / sb (by sight / by reputation) / how to do sth / that ... - as far as I know - to know about sth* (être un peu au courant de)
learn	apprendre	*to learn sth / how to do sth / that ... - to learn about sth / sb* (apprendre des choses sur)
swot	bûcher, potasser	*to swot for an exam - to swot up on a subject / maths*

Exercices sur le chapitre 2 (1.4)

1. Testez vos connaissances en traduisant les mots ci-dessous :
A / to swot - B / scholar - C / field - D / inkling

2. Traduisez :
A / Il n'a aucune idée de ce qu'est la grammaire de l'anglais, bien qu'il prétende posséder des connaissances suffisantes de cette langue. B / Peu de gens connaissent les subtilités (subtleties) de l'anglais mieux qu'elle. C / Je ne suis pas très savant en allemand, mais je ne suis pas non plus ce qu'on appelle un profane. D / Apprenez à vous servir de chaque mot de cette leçon.

3. Remettez les lettres dans l'ordre :
A / WOTS (v.)   B / WASHOLL (adj.)   C / NAYMAL (n.)   D / DEARNEL (adj.)

1.5. Remembering and forgetting

Collocations

■ *Noms*

memory	mémoire	*your memory may fail you* (peut vous faire défaut) - *to have a good memory for names* - *to suffer from loss of memory* - *to quote from memory*
	souvenir	*to have* (garder) *vivid memories of sth* - *sth may bring back memories*
memoirs ['memwɑːz]	souvenirs	*to write one's memoirs / a first volume of memoirs*
mind	esprit	*to bear sth in mind*
recollection	souvenir	*to have pleasant recollections of sth* - *to the best of my recollection* (autant que je me souvienne)
remembrance	souvenir	*to hold a service in remembrance of victims* - *Remembrance Day* (GB: journée du souvenir, le 11 novembre)
reminder	rappel	*to send sb a reminder that ... / to do sth* - *something may be a reminder of events past*
souvenir [ˌ--'-]	souvenir (objet)	*to bring back souvenirs from abroad as presents*

■ *Adjectifs*

oblivious	inconscient	*to be oblivious to a risk*
	oublieux	*to be oblivious to / of one's surroundings*
unforgettable [ˌ--'---]	inoubliable	*unforgettable memories / meal / event*

■ *Verbes*

forget	oublier	*to forget (sth / sb) - forget to do sth / that ...* - *not to forget to do sth* (ne pas oublier de faire qch) - *not to forget doing sth* (se rappeler avoir fait qch)
recall	se rappeler	*to recall sth / sb / doing sth*
recollect [ˌrekə'lekt]	se rappeler	*to recollect sth / sb / doing / that...*
remember	se rappeler	*to remember sth / sb / that...* - *to remember doing sth* - *to remember to do sth* (penser à faire)
remind	rappeler à qqn	*to remind sb / sb to do sth / sb that ...*
ring a bell	évoquer, dire qqch	*a name / the title of a book may ring a bell*

Exercices sur le chapitre 2 (1.5)

1. Testez vos connaissances en traduisant les mots ci-dessous :
A / to ring a bell - B / memoirs - C / memories - D / citer de mémoire

2. Traduisez en anglais :
A / Je ne me rappelle pas avoir dit cela. B / Rappelez-lui de m'appeler. C / Jamais je n'oublierai lui avoir parlé dans sa loge. D / Ce nom me rappelle quelque chose. E / Oublieux de ce qui se passait autour de lui, il évoquait les souvenirs inoubliables que le voyage lui avait rappelés. F / Tu as pensé à fermer le gaz?

1.6. Imagining

Collocations

■ *Noms*

fancy	imagination, fantaisie	*flight of fancy* (élan) - *realm* (royaume) *of fancy*
foreboding [fɔː'bəʊdɪŋ]	pressentiment, prémonition	*to have a gloomy* (sinistre) *foreboding that ...*
foresight	prévoyance	*lack of foresight - to have the foresight to do sth*
hindsight ['haɪndsaɪt]	analyse de l'événement après coup	*with the benefit / wisdom of hindsight*
hunch	intuition, pressentiment	*to have a hunch that ... - to act on / follow / play a hunch* (suivre une intuition)
imagination	imagination	*fertile / creative / feeble imagination - fire / excite sb's imagination - by a stretch of imagination* (en faisant un effort d'imagination)
insight	perspicacité aperçu	*to have / show remarkable insight* *to gain / provide / offer an insight into sth*
inventiveness	inventivité	*a writer with great inventiveness*
invention	invention	*sb's power of invention - sth may be just an invention - to come up with an ingenious invention*
misgiving [-'---]	doute, appréhension	*to have misgivings about sth / that ...*

■ *Adjectifs*

foreseeable	prévisible	*in the foreseeable future*
imaginary	imaginaire	*imaginary fears*
predictable	prévisible	*predictable outcome*
unforeseeable	imprévisible	*unforeseeable events*
unforeseen	imprévu, non prévu	*unforeseen circumstances*

■ *Verbes*

expect	s'attendre à	*to expect trouble*
	s'attendre à ce que, compter que	*to expect sb to do sth*
	attendre qn	*to expect sb* (prévoir l'arrivée)
	avoir de bonnes raisons de supposer que	*to expect that sb will do sth - to expect that sth will happen*
fancy	imaginer, s'imaginer	*to fancy that ... - to fancy oneself as an artist*

The mind and abstract relations

forebode	annoncer, présager	*clouds may forebode rain*
forecast	prédire	*to forecast the weather / that ...*
foresee	prévoir	*to foresee difficulties / that...*
foretell	prédire, prophétiser	*to foretell the future / how the world will end*
imagine	(s')imaginer	*to imagine doing sth / that... / how ...*
invent	inventer	*to invent a machine / a catchphrase*
predict	prédire	*to predict the future / that ...*
tell	savoir	*you can never tell*

Exercices sur le chapitre 2 (1.6)

1. Testez vos connaissances en traduisant les mots ci-dessous :

A / misgiving - B / foreboding - C / foresight - D / to forecast

2. Joignez une phrase de droite à une phrase de gauche :

A / Nobody expected
B / You can't foresee what will happen
C / You never can tell,
D / I just can't imagine what will
E / You need a great deal of inventiveness
F / Why does he fancy

1. happen in the foreseeable future.
2. he will pass the exam this year?
3. to invent such an excuse.
4. her to predict the future.
5. no more than I can forecast tomorrow's weather.
6. as the unforeseen tends to always happen.

3. Trouvez la lettre manquante en début et en fin de mot :

A / _ORESE_ (v.)   B / _EL_ (v.)   C / _UNC_ (n.)   D / _ANC_ (v.)   E / _INSIGH_ (n.)

1.7. Believing

Collocations

■ *Noms*

assumption	supposition, hypothèse	*on the assumption that ...* (en supposant que) - *to make erroneous / valid assumptions about sth / that ...*
belief	croyance, foi	*to hold strong beliefs* (avoir des opinions arrêtées) - *belief in sth / in God* - *beyond belief* (incroyablement)
	foi, confiance	*to shake* (ébranler) *sb's belief in sth* - *in the (mistaken) belief that ...* (croyant (à tort) que)
bias ['baɪəs]	préjugé	*to show (a) deep-rooted bias against sth / sb* - *to be without bias*
disbelief [ˌ--'-]	incrédulité	*to look at sb in disbelief* - *to react with disbelief* - *to suspend disbelief* (faire taire son incrédulité)
doubt	doute	*beyond doubt* - *to raise* (provoquer) */ entertain* (nourrir) */ dispel* (dissiper) *doubts about sth / as to whether ...* - *to be in doubt* - *there is no doubt (but) that ...* - *there is room for doubt* (le doute est permis)
hypothesis [haɪ'pɒθəsɪs]	hypothèse	*to advance / formulate the hypothesis that ...*
odds	chances	*the odds are that ...* (il y a des chances pour que ...) - *against all the odds* (contre toute attente) - *the odds are for / against sth happening* (il y a de fortes chances / peu de chances que qch arrive)

opinion	opinion	*to express / venture / form a frank / personal / negative / strong opinion about sth / sb - to be of opinion that ...*
point of view / viewpoint	point de vue	*to look at sth from a particular point of view / viewpoint*
prejudice ['predʒudɪs]	préjugé	*to arouse* (susciter) */ break down* (briser) */ have / hold / express deep-rooted prejudices*
riddle	énigme	*to solve a riddle - to speak in riddles*
view	opinion, avis	*to express / hold / advocate* (préconiser) *outdated / slanted* (tendancieux) *views about / on sth*

■ *Adjectifs*

biased / prejudiced	qui a un préjugé, partial	*to be strongly biased / prejudiced against sb / sth*
certain / sure	certain, sûr	*to be certain about sth / that ... - she is sure to win* (il est certain qu'elle va gagner)
conspicuous [-'---]	évident; voyant	*to be conspicuous / make oneself conspicuous for one's qualities* (se faire remarquer)
credible ['kredəbl]	croyable	*a barely credible story*
credulous	crédule	*credulous audience*
definite ['---]	certain, définitif clair, net catégorique	*definite answer* *definite improvement / standards* *to be definite about sth / that ...*
doubtful	incertain	*it is doubtful whether* (il n'est pas certain) */ it is doubtful that ...* (il est peu probable)
	douteux	*sth may be in doubtful taste*
incredible / unbelievable	incroyable	*it is incredible that...*
noted	réputé, célèbre	*to be noted for sth*
obvious	évident	*it is obvious (to sb) that ...*

■ *Verbes*

assume	supposer, présumer	*to assume sth / that ... - to be assumed innocent*
believe	croire être partisan de	*to believe sth / that ... / in sth / in sb* *to believe in doing sth*
conclude	conclure	*to conclude that ... / a meeting*
deem	considérer	*it is deemed safe to do sth*
doubt	douter de qch douter que ne pas douter que	*to doubt sb's word / abilities* *to doubt if / whether ...* *not to doubt that ...*
ensure	(s')assurer (que)	*to ensure that ...*
feel	considérer, estimer que	*to feel that ...*
figure	penser, supposer	*to figure that... - it figures* (ça va de soi)
figure out	arriver à comprendre	*to figure sb / sth out - to figure out how ...*
justify	justifier	*to justify sth / oneself / doing sth*
make sure	s'assurer (que)	*to make sure (that ...)*
overrate [,--'-]	surestimer	*to overrate sb's abilities*
presume	supposer (que ...)	*to presume (that ...)*
reckon	supposer (que)	*to reckon that... - I reckon not* (je suppose que non)
reckon	estimer que	*to reckon sth / sb to be ...*
regard [-'-]	considérer (comme)	*to regard sth / sb as the best ...*
set little / great store by	faire grand cas / peu de cas de	*to set much / great / little store by sth*

think highly / well / poorly of	avoir une haute / mauvaise opinion de	*to think highly / well / poorly of sth / sb*
underrate [,--'-]	sous-estimer	*to underrate sb's abilities / the importance of sth*
wonder	se demander	*to wonder (if / whether ...)*
	s'étonner	*to wonder / not to wonder that ...*

Exercices sur le chapitre 2 (1.7)

1. Testez vos connaissances en traduisant les mots ou expressions ci-dessous :

A / bias - B / disbelief - C / riddle - D / obvious - E / biased - F / to regard - G / to underrate H / to assume

2. Joignez une phrase de gauche à une phrase de droite :

1. He could only be presumed innocent
2. She did not believe in
3. It is very doubtful
4. He's made himself
5. She is not certain
6. He was deemed to
7. I just can't figure out
8. He was reckoned to be
9. He is thought very
10. I do not wonder

A. conspicuous for his qualities as a researcher.
B. to win the race.
C. until he was proved guilty.
D. one the best football players in the world.
E. highly of by all his colleagues.
F. how he could have won the race.
G. whether he will win the race.
H. that he lost the race.
I. set great store by his wife's opinion.
J. criticizing others all the time.

3. Remettez les lettres dans l'ordre :

A / USER   B / TERCIAN   C / NIPONOI   D / WIVE   E / DOCUNCLE   F / HOSEPYSHIT

2. Abstract relations

2.1. Cause and effect

Collocations

■ *Noms*

cause	cause	*to try and find the cause of sth - to give cause for concern* (être inquiétant)
chance	hasard	*a game of chance - to happen by chance - as chance would have it* (le hasard a voulu que) *- leave sth to chance*
	risque	*to take a chance (of sth / of doing sth)*
consequence ['---]	conséquence	*as a consequence - to take / suffer* (accepter / subir) *the consequences*
effect [-'-]	effet	*to have a disastrous effect on sth*
likelihood	probabilité	*to increase the likelihood of sth happening - there is little / every likelihood that ...* (peu de / toutes les chances que ...)
origin	origine	*to be of humble origin - to trace the origin of sth to sth*
outcome	aboutissement, effet	*to predict the (likely) outcome of sth*
side effects	effets secondaires	*to be aware of the side effects of a drug*

tendency ['---]		tendance	to show a tendency to do sth / towards sth
trend		tendance, mode, vogue	to set / start a trend towards sth

■ *Adjectifs*

be bound to		devoir forcément	to be bound to hear about sth - sth is bound to happen
be due to		être dû à	sth may be due to bad weather / strike action
haphazard [hæp'hæzəd]		sans aucun plan, incohérent	haphazard manner / guess
hit-and-miss / hit-or-miss		approximatif, hasardeux	hit-and-miss / hit-or-miss methods / undertakings
liable ['laɪ_əbl]		sujet à	to be liable to asthma
		susceptible de, risquer de	it is liable to have unfortunate consequences
likely		probable	a likely result - it is likely that...
		qui a de fortes chances de	to be likely to win
original [-'---]		original, d'origine	original plan / manuscript
probable		probable	it is / it seems highly probable that ... - the probable outcome / cost of sth
		vraisemblable, crédible	sth may sound probable
random		aléatoire, au hasard	random check / test / selection
trendy		dans le vent, branché	trendy clothes / magazine / club
unlikely		peu probable, improbable	(voir les exemples de *likely*)
widespread		répandu, étendu, généralisé	widespread speculation / support

■ *Verbes*

arouse		provoquer, susciter	to arouse interest / anger / concern
bring about		amener, provoquer	to bring about an accident / a result / a miracle
cause		causer, faire que	to cause trouble / anxiety - sth may cause sb to do sth
chance		se trouver que	to chance to know sb / see sth
when it comes to		quand il s'agit de	when it comes to doing sth
come about		se produire, arriver se faire que	problems / changes come about - it may come about that...
come across		trouver par hasard	to come across sth
entail [ɪn'teɪl]		entraîner	sth may entail a change / expenses
evoke		provoquer, faire naître	sth may evoke surprise / resentment / pity / sympathy
imply		impliquer, provoquer	sth may imply sth / consequences / that ...
involve [ɪn'vɒlv]		impliquer	sth may involve sb / sth / doing sth
mean		signifier, entraîner	sth may mean sth / that ... / doing sth
spring from		provenir de	sth may spring from a cause / out of envy
stem from		avoir pour origine	sth may stem from a difficult childhood / a misunderstanding / boredom
tell		se faire sentir	age / stress tells
tell on		avoir un (mauvais) effet (sur)	sth may tell on you
tend		avoir tendance à	sb / sth may tend to do sth
trigger (off)		déclencher	sth may trigger (off) headaches / riots / a conflict

Exercices sur le chapitre 2 (2.1)

1. Testez vos connaissances en traduisant en anglais les mots ou expressions ci-dessous :
A / branché, dans le vent - B / d'origine - C / effet - D / cause - E / aléatoire

2. Traduisez en anglais :
A / Y a-t-il encore des chances qu'il trouve la réponse? B / Des méthodes aussi approximatives risquent d'entraîner des conséquences graves. C / Certains verdicts ont tendance à déclencher des émeutes. D / Le surmenage commence à se faire sentir. E / Quand il s'agit de faire un choix important, il essaie de deviner quels sentiments de colère ou d'approbation susciteront ses décisions.

3. Remettez les mots dans l'ordre :
A / bring claimed he about miracles could he. B / fascinating at book the across this library came I. C / all mismanagement stem the political country's from difficulties current.

2.2. Reality and appearance

Collocations

■ *Noms*

appearance [-'--]	apparence	*to / by all appearances - to judge by appearances*
aspect ['--]	aspect	*to cover / bring out every aspect of a question*
error	erreur	*to commit / overlook an error of judgement*
fake	faux imposteur	*a painting / an antique can be a (clever) fake* *a person can be a fake*
godsend	aubaine	*sth may be a real godsend to sb*
lack	manque	*for / through lack of sth - to show a complete lack of interest*
mishap ['--]	incident	*to pass without mishap (sans encombres) - a slight / serious mishap*
mistake	erreur, faute	*to make / rectify / forgive a bad / foolish / minor mistake (about sth) - by mistake*
possibility	éventualité possibilité, chance	*to consider (envisager) the possibility of sth* *there's a strong possibility that ...*
reality	réalité	*to be out of touch with reality - to become a reality - the grim / harsh reality of life*
shortage	manque, pénurie	*acute teacher shortage*
wrong	erreur	*to be in the wrong about sth (se tromper sur)*

■ *Adjectifs*

actual	réel, véritable	*actual cost / her actual words* (ses propres paroles)
dummy	d'imitation, factice	*dummy gun / perfume / bottle on display*
fake	faux truqué	*fake painting / passport* *fake trial / game*
genuine ['dʒenjuɪn]	authentique, véritable	*genuine jewel / attempt / concern / person*
impossible	impossible	*it is (almost / virtually) impossible that ... / for sb to do sth*
improbable	improbable invraisemblable	*it is (highly) improbable that ... - improbable consequence* *improbable coincidence / explanation*

to be lacking	manquer (de)	*to be (badly / sadly / utterly) lacking in sth (a quality) / to be lacking for nothing - reliable information is lacking*
made up	inventé, fabriqué de toutes pièces	*made up stories / accounts* (compte-rendu) */ document*
missing	manquant	*to be (reported) missing - to have a finger missing from one's hand*
misleading [mɪsˈliːdɪŋ]	trompeur	*grossly misleading advertisement / description*
mistaken	erroné	*a case of mistaken identity* (erreur sur la personne)
be mistaken	se tromper	*to be mistaken about sth / in doing sth*
possible	possible, éventuel	*possible risks / consequences - it is (perfectly) possible for sb to do sth / that ...*
probable	probable	*probable cause / effect / outcome - it is probable that ...*
real	réel	*real life / gold*
to be short of	être à court de	*to be short of money / ideas / coal*
telltale	révélateur, qui trahit	*telltale signs / bloodstains*
true to life	vrai, conforme à la réalité	*true to life portrait / story*

■ *Verbes*

appear	apparaître, donner l'impression	*to appear (to be) nervous / content - it appears that... / as if...* (on dirait que)
come up	se produire	*sth interesting may come up*
crop up	surgir, survenir	*a difficulty / problem / subject may crop up*
disappear [,--'-]	disparaître	*sth / sb may disappear mysteriously* (out of sight / into the crowd)
fake	falsifier, simuler, feindre	*to fake a document / surprise / interest in sth*
happen	arriver se trouver que	*accidents / things / events happen to happen to know sth / sb*
lack	manquer (de)	*to lack courage / confidence / space*
make up	fabriquer, inventer	*to make up a story / an excuse*
mislead [mɪsˈliːd]	tromper, induire en erreur	*to mislead sb (into doing sth)*
mistake	se tromper, confondre	*to mistake sth / sb for sth / for sb else*
occur [əˈkɜː]	arriver, se produire venir à l'esprit	*accidents / tragedies occur it occurs to sb to do sth / to sb that ...*
prove	se révéler	*to prove (to be) well-founded / unworkable / impossible*
rule out	exclure, éliminer	*to rule out a possibility*
seem	sembler, paraître	*it seems that ... - to seem very nice / pleased*
symbolize	symboliser	*sth / sb may symbolize sth / sb*
take place	avoir lieu	*demonstrations / meetings / weddings take place at a specific time*
vanish	disparaître	*things / people / animals may vanish* (into thin air: se volatiliser)

Exercices sur le chapitre 2 (2.2)

1. Vérifiez vos connaissances en traduisant les mots ou expressions ci-dessous :

A / godsend - B / mishap - C / genuine - D / misleading - E / to crop up - F / come what may

2. Traduisez en anglais :

A / Il m'est venu à l'esprit soudain d'envisager une éventualité que j'avais jusqu'ici exclue. B / Il l'a amenée, en l'induisant en erreur, à falsifier un document authentique dont elle croyait qu'il était fabriqué de toutes pièces et donc faux. C / Il lui manque un doigt à la main gauche. D / On

The mind and abstract relations

manque toujours de renseignements fiables. E / Ce dont vous manquez le plus, semble-t-il, c'est de tact. F / Quelles que soient les véritables et profondes raisons de son manque de courage, il apparaît clairement que dès que survient une difficulté inattendue, il se volatilise. G / Je me suis trompé sur ce pistolet factice en plastique: il peut se révéler utile en cas d'urgence. H / Le meurtrier feignit la surprise lorsqu'on lui montra les taches de sang révélatrices.

3. Remettez les lettres dans l'ordre :
A / KAFE (adj)   B / ARLE (adj)   C / PENAPH (v)   D / CALK (n / v)   E / MEKASTIN (adj)

2.3. Elements

Collocations

■ *Noms*

clue	indice	*to look for clues - to find clues as to sth*
core	cœur	*sth is at the core of sth else - to cut through to the core of sth - to be a Conservative to the core* (complètement)
detail GB ['--] / US [-'-]	détail	*to provide / disclose full / precise / sketchy details of sth*
element	élément	*elements making up a whole*
feature	trait caractéristique	*key / notable feature - feature common to a group*
gap	écart, différence lacune	*the generation gap - the gap between rich and poor* *a gap in sth - to bridge a gap* (combler)
gist [dʒɪst]	essentiel	*to get the gist - the gist of sth*
loophole	lacune, trou	*loopholes in a law / in income tax legislation*
part	partie	*an essential / unimportant part of sth*
particulars [-'---]	informations détaillées	*to note down / take down sb's particulars*
rest	reste	*to keep the rest (of sth) - the rest* (les autres) *ran away*
sample	échantillon	*to take a sample of sth - to test a representative sample of a group*
shred	parcelle, trace	*a shred of hope / evidence / credibility*
synthesis ['sɪnθəsɪs]	synthèse	*to make a synthesis*
token	signe, gage, symbole	*to give / provide a token of sth - in token of sth - to wear black as a token of one's grief*
withdrawal	retrait	*to make a withdrawal from an account - to carry out a withdrawal from an occupied country*

■ *Adjectifs*

basic ['beɪsɪk]	de base, fondamental	*basic salary / problem / principle*
made up	constitué (de)	*to be made up of various elements*
particular	spécial	*sth of particular importance*
separate	séparé	*to keep sth separate from sth else*
sole	seul, unique	*sole exception / purpose / responsibility / survivor*
spare	disponible	*spare key / parts / tyre - to have spare money / time*
sundry	divers	*sundry things / people - all and sundry* (tout le monde)

■ *Verbes*

analyse ['---]	analyser	*to analyse water for possible contamination - to analyse sth into its constituents*
consist	comprendre, inclure consister à	*sth may consist of various elements* *the solution may consist in doing sth*

define	définir	to define objectives / principles
embody [ɪmˈbɒdi]	donner corps à, appliquer	to embody one's principles in one's behaviour
go by	juger d'après, se fier à	to go by appearances
go on	se fonder sur, s'appuyer sur	not to have much to go on - to have no clue to go on
include	inclure	to include the service charge
make for	contribuer à, faciliter	large print makes for easier reading - to take measures making for a more efficient system
make up	constituer, inclure	road accidents make up a quarter of hospital patients
offset [ɒfˈset]	contrebalancer	to offset the effects of sth
omit [əʊˈmɪt]	omettre	to omit sth from sth - to omit to do sth
partake of [pɑːˈteɪk]	partager	to partake of a meal
	contenir un élément de	this stubborness partakes of insolence
partake in	participer à	to partake in festivities
remove	ôter, supprimer, enlever	to remove sth / stains from sth / one's clothes
root out	éradiquer, éliminer	to root out inefficiency / corrupt practices
separate [ˈ---]	séparer	to separate sth from sth
sever [ˈsevə]	séparer, rompre	to sever relations / ties
synthetise [ˈsɪnθətaɪz]	synthétiser	to synthetise sth
withdraw	(se) retirer, enlever	to withdraw from a race / an election

Exercices sur le chapitre 2 (2.3)

1. Testez vos connaissances en traduisant les mots ou expressions suivants :

A / detail - B / part - C / sample - D / sundry - E / feature - F / gap - G / item - H / token
I / to offset - J / to root out

2. Transcrivez, en alphabet phonétique, la prononciation des mots suivants :

A / detail - B / element - C / gist - D / item - E / particular (n.) - F / synthesis - G / separate (adj.)
H / separate (v.) - I / embody - J / omit - K / partake - L / redeem - M / sever - N / withdraw

3. Traduisez en anglais :

A / La police n'a encore trouvé aucun indice solide relatif au meurtre d'hier soir. B / Quelles qualités pourraient constituer, à votre avis, le caractère de l'homme idéal? C / Je ne me fie pas aux comptes-rendus des films dans la presse. D / C'est souvent une erreur de se fonder sur le récit fait par les témoins. E / Au cœur de la discussion se trouvait le désir de nombreux participants de faire une synthèse acceptable des différentes positions exprimées. F / La musique qu'il joue recèle une certain tristesse. G / Il s'est retiré de la prochaine élection, ce qui a contribué à une plus grande clarté et a contrebalancé les effets malheureux de ses premiers discours. H / Ceux-ci étaient constitués presque entièrement de propos racistes. I / Il a rompu ses relations avec l'extrême droite et éliminé les pratiques malhonnêtes de certains membres du parti. J / Il a donné un gage de ses bonnes intentions en participant aux festivités de la soirée. K / Les gens ont saisi l'essentiel de son dernier discours et ont pris bonne note des informations détaillées qu'il a fournies sur les lacunes et les trous de la législation actuelle. L / Il se propose de supprimer les inégalités sociales, ce qui est un trait commun à tous les discours électoraux.

2.4. Relations

Collocations

■ Noms

bearing	rapport, relation, incidence	sth may have a / some bearing on sth
comparison [-'---]	comparaison	to draw / make a comparison between sth and sth else - to stand / bear comparison with sth
connection	lien, rapport	to make a connection - sth may have a connection with sth
discrepancy [-'---]	contradiction, divergence	there is a discrepancy between sth and sth else
example	exemple	to set a good / bad example - to follow sb's example - to hold sb up as an example
likeness	ressemblance (plutôt physique)	to bear a strong likeness to sb (ressembler beaucoup à)
link	lien	to sever links with (couper tout lien avec) sth / sb - sth / sb may have a close / strong / weak link with / to sth / sb
precedence ['presɪdəns]	priorité	to have / take / give precedence over sth
relationship	relation(s), rapport(s)	to have a good / bad relationship (bien / mal s'entendre) - to establish a casual / close / intimate / solid relationship with sb - sth may bear no relation to sth (n'avoir aucun rapport avec qch)
relevance ['reləvəns]	rapport, pertinence, lien étroit	sth may have some / be of some relevance to sth
resemblance [rɪ'zembləns]	ressemblance (de tous ordres)	to bear (avoir) a close / strong resemblance to sth
series ['sɪəriːz]	série, séquence	an unbroken series
simile ['sɪməli]	comparaison (littérature)	'as white as a sheet' is a simile
specialist	spécialiste	a heart specialist - a specialist in old books / on Milton
spitting image	portrait tout craché	to be the spitting image of sb
stereotype ['sterɪˌətaɪp]	stéréotype	to perpetuate a stereotype

■ Adjectifs

common	commun, courant	it is common knowledge that... (il est bien connu que) - sth is common to many people
connected	qui a un lien, associé	sth / sb may be connected with sth - a series of connected events
different	différent	basically / hardly different from (US than) sth
identical	identique	identical with / to sth
irrelevant [-'---]	non pertinent, sans rapport	irrelevant to sth
mock	factice, simulé, feint	mock horror / surprise exam (examen blanc)
normal	normal	it is perfectly normal (for sb) to do sth
odd	bizarre	odd behaviour - it is odd that... / (of sb) to do sth
ordinary ['----]	ordinaire	the ordinary run of things (le cours normal des événements)
quaint	étrange	quaint idea / characteristic
queer	bizarre, suspect	queer person / goings-on - it is queer to do sth / that...
related	lié, apparenté	related sciences - sb / sth may be closely / loosely related to sth / sb
relevant	pertinent, en rapport avec	relevant fact / remark - sth may be relevant to sth
run-of-the-mill	ordinaire, banal	run-of-the-mill job / performance / politician
same	même	to be the same age as sb else
similar	semblable	similar to sth
special	spécial	to pay special attention to - special to (spécifique à) a country
specific	spécifique	specific example / instructions - to be specific about sth (être très précis)
strange	étrange, inconnu	it is strange (of sb) to do / that...

typical	typique, caractéristique	it is typical (of sb) to do / that...
unaccountable	inexplicable	unaccountable behaviour
uncanny	mystérieux, sinistre	uncanny place / atmosphere - it is uncanny that... / (of sb) to do sth
unlike	dissemblable; peu ressemblant	to be unlike each other / one's mother
unusual	inhabituel	it is unusual (for sb) to do / that
usual	habituel	it is usual (for sb) to do
weird [wɪəd]	mystérieux, surnaturel bizarre, peu ordinaire	weird atmosphere / old house weird ideas

■ *Verbes*

ape	singer	to ape sb / sb's manners
compare [-'-]	comparer être comparable	to compare sth with / to sth sth may compare favourably / unfavourably in price / quality
depend	dépendre; compter sur	sth may depend on sth - to depend on sb to do sth
differ	être différent, différer	sth / sb may differ from sth / sb
have / be to do with	avoir un rapport avec	sth has to do with sth else
imitate	imiter	to imitate sb / sth
look like	ressembler	to look like sb else
mimic	imiter; parodier, ridiculiser	to mimic sb / sb's voice
overlap [,--'-]	se chevaucher, se recouvrir	dates / responsibilities / systems may overlap
relate [-'-]	relier, établir un lien	to relate sth to sth else
resemble [rɪ'zembl]	ressembler	to resemble sb closely
set off	mettre en valeur	sth may set off sb's beauty
simulate ['sɪmjuleɪt]	simuler, feindre imiter, simuler	to simulate surprise / pain / pleasure to simulate a noise
specialize ['speʃəlaɪz]	se spécialiser	to specialize in sth / in doing sth
take after	tenir de, ressembler à	to take after one's mother / father

Exercices sur le chapitre 2 (2.4)

1. Testez vos connaissances en traduisant les mots ci-dessous :

A / simile - B / discrepancy - C / weird - D / to set off - E / to overlap

2. Traduisez en anglais :

A / "Doit-on donner la priorité au rendement ou aux conditions de travail?" "Cela dépend de beaucoup de facteurs". B / Je compte sur vous pour donner le bon exemple. C / Quelle idée bizarre de se spécialiser dans les sciences étroitement liées à l'étude de ces inquiétants extra-terrestres dont on dit qu'ils ressemblent vaguement à des êtres humains. D / N'est-il pas pertinent d'établir un lien entre le comportement inexplicable et un peu suspect des habitants de ce chateau et les rumeurs inhabituelles qui circulent à son sujet?

3. Joignez une phrase de droite à une phrase de gauche :

A. Must you specialize	1. the two sisters are quite unlike each other.
B. Identical twins	2. be connected with?
C. What type of make-up do you think	3. in mimicking your teacher's voice?
D. It is so typical of him	4. to do with some special science?
E. What can this very unusual series	5. normally look like each other, don't they?
F. Does what she works on have	6. overlap mine.
G. Your holiday dates are likely to	7. to simulate surprise.
H. Unlike the two brothers who both take after their father	8. could set off her beauty even more?

3
Feelings

1. Emotion

Collocations

■ *Noms*

concern [-'-]	inquiétude, souci	*sth / sb may show / express / cause / arouse great concern for / about / at sth*
excitement	excitation, agitation	*sth may arouse / create / stir up intense excitement*
feeling	sentiment, sensation	*sth may arouse / stir up a feeling (of awe / pleasure / anger) - to express / show / hide / repress one's feelings*
frame of mind	état d'esprit	*to be in the right frame of mind for sth*
frenzy	accès, crise	*in a frenzy of anger - to work oneself into a frenzy* (se mettre violemment en colère)
mixed feelings	sentiments mitigés	*to have mixed feelings about sth*
mood	humeur, disposition	*to be in a good / genial* (chaleureux) */ bad / sullen / foul mood* (humeur massacrante) *- to be in the mood for sth / to do sth*
pang	serrement de cœur	*a pang of sadness / regret - to feel pangs of conscience / guilt* (éprouver des remords)
trouble	ennuis, problèmes	*to be in / get into trouble for doing sth*
turmoil	trouble, émoi	*one's mind / a country / may be in (a) turmoil*

■ *Adjectifs*

carried away	transporté	*to be / get carried away by enthusiasm*
concerned	inquiet, soucieux	*to be concerned for / about sb's health*
emotional [-'---]	affectif, émotionnel sensible, émotif	*a child's emotional problems - to get emotional* (être bouleversé) *to be too emotional*
emotive [-'--]	chargé d'émotion, passionnel	*emotive use of language / concept of art*
excited	excité, enthousiasmé	*to be / get excited at / about sth / to do sth*
exciting	passionnant	*to have an exciting time - it is exciting to do sth*
frantic	affolé frénétique, affolant	*to be frantic with worry* *frantic activity / pace of modern life / rush*
moody	d'humeur changeante de mauvaise humeur, maussade	*a very moody person* *to be / appear to be moody for no reason at all*
moving	émouvant	*moving appeal / tale / account / speech - it is moving to do sth*
temperamental [,--'--]	changeant, capricieux	*temperamental person / car / machine*
troublesome	gênant, pénible, difficile	*troublesome child / cough - it is troublesome to do sth*
upset	contrarié, fâché, inquiet	*to be / get upset about sth / that...*
worked-up	très énervé, agité	*to be / get all worked-up about / over sth*

■ *Verbes*

care	se soucier, se sentir concerné, s'intéresser	*"Nobody cares!" " I do, I care" - For all I care!* (pour ce que j'ai à en faire!) *- not to care a damn - to care about people*

curb	refréner, maîtriser	*to curb one's emotions / one's enthusiasm*
experience [-'---]	éprouver	*to experience a feeling of fear / a great deal of shame*
feel	sentir, ressentir	*to feel great anger / shame / pleasure in sb's company*
	se sentir	*to feel happy / sad / worried*
move	émouvoir, toucher	*to move sb deeply / to tears*
stir	remuer, émouvoir	*to stir sb deeply*
stir (up)	provoquer	*to stir (up) anger / a feeling / excitement*
touch [tʌtʃ]	toucher	*to touch the right note* (la corde sensible) - *to touch to the quick* (piquer au vif)
upset	contrarier, fâcher, inquiéter	*it may upset sb to do sth / sb that … - sth / sb may upset sb greatly*

Exercices sur le chapitre 3 (1)

1. Testez vos connaissances en traduisant les mots ci-dessous :
A / moody - B / frantic - C / turmoil (n.) - D / temperamental - E / upset (adj.)

2. Remettez les lettres dans l'ordre :
A / NOCRERN B / DOOM C / RIST (v.) D / ZYNERF E / GANP F / COHTU G / RACE (v.)

3. Remettez les phrases dans l'ordre :
A / great the news excitement aroused. B / feelings repress his to tried he. C / to he never pangs seems any of feel guilt. D / trouble into got he letting for himself enthusiasm carried be away by excessive.

2. Love and hate

Collocations

■ *Noms*

appeal	attrait, charme	*sth / sb may have / hold a certain appeal for sb - to lose one's appeal for sb*
craze	engouement, folie	*sth may become a craze - the latest craze for sth*
crush	béguin	*to have a crush on a particular person*
dislike	aversion	*to have a dislike of sth / take a dislike to sb*
for sth's / sb's sake	pour (l'amour de) qqch / qn	*to do sth for the sake of sb - for the sake of talking* (pour le plaisir de parler) */ of argument* (pour le plaisir de discuter) - *for your own sake* (dans votre intérêt)
hate	haine	*to feel nothing but hate for sb*
hatred	haine	*to have an intense hatred of sb / sth*
likes and dislikes	préférences et aversions	*to try and guess sb's likes and dislikes*
love	amour	*to marry for love - love at first sight*
pity	pitié	*to have / take pity on sb - to feel great pity for sb*
terms	acceptation	*to come to terms with sth* (accepter)

Feelings

■ *Adjectifs*

to be fed up	en avoir marre	*to be thoroughly fed up with sb / sth / (with) doing / that ...*
fond	tendre, affectueux	*fond farewell / look*
to be fond of	bien aimer, être amateur de	*to be fond of sb / sth / doing*
hateful	odieux, abominable	*sb / sth may be hateful to sb* (faire horreur à qqn) - *it is hateful of sb to sth*
hooked	accro, mordu	*to be hooked on sth*
impassioned [-'---]	passionné, enflammé	*impassioned plea* (plaidoyer) */ speech*
keen	enthousiaste, passionné	*keen student / gardener*
be keen	être passionné de	*to be keen on sth / football / chess*
be keen	adorer (faire)	*to be keen on doing sth*
be keen	tenir beaucoup à (faire), avoir très envie de (faire)	*to be keen to do sth*
passionate ['---]	passionné, enthousiaste	*to be passionate about sth / to have a passionate interest in sth*
tender	tendre, affectueux	*tender farewell / heart / memories*
unbearable	insupportable	*unbearable person / heat / pain*
unrequited [,--'--]	non réciproque, non partagé	*unrequited love*

■ *Verbes*

appeal	plaire à	*sth / sb may appeal to sb*
attract	attirer, séduire, plaire à	*sth / sb may attract sb to sb / sth*
bear / stand	supporter, tolérer	*sb can't / couldn't bear / stand sb / sth / doing sth*
care about / for	aimer, être très attaché à	*to care about / for sb very much / a lot*
dislike	ne pas aimer	*to dislike sb / sth / doing sth very much*
dote on	être fou de	*to dote on / upon one's grandchildren*
fall for	se prendre de passion pour	*to fall for sb / each other / sth*
fall in love	tomber amoureux de	*to fall in love with sth / sb / doing sth*
go for	adorer, aimer à la folie	*to go for sth / sb*
go off	ne plus aimer / avoir envie de	*to go off sb / sth*
hate	détester	*to hate sth / sb / doing sth*
like	bien aimer, trouver sympathique	*to like sth / sb / doing sth very much / a lot*
loathe [ləʊð]	avoir en horreur	*to loathe sth / sb / doing sth deeply / intensely*
love	aimer, adorer	*to love sb / sth / doing sth*
pity	avoir pitié de	*to pity sb greatly*
put off	ôter l'envie, dégoûter	*sth may put somebody off sth / off sb / doing sth*
relish ['--]	apprécier, prendre grand plaisir à	*to relish an idea / a prospect / doing sth*

Exercices sur le chapitre 3 (2)

1. Testez vos connaissances en traduisant les mots et expressions ci-dessous :

A / en avoir marre - B / accro - C / engouement - D / avoir pitié de qqn

2. Traduisez en anglais :

A / Le projet a plu à beaucoup de gens. Pas à vous? B / Il adore la musique moderne. Et vous? C / " Il n'a plus envie de café pour le petit déjeuner." "Moi non plus." D / Elle ne supporte pas qu'on l'aime! Trop d'expériences d'amour non partagé l'ont complètement dégoûtée de l'amour. E / Le fils est encore très attaché à ses parents; la fille aussi, d'ailleurs. F / "Il aime bien aider les autres." "Pas moi!" G / Il tient beaucoup à l'emmener en voiture chaque weekend pour lui montrer son jardin à la campagne. H / Il ne prend de plaisir qu'au jardinage. Elle non, elle a cela en horreur. I / Les films de ce genre ont perdu beaucoup de leur attrait pour moi. J. Son aversion des traditions l'amène parfois à se prendre de passion pour des gens marginaux.

3. Complétez les voyelles manquantes :

A / L_V_   B / H_T_   C / S_K_   D / L_K_   E / L__TH_   F / C_AR_   G / H_TR_D

3. Preference, enthusiasm

Collocations

■ Noms

enthusiasm [ɪn'θjuːziæzəm]	enthousiasme	to show / express great / wild enthusiasm for sth
heart	cœur	after one's own heart (exactement comme on les aime)
mind	envie	to have a good / half a mind (avoir bien / presqu'envie) to do sth
longing	désir, envie nostalgie, regret	to feel a longing for sth to look at sth with longing
preference ['---]	préférence	to display / show / express a marked / strong / tireless preference for sth / sb
wish	souhait	to express / fulfil a wish for sth / to do sth - to respect sb's wishes - to have a wish come true (se réaliser)

■ Adjectifs

eager	passionné, ardent	an eager defender of the faith
eager for	très désireux d'obtenir	to be eager for success / rewards
eager to	être très désireux de	to be eager to succeed / help
enthusiastic [ɪnˌθjuːziˈæstɪk]	enthousiaste	enthusiastic person / applause - to be enthusiastic about sb / sth / doing sth
favo(u)rite	préféré	favo(u)rite friend / piece of music / movie / restaurant
half-hearted	peu enthousiaste	half-hearted effort / attempt / attitude / acceptance - to be half-hearted about sth / doing sth
partial	qui a une préférence	to be partial to sth (avoir un penchant pour)
reluctant	hésitant, peu disposé	to be reluctant to do sth
repellent / repulsive	répugnant	repellent / repulsive food / repulsive manners - sth may be repellent to sb
squeamish	délicat, facilement dégoûté	squeamish person - to be squeamish about sth / doing sth
weary	las	weary person / sigh - to be weary of sth / doing sth
wishful thinking	le fait de prendre ses désirs pour des réalités	to indulge in wishful thinking

■ Verbes

covet ['kʌvɪt]	convoiter, avoir très envie de	to covet sth / sb's good fortune / wealth
crave	avoir grande envie / besoin de (qch)	to crave (for) happiness / love / (for) a cigarette / stardom
enthral(l) [-'-]	captiver, fasciner	sth / sb may enthral(l) sb
feel like	avoir envie de	to feel like sth / doing sth

Feelings

long (for)	avoir très envie de, attendre avec impatience	*to long for sb / sth*
look forward to	se faire une joie de	*to look forward to sth / doing sth*
marvel	s'émerveiller	*to marvel at sth / that ...*
mind	voir un inconvénient à	*to mind / not to mind sth / sb / sth happening / doing sth / sb doing sth*
prefer	préférer	*to prefer sth to sth else - to prefer doing sth to doing sth else - to prefer to do sth rather than do sth else - I'd prefer him (not) to do sth*
repel [-'-]	rebuter, dégoûter	*sth / sb may repel sb*
want	vouloir, avoir besoin / envie de	*to want sth / sb / to do sth - to want sb to do sth*
weary	se lasser	*to weary of sth / of sb / of doing sth*
wish	souhaiter	*to wish sb sth / to do / sb to do / sth to happen*
	avoir très envie (que), regretter (que ne pas)	*to wish sb were here / did / could / would do sth*
	regretter (que)	*to wish sb were not here / didn't / couldn't / wouldn't do sth*
I would / I'd rather	je préfère(rais)	*I'd rather do sth / he did not do sth*
yearn	avoir la nostalgie	*to yearn for sth / to do sth / for sth to happen / for sb to do sth*

Exercices sur le chapitre 3 (3)

1. Testez vos connaissances en traduisant les mots ou expressions ci-dessous :

A / longing - B / to long - C / wishful thinking - D / to crave - E / to enthrall
F / to have half a mind to do sth - G / a child after one's own heart

2. Joignez une phrase de droite à une phrase de gauche :

A) I'd much rather
B) She will soon weary
C) However partial he may seem to be to wine
D) Although she is not particularly squeamsih
E) She hasn't found anybody after her own heart
F) Her half-hearted acceptance of the marriage
G) She is very eager to succeed in life and consequently
H) The ballet master wishes she'd sound more enthusiastic

1) that's why she is reluctant to marry him.
2) he does prefer beer to any other drink.
3) when he says he's yearning for her to become the British public's favourite dancer.
4) you didn't covet my wife's fortune.
5) of marvelling at his strength.
6) wishes he wouldn't ask her to marry him.
7) she finds his table manners repellent.
8) may have caused him to feel like giving up the idea of matrimony.

3. Traduisez en anglais :

A / Je me fais une joie de vous rencontrer. B / Ça vous ennuie que je fume? C / Je regrette qu'il soit venu. D / Je regrette qu'il ne soit pas là. E / J'ai très envie qu'il vienne le plus tôt possible.

4. Sadness

Collocations

■ Noms

grief	chagrin, douleur	to express / feel / suffer deep / overwhelming grief - to be / go mad / wild with grief (fou de douleur)
melancholy ['----]	mélancolie, tristesse	to feel great melancholy over sth / at doing sth
misfortune [-'--]	malchance, infortune	to have the misfortune of doing / to do sth
monotony [-'---]	monotonie	to break / relieve the monotony of sth / of doing sth
sadness	tristesse	to feel deep sadness over / at sth
sigh	soupir	to breathe / heave / let out a deep sigh of relief
sob	sanglot	with a sob in one's voice - sobs shaking one's body
sorrow /	peine, chagrin	to cause / feel sorrow - to express one's deep sorrow at / over sth at doing sth - sth may be a great sorrow to sb
tear	larme	to burst into / shed bitter tears / tears of joy - to be moved to tears - to bring tears to sb's eyes
unhappiness	malheur, peine	to cause sb great unhappiness
woe(s) (lit.) [wəʊ(z)]	malheur(s) malheur à …!	a scene / tale of woe - economic woes woe to me / woe betide anyone who kills a human being!

■ Adjectifs

alone	seul	to be alone in doing sth - to feel very alone
bleak	morne, désolé sinistre, lugubre, morne sombre rude	bleak heath / landscape / moor bleak person / voice / story bleak future / outlook / prospects bleak season / winter
dismal	lugubre, sombre	dismal weather / countryside / songs / prospect
drab	terne, morne	drab colour / life / surroundings
dreary	morne, monotone ennuyeux	dreary life / job / weather (maussade) - it is dreary to do sth dreary person
forlorn (lit.)	abandonné, délaissé	to have a forlorn look about one / on one's face
gloomy	triste, sombre, malheureux	gloomy person / news / outlook / prospect - to feel gloomy about / over sth
grim	sévère, dur sinistre, sombre déprimé, triste	grim look / reality / necessity / truth grim expression / news / prospect / story / situation to feel pretty grim
lonely	seul, isolé	lonely person / house / village - very / desperately lonely
lonesome (US) ['ləʊnsəm]	seul, esseulé, qui fait se sentir seul	to be / feel lonesome - a long lonesome road
melancholy ['----]	triste, mélancolique	melancholy mood / person / thought / news / sight
monotonous [-'---]	monotone	monotonous job / voice - it is monotonous to do sth
sad	triste	sad person / day / moment / news - it is sad to do sth / that...
sorry	désolé	to be sorry for / about sth / sb / to do sth / that...
unhappy	malheureux	unhappy person / event / moment / country - to be unhappy about / over sth / to do sth / that...
woeful (lit.) ['wəʊfl]	affligeant, consternant	woeful person / news / look / situation / lack of imagination

Feelings 45

■ *Verbes*

cry	pleurer	*to cry loudly / bitterly in / with frustration / for joy - to cry tears of joy / one's heart / eyes out*
grieve	avoir du chagrin	*to grieve over / about / at sth - it may grieve sb to do sth / that ...*
miss	ressentir l'absence de, manquer	*to miss sb / sth / home / the warm weather / doing sth badly / terribly / very much*
moan	gémir	*to moan feebly / loudly over sth - to moan with pain*
mope	broyer du noir, ressasser	*to mope about / over sth*
pine	(se)languir	*to pine after / for sth / home / to do sth*
sigh	soupirer	*to sigh with relief / despair / for sth*
sob	sangloter	*to sob bitterly - to sob (out) a few words / oneself to sleep*
weep	pleurer	*to weep bitter tears about / over sth / for joy / with vexation*
whimper	geindre	*to whimper from fear / with pain*
whine	gémir, se lamenter	*to whine (to sb) about sth*

Exercices sur le chapitre 3 (4)

1. Testez vos connaissances en traduisant les mots ou expressions suivants :

A / triste - B / malheureux - C / gémir - D / soupirer - E / soupir - F / sanglot

2. Traduisez en anglais :

A / "Je ne vous manque pas? Si, vous me manquez beaucoup." B / Il mène une vie terne, c'est peut-être cela qui fait de lui un homme si ennuyeux. C / Elle poussa un soupir de soulagement quand il la quitta.

3. Joignez une phrase de droite à une phrase de gauche :

A. When he heard the gloomy news
B. That bleak landscape
C. He felt lonely
D. He always felt sorry
E. A woeful sight it was
F. Wouldn't you shed tears of joy
G. She missed him so terribly

1. that she had to live alone, when he was available!
2. to see two youngsters crying their eyes out.
3. that she wept and sobbed all day long.
4. if you heard that the cold dismal winter was over at last?
5. he felt great sorrow.
6. even in the company of his friends.
7. never failed to make him feel melancholy.

5. Happiness

Collocations

■ *Noms*

bliss	félicité, grand bonheur	*it is sheer bliss to do sth - to enjoy marital bliss*
fun	amusement	*it is great / good fun to do sth - to do sth for fun / for the fun of it - to have fun*
happiness	bonheur	*to cause / give (sb) great happiness - a feeling of happiness - to have the happiness* (chance) *to do sth*

heart	courage		to take / lose heart (reprendre / perdre courage)
hope	espoir		to arouse / express / entertain / dash / give up (a) fond (fol) / high / slender hope(s) of sth / for sb / that... - in the hope of sth / doing sth
joy	joie		to express / feel boundless joy - to shout with / for joy - to the great joy of sb - it is a great joy to sb / to do sth
pleasure	plaisir		to cause / feel great / genuine pleasure - to give sb pleasure to do sth - to take pleasure in doing sth - to derive pleasure from sth / from doing sth - it is a pleasure to do sth
relief	soulagement		to express / feel great / instant relief at sth / to do sth / that... - to bring relief to sb - to one's great relief - it is an immense relief (to sb) to do sth - to find relief in doing sth
spirits	humeur		to be in good / high / low spirits (de bonne humeur / déprimé) - to keep one's spirits up (ne pas se laisser abattre) - to raise sb's spirits (remonter le moral)
thrill	forte émotion, frisson		to experience give / provide a thrill - to get quite a / a tremendous thrill out of sth / doing sth (être ravi) - it is a (real) thrill to do sth
well-being	bien-être		to give sb a sense of material / physical well-being

■ *Adjectifs*

cheerful	gai, joyeux	cheerful person / atmosphere / mood / colour / news
confident ['---]	confiant	confident smile / step - to be confident of sth / that...
delighted	ravi	to be delighted at / by / with sth / doing sth / to do sth / that...
enjoyable	agréable	a highly enjoyable evening / holiday - it may be enjoyable to do sth
fortunate ['fɔːtʃən_ət]	chanceux, heureux	to be fortunate in sth / in having sth / to do / in doing sth / that...
glad	heureux, content	to be glad about sth / to do sth / that...
happy	heureux	to be happy about sth / to do sth / that...
hopeful	plein d'espoir encourageant	to be hopeful of sth / that... hopeful signs of economic recovery
merry	joyeux, gai	merry fellow / smile - the more, the merrier
pleased	content, satisfait	pleased smile - to be pleased about sth / with sb / to do sth / that...
relieved	soulagé	to be / feel relieved at sth / to do sth / that...
satisfied	satisfait	to be satisfied with sb / about / with sth / to do sth / that...

■ *Verbes*

cheer up	reprendre courage réconforter	to cheer up at sth / a piece of good news sth / sb may cheer somebody up
enjoy	bien aimer, prendre plaisir à	to enjoy sth / doing sth very much / thoroughly
enjoy oneself	bien s'amuser	to enjoy oneself doing sth
enliven [ɪnˈlaɪvn]	animer, rendre vivant	illustrations may enliven a book
exhilarate [ɪɡˈzɪləreɪt]	exalter, griser	sth may exhilarate sb - it may exhilarate sb to do sth
hope	espérer	to hope for sth / to do sth / that...
rejoice	se réjouir	to rejoice at / over sth / to do sth
relieve	soulager	sb / sth may relieve sb - it may relieve sb to do sth that...
thrill	(faire) vibrer, fasciner	to thrill to sb's tales / voice - it may thrill sb to do sth / that...

Feelings

Exercices sur le chapitre 3 (5)

1. Testez vos connaissances en traduisant les mots ou expressions ci-dessous :
A / glad - B / merry - C / to lose heart - D / confident - E / relief

2. Choisissez les mots qui conviennent pour remplir les blancs :
CHEERFUL / DELIGHTED / ENJOY ONESELF / ENJOYABLE / HAPPINESS
RAISE SOMEBODY'S SPIRITS / RELIEVED / THRILL / UNFORTUNATE
A / What a _____ sight it was to see the children _____ _____ at the birthday party.
B / We spent a very _____ evening at the President's residence and it really gave us a _____ to be invited to the White House.
C / I think the First Lady was _____ to have us too.
D / We all watched a play put on by the State Department's personnel and were _____ when the show was over...
E / Nothing can _____ as much as the scraps of _____ I manage to give occasionally to all those _____ people on the streets.

3. A gauche une liste de définitions, à droite des mots. Faites coincider les mots et leur définition :

A / to make cheerful   1) BLISS
B / complete happiness   2) CHEER UP
C / lucky   3) WELL-BEING
D / to cause to become happier and more cheerful 4) EXHILARATE
E / personal and physical comfort   5) ENLIVEN
F / to fill with joy and excitement   6) FORTUNATE

6. Unhappiness

Collocations

■ *Noms*

agony ['---]	grande souffrance	*to feel / experience acute / deep / untold* (indicible) *agony at sth / at doing sth - to be in an agony of doubt / fear*
anxiety [æŋ'zaɪ_əti]	anxiété, souci	*to feel great / deep anxiety about sth / for sb*
despair	désespoir	*to experience / overcome utter despair at / over sth / at doing sth - to do sth out of* (par) *despair*
disappointment [,--'--]	déception	*to feel (a) great / bitter disappointment at / over sth / at doing / that...*
misery ['mɪzər_i]	malheur, tristesse	*to cause / alleviate / relieve deep / untold misery - it is sheer misery to do sth*
regret [-'-]	regret	*to feel / express / show deep / keen regret(s) at / over sth / at (not) doing sth*
remorse	remords	*to feel / express / show profound / bitter remorse at / over sth / at doing sth*
shame	honte	*to feel / express deep shame at sth / at doing sth - it is a shame to do sth*
spirits	humeur, moral, ardeur, enthousiasme	*to lift / raise* (remonter) */ dampen* (refroidir) *sb's spirits - to be in good / high / low spirits - sb's spirits may rise / droop*

trepidation	vive inquiétude	with some / no small amount of trepidation - to be in a state of trepidation
unhappiness	malheur	to cause / relieve sb's great / intense (feeling of) unhappiness
worry	souci	to cause / feel deep / serious worry about (doing) sth / over sth / sb - it may be a great worry to do sth
wretch	malheureux	a poor homeless wretch

■ *Adjectifs*

anxious	inquiet, anxieux chargé d'inquiétude	to be anxious about / over sth anxious look / day / time / question
ashamed	honteux	thoroughly ashamed of sth / of oneself / at having done sth / that... / to do sth
bleak [bli:k]	lugubre, déprimé	bleak prospects - to feel bleak
cut up	affecté	to be badly cut up about sth
desperate ['---]	désespéré prêt à tout pour	desperate effort / person / scream / situation to be desperate for money / recognition / to do sth
despondent [-'--]	abattu	despondent look - to be / look despondent about doing sth
dire	terrible, extrême	dire misery / poverty / straits (situation) / consequences / warnings
disappointed [,--'--]	déçu	to be disappointed about / at / with sth / in sb / to do sth / that...
dispirited [dɪs'pɪrɪtɪd]	découragé, abattu	dispirited person / look - to be / look / sound dispirited
distracted	fou, bouleversé	distracted look - to be / look distracted with grief / worry
downcast	abattu, démoralisé	to be / feel / seem downcast
gruesome	horrible, macabre	gruesome report / detail / scene
hopeless	désespéré, sans espoir	hopeless grief / sigh / situation - to feel hopeless about sth / that...
miserable ['mɪzər_əbl]	très malheureux épouvantable	miserable face / look / person - to feel / look miserable miserable day / living conditions / life - to be miserable to do sth
unfortunate [-'---]	malheureux, malchanceux	unfortunate accident / person / decision / investment - it is unfortunate to do sth / that... - to be unfortunate in one's friends
unhappy	malheureux	unhappy person / look / time - to be / feel / look unhappy
worried	inquiet	worried person / look - to be / feel / look worried about sth / sb / to do / about doing / that...
worrisome ['wʌrɪsəm]	inquiétant	worrisome affair / situation
worrying	inquiétant	worrying situation - to have a worrying time
wretched	misérable lamentable	wretched person - to feel / look wretched - it is wretched of sb (to do sth)

■ *Verbes*

break down	s'effondrer, craquer	to break down and cry / weep
despair	(se) désespérer	to despair of sth / of doing sth / of sb doing sth
dishearten	décourager	it disheartens sb to do sth / that...
fret	se faire du souci	to fret about sth / sb / for sb (réclamer)
frustrate	frustrer	it may frustrate sb that... / sb to do sth
get down	déprimer, abattre	sth may get sb down - it may get sb down to hear that...
let down	décevoir, faire faux bond	to let down sb badly
regret [-'-]	regretter	to regret sth / to do / doing sth / that... deeply / very much
repent	se repentir	to repent sth / doing sth - to have nothing to repent of
shame	couvrir de honte faire honte à	to shame sb to do sth to shame sb in front of sb else - to shame sb into / out of doing sth
worry ['wʌri]	se faire du souci tourmenter	to worry about / over sth / sb it worries sb to do sth / sb that... - to worry sb with sth

Feelings

Exercices sur le chapitre 3 (6)

1. Testez vos connaissances en traduisant les mots ci-dessous :
A / gruesome - B / miserable - C / wretch - D / anxious - E / to get sb down - F / to break down
G / to fret

2. Choisissez :
A / He was worrying / ashamed / wretched of himself for letting down / up / over his unfortunate friend.
B / The employment prospects looked so bleak / cut up / despondent that he regretted / shamed / disheartened having immigrated to France.
C / It would be a shame of being / to be / for being unkind to someone so downcast.
D / He never repented of / in / from / Ø his sins.

3. Remettez les mots dans l'ordre pour constituer des phrases correctes :
A / untold called agony he at felt a being liar. B / out he despair of himself killed. C / a Directors of the shamed Board he giving into employees the rise. D / spirits more raise would his nothing than out their others of misery helping. E / unhappiness cut up badly people's other was he about.
F / lived in he misery for dire life most his of.

7. Surprise

Collocations

■ *Noms*

bewilderment [bɪ'wɪldəmənt]	perplexité, grand étonnement	*to show bewilderment at sth - to one's complete bewilderment, ...*
surprise	surprise	*to achieve* (obtenir un effet de) */ express / show (a) complete / outright surprise at sth / at doing sth - it is a surprise to do sth / that...*
wonder	(sujet d')étonnement	*it is a wonder that... - to look around in wonder*

■ *Adjectifs*

astonished	étonné	*to be greatly astonished at / by sth / to do sth / that...*
dazed	abasourdi	*to be dazed at sth*
dumbfounded [-'--]	interloqué	*to be dumfounded by sth*
flabbergasted ['----]	sidéré	*to be flabbergasted at sth*
mystified	(rendu) perplexe	*to be mystified to do sth*
nonplussed [nɒn'plʌst]	dérouter	*to be nonplussed by sth*
startling	surprenant	*startling news - it may be startling to do sth*
stupendous	prodigieux	*stupendous sums of money / memory / silence*
surprised	surpris	*to be surprised at / by sth / to do sth / that...*
taken aback	déconcerté	*to be taken aback by sth*
unexpected	inattendu	*unexpected bit of news / arrival*

■ *Verbes*

baffle	dérouter	*it baffles sb to do sth / sb that...*
puzzle	laisser perplexe	*it greatly puzzles sb to do sth / sb that...*

startle	surprendre	*it startles sb to do sth / sb that...*
stun	abasourdir	*it stuns sb to do sth / sb that...*
surprise	surprendre	*it surprises sb to do sth / sb that...*
wonder	se demander	*to wonder when / how / why / if...*
	s'étonner	*to wonder at / about sth*
	s'émerveiller	*to wonder at sth*

Exercices sur le chapitre 3 (7)

1. Testez vos connaissances en traduisant les mots ci-dessous :

A / baffle - B / flabbergasted - C / mystified - D / startling - E / stun

2. Joignez une phrase de droite à une phrase de gauche :

1) It greatly puzzled him
2) I often wonder how
3) He showed understandable bewilderment
4) I don't wonder that you are startled
5) Nothing could puzzle her more than
6) The tourists wondered at
7) When he started learning German
8) By asking the Minister such a bold question

A) at her stupendous memory.
B) to find that she'd done it all by herself.
C) he certainly achieved complete surprise.
D) she manages to do all that she does.
E) by such tactlessness.
F) he was nonplussed by the complex conjugation system.
G) the guests' apparent unconcern about the poor quality of the food.
H) the beauty of the sight.

8. Fear

Collocations

■ *Noms*

awe [ɔː]	effroi respectueux	*to be / stand in awe of sb* (être impressionné et effrayé par) - *to inspire awe in sb*
cold feet	peur	*to get / have cold feet about sth / doing* (avoir la trouille)
creeps	peur, dégoût	*to give sb the creeps* (faire froid dans le dos / dégoûter)
dismay [-'-]	désarroi, consternation	*to be filled / speak with dismay - (much) to one's dismay, ...*
fear	peur, crainte	*to be overcome / shake with fear - a fear of sth - to express one's fear(s) that...*
fright	frayeur, peur	*to take fright at sth - to give sb a fright*
omen ['əʊmen]	augure, présage	*it is a good / bad omen that...*
portent ['pɔːtent]	signe, présage	*sth is a portent of sth*
scourge [skɜːdʒ]	fléau, peste	*the scourge of war - a person may be a scourge - a scourge to mankind*

■ *Adjectifs*

afraid	effrayé	*to be very much / terribly afraid of sth / sb / to do / of doing sth / that...*
amazed	stupéfait	*to be amazed at / by sth / to do sth / that...*

Feelings

appalling	épouvantable	*appalling conditions - it is appalling to do sth / that...*
awesome	impressionnant, terrifiant	*awesome responsibility / weapon / account / task*
forbidding	menaçant, rébarbatif	*forbidding appearance / look / manner / range of mountains*
formidable ['fɔːmɪdəbl]	redoutable, effrayant	*formidable person / voice / task / opponent*
horrendous	terrible, affreux	*horrendous murder / cost / weather*
ominous ['ɒmɪnəs]	inquiétant, de mauvais augure	*ominous sign / cloud / silence / crisis*
portentous [pɔːˈtentəs]	sinistre, grave solennel, pontifiant	*portentous consequences* *portentous face / manner - to indulge in portentous philosophizing*

■ *Verbes*

amaze	stupéfier	*it amazes sb to do sth / that...*
appal	choquer, scandaliser	*it appals sb to do sth / that...*
dismay	consterner	*it dismays sb to do sth / that...*
dread	redouter	*to dread sth / doing sth / sb doing sth / that...*
fear	craindre	*to fear sth / sb / to do sth / that...*
flinch	reculer	*to flinch from sth / doing sth*
frighten	effrayer, faire peur	*it may frighten sb to do sth - sb may be frightened to do sth / into doing sth / out of doing sth*
panic	paniquer, avoir / faire très peur (à)	*sth may panic sb / sb into doing sth / out of doing sth - sb may panic at sth / at having to do sth - it may panic sb to do sth*
recoil	reculer (devant la perspective de)	*to recoil at / from sth / from doing sth*
scare	(s') effrayer	*to scare easily at sth - to scare sb to do sth / sb into / out of doing sth - it scares sb that...*
shirk	éviter, se dérober à	*to shirk sth / doing sth*
shrink	reculer (devant la difficulté)	*to shrink from sth / from doing sth*
shun	éviter / fuir	*to shun sth / sb*

Exercices sur chapitre 3 (8)

1. Testez vos connaissances en traduisant les mots ci-dessous :

A / to scare - B / ominous - C / portentous - D / awe   E / to shirk

2. Choisissez le mot qui convient ou les mots qui conviennent :

A / He flinched / frightened / feared me into giving up smoking.
B / I dismay / appal / dread seeing him again.
C / It was an awesome / a formidable / an afraid task.
D / He recoiled / shunned / amazed from fighting such a strong man.

3. Traduisez en anglais :

A / La peur de l'avenir me fait froid dans le dos. B / Je prends peur au moindre signe inquiétant d'aggravation du chômage. C / Il recule devant ses obligations, il n'est pas le seul. D / Si ça continue, je vais devoir, en lui faisant très peur, l'amener à renoncer à cet horrible projet. E / Les guerres civiles sont devenues un fléau pour beaucoup de pays d'Europe et d'Afrique. F / Ce monarque redoutable inspire à ses sujets une crainte mêlée de respect.

4

Oral and written communication

1. Questions and answers

■ *Noms*

encyclopedia [ɪnˌsaɪklə'piːdi ə]	encyclopédie	**lexicographer**	lexicographe
lexicology [ˌ--'---]	lexicologie	**lexicon**	lexique
lexicologist	lexicologue	**reference work**	ouvrage de référence
lexicography	lexicographie	**work book**	manuel

Collocations

answer	réponse	*to make / give / provide a spoken / written / blunt / direct / straight / non-commital / unequivocal / vague / wise answer to sth / sb*
description [-'---]	description	*to give / provide a(n) accurate / clear / fist-hand / thorough / lively / matter-of-fact description of sth / sb*
detail GB ['--] / US [-'-]	détail	*to spare sb the details - to bring up / furnish full / minute / graphic / petty details - to go into detail*
dictionary	dictionnaire	*to consult / update an abridged / unabridged / bilingual / technical dictionary - look up a word in a dictionary*
double-dutch	charabia	*to speak / write double-dutch - sth may be double-dutch to sb*
drift	sens général	*to get / catch sb's drift / the drift of sth*
enquiry *(GB)* [ɪn'kwaɪ əri]	demande d'informations	*to make an enquiry (se renseigner)*
expression	expression expression	*the free expression of opinions - to give expression to one's feelings to use colloquial / hackneyed / slang expressions*
fact	fait	*to ascertain (s'assurer) / establish check / deny / confirm / interpret / distort / twist / embellish a hard / well-established / well-known / indisputable / unquestionable fact - to distinguish / tell fact from fiction*
gibberish ['dʒɪbər ɪʃ]	baragouin	*sth may be sheer gibberish - to talk gibberish*
information (U)	renseignements	*to give / provide / get / ask for / collect / leak / suppress confidential / misleading / second-hand information about sth / that...*
inquiry (GB / US)	enquête	*to make / conduct / hold a(n) exhaustive / official / thorough / discreet / inquiry about / into sth / sb's affairs*
meaning	sens	*to get / misconstrue (mal interpréter) the double / hidden / accepted / clear / obscure meaning of sth*
particulars [-'---]	détails spécifiques	*to go into particulars - in every particular (à tous égards)*
pun	jeu de mots	*to make a pun*
query ['kwɪəri]	question, doute	*to raise a query - to put / respond to a query about sth / sb*
question	question	*to ask / answer / raise a(n) awkward / blunt / relevant / irrelevant / leading / tricky question about sth / as to whether...*
quotation / quote	citation	*to give a direct quotation from a book / an author*

record ['--]	archive, trace	to keep an accurate / detailed / sketchy record of events - sth may be / go on record
	dossier, passé, bilan	to have an academic / excellent / poor record - medical / police / service record
reference ['---]	allusion	to contain / make a direct / indirect reference to sth / sb
rejoinder	réplique	sharp rejoinder from sb to sb
reply	réponse	to give / make a curt / immediate / unpleasant reply to sth
statement	déclaration	to issue / deny / make / withdraw a brief / detailed / false / sweeping (péremptoire) statement about sth / that...
summary	résumé	to give / make a brief / inaccurate / brilliant summary of sth
supposition	supposition, hypothèse	to make a supposition that... - on the mere supposition that...
tip	tuyau, renseignement	to give sb a tip on / about sth / about how to do sth - to take sb's tip
topic	sujet, thème	to bring up a controversial topic for discussion - a topic of conversation
understatement [,--'--]	affirmation atténuée, litote	to make an understatement - it is quite an understatement to say that...
wording	formulation	to change / argue over the wording of sth

■ Adjectifs

formal	soigné (style), cérémonieux	formal language / letter / wording
glib	volubile	glib salesman / talker
	désinvolte, superficiel	glib answer / excuse / promise
informal	familier	informal expression / language
noncommittal [,--'--]	réservé, prudent	to be noncommittal about sth
	qui n'engage pas	noncommital answer / letter
outspoken [-'--]	franc et ouvert	to be outspoken in / about sth - outspoken critic / criticism / statement
plain	simple, clair	plain language / statement / words - it is plain that...
quizzical ['kwızıkl]	perplexe, interrogateur	quizzical tone / voice
	ironique, narquois	quizzical look
speechless	muet, interloqué	speechless with surprise / joy / anger
straightforward [-'--]	direct, sans détours	straightforward answer / manner
	clair, simple	straightforward issue / set of instructions
topical	actuel, d'actualité	topical issue / question / report
uneasy [-'--]	gêné, mal à l'aise	uneasy silence - to feel uneasy about sth

■ Verbes

answer	répondre	to answer sb / a question that...
ask GB [ɑːsk]/ US [æsk]	demander	to ask sb a question - to ask for sth / to do sth / sb to do sth / how to do sth - ask about sth / about / after sb - ask the time / way
come out with	sortir, dire	to come out with sth / an explanation / the correct answer
convey	transmettre	to convey sth / a message / one's thanks to sb
describe	décrire	to describe minutely / vividly sth to sb / how... - to be described as sb / sth
enquire	se renseigner	to enquire about sb / about / into sth / how / where...
express	exprimer	to express one's feelings
	exprimer	to express sth / oneself in English
imply	laisser entendre	to imply (to sb) that...
indicate	indiquer	to indicate sth (to sb) / (to sb)that...

Oral and written communication 55

mean	signifier, vouloir dire	*to mean sth / that...*
mention	mentionner, indiquer	*to mention sth (to sb) / (to sb) that... / where / how / when...*
pretend [-'-]	affirmer, prétendre	*to pretend that... / to be / to do sth*
pun	faire des jeux de mots	*to indulge in punning on the different meanings of words*
quote	citer	*to quote sth from somebody / a book*
recap(itulate) ['ri:kæp] / [ˌri:kə'pɪtʃuleɪt]	récapituler	*to recap(itulate) sth briefly*
record [-'-]	noter, enregistrer	*to record sth / that*
refer	faire allusion	*to refer to sth / sb*
reply	répondre, réagir	*to reply to sth / sb / that...*
reword / rephrase	reformuler	*to reword / rephrase a sentence / statement*
show	montrer	*to show (sb) sth / sb how to do sth*
signify	signifier	*to signify sth / that...*
specify	préciser	*to specify sth / that...*
stand for	représenter, signifier	*to stand for sth / for quality*
state	déclarer, indiquer	*to state sth / that...*
stress	insister sur, mettre l'accent sur	*to stress sth / a fact / a detail*
	souligner que	*to stress that*
sum up	résumer	*to sum up the main points / all the arguments / a story*
summarize ['sʌməraɪz]	faire un résumé	*to summarize a plot / story*
suppose	supposer	*to suppose sth / that... - to suppose sb / sth to be... - to suppose so / not*
thank	remercier	*to thank sb for sth / for doing sth / that...*
tip off	avertir, prévenir	*to tip sb off about sth*

Exercices sur le chapitre 4 (1)

1. Testez vos connaissances en traduisant les mots ou expressions suivants :

A / to tip off - B / to reply - C / to feel uneasy - D / déclarer - E / indiquer - F / volubile
G / soigné (style) - H / familier (style) - I / vivant (détail) - J / insignifiant

2. Traduisez en anglais :

A / Répondez aux questions que je vous ai posées. B / Essayez de vous exprimer avec clarté et de transmettre votre message en quelques mots. C / Pas de charabia! Donnez-nous des renseignements précis, utilisez des mots simples. D / Décrivez-nous la scène, ce qui est arrivé. E / Nous saisissons le sens général de vos déclarations écrites antérieures dont vous pouvez encore modifier, si vous le souhaitez, la formulation. F / Je vous remercie des jeux de mots que vous faites à certains endroits. G / Mais ce que nous attendons de vous ce sont des détails spécifiques sur le sujet en question, sans litote ni humour; ce n'est pas notre genre. H / Insistez sur ce que vous supposez être le sens profond des événements. I / N'oubliez pas qu'il s'agit d'une enquête. J / Si vous devez citer les paroles d'un témoin, ce que nous voulons ce sont des citations précises, pas simplement des allusions vagues. K / Il est important que nous puissions garder la trace de ce qu'ont dit les gens. L / Donc, il faudra que vous précisiez certains points. M / Soyez franc et ouvert. Pas de sourires narquois. Pas de réponses qui n'engagent à rien. N / Nous voudrions savoir ce que représentent les lettres X et Y dans votre carnet d'adresses. O / Quelqu'un a versé 100 000 dollars sur votre compte le 17 juillet 1996.

3. Transcrivez la prononciation de :

A / PRETEND B / RECAP C / RECAPITULATE D / RECORD (n.) E / RECORD (v.)
F / REWORD G / SUMMARIZE H / SUPPOSE I / TOPICAL J / UNEASY

2. Grammar and punctuation

◼ Noms

adjective ['---]	adjectif	participle ['----]	participe
adverb ['--]	adverbe	passive voice	voix passive
adverbial particle	particule adverbiale	pattern	schéma, structure
adverbial phrase	locution adverbiale	phonetics [-'--]	phonétique
(round) brackets (GB) / parentheses (US)	parenthèses	phrasal verb	verbe composé
		phrase	expression
brackets (US) / square brackets (GB)	crochets	preposition [,--'--]	préposition, locution
		pronoun ['prəʊnaʊn]	pronom
circumflex	accent circonflexe	proverb ['prɒvɜːb]	proverbe
clause	proposition	PTO	T.S.V.P.
colon	deux points	punctuation	ponctuation
comma ['kɒmə]	virgule	question mark	point d'interrogation
comparative [-'---]	comparatif	quotes	guillemets
conjunction [-'--]	conjonction	reverse [-'-]	contraire
consonant ['---]	consonne	saying	dicton
dieresis	tréma	semi-colon [,--'--]	point-virgule
exclamation mark	point d'exclamation	sentence	phrase
four-letter word	gros mot	sign language	langage des signes
full stop / period (US)	point	slash / stroke	barre oblique
gender	genre	spelling	orthographe
grammar	grammaire	stress	accent
homonym ['hɒmənɪm]	homonyme	superlative [-'---]	superlatif
hyphen ['haɪfən]	trait d'union	syllable	syllabe
inverted commas	guillemets	synonym	synonyme
language	langue, langage	syntax ['--]	syntaxe
linguistics [-'--]	linguistique	tense	temps
motto	devise	verb	verbe
noun	nom	vocabulary [-'----]	vocabulaire
paragraph ['pærəgrɑːf]	paragraphe, "à la ligne"	vowel	voyelle

◼ Adjectifs

compound	composé	mute	muet
countable	dénombrable	reflexive	réfléchi
illiterate [-'----]	analphabète, illettré	substandard	peu soigné
literate ['---]	capable de lire et d'écrire; cultivé	synonymous [sɪ'nɒnəməs]	synonyme

Collocations

◼ Verbes

coin	fabriquer, inventer	*to coin new words / phrases*
misspell [-'-]	épeler de travers, mal orthographier	*to misspell a word / sb's name*
spell	épeler orthographier	*to spell a word slowly* *to spell a word correctly / wrongly*

Oral and written communication

Exercices sur le chapitre 4 (2)

1. Testez vos connaissances en traduisant les mots ou expressions ci-dessous :
A / to spell - B / to misspell - C / pattern - D / period - E / colon - F / hyphen

2. Joignez une phrase de droite à une phrase de gauche :

A. I know what can be mute
B. Of course, a sentence
C. I always use exclamation
D. Words are made up
E. You can't just put in commas,
F. Adverbial particles
G. Using slang is regarded
H. If you used sign language
I. I wish you'd stop
J. You love coining new
K. As you know, illiterate
L. The word 'car' is countable,

1. marks when I write four-letter words.
2. you wouldn't make so many mistakes.
3. semi-colons and full stops whenever you feel like it.
4. is the reverse of literate.
5. can contain more than one clause.
6. of consonants and vowels.
7. furniture isn't.
8. as substandard by some purists.
9. mottos and sayings.
10. using the phrase: 'quote' 'unquote'.
11. apart from vowels.
12. combined with certain verbs make up the phrasal verbs.

3. Conversation, talk and talks

Collocations

■ *Noms*

chat	conversation sans façon	*to have a nice / friendly chat about sth / sb*
comment ['kɒment]	commentaire	*to make a(n) appropriate / inappropriate / favourable / ironic / nasty / shrewd / sarcastic comment on sth / that...*
conversation	conversation	*to have / hold / carry a conversation with sb - to be in deep conversation - to have no conversation - to make conversation - to strike up (entamer) (a) conversation with sb - to run out of conversation (ne plus avoir rien à dire)*
delivery [-'---]	élocution, débit	*sb's clear / good / fast / slow / effective / pleasant / halting delivery*
dialogue	dialogue	*interesting / meaningful dialogue between two people - to seek / resume / interrupt (the) dialogue with sb*
farewell	adieu	*to bid (a) fond / sad farewell to sb - to make one's farewell*
to have the floor	avoir la parole	*to ask for / have / get / be given / take the floor*
grapevine	ouï-dire	*to hear sth on / through the grapevine*
hearsay	ouï-dire, propos rapportés	*it is only hearsay - hearsay evidence*
lisp	zézaiement	*to have a lisp*
loudspeaker	haut-parleur	*to hear sth over a / the loudspeaker*
monologue ['mɒnəlɒg]	monologue	*to recite / go into a long monologue*
officer ['---] / **official**	porte-parole	*a regional / trade-union / university / government officer*
orator ['ɒrətə]	orateur	*marvellous / famous public orator*
pronunciation [- ,--'--]	prononciation	*to acquire / develop / have a good / faulty / correct pronunciation*
rumour	rumeur	*to hear / confirm / deny / circulate / spread idle unfounded rumours about sth / sb / that... - rumours may circulate / spread*

slip of the tongue	lapsus	to make a slip - to be given to (making) slips
small talk	conversation de circonstance	to be good / bad at small talk / at making small talk
soap-box	tribune improvisée	soapbox orator
soliloquy [-'---]	soliloque	to indulge in frequent soliloquies
speech	discours	to make / deliver / give / improvise a speech
	parole	to lose the power of speech - clipped / impaired / slurred speech - speech defect
	élocution, façon de parler	sb's confused / unclear speech - sb's speech may become slurred / grow hesitant / show a trace of an accent
	langage, parler	the speech of local farmers - to be familiar / unfamiliar with Welsh speech
swearword	juron	to use frequent / a string of swearwords
talk(s)	conversation	to have a serious / long talk with sb about sth
talks	pourparlers	to conduct / hold / break off exploratory / high-level talks with sb about sth
talk(s)	conférence	to give a learned talk about / on sth
talk	paroles	sweet talk (flatteries) / double / fast talk (paroles trompeuses)
talk	rumeur, bruit	there is talk that... / of sb doing sth
tone	ton	to speak in an angry / arrogant / patronizing (condescendant) / serious / humorous / threatening tone
voice	voix	to say sth in a clear / dull / loud / shaking voice - to raise / drop / lose one's voice - sb's voice breaks / changes / drops - sb may have a thin (filet de voix) / high-pitched (aiguë) / piping (flûtée) / harsh / gravelly (rapeuse) / rasping (rocailleuse) / hoarse (enrouée) / hushy (rauque) voice
whisper	murmure	to speak in a whisper / in whispers

■ *Adjectifs*

articulate [-'---]	qui s'exprime bien, clair	articulate person - to be articulate
chatty	qui aime bien bavarder	chatty person - to be very chatty
	plein de petits détails	chatty letter - chatty speech / expression
colloquial [-'---]	familier, de conversation	to use a lot of colloquial expressions
halting	hâché, hésitant	halting voice / confession / English
high	aigu, haut	high sound / note
inarticulate [,--'---]	qui a du mal à s'exprimer, peu clair	inarticulate person - to be / become inarticulate (with anger)
low	bas	to speak in a low voice - a low note
loud	fort	loud noise - to speak loud
oral	oral	oral test / English
to be rumoured	être dit de qqn	to be rumoured to be / do sth / it is rumoured that...
silent	silencieux	silent film / person - to keep / remain silent
still	silencieux, calme	still night / atmosphere
talkative	bavard	talkative person

■ *Verbes*

cackle	caqueter, jacasser	to cackle away / to one's heart content
chat	bavarder gentiment	to chat about sth / with sb
chatter	bavarder, papoter	to chatter incessantly about sth
chuckle	glousser, rire	to chuckle about / over sth / to oneself / with glee (joie)

Oral and written communication　　　　　　　　　　　　　　　　　　　　　　　　　　　59

comment ['kɒment]	faire une / des remarque(s)	*to comment on sth / about / on sb / that...*
curse	jurer, blasphémer	*to curse violently / coarsely / unintelligibly*
deliver [-'--]	prononcer	*to deliver a lecture / a sermon / an emotional speech / a not guilty verdict*
drawl (out)	parler / dire d'une voix traînante	*to drawl out a few words lazily / indistinctly*
grumble	grommeler	*to grumble about sth*
hear	apprendre, entendre dire	*to hear that...*
hear of / about	entendre parler de	*to hear of sth / sb*
hear from	recevoir des nouvelles de	*to hear from sb*
hush (up)	se taire, faire taire	*to hush sb up - hush!*
lisp	zézayer	*to lisp awkwardly / affectedly / irritatingly*
mispronounce	mal prononcer	*to mispronounce a word badly / frequently*
mumble	marmonner	*to mumble one's apologies to sb / that...*
murmur	murmurer	*to murmur a name / agreement / at / against sth / that...*
mutter	grommeler	*to mutter sth to sb / / about sth / that...*
pronounce	prononcer	*to pronounce sth correctly / wrongly*
ramble (on)	radoter	*to ramble on about sth / sb ceaselessly / monotously / maddeningly*
repeat	répéter	*to repeat sth / insistently / tirelessly*
say	dire	*to say sth to sb / that...*
shake one's head	faire signe de la tête que non	*to shake one's head disapprovingly*
shout	crier	*to shout (sth) at / to sb - to shout to sb to do sth - to shout that...*
speak	parler	*to speak about sth to sb / with sb bluntly / candidly / quickly / slowly*
speak out	parler franchement	*to speak out on / against / for sth*
speak up	parler plus fort, plus clairement	*to speak up for sth* (défendre qch)
splutter	bredouiller	*to splutter in embarrassment*
stammer	bégayer, balbutier	*to stammer a few words to sb - to stammer badly*
stutter	bégayer, bredouiller	*to stutter a few words / with rage*
swear	jurer, proférer des jurons injurier	*to keep swearing coarsely / audibly* *to swear at sb*
talk	parler, discuter	*to talk about sth to sb / with sb*
talk it over	discuter	*to talk it over quietly / animatedly / informally*
tell	dire (à qqn)	*to tell a story / the news - to tell sb about sth / sb to do sth / that... / sb how to do sth / sb where to go*
utter	prononcer, proférer	*to utter a sound / a word / an oath to sb*
voice	exprimer, formuler	*to voice one's opinion / comment / criticism / anger*
whisper	chuchoter	*to whisper sth to sb / in sb's ear / about sth*

Exercices sur le chapitre 4 (3)

1. Testez vos connaissances en traduisant les mots ou expressions ci-dessous :
A / chat (n., v.) - B / to deliver - C / to mutter - D / to ramble on - E / officer - F / small talk
G / swearword

2. Remplacez, dans les trois courts textes ci-dessous, les blancs par un des mots proposés :

A / GRAPEVINE - HEARSAY - HUSH UP - LOUD - LOUDSPEAKER - TO BE RUMOURED - SPEAK OUT - VOICE (v.)
He __ _____ to have _____ the whole village's grievances, but, mind you, it's all _____, I only heard it on the _____ as it were. Nobody has _____ it _____ _____ over a _____ in a public place. Actually some people may have tried to _____ it all _____.

B / ARTICULATE - COLLOQUIAL - GRUMBLE (v.) - HALTING - INARTICULATE - LISP (v.) - LOW - SPEAK - VOICE (n.)
I don't mind you _____ in a _____, even _____ _____ or using _____ expressions but I can't stand having you _____ about everything in such an _____ fashion and _____ affectedly. Do try to be more _____ for a change.

C / COMMENT (n.) - DELIVERY (n.) - LISP (n.) - MUMBLE - ORATOR - SLOW - SOAPBOX - DRAWL (v.)
He _____ too lazily and _____ too incoherently to be called a great _____ _____. His deliberately _____ _____, due perhaps to a bad _____, draws unfavourable _____ from the crowds.

3. Traduisez en anglais :

A / J'ai entendu parler de lui, mais je n'ai jamais eu directement de ses nouvelles. B / Discutons-en. C / Ne prononcez pas mal mon nom, s'il vous plait. D / Caqueter et glousser, c'est tout ce vous savez faire! E / Je ne lui ai rien dit et lui non plus n'a rien dit. F / Vous pouvez bavarder entre vous, mais ne criez pas. G / Ce n'est pas poli de chuchoter des choses à l'oreille de son voisin.

4. Written communication

Collocations

■ *Noms*

card	carte	*calling / visiting / post / greeting card*
correspondence [,--'--]	correspondance	*to carry on / start / break off a correspondence with sb*
draft GB [drɑːft] / US [dræft]	brouillon	*to make / prepare a final / preliminary draft*
form	formulaire	*to fill in / out (GB) / up (US) a form*
handbook	manuel, guide	*a clear / comprehensive handbook for tourists / foreigners / car servicing*
highlighter *(pen)*	surligneur	*used for highlighting lines or paragraphs that are thought important*
letter	lettre	*to write / type / send / forward / send on* (faire suivre) *a business / an airmail letter*
note	note	*to make a note of sth / that...*
	courte lettre	*to write / drop / send sb a note*
notepad	bloc-note	*a small-sized notepad*
notepaper	papier à lettre	*lined / unlined notepaper*
notice	avis, notice	*to put up / paste a notice that...*
notice to quit	préavis	*to give sb a month's notice - at / on short notice - until further notice*
notice board	panneau d'affichage	*(US) bulletin board to stick notices on*
pen	plume, stylo	*ballpoint / (US) felt tip / (GB) fibre-tip / fountain pen*

Oral and written communication 61

pencil	crayon papier	*sharp / sharpened / blunt / lead (plomb) pencil*
penpal	correspondant	*also penfriend*
pocket book book	carnet	*to write down notes / addresses / things to do in one's pocket*
		- (US) pocket book also refers to a strapless handbag
quill	plume d'oie	*to write with a quill*
regards [-'-]	amitiés	*to give / send sb one's regards*
report [-'-]	rapport	*to write out / submit / make a(n) accurate / biased / unfavourable report on / about sth / sb - report card (US) / (GB) school report*
	reportage	*to write up / send in a report on sth*
scrawl	griffonnage, gribouillis	*to write / recognize / decipher sb's scrawl*
scribble	gribouillis	*hardly legible scribbles on walls*
shorthand	sténo(graphie)	*to write / take notes in shorthand*
signature ['sɪgnətʃə]	signature	*to affix / scrawl one's signature*
stationery	papeterie	*office stationery*
translation	traduction	*to make a close / free / loose translation from / into another / a foreign language - to do a translation*
translator [-'--]	traducteur	*to get a job as a translator of English into French*

■ *Adjectifs*

illegible [-'---]	illisible	*utterly / hopelessly / intentionally illegible*
legible	lisible	*perfectly / satisfactorily legible*
lined / ruled	réglé	*lined paper / pad*
unlined / unruled	uni	*unlined paper*

■ *Verbes*

decipher [dɪ'saɪfə]	déchiffrer	*to decipher documents / tablets / hieroglyphs*
draft	rédiger	*to draft a letter / bill / contract / speech*
	faire un brouillon	*to draft the first version of sth*
fill in / out (GB)	remplir	*(US) to fill up a form*
highlight	surligner	*to highlight sth with a coloured pen*
jot down	noter	*to jot down the main points / a few notes*
know	savoir, connaître	*to know sth / sb / how to do sth / that...*
look up	chercher	*to look up a(n) word / address / telephone number in a book*
notify	notifier, informer	*to notify sb of sth / that... - to notify a crime to the police*
report [-'-]	annoncer, déclarer	*to report a major discovery / profits / heavy casualties*
	faire un compte rendu	*to report a meeting / one's findings*
	faire un reportage	*to report on events / the situation*
scrawl	griffonner	*to scrawl a note / slogan*
scribble	gribouiller	*to scribble a few lines to sb*
sign	signer	*to sign one's name / a letter / a cheque*
tick	cocher, pointer	*to tick a name / a box (case)*
tick off	compter, énumérer	*to tick off items on one's fingers*
translate	traduire	*to translate from one language into another language*
underline [,--'-]	souligner	*to underline a word / one's signature*
write	écrire	*to write legibly*
write down	noter, mettre par écrit	*to write sth down - to write down what is being said*
write out	écrire, rédiger	*to write out a report*
	établir	*to write out a cheque*

Exercices sur le chapitre 4 (4)

1. Testez vos connaissances en traduisant les mots ou expressions ci-dessous :

A / greetings card - B / notepad - C / notice board - D / report - E / to report - F / to notify

2. Traduisez en anglais :

A / Envoyez une lettre courte, sur du papier à lettres, uni ou réglé, plutôt que le brouillon d'une longue lettre que personne ne peut déchiffrer, qui est illisible parce qu'écrite en sténo! B / Remplissez le questionnaire concernant le préavis; cochez les cases appropriées; consultez le manuel. C / Soulignez ou surlignez, comme vous voulez, les points essentiels que vous avez notés dans votre carnet. D / Cherchez les mots à traduire dans un dictionnaire. E / Transmettez mes amitiés à votre correspondant. F / Ne gribouillez pas votre signature. G) Et faites moi un chèque.

3. Remettez les lettres dans l'ordre :

WONK - NIGS - NEP - PLINCE - LIQUL

5. Arguing

Collocations

■ *Noms*

address [-'-]	allocution, discours	*to deliver / give a(n) formal / moving / inaugural address about sth to sb*
advice	conseil(s)	*to give / act on / follow / take / disregard sb's friendly / misleading advice*
argument ['---]	argument	*to drive home / put forward / refute a groundless / weak / strong / compelling / sound argument about / against sth / that...*
	vive discussion, dispute	*to have / get into / settle / start / break off a heated / passionate / loud argument - an argument breaks out about / over sth with sb*
blunder	gaffe, bourde	*to make / commit a fatal / glaring* (énorme) */ serious blunder - it may be a blunder to do sth*
brick	énorme gaffe	*to drop a brick or a clanger*
case [s]	cas	*as is the case - as the case may be - a case in point* (un exemple caractéristique)
claim	affirmation	*sb's claim that... - to make a bold / unfounded claim*
conversation	conversation	*to have / carry / join in / break off / start an animated / serious conversation about sth with sb - to bug / tap* (mettre sur écoute) *a conversation*
discussion	discussion	*to have / start / bring up / a lively / candid / serious discussion about sth*
explanation	explication	*to give / offer / provide / turn down a convincing / unconvincing / superficial explanation - sb's explanation for sth / that...*
hint	allusion	*to drop / give a broad / obvious / subtle hint (to sb / about sth) - to take a hint* (comprendre)
joke	plaisanterie	*to crack / tell / take / indulge in a poor / bawdy* (grivoise) */ coarse / sick / stale joke about sth / sb*

Oral and written communication 63

message	message	*to give / deliver / get / send / leave a clear / coded message from sb / that...*
messenger	messager	*to dispatch a messenger - messenger service* (messagerie)
point	fait	*to come to the point* (en venir au fait)
standpoint	point de vue	*from a practical / specific / narrow / broad / Western / French standpoint*
suggestion	suggestion, proposition	*to make / offer / have / call for / reject an appropriate / interesting / practical / impractical suggestion about sth / about doing sth / that...*

■ *Adjectifs*

blunt	brusque, direct	*blunt person / question / reply*
convincing [-'--]	convaincant	*convincing person / argument*
corny	banal, niais	*corny joke / behaviour*
be right	avoir raison	*to be right about sth / sb / to do sth*
satisfied	convaincu	*to be satisfied with sth / that...*
wrong	avoir tort, se tromper	*to be wrong about sth / sb / to do sth*

■ *Verbes*

account for	expliquer, rendre compte de	*to account for sth / sb / sb doing sth*
address [-'-]	s'adresser à	*to address sb as (Mr So and So)*
advise	conseiller	*to strongly advise sth / doing sth / sb / sb about sth / sb to do sth / sb that...*
argue ['--]	argumenter	*to argue about / for / against sth*
	discuter	*to argue calmly / heatedly about / over sth with sb*
	se disputer	*to keep arguing about sth with sb*
assert [-'-]	affirmer, maintenir	*to assert one's innocence / good faith / that...*
beg	supplier, demander	*to beg for mercy / forgiveness / sb to do sth / sth of sb*
beware	prendre garde, se méfier	*beware of the dog / sth / what you say / of doing sth!*
claim	prétendre, affirmer	*to claim to do sth / that...*
conceal	cacher, dissimuler	*to conceal sth from sb*
confirm	confirmer	*to confirm sth / that...*
convince	convaincre	*to convince sb of sth / that...*
discuss	discuter de	*to discuss sth with sb*
eavesdrop ['iːvzdrɒp]	écouter de façon indiscrète	*to eavesdrop on sb / on sb's conversation*
entice	séduire, attirer	*to entice sb with sth / sb into sth / into doing sth*
entreat	implorer, supplier	*to entreat sb to do*
explain	expliquer	*to explain sth to sb / that... / why... / how to do sth*
expound	exposer	*to expound sth to sb at some length*
hint	faire allusion, insinuer	*to hint at sth / that...*
infer	déduire	*to infer sth from sth / that...*
mention	mentionner, parler de	*to mention sth to sb / that... / where / how...*
persuade [-'-]	persuader	*to persuade sb of sth / sb to do sth / that...*
suggest [-'-]	suggérer, proposer	*to suggest sth to sb / doing sth / to sb that...*

Exercices sur le chapitre 4 (5)

1. Testez vos connaissances en traduisant les mots ou expressions ci-dessous :

A / satisfied - B / to mention - C / to confirm - D / address (n.) - E / messenger - F / to conceal
G / standpoint - H / to assert - I / beware - J / to persuade

2. Joignez une phrase de droite à une phrase de gauche (pour deux ou trois phrases, il peut y avoir deux possibilités, le bon sens cependant limite le choix) :

A. None of the arguments he put forward
B. I begged him to
C. Who can have enticed you into
D. I kept dropping hints about his tactlessness
E. I wish you'd come to the point
F. Beware of
G. Why don't you suggest
H. I would strongly advise you

1. but he obviously could not take a hint.
2. and account for your behaviour last night.
3. committing a fatal blunder.
4. proved very convincing.
5. addressing the rioters yourself?
6. to act on my friendly advice.
7. eavesdropping on a private conversation?
8. stop cracking corny jokes when there's company.

3. Mots croisés :

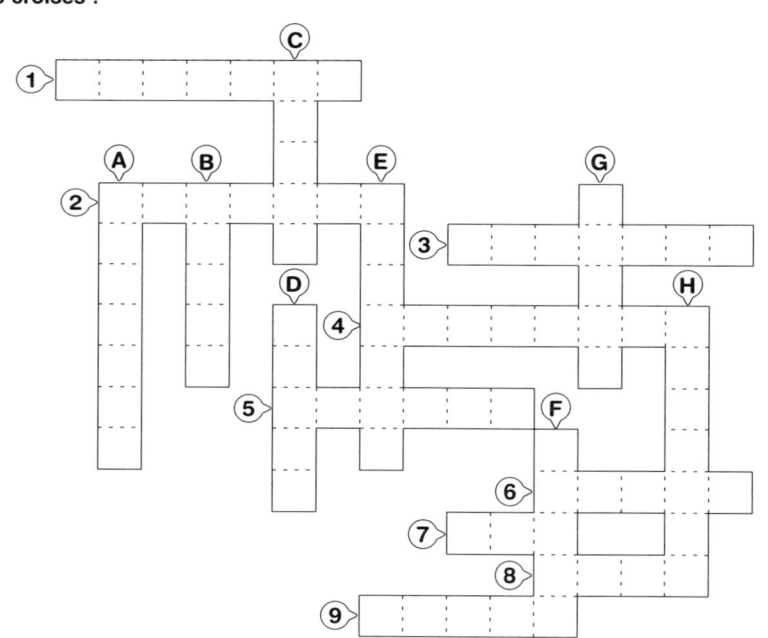

Clues :

<u>across</u> : 1. hide (v.) - 2. give a detailed explanation - 3. formal speech 4. persuade - 5. declare forcefully - 6. deduce - 7. ask with great eagerness - 8. suggest or mention indirectly - 9. frank, not trying to be polite

<u>down</u> : A. make things clear - B. to come to the ..... is to deal with what is being discussed - C. quarrel - D. affirm - E. to talk about sth with others - F. correct (adj.) - G. not correct - H. attempt to persuade sb to do sth

Oral and written communication

6. Agreeing

Collocations

■ *Noms*

acknowledgement(s) [ək'nɒlɪdʒmənt]	reconnaissance	*to make an acknowledgement of one's errors - in acknowledgement of sth*
	remerciements	*the acknowledgements at the end of a book*
agreement	accord	*to come to / carry out / work out / break / denounce a binding / tacit / tentative agreement on / about sth with sb*
approval [-'--]	approbation	*to give / show / meet with one's / sb's unqualified* (sans réserve) *approval of sth / to do sth*
point	argument	*to take / see sb's point* (voir où qqn veut en venir) */ to have got a point* (avoir de bons arguments) */ not to see the point of sth* (l'intérêt de qch) */ to make one's point* (exprimer clairement son point de vue)

■ *Adjectifs*

great	formidable	*great friend / idea*

■ *Verbes*

acknowledge [ək'nɒlɪdʒ]	reconnaître, admettre	*to acknowledge doing sth / sb to be sth / (to sb) that... - to acknowledge receipt of sth*
agree	être d'accord	*to agree on / about sth with sb / to do sth / that...*
apologize [-'---]	s'excuser	*to apologize to sb for sth / for doing sth*
approve	approuver	*to approve wholeheartedly / unreservedly of sth*
recognize ['---]	reconnaître	*to recognize that...*

■ *Adverbs*

admittedly	il faut bien l'admettre
great!	super!
"not at all"	"je vous en prie"

Exercices sur le chapitre 4 (6)

1. Testez vos connaissances en traduisant les mots ou expressions ci-dessous :

A / Merci mille fois — Je vous en prie.   B / Rencontrer l'approbation de qqn.
C / Accuser réception d'une lettre.   D / Voir où qqn veut en venir.

2. Traduisez en anglais :

A / Il a reconnu avoir volé l'argent. B / Il s'est excusé d'avoir succombé à la tentation auprès de ses parents qui, de toute façon, n'approuvaient pas la façon dont il vivait. C / Il est arrivé à un accord avec la police : s'il rendait l'argent plus des intérêts, il n'irait pas en prison. D / Tout le monde, il faut bien le reconnaître, n'était pas d'accord avec cette solution que lui trouvait formidable. E / Il avait sans aucun doute de bons arguments et que si on le laissait exprimer clairement son point de vue, il convaincrait les gens.

7. Disagreeing

Collocations

■ *Noms*

anger	colère	to arouse / feel / express / vent (donner libre cours) sb's / one's righteous / unbridled (incontrôlé) anger - a(n) fit / outburst of anger at sth / sb / at doing sth
claim	titre (à qch), revendication	to lay claim / stake (out) one's claim to sth (revendiquer)
critic	critique (personne)	a harsh / unkind / impartial art critic
criticism ['----]	critique	to arouse / come in for / express hostile / unsparing criticism - to level (diriger) criticism at (contre) sb
critique [-'-]	critique (écrit)	a scathing (acerbe) critique of society / of a political system
deadlock	impasse	to reach / come to / break a deadlock
denial [dɪˈnaɪ‿əl]	démenti	to issue a strong / unqualified denial of sth / that...
difference	différend	to settle / set aside minor / major unreconcilable differences
disagreement	désaccord	to express / resolve a marked / serious / slight disagreement
dispute [-'-]	conflit, dispute	to stir up / start / arbitrate / resolve a harsh / public / industrial / labour dispute
dissent [-'-]	désaccord, avis contraire	to express / brook (accepter) / tolerate no dissent from sb
emphasis [ˈemfəsɪs]	accent, importance	to lay particular emphasis on sth / on doing sth
exception	offense	to take strong exception to (s'offusquer) sth / to doing sth
exposé [ekˈpəʊseɪ]	révélations	to publish / publicize a lucid / complete exposé of sb's behaviour / doings
exposure	récit, révélation	public exposure of crime / hypocrisy / sb (dénonciation)
feelings	rancune	'no hard feelings' ("sans rancune")
feud [fjuːd]	querelle	to stir up a blood / family / personal feud
fit	accès, crise	a fit of anger - to have / throw a fit
innuendo [ˌɪnjuˈendəʊ]	insinuation	to cast / make a malevolent innuendo about sb / that...
mistake	erreur, faute	to make / rectify a serious / fatal / foolish / glaring / slight mistake
misunderstanding	malentendu	to cause / lead to / clear up a serious / slight misunderstanding about / over sth with sb
objection	objection	to make / raise / withdraw a strong objection to sth / (sb) doing sth
mind	état d'esprit	to speak one's mind / give a piece of one's mind
point	argument	to make one's point / to be off / to the point - a moot (controversé) point
qualification	réserve, nuance	to express strong qualifications - an approval without qualification
remark [-'-]	remarque	to make / drop a(n) inane (inepte) scathing (cinglant) / slanderous (calomnieux) / timely / witty remark
resentment	rancune	to arouse / feel / harbour / express bitter / deep resentment about / at sth / sb / that...
reservation	réserve, doute	to have / share a mental reservation about sth / sb
row [raʊ]	vive dispute	to have a terrible / family row over sth with sb
wrath [rɒθ]	(lit.) colère	to bring down / incur sb's wrath

Oral and written communication

■ Adjectifs

angry	en colère	to be angry at sth / sb / with sb / with sb for sth / with sb for doing sth
contradictory [,--'---]	contradictoire	contradictory promises / statements
disputable	contestable	disputable claims / statements
fierce	acharné	fierce discussion / argument
furious	furieux	to be furious about / over sth / at (US) / with sb / to do sth / that...
indignant [-'--]	indigné	indignant glance - to be / become indignant at / about sth / that...
mistaken	dans l'erreur	to be mistaken about sth
objectionable [-'-----]	inadmissible, désagréable	objectionable views / person / arguments / love scenes in a film
positive ['pɒzətɪv]	sûr, affirmatif	to be positive about sth / that...
questionable	contestable	highly questionable methods / activities / policy
resentful [rɪ'zentfl]	plein de ressentiment	to be resentful about sth (en avoir gros sur le cœur)

■ Verbes

challenge	contester, récuser	to challenge sb's authority / idea / plan
claim	réclamer, revendiquer	to claim responsibility for sth / one's innocence (clamer) / credit for sth / to own sth (affirmer posséder) / to be the owner / that...
contradict [,--'-]	contredire	to contradict sb / sth / everything
criticize ['---]	critiquer	to criticize sth / sb for sth / sb for doing sth
cry out	protester	to cry out against sth / sb doing sth
cut in	interrompre, couper	to cut in on sb
deny	démentir, nier	to flatly / categorically deny sth / doing sth / that...
differ	ne pas être d'accord	to differ on / about sth with sb
disagree	ne pas être d'accord	to completely disagree about / on sth with sb
disappprove [,--'-]	désapprouver	to strongly disapprove of sth / sb / sb doing sth
dispute [-'-]	contester	to dispute sth - not to dispute that...
dissent [-'-]	marquer son désaccord	to dissent from sth / sb's view / idea
emphasize	mettre l'accent sur, souligner	to emphasize sth / the importance / the necessity of sth / that...
explode	démontrer la fausseté de	to explode a(n) myth / theory / assumption
expose	démasquer	to expose sb / a scandal
fall out	se disputer	to fall out with sb over sth
grunt	grogner	to grunt a few words to sb / to sb that...
have it / sth out	s'expliquer	to have it out with sb
hit the roof	piquer une colère	to hit the roof frequently / over nothing
infuriate	rendre furieux	it infuriates sb to do sth
interrupt [,--'-]	interrompre	to rudely / abruptly interrupt sb
irritate	irriter	it greatly irritates sb to do sth
madden	mettre en colère	it maddens sb to do sth
misinterpret [,mɪsɪn'tɜːprɪt]	mal interpréter	to badly misinterpret sth / sb's words
mistake	confondre	to mistake sth / sb for sth / sb else
object [-'-] (to)	protester, s'élever contre	to strongly object to sth / sth being done / sb doing sth / that...
qualify	nuancer	to qualify one's opinion / a statement
question	mettre en doute	to question sth / sb / sb's good faith / right / whether...
remark [-'-]	faire remarquer, faire un commentaire	to remark on sth - to remark (to sb) that...
resent [-'-]	être contrarié de	to strongly / bitterly resent sth / doing sth / sb doing sth
squabble ['skwɒbl]	se quereller	to squabble endlessly about / over sth with sb

Exercices sur le chapitre 4 (7)

1. Testez vos connaissances en traduisant les mots ou expressions ci-dessous :

A / to qualify - B / to differ - C / to lay claim to sth - D / exposure - E / innuendo - F / to mistake
G / to be to the point

2. Mots croisés :

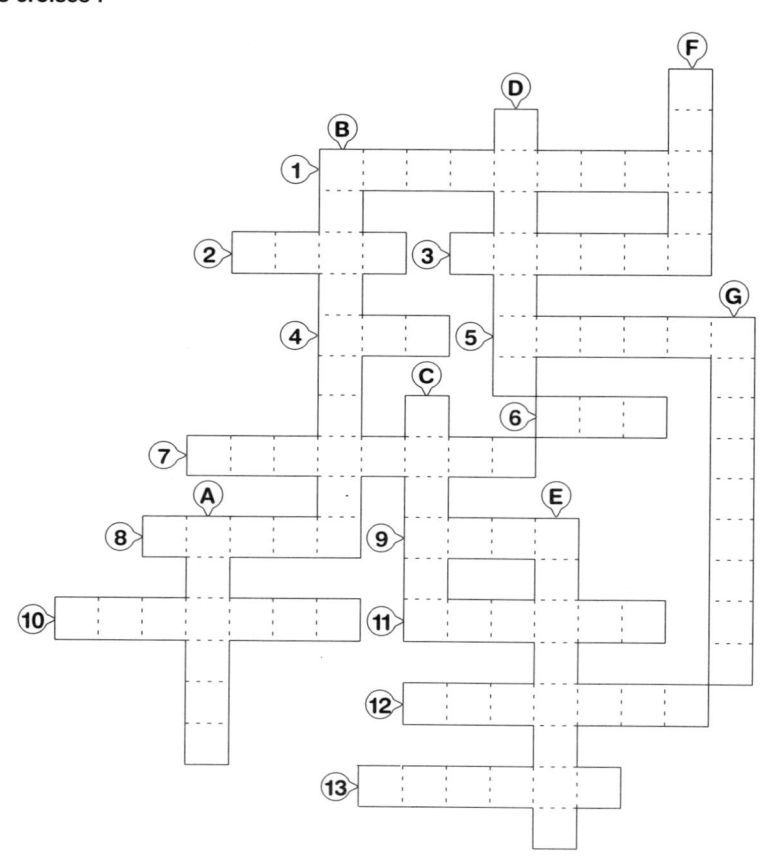

Clues :

<u>across</u> : 1. defy - 2. say that sth is not true - 3. passionate - 4. quarrel - 5. disclose, make public - 6. in good physical condition - 7. constructive - 8. express oneself in a low, guttural voice - 9. prolonged or bitter quarrel - 10. disagree - 11. say by way of comment - 12. to show sth to be false - 13. express opposition

<u>down</u> : A. be annoyed by sth - B. express the opposite of what sb says - C. have a different opinion - D. asserted, affirmed - E. a situation in which no progress is made by either party - F. give sb a ..... of one's mind is say what one really thinks of them - G. take ..... to sth is be annoyed and shocked by sth

3. Traduisez en anglais :

A / La critique très favorable écrite par ce critique contredit toutes les réserves, les insinuations malveillantes et les objections sur lesquelles il avait mis l'accent peu de temps avant dans un autre journal. B / Il avait dû nourrir une rancune profonde et amère et décidé alors de dire ce qu'il

Oral and written communication

avait sur le cœur. C / Puis il avait probablement réfléchi et il avait nuancé son jugement. D / Il n'était plus aussi furieux et indigné. E / Ce qui lui avait paru contestable, inadmissible ne l'était plus autant. F / Avait-il eu, avant le premier article, une violente dispute avec l'auteur? G / Les arguments de l'auteur lui avaient-ils paru hors de propos? H / Peut-être le critique, alors, ne pouvait-il pas supporter d'avis contraire de qui que ce soit? I / Quelqu'un avait-il réussi à régler leur différend? J / Y avait-il eu malentendu? K / De quoi le critique s'était-il offusqué? L / Qu'est-ce qui l'avait rendu furieux? M / L'auteur s'était-il attiré la colère du critique en l'interrompant au cours d'une conversation? N / Le critique avait-il alors piqué une colère? O / L'auteur avait-il menacé le critique de publier certaines révélations sur sa conduite privée? On ne le saura jamais.

4. Choisissez :

A / In a fit of anger / dispute / difference he disputed / disapproved / disagreed for / of / at the contents of the book. B / "I'll explode / fall out / remark his dangerous theories", he said. C / He must have misinterpreted / remarked / questioned on / at / about the shortcomings of that book and that was probably why they exploded / exposed / squabbled for days and days afterwards.

8. Quarrelling

Collocations

■ *Noms*

abuse (U) [ə'bjuːs]	insultes, injures	*to shower verbal abuse on sb - to hurl / shriek abuse at sb. - a hail of abuse*
bastard ['bɑːstəd]	salaud	*to be a bit of a bastard*
son of a bitch	fils de pute	*to call sb a son of a bitch*
names	insultes	*to call sb names*
curse	juron	*to utter / mumble a very bad / blasphemous curse*
insult ['--]	insulte	*to avenge* (venger) *a nasty insult on sb - to hurl an insult at sb* (accabler qqn d'injures) *- to add insult to injury* (dépasser les bornes)
nonsense ['--]	bêtise(s)	*to talk utter nonsense - it is nonsense to do sth*
oath [əʊθ]	juron	*to mutter / utter an oath*
passion	colère	*to get into a passion*
quarrel ['kwɒrəl]	querelle, dispute	*to start / pick / patch up / settle a bitter quarrel about sth with sb - a quarrel breaks out / starts / ensues*
rubbish	conneries	*to talk rubbish*
temper	humeur, colère	*to fly into a temper*
uproar ['ʌprɔː]	tumulte, tollé	*to create / cause / silence an unending uproar over sth - an uproar may mount / subside*

■ *Adjectifs*

bloody (GB)	foutu, sacré	*bloody fool / car / hell*
fucking (US)	de merde	*fucking idiot / car / hell*
damned (GB)	satané	*damned cheek* (culot)
hot-tempered	colérique	*hot-tempered person*
quarrelsome	querelleur	*quarrelsome person / temper*
quick-tempered	emporté	*quick-tempered person*

■ *Verbes*

abuse [ə'bjuːz]	insulter, injurier	*to shamefully / grossly abuse sb*
curse	maudire	*to curse sb for sth / for doing sth*
insult [-'-]	insulter	*to repeatedly / vilely / outrageously insult sb*
quarrel	se quereller	*to quarrel about / over sth with sb*
scold [skəʊld]	gronder	*to scold sb for sth / for doing sth*
shut up	faire taire	*to shut sb up*

Exercices sur le chapitre 4 (8)

1. Testez vos connaissances en traduisant les mots ou expressions ci-dessous :

A / to scold - B / to shut up - C / maudire - D / insulter - E / gronder - F / dire des bêtises G / conneries

2. Traduisez en français :

— Qu'est-ce qui a bien pu causer un tel tumulte? — Une querelle qui a éclaté entre deux hommes colériques qui se sont mis soudain en colère, se sont lancé à la tête des injures et des jurons grossiers, se sont insultés, se sont traité de sacrés salauds et de fils de pute de merde?

5
Degree

1. Important, unimportant

Collocations

Noms

climax ['klaɪmæks]	apogée, point culminant	*to reach / come to / work up* (s'acheminer vers) *to a dramatic* (spectaculaire) *climax - to bring matters to a climax*
degree	degré, proportion	*a job may demand a high degree of skill - there may be some degree of truth in sth - sth may increase to an alarming degree*
highlight	grand moment, événement	*the news highlights* (les grands titres) *- sth may prove to be the highlight of the day*
trifle	vétille, bagatelle	*to worry / quarrel over trifles*

Adjectifs

acute	aigu, vif	*acute pain / sense of guilt / distress*
chief	principal, qui vient en premier	*chief topic / interest / opponent / cause of sth*
comprehensive [,--'---]	complet, qui donne une vue d'ensemble	*comprehensive description / training / list*
definite ['---]	précis, net	*definite answer / time / place / view / plan / evidence*
drastic	radical, draconien	*drastic course of action / measures*
elementary [,--'---]	élémentaire	*elementary precautions / level / question*
essential	essentiel	*essential point / feature / characteristic - sth may be essential to sb - it is essential (for sb) to do sth / that ...*
excruciating [-'----]	extrêmement douloureux, intense	*excruciating fear / embarrassment / pain / cramp*
exhaustive	approfondi, qui épuise le sujet	*exhaustive inquiry / study / research*
extensive [-'--]	étendu, important	*extensive damage / knowledge / media coverage*
exquisite [-'--]	intense	*exquisite pain / pleasure / thrill*
foremost	premier, le plus en vue	*foremost expert / painter of his time*
full-blown	complet, total	*full-blown war / military operation / doctor* (diplômé)
full-length	en pied	*full-length portrait / mirror*
	long	*full-length dress / film / novel*
	de tout son long	*to lie full-length on the floor*
hard-and-fast	strict, absolu	*hard-and-fast rules*
immaterial [,--'---]	peu important	*sth is immaterial (to sb) - it is immaterial (to sb) what sb does - it is immaterial to do one thing or the other*
important	important	*important point / part* (rôle) */ book / news - sth may be important to / for sb - it is important (for sb) to to do sth / that ...*
leading	important, prépondérant	*leading man / lady* (premier rôle) */ industries* (de pointe) */ organisation / figure* (personnage)
main	principal, le plus important	*main course* (plat) */ entrance / reason / role*

major	principal, majeur	*major subject / problem / road / firm / role* (important)
minor	peu important	*minor issue / flaw / part / share*
momentous	capital, important, lourd de conséquences	*momentous occasion / change / decision / risk*
overall	global, d'ensemble	*overall impression / pattern of sb's life*
paramount ['---]	primordial	*paramount importance / interest / asset* (atout)
prevalent ['---]	dominant, général, courant, répandu	*the mood / atmosphere / theory / fashion / ideas prevalent at a certain time and place - sth may be very prevalent* (courant)
serious	grave, sérieux	*serious illnes / mistake / problem / threat*
sharp	net, bien défini	*sharp contrast / dividing line*
sheer	pur, à l'état pur	*sheer nonsense / coincidence - by sheer accident - to do sth through / out of sheer boredom*
significant [-'---]	très important	*significant discovery / event / change / damage / amount*
supreme [-'-]	suprême, remarquable	*supreme achievement / importance / effort / skill*
thorough ['θʌrə]	approfondi, minutieux	*thorough person / knowledge / search / cross-examination*
tremendous	considérable, très grand	*tremendous eater* (gros) */ meal* (énorme) */ success / improvement / help / feeling of pride*
trifling	insignifiant, peu important	*trifling error / value / matter / misunderstanding / sum of money*
trivial	banal, insignifiant, dérisoire	*trivial task / offence / loss / activity / information*
unimportant	sans importance	*relatively unimportant issue / feature of a system - sth may be / seem unimportant (to sb) - it is unimportant what sb does / how he does it*
utmost	le plus grand	*utmost seriousness / secrecy / respect / importance*
utter	absolu, total	*utter fool* (parfait imbécile) */ scandal / stranger / disregard of consequences - to talk utter rubbish*

■ *Verbes*

blow up	grossir, exagérer	*sth may be blown up out of all porportion*
enhance GB [ɪn'hɑːns] / US [ɪn'hæns]	améliorer, rehausser, mettre en valeur	*sth may enhance the beauty / value of sth / the beauty of sb / sb's reputation / chances / performance*
escalate ['---]	(s')intensifier, (s')aggraver	*a conflict / prices may escalate - sth may escalate a problem*
heighten ['haɪtn]	augmenter, accroître	*sb's interest in sth may heighten - sth may heighten the effect of sth / sb's interest in sth*
magnify	amplifier, grossir	*sb may try to magnify an incident / a problem - sb's fears may magnify the true dangers - problems may be magnified by poverty / racial tensions - sb's remarks may be magnified out of all proportion - sth may magnify a sound / vision*
matter	avoir de l'importance	*sth / sb / sb's attitude may matter very much (to sb) - it does not matter what sb thinks or says about sth*
prevail	régner, avoir cours	*rumours / conditions prevailing somewhere - a tradition / doctrine may prevail at a certain period*

■ *Adverbes*

as one man	unanimement, comme un seul homme, tous ensemble	*a crowd may rise to its feet as one man - as one man, the delegates made for the exit*
at all costs / at any cost	à tout prix	*sth must be done at all costs / not be done at any cost*
clean	complètment	*to clean forget sth - to go clean through sth - to get clean away* (disparaîtrre sans laisser de trace)
dead	exactement, en plein, complètement	*to be dead right / drunk - sth may be dead easy / slow*
far	de loin	*far better / worse - to be by far / far and away the better of the two*

Degree

flat	exactement	*to do sth in two minutes flat*
	complètement	*to be flat broke / out of money*
flat / flatly	catégoriquement	*to flatly refuse / deny sth - to turn sth down flat*
full-blast	à plein volume	*to turn on the radio full-blast*
a hell of a lot	énormément	*a hell of a lot of work / money*
hard	avec intensité, fort, dur	*to work / run / push / breathe / try / think hard*
like hell	vachement, comme un fou	*sth may hurt like hell* *to shout / run like hell*
jolly	rudement, drôlement	*jolly hard / good - to jolly well have to do sth* (ne pas avoir le choix)
nothing but	ne ... que, rien d'autre que	*nothing but a miracle / the best would do - to do nothing but sleep / cause trouble*
nothing short of sth	rien de moins que	*sb's action may have been nothing short of heroic - nothing short of a miracle can save him*
to a man	tous, sans exception	*all the senators present, to a man, voted in favour - people may discover, to a man, that ...*
with a vengeance	très fort, à tout va	*it may be raining with a vengeance - to work at sth with a vengeance*

Exercices sur le chapitre 5 (1)

1. Testez vos connaissances en traduisant les mots suivants :

A / excruciating - B / chief - C / utter - D / utmost - E / momentous - F / major

2. Choisissez l'adverbe ou la locution adverbiale qui convient :

A / It was raining - as one man / to a man / with a vengeance - on that day.
B / He was - scarcely / slightly / namely - drunk and could not walk straight.
C / She was - merely / flatly / full-blast - a child when her parents died.
D / He turned the offer - flat / dead / far.

3. Traduisez en anglais :

A / Cela n'a pas d'importance ce qu'il a dit hier soir. Pour moi, en tout cas, ce n'est pas important. B / Ce serait de la pure bêtise de donner à cet incident, à tout prix, une couverture médiatique étendue. C / Cela ne ferait qu'aggraver un problème suffisamment sérieux, étant donné l'atmosphère qui règne dans la galerie en ce moment. D / C'est vrai qu'il y a entre vous et ce peintre un malentendu qu'on aurait tort de considérer comme peu important. E / C'est vrai que cet artiste est un raseur absolu, un gros mangeur dont l'intérêt primordial dans la vie est la bouffe (grub). F / Mais c'est le peintre le plus en vue de notre époque; il a peint un nombre non négligeable de tableaux qui sont des réussites remarquables. G / L'impression générale de laisser-aller (scruffiness) qu'il donne est probablement la raison principale de l'aversion qu'on éprouve à son égard. H / Sa seule présence, la simple mention de son nom cause à certains un sentiment aigu de gêne. I / D'autres lui reprochent de gagner trop d'argent - comme si un artiste devait forcément avoir juste de quoi vivre et ne gagner que 500 dollars par mois. J / D'autres encore souhaiteraient le voir, victime d'une crise cardiaque avérée, étendu de tout son long dans son atelier. K / Dresser la liste complète de ses défauts, se livrer à une recherche minutieuse de tous ses actes, dénicher des preuves précises sur sa vie privée, savoir s'il a ou non un léger accent étranger, ce serait une tâche dérisoire. L / L'hostilité à son égard se calmera un jour... lorsqu'il sera mort.

2. Average, moderate, mere, standard

Collocations

■ *Noms*

average	moyenne	*on (an / the) average - sth may be above / below average - to work out* (calculer) *an average*
scale	échelle, étendue, envergure	*to do sth on a large / small scale - a map may be on a scale of one to ten*
standard	niveau, norme	*to reach a low / high standard - sth may raise / lower the academic* (universitaire) *standard - sth may be up to / below standard - sb / sth may set a standard - by any / anybody's standards* (indiscutablement)

■ *Adjectifs*

average	moyen	*average intelligence / size / marks* (notes) *- sth may be just average*
bare	tout juste suffisant, très faible, léger	*bare majority / possibility / minimum - to make a bare living* (gagner tout juste de quoi vivre)
faint	faible léger	*faint attempt / protest* *faint accent / sound / feeling of disgust*
fair	assez bon, passable	*to get a 'fair' at school - sth may be fair to middling* (pas mal) *- to have a fair chance of success - sth may be in fair condition* (en assez bon état)
	non négligeable	*fair amount / number / pace* (bonne allure) */ degree of competence / size*
gentle	léger, modéré	*gentle rain / exercise / movement / knock on the door*
intermediate [ˌ--'---]	intermédiaire de niveau moyen, peu avancé	*intermediate range* (portée) */ stage* (étape, phase) *intermediate student / course*
light	léger	*light reading / conversation / traffic / sleeper*
mere	simple, rien de plus que, rien d'autre que	*a mere coincidence - the mere thought / mention / presence of sth / sb may cause sb great distress - sb may still be a mere child - to earn a mere 500 dollars a month*
mild	léger, modéré	*mild puinshment / criticism / weather* (doux)
moderate	modéré, mesuré moyen, assez médiocre	*moderate person / drinker / view* (opinion) */ prices / increase* *moderate performance / ability*
near	très proche de, quasi-total	*near disaster / darkness - it was a near miss / thing* (on l'a échappé belle, il s'en est fallu de peu) *- near fall / tragedy*
sketchy	vague, sommaire superficiel	*sketchy description / research / work / memory* *sketchy knowledge of sth*
slight	léger, peu grave	*slight headache / accent / accident / incident / disadvantage*
standard	ordinaire, normal standard, courant, répandu	*standard size / height / procedure* *it may be standard practice to do sth*

■ *Verbes*

play down	minimiser	*to play down a danger / an incident / consequences / an aspect of sth*
subside	diminuer d'intensité, se calmer	*danger / a noise / pain / rage / anger / fear / hostility may subside after a time*

Degree

■ *Adverbes*

to a certain extent [-'-] / degree	dans une certaine mesure	to a large extent	dans une grande mesure
up to a point	jusqu'à un certain point	virtually	pratiquement

Collocations

barely	à peine, tout juste	*barely possible / fifty / sixty years old - to have barely done sth when ... - to be barely able to read and write - barely furnished room* (pauvrement meublée)
fairly	relativement, assez	*fairly good / certain / hard - to sing fairly well - sth may be fairly accurate / complicated*
	absolument, véritablement	*to be fairly mad with rage - sth / sb may fairly upset sb - to fairly blow up* (exploser de colère)
hardly	à peine	*he can hardly speak English - he hardly ever drinks coffee* (presque jamais) *- he hardly ate anything* (presque rien)
mainly	surtout, principalement	*mainly because of sth - mainly women and children*
merely	simplement	*not merely because ... but also because ... - to be merely a beginner* (simple débutant) *- to merely glance at sth* (se contenter de jeter un coup d'œil)
namely	à savoir, c'est-à-dire	*famous scientists, namely Smith, Robinson and Brown*
roughly ['rʌfli]	approximativement	*roughly 5 o'clock - to be roughly sb's age*
scarcely ['skeəsli]	à peine	*to be scarcely more than a child - to scarcely see sb - to scarcely have done sth when ...*
slightly	légèrement, un peu	*slightly drunk / better - to know sb only slightly* (vaguement)
a trifle	un peu	*a trifle easier than expected / too difficult - to be a trifle breathless*

Exercices sur le chapitre 5 (2)

1. Testez vos connaissances en traduisant les mots ou expressions ci-dessous:

A / faint - B / light - C / mild - D / to play down - E / barely - F / to a man - G / virtually H / sketchy

2. Traduisez les expressions ou phrases suivantes en vous reportant aux exemples et collocations données dans la colonne de droite du vocabulaire :

A / Il n'est pratiquement rien arrivé les cinq premières minutes. B / Seul un miracle pourrait le sauver. C / C'est un assez bon film. D / Il était absolument fou de rage. E / Il avait approximativement le même âge qu'elle. F / Grossir un problème. G / Minimiser un danger. H / Une découverte très importante. I / Un souvenir vague. J / Des prix modérés. K / Une prestation médiocre. L / De faibles protestations. M / Un léger coup à la porte. N / Intelligence moyenne. O / Atteindre un niveau élevé. P / Calculer une moyenne. Q / Un jour sur deux, en moyenne. R / Une punition légère. S / Il s'en est fallu de peu.

3. Traduisez en anglais :

A / Il avait le sommeil léger et même lorsque la circulation était fluide, il prenait, chaque soir, des précautions que lui considérait comme élémentaires mais que moi je trouvais un tantinet agaçantes. B / Mais à quoi bon se quereller pour des vétilles?

6
The world

1. Space

■ *Noms*

acid rain	pluies acides	**greenhouse effect** [-'-]	effet de serre
carbon dioxide [daɪˈɒksaɪd]	gaz carbonique	**oil-slick**	nappe de pétrole
ecology	écologie	**ozone layer** [ˈəʊzəʊn] [ˈleɪə]	couche d'ozone

Collocations

atmosphere ['---]	atmosphère	*rarefied / polluted atmosphere*
environment [-'---]	environnement	*to prevent / protect / clean up the environment*
fumes	vapeurs, fumées	*to inhale / breathe in gas (US) / petrol (GB) fumes*
inhabitant [-'---]	habitant	*a city of two million inhabitants*
moon	lune	*the new / full / half / quarter / moon wanes* (décroît) */ waxes* (croît)
moonlight	clair de lune	*to do sth by / in the moonlight*
nature	nature	*to harness* (exploiter) *the forces of nature*
planet	planète	*planets revolve / move round a star / the sun*
Pole	pôle	*the North / South Pole*
sky	ciel	*cloudless / overcast / dull / starry sky - the sky may cloud over / clear up*
star	étoile	*a bright / falling / shooting star shines / twinkles*
sun	soleil	*the blazing / hot sun rises / sets / shines / beats down* (taper) *- to sit in the sun*
surroundings	environnement	*to be indifferent to one's surroundings*
universe	univers	*in every part of the known universe*
waste (U)	déchets	*nuclear / radioactive / toxic waste*
wildlife	faune (et flore)	*wildlife park* (réserve naturelle)
world	monde	*to travel round the world - to believe in the next world*

south [saʊθ]	(le) sud	**eastbound**	qui se dirige vers l'est
north	(le) nord	**westbound**	qui se dirige vers l'ouest
southbound	qui se dirige vers le sud	**eastward**	vers l'est
northbound	qui se dirige vers le nord	**westward**	vers l'ouest
southward [ˈsaʊθwəd]	vers le sud	**eastern**	de l'est, oriental
northward	vers le nord	**western**	de l'ouest, occidental
southern [ˈsʌðn]	du sud, du Midi, méditerranéen	**in the east / north / south / west**	à l'est / au nord / au sud / à l'ouest
northern	du nord, nordique	**to the east / north / south / west**	à / vers l'est / au nord ou vers le nord / au sud ou vers le sud / le midi / à l'ouest ou vers l'ouest
east	(l') est		
west	(l') ouest		

the Middle East	le Moyen-Orient	
the Far East	l'Extrême-Orient	
the East End	quartiers pauvres et populaires de la partie est de certaines villes	
the West	l'Occident	

the Far West	le Far-West
the West End	quartier du centre-ouest de Londres; quartier des théâtres
out west (US)	dans l'Ouest des Etats-Unis

■ *Adjectifs*

			natural	naturel
lead-free [led] / unleaded	sans plomb		uninhabited [,--'---]	inhabité

Collocations

global	mondial	*global economy / trend / climatic changes*
worldwide	mondial	*worldwide reputation / famine*

■ *Verbes*

inhabit	habiter	*to inhabit a country / area / house*
pollute [-'-]	polluer	*an area may be polluted by waste products*

Exercices sur le chapitre 6 (1)

1. Testez vos connaissances en traduisant les mots ci-dessous:

A / moonlight - B / pole - C / surroundings - D / westbound - E / westward - F / southern

2. Remplissez la grille, à l'aide des définitions proposées; les lettres grisées, mises bout à bout feront apparaître un mot essentiel :

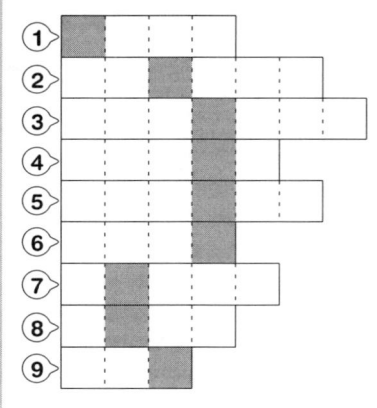

1 / there are the North ... and the South ... 2 / of, or concerning, the whole world. 3 / deals with how to protect the environment. 4 / you live in it, so do we all. 5 / it is around all of us. 6 / cardinal point. 7 / sun... and moon... cannot shine at the same time. 8 / in the sky at night. 9 / in the sky in the daytime.

3. En vous aidant des exemples et collocations de la colonne de droite du vocabulaire, traduisez les expressions ci-dessous:

A / Inhaler des vapeurs d'essence. B / Étoile filante. C / Habitant. D / Le soleil tapait. E / Un ciel triste, couvert. F / Le ciel se couvre, se dégage. G / Les régions habitées de l'univers.

The world 79

2. Land

■ *Noms*

clearing	clairière	oasis [əʊ'eɪsɪs]	oasis
crevice ['krevɪs]	fente, fissure	peak	pic, sommet
dale	vallon, vallée	plain	plaine
fen	marais, marécage	rock	pierre (US), rocher, rocs (GB)
grove	bosquet	slope	pente
heath [hi:θ]	lande, bruyère	wasteland	terrain vague
marsh	marécage, marais		terres en friche
moat [məʊt]	douve, fossé	wilderness ['wɪldənəs]	région sauvage et désolée
moor	lande	windmill	moulin à vent

Collocations

area	zone, région	*to close off / rope off* (isoler) *a built-up / distressed* (sinistré) *area*
bush	buisson, arbuste	*to prune* (élaguer) */ trim* (tailler) *bushes*
Bush	brousse	*to live (out) in the Bush*
cave	caverne, grotte	*to explore caves*
crevasse [krə'væs]	crevasse	*to fall down a crevasse*
desert	désert	*to reclaim an arid / trackless* (sans pistes) *desert*
ditch	fossé	*to dig a ditch*
earth	terre, sol	*to fall to earth / to the ground* (tomber par terre)
forest	forêt	*a virgin / rain forest* (pluviale)
glade	clairière	*a forest glade*
ground	terre, surface, sol, terrain	*firm / soft / high / holy ground - at ground level - to sit on the ground* (v. **earth**)
grounds	terrain, domaine, parc	*the hospital grounds*
hill	colline, coteau	*to go up a hill*
	pente	*a steep hill* (montée / descente raide / abrupte)
land	terre	*to live off the land* (vivre de la terre) *- to go / travel by land*
landscape	paysage	*a beautiful / gloomy landscape*
mainland	continent	*the British mainland*
mountain	montagne	*a chain / range of mountains*
path GB [pɑ:θ] / US [pæθ]	chemin, voie	*to make a path through the jungle*
	allée	*a garden path*
region ['ri:dʒən]	région	*a remote / unpopulated region*
scenery	paysage, cadre	*wild / picturesque scenery*
setting	cadre, décor	*a natural setting*
soil	terre, sol	*to till* (cultiver) */ cultivate a barren* (aride) */ fertile soil*
tunnel	tunnel	*to dig / bore a tunnel*
valley	vallée	*to live down in the valley*
view	vue	*a breathtaking / unhampered* (dégagée) *view*
volcano [vɒl'keɪnəʊ]	volcan	*active / dead volcanoes*
wood	bois	*to walk through the woods*
woodcutter	bûcheron	*woodcutters fell* (abattent) *trees*

■ *Adjectifs*

scenic ['si:nɪk]   pittoresque

■ *Verbes*

| **dig** | creuser | **fell** | abattre (des arbres) |
| **erupt** | entrer en éruption | **till** | cultiver |

Collocations

reclaim   reconquérir   *to reclaim land from the desert / forest*

■ *Adverbe*

inland   à / vers l'intérieur   *to go / travel inland*

Exercices sur le chapitre 6 (2)

1. Testez vos connaissances en traduisant les mots ci-dessous :

A / bush - B / cave - C / to erupt - D / valley - E / dale

2. Choisissez, pour chaque phrase, la ou les solutions possible(s) :

A / England is part of the British - landscape / plain / region / mainland.
B / He fell to the - soil / ground / earth / cave.
C / They endeavoured to reclaim the - ditch / land / desert / setting.
D / A grassy space without trees in a forest is called a - glade / clearing / moor / fen.
E / You may go up a - slope / hill / marsh / view.
F / They were busy digging a - ditch / windmill / tunnel / moat.
G / Some religious people hold certain places sacred as - holy moor / holy crevice / holy land / holy peak.

3. Sea

■ *Noms*

bank	berge, rive	**lock**	écluse
beacon ['bi:kən]	phare; fanal	**marsh**	marais, marécage
cliff	falaise	**ocean**	océan
coast	côte	**pebble**	caillou; galet
creek	crique	**pond**	étang, mare
foam	écume	**pool**	flaque, mare, pièce d'eau
ford	gué	**puddle**	flaque
gulf	golfe	**quay** [ki:]	quai (navires)
jetty	jetée	**quicksand(s)**	sables mouvants
lake	lac	**seashore**	rivage, bord de la mer
island	île	**seaweed**	algue
lifebelt	ceinture de sauvetage	**shingle** (U)	galets
lifeboat	bateau de sauvetage	**shore**	rivage, littoral
lighthouse	phare	**swamp**	marais, marécage
loch [lox]	lac (Ecosse)	**waterfall**	chute d'eau

The world

Collocations

beach	plage	*to sunbathe on a sandy / shingle beach*
buoy GB [bɔɪ] / US ['buː_i]	bouée	*to anchor a lifebuoy*
dam	barrage	*a dam may burst*
embankment	berge, talus	*a railroad / railway embankment*
harbour	port	*to clear* (quitter) *a natural port*
pier	jetée, embarcadère	*to meet sb at / on the pier*
port	port	*to make port* (arriver au port) - *to call at a port - put in(to) port*
reef	récif	*to strike a reef*
river	rivière, fleuve	*to dredge* (draguer) */ cross / ford* (passer à gué) *a river - a river flows / rises / overflows (its banks)* (sort de son lit) */ floods the countryside*
sea	mer	*to go to sea* (se faire marin) */ put out* (prendre la mer) *to sea / to sail the seas*
seaside	bord de (la) mer	*to go to / spend a week at the seaside*
stream	courant	*to go with / against the stream*
tide	marée	*the tide comes in / is in / goes out / is out / recedes / ebbs and flows* (monte et descend)
water	eau	*to walk in water up to one's thighs*

■ *Adjectifs*

choppy	un peu agité	*choppy sea / waves*
deep	profond	*a river may be three feet deep - to be ankle-deep in mud*
gentle	doux, graduel	*to go up a gentle slope*
rough	très agité	*rough sea - to have a rough crossing*
rugged ['rʌgɪd]	accidenté, escarpé échancré, découpé	*rugged area of land / mountains rugged coastline*
shallow	peu profond	*to ford / wade* (passer à gué) *a shallow river / pond*
sheer	abrupt, à pic	*a sheer cliff / drop* (dénivellation)
smooth	calme	*to sail on a smooth sea*
steep	raide, abrupt	*to climb up a steep hill / slope*

■ *Verbes*

climb	grimper, gravir, escalader	*to climb a mountain / up or down a hill / over a fence* (clôture)
ford	passer à gué	*to ford a river*

■ *Adverbes*

downstream	en aval		**upstream**	en amont

Exercices sur le chapitre 6 (3)

1. Testez vos connaissances en traduisant les mots suivants :

A / tide - B / shingle - C / pebble - D / pier - E / pond - F / embankment - G / puddle - H / pool

2. En vous aidant des exemples et collocations proposées dans la colonne de droite du vocabulaire, traduisez les expressions et phrases ci-dessous :

A / Passer à gué une rivière peu profonde. B / Avoir une traversée très agitée. C / Avoir de l'eau jusqu'aux chevilles. D / Escalader une chaîne de montagnes escarpées, une falaise abrupte. E / Aller au bord de la mer pour rester sur une plage de sable ou de galets à regarder la mer monter et descendre. F / Se faire marin à l'âge de seize ans. G / Faire escale dans un port. H / La rivière a débordé, inondé la campagne puis s'est retirée.

7

Posture and movement

1. Static

Collocations

■ *Noms*

back	arrière, fond	*at the back of the garden - to sit in the back of the car - in back of sth (US)* (derrière)
background	arrière-plan	*in the background*
corner	coin	*at / on the corner - round the corner*
front	devant, avant	*at / in the front of sth*
left	gauche	*on / to the left*
level ['levl]	niveau	*to be on a level with sth* (au même niveau que) - *at ground level*
location [ləʊ'keɪʃn]	emplacement, lieu	*to move to a new location - to be at an unknown location*
place	lieu, endroit	*a nice place for sth / to do sth - in this / that place*
position	place, position	*to change / shift position - to be in / take a(n) upright / sitting / lying / awkward / comfortable position*
posture ['pɒstʃə]	posture, position	*sb's posture may be very bad* (mal se tenir) - *some exercises may help develop a good posture - Humans have a naturally erect posture*
queue [kju:] / line (US)	queue	*to form / join / stand in a queue*
rear	arrière	*at the rear of a bus - at / in the rear of the garden - to attack sb from the rear*
right	droite	*to stand on the right - to move to the right*
room	place, espace disponible	*to find room enough for two - to take up too much room - to make room for sb*
shortcut	raccourci	*to take a shortcut to somewhere*
spot [spɒt]	endroit	*a peaceful / secluded beauty spot*
whereabouts	l'endroit où se trouve qqn ou qch	*to know sb's whereabouts*

■ *Adjectifs*

cramped	exigu, très étroit	*to be a bit cramped for space*
crawling	grouillant	*a place may be crawling with lice / bugs / police*
farther / further	plus loin, plus éloigné	*'How much farther is it?' - farther (to the) north - at the farther end of a room* (l'autre bout)
farthest / furthest	le plus éloigné	*the farthest depths of Africa* (le fin fond)
high	haut, élevé	*how high is it? - a building may be eight stories high*
left	gauche	*on the left (hand) side - to do sth with one's left hand*
level	au même niveau	*the top of a tree may be level with the window*
local	local, du quartier	*local traders / pub / women*
low	bas	*low ceiling / table / hill / wall*

motionless	immobile	to sit motionless - the motionless leaves
opposite ['---]	d'en face, opposé	opposite side / page / end
remote [-'-]	éloigné	sb / a place may be remote from another place
right	droit(e)	on the right (hand) side -to raise one's right hand
still	immobile	to be / stand / keep still

■ *Verbes*

coop up	enfermer (comme dans une cage)	to be cooped up all day in an office
hide	cacher	to hide sth from sb
lie	se trouver, être	a place may lie to the south of another
lie / lay (US)	être allongé	to lie flat / still
lurk	se tapir	to lurk behind sth
queue / stand in line (US)	faire la queue	to queue at a place for sth
sit	être assis; se trouver, être	to always sit at the same place - the village sits at the bottom of the valley
stand	être debout; se trouver, être	to stand near sth / leaning on sth - the church stands close to the river
stay	rester	to stay somewhere / (at) home / for dinner
stay put	ne pas bouger	to stay put in one job all one's life
wait	attendre	to wait for sb / for sth / for sb to do sth / until sth happens / until sb does sth

Exercices sur le chapitre 7 (1)

1. Testez vos connaissances en traduisant les mots ou expressions ci-dessous:

A / further - B / farthest - C / to stay put - D / rear - E / shortcut

2. Traduisez en anglais:

A / On manquait de place pour jouer à cache-cache. B / On y jouait quand même quand on restait enfermés toute la journée. C / On restait tapis sans bouger dans des coins obscurs ou dans des placards (où il n'y avait de la place que pour deux enfants de petite taille) grouillant d'insectes noirs. D / D'autres fois on sortait dans le jardin qui était de niveau avec le 1er étage: le soleil brillait, les feuilles étaient immobiles. E / Au fond du jardin, à gauche du perron (ou à droite, je ne me rappelle plus), il y avait un arbre de deux mètres de haut qui nous paraissait très haut. F / On s'asseyait dessous: c'était notre endroit préféré les jours de soleil.

3. Remettez les lettres dans l'ordre:

A. THRIG B. FELT C. OPSIOTEP D. NORTF E. TOILOCAN

2. Dynamic [daɪˈnæmɪk]

Collocations

■ *Noms*

| balance ['--] | équilibre | to keep / lose one's balance |
| haste | hâte | to act / do sth in great haste |

Posture and movement

motion	mouvement	*the gentle motion of a boat*
	mouvement, geste	*to make a motion as if to do sth - to do sth with a quick motion of one's hands*
move	mouvement	*with one move, he ... (en un éclair, il...) - to make a move as if to do sth - to be always on the move (se déplacer continuellement)*
	initiative	*to make (prendre) a move - to get a move on (se grouiller)*
movement	mouvement	*downward / jerky / soft movement - freedom of movement*
rush	précipitation	*to be / do sth in a rush - sth may be a bit of a rush - there may be a rush for sth / to do sth*
step	pas	*to take a step forward / back - step by step - to walk with quick / even / steady / long steps*
stop	arrêt	*to come / bring sth (a bus) to a stop - to make several stops*
track	trace, souvenir	*to keep / lose track of sth / sb*
trail	trace, marque	*to leave a trail of sth*
trap	piège	*to set / lay a trap for sb - to fall / lure sb into a trap*

■ *Adjectifs*

hasty ['heɪsti]	hâtif, irréfléchi	*hasty decision / conclusion*
swift	rapide, prompt, vif	*swift reply / revenge / temper - to be swift to do / in doing sth*
sharp	rapide, bien mené	*sharp piece of work - "look sharp!" (grouille-toi!)*

■ *Verbes*

dangle	(laisser) pendre	*keys dangling from a chain - to dangle sth in front of / before sb / at the end of sth*
hang	pendre, être accroché	*sth may hang from / on sth - sth may hang loose*
hang	pendre, suspendre	*to hang sth (hung / hung) - to hang sb (hanged / hanged)*
hasten ['heɪsn]	se hâter	*to hasten to do sth*
hurry (up)	se dépêcher	*to hurry home / back*
lay	poser, placer	*to lay sth on sth*
level ['levl]	diriger contre	*to level sth at sb*
lie down	s'allonger	*to lie down on the grass / a bed*
load	charger	*to load sth with sth / into sth*
make for	se diriger vers	*to make for a place*
motion	faire signe	*to motion (to) sb to do sth*
move	(se) déplacer	*to move / to move sth from a place to a place*
reach	atteindre	*to reach a place / for sth*
return [-'-]	rendre	*to return sth to sb*
rush	se précipiter	*to rush back / home / out / to a place*
	précipiter, emmener	*to rush things / sb to hospital (d'urgence)*
see sb (to)	accompagner	*to see sb home / out / to the door*
set	poser, mettre, préparer	*to set sth for sb / against sth*
shadow	suivre, filer	*to shadow sth / sb*
shift	déplacer, bouger	*to shift (sth / sb) from a place to a place - to shift gears - to shift the blame on sb*
show sb to	accompagner, faire visiter	*to show sb in / out / around / over a place*
show up	arriver	*to show up early / late / in time / on time / unexpectedly*
sit down	s'asseoir	*to sit down in / on sth / to a meal / to work*
slow down / up	ralentir	*to slowdown / up abruptly / gradually / gently*

squash [skwɒʃ]	écraser, serrer		to squash sth - to get squashed under / between two / several things / people
squeeze	presser, extraire (se) serrer		to squeeze sth out of / from sth to squeeze (sth) into a small space
step	avancer, marcher		to step forward / back / on sth
stop	arrêter, empêcher		to stop sth / sb / doing sth / sb doing sth
stretch	étirer, tendre		to stretch sth tight
take	prendre emporter, emmener		to take sth / sugar / milk to take sth / sb to a place / for a walk
track down	traquer, capturer		to track sb down
trap	piéger		to trap sb into sth / into doing sth
turn up	arriver, se présenter		to turn up drunk at / in a place
unload	décharger		to unload sth from a place

Exercices sur le chapitre 7 (2)

1. Testez vos connaissances en traduisant les verbes ci-dessous:

A / hurry - B / be on the move - C / get a move on - D / trail - E / slow down - F / move G / turn up

2. Joignez une phrase de droite à une phrase de gauche:

A. He motioned (to) him
B. She made for the door hastily
C. Be careful you don't step
D. I'm trying to keep track
E. Don't you try to trap me
F. He reached for the gun
G. The plastic surgeon' aim was to stretch tight

1. into shifting all the blame on myself.
2. of the luggage he says he's loaded into the car's boot.
3. the skin that used to hang loose over the cheek-bones.
4. as she feared he might show up any moment and level a loaded gun at her.
5. which I was dangling defiantly before him.
6. to lie down and keep still.
7. on the toys Junior has laid all over the floor

3. Choisissez, parmi les mots ci-dessous, celui qui convient pour compléter le sens de chaque phrase:

BALANCE   HASTEN   HASTY   RETURN
RUSH   SET (2 fois) SHADOW   SHARP
SHOW TO   SQUASH   SQUEEZE   STOP
SWIFT   TAKE   UNLOAD.

1. He lost his _____, as he was _____ing a ladder against a high wall. 2. He _____ to _____ the money to his unwanted visitor, then _____ him to the door. 3. He sat inadvertently on the bag and _____ the tomatoes in it. 4. He managed to _____ into the tiny car. 5. He always made _____, though not _____ decisions, which does not mean that he _____ things or anything like that. 6. _____ the boy home to _____ him getting into further trouble. 7. She _____ a cup full of steaming tea in front of him. 8. The police _____ the suspect and caught him _____ing the booty of a recent unsolved break-in. 9. That was a _____ piece of work said the Inspector.

Posture and movement

3. Body at work

Collocations

■ *Noms*

curtsy	révérence	*to make / drop / bob (GB) (sb) a curtsy (to sb)*
gait [geɪt]	démarche	*sb's habitual / steady / unsteady gait*
jolt [dʒəʊlt]	secousse, cahot	*to move along with a jolt*
twitch	contraction, tic	*a nervous twitch*

■ *Adjectifs*

brisk	rapide, vif	*to walk with a brisk step / at a brisk pace*
fidgety ['---]	nerveux, agité	*fidgety schoolboy*

■ *Verbes*

bend	plier, courber	*to bend one's arm / knees / head / a wire / a branch - to bend sth into shape*
	se pencher	*to bend down / over sth*
bow [baʊ]	(se) courber, saluer	*to bow one's head - to bow to an audience / before sb*
climb [klaɪm]	grimper	*to climb (up) a hill / on to sth / aboard / out / down*
crawl	ramper	*people / insects crawl in / out / about*
	aller lentement	*cars crawl along*
creep	se glisser	*to creep in / into / out / out of a place*
	ramper	*insects / snakes creep*
cringe [krɪndʒ]	reculer	*to cringe from sth / somewhere*
	ramper (servilement)	*to cringe to sb*
cuddle	(se) câliner	*to cuddle sb / up to each other*
dart	se déplacer comme une flèche	*to dart forward / from one place into / to another*
dash	se précipiter	*to dash around / out into the street - to dash for cover / shelter*
	jeter, lancer violemment	*to dash sth to the ground / to pieces*
edge	se déplacer lentement ou avec précaution	*to edge away from sb - to edge one's way to a place / through the crowd / past sb / sth*
fall	tomber	*to fall full length / in a heap on the floor / off a bike / from a tree / out of a window / over the edge*
fetch	aller chercher	*to fetch sth for sb / sb sth / sb from school / sb back*
fidget	gigoter, bouger sans arrêt	*to fidget about with impatience*
get about / around	circuler, se déplacer	*to get around a lot / by bus*
get along	partir, aller	*to get along to the office*
get away	partir, s'en aller	*to get away from sb / a place*
get back	revenir	*to get back home / to a place*
get in / into	entrer	*to get into (monter) a car / train*
get off	descendre	*to get off a bus / train / plane / boat*
get on	monter	*to get on a plane / boat*
get out	sortir	*to get out of a car*
go	aller, partir	*to go home / for good*
head for	se diriger vers	*to head for home / sb / sth*

jolt [dʒəʊlt]		cahoter, secouer	*the bumps on the road may jolt sb / to jolt along*
jostle		bousculer	*to jostle sb ruthlessly*
loiter		rôder, traîner	*to loiter on the way to / back from a place*
lurch		tituber	*to lurch to one's feet / towards sb / drunkenly*
		faire une embardée	*to lurch off the road*
plod		marcher lourdement	*to plod slowly / laboriously along*
prowl [praʊl]		rôder	*to prowl about / around in search of sth*
reel		chanceler	*to reel back into / off a place*
roam		errer, traîner	*to roam the streets / over the hills and plains / around town*
romp		s'ébattre	*to romp about joyfully*
saunter		flâner, marcher nonchalamment	*to saunter about / along / over from across a place*
scramble		se déplacer avec difficulté	*to scramble up / down a wall / over rocks*
		se déplacer précipitamment, de façon désordonnée	*to scramble away / to one's feet / out of the way*
shake		trembler violemment	*to shake uncontrollably with laughter / fear / cold - sb's voice may shake*
shiver ['ʃɪvə]		trembler, grelotter	*to shiver from / with cold / at the thought of sth*
shudder		trembler, frémir	*to shudder with fright / at the thought of sth / to do sth*
sit up		se tenir assis (bien droit)	*to sit up straight*
sneak		se glisser furtivement	*to sneak around / into / out of a place*
squirm		se tortiller, s'agiter	*to squirm with impatience*
		se dérober à	*to squirm out of sb's grasp / out of one's obligations*
stagger		tituber	*to stagger along / back / to / into a place*
stand up		se lever	*to stand up hurriedly / erect / upright*
stoop (down)		se baisser, se pencher	*to stoop down to pick sth up / over sth*
stray		vagabonder, s'égarer	*to stray onto a place / away from a group*
swagger		se pavaner	*to swagger in / out / about*
sweep		se déplacer majestueusement	*to sweep about / in / out*
totter		chanceler, vaciller	*to totter from / to / into / out of a place*
tremble		trembler	*to tremble with happiness*
trudge		marcher avec difficulté	*to trudge along / up a hill*
tumble		dégringoler	*to tumble down the stairs*
turn		tourner	*to turn abruptly / off the road / into a side street*
twist		tourner, tordre	*to twist one's hankie nervously / one's hair into a bun / sth into a certain shape / sth into a ball*
		se fouler	*to twist one's wrist / ankle*
twitch		se contracter	*one's hands may twitch convulsively*
		tirer sèchement	*to twitch sb's sleeve*
walk		marcher	*to walk slowly / fast / from / to a place*
wallow ['wɒləʊ]		se vautrer	*to wallow in the mud*
wander ['wɒndə]		errer	*to wander the streets / about / along*
wince		grimacer, se crisper	*to wince at a sound / at the memory / at the thought of sth / in pain*
wrestle		lutter, se battre	*to wrestle with sb / sb to the ground*
wriggle		se tortiller	*to wriggle about / one's toes / out of sb's grip*

■ *Adverbe*

gingerly ['dʒɪndʒəli]	précautionneusement	*to walk gingerly over sth*

Exercices sur le chapitre 7 (3)

1. Testez vos connaissances en traduisant les mots ou expressions ci-dessous:

A / fidgety (adj.) - B / to roam - C / to wince - D / to squirm - E / to trudge - F / to walk - G / to sit up

2. Remplir les blancs à l'aide des mots proposés ci-dessous. Les tirets dans les blancs indiquent le nombre de lettres du mot à trouver. Sauf indication contraire, tous les mots sont des verbes.

- MOTS DE QUATRE LETTRES:
  DART   DASH   JOLT   PLOD   REEL
- MOTS DE CINQ LETTRES:
  BRISK (adj.)   CRAWL   SNEAK   STOOP   SWEEP
- MOTS DE SIX LETTRES:
  CURTSY (n.)   FIDGET   JOSTLE   SHIVER   TUMBLE
- MOTS DE SEPT LETTRES:
  SAUNTER   SHUDDER   WRESTLE   WRIGGLE

A. She managed to _____ out of the threatening man's grip. B. He told him to stop _____ing at once. C. She _____ed down to pick up her handkerchief. D. She _____ed at the very thought of it. - E. The burglar _____ed out of the room unnoticed. - F. She'd _____ into my bedroom like a queen. - G. He _____ed with fright. H. A policeman on the beat _____ed over from across the street to find out what was going on. I. He _____d out of bed and ____ed into the bathroom. - J. They were badly ____ed by the bumps and holes of the uneven road. K. He'd ____ back home wearily after a hard day's work. - L. We were _____d about by the impatient crowd. M. He 'd ____ed back home at a fairly _____ pace, considering how drunk he was. N. Insects _____ed around all over the now unappetizing food. O. He ____ed past us as if he was being chased by a mad dog. P. She made a _____ to the queen, as she had been told to do. Q. They'd _____ on the hard floor for hours on end.

3. Les mots ont été curieusement coupés. Remettez de l'ordre:

A. It wit chedher slee vet ocat chherat tent ion.
B. Heus edtos wag geralot
C. Hewan dered thest reet saim les sly eve ryn ight.
D. Don otwall owinth emud!
E. Ied ged myw aytow ards thewin dow.

4. Choisissez:

A. He used to prowl / cringe / totter in search of something unattainable.
B. He cuddled / fell / fetched up to her before going to bed.
C. She bent / crept / staggered down to kiss the baby on the floor.

4. Arms and hands at work

4.1. Arms and hands (1)

Collocations

■ *Noms*

hug	étreinte	*to give sb a friendly / an affectionate hug*
sign	signe	*to communicate through signs - to make a sign (of approval) to sb / for sb to do sth - sign language - to give sb the thumbs up sign of approval* (donner son accord)
wave	geste de la main	*with a wave of the hand - to give sb a friendly wave*

■ *Verbes*

pinch	pincer	**prick**	piquer

Collocations

clasp GB [klɑːsp] / US [klæsp]	serrer, étreindre	*to clasp sb in one's arms / to one's breast / sb's hand*
hug	serrer dans ses bras	*to hug sb - to hug and kiss sb - to cuddle and hug sb*
lean	s'appuyer, se pencher	*to lean on sth / out (of sth) / over (sth) / across (sth)*
nudge	pousser du coude	*to nudge sb / sb to do sth*
shrug	hausser les épaules	*to shrug at sth*
wave	brandir	*to wave flags / placards* (pancartes)
	faire signe de la main	*to wave (back) at / to sb / sb goodbye / for silence - to wave on* (faire signer d'avancer) *the traffic*

Exercices sur le chapitre 7 (4.1)

1. Testez vos connaissances en traduisant les verbes ci-dessous:
A / clasp - B / hug - C / shrug - D / lean

2. Choisissez la ou les solutions possibles:
A. She nudged / leant / waved her friend to draw her attention.
B. She clasped / waved / hugged her friend goodbye.
C. She made a friendly sign / wave / hug to her friend.
D. She shrugged / nudged / clasped her to her breast.
E. Do give me a hug and a kiss / a hug and a wave / a hug and a sign.
F. Don't clasp / lean / shrug out of the window.

4.2. Arms and hands (2)

Collocations

■ *Verbes*

cast GB [kɑːst] / US [kæst]	jeter, lancer	*to cast sth / a net / a line*
drag	traîner, tirer	*to drag sth on / along*
draw	tirer	*to draw sb aside - to draw the curtains - to draw sth from a basket - to draw on one's socks* (enfiler)
drop	tomber	*temperatures / prices may drop / sth may drop suddenly - a horse may drop to third place*
	laisser tomber	*to drop sth by mistake or deliberately, e.g. bombs* (larguer)
	baisser	*to drop one's voice*
fling	lancer, jeter (avec force)	*to fling sth at sb / sth into the air / oneself on sth*
flip	envoyer (d'un petit coup sec)	*to flip sth in the air / sth into sth / sth open - to flip a coin - to flip through a book* (parcourir)
fumble	manier, chercher avec maladresse	*to fumble with sth / in(to) sth / into one's pocket for sth*
grab	saisir (brutalement)	*to grab sth / at sth / sb by the shoulders*

Posture and movement

hit	frapper, cogner	*to hit sth / a ball / sb in the face / sb on the head - to hit one's head on the ceiling*
hurl	jeter, lancer (avec violence)	*to hurl sth out of the window / sth at sb's face*
jab	piquer, enfoncer (avec vigueur)	*to jab sth into sth - to jab sth with sth - to jab sb in the ribs*
	montrer, pointer; taper sur	*to jab (at) sth (with one's finger / a knife) - to jab at the keys (touches) of a typewriter - to jab a finger at sb*
lash	battre, fouetter	*to lash sb's back - the sea lashes (against) the cliffs - the rain may lash (at / against) the windows*
pitch	lancer, jeter	*to pitch a ball / sth at sth*
poke	donner un coup ou une série de petits coups	*to poke at sb (pointer son index vers) with one's finger - to poke sb in the ribs / sb in the eye*
	pousser	*to poke sth at (vers) sth / sb*
	passer	*to poke one's head out / through (sth)*
	chipoter	*to poke at one's food*
prod	pousser à petits coups répétés	*to prod sth with sth / at sth*
	pousser, inciter	*to prod sb to do / sb into doing sth*
pull	tirer	*to pull sth / on / at sth - to pull sb out of bed / out of the water*
push	pousser	*to push on sth / sth into sth - to push a door open*
seize	saisir	*to seize sth / sb's arm / sb by the collar*
snatch	saisir, arracher	*to snatch sth / at sth / sth from sb's hand(s)*
throw	lancer, jeter	*to throw sth to / at sb / sth in / sth out / sth away*
thrust	enfoncer	*to thrust one's hands into one's pockets*
	pousser d'un geste brusque	*to thrust sth at / towards sb*
tip	incliner, pencher, basculer	*to tip one's head to one side / a chair back against a wall*
	renverser, faire tomber	*to tip sth into sth / sb off a chair*
toss	lancer, jeter, projeter	*to toss sth to sb / one's head back / a coin - to toss for it (tirer au sort) - the sea may toss a boat against the rocks*
	s'agiter, remuer	*to toss and turn in bed*
trundle	pousser, traîner (avec peine)	*to trundle sth along*
tug	tirer (fort) sur	*to tug sth / at sth*
wheel	pousser, tirer	*to wheel sth / sb about / into a room / up a hill*

Exercices sur le chapitre 7 (4.2)

1. Testez vos connaissances en traduisant les verbes ci-dessous:

A / cast - B / hurl - C / lash - D / pitch - E / seize - F / throw

2. Traduisez en anglais:

A / Il lança la ligne délicatement et sortit, en un rien de temps, un énorme poisson de la rivière. B / Il enfonça ses mains encore mouillées dans les poches de son imperméable. C / Il traînait, à grand peine, une brouette pleine de briques. D / Qui jouerait le premier? On tira au sort pour en décider. E / Elle le promena dans le jardin dans sa chaise roulante. F / Elle se jeta sur le canapé et fondit en larmes. G / Elle poussa le livre vers l'élève, d'un geste brusque. H / Elle renversa la tête en arrière. I / Je maniai les clefs si maladroitement que je les fis tomber. J / Dans un accès de colère, elle jeta violemment les livres à travers la pièce.

3. Joignez une phrase de gauche à chaque phrase de droite

1. I prodded and poked the dog
2. The doctor jabbed the needle
3. Their car hit a tree
4. A mugger hit the old lady
5. The team's captain flipped
6. I was so nervous that I fumbled
7. Little Jane kept tugging at
8. When they pushed the bookcase around,
9. Can't you just draw it along gently,
10. She quickly drew back

A) and the passengers had to be pulled out of the wreckage.
B) a coin to decide which team would bat first.
C) her mother's sleeve to catch her attention.
D) books dropped from the shelves.
E) when she saw the man was trying to snatch her purse.
F) do you have to drag it along so noisily?
G) to see if it would move.
H) into my arm.
I) on the head and grabbed her bag.
J) with my notes and dropped them.

4.3. Hands (only) at work

Collocations

■ *Noms*

hold [həʊld]	tenue, prise, emprise	*to get hold of sth - to catch / grab (a firm) hold of sth*
knock	coup	*give a knock on sth / at sth / on a door - to receive a nasty knock*
pat	tape (amicale)	*to give sb a pat on the back*
purchase ['pɜːtʃəs]	point d'appui, prise	*to be unable to get a purchase on sth*

■ *Adjectifs*

jerky	saccadé, cahotant	*jerky movement / playing / ride*

■ *Verbes*

spank	donner une fessée, fesser	**strangle**	étrangler (qqn)
stroke	caresser	**throttle**	étrangler, étouffer (qqn)

Collocations

bind	attacher	*to bind sb hand and foot / sb to sth*
	relier	*to bind a book in leather*
bounce	(faire) rebondir	*to bounce a ball against / off sth - a ball bounces*
carry	transporter	*to carry sth / sb into / from / to a place*
cling	s'accrocher	*to cling to sth / sb*
clutch	étreindre, serrer fortement	*to clutch sb's hand / sth in one's hand*
	s'agripper	*to clutch at sth / at straws / at a branch*
dip	tremper, plonger	*to dip sth into sth / one's hand in(to) water*
fold [fəʊld]	plier	*to fold sth / one's arms / sth in two*
frisk	fouiller (au corps)	*to frisk sb for sth*
grasp GB [grɑːsp] / US [græsp]	saisir, s'emparer de	*to grasp (hold of) a knife / at a rope / for sth*
grip	empoigner, saisir	*to grip sth / sb's hand / - fear may grip sb's heart*
grope	tâtonner, chercher à tâtons	*to grope around for sth - to grope one's way out of bed / into the kitchen in the dark*
hand	passer, donner	*to hand sth to sb*
hand (out)	distribuer	*to hand out leaflets / free meals / advice*
hold	tenir	*to hold sb close / tight / sb's hand - to hold hands with sb*

Posture and movement

jerk	cahoter	*a cart may jerk along / to a halt*
	secouer, tirer vivement	*to jerk a door open / sb to their feet*
knock	frapper, donner des coups	*to knock at / on a door - to knock sth into sth - to knock sb unconscious*
	faire tomber	*to knock sth off a table / sb off a bicycle*
	cogner	*to knock one's head on / against sth*
lift	soulever, lever, poser	*to lift sth (heavy) off a shelf / on to a table*
	lever	*to lift one's eyes*
lower	baisser, descendre	*to lower sth / sb into sth / on to sth*
	baisser	*to lower prices / one's voice / one's eyes*
pat	taper, tapoter	*to pat sth softly / sb's hand / sb on the back*
pick up	ramasser	*to pick sth up from the ground - to pick up the telephone* (décrocher)
	passer prendre	*to pick sb up from school / at the airport*
pinch	pincher	*to pinch one's fingers / sb awake / sb's arm*
point (at)	montrer (du doigt)	*to point the way / at sth - to point sb - to point one's finger at sb / sth*
point at	diriger, braquer	*to point a gun at sb*
point to	désigner, indiquer	*to point to sth / sb*
point out	attirer l'attention sur	*to point sth / sb out to sb*
press	presser, appuyer	*to press the button - to press one's nose against the window*
put	mettre, placer	*to put sth somewhere / on (to) a table / into a drawer*
put down	poser	*to put one's cup down (on the table)*
raise	soulever, lever, élever	*to raise a blind / a curtain / one's hand / one's voice*
reach	atteindre, parvenir à toucher	*to reach a place / sth / sb* (joindre qqn)
reach down	décrocher, descendre	*to reach sth down (for sb)*
reach for	tendre le bras pour prendre	*to reach for a packet of tea (from a shelf)*
reach out	tendre (le bras)	*to reach out to get sth - to reach out a helping hand*
rub	frotter, enduire	*to rub one's hands together / sth on sth / sth into sth*
	enlever, effacer, éliminer	*to rub the oil off with a cloth - to rub some words out*
rummage ['rʌmɪdʒ]	fouiller	*to rummage through a drawer / among books / for sth*
shake	trembler	*to shake with fear / cold / laughter*
	secouer	*to shake sb roughly / sb awake*
	brandir	*to shake one's fist at sb*
	obtenir un résultat en secouant	*to shake salt on one's food / the corn flakes out - to shake oneself free* (se dégager)
slam	claquer	*to slam a door (shut) - a door may slam*
slap	donner une tape, gifler	*to slap sb on the back / sb's face*
	poser brutalement	*to slap sth on a table - to slap down some money*
smack	donner une grande tape, taper violemment	*to smack sb's face / bottom*
smack down	poser avec un claquement sonore	*to smack a book down on a table*
stretch (out)	tendre	*to stretch a rope tight - to stretch one's arms upwards - to stretch (out) one's neck*
	étirer, élargir	*to try and stretch one's new shoes*
	s'étendre, s'étirer	*to stretch out and relax*
	s'allonger, s'élargir	*some fabrics (tissus) may stretch when put in the wash*
tickle	chatouiller	*to tickle sb (into a rage)*
	enchanter, ravir	*a plan may tickle sb pink / to death*
tie [taɪ]	nouer, attacher	*to tie one's shoe laces / a scarf over one's head - to tie sth in a knot* (faire un nœud à qch)
tie (up)	ficeler, ligoter, attacher	*to tie up a parcel - to tie a man to a post* (poteau)

twirl	faire tournoyer, tortiller	*to twirl one's hair / beard / sth in one's hand / round one's finger*
unfold	déplier	*to unfold a map / table / letter*
upset [-'-]	(se) renverser, (faire) chavirer	*a small boat may upset - sth may upset a boat - sb may upset a tin / cup*
wind [waɪnd]	enrouler	*to wind sth round sth*
	avancer (ligne sinueuse)	*to wind one's way home - to wind through a forest*
wind (up) [waɪnd]	remonter	*to wind a clock / watch*
wrench	tirer violemment, arracher	*to wrench sth off / away / open / (oneself) free*
	(se) tordre, fouler	*to wrench one's arm badly*
wring	tordre	*to wring one's hands* (se désespérer) *over sth - to wring sb's neck*
	arracher	*to wring money / details / the truth from / out of sb*

Exercices sur le chapitre 7 (4.3)

1. Testez vos connaissances en traduisant les verbes ci-dessous:
A / grip - B / wrench - C / press - D / raise - E / bind

2. Traduisez en anglais:
A / À tâtons, il cherchait la sortie. B / Elle distribuait des repas gratuits aux SDF. C / Il la tint serrée contre lui. D / Elle leva la main d'un geste brusque et frappa à la porte. E / Elle braqua un revolver sur le cambrioleur. F / Intéressée, elle leva les yeux, le vit, et baissa les yeux de nouveau. G / Elle décrocha le téléphone, le tint dans sa main droite quelques instants avant de répondre. H / Elle descendit le sac de l'étagère d'en haut. I / Arrêtez de fouiller dans mes tiroirs. J / Elle secoua la tirelire pour en faire sortir les pièces. K / Enlevez cette tache en frottant.

3. Joignez une phrase de droite à chaque phrase de gauche

1. He pressed button A
2. He shook him awake
3. The police officer twirled a key round his finger
4. He kept on tickling
5. He put down the cup
6. The police frisked the suspect
7. He upset his cup of tea
8. She wound wet cloths round
9. He slammed the door shut
10. He gripped her hand in fear

A. and clung to her sleeve all evening.
B and nearly knocked it off the table in the process.
C. when trying to unfold the morning paper .
D. and quietly pointed a gun at him.
E. his head which she patted soothingly.
F. and drunkenly wound his way home.
G. and the door jerked open.
H. who had been seen grabbing at the lady's bag.
I. and then very gently patted him on the back.
J. and pinching her all evening.

5. Feet and legs at work

Collocations

■ *Noms*

kick	coup de pied	*to give a ball a kick - to give sb a nasty / vicious kick*
jog	course (à petites foulées), jogging	*to break into a jog - to go for a jog*
jump	saut, bond	*to do* (réaliser) *a jump of two metres - to make a parachute jump - to get up with a jump*

Posture and movement

leap	bond, saut	*to make / take a leap for sth / at sth / on to a sofa*
limp	boîterie	*to have a slight / marked limp - to walk with a limp*
run	course (à pied)	*to go for a five-mile run - to break into a run - to arrive at a run (au pas de course)*
stride	enjambée, pas	*to take a few long strides - to cross a threshold with / in one stride*
stilt	échasse	*to walk on stilts*

■ *Adjectifs*

fast GB [fɑːst] / US [fæst] / **slow**	rapide / lent	*fast / slow runner / bowler* (lanceur au cricket) / *worker*
quick	rapide, vite expédié	*quick look / meal / answer*
	rapide, vif	*to have a quick eye for things - to be quick* (avoir vite fait de faire) *to do / to notice sth*

■ *Verbes*

follow	suivre		**scuttle**	courir à pas précipités, se précipiter
kneel	s'agenouiller			
sail	se déplacer d'un pas majestueux		**skip**	sautiller, sauter (à la corde)
			squat [skwɒt]	s'accroupir

Collocations

bounce	bondir (avec entrain)	*to bounce (up and down) on a bed - to bounce in*
bound	bondir, faire un / des bond(s)	*sb may bound into / out of a room - a dog may bound down a hill*
caper / frisk	gambader	*lambs capering / frisking about in the fields*
crouch [kraʊtʃ]	s'accroupir, se tapir	*to crouch (down) for protection / in readiness for sth / out of* (par) *fear*
glide	se déplacer sans bruit, avec grâce	*to glide (gracefully) in / out / past sb*
hop	sauter, sautiller	*to hop off / on to a bus - to hop about / in / out*
	aller à cloche-pied	*to hop over to a car after twisting one's ankle*
jog	courir à petites foulées	*to jog along - to jog to work*
jump	sauter, bondir	*to jump up and down for joy - to jump off a window / over a fence*
kick	donner un / des coups de pieds	*to kick a ball (into the net) - to kick a ball out - to kick at sth - to kick sb in the shins*
leap	sauter, bondir	*to leap (up) off / out of a place / on to sth - to leap (over) a gate*
limp	boiter, se déplacer en boîtant	*to (badly) limp along / back home*
pass GB [pɑːs] / US [pæs]	passer devant, par	*to pass sb / a place - to pass through a town*
	passer qch à	*to pass sth (out) to sb*
run	courir	*to run a race / a mile - to run up and down the stairs*
scamper	trottiner	*mice may scamper around in the attic*
	gambader, galoper	*children may scamper up and down the stairs*
shuffle	traîner, traînasser	*to shuffle around in one's slippers - to shuffle in / out - to shuffle one's feet*
slide	glisser, coulisser	*to slide down a bannister - a door may slide shut*
	faire glisser, faire coulisser	*to slide a door shut*
slip	glisser (accidentellement)	*to slip on sth - sth may slip out of your hands*
	se déplacer furtivement, se faufiler	*to slip in / out / through the traffic*

spring	bondir, sauter, surgir	*to spring on / at sb - to spring out of bed / to one's feet*
stalk [stɔːk]	rôder	*to stalk the streets*
	se déplacer, l'air hautain, à grands pas	*to stalk in / out*
stamp / stomp	taper du pied, marcher sur	*to stamp one's feet to keep warm - to stamp on an insect*
	se déplacer bruyamment ou avec colère	*to stamp around / out of a room in anger*
steal	se déplacer sans bruit	*to steal in / out of a room*
storm	se déplacer avec grande colère	*to storm off / in / out without saying a word*
stride	marcher à grandes enjambées, arpenter	*to stride confidently in / out / up to sb*
stumble	trébucher	*to stumble against / over a stone*
	se déplacer d'un pas mal assuré	*to stumble along / in / off*
tiptoe	marcher sur la pointe des pieds	*to tiptoe across a room / down the stairs*
tread	marcher (sur), parcourir	*to tread the streets* (battre le pavé) - *to tread on sb's toes* - *to tread* (prendre) *a path* - *to tread a cigarette end into the ground* (enfoncer)
trip	(faire) trébucher	*to trip sb (up) - to trip over sth*
	marcher d'un pas léger ou sautillant	*to trip in / out*

Exercices sur le chapitre 7 (5)

1. Testez vos connaissances en traduisant les verbes suivants:

A / tread - B / caper - C / hop - D / leap - E / squat - F / limp - G / scuttle - H / stride

2. Traduisez les expressions ou phrases ci-dessous en vous aidant des collocations et exemples de la colonne de droite:

A. Faire un saut de deux mètres. B. Faire un saut en parachute. C. Faire un bond pour atteindre qch. D. Se mettre à courir. E. S'accroupir par peur. F. Traverser une pièce sur la pointe des pieds. G. Se mettre debout d'un bond. H. Battre le pavé. I. Entrer sans bruit.

3. Dans les séries de mots proposés, indiquez lequel ne peut pas être un synonyme des autres:

A) LEAP / JUMP / STALK / BOUND
B) TRIP / STUMBLE / SAIL
C) TIPTOE / STOMP / STAMP
D) STRIDE / STALK / SAIL / LIMP
E) SCAMPER / SCUTTLE / STORM
F) SLIDE / SLIP / GLIDE / SHUFFLE

Posture and movement

6. Getting together

Collocations

■ *Adjectifs*

crowded	plein, bondé, encombré,	*crowded bus / city / street - a room may be crowded (out) with furniture / people - to have a crowded schedule* (emploi du temps chargé)
packed	bondé, comble, bourré	*a place may be packed with people - a leaflet may be packed with useful information*
	serré	*to be packed like sardines*
overcrowded	surpeuplé, bondé	*overcrowded cities / prisons / schools - a place may be overcrowded with tourists*

■ *Verbes*

cluster	se grouper, se regrouper	*to cluster around (sb) - to cluster together*
collect [-'-]	(se) rassembler	*to collect evidence / information - a crowd may collect*
	collectionner	*to collect stamps*
	passer prendre	*to collect sb in one's car / from the station*
gather	(se) réunir, rassembler	*to gather (round) - to gather round sb - to gather things / people together*
	ramasser, recueillir, récolter	*to gather wood / eggs / fruit - to gather in the corn*
huddle	se réunir, entrer en réunion	*to huddle (with sb) to discuss sth*
	se blottir	*to huddle round the fire*
squeeze in	réussir à (faire) entrer dans, (se) caser	*to squeeze into a car / into one's trousers - to squeeze sb / sth in(to) sth*
swarm [swɔːm]	pulluler, grouiller	*a place may be swarming with tourists*
	se déplacer en foule, déferler, envahir	*people may swarm in / out / round / through the gates / onto the football pitch*

Exercices sur le chapitre 7 (6)

1. Testez vos connaissances en traduisant les mots ci-desous:

A / crowded - B / overcrowded - C / to huddle - D / to cluster

2. Traduire en anglais:

A / L'entraîneur, après s'être lui-même réuni avec le président du club, avait réuni les joueurs pour une petite conversation amicale. B / La foule déferlait depuis deux ou trois heures dans le stade, maintenant comble. C / On avait eu du mal à caser les supporters de l'équipe visiteuse. D / Quand la partie commença, les joueurs se groupèrent de nouveau autour de leur capitaine.

8

People

1. Life

1.1. General

■ *Noms*

bloke	type, mec	**people**	gens
human being	être humain	**teenager**	adolescent (13 à 19 ans)
kid	enfant, môme	**youngster**	jeune

Collocations

background	milieu	*to be from / come from a certain / privileged / working-class background - to take into account sb's family background*
chap	type	*"Hello, old chap" - "Poor chap!"*
generation gap	écart, conflit de générations	*to bridge the generation gap*
guy	mec, gars, type	*a good / tough guy - this guy Johnson*
guys	mecs (hommes et femmes)	*"Come on, guys!"*
impression	imitation	*to do a good impression of sb*
mankind	humanité	*the future of mankind*
person	personne	*not to like sb as a person - to come in person*
privacy GB ['prɪvəsi] US ['praɪvəsi]	intimité, vie privée	*to value one's privacy - to hate the lack of privacy of a situation*

■ *Adjectifs*

rootless ['ru:tləs]	sans racines	

Collocations

private ['praɪvət]	privé	*sb's private life - to keep sth private*
public	publique, du public	*to attract public support - to be a hazard to public health / property*

■ *Verbes*

impersonate [-'---]	imiter	*to be able to impersonate sb on demand*

Exercices sur le chapitre 8 (1.1)

1. Testez vos connaissances en traduisant les mots ci-dessous:

A / private - B / public - C / kid - D / human being - E / background

2. Traduisez en anglais:

A / Enfant, il savait imiter tous ses professeurs à la demande. B / "Alors, les mecs? On y va!" C / C'était un brave mec, et le gars Johnson lui disait parfois: "Alors, vieux, ça va?" D / Certains adolescents constituent, dit-on, un danger pour la propriété privée. E / Peut-être est-ce parce que beaucoup de ces jeunes sont sans racines et n'ont nulle part où aller. F / Soyez indulgents envers eux: tous ne viennent pas d'un milieu aussi privilégié que le vôtre.

1.2. Stages of life

■ *Noms*

way of life	façon de vivre	**pro-lifer**	adversaire de l'avortement

Collocations

age	âge	*at the age of forty - to be / act one's age - to be underage / overage / of age - to come of age - old age pensioner* (OAP) (retraité) *- to act / feel / look one's age - to live to a ripe old age*
life	vie	*to live a busy / hard / uneventful / happy life - to save sb's life - to take one's own / sb's life - to have a long life expectancy - life and death - to devote one's life to sth / to sb / to doing sth*
lot	sort, destin	*to cast / throw in one's lot with sb - to fall to one's lot to do sth*
ups and downs	hauts et bas	*to experience ups and downs in (one's) life*

■ *Adjectifs*

immortal	immortel	**mortal**	mortel

Collocations

alive	vivant	*to be still / no longer alive*
eventful	mouvementé, fertile en événements	*eventful day / life*
live	en direct	*live broadcast / telecast / performance*
living ['lɪvɪŋ]	vivant, existant	*the living and the dead - the best living performance*
uneventful [,--'--]	terne, sans histoires	*uneventful day / life*

■ *Verbes*

exist [-'-]	exister, subsister	*to exist on bread and butter*
live	vivre	*to live very simply / in poverty / to a ripe old age - to live on love / on a low salary / off one's parents - to live to regret sth / doing sth* (finir par regretter)

1.3. Early stages

■ *Noms*

baby	bébé	**puberty**	puberté
incubator	couveuse	**toddler**	tout petit enfant
infancy ['---]	toute petite enfance	**newborn**	nouveau-né
infant	tout petit enfant	**menstruation**	menstruation
midwife	sage-femme	**(pair of) forceps**	forceps

Collocations

birth	naissance	*to be of noble birth - to give birth to a child - to be French by birth*
caesarian [sɪ'zeərɪ_ən]	césarienne	*to have a caesarian - a baby may have been born by a caesarian*

People 101

child		a child of five / aged five - to conceive / bear / bring up / feed / nurse / train / (toilet) train a child (apprendre à être propre)
childbirth	accouchement	to die in childbirth (en couches) - to attend childbirth classes (cours d'accouchement sans douleur)
delivery [-'---]	accouchement	to have a(n) easy / normal / breech (par le siège) delivery
junior	cadet	to be sb's junior by a few years
labour	travail	to induce (déclencher) labour - to go into / be in labour - to feel the labour pains
miscarriage	fausse-couche	to have a miscarraige
pregnancy	grossesse	to terminate (mettre fin à) an unwanted / pregnancy - an ectopic (extra-utérine) / false / phantom (nerveuse) pregnancy
still-birth	enfant mort-né, mort à la naissance	to have / recover from a still-birth
teens	adolescence	to be still in one's (early / late) teens
youth [ju:θ]	jeunesse jeune homme les jeunes	in one's (gilded) youth - in the prime of youth (en pleine jeunesse) a youth / several youths the youth of this country is / are ...

■ *Adjectifs*

newborn	récent, tout nouveau	**pubescent** [pju'besnt]	pubère
precocious [-'--]	précoce	**unborn**	qui n'est pas encore né, à venir

Collocations

born	né	he was born French - born and bred (élevé) in England - born of poor parents / to wealth (être né riche)
expectant	qui attend un bébé	expectant mother
grown-up	grand, mûr	sb's grown-up children - to be very grown-up at 11 years old
junior	jeune, inexpérimenté débutant, de statut inférieur	to be too junior to apply for a job junior doctor / partner / minister / school (primaire)
new-born	nouveau-né, récent	new-born baby / democracy
pregnant	enceinte	to be five months pregnant - to be / become / get pregnant with twins - to get a woman pregnant
premature ['premətʃə]	prématuré	a baby may be (born) two months premature - to have a premature baby
still-born	mort-né	still-born baby / plan
young	jeune	to be young at heart (avoir la jeunesse du cœur) / in spirit
youthful	de jeunesse	youthful prank (bêtise) / mistake / indiscretion (péché) / offender (jeune délinquant)

■ *Verbes*

menstruate ['menstrueɪt]	avoir ses règles	**have one's periods**	avoir ses règles

Collocations

be born	naître	to be born of sb - to be born to wealth / to poor parents / to do sth - I was born on March 2nd
deliver [-'--]	accoucher	a midwife helps to deliver a child - to be delivered of a daughter (old use) - to be delivered of a baby girl

1.4. The intermediate stage

■ *Noms*

adult ['--]	adulte	**menopause** ['menəupɔːz]	ménopause
grown-up	grande personne		

Collocations

middle age cinquantaine	*to be in early / late middle age - middle age spread* (embonpoint)

■ *Adjectifs*

adult ['--]	(d')adulte	**middle-aged**	qui a la cinquantaine
grown-up	(de) grande personne		

Collocations

mature [-'-] mûr, mature	*to be mature for one's age*
mellow serein, moins entier	*to grow more mellow over the years*

■ *Verbes*

break up rompre, ne pas marcher	*to break up with sb - sb's marriage may break up*
go through passer par	*to go through sth / a lot / a stage / a hard time*
grow up grandir	*to grow up to be sb / into a fine young woman*

1.5. Later stages

■ *Adjectifs*

elderly	âgé	**old**	vieux, ancien

Collocations

■ *Noms*

elderly personne âgée	*new housing for the elderly*
old age vieillesse	*to save money for one's old age* (ses vieux jours) - *to be stil active in one's old age*
senior ['siːnɪə] aîné	*to be sb's senior by a few years*
aged âgé / âgé, vieux	*a man aged 50* / *sb's aged uncle - the aged*
senior supérieur, responsable	*senior officials / management / cabinet / post* (portefeuille ministériel) */ executive*

■ *Verbes*

age vieillir	*to age fast / suddenly / a lot ¬ sth may age sb*

2. Death

■ *Noms*

cemetery ['semətri]	cimetière (ville)	**hearse** [hɜːs]	corbillard
churchyard	cimetière (campagne)	**orphanage** ['ɔːfənɪdʒ]	orphelinat
graveyard	cimetière (campagne)	**vault**	caveau

People

undertaker /	entrepreneur des pompes	**wreath** [ri:θ]	couronne (mortuaire)
mortician (US) [-'--]	funèbres	**grave-digger**	fossoyeur
widowhood	veuvage		

Collocations

burial ['berɪəl]	enterrement	*a burial is done / takes place - a burial service is held*
coffin	cercueil	*to gently lower sb's coffin into the grave*
death	mort	*to die a horrible / violent death - sth may cause sb's death - to face / meet one's (own) death - to pay the death duties*
deceased	défunt	*the name of the deceased (sg / pl)*
euthanasia [ˌju:θə'neɪzɪə]	euthanasie	*to practise / oppose / campaign for euthanasia*
funeral	obsèques	*to attend sb's funeral*
grave	tombe	*to lay sb's body into a grave*
mortality	mortalité	*infant mortality - mortality rate*
mourner	proche (du défunt)	*the mourners pay their last respects to the dead person*
mourning	deuil	*to be in / go into mourning for sb - to declare / observe a period of national mourning - to wear mourning (clothes)*
obit(uary)	rubrique nécrologique	*sb's obituary / obituary notice in a paper*
orphan	orphelin	*to be / become / be left an orphan - an orphan girl*
post-mortem	autopsie	*to do / carry out a post-mortem (examination) to establish the cause of death*
shroud	linceul	*to be wrapped up in a shroud*
suicide	suicide personne qui se suicide	*to contemplate / attempt / commit suicide* *the suicide's death may come as a shock*
tomb [tu:m]	tombe	*to lay sb to rest in a tomb*
tombstone	pierre tombale	*to have the dead person's name engraved on a tombstone*
widow / widower	veuve / veuf	*to be / become / be left a widow*
will	testament	*to make (out) / draw up / execute / challenge a will*

■ *Adjectifs*

bereaved	endeuillé	*bereaved person - the bereaved* (la famille et les amis)
dead	mort	*to drop dead - to rise from the dead - the quick and the dead* (les vivants et les morts)
deceased	décédé	*one / two deceased person(s) - to pay a tribute to the deceased*
late	défunt, feu	*sb's late husband - the late King - late Mr Jones*

■ *Verbes*

bury ['beri]	enterrer	*to bury sb alive*
die	mourir	*to die a natural death / intestate / in action* (au combat) */ of an illness*
mourn	pleurer	*to mourn (for) sb / sb's death / over lost opportunities*
outlive	survivre	*to outlive sb by 10 years*
pass away	s'en aller, mourir	*to pass away suddenly*
survive	survivre	*to survive sth / a disaster / sb*

Exercices sur le chapitre 8 (1.2 à 1.5 et 2)

1. Testez vos connaissances en traduisant les mots ci-dessous:

A / coffin - B / to bury - C / death duties - D / grave

2. Traduisez en anglais:

A / Elle a survécu à l'incendie, non? B / Elle pleure la mort de son père — Nous aussi. C / Il a beaucoup vieilli récemment, elle non. D / Il en a vu, pendant sa jeunesse, le pauvre! — Moi aussi. E / Elle est restée orpheline à 6 ans. — C'est ça. F / Ils n'ont pas pratiqué d'autopsie? — Bien sûr que si. G / Il ne s'est finalement pas suicidé et elle non plus, d'ailleurs. H / Il n'a pas assisté à l'enterrement au cimetière du village. — Elle, si. I / Elle est encore en deuil, lui non.

3. Quelle définition de gauche va avec quel mot de droite?

1. to live longer than someone else
2. to die
3. with nothing very much happening
4. old
5. a vehicle used for carrying a coffin
6. period during which one is a widow
7. the painless killing of sb very old or incurable
8. a very, very young child

A. euthanasia
B. infant
C. to pass away
D. to outlive
E. widowhood
F. uneventful
G. elderly
H. hearse

4. En consultant les exemples d'emploi et de collocation des mots de la colonne de droite, traduisez:

A / Trouver la mort dans un accident. B / Être majeur. C / Vivre très vieux. D / Une vie sans histoires. E / Être de 15 ans plus âgé que quelqu'un. F / Mettre fin à ses jours. G / Partager le sort de quelqu'un. H / Avoir la cinquantaine. I / Consacrer sa vie à quelqu'un. J / Rendre un dernier hommage au disparu. K / Payer les droits de succession.

5. Remettez dans un ordre cohérent les fragments de quatre phrases répartis dans les quatre lignes ci-dessous:

A. This brought about / He saved / It fell / The firm's
B. junior manager / the break-up / to my lot
C. her life / is an expectant / to write
D. of their marriage / the deceased's obituary / on two occasions / mother

6. La colonne A (comme ANSWER) vertical, vous donnera un mot désignant ce que nous avons tous été au début de notre vie.

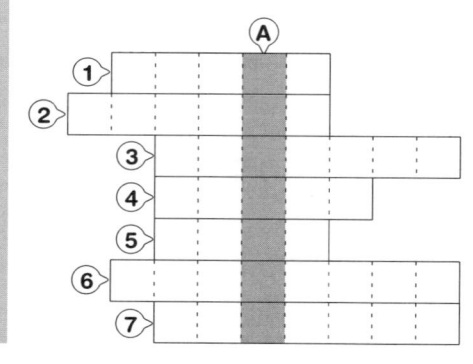

1. The end of it all.
2. Younger and not so competent.
3. Old.
4. Sb whose husband is dead.
5. a dead man's wishes.
6. having lost sb dear to one.
7. to manage to live in spite of extreme danger.

People

3. Identity and status

■ *Noms*

changeling	enfant substitué à un autre (par les fées)	childhood	enfance
		family record book	livret de famille

Collocations

bachelor	célibataire	to remain a bachelor - to lead a bachelor's life - to be a(n) confirmed / eligible bachelor
boy	garçon	when a boy (quand il était petit), he ... - a good / naughty little boy - a mother's boy
	élève	an old boy (un ancien élève)
boyhood	enfance	sb's boyhood dream - in / during one's boyhood
fame	célébrité	to seek / achieve international / undying fame - to rise to fame - sth may bring sb fame
fate	destin	to decide one's own fate - to meet one's fate - a stroke of fate - a certain fate may befall sb (être réservé à)
foundling ['faʊndlɪŋ]	enfant trouvé	to adopt a foundling
girl	fille	a good / naughty little girl
girlhood	enfance	in / during one's girlhood
honour	honneur	it is a great / dubious honour to do sth - to do / bring sb honour
ID [aɪ'diː]	papiers (d'identité)	not to have any ID
identity	identité	to hide / conceal / reveal one's identity - to establish sb's identity - a case of mistaken identity
lad	gars, copain	a good / bad lad - "Hi, lad!"
lass / lassie	fille / fillette	"lads and lasses!"
maid / maiden	jeune fille, demoiselle	maidens wearing crowns of flowers
male	homme	two British males - a particularly eligible male
man	homme	it is man's fate to do sth - a handsome / ugly / family / married / single / divorced man
manhood	âge d'homme	to reach manhood - in one's early manhood
name	nom	sb's Christian / first (prénom) / middle / family / last name (nom de famille)
namesake	homonyme	to be sb's namesake
nickname	surnom	to give / be given / earn a nickname
renown	célébrité, renom	to achieve / attain great renown - sb's renown may spread across a country - sb of great renown
reputation	réputation	to have / hold the reputation of doing sth - to acquire an enviable reputation for doing sth - to live up to one's reputation
status ['steɪtəs]	statut	to achieve / enjoy / have legal / marital status
surname	patronyme, nom de famille	to drop / take one's husband's surname
woman	femme	a pretty / fine-looking / divorced / married / single woman
womanhood	féminité	to reach womanhood - to be the image of womanhood

■ *Adjectifs*

famous ['feɪməs]	célèbre	to be famous as a writer / for sth / for being sth / for doing sth
female	féminin, de(s) femme(s)	female characteristic / equality

foster	d'accueil, de placement	*foster parents / home*
honourable	honorable, respectable	*honourable person / agreement / intentions - it is honourable to do sth*
male	masculin, d'homme(s)	*male student / attitude / population / role*
manly	masculin, viril	*manly figure / laugh / voice - it is manly to do sth*
mannish	masculin (homasse)	*mannish voice / manners - to look / sound mannish*
renowned	renommé, réputé	*to be renowned as a painter / for sth / for being / doing sth*
reputable	qui a bonne réputation, honorable	*reputable company / wine / conduct / scientist*
respectable	respectable, comme il faut	*respectable person / home / profession*
so-called	soi-disant, prétendu	*sb's so-called friends / uncle*
underage	mineur	*underage sex / drinking - to be underage*
womanish	efféminé	*womanish reaction / look / voice - to look / sound womanish*
womanly	féminin	*womanly virtues - it is womanly to do sth*

■ *Verbes*

identify	(s')identifier	*to identify sth / sb as being sth - to identify with sb / sth*
name	nommer	*to name a child after / for (US) his grandfather*
	fixer, indiquer	*to name the day for a ceremony*
register ['---]	(s') inscrire, enregistrer	*to register for work / for a course / as sb / as sth - to register (sb / sth) with the authorities / with the police - to register a birth* (déclarer)

Exercices sur le chapitre 8 (3)

1. Testez vos connaissances en traduisant les mots ci-dessous:

A / namesake - B / nickname - C / lass - D / ID - E / so-called - F / womanly - G / womanish

2. Traduisez en anglais:

A / Il a une voix efféminée — Ah, bon vous trouvez? B / Vous vous identifiez trop à votre père — Mais non! C / C'est un père de famille tout à fait digne de respect — En effet. D / On vous a appelé Leonard d'après de Vinci? — Mais oui. E / Il faut que je m'inscrive à l' ANPE — Moi aussi. F / Jane a eu une enfance heureuse — Ce n'est pas le cas de toutes les femmes. G / Elle cherche la célébrité — Pas vous? H / Il est resté célibataire toute sa vie — Pas vrai! — Si! I / On croit que Patricia est une enfant substituée à la naissance — Et ce n'est pas le cas? — On n'est pas sûr — En tout cas, c'est une enfant trouvée.

3. Remplacez dans chaque phrase le mot souligné par un des mots en majuscules proposé ci-dessous:

ACHIEVE   DROP   FAMOUS   FOSTER   HONOURABLE   IDENTITY   NICKNAME   RENOWNED   REPUTABLE   STATUS   SURNAME

A. He was <u>female</u> for being witty. B. He was given a <u>namesake</u> by his school-pals. C. He could hardly remember his <u>lassie</u> parents. D. He was an <u>underage</u> scientist who wrote in all the <u>manly</u> scientific journals. E. He tried to hide his real <u>manhood</u> for unexplained reasons. F. She had <u>identified</u> such <u>a</u> personal <u>namesake</u> that she could <u>register</u> her husband's <u>womanhood</u> when she married.

People

4. Behaviour and morals — Qualities and defects ['--]

4.1. General

Collocations

■ *Noms*

attitude	attitude	*to take / strike* (affecter) *a casual attitude about sth / towards sb*
behaviour	comportement	*to exhibit a strange / model / scandalous / unruly behaviour about sth / towards sb - to be on one's best behaviour*
character ['---]	caractère	*to form / reflect sb's strange / true / disreputable character - to lack character - a person of great character - sth may be in / out of character* (bien / ne pas bien correspondre à) *(with sth)*
defect	défaut, défectuosité	*it may be a character defect in sb that... - to try and correct a birth defect*
failing	défaut, insuffisance	*to have little / many failings*
fault	faute, défaut	*it / sth may be your fault - it may be through no fault of yours that... - to be at fault for / in not doing sth - to know one's faults*
habit	habitude	*to be / get into / get out of a good / bad / ingrained habit of doing sth - to form a habit - to make a habit of sth / of doing sth - to break sb of a habit*
moral ['mɒrəl]	morale	*the moral of a story*
morale [mə'rɑːl]	moral, optimisme	*to raise / undermine sb's morale - sb's morale may be low / high*
morals ['mɒrəlz]	sens moral, moralité	*to have loose / strict / no morals - to protect / corrupt sb's morals*
personality [,--'---]	personnalité, caractère	*wonderful / amusing / forceful charismatic personality - to form / shape sb's personality - to lack personality*
principle	principe	*to have high / no principles - to be a person of principle - to lay down / betray / apply / stick to one's principles*
quality	qualité	*to have / possess / show outstanding qualities of patience and understanding*
shortcoming	défaut faiblesse	*to be conscious of one's shortcomings*
temper	caractère, tempérament humeur, colère	*to have an even / quick / hot temper to be in a good / bad / dreadful temper - to be in a temper / out of temper* (en colère) *- to keep / lose / fly into a temper* (se mettre en colère)
temperament ['---]	tempérament	*artistic / excitable temperament - to be quiet by temperament - a person of conservative temperament*
value	valeur, principe valeur, prix	*to cherish / foster / return to traditional moral values to attach value to sth - to put / set high value on something*
vice	vice	*to fight / wipe out* (éradiquer) *vice*
virtue	vertu	*to promote / reward / extol the virtues of sth / sb* (chanter les louanges) *- to have many virtues and few faults*
weakness	faiblesse, point faible	*to have a weakness for sth - to reveal / show weakness - the strengths and weaknesses of sth / sb*

■ *Adjectifs*

apt	qui a tendance à	*to be apt to be lazy - to be apt to do sth*
bad-tempered	qui a mauvais caractère de mauvaise humeur	*bad-tempered person / child to be bad-tempered on frequent occasions*
even-tempered	au caractère égal	*a happy, even-tempered woman*
immoral [-'---]	immoral	*immoral behaviour / person - it is immoral to do sth*

innate [ɪ'neɪt]	inné	*to have / show (an) innate talent / goodness*
moral	moral	*moral obligation / judgement / person / grounds / support*
prone to	sujet, enclin à	*to be prone to accidents / to illness / to do sth*
proper ['prɒpə]	convenable, approprié, qui convient	*proper place / clothes / thing to say - sth may be proper for sth / for doing sth - it is proper to do sth / that...*
right	bien (moralement)	*to do what is right - it is right to do sth / that...*
shameful	honteux, indigne	*shameful waste / lack / performance - it is shameful to do sth / that...*
temperamental [,--'--]	capricieux, lunatique inné, viscéral	*temperamental person / behaviour* *temperamental dislike / difference* (différend)
used to	habitué à	*to be used to sth / to doing sth*
vicious	vicieux, pervers méchant, malveillant brutal, violent, cruel	*vicious person* *vicious person / look / words* *vicious attack / killer / system*
virtuous	vertueux	*virtuous person - to feel virtuous*
well-behaved	bien élevé	*well-behaved child / crowd*
well-bred	cultivé, poli	*well-bred child / voice*
worthy	digne	*worthy person / winner of a prize - to be worthy of sth / to do sth*
wrong	mal (moralement)	*wrong action - it is wrong to do sth / that...*

■ *Verbes*

act	agir, se comporter	*to act on impulse / like a child / without thinking / as if...*
behave	se conduire	*to behave well / badly / strangely / responsibly*
deserve	mériter	*to deserve sth / to do sth / being discussed*
mend one's ways	s'amender	*to promise to mend one's ways*

Exercices sur chapitre 8 (4.1)

1. Testez vos connaissances en traduisant les mots ou expressions ci-dessous:

A / to strike an attitude - B / sb's many failings - C / habit - D / moral (n.) - E / morale - F / morals

2. Traduisez en anglais:

A / Elle a échoué, mais ce n'était absolument pas de sa faute. B / Le docteur est coupable de ne pas avoir envoyé son malade à l'hôpital plus tôt. C / La morale de cette histoire est qu'on ne peut pas aisément remonter le moral de quelqu'un lorsque des échecs répétés l'ont sapé. D / Il s'est mis en colère, et pourtant c'est une personne au caractère égal dont les vicissitudes de la vie ont forgé le caractère. E / Homme au sens moral très strict, il veut éradiquer le crime, le vice et la violence. Noble tâche. F / Son œuvre mérite d'être largement reconnue. G / Elle m'a servi d'interprète aux USA. H / Arrête d'agir comme le gosse capricieux que tu es. I / C'était un jeune homme bien élevé dont le talent inné pour la musique le rendrait un jour digne de jouer dans les grands orchestres.

3. Remplissez les blancs à l'aide des mots de la double pyramide ci-dessous:

A. He's lost his bad _____ of drinking too much. B. He is not perfect - he has many _____s C. She is a woman of _____. D. He behaves in an _____ way. E. He prefers _____s to _____s: which is a natural inclination in many of us. F. His strange _____ sometimes surprises me. G. Is he conscious of his _____s? H. He sometimes strikes an _____ that I do not approve of. I He is a man who _____s praise. J He is _____ to accidents. K. He lacks _____. L. He is often _____ although he is _____ to deny it. M. He tends to _____ like a child.

1.		APT
2.		HABIT
3.		FAILING
4.		CHARACTER
5.		PERSONALITY
6.		PRINCIPLES
7.		VIRTUES
8.		WRONG
9.		IMMORAL
10.		BEHAVIOUR
11.		SHORTCOMING
12.		ATTITUDES
13.		DESERVE
14.		PRONE
15.		ACT

4.2. Pride / Self-confidence / Diffidence

Collocations

■ *Noms*

conceit [kən'si:t]	vanité, suffisance	*sb's incredible conceit - to be full of conceit*
confidence (U) ['---]	confiance	*to have confidence (in oneself / in sb) - to gain / win / betray sb's confidence - to place / misplace one's confidence - to have every confidence* (être sûr) *that ... - to lack confidence* (confiance en soi) *- to inspire confidence in sb*
confidence (C)	confidence	*to take sb into one's confidence - to exchange confidences - to violate a confidence - to tell sb sth in strict confidence*
dash	panache	*to carry off a situation with dash - to cut a dash* (faire grosse impression)
diffidence ['---]	manque de confiance en soi	*to do sth with some / great diffidence*
nerve	courage, assurance culot	*it takes a lot of nerve to do sth - to lose one's nerve* *"you've got a bloody nerve!" - "the nerve of it!" - "what a nerve!"*
pride	fierté, vanité	*sth may be a blow to one's pride - to take pride in sth / in doing sth - sth may hurt sb's pride*
self-confidence	confiance en soi	*to lack self-confidence - not have the self-confidence to do sth - to acquire / develop / have / display / show self-confidence - sth / sb may restore / undermine sb's self-confidence*
spirit	courage, énergie, fougue	*a man of spirit - to lack spirit - to break sb's spirit*

■ *Adjectifs*

assertive [-'---]	assuré, péremptoire	*assertive person / act - to need to be more assertive*
conceited [-'---]	vaniteux, suffisant	*conceited person - to be / sound conceited about sth*
confident	assuré, confiant	*confident person / tone / manner - to be confident of / about sth / that...*
diffident	qui manque de confiance en soi	*diffident person / manner - to be diffident about sth / about doing sth*
gentle	doux	*gentle person / manner / nature / voice / method - to be gentle with sb - to try gentle persuasion on sb*
humble	humble, modeste	*humble background / birth / origins / apologies - in my humble opinion*

insecure	peu sûr (de soi)	*insecure person / period / future - to feel insecure about sth / about doing sth*
proud	fier	*proud owner / parents - to be proud of sth / of sb / to do sth / that...*
righteous ['raɪtʃəs]	juste, vertueux	*righteous man / anger*
self-collected / possessed	qui garde son sang froid	*self-collected person / public speaker - to remain self-collected*
self-confident	sûr de soi	*aggressively self-confident person*
self-conscious	timide, gêné	*self-conscious person - to feel self-conscious about sth / about doing sth / that...*
self-righteous	sûr du bien-fondé de ses valeurs	*self-righteous person / indignation*

■ *Verbes*

boast [bəʊst]	se vanter s'enorgueillir de posséder	*to boast of / about sth / about doing sth / that... the town boasts three theatres*
brag	se vanter bruyamment	*to brag about sth / about doing sth / that..*
pride oneself (on)	s'enorgueillir (de)	*to pride oneself on sth / on doing sth / that...*

Exercices sur le chapitre 8 (4.2)

1. Testez vos connaissances en traduisant les mots ci-dessous:

A / dash (n.) - B / gentle - C / conceited - D / assertive - E / righteous

2. Choisissez:

A. He prided himself of / from / on / over / in his achievements.
B. He takes pride of / in / on / from / at the success of his children.
C. He did not have the pride / dash / nerve / conceit to contradict anyone.
D. He was so self-conscious / self-righteous / self-possessed / assertive that he blushed every time he was spoken to by a woman.

3. Traduisez:

A. Son incroyable suffisance rendait cet homme vertueux antipathique à tous. B. Sur la promenade, ses habits dernier cri faisaient grosse impression. C. Il faut beaucoup de courage pour surmonter un tel coup porté à son orgueil. D. Que peut une femme peu sûre d'elle-même face à un homme aussi sûr de lui? E. Les attentats terroristes sont destinés à faire perdre courage aux populations visées. F. De quoi se vante-t-il ainsi? G. De quoi s'enorgueillit-elle?

4.3. Shyness and insolence / Curiosity / Wisdom and folly

■ *Noms*

foolishness	stupidité	**madness**	folie, aliénation
folly (U)	folie, sottise	**insolence** (U)	insolence

Collocations

consistency [-'---]	cohérence, logique	*to lack consistency - to show great / little / no consistency*
exhibition	démonstration	*an exhibition of rudeness / arrogance / musicianship / skill - to make an exhibition of oneself* (se donner en spectacle)

People

fool	imbécile, sot	*to be a fool / fool enough to do sth*
imp	coquin, espiègle	*an imp of a child*
wisdom	sagesse	*a person of great wisdom - to doubt / question sb's wisdom - to have the wisdom to do sth*

■ *Adjectifs*

cheeky	insolent	*cheeky brat (gamin) / self-confidence*
consistent	cohérent	*sth may be consistent with sth*
	régulier	*consistent person / improvement / loyalty*
coy	faussement timide	*coy voice / smile*
	secret, réservé	*to be coy about sth / about doing sth*
cranky	bizarre, excentrique	*cranky person / ideas / habits*
crude	grossier, vulgaire	*crude person / behaviour / joke*
curious	curieux	*to be curious about sth / to do sth - it is curious that...*
down-to-earth	terre à terre	*down-to-earth person / manner / explanation*
familiar	familier	*familiar name / face - there is sth familiar about sth / sb*
	au courant	*to be familiar about sth - sth may be familiar to sb*
forthright	direct, franc	*forthright person / manner / opposition*
fresh	impertinent, qui prend des libertés	*to be / get fresh with sb*
gushing	exubérant, excessivement enthousiaste	*gushing person / praise*
inquisitive [-'---]	curieux, indiscret	*inquisitive person / mind - to be / to sound inquisitive about sth / sb*
lively ['laɪvli]	vivant	*lively person / conversation - to be lively company*
matter-of-fact	pratique, prosaïque	*matter-of-fact approach / voice / ideas*
meek	doux, docile	*meek person - to look / sound meek*
mild	doux	*mild person / manner / voice*
modest ['mɒdɪst]	modeste	*modest salary needs / house - to be modest about sth*
	modéré, peu marqué	*modest improvement / recovery / gains in the elections*
	pudique, réservé, simple	*modest person / clothes / manner / walk*
no-nonsense	direct, franc, raisonnable	*no-nonsense person / manner / approach*
nosy	curieux, indiscret	*nosy person - to be nosy*
open-minded	ouvert, sans préjugés	*open-minded person - to be open-minded about sth*
peaceful	paisible	*peaceful person / place / afternoon - to feel / look peaceful*
practical	pratique, réaliste	*practical person / problem / experience - for all practical purposes (à toutes fins utiles)*
quiet	calme paisible	*quiet person / village / life*
	tranquille, silencieux	*to keep quiet about sth*
reasonable	raisonnable	*reasonable person / price - to be reasonable about sth - it is reasonable to do sth*
restless	agité, impatient	*restless person / night - to feel / get restless*
saucy	effronté	*saucy boy / remark - to be saucy about sth*
sensible	judicieux, sensé	*sensible person / decision / idea - it is sensible to do sth*
	pratique	*sensible clothes / shoes / way of dealing with sth*
	conscient	*to be sensible of sth*
sensitive	sensible à	*to be sensitive to sth*
	susceptible	*to be sensitive about sth*
	délicat	*sensible issues / area*

shy	timide	shy person / smile
	intimidé, craintif	to be shy of sb / of doing sth
straightforward	direct, franc	straightforward person / answer / account / manner - to be straightforward about sth
	simple, pas compliqué	straightforward instructions / issue
subdued [-'-]	contenu, retenu	subdued laughter / cheers / feeling
	morose, replié sur soi	subdued person
timid	timide, apeuré	timid person / attempt
unassuming [,--'--]	modeste, sans prétentions	unassuming person / manner
unreasonable	peu raisonnable, déraisonnable	unreasonable person / request - it is unreasonable (of sb) to do sth
wise	sage, avisé	wise person / decision - to be wise to do sth -it is wise (of sb) to do sth

■ *Verbe*

show off	se faire remarquer	to show off in front of people
	exhiber	to show off one's new car / knowledge

Exercices sur chapitre 8 (4.3)

1. Testez vos connaissances en traduisant les mots suivants:
A / meek - B / peaceful - C / open-minded - D / sensible - E / sensitive

2. Choisissez:
A. It would be shy / restless / sensible to buy new shoes, I think.
B. He gave a straightforward / subdued / meek account of the event.
C. As he was a timid person, he often spoke in a nosy / subdued / practical voice.
D. What he said was quite cheeky / consistent / cranky with what he'd said before.

3. Traduisez:
A / Arrête de faire étalage de tes connaissances. B / Est-il idiot au point de croire cela? C / J'aime sa façon pratique d'aborder les problèmes. D / Il a présenté ses arguments à sa façon directe habituelle. E / Il est un peu trop curieux de ce qui arrive à ses voisins. F / Je mets en doute sa logique et sa sagesse.

4. Crossword puzzle

Across:
1. used for walking - 2. (jumbled) informal for 'earthquake'; two cardinal points - 3. alleys to a house; negation - 4. preposition (see: 3 and 7 down) - public show of objects 5. (jumbled) full of wisdom; south-east - 6. unduly inquisitive ; hard hat (in a tropical climate) - 7. (jumbled) not a nice place for a bird - 8. (jumbled) in a bank or wine cellar; suffix - 9. (jumbled) music with a steady beat; eager to know about sth - 10. pretending to be shy - 11. personal pronoun; (jumbled) insolent

Down:
1. take no notice of - 2. French personal pronoun. - 3. not up (see: 4 across and 7 down); net-like decorative cloth made of very fine thread - 4. adverb; conjunction - 5. insolent - 6. full of life; Trade Union - 7. prefix connected with formerly; we all live on it - 8. excessively enthusiastic - 10. British Standard; vulgar - 11. calm and silent - 12. all right; with vinegar - 13. little devil -14. (jumbled) snow - 15. absurdity.

People 113

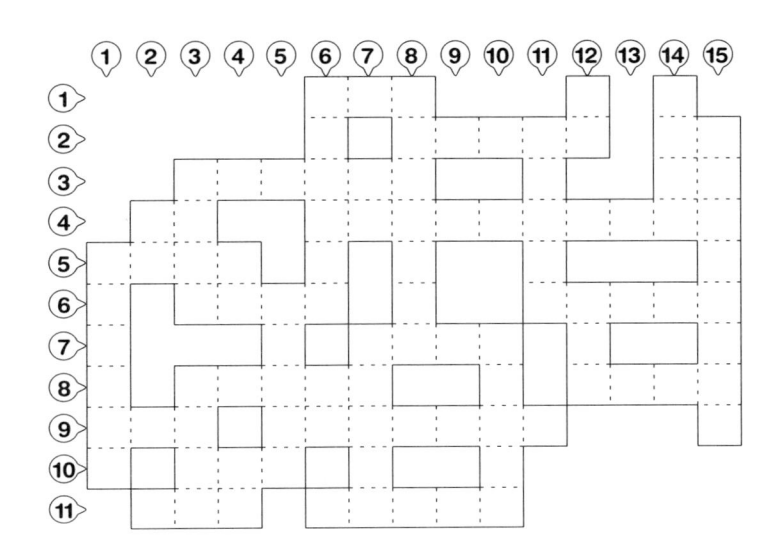

4.4 Awkward / Helpless / Obstinate / Whimsical

Collocations

■ *Nom*

whim	caprice, fantaisie	*to indulge a whim* - '*as the whim takes him*' ('comme l'idée lui prend') - *to do sth at* (selon) *the whim of sb / on a whim*

■ *Adjectifs*

awkward ['ɔːkwəd]	difficile, peu commode	*an awkward person to live with - the awkward age* (ingrat) - *sth / sb may make things awkward for sb - it is awkward to do sth*
	gêné, embarrassé	*awkward silence / smile - to feel awkward*
	gênant	*awkward situation - it is awkward to do sth*
	maladroit, gauche	*awkward person / gesture*
choos(e)y	difficile	*to be choosy about sth / about doing sth*
demanding GB [dɪˈmɑːndɪŋ] / US [dɪˈmændɪŋ]	exigeant	*demanding job / public / child*
dogged ['dɒgɪd]	tenace, persévérant	*dogged person / determination*
	obstiné	*dogged refusal*
easy-going	facile à vivre, décontracté	*easy-going person / attitude / manner*
edgy	nerveux, sur les nerfs	*to be / seem / sound edgy*
fastidious [-'--]	tatillon, méticuleux	*fastidious person - to be fastidious about sth*
	minutieux	*fastidious work*
headstrong	têtu, entêté	*headstrong person*
	imprudent	*headstrong actions*
helpless	impuissant, qui ne peut agir	*helpless person / attitude / feeling - to be helpless to do sth* (incapable)
	désespéré	*to give sb a helpless look*
	sans défense	*helpless children*
highly-strung	nerveux, tendu	*highly-strung person*
hopeless	désespéré	*hopeless person / case / love / attempt*
	invétéré	*hopeless drunk / liar*
	incompétent	*hopeless dancer - to be hopeless at sth / at doing sth / as a dancer / with one's hands*

jumpy	nerveux, effrayé	*jumpy person - to be / get jumpy about sth / about doing sth*
narrow-minded	étroit d'esprit, borné	*narrow-minded person / approach / opinion*
obstinate	têtu, obstiné tenace	*obstinate person / refusal - to be obstinate about sth obstinate resistance / belief in sth*
stern	sévère austère	*stern person / measure / warning / rebuke stern appearance / look (regard) / voice*
stubborn	têtu obstiné, acharné	*stubborn person stubborn silence / refusal / opposition / resolve*
touchy	susceptible délicat	*touchy person - to be touchy about sth touchy subject / issue / point*
uncompromising [-'----]	intransigeant ardent, convaincu	*uncompromising attitude / party men uncompromising opponent / commitment*
uneasy	mal à l'aise	*to be / feel / sound uneasy about sth / about doing sth / that ...*
vulnerable	vulnérable	*vulnerable person - to be vulnerable to sth*
wayward ['weɪwəd]	têtu, peu souple imprévisible	*wayward person wayward behaviour / reaction*
whimsical ['wɪmzɪkl]	capricieux, fantasque étrange, insolite	*whimsical person / behaviour / way whimsical idea / air / smile*

Exercices sur le chapitre 8 (4.4)

1. Testez vos connaissances en traduisant en anglais les mots ou expressions ci-dessous:

A / se sentir gêné - B / refus obstiné - C / facile à vivre - D / sur les nerfs - E / personne tatillonne
F / travail minutieux - G / cas désespéré - H / nerveux, tendu - I / capricieux - J / intransigeant

2. Joignez une phrase de droite à chaque phrase de gauche:

A. You really are a headstrong person
B. You shouldn't be so demanding
C. He is a hopeless drunk
D. I always get jumpy about people
E. He is a pretty awkward person
F. He bought his new car
G. You're so helpless at doing the simplest things of daily life
H. I know you're a dogged person

1. so I don't see why you call his drinking behaviour wayward.
2. to live with because he's so edgy.
3. but I do wish you were a little less obstinate at times.
4. but need you always show such stubborn insistence on having people indulging your every whim?
5. that you can't afford to be choosey about who offers to help you.
6. as you know he is pretty hopeless at this.
7. who speak in such a stern voice.
8. on a whim and now regrets he did so.

4.5. Courage and cowardice

Collocations

■ *Noms*

courage	courage	*to show great / grim (à toute épreuve) courage - to pluck up enough courage / to lack the courage to do sth - it takes courage to do sth*
coward ['kaʊ_əd]	lâche	*to call sb a dastardly (infâme) coward*
cowardice ['kaʊ_ədɪs]	lâcheté	*to do sth out of (par) cowardice - to detect a streak (tendance) of cowardice in sb*

People

daredevil	casse-cou	*to be a bit of a daredevil - a daredevil rider / stuntman* (cascadeur)
grit	cran	*to show true grit - it takes grit to do sth - to have the grit to do sth*
gut(s)	courage	*it takes a lot of guts to do sth - to have the guts to do sth*
pluck	courage	*to show a lot of pluck - it takes pluck to do sth - to have the pluck to do sth*
tomboy	garçon manqué	*to be a bit of a tomboy*

■ *Adjectifs*

bold [bəʊld]	hardi, intrépide, audacieux	*bold person / gesture / move - to put a bold face* (faire face) *on sth - to be / make so bold as to do sth*
courageous [kəˈreɪdʒəs]	courageux	*courageous person / attempt / behaviour - it is courageous (of sb) to do sth*
cowardly	lâche	*cowardly person / behaviour / attack - it is cowardly (of sb) to do sth*
daring	audacieux, hardi, risqué provoquant	*daring person / climb / move* (initiative) */ rescue operation daring skirt / dress*
fearful	peureux, craintif	*to be fearful of sth / of doing sth / that*
fearless	intrépide, sans peur	*fearless person / reporter - to be fearless of sth*
gallant	courageux, vaillant	*gallant person / effort / fight / stand* (position) *against sth*
game	prêt (à tout) courageux	*to be game for anything to be game to the end*
manly	mâle, d'homme, viril	*manly person / laugh / activities - it is manly to do sth*
plucky	qui a du cran	*plucky person - it is plucky of sb to do sth*
poor	médiocre	*poor violin-player / result - to be in poor health - to come only a poor second* (n'occuper que la seconde place)
puny	misérable, pitoyable	*puny person / efforts / little engine - a puny 10 % vote* (voix)

■ *Verbes*

challenge	défier, mettre au défi	*to challenge sb to a game of chess / sb for the leadership / sb to do sth*
court	risquer, aller au devant de	*to court death / disaster / arrest*
dare	oser	*to dare (to) do sth - "I dare not do sth" - "dare you answer back?"*
	défier	*to dare sb to do sth*
dodge	(s')esquiver, se faufiler	*to dodge sth / doing sth - to dodge into / out of a place*
hide	cacher	*to hide sth / sb from sb - to hide (oneself)*
hold out	tenir le coup	*to hold out for a period of time*
stick out	tenir jusqu'au bout	*to stick out an evening course - to stick it out*

Exercices sur le chapitre 8 (4.5)

1. Testez vos connaissances en traduisant les mots ci-dessous:

A / craintif - B / intrépide - C / cowardice - D / grit - E / game (adj.) - F / plucky - G / to stick it out

2. Traduisez:

A / Comment a-t-il osé défier un homme aussi vaillant? B / Ne me cachez pas la vérité, en esquivant mes questions. C / Il faut du cran pour aller au devant d'une arrestation quasi certaine. D / Il y a dans ce personnage une tendance à la lâcheté qu'on ne trouve pas chez certains héros virils des romans d'amour à quatre sous. E. Il n'a remporté que 15% des voix - résultat médiocre. F / Ne traitez pas de lâche un cascadeur casse-cou qui, pour une fois, se demande s'il tiendra jusqu'au bout. G / Il a eu l'audace de la contredire.

4.6. Kindness

Collocations

■ *Noms*

consideration	considération, estime, égard	*to show consideration for sb's feelings* (ménager les susceptibilités) - *to do sth out of* (par) *consideration for sb*
devotion	dévouement attachement	*to show blind / great / utter devotion to sth / to sb sb's selfless devotion to sb*
kindness	bonté	*to display great kindness to sb - to do sth out of* (par) *kindness - to do sb a kindness* (rendre service)
mercy	pitié, indulgence	*a mercy flight / mission* (humanitaire) - *to show infinite mercy towards sb - to have mercy on sb*
	merci	*to beg for mercy - to be at sb's mercy*
patience	patience	*to lose one's / run out of / show infinite patience - sb's patience may wear thin* (avoir des limites) - *it takes a lot of patience to do sth*
thoughtfulness	prévenance, considération	*to show great thoughtfulness towards sb / about sth*
tolerance	tolérance	*to have / show great tolerance for sth / towards sb*
understanding [‚--'---]	compréhension	*to have good understanding* (comprendre vite) - *to have a good understanding of sb's problems - sth may be beyond understanding* (dépasser l'entendement)

■ *Adjectifs*

considerate [-'---]	prévenant	*to be considerate of sb - it is considerate (of sb) to do sth*
decent ['di:snt]	convenable, décent	*decent person / wage / home - it is decent* (sympathique) *(of sb) to do sth*
devoted	dévoué ardent	*devoted person - to be blindly devoted to sth / sb devoted research / care*
dutiful	consciencieux, obéissant	*dutiful person / son / attendance at church*
even-handed	impartial, équitable	*even-handed person / treatment of sb*
fair	juste, équitable	*a scrupulously fair person / decision / share - to be fair to sb - sth is / is not fair on sb - it is fair (of sb) to do sth - "fair enough!"* (très bien!, d'accord!)
faithful	fidèle	*faithful friend / translation / customer - to be faithful to sb*
forbearing	patient, tolérant	*forbearing person / nature - to be forbearing with sb*
generous	généreux	*generous person / donation - it is generous (of sb) to do sth - to be generous in one's praise / with one's time / with one's money*
humane [hju'meɪn]	humain	*humane action / treatment*
merciful	clément, charitable	*merciful person / release* (libération) - *to be merciful to sb - it is merciful (of sb) to do sth*
kind	bon, aimable	*kind person / review / behaviour / eyes - to be kind to sb - it is kind (of sb) to do sth - to be so kind as to do sth*
kindly	bon, bienveillant	*kindly person / interest in sth / attitude*

People

lavish ['lævɪʃ]	généreux, magnanime	*lavish gift / portion / promise - to be lavish in doing sth / in one's praise / with money*
obliging	serviable, complaisant	*to be obliging to sb - it is very obliging of sb (to do sth)*
patient	patient	*patient person / sigh - to be patient with sb*
sweet	gentil, doux adorable	*sweet person / voice - it is sweet of sb to do sth a sweet old lady / little house*
sympathetic [,--'---]	compatissant compréhensif	*sympathetic words - to be sympathetic to be sympathetic to / towards sb / to sb's grievances*
thoughtful	prévenant, attentionné réfléchi, sérieux	*thoughtful person / behaviour - it is thoughtful of sb to do sth thoughtful decision / remark / work / study*
tolerant ['---]	tolérant	*to be tolerant of others / of criticism*
understanding	compréhensif, bienveillant	*to be understanding (of / about sth) - understanding person / boss / smile*
whole-hearted	sans réserve	*whole-hearted support / sympathy / efforts*

■ *Verbes*

look up to sb	avoir du respect pour qqn	**treat sb well**	bien traiter qqn
relent	se laisser fléchir	**sympathise with sb**	plaindre qqn, compatir avec qqn

Collocations

devote	consacrer, donner	*to devote time / money / oneself to sth / to sb / to doing sth*
lavish	prodiguer	*to lavish money / time / effort / praise / one's attention on sb*
oblige	rendre service (à), obliger	*to do sth to oblige (sb) - to oblige sb with sth* (prêter) - *to oblige sb by doing sth*

4.7. Unkindness

Collocations

■ *Noms*

malice	méchanceté, malveillance	*an act of sheer malice - to do sth from / through malice - to bear sb malice* (en vouloir à qqn) - *with malice aforethought* (avec préméditation)
meanness	manque de cœur, mesquinerie	*to show meanness with / about sth / to sb - to do sth out of* (par) *meanness*
unkindness	manque de gentillesse, méchanceté	*sb's incredible unkindness to sb else*

■ *Adjectifs*

beastly	insupportable, infect bestial, brutal	*beastly child / day - to be beastly to sb beastly person / behaviour*
cruel	cruel	*cruel person / world / winter / remark - to be cruel to / towards sb - it is cruel (of sb) to do sth*
harsh	dur, sévère	*harsh person / upbringing / life / punishment / voice - to be harsh with / to sb*
insensitive [-'---]	insensible	*insensitive remarks - to be insensitive to sth - it is insensitive of sb to do sth*
malicious	méchant, malveillant	*malicious look / gossip* (médisances) */ telephone call - to be malicious towards sb*

mean	mesquin, méchant	*to be mean to sb - to feel mean about sth* (avoir honte) - *it is mean of sb (to do sth)*
nasty GB ['nɑːsti] / US ['næsti]	désagréable, déplaisant horrible, méchant	*nasty person / remark / temper / weather nasty man / trick - to be nasty to sb - it is nasty of sb (to do sth)*
ruthless	impitoyable, implacable	*ruthless person / ambition / determination / efficiency*
thoughtless	peu délicat, qui manque d'attention irréfléchi	*thoughtless person / behaviour / action - it is thoughtless (of) sb to do sth thoughtless remark / decision / action*
unfaithful	infidèle	*unfaithful husband - to be unfaithful to sb*
unfeeling	insensible, dur	*to be unfeeling towards sb / sth - it is unfeeling of sb to do sth*
unkind	peu aimable, désobligeant, pas gentil	*unkind person / remarks - to be unkind to sb - it is unkind (of sb) to do sth*
unsympathetic	insensible, incompréhensif, hostile	*to be unsympathetic to sth / to a cause*

■ *Verbes*

grind down	écraser, réprimer	**oppress**	opprimer
ill-treat sb	maltraiter qqn	**wrong sb**	porter préjudice à qqn
molest [mə'lest]	importuner, harceler		

■ *Adverbes*

kindly	aimablement, obligeamment favorablement	*to kindly offer to help to look kindly on sth / think kindly of sb - not to take kindly to sth / to doing sth*
whole-heartedly	de tout cœur	*to agree to sth / to support sth / sb wholeheartedly*

Exercices sur le chapitre 8 (4.6 et 4.7)

1. Testez vos connaissances en traduisant les mots ci-dessous:

A / kindly (adj.) - B / wholeheartedly - C / to relent - D / lavish (adj.) - E / to lavish

2. Traduisez en anglais:

A / C'est très attentionné de votre part de consacrer tout votre temps libre à aider les autres. B / Que c'est gentil à vous de me prêter de l'argent. C / J'apporte à votre généreux projet mon soutien sans réserve. D / Il ne tarit pas d'éloges sur mes romans. E / C'est très sympa de faire montre d'une telle abnégation. F / Je fais cela par pure bonté. G / Ma patience a des limites. H / Consciencieux et prévenant, voilà deux mots qui décrivent bien cet homme éminemment humain, connu par ailleurs pour être un mari fidèle.

3. Remplacer chaque mot souligné par un des mots en majuscules ci-dessous:

DECENT   TO DEVOTE   DEVOTED   DUTIFUL   EVEN-HANDED   LAVISH
TO LOOK UP TO   THOUGHTLESS

A / He received <u>forbearing</u> treatment in the distribution of the old man's legacy. B / He was <u>merciful</u> with his own as well as with other people's money. C / It was most <u>thoughtful</u> of him to have kept the old woman waiting outside in the cold. D / He <u>looked up to</u> his whole life to helping others. E / She earned a <u>ruthless</u> salary from the start. F / She cared for him in his old age as a <u>cruel</u> daughter should. G / He spent years of <u>lavish</u> care by the side of his ailing mother. H / The only person he ever <u>relented</u> was his grandfather.

People

4.8. Prudence / Imprudence

Collocations

■ *Nom*

discretion	discrétion	*to be the soul of discretion*
	bon sens, raison	*to show / lack discretion / use one's own discretion - to reach the age of discretion*

■ *Adjectifs*

cautious	prudent, circonspect	*cautious person / driver / approach - to be cautious about sth / of sb / about doing sth / in doing sth*
discreet [-'-]	discret	*discreet person / distance* (respectueuse) */ enquiries - to be discreet about sth*
imprudent [-'--]	imprudent	*imprudent person / behaviour - it is imprudent (of sb) to do sth*
prudent	prudent	*prudent person / behaviour / choice - it is prudent (of sb) to do sth*
punctual	ponctuel	*punctual person / start of sth - to be punctual in sth / in doing sth*
rash	imprudent, irréfléchi	*rash person / move / decision - it is rash (of sb) to do sth - in a rash moment*
reckless	imprudent, téméraire	*reckless person / driving / disregard for sth - it is reckless (of sb) to do sth*
wary ['weəri]	sur ses gardes, méfiant	*wary person - to be wary of sb / of / about doing sth - keep a wary eye on sb*

■ *Adverbe*

warily	avec circonspection	*to do / eye sth warily*

Exercices sur le chapitre 8 (4.8)

1. Testez vos connaissances, en traduisant les mots ci-dessous:

A / wary - B / rash (adj.) - C / reckless

2. Traduire en anglais:

A / Elle le regardait toujours avec circonspection. B / L'experience lui avait appris à être prudente dans le choix de ses partenaires. C / Il serait imprudent, pensait-elle, irréfléchi, téméraire même d'accepter sa proposition d'entrée de jeu. D / Comme elle hésitait! On lui avait si souvent reproché de manquer de bon sens. E / Elle se méfiait des hommes ponctuels, discrets: trop parfaits.

4.9. Reliability and deceit

Collocations

■ *Noms*

cad	goujat	*to behave like a cad*
conscience	conscience	*to appeal to sb's / ease one's conscience - to have a clear / easy / bad / guilty conscience*
craft GB [krɑːft] / US [kræft]	ruse	*to show / use subtle political craft - to obtain sth by craft*

deceit [-'-]	tromperie, duperie, fausseté	*to practice deceit - to expose* (dénoncer) *sb's deceit*
deception	fraude, subterfuge, abus de confiance	*credit card deceptions - to practise / resort to deliberate / calculated deception*
prig	pharisien, prétentieux	*a self-righteous / offensive* (répugnant) *prig*

■ *Adjectifs*

crafty GB ['krɑːfti] / US ['kræfti]	rusé, malin, astucieux	*crafty person / tactics / politician / idea*
deceitful	trompeur, sournois	*deceitful person / attempt - it is deceitful to do sth*
deceptive	trompeur	*deceptive impression / appearance*
dependable	fiable, sérieux	*dependable person / car*
gullible	crédule, naïf	*gullible person*
honest ['ɒnɪst]	honnête	*honest person / living - to be honest about sth - it is honest to do sth*
ingenuous [-'---]	ingénu, candide	*ingenuous person / expression / apology*
naive [naɪ'iːv]	naïf	*naive person / belief / hope - it is naive (of sb) to do sth*
plain-spoken	qui a son franc parler	*plain-spoken person - to be plain-spoken about sth*
prim	guindé, prude très comme il faut	*prim person / behaviour - to be prim and proper* (collet-monté) *prim voice*
reliable	sûr, sérieux	*thoroughly reliable person / evidence*
scrupulous	scrupuleux	*scrupulous person / scholarship* (érudition) *- to be scrupulous about sth / about doing sth*
sly	rusé, dissimulé espiègle	*sly person / smile / remark - to do sth on the sly* (en douce) *- sly little girl*
smug	suffisant, content de soi	*smug person / satisfaction - to be / sound (damned) smug about sth*
spontaneous [-'---]	spontané	*spontaneous person / reaction / enthusiasm*
square	ennuyeux, vieux jeu honnête franc, clair et net	*square person / haircut square person - to give / get a square deal square answer / person*
steadfast	constant, inébranlable loyal, dévoué	*steadfast friend / opponent / admiration to be steadfast in one's support*
straight	traditionnel, conventionnel franc, droit clair, simple	*straight person / theatre / play straight person / talk - to be straight with sb straight answer / choice*
underhand	sournois	*underhand person / dodge* (combine) */ way / attempt*
unscrupulous	peu scrupuleux	*unscrupulous person / methods*
upright	droit, honnête	*upright person / citizen*

■ *Verbes*

deceive	tromper	*to deceive sb (into doing sth) - to deceive oneself* (se mentir à soi-même)
depend on	compter sur	*to depend on sb for sth / on sb to do sth*
exaggerate	exagérer	*to exaggerate sth grossly / greatly*
rely on	faire confiance à qqn	*to rely on sb for sth / on sb to do sth*

Exercices sur le chapitre 8 (4.9)

1. Testez vos connaissances en traduisant les mots ci-dessous:

A / underhand - B / upright - C / to deceive - D / deception - E / cad - F / crafty

2. Remplir les blancs à l'aide des mots des pyramides ci-dessous:

1. self-satisfied in an unpleasant way. 2. trust (that sb will do sth to help you) 3. with honesty 4. you may have a clear or a guilty _____. 5. sb who has no scruples is _____. 6. to make sth appear more important than it really is. 7. a _____ answer or choice is simple and clear. 8. a _____ style of dress is old-fashioned 9. a _____ person is easily shocked. 10 too clever to be honest. 11. somebody you can count on is _____. 12. same as 11. 13. sb who is _____ says exactly what they think. 14. sb who has scruples is _____. 15. willing to believe everything other people say. 16. behaviour that is deliberately intended to make people believe sth which is not true. 17. sb who thinks they behave better than other people. 18. sb who deceives and treats women (especially) badly. 19. a form of deceit. 20. if you make sb believe that sth is true, which is not, you _____ them. 21. sb who deceives other people is _____. 22. not planned or arranged in advance. 23. naive and innocent. 24. a moral, honest person is _____. 25. foolishly credulous. 26. crafty.

1. _ _ _ _
2. _ _ _ _ _ _
3. _ _ _ _ _ _ _
4. _ _ _ _ _ _ _ _ _
5. _ _ _ _ _ _ _ _ _ _ _ _
6. _ _ _ _ _ _ _ _ _ _
7. _ _ _ _ _ _ _ _ _ _
8. _ _ _ _ _ _
9. _ _ _ _
10. _ _ _ _ _ _
11. _ _ _ _ _ _
12. _ _ _ _ _ _ _ _ _ _
13. _ _ _ _ _ _ - _ _ _ _ _ _
14. _ _ _ _ _ _ _ _ _ _
15. _ _ _ _ _ _ _ _
16. _ _ _ _ _ _
17. _ _ _ _
18. _ _ _
19. _ _ _ _ _
20. _ _ _ _ _ _
21. _ _ _ _ _ _ _ _ _
22. _ _ _ _ _ _ _ _ _ _ _ _ _
23. _ _ _ _ _ _ _ _ _
24. _ _ _ _ _ _ _
25. _ _ _ _ _
26. _ _ _

4.10. Earnestness and negligence

Collocations

■ *Noms*

earnest ['ɜːnɪst]	sérieux	*to be / begin in deadly earnest - it is raining in earnest* (pour de bon)
indulgence	indulgence	*to treat sb with indulgence*
	assouvissement, laisser-aller	*indulgence of one's every desire - indulgence in bad habits*
	satisfaction, gâterie	*to allow / deny oneself any unjustifiable indulgence / a few indulgences*
responsibility [- ,--'---]	responsabilité	*to dodge* (esquiver) */ claim / disclaim / share / assume / be given / take (over) full / the ultimate responsibility for sth*
talent (U)	talent	*a person of great / considerable talent - to have / display / develop / squander* (gâcher) *(a / one's) great / natural / mediocre / outstanding talent for sth / for doing sth*
	personne(s) de talent	*to look for new / young / local talent*
zeal	zèle, ardeur	*to show great / excessive zeal for sth*

■ *Adjectifs*

absent-minded	distrait	*absent-minded person / way*
casual	désinvolte, nonchalant	*casual person / attitude - to be / appear / sound casual about sth*
complacent [kəm'pleɪsnt]	satisfait, content de soi	*complacent person / attitude / smile - to be complacent about sth*
earnest ['ɜːnɪst]	sérieux	*earnest person / attempt - to be earnest about sth*
	ardent, fervent	*earnest hope / desire*
energetic [,--'---]	énergique, dynamique	*energetic person / activity / programme - to feel energetic*
giddy ['gɪdi]	écervelé, léger	*giddy person / show*
lazy	paresseux	*lazy person / excuse / smile / way*
listless	indolent, apathique	*listless person / attitude / voice*
neglectful	négligent	*neglectful person / attitude - to be neglectful of sth / of sb / of one's duty / of one's appearance*
off-hand	désinvolte, cavalier	*off-hand manner / approach / remark - to be off-hand with sb*
painstaking	consciencieux, soigneux	*painstaking person / journalist / worker*
	rigoureux, méticuleux	*painstaking research / care*
remiss	négligent	*to be remiss in / about sth / in / about doing sth - it is remiss of sb (to do / not to do sth)*
responsible	responsable	*responsible person / decision - to be responsible (to sb) for sth / for doing sth - to hold sb responsible*
	de responsabilité	*responsible job / activity / post*
slack	négligent, peu sérieux	*slack person / worker - to be slack about sth / about doing sth*
	négligé, relâché	*slack work / discipline / procedure*
talented ['---]	doué, talentueux	*talented person*
versatile GB ['vɜːsətaɪl] / US ['vɜːsətl]	souple, aux talents variés	*versatile person / mind*
wanton	immoral, dissolu	*wanton person / behaviour / thoughts*
	injustifié	*wanton cruelty / action*
zealous ['zeləs]	zélé, acharné	*zealous person - to be zealous in doing sth*

■ *Verbes*

help	aider	*to help sb with sth - to help (sb) to do sth*

People

indulge	se permettre (un plaisir), s'adonner à	*to indulge in drink / day-dreaming / fantasies*
	gâter, faire plaisir	*to indulge sb / sb with sth / oneself*
	satisfaire	*to indulge a passion / sb's every whim*
pull oneself together	se reprendre	*to need to pull oneself together*
see sb through	aider à tenir le coup	*to see a friend through hard times - enough money to see sb through the week*

Exercices sur le chapitre 8 (4.10)

1. Testez vos connaisssances en traduisant les mots ci-desous:

A / casual - B / wanton - C / zealous - D / slack (adj.)

2. Traduire en français:

A / The interview will begin in dead earnest when the head of the department joins the interviewing team. B / You can't expect to take over the responsibility of that department if you're not a sufficiently responsible person. C / Do try not to sound too casual when answering the questions. D / A complacent smile would be out of place. E / Don't speak in a listless voice if you want to convince your prospective employer. F / Only an applicant with a clearly versatile mind stands a chance of getting the job. G / Never be slack about the apparently small details like your personal appearance. H / Some applicants are remiss in sending in all the relevant information about themselves in time. I / The firm is looking for young, artistic talent. J / Make sure you don't look absent-minded during the interwiew. K / Showing that you are an earnest, energetic, not a lazy, giddy person will get you the job. L / Pull yourself together, don't just for this once indulge (in) your usual offensive nose-picking habit! M / The interviewer won't be using wanton cruelty. Well, at least, I hope he won't! N / This is an exceptional occasion — you will have to deny yourself some of your favourite indulgences, like smoking if you're not clearly permitted to do so.

9

The family and family life

1. Parents and relatives

■ *Noms*

aunt	tante	great grandfather	arrière grand père
baby	bébé	infant	tout petit enfant
brother	frère	nanny (GB) /	nourrice, bonne d'enfants
daughter	fille	child's nurse (US)	
father ['fɑːðə]	père	nephew	neveu
folks [fəʊks]	parents, famille	niece	nièce
gran / granny	grand'mère	pacifier ['pæsɪfaɪ ə]	tétine
grand(d)ad(dy)	grand'père	son	fils
grandfather	grandpère	uncle	oncle

Collocations

child	enfant	*to be a spoiled / latchkey* (livré à lui-même) */ an only / adopted / child - to toilet-train a child*
childhood	enfance	*childhood memories*
cousin	cousin	*first cousin* (germain) */ first cousin once removed* (issu de germain)
family	famille	*large / nuclear / close / broken / extended family*
home	maison, foyer, chez soi	*to make one's home at / in a place - to be (at) home / go home*
household	maison, famille, foyer	*most households own television sets - sb may have to manage the whole household - to do the household chores* (tâches ménagères)
kin (pl)	parents, famille	*all of sb's kin may be dead*
next of kin (pl)	parents les plus proches	*sb's next of kin may be informed of their death*
lullaby ['lʌləbaɪ]	berceuse	*to sing lullabies to a baby to help him / her to go to sleep*
maternity	maternité	*maternity home / leave* (congé) */ benefit / allowance*
mother ['mʌðə]	mère	*expectant / unwed / surrogate* (porteuse) */ foster* (adoptive) *mother*
motherhood	maternité	*motherhood may or may not suit sb*
offspring (pl. inv.)	progéniture, rejetons	*to have / produce one / several offspring*
parent	parent (père ou mère)	*loving / strict / permissive / parent*
relation / relative ['---]	parent (autre que père ou mère)	*close / distant relatives*
twin	jumeau	*twinboy(s) / girl(s) / brother(s) / sister(s)*
upbringing ['---]	éducation	*to be given a(n) easy-going / strict / religious upbringing*

■ *Adjectifs*

hen-pecked	mené par le bout du nez	**single / unmarried**	célibataire

Collocations

elder	aîné, plus âgé		to be sb's elder by two years
eldest	aîné (de plus de deux)		to be the eldest of four children
homesick	nostalgique		to be homesick for sb / sth

Verbes

bottlefeed	nourrir au biberon	support	subvenir aux besoins de
breastfeed	nourrir au sein	look after	s'occuper de
spoil	gâter		

Collocations

bring up (GB) / raise (US)	élever	to bring up a child strictly / in the catholic faith
gather	(se) réunir	to gather around sb - to gather all of one's children
look after	s'occuper de	to look after one's children and home
lull [lʌl]	faire dormir, endormir	to lull a baby to sleep
	endormir la méfiance de qqn	to lull sb into doing sth

Exercices sur le chapitre 9 (1)

1. Testez vos connaissances en traduisant les mots ci-dessous:
A / lullaby - B / surrogate mother - C / motherhood - D / relatives - E / kin - F / next of kin

2. En vous aidant des collocations et exemples de la colonne de droite, traduisez les expressions ou phrases ci-dessous:

A / Endormir un bébé en le berçant. B / Subvenir aux besoins de ses neveux et nièces. C / S'ennuyer de quelqu'un. D / Recevoir une éducation sévère ou libérale. E / Il ne me reste, comme famille, que quelques parents éloignés. F / Ce sont des parents permissifs qui ne s'occupent guère de leurs rejetons. G / En endormant sa méfiance, il lui a fait faire les choses les plus horribles. H / Un enfant livré à lui-même

2. Married life / Divorce / Inheritance

Noms

best man	garçon d'honneur	godchild	filleul
birthday	anniversaire	groom	(jeune) marié
break-up	rupture, échec (mariage)	henparty	soirée entre femmes
bride	(future / jeune) mariée	in-laws	beaux-parents, belle-famille
bridegroom	(futur / jeune) marié	mother-to-be	future mère
bridesmaid	demoiselle d'honneur	old maid	vieille fille
courtship	cour (période où on fait la cour à qqn)	spinster (terme administratif)	célibataire (femme)
daughter-in-law	belle-fille	stag party	soirée entre hommes

The family and family life 127

stepfather / mother	beau-père, belle-mère; etc	**Valentine card**	carte de vœux (de la Saint-Valentin)
stepson	beau-fils (remarriage)		
sweetheart	petit(e) ami(e)		

Collocations

bachelor	célibataire	*to be a(n) confirmed / eligible bachelor* (bon parti)
bequest [-'-]	legs	*to make a bequest to sb*
care	placement	*to take / put sb into care* (placer dans un établissement ou famille d'accueil)
cuckold ['kʌkəʊld]	cocu	*to be made a cuckold*
custody	garde	*to gain / receive / get / be given / awarded / granted custody of sb*
death duties	droits de succession	*to have to pay heavy death duties / death tax (US)*
divorce [-'-]	divorce	*to get / grant a divorce - to sue* (entamer une procédure) *for an undefended* (non contesté) *divorce / for divorce by mutual consent*
dowry ['daʊri]	dot	*provide a dowry for sb*
engagement	fiançailles	*to announce / break off one's engagement to sb*
executor [-'---]	exécuteur testamentaire	*to appoint an executor*
godfather/mother	parrain, marraine	*to be godfather to a child*
guardian	tuteur	*to appoint sb guardian to sb*
heir [eə] / **heiress** ['eəres]	héritier, héritière	*to be / fall the rightful / sole heir to sb's property*
honeymoon	lune de miel	*to be / go on one's honeymoon*
husband	mari	*to leave one's faithful / unfaithful husband*
inheritance (U)	héritage	*to come into an inheritance*
legacy	legs	*to leave / get a legacy*
marriage	mariage	*to arrange / annul / break up a civil / common-law marriage* (concubinage) *- sth / sb may cause the break-up of a marriage - a marriage may fall apart* (se désagréger)
polygamy	polygamie	*to practice polygamy*
pregnancy	grossesse	*the early / late stages of pregnancy - to get a pregnancy test - to wish to terminate an unwanted pregnancy*
proposal	demande en mariage	*to receive / turn down a proposal from a man - to make a proposal to a woman / a woman's parents*
ward(-of-court)	pupille	*to be made ward-of-court*
wedding	mariage	*to celebrate one's wedding anniversary - to be present at / attend the wedding ceremony - to officiate at / perform* (célébrer) *a wedding*
wife	femme, épouse	*to beat / desert one's wife - a battered / jealous / common-law wife* (concubine) *- to have two children by one's former wife*
will	testament	*to draft / draw up / make out / challenge* (contester) */ execute a will*

■ *Adjectifs*

adopted	adopté	**adoptive**	adoptif

Collocations

broken	désuni, brisé	*broken home / marriage*
divorced	divorcé	*to get divorced from sb*

engaged	fiancé	*to be / become engaged to sb*
foster	d'accueil, de placement	*foster parents / family / home*
married	marié	*to be married to sb - to be married with two children*
pregnant	enceinte	*to get pregnant (by sb) - to be three months pregnant with a little girl*

■ Verbes

adopt	adopter		**disinherit** [ˌdɪsɪn'herɪt]	déshériter
baptize / christen ['krɪsn]	baptiser		**woo** [wuː]	courtiser
celebrate	fêter			

Collocations

bequeathe / leave	léguer, laisser	*to bequeathe all of one's property* (biens) *to one particular heir*
break up	rompre, ne pas marcher	*to break up with sb - sb's marriage may break up*
cheat	tromper	*to cheat on one's wife / on one's husband*
court	faire la cour	*to court a girl*
elope [-'-]	s'enfuir de chez soi	*to elope with a man (to marry him)*
divorce	divorcer	*to divorce sb*
foster	accueillir	*to foster a child into one's home*
foster out	placer	*to foster a child out to a foster home*
inherit [-'--]	hériter	*to inherit sth from sb*
look after	s'occuper de	*to look lovingly after sb*
marry	(se) marier,	*to marry sb - to marry off one's daughter to sb*
propose	demander en mariage	*to propose to sb*
separate	se séparer	*to separate (from sb)*
split	se séparer, rompre	*to split (with sb)*
succeed	succéder à	*to succed sb*
wed	(se) marier, épouser	*to wed (sb) - to get wed at an early age*
wish	souhaiter	*to wish sb many happy returns of the day* (souhaiter à qqn un bon anniversaire)

Exercices sur le chapitre 9 (2)

1. Testez vos connaissances en traduisant les mots suivants:

A / best man - B / foster (adj.) - C / custody - D / spinster - E / to elope - F / to split

2. En vous aidant des collocations et exemples de la colonne de droite, traduisez les expressions ci-dessous:

A / Un foyer désuni. B / Placer un enfant dans un foyer d'accueil. C / Hériter de quelqu'un. D / Tomber enceinte d'un inconnu. E / Être enceinte de trois mois. F / Être enceinte d'une petite fille. G / Entamer une procédure de divorce. H / Fêter un anniversaire de mariage. I / Un célibataire endurci. J / Être fiancé / marié avec quelqu'un.

10
Social and human relations

1. Social relations

1.1. General

Collocations

■ *Noms*

acquaintance [-'--]	connaissance, relation	to be an acquaintance of sb's - to make sb's acquaintance - to have / strike / keep up an acquaintance with sb - sb may be just a nodding / passing acquaintance
form	usage	it is good / bad form to do sth (ça se fait / ça ne se fait pas)
call	visite	to pay / make a call on sb - a doctor may make house calls (se déplacer)
caller	visiteur	to be a(n) usual / casual caller
crowd	foule	sth / sb may attract / draw a disorderly / an enormous crowd - a crowd may collect / gather / break up / disperse / mill around (se presser nombreuse)
	bande	to mix with the wrong crowd - to run around (traîner) with a fast crowd (de fêtards) / with a wild (déchaînée) crowd
encounter	rencontre	to have a brief encounter with sb
function	réception, cérémonie	to attend / a(n) annual / social (mondaine) function
go-between	intermédiaire	to act as a go-between
greeting(s)	accueil	to extend a friendly / warm greeting to sb
	bon souvenir, carte	to send holiday / the Season's (de vœux) / one's best greetings
guests	invités, visiteurs, gens	to invite guests to dinner - to have unexpected guests over the weekend
host [həʊst]	hôte, invitant	to act the dutiful host - to play host to the Olympic Games
introduction	présentation	to make a formal introduction of sb - to need no introduction
invitation	invitation	to send out invitations - to do sth at sb's invitation - 'by invitation only'
manners	manières	to have good / charming / bad / awful manners - to mind one's manners - to learn some manners - it is bad manners to do sth
mixer	personne sociable ou peu sociable	to be a good / bad mixer
name-dropping	mention de noms de gens connus	to be fond of name-dropping - there was a lot of name-dropping over dinner
newcomer ['---]	nouveau venu	to be a newcomer to sth / to computing / to a town
party	réception, fête	to attend / crash (entrer sans être invité) / throw (organiser) a singles party (pour célibataires)
pomp	pompe	to open a new shop with pomp and circumstance (grand apparat)
throng [θrɒŋ]	foule, multitude	throngs of people - a patient throng
touch	contact	to get / keep in touch with sb / lose touch (se perdre de vue)

treatment (U)	traitement	*to complain of ill-treatment - to get good / inhumane treatment*
venue ['venju:]	lieu de réunion ou de rendez-vous	*to decide on the venue for sth*
visit	visite	*to make / pay / cancel a formal / friendly / state visit to a place / a country - to be on a visit*
visitor	visiteur, personne en visite	*to show in / out a visitor - to be a frequent visitor from / to a country*
welcome	bienvenue, accueil	*to bid sb* (souhaiter) *welcome - to give sb a hearty / warm / cool welcome - to receive an enthusiastic welcome home*

■ Adjectifs

crowded	bondé, encombré, plein de monde	*crowded streets / shops - a room may be crowded with furniture / people*
formal	solennel, de cérémonie officiel soigné, guindé	*formal dinner / occasion / dress / ball* *formal agreement / denial* (démenti) */ talks* *formal person / style / language*
informal [-'--]	décontracté, informel officieux	*informal dress / dinner / gathering* *informal visit / talks*
non-U	peu raffiné, "pas classe", commun	*non-U (non upper-class) table manners / language / behaviour*
odd man out / odd one out	exclu, intrus	*to be / feel the odd one out*
unanimous [-'---]	unanime	*unanimous agreement / vote - to be unanimous in sth / in one's dislike of sth / in doing sth*
unsociable	peu sociable, sauvage	*unsociable person - to appear unsociable*
U	distingué, 'classe'	*it may not be very U to do sth*
welcome	bienvenu bienvenu, opportun	*welcome person - to be / feel welcome to sth - to make sb welcome* *welcome news / offer / relief*

■ Verbes

call	passer	*a postman / doctor may call everyday / every now and then*
call by	passer (US)	*to intend to call by later on*
call for	passer prendre	*to call for sb / sth at a certain place*
call (in) at	passer chez / à	*to call (in) at the grocer's*
call in / into	passer chez / à	*to ask somebody to call in again later on - to call into the office to pick some papers up*
call on	rendre visite à	*to call on sb*
crowd	se presser en foule	*to crowd about / round sb to do sth - to crowd the shops*
crowd in	s'entasser	*to crowd in / into a place*
drop in	passer rapidement	*to drop in (on sb)*
expect sb	attendre (la venue de qqn) s'attendre à ce que compter sur qqn	*to expect friends for dinner* *to expect that...* *to expect sb to do sth*
get along / on	s'entendre	*to get on well with sb / not to get on together*
get together	se réunir	*to get together with some friends*
greet	saluer accueillir	*to greet sb with a wave of the hand* *to greet sb with open arms - to greet a piece of news with great relief*
introduce [,--'-]	présenter	*to introduce sb / oneself (to sb)*
invite	inviter	*to cordially invite sb to a party / sb to do sth*

Social and human relations

join	rejoindre	*to join sb at a place / later on*
	se joindre à	*to join sb for / in a drink / in doing sth*
look sb up	passer voir	*to look sb up that one has lost track of*
	se renseigner sur, chercher	*to look sb up in a directory / phone book*
meet	(se) rencontrer	*to meet (sb) regularly - to meet up with sb (US)*
misbehave [,--'-]	se conduire mal	*to misbehave repeatedly / in public*
participate [-'---]	participer	*to participate in sth / in doing sth*
socialize ['---]	fréquenter qqn, être sociable	*to socialize with sb - to find it difficult to socialize*
summon	appeler, convoquer	*to summon sb as a witness / sb to do sth*
unite	unir, s'unir	*to unite in sth / in doing sth / to do sth*
visit	rendre visite	*to visit sb / to visit with sb (US)*
welcome	accueillir	*to warmly welcome sb / sb in / sb home*
	accueillir, accepter	*to welcome an opportunity / news / sb's*
	avec plaisir	*marriage / a cup of tea*

Exercices sur le chapitre 10 (1.1)

1. Testez vos connaissances en traduisant les mots ou expressions ci-dessous:
A / to greet - B / caller - C / encounter - D / to misbehave - E / to unite - F / venue

2. Traduisez en anglais:
A / Votre médecin se déplace-t-il? B / Ça ne se fait pas de ne pas rendre visite à des voisins qui sont nouveaux venus dans le quartier: il faut leur réserver un accueil chaleureux. C / Se rendre à des réceptions, porter une tenue de soirée adaptée à chaque occasion, parler un langage soigné, faire attention à bien se tenir, se joindre à des gens qu'on connaît à peine pour ne pas se sentir exclu, présenter les invités les uns aux autres (sauf ceux qui, connus de tout le monde, n'ont pas besoin d'être présentés), participer aux jeux, s'il y en a, tout cela, c'est plus qu'une personne peu sociable comme moi peut supporter. D / Jouer les hôtes, accueillir les invités à bras ouverts, servir d'intermédiaire entre les gens, faire se rencontrer Monsieur Lebrun et Madame Lepetit, se plier au jeu des noms connus qu'on cite comme ça en passant, veiller à ce que les dames s'entendent bien entre elles et souhaitent ensuite se fréquenter; dans le grand monde, on compte sur vous pour faire tout cela. E / Organiser soi-même les soirées, dégager (ou faire dégager) les pièces encombrées de meubles afin que les invités puissent danser, faire attention à qui est invité, passer voir les voir les amis de ses parents à l'étranger, envoyer à sa famille, sans oublier personne, un carte de bon souvenir, rester en contact avec des gens qu'on a perdus de vue depuis l'école, en les invitant à dîner: telles sont les obligations des jeunes filles de bonne famille.

1.2. Feasts, festivals and festivities

■ *Noms*

All Saints' Day	Toussaint	**hot cross buns**	brioches du Vendredi Saint
All Souls' Day	Jour (ou Fête) des Morts	**Palm Sunday** [pɑːm]	Dimanche des Rameaux
bonfire	feu de joie	**Pancake Day**	Mardi-Gras
Easter	Pâques	**Passover**	Pâque Juive
Good Friday	Vendredi Saint	**Shrove Tuesday** [ʃrəʊv]	Mardi-Gras
festival	fête, festival	**Whitsun(tide)**	Pentecôte
festivity	festivités, réjouissances	**Xmas**	Noël
feast	fête, jour de fête		

Collocations

Boxing Day [ˈbɒksɪŋ]	26 ou 27 décembre, jour des cadeaux	*the first weekday after Christmas*
carol	chant (joyeux)	*to sing Xmas carols*
Christmas	Noël	*to celebrate / stay over Christmas / give Christmas boxes* (cadeaux) *on Christmas Eve or on Christmas Day - to pull* (apart) *Christmas crackers* (diablotins) *- Father Christmas / Santa Claus (US)*
feast	fête, jour de fête	*to keep feasts like Easter - feast days - movable* (mobile) */ immovable feasts*
	festin	*to be given / treated to a feast*
Guy Fawkes' night [gaɪˈfɔːks]	nuit de Guy Fawkes	*to burn the guy* (effigie) *of Guy Fawkes, in memory of his failed attempt to blow up Parliament in 1605*
Halloween [ˌhæləʊˈiːn]	veille de la Toussaint	*on Halloween children dress up as ghosts or witches and make lanterns out of pumpkins* (citrouilles)
maypole	mât de mai	*a painted, flower-decked pole to dance around on May 1st*
New Year	Nouvel An	*New Year's Day / Eve - Happy New Year!*
red-letter	très important, mémorable	*red-letter occasion / day*
Thanksgiving (day)	fête nationale américaine, jour d'action de grâce(s)	*4th Thursday in November*

■ *Verbes*

feast	festoyer	*to feast on / off smoked salmon*

Exercices sur le chapitre 10 (1.2)

1. Testez votre compréhension en traduisant les mots ci-dessous:

A / bonfire - B / Halloween - C / festival - D / Passover

2. Traduisez en anglais:

A / N'allumez pas de feu de joie dans votre jardin le Vendredi Saint, le jour des Morts ou à la Toussaint. B / Ne chantez pas de chants de Noël, ne donnez pas d'étrennes ou de diablotins aux enfants le jour de Pâques. C / Au mois de mai, on danse, dans certaines régions d'Angleterre autour d'un arbre de mai: ne vous trompez pas de jour! D / La Pâque juive, la Pentecôte, le Nouvel An chrétien ne sont pas des fêtes qui risquent de se chevaucher. E / Vous avez de meilleures chances de vous régaler de dinde rôtie lors de la fête du 4ème jeudi de novembre aux Etats-Unis qu'au Mardi gras, jour des crêpes. F / Le jour où vous vous êtes déguisé en Père Noël a-t-il vraiment été le plus grand jour de votre vie?

1.3. Fun

■ *Noms*

gossip(er) (C) [ˈgɒsɪp]	commère		**dirt** (U) (US)	ragots

Collocations

anecdote	anecdote	*to tell a witty / dull anecdote*
fun (U)	amusement, plaisir	*to have great fun - it is good fun to do sth - to poke fun* (se moquer) *at sb / make fun of sb - what fun!*

Social and human relations

gossip (U)	commérages	*to spread a piece / a tidbit of gossip / idle gossip* (ragots) */ malicious* (malveillant) *gossip / silly gossip about sb / that ...*
guffaw [gʌ'fɔː]	rire bruyant	*to give / let out a guffaw*
hell	amusement emploi comme intensif expression de colère	*to do sth for the hell of it* *to have a hell of a good time* (s'amuser vachement) *to raise hell* (gueuler) *- to tell sb to go to hell - to hell with it!*
humour	humour	*to have a sense of humour - dry* (mordant) */ deadpan* (pince-sans-rire) */ slapstick* (gros) *humour*
impression	imitation	*to do a funny / really good impression of sb*
jest	plaisanterie	*to say sth in jest - sth may be no jest* (à prendre sérieusement)
joke	plaisanterie, jeu de mots	*to tell / crack* (sortir) *a joke - to make a joke of / about sth / sb* (plaisanter sur) *- not to get / see the joke - some people can't take* (ne pas comprendre) *a joke*
	tour	*to play a joke / a practical joke* (farce) *on sb*
laugh GB [lɑːf] / US [læf]	rire	*to have a good laugh / the last laugh* (être celui qui rit bien le dernier) *- to stifle a laugh*
laughter (U) GB ['lɑːftə] / US ['læftər]	rire, rires	*there was a lot of laughter / a burst of contagious / loud / subdued* (contenu) *laughter - sth may cause laughter - sb may roar with laughter*
life	vie	*to be full of life - to live life to the full - to be the life and soul of a party* (mettre de l'ambiance)
mirth	rires, gaieté	*to provoke general mirth*
pun	jeu de mots	*to make a very bad pun*
quip	mot d'esprit, quolibet	*to make a nasty quip about sb*
scandal (U)	médisances, calomnie scandale	*juicy bit of scandal - to spread / specialise in scandal* *to cause / create / hush up / uncover a juicy scandal - a scandal may burst out - it is a scandal that ...*
smile	sourire	*to give (sb) a cheerful / sad smile - to repress / crack* (esquisser) */ flash* (adresser) *a smile at sb*
time	temps, période	*to have a nice time* (s'amuser) */ have a bad time* (moments difficiles) */ go through bad times*

■ *Adjectifs*

amusing	amusant	*amusing person / story / situation - it is highly amusing to do sth / to sb / that ...*
funny	drôle	*genuinely funny person / joke / situation - it is excruciatingly funny to do sth / to sb / that ...*
humorous	plein d'humour	*humorous person / book / way of looking at things*

■ *Verbes*

giggle	ricaner	*to giggle at sth*
gossip ['gɒsɪp]	papoter	*to gossip about sth / with sb*
guffaw [gʌ'fɔː]	rire bruyamment	*to guffaw coarsely / rudely*
jest	plaisanter, ne pas parler sérieusement	*to (foolishly) jest about sth / with sb*
joke	plaisanter	*to joke about sth / with sb / that ...*
laugh GB [lɑːf] / US [læf]	rire	*to laugh heartily at a joke - to laugh at sb / sth* (se moquer) *- to laugh one's head off*
smile	sourire	*to smile at sb / one's approval / one's thanks*
smirk	sourire avec suffisance	*to smirk unpleasantly at sth*
tease	taquiner	*to tease sb about sth / sb for doing sth*

Exercices sur le chapitre 10 (1.3)

1. Testez vos connaissances en traduisant les mots suivants:
A / mirth - B / quip - C / jest (n. / v.) - D / pun - E / to smirk - F / to tease

2. Remplacez les mots soulignés par un des mots en majuscules ci-dessous:
GIGGLE   GUFFAW   HELL   PUN   SCANDAL
A / It's a real <u>anecdote</u> that you <u>tease</u> at every supposedly funny thing she says. B / Why must you <u>hell</u> so coarsely all the time? C / He sometimes made very poor <u>laughs</u>. D / "Go to <u>fun</u>!" he shouted.

3. Traduisez les expressions ci-dessous, en vous aidant des exemples et collocations figurant dans la colonne de droite du vocabulaire:
A / Un scandale éclate. B / Répandre des médisances. C / Esquisser un sourire. D / Connaître des moments difficiles. E / Des rires contenus. F / Sortir une plaisanterie. G / Laisser échapper un rire bruyant. H / Se moquer de quelqu'un (avec le mot: fun). I / Commérages malveillants. J / S'amuser vachement (avec le mot: hell). K / Plaisanter bêtement de tout. L / Montrer d'un sourire qu'on approuve.

1.4. Boredom / Annoyance

Collocations

■ Noms

annoyance (U)	contrariété	*to feel / show annoyance at sth / with sb / that ...*
boredom	ennui (qu'on éprouve)	*out of* (par) *sheer / utter boredom - to experience a feeling of boredom*
bother ['bɒðə]	ennui, problème	*to have a bit of bother with the police - sth / sb may be (a bit of) a bother to sb*
dullness	ennui (dégagé par qch)	*the dullness of one's life / of a repetitive task*
fuss	histoires (que l'on fait)	*to make / kick up a fuss about / over sth*
matter	question, problème	*legal matters - it's a matter of life and death / quite a different matter - it's just a matter of doing sth - to do sth in a matter of minutes - what is the matter (with sb)? - there is sth / nothing the matter (with sb / sth)*
mischief ['--]	espièglerie, malice, bêtises	*to be / get up to some mischief - to keep sb out of mischief* (empêcher qqn de faire des bêtises) *- to do sth out of sheer mischief*
nuisance	ennui, embêtement empoisonneur, fléau	*what a nuisance! - it is a nuisance doing sth / that ... to be nothing but a nuisance - to make a nuisance of oneself*
routine [-'-]	routine	*to go through the daily / business routine*
trick	tour, blague	*to play a dirty trick on sb*

■ Adjectifs

bored	qui s'ennuie, d'ennui	*bored expression / look - to be / get bored stiff / to death with sth / with doing sth*
cross	fâché, de mauvaise humeur	*cross expression on sb's face - to be / get / look cross (with sb) - to make sb cross*
crossed	contrarié	*to be crossed in love*

Social and human relations   135

dull	ennuyeux	*dull person / book / task*
fussy	difficile, tatillon	*to be fussy about sth*
humdrum	monotone, routinier	*humdrum life / existence / task*
mischievous ['---]	espiègle	*mischievous child / smile*
provoking [-'--]	contrariant, agaçant	*provoking person / remark / situation*

■ *Verbes*

annoy	agacer, contrarier	*to annoy sb - it annoys me very much that ...*
bother ['bɒðə]	inquiéter	*to bother oneself about sth - to be bothered about sb / sth / that ...*
	embêter, déranger	*to bother sb (with sth) - it bothers me to do sth / that ...*
	se donner la peine	*not to bother (to do sth)*
disturb	déranger, troubler	*to disturb sb - it disturbs me to do sth / that ...*
exasperate [-'---]	exaspérer	*it exasperates me that ...*
fuss	faire des histoires	*to fuss about sth / over sb* (être aux petits soins)
	se tracasser, s'en faire	*to keep fussing about sth / about doing sth*
intrude	déranger	*to hope that one is not intruding*
	interférer avec	*sth may intrude on sb's private life / on one's good mood* (gâcher)
mess about / around	traîner	*to mess about idly*
	bricoler	*to mess around (in) the garden / the house*
	tripatouiller	*to mess about with sth*
	embêter, harceler	*to mess about with sb*
provoke [-'-]	provoquer	*to provoke sb into doing sth - to provoke an outcry* (protestation)
trick	tromper, amener à	*to trick sb into doing sth*
	escroquer, soutirer	*to trick sth out of sb*

Exercices sur le chapitre 10 (1.4)

1. Testez vos connaissances en traduisant les mots ci-dessous:

A / trick (n.) - B / to fuss - C / bored - D / boredom - E / fussy

2. Traduisez en anglais:

A / Qu'est-ce qu'il y a qui ne va pas? B / Je ne suporte plus la monotonie de mon emploi de bureau. C / Je comprends que ce soit un petit problème pour toi. D / Petit problème! Ça devient une question de survie! E / Tu exagères. Ne fais pas tant d'histoires: tu pourrais être au chômage. F / Je m'ennuie, alors je fume trop, par pur ennui; j'ai envie par moments de faire des bêtises! G / A ton âge? Ton patron est un vrai empoisonneur, je te l'accorde, mais ... H / J'ai envie de lui jouer un tour, un sale tour... I / Ne fais pas ça: il va croire que tu te venges d'un amour non partagé et que tu cherches à semer la zizanie dans le bureau. J / Ce que tu peux être agaçant! Je crois que tu m'agaces exprès pour provoquer ma colère. K / Mais non. J'ai une idée: sois aux petits soins pour lui. L / Pas question! Il me met en colère du matin au soir. M / Il te harcèle? N / Non. Mais il me gâche ma bonne humeur. O / Drôle de façon de s'exprimer. P / Il m'exaspère, si tu préfères. Ça me donne envie de lui escroquer de l'argent! Q / Lequel des deux se rend le plus insupportable? Je me le demande, parfois!.

2. Human relations

2.1. Good relations

Collocations

■ *Noms*

bond	attachement, lien	*close / strong marriage / family bonds - to form / strengthen / undo one's bond with sb - bonds of friendship*
boy / girl friend	petit(e) ami(e), copain / copine	*to have a steady girlfriend - to jilt (plaquer) / walk out on (quitter) one's boyfriend*
chum	copain	*childhood / school chums*
favour	service	*to ask a favour of sb - to do sb a favour*
gift	cadeau	*lavish / extravagant / farewell gift - to give sth as a gift*
guidance	conseils	*to seek / need guidance - vocational guidance* (professionnel) *- for sb's guidance* (à titre d'information)
hand	coup de main, aide	*to give / lend sb a hand - not to lift a hand with sth*
help	aide	*to give / offer help to sb (with sth) - to be of great help / a great help to sb*
pal [pæl]	pote, "mec"	*to be sb's pal - "Come on, pal!"*
present ['--]	cadeau, présent	*to give sb sth as a birthday / Christmas present*
promise ['prɒmɪs]	promesse	*to make / keep / fulfill / break a promise to do sth / that...*
relief [-'-]	soulagement	*to express / feel / bring / give relief to sb - it is a great relief to sb to do sth / that... - to find relief in doing sth*
request [-'-]	demande, requête	*to make / grant / meet* (satisfaire) */ turn down sb's reasonable request for sth / to do sth*
share	part	*to do one's share of sth - to give sb a fair share - to pay one's share*
side	côté, camp	*to be on sb's / take sb's side - to change / take / pick / choose sides*
solace ['sɒləs]	consolation	*to seek / find solace in sth / in doing sth - to be a solace to sb*
solidarity [ˌ--'---]	solidarité	*to do sth in solidarity with sb - a spontaneous show of solidarity*
support [-'-]	soutien, appui	*to enlist* (mobiliser) */ give / provide / seek / get whole-hearted support for sth*
sympathy ['---]	compassion, soutien	*to arouse / express / feel / have deep / heartfelt sympathy for sb / sth - to do sth out of sympathy for sb*
treat	gâterie, petit cadeau, sortie bonne surprise	*to go somewhere as a special treat - to have got a treat for sb - to give sb a treat*
turn	service	*to do sb a good turn / a bad turn* (mauvais tour)
word	parole	*to keep / give / break one's word - to go back on one's word - to hold / keep sb to their word - my word is my bond* (m'engage)

■ *Adjectifs*

alone	seul, à l'écart	*to stand / remain alone from other people - not to be alone in doing sth - to feel very alone*
congenial [kən'dʒiːni̯əl]	sympathique, agréable, qui présente des affinités	*congenial company / surroundings / weather - to find sb very congenial*

Social and human relations

encouraging [-'---]	encourageant, d'encouragement	*encouraging word / sign - it is encouraging to do sth / that...*	
genial ['dʒiːni̯əl]	sociable, aimable, cordial, chaleureux	*genial person / comment / smile - to be genial to / towards sb*	
hearty	chaleureux, gai, jovial, plein de vie	*hearty person / laugh / song / welcome*	
helpful	serviable; d'un grand secours, utile	*helpful person / suggestion / medication - it is helpful to do sth - sth may be helpful to sb*	
polite	poli	*to be polite to sb - it is polite (of sb) to do sth*	
sympathetic [,--'--]	compatissant, compréhensif, bien disposé à l'égard de	*sympathetic words / smile / handshake - to be sympathetic over sth / to sb*	
tactful	plein de tact	*tactful person / inquiry - it is tactful (of sb) to do sth - to be tactful with sb*	
vicarious [vɪ'keəri̯əs]	indirect, par procuration	*vicarious satisfaction / pride / enjoyment of sth*	

■ *Verbes*

give	donner	**make (it) up with**	se réconcilier avec
give out	distribuer	**mean well**	avoir de bonnes intentions
hit it off (with)	s'entendre (avec)		

Collocations

coax	cajoler, enjôler	*to coax sb into doing sth / sb out of sth* (extorquer habilement)
count sb in	inclure, faire partager	*to count sb in / sb in on sth*
encourage [-'---]	encourager	*to encourage sth - to encourage sb to do sth*
help	aider	*to help sb with / in sth / sb to do sth - to help sb down (the stairs) / sb with their luggage / sb into a car*
incite	inciter, entraîner pousser, inciter à	*to incite sb to sth / sb to do sth* *to incite sth / racial hatred*
induce	persuader entraîner, provoquer	*to induce sb to do sth* *to induce sleep / a sense of failure / an emotion*
lure	séduire, persuader	*to lure sb into doing sth / sb away from sth / sb away from sb* (éloigner de)
offer	offrir proposer	*to offer sth / sb sth* *to offer to do sth*
pal up	devenir copains	*to pal up (with sb)*
present [-'-]	offrir en cadeau	*to present sth / sb with sth*
promise ['promɪs]	promettre	*to promise sth / sb sth / to do sth / that...*
put up with	supporter	*to put up with sb / sth*
reconcile ['---]	réconcilier	*to reconcile sb with sb - to be reconciled*
relieve [-'-]	soulager	*to relieve sb of sth - it may relieve sb to do sth*
request [-'-]	demander, prier	*to request a favour from sb - to request that...*
return	rendre, rapporter	*to return sth to sb - to return sb's love*
share	partager, participer	*to share sth with sb / in sth / in doing sth*
side	prendre parti	*to side with / against sb*
solace ['sɒləs]	consoler	*to solace sb as best one can*
soothe	apaiser, calmer	*to soothe sb / sb's anger / fears / pain*
spur (on)	inciter, aiguillonner	*to spur sb on to do sth*
support [-'-]	soutenir	*to support sb / sth / a cause*
sympathize ['---]	comprendre, compatir	*to deeply sympathize with sb / sth*

treat	s'offrir qch / offrir qch à qqn	*to treat sb to sth - to treat oneself (to sth)*
urge	vivement conseiller, pousser	*to urge sth / caution / sb to do sth*
vouch for	répondre de	*to vouch for sth / for sb / for sb's honesty*
vow [vaʊ]	jurer, s'engager	*to vow obedience / secrecy - to vow to do sth*
wait on sb	se mettre au service de	*to wait on sb (hand and foot) - to wait on tables* (servir à table)

■ *Preposition*

on behalf of /	au nom de, de la part de
in behalf of (US)	

■ *Adverbe*

to be well in with sb	être en bons termes avec qqn

Exercices sur le chapitre 10 (2.1)

1. Testez vos connaissances en traduisant les mots ou expressions ci-dessous:

A / bond - B / to hit it off - C / relief - D / share - E / side - F / sympathy - G / to give out H / to put up with

2. Joignez une phrase de droite à chaque phrase de gauche:

A. He never failed to do her
B. Her sympathetic attitude to people in pain
C. She found relief and solace
D. Giving guidance only when requested
E. Workers need to be well in with the trade-unions
F. He requests no favour from anybody
G. She got a vicarious kick
H. She coaxed her boy-friend
I. Once you give your word
J. It relieved the boy to hear that

1. you can't go back on it.
2. although he always offers to help them.
3. does more to strengthen the bonds of friendship than anything else.
4. a good turn in his usual tactful way.
5. into counting her in on the job (sur le coup).
6. his parents had made up and hit it off again.
7. to enlist their support when starting a strike.
8. used to lure people into confiding in her.
9. in the congenial company of her mother.
10. out of hearing of a woman triumphing over a man in a chess contest.

3. En consultant les exemples et les collocations figurant dans la colonne de droite des mots présentés, traduisez les expressions ci-dessous:

A / Inciter qqn à la violence. B / Extorquer habilement de l'argent à qqn. C / Persuader qqn de faire qqch. D / Être en compagnie sympathique. E / Sourire chaleureux. F / Des cadeaux somptueux. G / Plaquer son petit ami. H / Tenir / ne pas tenir ses promesses. I / Eprouver du soulagement à faire qqch. J / Se montrer compréhensif sur un point particulier. K / Apaiser la colère de qqn. L / Un rire jovial. M / Jurer obéissance et secret. N / À titre d'information.

2.2. Hostile relations

Collocations

■ *Noms*

feelings	sentiments	*to hurt sb's feelings* (blesser) - *no hard feelings!* (sans rancune!)
grudge [grʌdʒ]	rancune	*to bear / have / hold a grudge against sb* (en vouloir à qqn) - *to pay off a grudge* (prendre sa revanche) *against sb*

Social and human relations

malice ['--]	méchanceté, malveillance	*to bear sb malice* (vouloir du mal) - *to do sth out of sheer malice*
offence [-'-]	offense	*to give / cause offence to sb* (blesser) - *to take offence (at sth)* (s'offusquer)
rival ['raɪvl]	rival, concurrent	*to be sb's rival for / in sth*
rivalry ['raɪvəlri]	rivalité	*to stir up keen / strong rivalry with sb / between people*

■ *Adjectifs*

impolite [,--'-]	impoli	*to be impolite to sb - it is impolite (of sb) to do sth*
inconsiderate [,--'---]	qui ne tient pas compte de	*to be inconsiderate of sb's feelings - it is inconsiderate (of sb) to do sth* (c'est un manque d'égards)
malicious [-'---]	malveillant méchant	*malicious talk / comment / behaviour*
offensive [-'---]	offensant, choquant	*offensive language / remark - sth may be offensive to sb - it is offensive to do sth*
rude	grossier, mal élevé	*rude person / remark / joke / gesture - to be rude to sb / look rude - it is rude (of sb) to do sth*
sulky	maussade, boudeur	*sulky person / face / silence - to be sulky about sth*
sullen	renfrogné, maussade	*sullen person / face / obstinacy*
tactless	qui manque de tact, indiscret	*tactless person / remark - it is tactless (of sb) to do sth*
unfriendly	inamical, hostile	*unfriendly attitude / remark - to be unfriendly to / towards sb - to look unfriendly*
wild	déchaîné, délirant, extravagant	*wild applause / person / scheme / promise / dream / party*
	fou, furieux	*to be wild with grief / jealousy - sth may drive sb wild*
	fou, dingue	*to be wild about sth / sb*

■ *Verbes*

cut sb dead	faire semblant de ne pas voir qqn	**harass** ['--]		harceler
		jilt		quitter, plaquer

Collocations

compete (with) [-'-]	être / entrer en concurrence (avec)	*to compete with / against sb for sth / to do sth*
count sb out	ne pas associer, exclure	*to count sb out (of sth)*
discourage	décourager	*to discourage sb from doing sth*
discriminate [-'----]	établir une discrimination	*to discriminate against / in favour of sb*
do sb in	liquider, trucider	*to do sb in (in a nice, clean way)*
go for	attaquer violemment	*to go for sb / for sb's throat / for sb's work*
grudge [grʌdʒ]	donner à regret	*to grudge one's money / support*
	rechigner	*to grudge doing sth*
ignore [-'-]	ne pas tenir compte de	*to ignore warnings / requests / objections*
	ne pas prêter attention à	*to ignore sb / remarks*
inflict	infliger, imposer	*to inflict pain / punishment / defeat / oneself / one's company on sb*
nag	harceler, embêter tourmenter	*to nag sb into doing sth - to nag at sb to do sth*
		sb's conscience may nag them
offend [-'-]	offenser, blesser, choquer	*to offend sb / sb's sense of justice*
rival ['raɪvl]	rivaliser, égaler	*to rival sb / sb in sth / sb's talent / sb's stubborness* (entêtement)
stand	supporter	*sb can't stand sth / sb / doing / to do sth*
stick	supporter, tenir	*sb can't stick sb / sth / sb doing sth / three years of the same thing*
sulk	bouder	*to sulk about / over sth*

threaten	menacer	to threaten sb / sb with sth / to do sth / that...
vex	contrarier, ennuyer	to vex sb - it vexes sb to do sth / that...
vie	rivaliser	to vie against / with sb (for sth) / with sb to do sth

Exercices sur le chapitre 10 (2.2)

1. Testez vos connaissances en traduisant les mots ou expressions ci-dessous:

A / sulk - B / sullen - C / rivalry - D / to vie - E / to discourage - F / to harass

2. Corrigez l'erreur d'orthographe que contient chacune des phrases suivantes:

A / Why must you keep sucking all day? B / I wish you weren't lying with her all the time. C / Nothing sexes people more than offensive remarks like that. D / Did you have to jolt your girlfriend so abruptly? E / You mustn't bag her into doing things she doesn't want to do.

3. Traduisez en anglais:

A / Elle devait être folle de ce type pour tenir dix ans avec quelqu'un d' aussi grossier, elle qui ne supporte pas de vivre avec des gens malpolis et sans tact! B / Elle a bien dû s'offusquer, dès qu'elle l'a connu, de ses remarques malveillantes, de son langage choquant, de son attitude peu amicale envers ses amis? C / Elle a dû être folle de jalousie lorsqu'il l'excluait des soirées délirantes auxquelles il se rendait seul. D / Qu'a-t-elle pu éprouver lorsqu'il rentrait à demi-ivre et qu'il l'attaquait physiquement et verbalement? E / Comment n'aurait-elle pas eu envie de le liquider, lorsqu'il menaçait de l'étrangler ou simplement lorsqu'il faisait semblant de ne pas la reconnaître dans la rue (ce qu'il faisait par pure méchanceté) ou lui donnait, à contre-cœur, cinq livres par semaine d'argent de poche?

2.3. Friendship and love

■ *Noms*

buddy	copain, pote	roommate	camarade de chambre (pensionnat); personne avec qui on partage un appartement
chum	copain, camarade		
lady-killer	bourreau des cœurs		
pal	copain	(old) china (GB)	pote, copain
eunuch ['juːnək]	eunuque	lecher ['letʃə]	débauché
mate	camarade		

Collocations

affair [-'-]	aventure, liaison	to have / carry on a casual / secret affair with sb
chick	petit chou	"Hi there, chick!"
crush	béguin	to have a (school girl's) crush on sb
date	rendez-vous petit(e) ami(e)	to have / make / go out on a date with sb to go out with / bring a regular date along
friend	ami(e)	to make friends (with sb) - a bosom / close / staunch / false - to be a good friend to sb - 'a friend in need is a friend indeed' (c'est dans le besoin qu'on connait ses amis)
friendliness	gentillesse	sb's friendliness towards sb
friendship	amitié	to form / strike up / break up a close / lifelong friendship with sb
honey	"mon ange!"	"Hi there, honey!"

Social and human relations

intimacy ['----]	intimité	to preserve / wish for intimacy
kiss	baiser	to give sb a kiss - to throw / blow (envoyer) a loving kiss to sb
lover	amant, maîtresse	to take / jilt an unfaithful lover
mate	camarade, compagnon	to spend more time with one's schoolmates than with one's family - "Look here, mate"! - a plumber's mate
romance [-'-]	idylle, roman d'amour grand amour	to have a romance with sb a dream of ever-lasting romance
sexism	sexisme	to eradicate / practise sexism

■ *Adjectifs*

inveterate [-'---]	invétéré	**virgin**		vierge
sensual	sensuel			

Collocations

beloved adj. épithète [bɪ'lʌvɪd] / adj. attribut du sujet : [bɪ'lʌvd]	cher, chéri, aimé(e)	to be beloved to all one's friends - sb's beloved parents
friendly	aimable, gentil, amical	to be friendly to / towards sb - it is friendly (of sb) to do sth
intimate	intime	to be intimate (with sb) (être intime ou avoir des relations intimes) - to be on intimate terms (with sb)
romantic	romantique, romanesque	romantic love / attachment romantic ideas / outlook on life
rude	cru, obscène	rude joke / language / word
seductive	séducteur, séduisant	seductive person / argument / offer / voice

■ *Verbes*

cuddle	(se) câliner	to kiss and cuddle - to cuddle a baby
cuddle up	se blottir, se pelotonner	to cuddle up (close to sb) (tout contre qqn)
date	sortir (avec qqn)	to date (sb)
hug	serrer dans ses bras, étreindre	to kiss and hug - to cuddle and hug - to hug sb
kiss	(s')embrasser	to kiss / sb passionately / sb good-night
lust after / for	désirer, convoiter	to lust for one's best friend's wife
make eyes at	faire les yeux doux à	to make eyes at sb
pick sb up	draguer	to pick up a woman
seduce	séduire amener, entraîner	to seduce sb to seduce sb away from sth / sb into doing sth
snuggle	se blottir, se pelotonner	to snuggle into a corner - to snuggle close to sb - to snuggle down into one's warm duvet
take to sb	se prendre d'amitié pour / prendre goût à	to take to sb - to take kindly to sth (regarder favorablement)

Exercices sur le chapitre 10 (2.3)

1. Testez vos connaissances en traduisant les mots ou expressions ci-dessous:

A / to blow a kiss - B / friendliness - C / friendship - D / séduisant

2. Remplacez la lettre en gras des mots ou expressions ci-dessous par une autre lettre de façon à ce que les mots nouveaux correspondent aux définitions données:

A. **S**LOW A KISS
B. **H**ISS
C. **R**UST FOR
D. **B**AKE TO
E. **F**ATE
F. **N**ICK UP
G. **N**UDE
H. **M**ONEY
I. **C**RICK

A. to send a kiss.
B. to touch with the lips.
C. to desire sb / sth very strongly.
D. to feel a liking for sb especially at once.
E. to go out with a boy / girlfriend.
F. to talk to sb with sexual intentions.
G. obscene.
H. you say this to a girl that you are very fond of.
I. same definition as above.

3. Traduisez en anglais:

A / Elle refuse de sortir avec des hommes qu'elle soupçonne d'être des débauchés invétérés. B / Son petit ami a le béguin pour moi. C / Il n'arrête pas de me faire les yeux doux. D / Mais je ne me laisse pas draguer pour une petite liaison de passage. E / Il essaie, par la séduction, de m'amener à avoir avec lui des relations intimes. F / De toute façon, c'est dans le besoin (pas dans le lit) qu'on connaît ses vrais amis.

2.4. Sex

■ *Noms*

birth control	contrôle des naissances	lesbian	lesbienne
(the) coil	stérilet	an easy lay	qqn qui couche facilement
contraception	contraception	sperm	sperme
contraceptive [,--'--]	contraceptif	a good lay	qqn qui baise bien
diaphragm	diaphragme	virgin	vierge (homme ou femme)
(Dutch) cap	diaphragme	virginity	virginité
intra-uterine device / IUD	stérilet	red-light area	quartier chaud
loop	stérilet	brothel ['brɒθl]	bordel
erection	érection	pimp	souteneur
hard-on	érection (fam.)	prostitute	prostitué(e)
coitus	coït	sexuality	sexualité
boyfriend	petit ami	one-night stand	aventure d'un soir
girlfriend	petite amie	whore	putain
lover	amant	French letter	capote anglaise *(old use)* (GB)
mistress	maîtresse	one-night stand	aventure d'un soir
(love) affair	liaison	soliciting	racolage
gay	homosexuel	procurer	entremetteur, proxénète
lecher	débauché		

Collocations

condom / rubber (US)	préservatif	*to use / wear a condom*
foreplay (U)	préludes amoureux	*to indulge in prolonged foreplay*
homosexual	homosexuel(le)	*a homosexual may decide to come out (of the closet)* (dire qu'il est homosexuel)
intimacy	relations sexuelles	*intimacy may take place on the first date*
intercourse ['---]	relations sexuelles	*to have (sexual) intercourse with sb*
lust	désir sexuel, luxure	*to arouse / feel uncontrollable lust for sb - to satisfy one's lust*

Social and human relations

orgasm ['---]	orgasme	*to achieve orgasm - to have / reach an orgasm*
petting	caresses, pelotage	*to indulge in heavy petting* (poussé)
pill	pilule	*to be on / come off the pill* (prendre / ne plus prendre)
prostitution	prostitution	*to ban / decriminalise / engage in prostitution*
queer	homosexuel	*'queer' is an old-fashioned word for gay*
sex	relations sexuelles	*to have extra-marital sex (with sb) - to practice safe sex* (sans riques)

■ *Adjectifs*

bawdy	paillard	**lustful**	lascif, luxurieux
chaste	chaste	**ribald**	grivois
gay	homosexuel	**smutty**	grossier, cochon
lesbian	lesbien	**virgin**	vierge

Collocations

intimate ['---]	sexuel	*to have intimate relations with sb - to be intimate (with sb)* (avoir des rapports intimes)
lecherous ['letʃər_əs]	lubrique	*lecherous person / expression / gleam in sb's eyes*
lewd [luːd]	obscène	*lewd entertainment / joke / language*
promiscuous [-'---]	aux mœurs légères	*promiscuous person / sexual behaviour - to be very promiscuous* (coucher facilement)
queer	homo (homme)	*a supposedly queer person / voice / manner*
sexual	sexuel	*sexual abuse / harassment*

■ *Verbes*

bonk	s'envoyer en l'air	**lust after / for**	désirer, convoiter
castrate [-'-]	castrer	**make a girl**	se faire une fille
come	jouir	**make love (with)**	faire l'amour (avec)
conceive	concevoir	**masturbate (sb)**	se masturber; masturber qqn
ejaculate [-'---]	éjaculer	**neck**	se peloter, se bécoter
emasculate [-'---]	émasculer	**pat**	tapoter, toucher légèrement
go to bed (with)	coucher (avec)	**seduce**	séduire
knock off a girl	s'envoyer une fille	**pet**	(se) caresser (l'un l'autre)
make out (with)	se peloter; peloter qqn	**score a girl**	lever une nana
to have it off (with sb)	coucher (avec qqn)	**screw**	tringler, s'envoyer une nana
knock up a girl	mettre une fille en cloque	**sleep with sb**	coucher avec qqn
lay a girl	sauter une nana	**sleep around**	coucher à gauche et à droite

Collocations

caress [-'-]	caresser	*to caress sb lovingly / gently*
fondle	caresser	*to fondle sb's breasts / ear - to fondle a baby*
fuck	baiser	*to fuck sb - fuck it!* (merde!) *- fuck off!* (tire-toi, connard!)
stroke	caressser	*to stroke sb's arm / hair / back of their hand*
turn on	exciter	*sth / sb may turn sb on*

Exercices sur le chapitre 10 (2.4)

1. Testez vos connaissances en traduisant les mots ci-dessous:
A / brothel - B / lecher - C / cap - D / whore - E / paillard - F / grivois - G / lascif - H / lubrique

2. Choisissez la solution qui convient au contexte de cette section:
A. To want to have it up / off / out / down with a girl
B. To try to knock a girl up / down / in / out
C. To ask somebody to do / take / have / make love with you.
D. Some clothes tend to arouse a man's lust / gust / rust / must
E. Some people indulge in prolonged fourplay / fiveplay / foreplay / moreplay
F. To boast of having sexual intermeal / interdessert / intercourse / interdish with all well-known models
G. To boast of having frequent harsh-ons / hard-ons / heart-ons / hurt-ons

3. Power games

3.1. Permission

Collocations

■ *Noms*

compliance [kəm'plaɪ̯ əns]	conformité	*in compliance with sth*
	acceptation (sans discussion)	*sb's compliance with sth*
leave	permission, autorisation	*to ask leave (from sb) to do sth*
	congé	*to be / go on leave - to be on sick leave - to take leave of sb*
permission [-'--]	permission	*to give / refuse / ask (sb's) permission for sth / to do sth*
power game	jeu de pouvoir	*to engage in / indulge in the power game.*
power play	coup de force, offensive concentrée	*to work a successful power play*
settlement	règlement	*to seek a fair / speedy / tentative (provisoire) settlement of sth*
showdown	épreuve de force	*to seek a final showdown over sth with sb - it may be time for a showdown for sb*
understanding [,--'--]	accord	*to arrive at / come to a secret / tacit understanding with sb about sth / with sb to do sth*

■ *Adjectifs*

allowed	autorisé	*to be allowed to do sth / some extra luggage*
dependent [-'--]	dépendant	*to be dependent on sth / sb*
independent [,--'--]	indépendant	*independent person - to be independent of sb*
obedient [ə'biːdi ənt]	obéissant	*obedient person - to be obedient to sb / to sb's orders*

■ *Verbes*

accept [-'-]	accepter qch	*to readily accept sth / sb's whims (caprices)*
	reconnaître que	*to accept that ...*

Social and human relations 145

allow	accorder	*to allow (sb / oneself) sth - to allow oneself small indulgences (plaisirs)*
	autoriser	*to allow sb to do sth - to allow sb in / out / past - not to allow smoking*
comply	se conformer	*to comply with sth / with the law*
	accepter (sans discuter)	*to comply with sb's wishes / whims*
consent [-'-]	consentir	*to consent to sth / to do sth*
dance attendance on GB [dɑːns] / US [dæns]	se mettre entièrement au service de	*to dance attendance on one's immediate superiors*
give in	céder	*to give in to sb / to sth / to threats*
give way	céder	*to give way to sb's demands*
	se laisser aller à	*to give way to anger / tears*
grant GB [grɑːnt] / US [grænt]	accorder	*to grant sb sth / permission / leave / a visa*
lead	mener, diriger, amener	*to lead everything / the conversation / a demonstration / a political party - to lead sb to think that... - to lead sb somewhere*
let	laisser, autoriser	*to let sb do sth*
obey	obéir	*to obey sb / sb's orders*
permit	permettre	*to permit sth / smoking - to permit access to sth - to permit sb to do sth - to permit oneself a glass of champagne*
permit of	admettre	*sth may permit of several interpretations*
put one's foot down	faire preuve de fermeté	*to put one's foot down and oppose sth*
satisfy	satisfaire, réaliser	*to satisfy sb's desires*
vouchsafe [vaʊtʃ'seɪf]	condescendre à accorder	*to vouchsafe an answer / a secret / peace*
	condescendre à faire	*to vouchsafe to do sth*
yield [jiːld]	céder	*to yield sth / to sb - to yield a point to sb* (concéder un point)

3.2 Abuse, force

■ *Noms*

abuse (C) [ə'bjuːs]	abus	*sth may be open to abuse - to try and remedy abuses - the abuse of alcohol*
abuse (U)	mauvais traitements, violences	*child / sexual abuse*
ban	interdiction	*to impose / place a ban on sth - to lift a ban from sth*
influence	influence	*to exert / use one's positive / strong influence - to curb* (limiter) *sb's baneful* (nuisible) *influence*
law	loi	*to lay down the law* (faire la loi)
order	ordre	*to issue / carry out / obey / cancel an order to do sth*
pressure	pression, tension	*to bring pressure to bear on sb - to feel / relieve / ease / resist (the / sb's) strong / relentless pressure (from sb)*
refusal	refus	*to meet with a flat / outright* (absolu) *refusal of sth / to do sth*
scapegoat	bouc émissaire	*to make sb a scapegoat - to be in search of a scapegoat*
showdown	épreuve de force	*to have / seek a showdown with sb*
veto ['viːtəʊ]	veto	*to put a veto on sth - to override* (passer outre) *a veto over sth - a country's power of veto*

■ Adjectifs

compulsory [-'---]	obligatoire	*compulsory education for everyone - it is compusory (for sb) to do sth*
disobedient [ˌdɪsə'biːdiənt]	désobéissant	*disobedient child - to be disobedient to sb*
high-handed	autoritaire, cavalier	*high-handed manner / behaviour - to be highhanded with sb - it is highhanded to do sth*
patronizing ['----]	condescendant	*patronizing tone / arrogance / behaviour*
strict	sévère	*to be strict about sth / towards / with sb*

■ Verbes

abuse [ə'bjuːz]	abuser de	*to abuse one's authority*
	maltraiter	*to abuse a child*
ban	interdire	*to ban sth / sb / sb (from) doing sth*
bid	ordonner	*to bid sb (to) do sth*
bully ['bʊli]	intimider, persécuter	*to bully sb into doing sth*
challenge ['--]	mettre au défi	*to challenge sb / sb to do sth*
compel	obliger, contraindre	*to compel sb to do sth*
demand GB [dɪ'mɑːnd] / US [dɪ'mænd]	exiger	*to demand sth from sb - to demand to do sth / that ...*
disobey [ˌ--'-]	désobéir	*to disobey sb / sth*
exact	exiger (de façon abusive)	*to exact sth from sb*
foil	déjouer, contrecarrer	*to foil sb's plan / attempt / a plot*
forbid	défendre, interdire	*to expressly forbid sth / sb sth / sb to do sth*
force	forcer, imposer	*to force sth on sb / sb to do sth*
get	obtenir que, faire faire	*to get sb to do sth*
hold one's own	faire bonne figure	*to hold one's own with sb / in public*
	tenir bon	*to hold one's own against attacks*
influence	influencer	*to deeply influence sb in sth / sb to do sth*
insist	tenir absolument	*to insist on sth / on doing sth / on sb doing sth / on sth being done - to insist that ...*
	bien préciser que	*to insist that...*
interfere [ˌɪntə'fɪə]	s'immiscer, intervenir	*to interfere in sth / with sb*
	procéder à des attouchements	*to interfere with a child*
intervene [ˌɪntə'viːn]	intervenir	*to intervene in sth*
make	obliger, faire faire	*to make sb do sth - to be made to do sth*
meddle	se mêler	*to meddle in sth / with sb's plans*
monopolize [-'---]	monopoliser, occuper complètement	*to monopolize sth - sb's mind may be monopolized by sth*
oblige	obliger, contraindre	*to oblige sb to do sth*
	obliger (rendre service)	*to oblige sb by (not) doing sth*
oppress [-'-]	opprimer, oppresser	*sb may oppress sb - heat may oppress sb*
order	ordonner	*to order sth / sb to do sth / that... - to order sth done / sb out / sb home / sb to bed*
put one's foot down	faire acte d'autorité	*to put one's foot down about sth*
refuse [rɪ'fjuːz]	refuser	*to outright / flatly refuse sth / sb sth / to do sth*
restrain	retenir, empêcher	*to restrain sb from doing sth*
restrict	restreindre, limiter	*to restrict access / smoking / sb's freedom / oneself to five cigarettes a day / a discussion to a few items*
step in	intervenir	*to step in and do sth*

Social and human relations   147

stop	empêcher	to stop sb doing sth
suppress	interdire, mettre fin à	to suppress dissent / newspapers / revolt
	cacher, étouffer	to suppress the truth / a scandal
	réprimer, retenir	to suppress one's feelings / one's sobs / a smile
veto	opposer son véto	to veto a plan
withhold	taire, cacher	to withhold sth from sb
	refuser	to withhold payment / one's consent

Exercices sur le chapitre 10 (3.1 et 3.2)

1. Testez vos connaissances en traduisant les mots ou expressions ci-dessous:

A / scapegoat - B / compliance - C. to grant - D / settlement - E / to vouchsafe - F / to yield

2. Traduisez en anglais:

A / Ne laissez pas les enfants faire la loi! B / C'est bien que les enfants deviennent, peu à peu, indépendants de leurs parents, mais il ne faut pas leur permettre de fumer, sous prétexte que vous aussi, vous fumez. C / Il faut que vous les fassiez obéir à vos ordres; il faut qu'ils apprennent à être obéissants dès l'enfance. D / Les enfants essaient souvent de mettre leurs parents au défi de les punir. E / Ils espèrent obtenir de vous que vous consentiez à la réalisation de tous leurs désirs, que vous acceptiez, sans discuter, tous leurs caprices, en bref, que vous leur cédiez. F / Déjouez leurs plans à temps, sinon ils vont vous imposer une épreuve de force. G / Tenez bon contre leurs assauts! H / Faites preuve d'autorité. I / Pourquoi n'acceptez-vous pas cette évidence: ce sont les enfants qui obéissent, pas les parents. J / Aucun père sain d'esprit ne laisse, par exemple, ses enfants lui interdire d'entrer dans leur chambre!

3. Remplacez chaque mot en italique par un des mots en majuscules ci-dessous, pour que les phrases aient un sens:

BRING TO BEAR	BULLY	DEMAND
FORBID	FORCE	HIGHHANDED
INSIST	INTERVENE	ISSUE (v.)
MEDDLE	ORDER (n.)	PATRONISING
REFUSE	STOP	SUPPRESS

A. Nobody can suppress. me to restrict if I don't want to. B. I wish you would bid her smoking so much. C. The governement is trying to force the freedom of the Press. D. I must abuse on your not obliging in my private affairs. E. I wish you weren't so compulsory with your students. F. He ordered to let himself be vetoed into doing it. G. I restrain you to put on that disobedient manner with me. H. I withhold that pressure be oppressed on him so that he will cancel the most unfair influence he has just compelled.

4. Attitudes

4.1. Admiration, respect, attention, gratitude

Collocations

■ *Noms*

attitude	attitude	to adopt a threatening attitude - sb's attitude to / towards sth / sb may surprise one - to take the attitude that ... (considérer que) - to resent sb's attitude - to undergo a change of / in attitude - to strike (prendre) an attitude of offended dignity
	confiance en soi, parfois déplaisante	sb may have attitude (très sûr de soi)

regard [-'-]	attention, considération respect, égards	*to pay great / scant regard to sth* (tenir compte) *to have great regard for sb - to do sth out of regard for sb*
regards	bon souvenir	*to give / send sb one's (best) regards*
tribute ['trɪbjuːt]	hommage	*to pay sb (a) moving / fitting* (juste) *tribute*

■ *Adjectifs*

grateful	reconnaissant	*to be grateful to sb / for sth / for doing sth / that...*
impressive	impressionnant	*impressive film / list / achievement - sth may be impressive for its beauty, etc*
thankful	reconnaissant, content	*to be thankful to sb / for sth / to be alive / to have escaped / that ...*

■ *Verbes*

admire	admirer	*to greatly admire sb for sth (a quality) / sb for doing sth*
congratulate [-'---]	féliciter	*to congratulate sb on sth / sb on doing sth*
flatter	flatter	*to flatter sb / oneself about / on sth / about / on doing sth - to flatter sb into doing sth - it may flatter sb that ... / sb to be asked sth*
impress [-'-]	impressionner	*to favourably / unfavourably impress sb / sb with sth (a quality) - it may impress sb to be asked sth / that...*
look up to	avoir respect et admiration pour	*to look up to sb / one's parents / one's teachers*

Exercices sur le chapitre 10 (4.1)

1. Testez vos connaissances en traduisant les mots ci-dessous:
A / regards - B / tribute - C / thankful - D / to look up to - E / to impress

2. Traduisez en anglais:
A / Ma mère se flatte d'être une mère exceptionnelle. B / On lui fait croire, en la flattant, qu'elle a un fils plein de talent. C / On l'admire d'avoir consacré sa vie à ce fils unique. D / Je suis bien heureux d'être venu au monde, bien sûr. E / Ma mère impressionne les gens par son amour pour moi. F / Dois-je, pour autant, lui être reconnaissant toute ma vie de m'avoir mis au monde? G / "Je ne cesse de me féliciter d'avoir mis au monde ce petit génie," dit-elle. H / Tout le monde la respecte et lui rend hommage, à elle. Et moi, dans tout ça?

4.2. Contempt / Mockery

Collocations

■ *Noms*

contempt [-'-]	mépris	*to feel (nothing but) contempt for sb / sth - to hold sb in contempt - sth may be beneath contempt* (méprisable)
irony	ironie	*to detect a tinge* (pointe) *of irony in sb's tone - to speak with (slight / heavy) irony / without irony - the irony of it is that ...*
jeer	raillerie, lazzi	*to heap / pour jeers on sth / sb's ideas - to greet sth with jeers*
laughing stock	risée	*to be / to be made the laughing stock of the neighbours*
scorn	mépris, dédain	*to feel scorn for sth / sb - to speak with scorn in one's voice*
sneer	ricanement, raillerie	*to say sth with a sneer - to draw sneers from sb*

Social and human relations

■ *Adjectifs*

contemptible [-'---]	méprisable	*contemptible remark / person - it is contemptible (of sb) to do sth*
contemptuous [-'---]	méprisant	*contemptuous tone of voice - to be contemptuous of sth / of sb*
despicable [-'---]	méprisable	*despicable behaviour - it is despicable to do sth*
ironic(al) [-'--(-)]	ironique	*ironical remark - it is ironical that...*
ludicrous ['luːdɪkrəs]	ridicule, risible	*ludicrous person / attempt - it is ludicrous to do sth / that...*
scornful	dédaigneux, méprisant	*scornful person / attitude / laughter - to be scornful of / about sth*
ungrateful	ingrat, sans reconnaissance	*to be ungratefful to sb / for sth*

■ *Verbes*

despise	mépriser	*to despise sb for sth / sb for doing sth*
disparage [-'--]	dénigrer, décrier	*to disparage sth / sb / sb's efforts / ideas*
jeer at	railler	*to jeer at sb for sth / at sb for doing sth*
laugh at	rire de, trouver amusant, se moquer de	*to laugh at a good joke* *to laugh at sth / sb / sb's behaviour / clothes*
scorn	mépriser refuser avec mépris	*to scorn sth / sb for doing sth* *to scorn to do / doing sth*
sneer at	sourire, rire avec mépris de	*to sneer at sth / sb / sb's suggestions*
snigger / snicker	ricaner	*to snigger at sth*
spurn	dédaigner, repousser avec dédain	*to spurn sb / sb for doing sth - a spurned lover* (éconduit)

Exercices sur le chapitre 10 (4.2)

1. Testez vos connaissances en traduisant les mots suivants:

A / to jeer - B / scorn - C / ludicrous - D / laughing stock - E / to snigger - F / to spurn

2. Remettez les mots dans l'ordre pour constituer des phrases cohérentes:

A / she why sneering and keep does sniggering I everything at say?
B / contempt but nothing feels she him for and to fails never disparage to efforts public in his.
C / suggestions his of contemptuous is she, though they even appear to don't ludicrous or be despicable.

3. Parfois une lettre ou un bloc de trois ou quatre lettres s'est déplacé d'un mot sur un autre. Rétablissez:

A. IRONFUL   B. SCORNIC   C. UNGRATIBLE   D. CONTEMPTFUL   E. LUDICABLE
F. DESPICROUS   G. SCURN   H. SPORN

4.3 Trust / Confidence / Truth

Collocations

■ *Noms*

confidence	confiance	*to have / feel / express absolute confidence in sb / sth / that ...* *- to gain sb's confidence - to place / misplace one's confidence*
	confidence	*to violate sb's confidences* (trahir un secret) *- to exchange confidences - in strict confidence* (sous le sceau du secret)

pledge	promesse, engagement		*to make / take a solemn pledge to do sth - to give (sb) / fulfil / honour one's pledge*
promise ['promɪs]	promesse		*to make / keep / fulfill / break a promise to do sth / that ...*
trust	confiance		*to abuse / betray sb's trust - to put one's trust in sb / sth / in doing sth*
truth	vérité		*to establish / face / find / reveal / seek / tell the plain / naked truth*

■ Adjectifs

honest ['ɒnɪst]	honnête	*honest person / dealings - to be honest about sth - it is (not) honest (of sb) to do sth*
reliable	sérieux, sur qui / quoi on peut compter, fiable	*reliable person / employee / information / memory*
true	vrai	*true fact / statement - it is true that... - a dream may come true (se réaliser)*
trustworthy ['---]	digne de confiance	*trustworthy person / friend*
truthful	sincère, qui dit la vérité, véridique	*truthful person* *truthful statement / account / story*
unreliable	peu fiable, sur qui / quoi on ne peut pas compter, douteux	*unreliable person / machine / information*
untrue	inexact, faux, infidèle	*untrue belief / statement - it is untrue that...* *to be untrue to sb*
untrustworthy	indigne de confiance, peu sûr	*untrustworthy person / witness / source of information*
untruthful	qui ne dit pas la vérité, mensonger	*untruthful person* *untruthful statement / account*

■ Verbes

confide (in)	(se) confier (à)	*to confide a secret to sb - to confide in sb*
entrust	confier	*to entrust sth / money to sb / sb with sth*
pledge	promettre (s') engager	*to pledge (one's) support / allegiance / money to sb* *to pledge sb / (oneself) to sth / to do sth / that... - to pledge one's word*
promise ['promɪs]	promettre	*to promise sth / sb sth / to do sth / that ...*
rely	compter sur, se fier à	*to rely on sb (for sth / for doing sth) - to rely on sb to do sth / on sth happening / on trains being on time*
tell on sb	cafarder, dénoncer	*it's not nice to tell - to tell on sb (for doing sth)*
trust	avoir confiance / foi en, faire confiance à, confier	*to blindly trust sb / in God* *to trust sb with sth / sb to do sth*
undeceive [ˌ--'-]	détromper	*to undeceive sb about sth*

Exercices sur le chapitre 10 (4.3)

1. Testez vos connaissances en traduisant les mots ci-dessous:

A / truth - B / truthful - C / trustworthy - D / to confide - E / to entrust - F / to undeceive

2. En vous reportant aux expressions et collocations figurant dans la colonne de droite, traduisez les expressions suivantes:

A / Faire confiance à quelqu'un pour découvrir la vérité. B / Se réaliser (rêve). C / S'engager à quelque chose. D / Donner sa parole. E / Gagner / trahir la confiance de quelqu'un. F / Il n'est pas honnête de trahir un secret. G / Confier un secret. H / Mal placer sa confiance. I / Confier son argent à quelqu'un.

Social and human relations

4.4 Lies

Collocations

■ *Noms*

excuse [ɪk'skjuːs]	excuse, prétexte	*to find / make up a lame / poor excuse for sth / for doing sth - it's just an excuse to do sth - to accept / reject the excuse that ...*
falsehood	faux, fausseté	*truth and falsehood (le vrai et le faux) - to expose the falsehood of a statement*
	mensonge	*to tell / explode a downright falsehood*
fib	petit mensonge	*to tell (sb) fibs*
fraud	escroquerie, fraude	*to be charged with blatant (avéré) / shameful / (tax) fraud*
	imposteur	*to be a notorious fraud*
hoax	canular	*to contrive a hoax / a hoax call - a hoax may mystify (tromper) / ridicule / scare sb*
humbug	charlatan, imposteur	*to be / expose a humbug of a doctor*
	fumisterie, tromperie, supercherie	*to practise / contrive (forger) an intolerable humbug*
	balivernes	*to talk a lot of humbug (old use)*
hypocrite ['hɪpəkrɪt]	hypocrite	*consummate / pompous hypocrite*
liar	menteur	*to call sb a notorious / monstrous liar*
lie	mensonge	*to tell a white (pieux) lie / a pack of lies*
monkey business	affaire pas nette, combines	*some monkey-business may have been going on for some time*
pretence [-'-]	faux-semblant	*to make a pretence of doing sth / that... (faire semblant de / que) - it's only / all pretence (de la comédie)*
	prétexte	*under false pretences*
put-up job	coup monté	*to do / pull a put-up job*
untruth	contre-vérité, invention	*to tell an untruth*

■ *Adjectifs*

dishonest [dɪs'ɒnɪst]	malhonnête	*dishonest person / behaviour - to be dishonest in sth / in doing sth - it is dishonest (of sb) to do sth*
false	erroné, faux	*false note / statement / move (faux pas) / idea*
	faux, mensonger	*false witness / report / promises*
	perfide, déloyal	*false friend - to be false to sb*
hypocritical [,-'---]	hypocrite	*hypocritical person / attitude - to be hypocritical about sth - it is hypocritical to do sth*

■ *Verbes*

betray	trahir	*to betray sb / one's country / sb's trust*
cheat	tricher	*to cheat at games / on an examination*
cheat on sb	tromper qqn	*to cheat on one's wife*
cheat sth out	extorquer qch	*to cheat money out of sb*
distrust	ne pas avoir confiance en	*to distrust sb / sth*
double-cross	trahir, doubler	*to double-cross sb*
explode	enlever toute crédibilité à	*to explode a(n) myth / theory / argument*
expose	révéler, démasquer	*to expose a person / plot / secret / scandal*
fool	tromper, duper	*to fool sb - to fool sb into doing sth / sb out of sth - to have sb fooled*

give away	trahir, révéler (la vraie nature de)	to give away sb's manners - sb's clothes may give her / him away
	révéler (volontairement ou non) dénoncer	to give away a secret / where sth is
		to give sb away to the police
lie	mentir	to lie shamelessly about sth to sb
make believe	imaginer, faire semblant que	to make believe that...
mistrust	douter, se méfier de	to mistrust sb / sth / one's own abilities
pretend	faire semblant	to pretend to be / to do sth / that...
reveal	révéler	to reveal sth to sb / (to sb) that...
take in	tromper, rouler	to take sb in - to be taken in by sb's good appearance / sleek (mielleux) talk
traduce	calomnier, diffamer	to traduce sb / a country

Exercices sur le chapitre 10 (4.4)

1. Testez vos connaissances en traduisant les mots ci-dessous:

A / to mistrust - B / untruth - C / hoax - D / humbug - E / to double-cross - F / to distrust - G / to distrust

2. Choisissez le mot qui convient:

A. He made a humbug / a pretence / a hoax that he could find all the money necessary for the trip.
B. He keeps telling the sweet old ladies frauds / fibs / monkey business.
C. He always manages to distrust / lie / fool sweet old ladies into giving him money.
D. He has revealed the liar / falsehood / put-up job of that statement.
E. He lied on / cheated on / pretended on his wife.
F. It is not always easy not to be taken in / hoaxed / traduced by his suave manners.

4.5 Excusing / forgiving

Collocations

■ *Noms*

| excuse [ɪk'skjuːs] | excuse, prétexte | to find / make up a lame (piètre) / poor excuse for sth / for doing sth - sth may be just an excuse not to do sth - to accept / reject the excuse that ... |
| reward [-'-] | récompense | to claim / receive a well-deserved reward for sth / for doing sth |

■ *Adjectif*

| lenient ['liːni‿ənt] | indulgent | to be purposely / unduly lenient to / towards / with sb |

■ *Verbes*

excuse [ɪk'skjuːz]	excuser	to excuse sb for sth / for doing sth - to be excused (dispensé) from sth / from doing sth
forgive	pardonner	to forgive sb sth / sb for sth / sb for doing sth
overlook [,--'-]	laisser passer, fermer les yeux sur	to deliberately overlook an error / sb's unkind attitude / the fact that...
reward [-'-]	récompenser	to reward sb with sth for sth / for doing sth

Social and human relations   153

spare   épargner   *to spare sb / sb's life / sb's feelings* (ménager) - *to spare oneself*
                                                      the trouble of doing sth
                     éviter (à qqn)   *to spare sb sth / sb embarrassment / sb the details / sb the shame*
                                                      of sth

Exercices sur le chapitre 10 (4.5)

1. Testez vos connaissances en traduisant les mots ci-dessous:
A / excuse (n.) - B / reward (n.) - C / to overlook - D / to spare

2. Joignez à chaque mot de droite la définition de gauche qui s'y rapporte:

A. to ignore or disregard sth   1. lenient
B. to pardon   2. reward
C. not disposed to severity   3. overlook
D. give somebody something to show one's appreciation 4. spare
E. to save somebody something usually unpleasant   5. to forgive

3. Choisissez la / les solutions possible(s):

A. To forgive sth to sb / sb sth / sth sb / sb for sth
B. To excuse sb sth / sb for sth / sb from sth / sth at sb
C. To reward sb of sth / sb with sth / sth to sb / sb sth

4.6. Complaint / revenge

Collocations

■ *Noms*

complaint [-'-]   réclamation, plainte   *to express / make a complaint about sth / (to sb) that ... - to file /*
                                                          lodge a complaint (porter plainte) *with sb* (auprès de) *against*
                                                          sb - to take into account / disregard a justified complaint
grievance   sujet de plainte, grief,   *to voice* (formuler) */ submit / settle / nurse* (nourrir) *a grievance*
                             revendication   *against sb*
representations   protestations (officielles) *to make* (adresser) *representations to sb*
retribution   châtiment   *to visit divine retribution on sb* (faire porter à qqn le poids de)
revenge [-'-]   vengeance   *to get / take / wreak* (assouvir) *(one's) vengeance on sb for sth*

■ *Verbes*

avenge   venger   *to avenge sb's death / oneself on sb for sth*
blame   reprocher, en vouloir à   *to unfairly blame sb for sth / sb for doing sth - to blame sth on sb*
                                                          (mettre sur le dos de)
chide   gronder, réprimander   *to chide sb for sth / sb for doing sth*
complain   se plaindre   *to bitterly complain about sth to sb / to sb that...*
have it in   en vouloir à mort   *to have it in for sb for no good reason*
punish   punir   *to lightly / severely punish sb for sth / sb for doing sth*
rail at / against   s'en prendre à, invectiver   *to relentlessly rail at sb*
rebuke   réprimander   *to mildly / cuttingly rebuke sb for sth / sb for doing sth*
reproach   reprocher, faire des   *to fiercely reproach sb for / with sth / sb for doing sth*
                             reproches à

revenge [-'-]	venger	*to revenge oneself on sb for sth*
scold [skəʊld]	gronder	*to harshly scold sb for sth / sb for doing sth*
tell off	attraper	*to tell sb off for sth / sb for doing sth*

Exercices sur le chapitre 10 (4.6)

1. Testez vos connaissances en traduisant les mots ci-dessous:

A / to chide - B / to rail at sb - C / retribution - D / representations

2. La première lettre de chaque verbe dans les phrases ci-dessous a été omise ou indûment remplacée par une autre. Rétablissez la situation:

A / He's been COLDING the poor child all morning. B / Stop MAILING AT her so sarcastically. C / Why did you SELL him OFF so sharply? D / There's no point in HIDING the kid all the time. E / Don' FLAME everything ON me, please!

3. Traduisez en anglais:

A / Quel épouvantable grief nourrit-elle en son cœur? B / La mort de qui veut-elle venger? C / A qui se plaint-elle et de quoi se plaint-elle? Auprès de quels dieux porte-t-elle plainte? D / De qui veut-elle se venger? E / A qui en veut-elle ainsi à mort? F / Sur qui demande-t-elle que pèse le poids du châtiment divin?

11
Education

A. Primary and secondary education

1. Schools

■ *Noms*

boarding school	pensionnat, internat	**high school diploma**	baccalauréat
child care centre (US) / creche / day nursery	crèche	**high school** (GB)	lycée
		comprehensive school [,--'---]	établissement secondaire polyvalent
co-educational school	établissement scolaire mixte		
daycare (centre)	garderie	**denominational school**	établissement confessionnel
infant school	CP et CE 1	**junior high (school)** (US)	collège
nursery school	école maternelle; jardin d'enfants (privé)	**primary / elementary** (US) [,--'----] / **grade** (US) school	école primaire
kindergarden	jardin d'enfants		
prep school / preparatory [-'----] **school** (GB)	école primaire privée	**secondary school**	lycée
		senior high school (US)	lycée
playgroup / playschool	garderie	**senior year** (US)	(classe) terminale
prep school / preparatory school (US)	lycée privé	**public school** (US / GB)	école publique
		Public School (GB)	'Public School'
private school / independent school	école privée	**state school** (US / GB)	école publique
junior school (GB)	école primaire (7 à 11 ans)	**training college**	école professionnelle
high school (US)	collège (ou lycée)	**teacher training college**	IUFM

Collocations

education	enseignement, études	*to provide / be given / receive a classical / scientific education - to complete one's education abroad*
form (GB)	classe	*first* (sixième) / *lower sixth* (première) / *upper sixth* (terminale) *form*
grade (US)	classe	*sixth* (sixième) / *seventh* (cinquième) / *tenth* (seconde) / *junior* (première) / *senior* (terminale)
grammar school	lycée	*used to be reserved for the more academically able*
school	école, classe	*to go to / attend school / a good school - school may start or begin at 9 and finish at 5 - to start / begin school at (the age of) 5 and finish school at (the age of) 16 - to enter a private school - to graduate from school* (sortir avec un diplôme) *at 17 - to drop out of school* (abandonner ses études) *- to still be at / in (US) school - to teach school in New York (US:* être prof*)*

schooling	instruction, études	*to receive very little formal schooling* (faire peu d'études) - *schooling may be compusory from 4 to 16 - to lose a year's schooling* (perdre une année)
school fees / tuition fees	frais de scolarité	*to pay / be exempted from paying the tuition fees*

■ *Verbe*

educate	instruire, former	*to educate sb for sth / sb to do sth*

2. School activities / discipline / exams

Collocations

■ *Noms*

A-level	niveau Bac	*to take A-level French*
A levels / high school diploma (US)	baccalauréat	*to pass / get one's A-levels - several A-levels may be required for entrance to university*
caning	châtiments corporels	*to abolish / stand for* (défendre) *caning*
composition [,--'--]	rédaction (GB)	*to do / write a composition*
course / program (US)	cursus	*to take a one-year course in French*
curriculum [kə'rɪkjʊləm]	programme (d'une classe)	*core curriculum* (tronc commun)
detention	retenue	*to be kept in detention for cheating*
dictation	dictée	*to give / take down a dictation*
discipline	discipline	*to enforce / maintain discipline*
drill	exercice	*to conduct grammar drills*
environmental studies [ɪn ˌvaɪrən'mentl]	science de l'environnement	*to go in for environmental studies*
essay / theme (US)	dissertation	*to do / write an essay on / about sth*
exam(ination)	exam(en)	*to take / sit / pass* (réussir) *an examination in sth*
exercise	exercice	*to do an exercise*
GCE (A-level)	Baccalauréat	*to take six subjects for GCE (General Certificate of Education) (A-level)*
GCSE (O-level)	Brevet	*to have eight GCSEs (General Certificate of Secondary Education) (O-level)* (le brevet dans 8 matières)
grade (US)	classe, année note, niveau	*to be in the fifth grade* (CM2) *to get good grades in French - to be a grade A student* (excellent)
homework / assignment(s) [ə'saɪnmənt(s)] (US)	devoirs, tâches	*to be set some homework to do - to be given a lot of heavy reading assignments*
make-up	examen de rattrapage	*to take a make-up in two subjects*
mark / score (US)	note	*average / high / low mark - to get 11 out of 20*
mistake	erreur, faute	*to make / rectify / excuse a bad / serious / minor / slight mistake*
mock exam / practice test (US)	examen blanc	*to sail through* (se tirer brillamment) *a mock exam*
O-level	niveau Brevet (examen, résultat)	*to take O-level English to get four O-levels*
oral test	contrôle oral	*to fail the oral test in German*
paper	(sujet d') examen travail à rendre	*the German paper may be hard* *to set the students a paper - to hand in one's paper*

Education 157

pass GB [pɑːs] / US [pæs]	moyenne	*to get a pass* (obtenir la moyenne)
physical training (PT) / education	éducation physique	*to attend / be excused from physical training / to attend physical education lessons*
précis(-writing) ['preɪsiː]	compte rendu de lecture	*to write a précis of the main points*
prep	étude (sur place) devoirs	*a teacher may have to supervise prep* *not to have much prep to do*
prize	prix	*to give sb / award sb / receive a prize for chemistry*
prose	traduction (thème)	*to do a prose*
quiz	contrôle	*to give / take* (subir) *a quiz*
(school) report / report card (US)	bulletin scolaire	*to receive a favourable / unfavourable end of term report*
row [raʊ]	chahut, tapage	*to start a row*
sandwich course	enseignement alterné	*to attend a sandwich course*
school outing / visit	sortie scolaire	*to go on / take students on an outing*
school record ['rekɔːd] / student file (US)	dossier scolaire	*to consult / look at a student's file*
syllabus ['sɪləbəs]	programme (d'une matière)	*sth may be on the syllabus*
test	contrôle	*to give / set a class a test - a class may take / pass / fail a test*
written test / quiz (US)	épreuve écrite, interrogation écrite	*to pass the written test and fail the oral / the oral test*

■ *Adjectifs*

make-up	de rattrapage	*make-up class / exercise / exam*
optional	facultatif	*optional subject*
remedial [rɪˈmiːdiəl]	de soutien, de rattrapage	*remedial course*

■ *Verbes*

correct	corriger (les erreurs)		**play up**	chahuter
erase / rub out	effacer		**prep** (US)	faire ses études dans une école privée
expel	expulser			
go over sth	revoir, réviser qch		**review** (US) / **revise**	revoir, réviser
jot down	noter, prendre en note		**stay down**	rester dans la même classe, redoubler
note down	noter			

Collocations

drill	faire (faire) des exercices	*to drill students in grammar / in the use of the past tenses - to drill the subtleties of grammar into the first-year students - to be drilled* (entraîné) *into doing sth*
examine [-'--]	faire passer un examen, interroger	*to examine a student for the oral test*
fail	échouer, rater coller	*to fail an exam / in the maths test* *to fail a candidate*
grade (US)	noter, donner une note	*to grade homework*
make up	rattraper	*to make up a course / an examination*
mark	corriger et noter	*to mark papers*
move up	(faire) passer dans la classe supérieure	*to move (sb) up into the next class*
pass GB [pɑːs] / US [pæs]	réussir	*to pass an exam / in English*

repeat	redoubler	*to repeat a year*
quiz / test	donner un contrôle	*to quiz the pupils in maths*
sit / take	passer, se présenter	*to sit / take an exam*
sit for	se présenter	*to sit for one's O-level*

Exercices sur le chapitre 11 A (1 et 2)

1. Testez vos connaissances en traduisant les mots ci-dessous :

A / junior high (US) - B / playschool - C / prep school (GB) - D / first form - E / curriculum
F / sandwich course

2. Traduisez en vous aidant des exemples et collocations de la colonne de droite du vocabulaire :

A / Terminer ses études à l'étranger. B / Être exempté des frais de scolarité. C / Redoubler la classe de CM2. D / Faire faire des exercices de grammaire à des étudiants. E / Passer dans la classe supérieure. F / Rattraper une série de cours. G. Se présenter à un examen. H / Corriger un devoir.

3. Remplissez la grille ci-dessous à l'aide des définitions proposées :

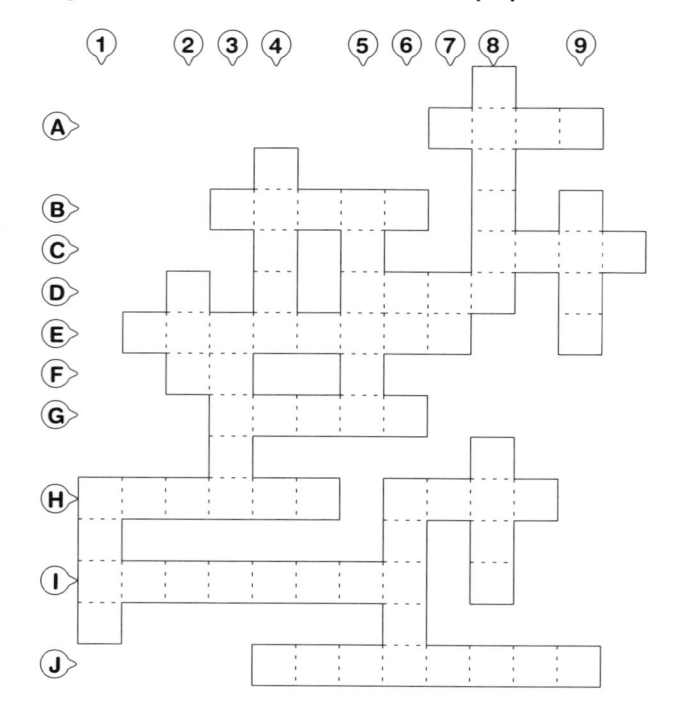

Horizontalement : A / interrogation écrite - B / thème - C / suite de l'écrit - D / 60 minutes - E / devoirs - F / nous - G / exercice - H / résumé - examen - I / programme - J / redoubler
Verticalement : 1 / réussir - 2 / chahut - 3 / abréviation de 'medical doctor' - 4 / note (US) - 5 / école - 6 / conjonction - dissertation - 7 / Royaume-Uni - 8 / primaire (école) - note (GB) - 9 / échouer

Education

3. Periods

■ *Noms*

half-term	vacances de mi-trimestre	**period** ['pɪəri_əd]	"heure" de cours
midterm	(vacances de) mi-trimestre		

Collocations

attendance [-'---]	présence	*attendance at classes is compulsory - to take attendance* (faire l'appel)
break / recess (US) [-'-]	récréation, courtes vacances	*to have a ten-minute break - to discuss sth during break - the Easter break*
class GB [klɑːs] / US [klæs]	classe	*to attend / take* (enseigner) *a Latin class*
holiday(s)	vacances	*to go on holiday - during the Xmas holidays*
lesson	cours	*to teach an afternoon biology lesson*
sick note	mot d'excuse	*to send in a sick note*
term	trimestre	*autumn / (US) fall / spring / summer term*
timetable	emploi du temps	*to make up / follow a timetable*
vacation (US)	vacances	*to go on vacation - the summer / (US) long vacation*

■ *Adjectifs*

compulsory [-'---]	obligatoire	*compulsory attendance / subject - it is compulsory (for sb) to do sth*
optional ['---]	facultatif	*optional subject / homework - it is optional (for sb) to do sth*

■ *Verbes*

go back to school	reprendre l'école, la classe, rentrer	**cut a class** GB [klɑːs] / US [klæs]	sécher un cours
call in sick	téléphoner qu'on sera absent	**play truant / hooky** (US)	faire l'école buissonnière, sécher les cours

Collocations

attend	assister	*to attend school / lessons*
break up	s'interrompre, être en vacances	*school breaks up - the students break up*

4. Supplies and equipment

■ *Noms*

ballpoint / biro	stylo à bille, bic	**eraser / rubber**	gomme
bookcase ['bʊk keɪs]	bibliothèque (meuble)	**exercise book**	cahier d'exercices ou de devoirs
calculator ['----]	calculatrice		
compass / pair of compasses ['kʌmpəsɪz]	compas	**felt-tip pen**	feutre
		form	banc (d'école)
copybook	cahier d'écriture	**notebook**	cahier, carnet
desk	bureau	**notice / bulletin** (US) ['bʊlətɪn] **board**	tableau d'affichage
duster	chiffon		

overhead projector	rétro-projecteur	**sponge** [spʌndʒ]	éponge
pencil	crayon papier	**teaching aids**	matériel pédagogique
protractor	rapporteur	**textbook**	manuel scolaire
rostrum ['rɒstrəm]	chaire, estrade	**workbook**	cahier ou livret d'exercices
ruler	règle	**magnifying** ['----] **glass**	loupe
set square	équerre (à dessin)	(GB [glɑːs] / US [glæs])	
sheet	feuille de papier	**supplies** [-'-]	fournitures
slide projector	projecteur de diapositives		

5. Premises

■ *Noms*

cafeteria (US) [ˌkæfə'tɪəri̯ə] / **dining hall** (GB)	cantine, réfectoire	(**assembly** [-'--]) **hall**	salle de réunion (profs et élèves)
refectory [-'---]	réfectoire	**laboratory** GB [-'----] / US ['-----]	laboratoire
dormitory ['---]	dortoir	**playground**	cour de récréation
gymnasium [-'---]	gymnase	**playing field**	terrain de jeux / de sports

Exercices sur le chapitre 11 A (3, 4, 5)

1. Testez vos connaissances en traduisant les mots ci-dessous :

A / premises - B / supplies - C / dortoir - D / feutre - E / chiffon - F / chaire, estrade
G / équerre - H / trimestre

2. Joignez une phrase de droite à chaque de phrase de gauche :

1 / I always use a ballpoint
2 / He rarely attends biology lessons
3 / It is optional for students
4 / It is better to send in
5 / All teachers do not take
6 / Attendance at classes is not compulsory
7 / The holidays begin
8 / To rub things out

A / you may use an eraser or a sponge.
B / a sick note than to call in sick.
C / to write notes in my notebook.
D / during the long vacation, of course!
E / when school breaks up.
F / to take subjects that are not compulsory!
G / and often cuts the French class.
H / attendance after the lunch-time break.

6. Pupils / Students

■ *Noms*

beginner [-'--]	débutant	**cheat**	tricheur
boarder	pensionnaire, interne	**low achiever**	élève médiocre
dunce [dʌns]	cancre	**old boy**	ancien élève ('preppie')
former pupil	ancien élève	**playfellow / mate**	camarade de jeux

Education 161

prefect	moniteur, surveillant	**school chum / mate / pal**	copain
preppie	élève d'une 'prep school'	**student** (US)	élève
pupil (GB)	élève	**day-pupil**	externe
school leaver	élève en fin de scolarité		

Collocations

classmate	camarade de classe	*to get on well / badly with one's classmates*	
scholarship / school maintenance allowance	bourse (selon les revenus ou les résultats)	*to be given / granted a scholarship*	
old boy	ancien élève (de Public School ou d'Université)	*to arrive on the board* (conseil d'administration) *through the old boy network* (réseau d'anciens élèves)	

■ *Adjectifs*

held back / kept down	obligé de redoubler	**talkative**	bavard
kept in	gardé en retenue	**hardworking**	travailleur
restless	remuant		

■ *Verbes*

drop out (of school)	abandonner les études	**keep still / quiet**	rester tranquille, se taire
haze	bizuter		

Collocations

bully ['bʊli]	brutaliser, bizuter	*to bully sb into sth / into doing sth*	
cheat	tricher, copier	*to cheat on an examination*	

7. Staff

■ *Noms*

inspector of schools	inspecteur	**librarian** [laɪˈbreərɪ ən]	bibliothécaire, documentaliste
director [dəˈrektə] **/ commissioner** (US) **of education**	recteur d'académie	**principal / head**	principal, chef d'établissement
		vice-principal	directeur-adjoint, censeur
bursar [ˈbɜːsə]	intendant	**master** GB [ˈmɑːstə] / US [ˈmæstər]	maître d'école, professeur
accreditation officer	inspecteur (US)	**mistress**	maîtresse d'école, professeur
headmaster GB [hedˈmɑːstə] / US [hedˈmæstər]	proviseur, directeur	**the latin master**	le prof de latin
		teacher	enseignant
		trainee teacher	stagiaire
year head / dean (US)	conseiller d'éducation	**the English mistress**	la prof d'anglais
headmistress	directrice	**school marm / school ma'am** (US)	institutrice (de campagne)
deputy head / deputy	censeur, directeur		

Collocations

careers [-'-] **adviser / counselor** (US) [ˈkaʊnsl ə]	conseiller d'orientation	*to seek / get sound advice from the counselor*	
private tuition	cours particuliers	*to pay for private tuition*	

staff GB [stɑːf] / US [stæf]	personnel enseignant	*the school's staff is / are excellent*
sub / substitute ['---] / supply teacher	remplaçant	*a sub may substitute for the permanent teacher*

■ *Verbes*

coach	préparer	*to coach a student for an exam*
take a class	enseigner, faire cours	*to take the lower fifth in French*
teach	enseigner	*to teach sb a subject / sb (how) to read*
train	former, préparer	*to train sb for sth / for an exam / sb to do sth*
tutor	donner des cours particuliers	*to tutor sb in maths*

8. Subjects

■ *Noms*

arithmetic [-'---]	arithmétique		**square**	carré
geometry	géométrie		**parallelogram** [,--'---]	parallélogramme
algebra ['ældʒɪbrə]	algèbre		**triangle**	triangle
mathematics [,--'---]	mathématiques		**trapezium** [trə'piːzi̯əm]	trapèze
maths / math (US)	maths		**diameter** [daɪ'æmɪtə]	diamètre
trigonometry [,--'---]	trigonométrie		**radius** ['reɪdi̯əs]	rayon
quadrilateral [,kwɒdrɪ'lætrəl]	quadrilatère		**circumference** [-'---]	circonférence
			cone	cône
acute [-'-] **angle**	angle aigu		**sphere**	sphère
obtuse [əb'tjuːs] **angle**	angle obtus		**arc**	arc
right angle	angle droit		**tangent**	tangente
degree [-'-]	degree		**set**	ensemble
pi [paɪ]	pi		**computer science /** **computing**	informatique
theorem ['θɪərəm]	théorème			
cosine ['kəʊsaɪn]	cosinus		**subset**	sous-ensemble
sine [saɪn]	sinus		**science**	science
rectangle ['---]	rectangle			
art	art, études d'art		**Greek**	grec
the arts	les (beaux-)arts		**gymnastics**	gymnastique
drawing	dessin		**handicraft**	artisanat, travail manuel
arts	les lettres		**history**	histoire
crafts GB [krɑːfts] / US [kræfts]	travaux manuels		**home economics**	économie domestique
			languages	langues
current affairs	les grands problèmes actuels		**Latin**	latin
dancing GB ['dɑːnsɪŋ] / US ['dænsɪŋ]	danse		**modern / foreign** **languages**	langues vivantes / étrangères
games	sports, activités de plein air		**music**	musique
domestic science	arts ménagers		**RE / RI** [ɑːr'iː] / [ɑːr'aɪ]	instruction religieuse
geography	géographie		**physical education** (PE) **/ physical training** (PT)	éducation physique
general knowledge	culture générale			
grammar	grammaire			

Education

Collocations

religious education / instruction	instruction religieuse	*to receive religious education (RE) / instruction (RI) at school*
spelling	orthographe	*to improve one's deficient spelling*
sport(s)	sport	*to do / go in for sport(s)*
technical education	travaux manuels	*to be given a thorough technical education*
the three Rs	lecture, écriture et calcul	*to be taught Reading / Writing / Arithmetic*

■ *Verbes*

add up	additionner	*not to know how to add up two and two*
divide	diviser	*to divide a number by four*
go in for / take up	choisir, s'orienter vers	*to go in for / take up modern languages*
multiply	multiplier	*to multiply a number by three*
spell	épeler	*to spell a word aloud*
	orthographier	*to spell a word correctly / incorrectly*
subtract [-'-]	soustraire	*to substract a number from another number*

Exercices sur le chapitre 11 A (6, 7, 8)

1. Testez vos connaissances en traduisant les mots ci-dessous :

A / élève en fin de scolarité - B / copain (de classe) - C / abandonner ses études
D / recteur d'académie - E / cosinus - F / sinus - G / informatique - H / travaux manuels

2. Joignez une phrase de droite à chaque phrase de gauche :

1 / Only the more hardworking students	A / often end up being kept in or even kept down.
2 / Beginners often get hazed and bullied	B / tutorials to a small number of students.
3 / Restless, talkative students	C / if you can't spell, or can you?
4 / Some boarders get on	D / are granted scholarships.
5 / A tutor's job consists in giving	E / by older dunces and the low achievers.
6 / Although he can't add up properly	F / taught by a bursar or the librarian.
7 / You can't go in for teaching	G / badly with their playmates.
8 / RE and RI are not subjects usually	H / he is good at maths.

B. Higher education

1. Places and organisation

■ *Noms*

alma mater [ˌælmə'mɑːtə]	université où on a obtenu ses diplômes		**dormitory** (GB) ['----]	dortoir
art college	école des beaux-arts		**dormitory** (US) / **hall of residence** (GB)	résidence universitaire
college of education	IUFM		**fraternity** [-'---]	confrérie (d'étudiants)

graduate school. / postgraduate school (US)	3ᵉ cycle	lecture hall	amphithéâtre
		poly(technic)	IUT
higher education	enseignement supérieur	sorority [-'---]	club / cercle d'étudiantes
Ivy League Universities (US)	universités du nord-est (réputées)	teacher training college	IUFM
		training scheme	programme de formation
laboratory GB [-'----] / US ['-----]	laboratoire		

Collocations

college (US)	université	college covers the first three years - to go to college (faire des études)
education	études	sb's education may have been interrupted / neglected
fraternity	club / cercle d'étudiants	to join (devenir membre) a fraternity
further education	enseignement postscolaire	to promote further education
tuition	scolarité	to pay 1000 dollars tuition per semester
tuition fees	frais de scolarité	to pay the tuition fees - to be exempted from the tuition fees
university	université	to be at / study at a university (faire des études universitaires) - to go to (a) university

■ *Adjectifs*

academic [,--'---]	universitaire	academic year - academic officers (US) (enseignants et administratifs)
educated at	qui a fait ses études à	sb may have been educated at Oxford

2. Staff

■ *Noms*

academic	universitaire	proctor (US)	surveillant (examen)
dean (of the faculty)	doyen	president (GB) / vice-chancellor (US)	président
careers [-'-] officer / adviser	conseiller d'orientation	professor / college professor (US)	professeur
Faculty Board	conseil de Faculté		
fellow (US)	boursier	researcher / research worker	chercheur
governing body	administrateurs	scholar	chercheur, érudit
fellow (GB)	chargé de cours	senior lecturer / assistant professor [-'---] (US)	maître de conférences
junior lecturer / instructor (US)	assistant		
		summer school / summer institute (US)	université d'été
lecturer	maître de conférences		
proctor (GB)	responsable de la discipline	staff (GB [stɑːf] / US [stæf])	personnel enseignant

Collocations

don	professseur	especially at Oxford and Cambridge
faculty	corps enseignant, enseignants	to be on the faculty - the faculty meet(s) at regular intervals
Faculty	Faculté	the Law Faculty - the Faculty of Arts
lecture	conférence	to attend / give / deliver a lecture
paper	exposé, communication	to give / read a paper on sth
research	recherche	to conduct / supervise / do thorough / original research on / into sth

Education

seminar ['seminɑː]	séminaire	to conduct / hold a seminar on sth
talk	exposé oral; causerie	to give an informal talk about sth
tenure ['tenjə]	titularisation	to have / get tenure (être titulaire / titularisé) - to be on the tenure track (être titularisable)
tutor	directeur d'études	to be a course tutor to sb
tutorial [-'---]	travaux dirigés	to give sb / have a tutorial with sb on sth
vacation	vacances (universitaires)	to be away on vacation

■ *Adjectifs*

learned ['lɜːnɪd]	savant, cultivé	learned person / book
scholarly	savant, érudit	scholarly person / work
tenured	titulaire	tenured professor

■ *Verbe*

tutor	diriger (les travaux)	to tutor sb in Greek

3. Students

■ *Noms*

apprentice	apprenti	registrar's office	service de la scolarité
alumnus / alumna [-'---] / former student	ancien(ne) étudiant(e)	registration	inscription (GB)
		second year student / sophomore (US)	étudiant de seconde année
bullying ['bʊliɪŋ]	brimades, brutalités		
fresher (GB) / freshman (US)	étudiant de première année	student card	carte d'étudiant
		trainee [-'-]	stagiaire
graduate	licencié, diplômé	undergraduate [ˌ--'---]	étudiant de premier cycle
hazing	bizutage	vocational training	formation professionnelle
postgraduate	étudiant de troisième cycle	internship	stage en entreprise
rag mag	magazine humoristique	traineeship	stage d'emploi-formation
ragging	canulars, farces		

Collocations

apprenticeship	apprentissage	to fill / serve an apprenticeship
course	cursus	to take / sign up for / complete a course in sth
attendance [-'--]	assiduité, fréquentation	sb's attendance record (bilan d'assiduité) may be good or bad - attendance at some classes may be low or high
dropout	abandon	an alarming dropout rate
	étudiant qui abandonne	first-year drop-outs
enrolment	inscription	open enrolment in / registration for a course
	effectifs	to record an enrolment of 3000 as against 2600 the preceding year
rag	divertissements au profit d'œuvres charitables	to be on the rag committee - to organize a fancy dress parade for rag week
student	étudiant	outstanding / poor (médiocre) / full / part time student
studies	études	to start / pursue / complete (achever) advanced studies in sth
study	étude	to make / conduct an exhaustive study of sth

■ Verbes

drop out	abandonner (ses études)	*to drop out of a course / college*
enrol	(s')inscrire	*to enrol for a course - to enrol students in a course*
major in	se spécialiser en, choisir une filière de	*to major in linguistics* (prendre linguistique en dominante)
minor in	prendre en sous-dominante	*to minor in chemistry*
orientate ['ɔːrɪ‿ənteɪt]	orienter	*to orientate oneself to / towards sth*
read	faire des études de	*to read modern languages / for the bar* (droit)
register ['---]	(s')inscrire	*to register (students) for / in a course*
study	étudier	*to study hard for a degree - to study a subject / book*
transfer [-'-]	changer (d'établissement / d'orientation)	*to transfer to another college / to another course / subject*

4. Subjects

■ Noms

art	art, matières artistiques	**computer science / computing**	informatique
arts / liberal arts	lettres et sciences humaines	**science**	science
business management	administration, gestion	**technology**	technology

Collocations

law	droit	*to read / go in for law* (faire des études de droit)

5. Exams [-'-] and degrees [-'-]

■ Noms

art degree	diplôme de l'école des Beaux Arts	**doctorate** ['dɒktərət]	doctorat
		Ph.D.	thèse docteur
commencement [-'---] **/ graduation** (US)	remise des diplômes	**honours degree**	licence avec mention
credit / unit	UV (unité de valeur)	**upper second**	mention Bien
(doctoral) dissertation / thesis	thèse de doctorat	**lower second**	mention Assez Bien
		first-class honours	mention Très Bien

Collocations

BA / arts degree	licence ès lettres	*BA stands for Bachelor of Arts*
BSc degree	licence ès science	*BSc stands for Bachelor of Science*
degree	licence	*to do a degree in linguistics*
MA	maîtrise ès lettres	*MA stands for Master of Arts degree*
MSc	maîtrise ès sciences	*MSc stands for Master of Science degree*
resit ['riːsɪt]	deuxième session	*to have a resit in law - to have to do a resit in / for French* (repasser l'examen)

Education

■ *Verbes*

graduate	obtenir un diplôme	*to graduate in linguistics*
do research	faire de la recherche	*to do research in / into sth*
fail	échouer, rater	*to fail an exam / a degree / in a subject*
	recaler, coller	*to fail a student*
flunk	coller,	*to flunk a candidate*
	être collé (à, en)	*to flunk - to flunk an exam / a subject*
pass / get through	réussir	*to pass / get through - to pass an exam*
GB [pɑːs] / US [pæs]		
pass	admettre, recevoir	*to pass a student*
research	faire des recherches	*to research on / into sth*
	réunir des documents sur	*to research a subject / sb's background*
resit [riːˈsɪt]	se représenter	*to have to resit in French / resit an exam*
sit / take	se présenter à (examen)	*to sit an exam*
sit for	se présenter à (diplôme)	*to sit for one's BA degree*

Exercices sur le chapitre 11 B (1 à 5)

1. Testez vos connaissances en traduisant les mots ci-dessous :

A / alma mater - B / fraternity - C / polytechnic - D / tenured - E / vacation - F / academic (n.) G / attendance record - H / rag mag

2. Rétablissez l'ordre des lettres :

A / TIRES - B / DUSTY - C / NOD - D / TAR - E / DANE - F / TROUT - G / PREAP - H / GAR

3. Rétablissez l'ordre des mots :

A / he been has a very subject researching for scholarly years five twenty. B / in up took a course he arts and to transferred then art. C / linguistics in for went he and a course one-year for registered in well computing as. D / in his degree BA sat he for June, exam failed the and to September in resit had it.

4. Traduisez en vous aidant des exemples et collocations donnés dans la colonne de droite du vocabulaire :

A / Faire des études. B / Devenir membre d'un club d'étudiantes. C / Les enseignants se réunissent une fois par semaine. D / Donner une conférence. E / Tenir un séminaire. F / Faire de la recherche. G / S'orienter vers les sciences. H / S'inscrire à un cours. I / Taux d'abandon. J / Faire des études de droit.

12

The media, culture and science

A. The media

0. General

■ *Noms*

media ['miːdi ə] event [-'-]	événement médiatique	media hype [,--'-]	promotion dans les médias

Collocations

media (sg / pl)	médias, presse écrite et parlée	*the local / national / news media - to get fair media attention*
media coverage ['---]	couverture médiatique	*to get heavy / massive media coverage - to get good media report* (être bien couvert)
medium	support, véhicule, moyen d'expression	*television can be a medium for giving information and for amusing people - sb's opinion can be best expressed through the print or the broadcasting medium - the theatre may be sb's favourite medium - sb's talent in mediums other than photography*

1. The radio

■ *Noms*

broadcast ['--]	émission, programme	wave(band)	(bande des) fréquences
FM	modulation de fréquence	wavelength	longueur d'onde
frequency	fréquence	wireless (set)	(poste de) TSF
listener	auditeur	jingle	refrain publicitaire
loud speaker	haut-parleur	news broadcast	journal parlé
pirate radio	radio-pirate	announcer	speaker(ine)
radiocar	voiture de reportage	charts	hit parade
radioplay	pièce radiodiffusée pièce pour la radio	sportscaster	journaliste sportif
radio / radio set	(appareil de) radio	newscaster	présentateur du journal
radio station	station de radio	short / long / medium wave	ondes courtes / grandes ondes / ondes moyennes
transmitter [-'--]	émetteur		

2. Television

2.1. Equipment

■ *Noms*

autocue ['ɔːtəʊkjuː]	téléprompteur	instant replay	retour sur image
film library	cinémathèque	keying	incrustation électronique

lavalier / clip on [ˌlævəˈlɪə] **microphone**	micro-cravate	**file footage** (US) / **record(s)** (US)	images d'archives
library pictures (GB)	images d'archives	**mobile** [ˈməʊbaɪl] **studio**	voiture de reportage
microphone	microphone	**monitor screen**	écran de contrôle
mike	micro	**network**	réseau
static (U) [ˈstætɪk]	parasites	**slow motion**	ralenti

Collocations

interference (U) [ˌ--ˈ--]	parasites	*to try and prevent interference produced by various sources*
television [ˈ----]	télévision	*to watch (too much) television - to turn on / turn off / turn up / turn down the television*

2.2. Production

■ Noms

broadcast [ˈ--]	émission	**quiz / quiz program** (US) / **quiz show**	jeu concours (radio / télévision)
call-in (program) (US) / **phone-in** (GB)	émission à ligne ouverte	**recording** [-ˈ--]	enregistrement
program(me)	émission, programme	**repeat** [-ˈ-] / **rerun** [ˈ--]	rediffusion
coverage [ˈ---]	couverture	**report** [-ˈ-]	reportage
feature film	film de la soirée	**sitcom**	comédie de situation
game show	jeu télévisé ou radiophonique	**soap opera** [ˈ---]	feuilleton (grand public)
headlines	titres du journal télévisé	**talk show**	débat, talk show
news bulletin / **newscast** (US)	bulletin d'informations	**newsbreak**	nouvelle importante
newsflash	flash d'informations	**telecast**	émission
prime time (US) / **peak viewing hours** (GB)	heures de grande écoute	**time-slot**	créneau horaire
		weather forecast	bulletin météo
variety show	émission de variétés	**chat show**	causerie télévisée

Collocations

documentary [ˌ--ˈ---]	documentaire	*to show* (faire passer) *a documentary on sth*
credits	générique	*the credits may roll at the beginning and / or at the end of a film*
entertainment [ˌ--ˈ--]	distraction(s)	*television provides entertainment*
footage (U)	séquences	*to show previously unseen footage on / about sth*
news (U)	informations, nouvelles	*to listen to / watch the latest news - to be in the news* (sur le devant de l'actualité) *- to hear sth on the news*
prize	prix	*to win / be awarded a prize in a quiz show*
programme / program (US)	programme, émission	*to bill* (programmer) */ pick* (choisir) *a program*
running commentary	commentaire suivi	*to give a running commentary on sth*
serial [ˈsɪəri‿əl]	feuilleton (à histoire suivie)	*to make a novel into a television serial*
series [ˈsɪəriːz]	feuilleton, série (à épisodes indépendants)	*a documentary series on sth - a funny comedy series set in Manchester*
show	émission	*to be on Mr So-and-so's show* (passer chez)

2.3. Staff

■ Noms

anchorman/woman	présentateur / présentatrice	**broadcaster** [ˈ---]	animateur, journaliste
announcer	speaker(ine)	**channel**	chaîne

The media, culture and science   171

commentator ['----]	commentateur	newscaster / newsreader	présentateur (journal télévisé)
commercial	publicité	sportscaster	journaliste sportif
commercial break	pause / page de publicité	quiz master GB ['mɑːstə] / US ['mæstər]	animateur de jeux
compere ['kɒmpeə] / host [həʊst]	animateur	producer	réalisateur
interviewer ['----]	intervieweur	MC / emcee	animateur

2.4. Viewers

■ *Noms*

antenna (US) [æn'tenə] / aerial (GB)	antenne	subscriber	abonné
audience ratings / figures	indice d'écoute, audimat	subscription television	télévision à péage
box / tube	'télé', 'téloche'	television set	poste de télévision
cable television	télévision par câble	telly	télé
channel hopping	zapping	boob tube (US)	télé (familier)
channel jumper	zappeur	giveaway	jeu (radio ou télé) doté de prix ou cadeaux
couch potato	abruti de télé	TV	télé
(satellite) dish	antenne parabolique	VCR / video cassette recorder	magnétoscope
high definition	haute définition	viewer	téléspectateur
pay TV	chaîne à péage / cryptée	videotape	bande / cassette vidéo
remote control [-,--'-]	télécommande	viewership / viewing figures / viewing ratings	indice d'écoute
satellite-television	télévision par satellite		
screen	écran	cablevision	télévision câblée

Collocations

license fee	redevance	*to pay / be exempt from paying the license fee*	
ratings	indices, audimat	*to have / get good / bad / poor* (médiocre) *ratings*	

■ *Adjectifs*

bias(s)ed ['baɪ əst]	partial	unbias(s)ed [ʌn'baɪ əst]	impartial
live	en direct	pre-recorded	en différé
recorded	enregistré		

Collocations

■ *Adverbes*

on FM / on frequency modulation	sur modulation de fréquences	*to get a station on FM as well as on medium wave*
on the air	à l'antenne	*to be / go on the air* (être / passer à l'antenne)
on the radio	à la radio	*to be* (passer à) *on the radio - to hear the news on the radio / on television*
on television	à la télévision,	*to go on television* (passer)
on the telly / on TV	à la télé	*to watch a program on the telly / on TV*

■ *Verbes*

interview ['---]	interviewer	**pick up**	capter, recevoir

repeat [-'-] / rerun [-'-]	rediffuser, repasser	video tape	enregistrer (magnétoscope)
switch channels	zapper	turn up / down	monter / baisser (le son)
switch on / off	allumer / éteindre	watch	regarder, suivre
tape	enregistrer (radio)	emcee a show	présenter une émission
telecast / televise	téléviser	rerun / repeat	rediffuser, passer de nouveau
transmit [-'-]	émettre	serialize	adapter en feuilleton
tune in to	prendre, écouter (une station) / se brancher (sur une chaîne)	anchor	introduire (une émission)
		emcee	animer (une émission)

Collocations

broadcast ['--]	diffuser	*to broadcast live from the Palace*
comment ['--] on	commenter	*to comment on current events*
compere ['kɒmpeə]	animer	*to compere a show*
cover	couvrir, assurer la couverture de	*to cover the Olympic Games*
host [həʊst]	animer	*to host a show*
jam	brouiller	*to jam broadcasts from foreign stations*
report sth [-'-]	faire un reportage, une enquête sur qch	*to report sth / that ...*

Exercices sur le chapitre 12 A (0, 1, 2.1 à 2.4)

1. Testez vos connaissances en traduisant les mots ci-dessous :

A / credits - B / wavelength - C / wireless set - D / radiocar - E / mike - F / time-slot - G / serial H / series

2. Traduisez en vous aidant des exemples et des collocations de la colonne de droite du vocabulaire :

A / — On a parlé de vous aux nouvelles de 13 heures. B / — C'est vrai? C / — Ils ont montré une séquence de votre visite chez la Reine. D / — Vraiment? E / — C'était une émission à ligne ouverte. Tous les téléspectateurs d'Angleterre ont dû allumer leur poste et téléphoner! Et l'indice d'écoute a dû monter en flèche. F / — Et bien, non. Il semble que les gens aient zappé et se soient branchés sur une autre chaîne. G / — Ce n'est pas possible! Ils vont repasser l'émission! H / — Cela m'étonnerait!

3. Joignez une phrase de droite à chacune des phrases de gauche :

1 / I offered to compere a quiz game
2 / I have a radio and turn it on
3 / I much prefer live reports
4 / I watch the 9 o'clock news because
5 / Why don't you turn down the sound
6 / I like the way they cover sports
7 / I was on Johnson's show last week
8 / The remote control is a great help

A / to library pictures.
B / when the credits begin to roll?
C / but I did not get heavy media coverage.
D / but they said I got too poor ratings.
E / but I don't like the way they comment on current events.
F / for channel jumpers like me.
G / I rather like the face of the newscaster.
H / to listen to radio plays.

The media, culture and science   173

3. Newspapers

3.1. Staff / people

■ *Noms*

cartoonist [-'--]	caricaturiste	managing editor	rédacteur en chef, directeur de la rédaction
legal correspondent	chroniqueur judiciaire	newspaper man	journaliste de la presse écrite
chief editor	rédacteur en chef	pressman (GB)	journaliste, reporter
City editor (GB)	chroniqueur financier	reporter [-'--]	reporter
city editor (US)	journaliste local	press baron / lord	magnat de la presse
columnist	chroniqueur	sub-editor	secrétaire de la rédaction
copyreader	correcteur-rédacteur	press officer	attaché(e) de presse
journalist	journaliste	press secretary ['----]	porte-parole
leader writer (GB)	éditorialiste	newspaper tycoon [taɪˈkuːn]	magnat de la presse

Collocations

correspondent [,--'---]	correspondant	*special / legal / foreign correspondent*
critic	critique	*to be an unkind / impartial art / drama / music / theatre / literary critic for a paper*
editor	responsable d'une section, rédacteur	*the sports / fiction editor*
press corps	les journalistes (accrédités)	*the White House press corps*

3.2. Content of a newspaper

■ *Noms*

advert ['--] / ad / advertisement [-'---]	annonce, publicité	current events [,---'-]	actualité
		feature article	article de fond
advertorial	publi-reportage	double spread	double page
piece	court article	full-page spread	page entière
agony ['---] column	courrier du cœur	gossip column	chronique à scandales
banner headlines	gros titres	leader / leading article / editorial	éditorial, article de tête
caption	légende		
comic book	magazine de BD	muckraking	révélation de scandales
cartoon [-'-]	caricature, dessin humoristique bande dessinée	news in brief	faits divers, brèves
classified ads	annonces classées	stop-press news	nouvelles de dernière minute
column	rubrique	strip cartoon	bande dessinée
comic strip / comics	bande dessinée	wanted ads / small ads (US) / want ads (US)	petites annonces
content ['--]	contenu		
court circular	bulletin de la Cour	situations wanted	demandes d'emploi
critique [-'-]	critique (article)	situations vacant	offres d'emploi

Collocations

advertisement [-'---]	annonce	*a newspaper may run* (faire passer) *an advertisement for sth - sb may place / put in an advertisement*

announcement	annonce	*to issue / make a public announcement about sth / that...*
article	article	*to write / publish an article on sth / on sb - a newspaper may carry an interesting article on vegetarianism*
comment ['--]	commentaire	*sth may arouse / evoke a(n) favourable / unfavourable / scathing (acerbe) comment in some papers*
criticism ['----]	critique	*a book may get adverse criticism - it may come in for a great deal of criticism*
crossword (puzzle)	mots croisés	*to do the crossword (puzzle) in the newspaper*
front page	une	*some news may get banner headlines across the front page (faire cinq colonnes à la une)*
heading	en-tête, chapeau	*not all news comes under the same heading*
headlines	titres	*some news hits the headlines, some does not*
interview	interview	*to give / grant / conduct an interview with sb*
item (of news)	nouvelle	*to read about a surprising item of news*
lay-out	maquette, présentation	*to modify the lay-out for greater clarity*
news	nouvelles, actualité	*to make news* (défrayer la chronique) *- to break* (annoncer) *major / minor news / an interesting bit of news to sb - the news of sth / that ... may break* (être annoncée)
notice	compte-rendu, critique	*a book may get mixed / enthusiastic notices*
obituary [-'----] **notice / obit**	nécrologie	*to write the obit of sb*
obituary (column)	rubrique nécrologique	*the obituary page of a paper*
op-ed page [ˌɒpedˈpeɪdʒ]	page comprenant lettres, commentaires et chroniques	*op-ed is short for opposite editorial page - an op-ed piece / column / page*
personal column	petites annonces (personnelles)	*to put an ad in the personal column*
report [-'-]	reportage, enquête	*to send in a(n) detailed / slanted* (tendancieux) */ unbiassed report from abroad*
review [-'-]	article, critique	*to write / do a negative / enthusiastic review of a book / play*
story	reportage, affaire, article	*a newspaper may print* (publier) */ run / carry a story about sth*

3.3. Management and sale

■ *Noms*

back issue	vieux, ancien numéro		**newspaper owner**	propriétaire de journal
bookstall	kiosque à journaux étalage de bouquiniste		**newsprint** (U)	papier journal
			newsroom	salle de rédaction
censor	censeur		**news stand**	kiosque à journaux
censorship ['---]	censure		**newsvendor**	vendeur de journaux
daily	quotidien		**paperboy**	livreur / vendeur / crieur de journaux
fashion magazine	journal de mode			
the fourth estate	le quatrième pouvoir (la presse)		**paper shop**	marchand de journaux
weekly	hebdomadaire		**pass-on readership**	lectorat par exemplaire
freedom of the press	liberté de la presse		**press briefing**	point de presse
girlie magazine	revue sexy		**press card**	carte de presse
gutter press	presse à scandale(s)		**press release**	communiqué de presse
journalism	journalisme		**press run**	tirage (revue)
monthly	mensuel		**quality paper**	journal de qualité
newsagent	dépositaire		**quarterly** [ˈkwɔːtəli]	publication trimestrielle
news agency / news service	agence de presse		**skin / porn magazine**	revue porno

The media, culture and science

sports magazine	magazine sportif	**tabloid**	tabloïde, journal
syndicate ['---]	agence de distribution d'articles ou reportages	**wanted ads** / (US) **small ads**	petites annonces
		women's magazine	magazine de femmes

Collocations

censorship ['---]	censure	to impose / exercise / lift censorship of / over sth
circulation [,--'--]	tirage	an event may raise the circulation from 40 000 to 50 000 copies a day - a newspaper may attain a nation-wide circulation / have a circulation of over 100 000
correction	rectificatif	to make / publish / insert a correction
issue ['ɪʃuː]	numéro	to bring out / publish a special issue on sth - an issue with photographs may come out (sortir)
journal	journal, revue (spécialisée)	a trade journal (professionnel)
journalism ['----]	journalisme	to go into print journalisme (presse écrite) / into broadcast journalism (reportage radiodiffusé ou télévisé)
magazine	magazine	fashion / glossy (de luxe) / popular magazine
news / press conference	conférence de presse	to hold a news conference
(news)paper	journal	to work as a reporter on the local paper
paper round	livraison à domicile	to do a paper round every morning
piece	(court) article	to write a piece about snow / a snow piece
press	presse	to fight for the freedom of the press
	les journalistes	the press were there for the inauguration
press cutting / clipping	coupure de presse	press cutting agency (argus de la presse)
press release	communiqué de presse	to put out a press release about sth
press statement	déclaration à la presse	to issue a press statement
print (U)	caractères	some news may appear in large / small / bold (gras) print
print	presse écrite	a debate may be raging both in print and on radio and television - to work in print journalism
reader	lecteur	to be a regular reader of tabloids - some readers write in and give their views - to conduct a reader survey (sondage)
readership	lectorat, nombre de lecteurs	a newspaper may have a right-wing readership / a readership of 12 000
subscriber	abonné	to be a subscriber to a magazine
subscription [-'--]	abonnement	to enter / renew / cancel one's subscription to a newspaper

■ *Adjectifs*

syndicated	publié simultanément dans plusieurs journaux	syndicated column / cartoon / article / journalist (journaliste d'agence)

■ *Verbes*

advertise sth	faire connaître qch	**publish**	publier, faire paraître
advertise sth ['---]	faire de la publicité pour qch	**serialize**	publier en feuilleton
print	imprimer		

Collocations

be published / come out	paraître	a daily is published every day of the week, except Sunday
keep abreast of / keep up (with)	se tenir au courant	to try to keep abreast of / to keep up with the news (actualité)
lay out	disposer, présenter	to lay out the major news so as to attract notice to it

leak out	filtrer, transpirer	*a secret may leak out through the press*	
renew [-'-]	renouveler	*to renew a subscription*	
report [-'-]	faire un reportage	*to report on sth / that*	
review [rɪ'vjuː]	faire la critique, écrire un article sur	*to review a play / a book*	
run	diriger	*to run a paper*	
subscribe [-'-]	s'abonner	*to subscribe to a magazine*	

Exercices sur le chapitre 12 A (3.1 à 3.3)

1. Testez vos connaissances en traduisant les mots ci-dessous :

A / the fourth estate - B / the gutter press - C / newsroom - D / press run - E / issue (n.) F / paper round - G / readership - H / subscriber

2. Traduisez en vous aidant des exemples et des collocations de la colonne de droite du vocabulaire :

A / Faire les mots croisés. B / Défrayer la chronique. C / Faire passer une annonce. D / Voilà une nouvelle importante qui va provoquer des commentaires acerbes dans certains journaux. E / L'article a été critiqué. F / Toutes les nouvelles ne font pas la une. G / La nouvelle de sa mort vient d'être annoncée et va probablement faire monter le tirage des journaux. H / Entrer dans la presse écrite. I / Annoncer une nouvelle de peu d'importance comme si elle méritait un article de tête.

3. Eliminez celui des quatre mots qui n'est pas étroitement lié aux autres :

A / daily - syndicated - weekly - monthly - B / papershop - newsagent - news stand - censor - C / issue - piece - article - leader - D / double spread - op-ed page - stop-press news - full-page spread

4. Choisissez les mots ou groupes de mots qui conviennent :

A / The *managing director / city editor / columnist / copy-reader* runs the paper.
B / The paper *ran / published / placed / put in* the advert as required.
C / The news *came out / leaked out / laid out / published* last night.
D / The *cartoonist / press officer / press secretary / theatre critic* *reviewed / reported on / subscribed / printed* the play.

B. Culture

1. Literature

1.1. Books and publishing

■ *Noms*

author	auteur	bookbinder	relieur
blurb	texte de présentation	bookseller	libraire
distributor [-'---]	diffuseur	bookshop / bookstore	librairie

The media, culture and science

capitals	majuscules	**novelist**	romancier
capital letter	lettre majuscule	**paperback**	livre de poche
character ['---]	caractère d'imprimerie	**pen name**	pseudonyme
collected works	œuvres complètes	**poet**	poète
content ['--]	contenu	**printer**	imprimeur
(dust) jacket	jaquette	**proof-reading**	relecture d'épreuves
editor ['edɪtə]	responsable de publication	**publishing house**	maison d'édition, éditeur
excerpt ['--]	extrait	**soft cover book**	livre broché
foreword	avant-propos	**publisher** ['---]	éditeur
ghost-writer	'nègre'	**small letter**	minuscule
handbook / manual	manuel	**textbook**	manuel scolaire
hardback	livre relié	**typescript**	manuscrit dactylographié
misprint	faute d'impression		

Collocations

book	livre	to bring out / put out (sortir) / publish a book - to autograph (dédicacer) a book for sb - a book is printed / goes into print (est mis en fabrication) / goes out of print / is sold out (est épuisé) - a book appears / is publihed / comes out
chapter	chapitre	to refer sb to / point out sth in chapter 12
contents ['--]	table des matières	also called: table of contents
copy	exemplaire	to run off (tirer) / print 10000 copies of a book
footnote	note de bas de page	to add / append a footnote to a page
literary ['---] **prize**	prix littéraire	to be awarded a prize for best novel of the year
page	page	to find sth on the sports page
preface ['--]	préface	to write a preface to a book
printed word	l'écrit, tout ce qui est imprimé	to have no interest in the printed word (books, newspapers, etc)
reader	lecteur	not to be much of a reader - to be a keen reader of novels
print (run)	tirage	a book may have a print of 5000
reprint	réimpression	to issue a reprint of a book
royalties	droits d'auteur	to be paid / receive royalties on a book - a book may bring in / earn the author handsome royalties
type (U)	caractère	a book may be printed in small / large / bold (gras) / italic type
work (C)	œuvre, ouvrage	to bring out a new work on England - not all of his works have come out yet
writer	écrivain	a writer may be a hack (écrivaillon) / a well-known fiction / crime / textbook / screen (scénariste) / software / speech writer

■ *Adjectifs*

annotated	annoté	**out of print**	épuisé
in print	disponible	**secondhand**	d'occasion

Collocations

bound	relié	a cloth-bound volume - a Bible bound in leather - a book may be bound with paper / paperbound (broché)
edited ['---]	préparé	a new edition edited by a well-known professor
printing	en réimpression, à l'impression	a book may be printing and shortly to come out

Verbes

bind	relier	**edit** ['--]	préparer, mettre au point
bring out	faire paraître		diriger la publication, assurer
come out	paraître, sortir		la rédaction
print	imprimer	**publish** ['--]	publier

Collocations

run out   manquer, être épuisé   *a bookseller may run out of a bestseller - a book may run out*

Exercices sur le chapitre 12 B (1.1)

1. Testez vos connaissances en traduisant les mots ci-dessous :

A / textbook - B / pen name - C / hardback - D / (dust)jacket - E / proof-reading - F / foreword
G / ghost-writer - H / character

2. Joignez une phrase de droite à une phrase de gauche :

1 / Books are printed
2 / The editor is in charge of
3 / No publishing house has yet dared
4 / A popular book's first print-run
5 / When an unknown novelist's first novel goes into print
6 / Although I am not much of a novel reader
7 / He is nothing more than a hack
8 / The table of contents of a book

A / the publisher hardly ever runs off more than 5000 copies.
B / I always buy books that are awarded prizes.
C / and his books don't earn him handsome royalties.
D / may not give you a fair idea of the content of that book.
E / to publish his collected works.
F / may run out or be sold out within two weeks.
G / then bound with paper or in leather.
H / editing the book.

1.2. Literary production

Noms

allegory ['----]	allégorie	**narrative** ['---]	histoire, récit
blank verse	vers non rimés	**narrator** GB [nə'reɪtə] / US ['næreɪtər]	narrateur
detective novel	roman policier		
cloak and dagger story	roman de cape et d'épée	**novel**	roman
epic ['epɪk]	épopée	**nursery rhyme**	comptine
fairy tale	conte de fées	**poem**	poème
fiction	fiction	**poetry**	poésie
figure of speech	figure de rhétorique	**satire** ['sætaɪə]	satire
hero	héros	**short story**	nouvelle
heroine ['---]	héroïne	**stanza / verse**	strophe
image	image	**story**	histoire, nouvelle
limerick ['lɪmərɪk]	poème humoristique de cinq vers	**symbol**	symbole
		theme [θiːm]	thème
literature ['lɪtrətʃə]	littérature	**title**	titre
metaphor ['metəfə]	métaphore		
narration [-'--]	narration	**whodunnit** [-'--]	roman policier

The media, culture and science

Collocations

biography [-'---]	biographie	*to write an authorised / unauthorised biography*
character ['---]	personnage	*to portray / draw* (dépeindre) *a character*
diary	journal (intime)	*to keep a diary*
essay ['--]	essai	*to write an essay about / on sth*
line (C)	vers	*to quote a line from a poet*
plot	intrigue	*a novel may have a straightforward / contrived* (peu naturelle) */ simple plot*
portrait	portrait	*to give / paint a very vivid portrait of sb*
prose	prose	*to write in prose*
quotation	citation	*to give a quotation from a poem*
rhyme	rime	*a poem may have a fixed rhyme scheme*
	court poème	*especially verse written for children - nursery thymes*
simile ['sıməli] (U / C)	comparaison	*a poem may be rich in simile / contain many similes*
stress	accent	*sentence / word stress*
tale	conte	*to narrate a tale*
verse	vers, poésie; strophe, verset	*to compose verse - to write in verse*
writings	écrits	*to publish sb's collected writings*

■ Adjectifs

commonplace	banal		**far-fetched**	tiré par les cheveux, invraisemblable
drab	terne		**fine**	bon, de qualité
dull	ennuyeux, fade		**hackneyed** ['hæknıd]	rebattu, galvaudé
engrossing [ın'grəusıŋ]	absorbant		**uninteresting**	sans intérêt
exciting	passionnant		**poor**	médiocre, assez mauvais

■ Verbes

declaim	déclamer		**narrate** [-'-]	narrer, raconter
describe	décrire		**plagiarize** ['pleıdʒəraız]	plagier
entitle [-'--]	intituler			

Collocations

deal with	traiter de, avoir pour sujet	*a book may deal with rail travel*
flip through	parcourir	*to flip through a magazine*
portray	faire le portrait	*a writer may excel at portraying working-class people*
quote	citer	*to quote lines from a poem / from Shelley*
read	lire	*to read (sth) to sb*
recite	réciter	*to recite verse from memory*
thumb through	feuilleter	*to thumb through a book / the pages*
turn over	tourner	*to turn over the pages quickly*

■ Adverbe

PTO	TSVP	*"please, turn over."*

Exercices sur le chapitre 12 B (1.2)

1. Testez vos connaissances en traduisant les mots ci-dessous :
A / whodun(n)it - B / tale - C / simile - D / stanza - E / quotation - F / engrossing - G / to entitle H / cloak and dagger story

2. Traduisez en vous aidant des exemples et des collocations de la colonne de droite du vocabulaire :
A / Je préfère que vous me lisiez le sonnet tout entier plutôt que de m'en citer deux ou trois vers rebattus ou médiocres. B / Le risque de tomber sur des comparaisons tirées par les cheveux, des descriptions ternes et banales, de longs passages sans intérêt, est moins grand dans une nouvelle que dans un roman. C / Il y a des romans que je ne fais que feuilleter ou parcourir, les vôtres par exemple.

3. Rectifiez les mots qui suivent (lettres interverties : I; lettre à ajouter : +; lettre à enlever : -; lettre à changer : C) :
1 / DAIRY (I) ; 2 / STOREY (-) ; 3 / MAGE (+) ; 4 / ZERO (C); 5 / LOT (+) ; 6 / MINE (C); 7 / HOVEL (C).

2. Cinema

2.1. Staff / People

■ *Noms*

actor	acteur	extra	figurant
actress ['--]	actrice	**film fan**	cinéphile
best boy	électricien	**film-goer**	cinéphile
boom operator	perchiste	movie-goer	amateur de cinéma
cast GB [kɑːst] / US [kæst]	distribution, acteurs	movie maker / film-maker	cinéaste
continuity girl	scripte	producer	producteur
crew	équipe technique	**stage hand**	assistant de plateau
director [-'--]	réalisateur	**screen / script writer**	scénariste
dresser	habilleuse	**stand-in / understudy**	doublure
editor ['---]	monteur, monteuse	stuntman	cascadeur
effects [-'-] man	bruiteur	**supporting actor**	second rôle
gaffer	chef électricien	**usherette** [,--'-]	ouvreuse
head grip	chef machiniste	art director	décorateur
prop man	accessoiriste		

2.2. Types of films

■ *Noms*

art film	film d'art et d'essai	**feature (film)**	grand film
cartoon [-'-]	dessin animé	**full-length film**	long métrage
cinema	cinéma	horror film	film d'horreur

The media, culture and science

science fiction film	film de science fiction	sound / talking film / movie	film parlant
newsreel	actualités filmées	thriller	film à suspense
short (film / feature)	court métrage	talkie	film parlant
silent film	film muet	continuous [-'---] performance [-'---]	spectacle permament
skin flick	film porno		

2.3. Film-rating

■ *Noms*

A film	présence des parents souhaitée	X-rated movie	interdit aux mineurs moins de 17 ans (US) / moins de 18 ans (GB)
AA film	interdit aux moins de 14 ans		
film-rating	classement des films		

Collocations

G movie	film tous publics	*G stands for general*
PG film / movie	film pour adultes et adolescents	*PG stands for parental guidance*
R movie	film interdit aux moins de 17 ans non accompagnés	*R stands for restricted*
U film (GB)	film tous publics	*U stands for universal*

2.4. The film industry

■ *Noms*

box-office takings / receipts [-'-]	recettes	global receipts [-'-]	recettes mondiales
		movie (US)	film
drive-in cinema	cinéma de plein-air	movie house / theater (US)	cinéma
double feature	séance avec projection de 2 films	press view / preview	avant-première
		news theatre	cinéma / salle d'actualités
film rights	droits d'adaptation	rushes / dailies	séquences non encore montées

Collocations

award [ə'wɔːd]	récompense	*to win the Academy Award for best director*
cinema (U)	le cinéma	*to be fond of French cinema*
cinema (C)	un cinéma	*a cinema may be crowded*
film	film	*to make / shoot a film*
film / movie industry ['---]	industrie cinématographique	*the 20th century American movie industry*
flick	film	*to go to the flicks (in the 1950's)*
picture	film	*to be in a Spielberg picture*
pictures	cinéma	*to go to the pictures*
release [rɪ'liːs]	sortie (d'un film)	*a film may be on general release* (non limité à quelques salles)

2.5. Equipment / technique

■ *Noms*

boom	perche	dissolve [dɪ'zɒlv]	fondu-enchaîné
crane	grue	dolly	chariot

fade-in	ouverture en fondu	clapper board	clap
fade-out	fermeture en fondu	film library	cinémathèque
film / movie camera	caméra	library pictures / file footage (US)	images d'archives
long shot	plan large	performance [-'---]	séance
range finder	télémètre	subtitles	sous-titres
take / shot	prise de vue	view finder	viseur
trolley	chariot mobile	continuous [-'---] performance	spectacle permanent
reel	bobine		

Collocations

close-up	gros-plan	*to take a close-up of sb's face*
credits	générique	*the credits usually roll at the end of a film*
editing / montage [mɒn'tɑːʒ]	montage	*to do the editing - to be in charge of the editing*
footage (U)	séquences	*to feature / screen up-to-now unknown footage of sth*
location (U)	extérieurs	*to shoot on location*
score	musique d'un film	*to write the score of a film*
screen	écran	*to write for / adapt sth to the screen*
screenplay / movie script	scénario	*to do / write the screenplay for / of a film*
set	plateau	*to spend several days on the set*
shot / take	prise de vues, plan	*a film may contain some shots of street fighting*
sound track	bande sonore	*to play the soundtrack record of / from a film*
stand-in	doublure	*to act as stand-in for sb*
studio	studio	*to shoot in the studio* (en studio)
stunt	cascade	*a stuntman may perform driving stunts*
trailer	bande-annonce	*to show the trailers for the forthcoming films*

■ *Verbes*

dub	doubler	release [rɪ'liːs]	(faire) sortir (un film)
subtitle	sous-titrer	screen	porter à l'écran

Collocations

act	jouer, tenir un rôle	*to act (the part of) Hamlet*
feature ['fiːtʃə]	avoir pour vedette	*a film may feature Robert Redford*
	présenter	*a film may feature exceptional newsreel footage*
film	filmer	*sb may be good at filming interiors*
	bien rendre, bien passer à l'écran	*sth may film well / beautifully - sb may film well* (être photogénique)
play	jouer	*to play the lead role / a minor role*
shoot	tourner	*to shoot a film on location*
show	passer (un film)	*to show a French film at the local cinema - a French film may be showing at the Odeon*

The media, culture and science

Exercices sur le chapitre 12 B (2.1 à 2.5)

1. Testez vos connaissances en traduisant les mots ci-dessous :
A / fade-in - B / fade-out - C / newsreel - D / understudy - E / film-rating - F / X-rated
G / PG movie - H / press view / preview

2. Indiquez si ce qui est dit dans chaque phrase est vrai ou faux; choisissez le mot qui convient ou rectifiez, si nécessaire :
A / Stuntman is another word for an effects man. B / A stand-in is a substitute for an actor. C / An usherette does stunts off screen. D / The crew consists of a worst boy / a gofer / a footgrip / a propman / a stageman. E / You look at the rushes only after the film has been released. F / A feature film is a film with close-ups of people's faces. G / A continuity girl shows people into the cinema. H / A skin-flick is a film with policemen in the nude in it.

3. Theatre and stage

3.1. Various forms of stage entertainment

■ *Noms*

chorus girl	girl	show-business / showbiz	le monde du spectacle
chorus line	troupe (d'une revue)	stand-up (comedian)	comique, raconteur d'histoires
entertainer [,--'--]	artiste de variétés	variety / vaudeville	spectacle de music-hall, revue
show	spectacle	show (US)	

Collocations

entertainment [,--'--]	spectacle	*to provide musical entertainments*
	distraction	*to provide both entertainment and education*

■ *Verbe*

entertain [,--'-]	amuser, divertir	*a play may fail to entertain its audience*

3.2. Dancing

■ *Noms*

ballroom	salle de bal	dance step	pas de danse
dance floor	piste de danse	tap-dancing	claquettes
dance hall	(grande) salle de bal	fancy-dress ball	bal déguisé

Collocations

ball [bɔːl]	bal	*to hold / organise a ball*
dance GB [dɑːns] / US [dæns]	danse	*to do a dance - to ask if one may have the next dance*
	danse (art)	*to be masters of dance and theatre*
dancing	danse (activité)	*to go dancing - to be fond of dancing*

3.3. Ballet dancing

■ Noms

ballet	ballet	choreography [,--'---]	chorégraphie
ballet dancing	danse classique	dancer	danseur
ballet master / mistress	maître / maîtresse de ballet	leotard ['liːətɑːd]	collant (de danseur)
GB ['mɑːstə] / US ['mæstər]		principal dancer	danseur étoile
ballet shoe	chausson de danse	prima ballerina	danseuse étoile
ballet skirt	tutu	[ˌpriːməbæləˈriːnə]	
choreographer [,--'---]	chorégraphe	tights	collant (de danseuse)

■ Verbe

be on points / dance on points	faire des pointes

3.4 Plays

■ Noms

character ['---]	personnage	monologue ['---]	monologue
character part / role	rôle de composition	pantomime	spectacle de Noël pour enfants
comedy	comédie	plot	intrigue
low comedy	farce	show	spectacle
tragedy	tragédie	slapstick	grosse farce
comedy of manners	comédie de mœurs	soliloquy [-'---]	soliloque
coup de théâtre	coup de théâtre	stage effects [-'-]	effets scéniques
denouement	dénouement	stage directions	indications scéniques
GB [deɪˈnuːmɒ̃] / US [ˌdeɪnuːˈmɑ̃ː]			

Collocations

aside	aparté	to say sth in an aside
business	jeux de scène	to introduce some stage business into an otherwise rather dull play
comedy	comédie	situation / black / light / slapstick (grosse farce) comedy - a play may have plenty of melodrama and excitement as well as comedy
drama ['drɑːmə]	art dramatique, théâtre drame, pièce dramatique	to teach drama in a drama school epic drama - to act in a drama
leading role / lead	rôle principal, premier rôle	to be the male / female lead
mime	mime	to study mime to become a mime
part	rôle	to play a part
play	pièce de théâtre	a play opens / runs for some time / closes (ferme, fait relâche) - to put on / stage / present / produce / perform / rehearse a play
plot	intrigue	to build / construct a contrived (peu naturelle) / simple plot - the plot may thicken (se corser)
rep / repertory ['----]	troupe ou théâtre de répertoire	to act in / play repertory - to do several years in rep
role	rôle	to perform / understudy a role

The media, culture and science

situation comedy / sitcom	comédie de situation, sitcom		to be a first-rate sitcom actress
skit	parodie, satire		to do a skit on sb
speech	monologue, tirade		to have to say Hamlet's long speech
theatre	théâtre, pièce		to go to the theatre - there is good and bad theatre
	théâtre, activité théâtrale		to have been in the theatre all one's life
tour	tournée		to be / go on tour
villain ['--]	méchant		to specialize in playing villains

3.5. People and people's activities

■ *Noms*

actor	acteur	ham (actor)	cabot
actress	actrice	playgoer	amateur de théâtre
ballerina [,--'---]	ballerine	playwright	auteur dramatique
ballet dancer	danseur de ballet	prompter	souffleur
conductor	chef d'orchestre	stage hand	machiniste
performer [-'--]	artiste, interprète	stage manager	régisseur
character actor	acteur de genre	understudy ['----]	doublure
crew	équipe technique	dry run	répétition de toute la pièce
comedian [-'---]	comédien, acteur comique, chansonnier	blocking rehearsal	filage, mise en place
		producer	metteur en scène
dress-rehearsal	générale	singer	chanteur
director [-'--]	metteur en scène	stage designer	décorateur
dresser	costumière	walk-on	figurant

Collocations

acting	métier d'acteur, interprétation, jeu	to do a bit of acting - to want to get into acting — the acting may be good or poor
amateur dramatics	théâtre amateur	to engage in / go in for amateur dramatics
applause (U)	applaudissements	to win / get an enthusiastic round (salve) of applause from the audience - to burst into loud applause
audience	spectateurs, public	there may be a large audience at a play - some members of the audience may be shocked by scenes of violence
audition	audition, essai	to give sb an audition (auditionner) - to hold auditions (organiser) - to do (passer) an audition
bow [baʊ]	salut	to take a bow (saluer) to the audience
cast GB [kɑːst] / US [kæst]	distribution, acteurs	to select / head an all-English cast
cue	réplique, signal	to give sb their cue (signal de parler) - to take one's cue (commencer à parler)
curtain call	rappels	to take three curtain calls (être rappelé 3 fois)
encore ['--]	bis, rappel	to call for an encore (bisser) - to give an encore of a song
line	réplique, texte	to deliver one's lines
rehearsal	répétition	to hold / schedule a rehearsal
run-through	filage	to have a last run-through
stage fright	trac	to have stage fright

3.6. The house

■ *Noms*

aisle [aɪl] **/ gangway**	allée	**greenroom**	foyer des artistes
apron stage	avant-scène	**interval / intermission** (US)	entracte
balcony / circle	balcon	**matinée**	matinée
box	loge (spectateur)	**gallery / gods**	dernier balcon, poulailler
dress circle	corbeille	**properties / props**	accessoires
dressing-room	loge (acteur)	**orchestra** ['---] **pit**	fosse d'orchestre
footlights	rampe	**proscenium**	avant-scène
foyer	foyer (pour le public)	**stage-door**	entrée des artistes

Collocations

backstage	coulisse(s)	*to go backstage*
bill	affiche	*to head / top the bill*
boards	planches, théâtre	*to tread the boards* (monter sur les planches)
full house	salle comble	*to play to a full house*
gods	poulailler	*to be sitting in the gods*
house	salle, nombre de spectateurs	*to bring the house down* (faire crouler la salle sous les applaudissements) - *there may be a good / decent* (moyenne) *house*
	représentation	*the first house may be sold out*
limelight	feux de la rampe	*to be in the limelight*
performance [-'--]	représentation	*to give an afternoon and evening performance*
playhouse	théâtre	*to see a show at the local playhouse*
run	série de représentations	*a play may have a triumphant / two-year run*
scenery ['siːnəri] **/ set**	décor	*to shift / design the scenery - a change of scenery / sets*
seat	place (assise)	*to secure a seat in the stalls*
set	scène	*to be late on (the) set*
spotlight	projecteur	*to train the spotlight on to sth - to direct it at sth*
stage	scène	*to go on stage* (entrer en scène) - *to go on the stage* (faire du théâtre)
stalls [stɔːlz] **/ pit**	orchestre	*to book a seat in the stalls*
wings	coulisses	*to wait in the wings*

■ *Adjectifs / adverbes*

off-Broadway	d'avant-garde	**downstage / upstage**	sur le devant / au fond de la scène

Collocations

comic	comique, de comédie	*comic writer / performance / actress*
comical	comique, drôle	*comical hat*
dramatic	dramatique, théâtral spectaculaire	*dramatic entry / effect / works* *a dramatic accident on the stage*

■ *Verbes*

clap one's hands	applaudir	**ham it up**	cabotiner
direct	mettre en scène, diriger (les acteurs)	**memorize**	mémoriser
dramatize ['---]	adapter pour la scène	**mime**	faire du mime
dry up	avoir un trou	**rant** [rænt]	déclamer

The media, culture and science 187

rehearse	répéter (une pièce)	**stage**	monter, mettre en scène
run through	filer (une pièce)	**understudy** ['----]	doubler (un acteur)

Collocations

act	jouer, interpréter	*to act (the part of) Macbeth / in a play*
applaud	applaudir	*to applaud (sb) heartily / enthusiastically*
audition	auditionner	*to audition (sb) for a part / (sb) to be Macbeth*
boo	conspuer	*the audience may boo an actor off the stage*
bow [baʊ]	saluer	*the actors bow to the audience at the end of the performance*
cast GB [kɑːst] / US [kæst]	distribuer	*to be cast as the villain / in the role of the villain*
encore	bisser, rappeler	*to encore an actor / a song*
overdo [,--'-]	exagérer, surjouer	*some scenes in a play may be a bit overdone*
perform	jouer, interpréter	*a play may be performed by an all-English cast*
play	jouer	*to play the (part of the) villain / Hamlet*
prompt	souffler	*the prompter may prompt (an actor) when necessary*
produce	produire, donner, monter	*producing a play involves organizing everything for the play to be shown to the public*
	mettre en scène	*producing a play may also mean just directing*
put on	monter	*to put a play on at school*
tour	être / partir en tournée	*to tour a country / abroad*

Exercices sur le chapitre 12 B (3.1 à 3.6)

1. Testez vos connaissances en traduisant les mots ci-dessous :

A / leotard - B / stand-up - C / principal (dancer) - D / character - E / lead - F / plot
G / character actor - H / prompter - I / stagehand - J / props

2. Remplissez la grille à l'aide des définitions proposées; les lettres grisées mises bout à bout font apparaître un mot du domaine de la danse :

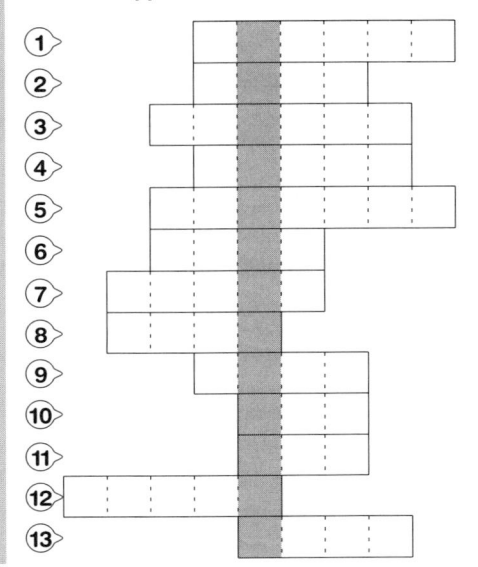

1 / the art of playing a part - 2 / a performance - 3 / .....-girls are singers and dancers - 4 / plays considered as a form of literature - 5 / person in charge of the actors' clothes - 6 / events in a play - 7 / plays are performed on it - 8 / an actors' company's journeying - 9 / actors in one particular play - 10 / another word for stalls - 11 / ..... it up means to overdo it on the stage - 12 / passage between rows of seats - 13 / to say one's lines in a loud, unnatural way.

3. Vous trouverez ci-dessous des amorces de phrases (A à H). Vous trouverez aussi des phrases qui font suite à ces amorces (1 à 12). Indiquez par une lettre et un ou deux chiffres la séquence logique des phrases. (Un point d'exclamation (!) indique la fin d'une phrase).

A / He dreams of acting
C / The actor who played the villain
E / Not many plays
G / It is not the dresser's job

B / If an actor hams it up
D / Not all ballet dancers
F / People clap their hands
H / They hardly ever played

1. expected to be booed
3. to shift the scenery or to
5. the part of Hamlet!
7. run for more than two years!
9. see to the spotlights!
11. and were never encored!

2. the minute he walks on
4. to a full house
6. and hardly ever stop applauding!
8. and much to his surprise, got enthusiastic applause!
10. some scenes are bound to be a bit overdone!
12. can dance on points the way she does!

4. Music

4.1. Tapes and records

■ *Noms*

amplifier	amplificateur	**loudspeakers**	enceintes, baffles
cassette [-'-]	cassette	**record-player**	tourne-disques
cassette-player	lecteur de cassettes	**single**	45 tours
cassette desk	platine à cassettes	**cassette recorder**	magnétophone à cassettes
CD-player	platine laser	**tape**	bande magnétique, cassette
CDV (compact disc video)	CDV	**tape recorder**	magnétophone
disc (US)	disque	**turntable**	platine
headphones	écouteurs	**record** (GB)	disque
long player, LP	33 tours		

4.2 Performers

■ *Noms*

accompanist [-'---]	accompagnateur	**musician**	musicien
cellist	violoncelliste	**organ-grinder**	joueur d'orgue de Barbarie
composer [-'--]	compositeur	**organist**	organiste
conductor [-'--]	chef d'orchestre	**singer**	chanteur
leader / first violin	premier violon	**performer** [-'--]	exécutant, interprète

Collocations

soloist	soliste	*soloists perform solo* (en solo) / *solos* (des solos)
violinist	violoniste	*a violinist draws a bow across the strings*

4.3. Concerts and singing

■ *Noms*

anthem	motet	**band**	orchestre (jazz)
antiphon	antienne	**baton**	baguette, baton

The media, culture and science

brass band GB [brɑːs] / US [bræs]	fanfare	**lyrics** ['lırıks]	paroles de chanson
burden / chorus	refrain	**opera house**	opéra (lieu)
canticle	cantique, hymne	**orchestra pit**	fosse d'orchestre
carol ['--]	chant joyeux	**piece (of music)**	morceau (de musique)
chant GB [tʃɑːnt] / US [tʃænt]	chant scandé, mélopée	**verse**	couplet
		prom / promenade concert	concert avec places assises et debout (Londres)
concert hall	salle de concert	**roundelay**	rondeau (mis en musique)
counterpoint	contrepoint	**words**	paroles
ditty	chansonnette	**quartet**	quatuor
hit song	tube	**quintet**	quintette
libretto	livret (opéra)	**shanty**	chanson de marins
lullaby ['lʌləbaı]	berceuse	**song**	chant, chanson

Collocations

acoustics (v. pl.)	acoustique	*the acoustics in this concert hall are very good*
bar	mesure	*to hum a few bars of a well-known tune*
choir ['kwaɪ_ə]	chœur, chorale	*to sing in / form / lead a choir*
chorus ['kɔːrəs]	refrain	*to join in* (reprendre) *the chorus*
	choral	*to sing a chorus*
	chœur, chorale	*the Brighton Festival Chorus*
	troupe, chœur	*to be in the chorus of a musical*
concert	concert	*to give / stage* (organiser) *a concert*
music	musique	*to dance to the music of a big band*
musical	comédie musicale	*to produce / stage a musical*
opera	opéra	*to stage a comic / light opera*
orchestra ['---]	orchestre	*chamber / symphony / pop orchestra*
performance [-'--]	exécution, interprétation	*to give an inspired performance of a piece*
rhythm	rythme	*to dance to the rhythm of the drums*
scales	gammes	*to practise* (faire) *scales*
strain	accord, accent	*to hear the strains of a piece of music - to march to the strains of a military song*
tune	air	*to remember the words but not the tune of / to a song*

4.4. Notes and instruments

A	la		E	mi
B	si		F	fa
C	do		G	sol
D	ré			

■ *Noms*

baby grand (piano)	demi-queue	**bow** [bəʊ]	archet
bagpipes	cornemuse	**brass** GB [brɑːs] / US [bræs]	cuivres
upright (piano)	piano droit	**cello** ['tʃeləʊ]	violoncelle
grand (piano)	piano à queue	**clavichord**	clavicorde
harpsichord	clavecin	**double bass** [beıs]	contrebasse

drums	batterie	**organ**	orgue
fiddle	violon (musique populaire)	**recorder**	flûte à bec
flat	bémol	**sharp**	dièse
flute	flûte	**sheet music**	partitions
harp	harpe	**staff / stave**	portée
horn	cor	**violin**	violon
keyboard	clavier	**music lover**	mélomane
oboe ['əʊbəʊ]	hautbois		

Collocations

chord	accord	*to play chords - to strike up the opening chords*
drum	tambour	*to beat / roll a drum*
ear	oreille	*to have a good ear* (avoir l'oreille juste, de l'oreille) / *no ear for music*
guitar [gɪ'tɑː]	guitare	*to strum* (gratter) *(a tune on) a guitar*
key	touche	*to press / strike a key*
	ton	*to play in the key of C - to play in key / off key*
piano	piano	*to play the piano*
pitch	ton	*to have perfect pitch* (avoir l'oreille absolue)
score	partition	*to follow the score*
strings	cordes	*to pluck at* (pincer) *the strings of a guitar*
	les cordes (instruments à cordes)	*the strings may be too loud*
wind(s)	instruments à vent	*the wind is / are sometimes too loud*

■ *Adjectifs / adverbes*

catchy (tune)	facile à retenir (air)	**music loving**	mélomane

Collocations

flat	en dessous du ton	*to be / sing flat*
	bémol	*a piece in E flat*
in tune	juste	*to play / sing in tune*
	accordé	*a violin may be or not be in tune (with the piano)*
melodious	mélodieux	*melodious sound / voice*
musical	musicien	*to be musical*
out of tune	faux	*to play / sing out of tune*

■ *Verbes*

accompany	accompagner	**have an ear for music**	avoir de l'oreille
be in the charts	figurer au hit-parade	**hum**	fredonner
beat time	battre la mesure	**keep time**	rester en mesure
chant GB [tʃɑːnt] / US [tʃænt]	psalmodier	**set to music**	mettre en musique
conduct [kən'dʌkt]	diriger	**sing**	chanter

Collocations

perform [-'-]	exécuter, interpréter	*to perform a piece beautifully*
play	jouer	*to play a tune to sb on the piano*

The media, culture and science

strike up	attaquer	*to strike up the national anthem*
string	mettre des cordes	*to string a guitar / violin*
tune	accorder	*to tune the strings to a key of G*

Exercices sur le chapitre 12 B (4.1 à 4.4)

1. Testez vos connaissances en traduisant les mots ci-dessous :
A / to string - B / to tune C / flat (adj.) - D / chord - E / recorder - F / horn - G / keyboard H / clavichord

2. Traduisez en vous aidant des exemples et des collocations de la colonne de droite du vocabulaire :
A / Danser sur une musique de jazz. B / Faire des gammes. C / Accompagner un violoncelliste. D / Attaquer l'hymne national. E / Avoir l'oreille juste. F / Chanter faux un air facile à retenir. G / Ce violon n'est pas accordé avec le piano à queue. H / Jouer du violoncelle avec un archet de mauvaise qualité.

5. Painting and the arts

5.1. Art, the arts, arts and craft

■ *Noms*

art school / college	école des beaux-arts	**handicraft** (U)	artisanat (art)
the (fine) arts	les beaux-arts	**handicraft** (C)	objet artisanal
arts and craft GB [krɑːft] / US [kræft]	artisanat (d'art)	**weaving**	tissage

Collocations

art	art	*to study art* (faire des études d'art) / *go to art classes* (cours de dessin)
arts	lettres (et sciences humaines)	*to be an arts student with an arts degree - to take up arts at college*
craft	art, métier	*you can tell if someone knows their craft.*
craftsmanship	art, habileté qualité, fini	*a fine example of craftsmanship* *to admire the craftsmanship of an object*

5.2. People

■ *Noms*

artist	artiste		**painter**	peintre
auctioneer [ˌ--'-]	commissaire priseur		**potter**	potier
craftsman	artisan		**sculptor**	sculpteur
curator [kjuˈreɪtə]	conservateur (musée)		**sculptress**	sculpteur (femme)
drawer	dessinateur		**sitter**	modèle

5.3. Tools and materials

■ *Noms*

brush	pinceau	easel	chevalet
canvas	toile	enamel [ɪ'næml]	émail
charcoal	fusain	frame	cadre, encadrement
china / porcelain	porcelaine	kiln	four
china clay	kaolin	paint	peinture
chisel ['tʃɪzl]	ciseau; burin	plaster GB ['plɑːstə] / US ['plæstər]	plâtre
clay	argile	sketchbook	carnet à dessins
crayon	crayon de couleur	stoneware	grès
drawing paper	papier à dessin	studio	atelier
drawing board	planche à dessin	(potter's) wheel	tour (de potier)

5.4. Production

■ *Noms*

art gallery	galerie (d'art)	painting	peinture
the art market	le marché de l'art	picture	tableau
ceramic [-'--]	céramique (objet)	pot (C)	pot, poterie
ceramics	céramique (art)	pottery	poterie
daub	'croûte'	preview / private view	vernissage
work of art	œuvre d'art	print	gravure, estampe
enamelling [ɪ'næmlɪŋ]	émaillage	sketch	croquis, esquisse
engraving	gravure	still life	nature morte
etching	eau-forte	waxworks	musée de cire
earthenware / terra cotta	terre cuite	waxwork	objet / statue en / de cire
exhibit	objet, pièce exposé(e)	work	œuvre
exhibition	exposition	woodcutting	gravure sur bois
handicrafts	objets artisanaux	a piece of pottery	une poterie
museum	musée		

Collocations

auction (sale)	vente aux enchères	*to put sth up for auction - to sell a painting by auction*
cast GB [kɑːst] / US [kæst]	moulage	*to make a bronze cast of a statue*
oil	peinture à l'huile, huile	*to do a portrait in oils*
pot	pot, poterie	*to throw a pot* (tourner, faire)
sculpture	sculpture	*to do some sculpture - to exhibit a fine (piece of) sculpture*
statue	statue	*to put up / erect a statue to sb*
watercolour	aquarelle	*to do some lovely watercolour sketches*

■ *Verbes*

fashion	façonner, modeler	glaze	vernisser
fire	cuire	mo(u)ld [məʊld]	mouler

The media, culture and science

Collocations

be on show	être exposé	*to go and see the paintings on show*
bid	offrir, faire une offre	*to bid 10000 dollars for a painting*
carve	sculpter (dans du bois)	*to carve sth out of wood*
cast GB [kɑːst] / US [kæst]	mouler; couler, fondre	*to cast a statue / metal / plaster*
chisel	ciseler, enlever au couteau	*to chisel sth out of wood or metal*
draw	dessiner	*to be able to draw (sth)*
exhibit	exposer	*to exhibit (one's works)*
illustrate	illustrer	*to illustrate a book with pictures*
mould [məʊld]	mouler	*to mould sth in / from / out of clay*
paint	peindre	*to paint in oils / in watercolours*
sit	poser	*to sit (for a painter)*
sketch	faire un croquis	*to be fond of sketching trees*
sketch in	ajouter, dessiner	*to sketch in animals in the background*
sketch out	esquisser, ébaucher	*to sketch out a design for a new school*
throw	tourner	*a potter throws pots on the wheel*

Exercices sur le chapitre 12 B (5.1 à 5.4)

1. Testez vos connaissances en traduisant les mots ci-dessous :

A / handicraft - B / curator - C / auctioneer - D / charcoal - E / waxworks - F / to glaze
G / to mould - H / drawer

2. Choisissez le mot qui convient :

A / He studied *arts / art / weaving* and became a painter. B / He knows his *craft / craftsmanship / curator* well. C / A potter's job consists mainly in *sketching in / throwing / casting pots / pans / plates* on the *brush / wheel / kiln*. D / A professional sitter *can glaze / sit / mould* for hours on end.

C. Science

1. Science and technology

1.1 The sciences

■ *Noms*

anatomy [-'---]	anatomie	**chemistry**	chimie
applied sciences	sciences appliquées	**experimental sciences**	sciences expérimentales
biochemistry [,--'---]	biochimie	**genetics** [-'---]	génétique
biology [-'---]	biologie	**mathematics** [,--'---]	mathématiques
botany	botanique	**medicine**	médecine

microbiology [,---'---]	micro-biologie	physiology	physiologie
speleology [,--'---]	spéléologie	zoology	zoologie
natural sciences	sciences naturelles	eugenics	eugénisme
physics	physique		

Collocations

mathematics [,--'---]	mathématiques	sb's mathematics / maths (GB) are / is weak - sb's math (US) is weak
science (U / C)	science	to study / go in for / go into science - mathematics is an exact science - to be interested in pure / applied / modern / political science
the sciences	les sciences, branches du savoir	government support for the sciences - to be more interested in the arts (lettres) than in the sciences

1.2. People

■ *Noms*

astronomer [-'---]	astronome	physicist	physicien
astrophysicist [,--'---]	astrophysicien	researcher	chercheur
biochemist	biochimiste	scientist	savant, scientifique
biologist	biologiste	speleologist	spéléoloque
botanist	botaniste	technician [-'--]	technicien
chemist	chimiste	zoologist	zoologiste
mathematician [,---'--]	mathématicien	electronics engineer	électronicien

1.3. Science at work

1.3.1 Chemistry, biology and genetics

■ *Noms*

acid	acide	burette	burette
ammonia	ammoniaque	test tube	éprouvette
base	base	element	élément
chemical	produit chimique	formula	formule
chlorine ['klɔːriːn]	chlore	funnel ['fʌnl]	entonnoir
crucible ['kruːsəbl]	creuset	lab / laboratory	laboratoire
clone	clone	litmus paper	papier tournesol
gene	gène	lens	lentille
chromosome	chromosome	mass	masse
carbon	carbone	nitrate ['naɪtreɪt]	nitrate
nitrogen	azote	precipitate [-'---]	précipité
corpuscule	corpuscule, globule	retort	cornue
genetic inheritance	patrimoine génétique	still	alambic
protein	protéine	test tube	éprouvette
tissue	tissu	vat	cuve
catalyst	catalyseur	microscope ['maɪkrəskəʊp]	microscope

1.3.2. Physics, electricity and electronics

■ *Noms*

circuit	circuit	radar ['reɪdɑː]	radar
coil	bobine	robot	robot
conductivity [ˌ--'---]	conductivité	robotics [rəʊ'bɒtɪks]	robotique
conductor	conducteur	voltage	voltage
dynamo	dynamo	physics	physique
electricity	électricité	electronics	électronique
generator	groupe électrogène	acoustics	acoustique
fuse	fusible	aerodynamics	aérodynamique
(power) grid	réseau électrique	atom	atome
laser ['leɪzə]	laser	electrode	électrode
laser beam	rayon laser	neutron	neutron
magnet	aimant	wave mechanics	mécanique ondulatoire
magnetism	magnétisme		

Collocations

battery	pile, batterie	*a battery may be / go flat - to put a battery on charge - to charge / discharge a battery*
breakthrough	découverte importante, percée	*to achieve / make a breakthrough*
cell	cellule	*cancer / blood cells - cells divide*
current	courant	*current may be AC (alternating) or DC (direct)* (continu)
discovery	découverte	*to make a(n) outstanding / startling discovery*
electricity	électricité	*to generate electricity - to run a car on electricity*
experience	expérience (acquise)	*to acquire / gain experience - to know sth from / by experience*
experiment	expérience (scientifique)	*to make / carry out a successful experiment*
magnet	aimant	*a magnet attracts iron*
microscope ['maɪkrəskəʊp]	microscope	*to examine sth through / under a microscope*
power	énergie	*hydroelectric / nuclear power*
	courant	*power cut* (coupure) */ failure* (panne) *- power line* (à haute tension) */ power station* (centrale électrique)
practise	pratique	*to put a theory into practise*
technique [-'-]	technique	*to acquire / develop / perfect a technique*
technology (C / U)	technologie	*to advocate* (préconiser) */ develop / expand / launch modern technology - to know the technology to do sth - to keep pace with the advances in modern technology / with western technologies of housing / with industry / health / computer technologies*
telescope	téléscope	*to focus* (diriger) *a telescope on a star*
test	essai	*to conduct / carry out a test*
theory	théorie	*to present / confirm / formulate / test / develop a theory*

■ *Adjectifs*

artificial	artificiel	imitation	simili
atomic	atomique	magnetic	magnétique
chemical	chimique	man-made	artificiel (lac); synthétique (fibre)
experimental	expérimental, au stade expérimental	mathematical	mathématique

microscopic [,--'---]	microscopique	**scientific**	scientifique
nuclear	nucléaire	**synthetic**	de synthèse, synthétique
plastic	plastique	**theoretical** [-'---]	théorique
practical	(d'ordre) pratique		

Collocations

electric	électrique, mû à l'électricité	*electric bulb / fire / motor / fan / blanket / chair*	
electrical	electrique	*electrical appliance / component* (élément) */ equipment / fittings* (installations) */ energy*	

■ *Verbes*

analyse	analyser	**research into**	faire des recherches sur
discover	découvrir	**search for**	chercher
electrify	électrifier	**synthetize**	synthétiser
experiment on sth	expérimenter qch, faire des expériences sur qch	**test**	tester
		try out	essayer, faire l'essai de
generate	générer, produire	**attract**	attirer
oxidize	(s')oxyder	**repel**	repousser
purify	purifier	**clone**	cloner
react (with)	réagir (avec)	**mutate**	(faire) subir une mutation

2. Computer science

■ *Noms*

bit	bit	**electronics**	électronique
bug	bogue	**expert system**	système expert
byte	octet	**floppy (disc)**	disquette
chip	puce	**file**	dossier
computer	ordinateur	**hacker**	pirate
computer science	informatique	**hardware** (U)	matériel
computing	informatique	**home computer**	ordinateur portable
computerization	informatisation	**interface**	interface
diskette [-'-] **/ disc**	disquette	**laptop computer**	ordinateur portable
computer scientist	informaticien	**keyboard**	clavier
computaholic [-,--'---]	un dingue de l'informatique	**keyboard operator** ['----]	claviste, pupitreur
data ['deɪtə]	données	**mainframe**	unité centrale
data processing	traitement de données	**light pen**	crayon optique
data processor	machine de traitement de données	**megabyte**	méga-octet
		memory	mémoire
data processor	informaticien	**memory chip**	puce à mémoire
data base	base de données	**machine** [-'-] **language**	langage machine
desk-top computer	ordinateur de bureau	**microchip**	puce (électronique)
(hard) disc	disque dur	**printer**	imprimante
disk drive	lecteur de disquettes	**microprocessor**	micro-processeur
electronic mail	courrier électronique	**modem** ['məʊdem]	modem

The media, culture and science   197

monitor	moniteur	programmer ['prəʊgræmə]	programmeur
multi-user system	configuration multiposte	ROM (read only memory)	mémoire morte
peripheral [pə'rɪfr̩əl]	périphérique	software (U)	logiciel(s)
motherboard	carte mère	telematics	télématique
(software) package	progiciel	systems analyst	analyste-programmeur
personal computer	PC	terminal	terminal
screen	écran	virus	virus
print-out	tirage; sortie papier	visual display unit	console de visualisation
program	programme	word processor ['----]	machine de traitement de texte
RAM (random access ['--] memory)	mémoire vive	word processing ['----]	traitement de texte

■ *Adjectif*

| user-friendly | convivial |

■ *Verbes*

computerize [-'---]	informatiser	load	charger
debug [diː'bʌg]	mettre au point, déboguer	print out	imprimer
delete / erase [dɪ'liːt]	effacer	process ['--]	traiter
design	concevoir (un programme)	program	programmer
display	afficher	retrieve	récupérer
feed data into a computer	alimenter un ordinateur en données	save	sauvegarder
		unload	décharger
hack into a system	pirater un système	download	télécharger
key in a data	saisir une donnée	sort	trier

Exercices sur le chapitre 12 C (1.1, 1.2, 1.3.1, 1.3.2 et 2)

1. Testez vos connaissances en traduisant les mots ci-dessous :
A / still (n.) - B / vat - C / lens - D / nucleus - E / nuke - F / cell - G / chip - H / unmanned
I / disquette - J / mémoire morte - K / logiciel - L / progiciel - M / récupérer - N / pirater un système

2. Traduisez en vous aidant des exemples et collocations indiqués dans la colonne de droite du vocabulaire :

A / Concevoir un programme. B / Saisir une donnée. C / Mettre au point une technique. D / Mettre en pratique une théorie. E / Effectuer un essai. F / Effectuer une expérience. G / Acquérir de l'expérience. H / Réussir une percée. I / Une batterie peut se décharger. J / S'intéresser davantage aux lettres qu'aux sciences. K / Télécharger un programme.

3. Space technology

■ *Noms*

aerospace ['eərəʊspeɪs] industry ['---]	industrie aéro-spatiale	astronomer [-'---]	astronome
		astronomy	astronomie
astronaut ['---]	astronaute	astrophysics [,--'--]	astrophysique

astrophysicist [,--'---]	astrophysicien	re-entry	rentrée (dans l'atmosphère)
cosmonaut	cosmonaute	retrorockets	rétrofusées
countdown	compte à rebours	rocket	fusée
flying saucer	soucoupe volante	satellite	satellite
launch	lancement	shuttle	navette
launch(ing) pad	rampe de lancement	skylab(oratory)	laboratoire spatial
launching site	site de lancement	splashdown	amerrissage
launch vehicle	fusée de lancement	stage	étage (de fusée)
lift-off	décollage	weightlessness	apesanteur
lunar vehicle	véhicule lunaire	touchdown	atterrissage
orbit	orbite	weather satellite	satellite météorologique
moon landing	alunissage	spaceman	astronaute, cosmonaute

Collocations

space	espace	*space craft* (vaisseau spatial) / *flight* / *probe* (sonde) / *suit* (combinaison) / *ship* / *station* / *travel - to stare into space* (regarder dans le vide)	
UFO	OVNI	to sight a UFO (Unidentified Flying Object)	

■ *Adjectifs*

manned	habité	weightless	en état d'apesanteur
unmanned	inhabité	remote-controlled	télécommandé

■ *Verbes*

dock	arrimer	revolve	tourner
launch	lancer	splash down	amerrir
lift off	décoller	touch down	atterrir
orbit	être placé sur orbite, graviter	spacewalk	marcher dans l'espace

Exercices sur le chapitre 12 C (3)

Testez vos connaissances en traduisant les mots ci-dessous :

A / splashdown - B / shuttle - C / rocket - D / countdown - E / lift-off - F / remote-controlled
G / habité - H / combinaison spatiale - I / voyages interplanétaires - J / atterrir
K / compte à rebours - L / arrimer - M / alunissage - N / étage - O / navette

4. The social sciences

4.1. General

■ *Noms*

anthropology	anthropologie	history ['hıstrı]	histoire
economics (sg) [,--'--]	économie (science)	humane [-'-] studies	humanités, sciences humaines
economy [-'---]	économie (d'un pays)	philosophy	philosophie
geography	géographie	politics ['---]	politique

The media, culture and science

psychology	psychologie	**human sciences**	sciences humaines
social science(s)	sciences humaines	**ethics**	éthique
social studies	sciences sociales	**linguistics**	linguistique
sociology	sociologie	**ethnology**	ethnologie
statistics (pl)	statistiques (données)	**ethnography**	ethnographie
statistics (sg)	statistique (science)		

Collocations

economics (sg) [,--'---]	économie (science) organisation économique	*to have a degree in / study economics* *the economics of the timber trade*
economy (C)	économie, situation économique	*(the state of) a country's economy may be sound / worrying* *- Western economies - the economy of Great Britain* *- the British economy*

4.2 people

■ *Noms*

anthropologist [,--'---]	anthropologue	**philosopher**	philosophe
economist	économiste	**psychologist**	psychologue
geographer	géographe	**sociologist**	sociologue
historian [-'---]	historien	**statistician** [,--'---]	statisticien

4.3. History

■ *Noms*

the ancient world	l'Antiquité	**keep**	donjon
castle	château fort	**knight**	chevalier
century	siècle	**the Middle Ages**	le Moyen-Âge
battlements	créneaux	**moat**	fossé, douve
chivalry ['ʃɪvlri]	chevalerie	**modern times**	les temps modernes
coat of mail	cotte de mailles	**the Reformation**	la Réforme
conspiracy [-'---]	conspiration	**the Renaissance** [-'--]	la Renaissance
crusader [-'--]	croisé	**revolution**	révolution
drawbridge	pont-levis	**slave**	esclave
dungeon ['dʌndʒən]	cachot	**statesman**	homme d'état
the (Age of) Enlightenment	le Siècle des lumières	**sovereign** ['sɒvrɪn]	souverain
tower	tour	**tournament**	tournoi

Collocations

collapse [-'-]	effondrement	*sth may bring about the total collapse of a country's economy*
crusade [-'-]	croisade	*to go on / join a crusade*
defeat	défaite	*to suffer a defeat at the hands of sb - to inflict a defeat on sb*
downfall	chute	*sth may bring about sb's downfall - to head for a downfall*
event [-'-]	événement	*to predict / forecast / hasten an event - an event occurs / takes place*
plot	complot	*to devise / hatch* (fomenter) */ foil / thwart* (contrecarrer) */ expose* (dénoncer) */ uncover / discover a cunning plot against sb / to* *do sth*

riot	émeute	*to foment / incite a riot - sth may touch off* (déclencher) / *spark (off) / lead to a riot - to put down* (réprimer) / *crush a riot - a riot may break out / erupt*
slavery	esclavage	*to abolish / introduce slavery - to be sold into / freed from slavery*
victory	victoire	*to achieve / win a decisive / resounding* (retentissante) *victory over sb*
war	guerre	*to win / lose a(n) all-out / defensive / local / revolutionary war - to conduct a war of aggression / of attrition* (d'usure) *against sb - to be at war with sb - to wage war / declare war on sb - to go (off) to war - to make war on sb - to take / carry war into enemy territory - a war may break out / rage / spread to another country / come to an end*

■ *Adjectifs*

medieval [ˌmedi'i:vl]	médiéval	**psychological**	psychologique
philosophical	philosophique	**revolutionary** [ˌ--'----]	révolutionnaire

Collocations

ancient ['eɪnʃənt]	ancien, antique, historique	*ancient Greece / monument / times*
eventful [-'--]	fertile (en événements) mémorable	*eventful period / social life* *eventful journey / day*
historic	historique, marquant	*historic change / compromise*
historical	historique	*historical event / process / fact*
uneventful	sans histoires, calme	*uneventful period / career / day / life / journey*

■ *Verbes*

defeat	défaire, vaincre	**overthrow** [ˌ--'-]	renverser
enslave	réduire en esclavage		

Collocations

happen	arriver se trouver	*sth happens (to sb) - it may happen that ...* *to happen to know sb*
occur [-'-]	se produire, se présenter venir à l'esprit	*changes / difficulties / opportunities may occur* *it may occur to sb to do sth / to sb that ...*
take place	avoir lieu	*a meeting takes place at a certain time*

Exercices sur le chapitre 12 C (4.1 à 4.3)

1. Testez vos connaissances en traduisant les mots ci-dessous :

A / century - B / castle - C / battlements - D / dungeon - E / keep - F / moat - G / drawbridge

2. Traduisez en vous aidant des exemples et des collocations de la colonne de droite du vocabulaire :

A / Qui aurait pu prévoir un tel événement? B / Comment ont-ils gagné une guerre d'usure? C / Qu'est-ce qui a déclenché les émeutes? D / Comment ont-elles été réprimées? E / Qui a remporté une victoire retentissante? F / La guerre a fait rage pendant dix ans. G / Elle a éclaté il y a dix ans. H / Elle s'est étendue aux pays voisins. I / Elle s'est achevée le mois dernier. J / Qui avait fomenté le complot qui devait renverser le roi et amener la chute du gouvernement? K / Le pays vaincu, qui a subi une défaite humiliante, cherche maintenant à infliger une défaite écrasante à son ennemi. L / C'est ça, l'histoire des hommes?

13

Towns, the environment, the country

A. Towns, housing and transport

1. Towns

■ *Noms*

borough ['bʌrə]	municipalité; arrondissement circonscription électorale	lower town	ville basse
burgh ['bʌrə]	(Ecosse) ville (avec charte)	major city / metropolis [-'---]	métropole
capital (city)	capitale	market town	bourgade
cityscape	paysage urbain	hood	quartier (argot, US)
commuter belt	périphérie	outskirts	périphérie, environs
council estate ['kaʊnsl] / [-'-]	cité (de logements sociaux)	pedestrian [-'---] precinct ['priːsɪŋkt]	zone piétonne
country town ['kʌntri]	ville de province		
county town / ['kaʊnti] county seat (US)	chef-lieu	red light district / area	quartier des prostituées
		resort [rɪ'zɔːt]	lieu de séjour, de vacances
council ['kaʊnsl]	conseil municipal	row of houses	rangée de maisons
dormitory ['---] / satellite town (US)	ville-dortoir	settlement	habitations, lieu d'implantation
		townscape	paysage urbain
(housing) estate [-'-] / project (US)	lotissement, cité	upper town	ville haute
		urban blight / decay	dégradation des centres villes
industrial estate [-'-] / [-'---] industrial park (US)	zone industrielle	speed zone	zone à vitesse limitée
		mushroom town	ville-champignon
housing development [-'----] (US)	ensemble immobilier privé	township	commune, municipalité
		townhall (GB)	hôtel de ville
inner-city (areas)	quartiers déshérités (du centre-ville)	urban centre	centre urbain

Collocations

area ['eəri̯ə]	zone, quartier	*to close off / cordon off / rope off a residential area - speed zone in a built-up area* (agglomération)
block	pâté de maisons	*to live two blocks away* (deux rues plus loin)
city	grande ville	*life in the modern city - city life - to run / manage a sparsely / densely populated city*
city hall	(US) hôtel de ville; mairie, administration municipale	*to march to City Hall to lodge one's demands - to blame City Hall for mismanagement*
district	quartier, arrondissement	*rich / middle-class / working-class district*
neigbourhood ['neɪbəhʊd]	voisinage, quartier	*to live in a(n) nice / unsafe / changing neighbourhood / in the neighbourhood of the church - to be well-known in an ethnic / multicultural neighbourhood for sth / for doing sth - to run a neighbourhood watch* (comité de surveillance)

quarter ['kwɔːtə]	quartier, partie		the student / Muslem / commercial quarter
spa	ville de cure / d'eaux		to take the waters (faire une cure) in a spa
suburbia [sə'bɜːbiə]	banlieue (entité)		to come from / live in suburbia
suburbs	banlieue		to live in the outer suburbs (grande banlieue)
town	ville		to live in (a) rambling (construite sans plan précis) town - to be from out of town - to go in(to) town / downtown - to go out on the town (faire une virée)
ward [wɔːd]	section électorale		for local elections on local council boards

■ *Adjectifs / Adverbes*

downtown	dans le centre, en ville, dans le quartier commerçant	to live downtown - to visit downtown Chicago (le centre de Chicago)
uptown	dans les quartiers chics, des quartiers chics	to live uptown - to visit uptown New York

Exercices sur le chapitre 13 A (1)

1. Testez vos connaissances en traduisant les mots ci-dessous :

A / pedestrian precinct - B / resort (n.) - C / speed zone - D / estate - E / borough
F / council estate - G / spa - H / suburbia

2. Traduisez en anglais :

A / Vivre deux rues plus loin. B / Reprocher à l'administration municipale son incurie. C / Administrer une ville à forte densité de population. D / Diriger le comité de surveillance d'un quartier. E / Aller en ville. F / Vivre à la périphérie d'une ville sans plan précis. G / Prendre les eaux dans une ville d'eau.

2. Buildings, houses and flats

■ *Noms*

bed sit(ter)	studio (très simple)		flat (GB)	appartement
block of flats	immeuble d'habitation		flatlet (GB)	studio
building	bâtiment		low-rise building	immeuble à hauteur limitée
bungalow	petit pavillon (en rez-de-chaussée)		high riser (US)	tour
castle	chateau (fort)		detached house	maison individuelle, pavillon
condominium (US) / condo (colloquial) [ˌkɒndə'mɪniəm]	appartement ou immeuble, en copropriété		hovel ['hɒvl]	taudis, masure
			manor (house)	manoir, gentilhommière
			mansion ['mænʃn]	hôtel particulier
dwelling	habitation, résidence		office block	immeuble de bureaux
council house	immeuble HLM		investment property	immeuble de rapport
lodging house	pension (terme daté)		one-room flat	studio
rooming house (US)	immeuble locatif		palace	palais
duplex (GB) ['djuːpleks]	duplex, double appartement		residence	résidence (officielle)
duplex house (US)	maison jumelée		semidetached (house)	maison jumelle (mitoyenne)
efficiency [-'---] apartment	studio (US) (souvent meublé)		shack	cabane, baraque

Towns, the environment, the country

studio flat (GB)	studio	**town house**	hôtel particulier ; maison mitoyene
studio	atelier d'artiste		
penthouse (US)	appartement avec terrasse au dernier étage (hôtel ou immeuble d'habitation)	**villa**	pavillon (en ville) maison (de campagne ou à la mer), villa
maisonette [ˌmeɪzəˈnet]	(appartement en) duplex	**(weekend) cottage**	maison de campagne
skyscraper	gratte-ciel	**war memorial**	monument aux morts
main home	résidence principlae	**frame house** (US)	maison à charpente de bois
second home	résidence secondaire	**pile dwelling**	maison sur pilotis
thatched cottage	chaumière	**all mod cons / modern conveniences** [-'----]	tout le confort
tower block (GB)	immeuble-tour		
tower (US)	immeuble-tour	**lot** (US)	terrain à bâtir
terraced houses	maisons mitoyennes	**plot / lot**	parcelle, lotissement
half board	demi-pension	**boarding house**	pension (de famille)
full board	pension complète	**board and lodging**	(chambre avec) pension

Collocations

abode	demeure (lit. jur.)

place of abode - to take up one's abode (élire résidence) *- to have no fixed abode*

apartment (US)	appartement
apartment (GB)	chambre, pièce

self- contained (indépendant) */ unfurnished apartment*
furnished apartments (meublé)

comfort (U) [ˈkʌmfət]	confort (d'une maison)
comforts	confort matériel

a house may have every (modern) comfort
to like home comforts (aimer ses aises)

home	maison, foyer, chez soi

to leave / come back home - one's home may be near a large town - to make one's home (s'installer) *somewhere - to come from a good home* (famille, milieu) */ from a broken home* (foyer désuni) *- to be away from home*

house	maison

to build / pull down / tear down / renovate / occupy / live in / leave / (US) rent out / let / own a house - a house may be ramshackle / dilapidated (délabrée) *- to keep house* (tenir la maison) *- to keep open house* (tenir table ouverte)

luxury (U)	luxe
luxury (C)	luxe, plaisir

to live in (the lap of) great luxury - to lead a life of ease and luxury
to enjoy the luxury of a bath after a long walk - buying sth expensive may be a luxury - to spend money on luxuries - it is an unknown / a real / sheer / pure luxury to do sth

■ *Adjectifs*

comfortable [ˈkʌmftəbl]	confortable	**homely**	accueillant
convenient [-'---]	pratique	**large**	grand
cosy	douillet	**luxurious** [lʌgˈzjʊəri‿əs]	luxueux
dilapidated [-'----]	délabré	**ramshackle**	branlant, délabré
comfy	agréable, confortable	**shabby**	miteux
functional	fonctionnel	**spacious** [ˈspeɪʃəs] / **roomy**	spacieux
drafty GB [ˈdrɑːfti] / US [ˈdræfti]	plein de courants d'air	**snug**	confortable, douillet
commodious [kəˈməʊdi‿əs]	vaste, spacieux	**well-built**	bien construit, solide

Exercices sur le chapitre 13 A (2)

1. Testez vos connaissances en traduisant les mots ci-dessous :

A / condo - B / homely - C / dilapidated - D / roomy - E / comfy - F / pile dwelling - G / abode
H / lodging house - I / shack

2. Joignez une phrase droite à chaque phrase de gauche :

1. They're pulling down the very house
2. The self-contained apartment he owned
3. He liked home comforts and longed for
4. He did not live in the lap of luxury
5. He dreamt of renting a penthouse
6. She dreamt of a thatched cottage

A. but enjoyed the luxury of a bath after work.
B. a good woman to keep house for him.
C. or a snugmaisonnette.
D. even if it were shabby and ramshackle.
E. he had planned to make his home in.
F. had every modern comfort.

3. People

■ Noms

boarder	pensionnaire	**mayor**	maire
paying guest	hôte payant	**mayoress** GB [ˌmeər'es] / US ['meɪ̯ərəs]	mairesse; épouse du maire
city dweller / town dweller	citadin		
commuter [-'--]	banlieusard (travaillant en ville)	**suburbanite** [sə'bɜːbənaɪt]	habitant de la banlieue
councillor / council man (US)	conseiller municipal	**the people next door**	les voisins d'à côté
		townee / townie (US)	pur citadin (familier)
inhabitant	habitant	**vigilante** [ˌvɪdʒɪ'lænti]	membre d'un groupe d'auto-défense
local	personne du pays (du coin, du quartier)		
		flatmate / roommate (US)	personne avec qui on partage un appartement
lodger / roomer (US)	locataire (ou pensionnaire)		

Collocations

colony	colonie	the British colony in Spain has / have their own newspaper
neighbour	voisin	to call on / make friends with / visit / visit with (US) / look up (passer voir) a neighbour - to be a good neighbour to sb
stranger	étranger	to be a stranger to London (ne pas connaître) / to politics

■ Adjectifs

civic	municipal; administratif	**suburban** [-'--]	de banlieue
self-contained (flat)	indépendant	**urban**	urbain, de ville
streetwise	conscient des dangers de la rue et débrouillard		

■ Verbes

commute	faire le trajet de chez soi à son travail et vice versa	**get lost**	se perdre
		settle	s'installer, s'établir (colons)

Collocations

ask the way	demander son chemin	to ask the way to a place of (à) a passer-by
settle down	s'installer, se fixer	sb may not be able to settle down anywhere
settle in	s'installer, s'adapter	it may take sb some time to settle in

Towns, the environment, the country

■ Adverbes

downtown	en ville, dans le centre des affaires	**midtown**	entre le centre et la périphérie
uptown	dans les quartiers résidentiels		

Exercices sur le chapitre 13 A (3)

1. Testez vos connaissances en traduisant les mots ci-dessous :
A / boarder - B / townee - C / flatmate - D / vigilante - E / lodger - F / roomer (US) - G / commuter

2. Traduisez en anglais :
A / Rendre visite à un voisin. B / Ne pas connaître une ville. C / Demander son chemin à un passant. D / Pouvoir se fixer, s'installer n'importe où. E / S'adapter facilement.

4. Building a house

4.1. Materials

■ *Noms*

breeze-block	parpaing	**plaster** GB ['plɑːstə] / US ['plæstər]	plâtre
brick (U / C)	brique		
cement [sə'ment]	ciment	**reinforced concrete** [ˌriːɪn'fɔːst] - ['kɒŋkriːt]	béton armé
concrete ['kɒŋkriːt]	béton		
glass GB [glɑːs] / US [glæs]	verre	**slate** (U / C)	ardoise
laminated glass	verre feuilleté	**stone** (U / C)	pierre
lumber (US)	bois de charpente	**tile** (U / C)	tuile (toit); carreau (sol)
mortar	mortier	**tiling**	tuiles; carrelage (sol)
paint	peinture	**timber**	bois de charpente

4.2. Machines / tools

■ *Noms*

board / plank	planche	**ladder**	échelle
brush	pinceau	**nail**	clou
bucket	seau	**pail**	seau
concrete ['kɒŋkriːt] **mixer**	bétonnière	**pick / pickax(e)**	pioche, pic
crane	grue	**plane**	rabot
electrical wiring	installation électrique	**pneumatic** [nju'mætɪk] **drill / jack hammer**	marteau-piqueur (US)
excavator ['----]	pelleteuse		
file	lime	**screw**	vis
frame	cadre (fenêtre)	**screwdriver**	tourne-vis
hammer	marteau	**shovel** ['ʃʌvl]	pelle
hand drill	perceuse à main	**vice**	étau

Collocations

scaffolding (U) ['skæfəʊldɪŋ]	échafaudage(s)	*to erect / take down scaffolding - some public buildings may be covered in scaffolding and closed to the public*

Exercices sur le chapitre 13 A (4.1 et 4.2)

1. Testez vos connaissances en traduisant les mots ci-dessous :

A / scaffolding - B / shovel - C / mortar - D / tiling - E / frame

2. Appariez chaque mot de gauche avec la définition de droite qui convient :

A. concrete
B. breeze-block
C. lumber
D. crane
E. vice
F. brush
G. file
H. timber
I. pick
J. slate

1. used by painters.
2. building material.
3. covers roofs.
4. large pointed tool for breaking up roads, etc.
5. a light brick for building.
6. used for lifting heavy objects.
7. American English for timber.
8. holds sth firmly so that it can be worked with both hands.
9. wood for building.
10. used for rubbing or making smooth.

4.3. Parts of a house

■ *Noms*

beam	poutre	joist	solive
ceiling	plafond	basement	sous-sol
floor	sol, plancher	topfloor	dernier étage
stone floor	sol dallé	floor space	surface au sol
floor board	latte (de plancher)	panel	panneau
floor covering	revêtement de sol	pipe	tuyau
flooring	revêtement; parquet	rafter	chevron
first floor	premier étage (GB); rez-de-chaussée (US)	roof	toit
foundations	fondations	girder	poutre, poutrelle
front / facade [fə'sɑːd]	façade, devant	single-storey house (GB)	maison à un étage
gable	pignon	two-storied house (US)	maison à un étage
gutter	goutière	upper story	dernier étage
groundfloor (GB)	rez-de-chaussée	storey (GB) / story (US)	étage
groundfloor (US)	premier étage	wall	mur

4.4. People

■ *Noms*

architect ['---]	architecte	builder's labourer	ouvrier du bâtiment
bricklayer	maçon	building contractor (US)	entrepreneur (en bâtiment)
builder	entrepreneur; maçon	carpenter ['---]	charpentier

Towns, the environment, the country

civil engineer [,--'-]	ingénieur des travaux publics
draftsman (US) / draughtsman (GB)	dessinateur industriel
(property) developer [-'---]	promoteur
electrician	électricien
glazier ['gleɪzi ə]	vitrier
joiner	menuisier
locksmith	serrurier
mason ['meɪsn]	maçon
paper hanger	tapissier
plumber ['plʌmə]	plombier
slater	couvreur
stone mason	tailleur de pierres
surveyor	expert ; géomètre
tiler	couvreur ; carreleur
town planner	urbaniste
clerk of works GB [klɑːk] / US [klɜːk]	conducteur de travaux

■ **Verbes**

design	concevoir, faire le plan de
develop [-'---]	aménager (terrain)
drive in	enfoncer (clou)
fit	installer (serrure)
file	limer
paint	peindre
paper	tapisser
plane	raboter
plaster GB ['plɑːstə] / US ['plæstər]	plâtrer
saw	scier
plan	dresser les plans de
slate	ardoiser
tile	couvrir de tuiles ; carreler
whitewash	blanchir à la chaux, chauler

Collocations

bore	forer, percer	*to bore a hole with a drill / through solid rock*
build	construire, bâtir	*a house may be built of stone / by the river / near the town / into the hillside* (à flanc de colline) */ out of wood* (en bois)
dig	creuser	*to dig the foundations - to dig into the ground - to dig a hole with a pickaxe and shovel*
screw	visser	*to screw sth down or up* (à fond) */ sth off* (dévisser) */ sth on* (fixer avec des vis)

Exercices sur le chapitre 13 A (4.3 et 4.4)

1. Testez vos connaissances en traduisant les mots ci-dessous :

A / to bore - B / to screw - C / file (n.) - D / to develop - E / gable - F / gutter - G / joist
H / draughtsman

2. Remplacez les mots en italiques des phrases par l'un des mots ci-dessous :

ARCHITECT - BUILDER'S LABOURER - BUILDING - DESIGN (v.) - DIG (v.) - FIT (v.) - FOUNDATIONS - LOCKSMITH - PAPER (v.) - PAPER HANGER - PLASTER (v.) - ROOF - TILE (n.)

A / He asked a *bricklayer* to *drive in* the plans of a new *contractor*. B / He covered the *gable* with *joists*. C / The *glazier sawed* and *slated* the walls. D / The *joiner whitewashed* the locks.
E / A young *developer* was busy *tiling* the *pipes*.

5. Housing

5.1. Housing and rehabilitation

■ Noms

hostel	foyer (travailleurs, étudiants, jeunes filles)	lodgings	chambre (meublée); pension
youth hostel	auberge de jeunesse	lodging (U)	logement, hébergement
redecoration	réfection (peintures, papiers peints)	renovation / restoration	rénovation, restauration
		restoration	rénovation (d'un immeuble)
refurbishment [-'---]	remise à neuf	sewer	égout
rehabilitation	restauration	sewerage system	système / réseau d'égouts
		repairman	réparateur

Collocations

accommodation (U, GB) — hébergement / logement
to provide accommodation
accommodations (US) - to seek / find decent / suitable / cheap / temporary accommodation

habitation — habitation
a house may show signs of habitation / may be unfit / fit for habitation

■ Adjectifs

uncomfortable [ʌnˈkʌmftəbl]	inconfortable	roomy	spacieux (appartement)
		spacious ['speɪʃəs]	spacieux (pièce)
large	grand		

Collocations

cramped — étroit, petit
cramped room / house - to be cramped for space (manquer de place)

crowded — plein, encombré
a room may be crowded with furniture

crammed — entassé, bourré
to be all crammed into one room - a drawer crammed with letters

■ Verbes

convert [-'-] (into)	transformer (en)	put in	(faire) installer (chauffage, double vitrage)
give a face-lift	ravaler; retaper		
modernize	moderniser	redevelop [,--'---]	rénover, réaménager
extend (a house)	agrandir	refurbish [-'--]	remettre à neuf
knock down	démolir, abattre (cloison)	restore	rénover (immeuble)
redecorate	refaire (une pièce), repeindre, retapisser	rehabilitate [,--'---]	restaurer, rénover (bâtiment ou quartier)
		renovate ['---]	rénover (maison)

Collocations

build in / into — encastrer
to build a cupboard into a wall

convert [-'-] — transformer
to convert two rooms into one

partition off — séparer par une cloison
to partition off rooms from an original larger room - to partition off a large room into several smaller ones

Exercices sur le chapitre 13 A (5.1)

1. Testez vos connaissances en traduisant les mots ci-dessous :
A / refurbishment - B / sewer - C / hostel - D / accommodation - E / to give a face-lift - F / cramped
G / to redecorate

2. Traduisez en anglais :
A / Manquer de place. B / Chercher un logement correct. C / Une pièce encombrée de meubles.
D / Un tiroir bourré de lettres. E / Encastrer un placard. F / Séparer une pièce par une cloison.
G / Abattre une cloison. H / Installer le chauffage.

5.2. The housing problem

5.2.1. Places

■ *Noms*

cabin ['kæbɪn]	cabane, hutte	shack	cabane, hutte
cardboard city (U)	abris de carton des SDF	shanty	baraque, bicoque
dosshouse / flophouse (US)	asile de nuit	shantytown	bidonville
hovel	taudis, masure	shed	abri; hangar, appentis
hut	hutte, baraque		

Collocations

housing (U)	logement(s)	*subsidized / low-cost / low-income housing* (HLM) - *to live in bad housing conditions* - *to implement* (mettre en œuvre) *a government housing policy designed to provide more cheap housing in order to remedy the housing shortage*
shelter (U)	abri	*to offer / seek shelter from the cold* - *to take shelter / get under shelter*
slum	taudis	*to live in the slums* (zone, quartiers pauvres) *in a slum area - to promote a slum clearance programme*

5.2.2. People

■ *Noms*

bum	bon à rien, fainéant	squatter ['skwɒtə]	squatteur
dosser	clochard (habitué des foyers)	tramp	chemineau; clochard
hobo	vagabond, itinérant	vagabond	vagabond
homeless	SDF	vagrant	vagabond, clochard

■ *Adjectifs*

destitute	sans ressources	needy	dans le besoin
down-and-out	indigent	out of work	sans emploi
homeless	sans domicile fixe	unemployed [,--'-]	au chômage
jobless	sans travail		

Verbes

lodge	loger, héberger	**sleep rough**	coucher dehors, dormir sous les ponts
put sb up	loger, dépanner qqn	**squat** [skwɒt]	squatter

Collocations

accommodate [-'---]	loger, héberger contenir, recevoir	to be unable to accommodate one's own friends a cottage may accommodate up to six people
shack up	crécher	to be shacked up with sb (être à la colle) - two people may shack up together
shelter	abriter recueillir, donner asile à	to shelter sb from the cold to shelter the homeless

Exercices sur le chapitre 13 A (5.2.1 et 5.2.2)

1. Testez vos connaissances en traduisant les mots ci-dessous :

A / dosshouse - B / shantytown - C / bum - D / hobo - E / destitute (adj.) - F / down-and-out G / to shack up

2. Traduisez en anglais :

A / Promouvoir un programme d'aménagement des quartiers pauvres. B / Un appartement qui peut accueillir cinq personnes. C / S'abriter du froid. D / Chercher abri. E / Se mettre à l'abri. F / Mettre en œuvre une politique de logement audacieuse. G / Remédier à la crise du logement. H / Loger un ami pour la nuit. I / Dormir sous les ponts.

5.2.3. Architecture and town planning

Noms

building permit	permis de construire	**planning permission**	permis de construire
building land	terrain à bâtir	**playground**	aire de jeux
builder's yard	chantier de construction	**prefab**	maison préfabriquée
building site	chantier de construction	**public garden**	square
contractor's yard	dépôt de matériaux de construction	**public park**	jardin public
		real estate [-'-] (US)	l'immobilier
development [-'---] **area**	zone urbaine prioritaire (ZUP)	**sandlot** (US)	terrain vague et / ou de jeux
green belt	ceinture verte	**site for sale**	terrain à bâtir
green areas / spaces	espaces verts	**town planning**	urbanisme
listed building	monument classé ou historique	**town-and-country planning**	aménagement du territoire
lot (US)	terrain (à construire)	**waste ground / land**	terrain vague
plot of land	terrain (à cultiver)	**urban development** [-'---]	zone d'aménagement concerté
mews (C)	ruelle, venelle écuries rénovées	**vacant lot**	terrain inoccupé

Collocations

architecture ['ɑːkɪtektʃə]	architecture	to admire / be a student of modern / Gothic / Roman architecture / the architecture of ancient Greece
development [-'---]	exploitation, aménagement zone	to provide money for the development of a region to finance industrial / housing development(s)

Towns, the environment, the country

planning	planification	*to believe in long range / short term planning*
premises ['premɪsɪz]	locaux, lieux	*the food may have to be eaten on the premises* (sur place) - *to move to new premises*
property (U) ['---]	biens immobiliers propriété	*also referred to as: real property - in the US: real estate sth may be sb's property - sb's personal property* (biens mobiliers)
site	emplacement, chantier	*'protective helmets must be worn on site'*

Exercices sur le chapitre 13 A (5.2.3)

1. Testez vos connaissances en traduisant les mots ci-dessous :

A / listed building - B / development area - C / urban development - D / premises - E / mews

2. Remplissez les blancs avec les mots ci-dessous :

ARCHITECTURE - BUILDING PERMIT - BUILDING LAND - CONTRACTOR - GREEN AREAS - PREFAB - PREMISES - PUBLIC GARDEN - SANDLOT - SITE - PROPERTY - WASTE GROUND

A / After he found _____ and obtained a _____ close to quite a nice _____, he felt relieved. B / He loved _____ away from the _____ of his childhood. C / He longed to move to new _____. D / He was a building _____ and spent most of his time on the _____ he was in charge of. E / He was a great admirer of Greek _____. F / But he never planned to turn his newly-acquired _____ into a Greek temple. G / He was happy to be able to forget about the _____ and _____ of not so long ago.

6. Streets

6.1. Types of streets

■ *Noms*

alley(way) ['æli(weɪ)]	ruelle	**thoroughfare**	voie, artère
avenue ['---]	avenue	**walkway** (GB)	sentier pédestre
boulevard ['buːləvɑːd]	boulevard	**pedestrian street / way / precinct** [pə'destri‿ən] / ['priːsɪŋkt]	rue piétonnière
crescent ['kreznt]	rue semi-circulaire		
"cul-de-sac" ['kʌldəsæk]	voie sans issue		
dead end	impasse	**walkway** (US)	passage pour piétons, passerelle (entre 2 bâtiments)
high street	grand'rue; rue principale	**catwalk**	passerelle (de manœuvre)
lane	ruelle	**signboard**	panneau publicitaire
main street	rue principale	**hoarding**	palissade; panneau d'affichage
Main Street (US)	rue commerçante les petits commerçants	**standard lamp / lamp-post**	lampadaire
		ring road / beltway (US)	boulevard périphérique
mall [mɔːl]	rue piétonnière, centre commercial	**taxi rank / stand** (GB) / **cabstand** (US)	station de taxis
side street	petite rue; rue transversale	**tokaway zone**	zone d'enlèvement

6.2. Traffic

Collocations

■ *Noms*

street	rue	*to see sb in the street* - *to be out on the street(s)* (être à la rue, sans abri) - *to be / work on the streets* (faire le trottoir) - *to put / turn sb (out) into the street* (mettre qqn à la rue)
traffic (U)	circulation	*heavy / light / rush-hour / outbound traffic - the traffic may build up* (un bouchon se forme) - *to announce a traffic build-up / tailback (GB) / hold-up (US)* (ralentissement) */ jam*
(traffic) lights	feux de signalisation	*to go through / jump the traffic lights - to run a red light (US)* - *to drive through* (passer à) *the yellow / amber light - there may be a new set of traffic lights at the crossroads*

■ *Verbes*

knock sb down	renverser qqn	**run over sb**	écraser qqn

Collocations

cross (over)	traverser	*to cross the road from one side to the other*

6.3. Roadway and pavement

■ *Noms*

causeway	chaussée		**pedestrian crossing**	passage pour piétons
cobble stones	pavés ronds		**rubbish** (GB) (U)	ordures
cleansing truck ['klenzɪŋ]	balayeuse		**rubbish heap**	tas d'ordures
collection	ramassage		**rubbish bin**	boîte à ordures, poubelle
cycle lane / track	piste cyclable		**rubbish tip / dump**	décharge publique
crossroads	croisement		**refuse** (US) (U) ['refjuːs]	ordures, déchets
crosswalk (US)	passage clouté		**household rubbish**	ordures ménagères
curb (US)	bord du trottoir		**pileup**	carambolage
drains	égouts (ville); canalisation (maison)		**speed zone**	zone à vitesse limitée
			square	place
kerb (GB)	bord du trottoir		**street**	rue
embankment	quai (fleuve)		**tar**	goudron
garbage (US) (U) ['gɑːbɪdʒ]	ordures		**underpass** (US)	passage souterrain
garbage dump ['gɑːbɪdʒ]	décharge publique		**subway** (GB)	passage souterrain
dog dirt / mess / muck (U)	crottes de chien		**subway** (US)	métro
gutter	caniveau		**trash can** (US)	poubelle, boîte à ordures
garbage can	poubelle		**skip**	benne (à ordures)
pavement (GB)	trottoir		**sewer** (C)	égout
pavement (US)	chaussée		**sewerage** (U)	égouts
paving stone	pavé		**mains drainage**	tout-à-l'égout
railings	grilles		**tip** (GB)	décharge
roadway	chaussée; tablier (de pont)		**street lighting**	éclairage public
tip lorry / tipper / dump(ing) truck (US)	benne à ordures		**street lamp** (US)	réverbère
zebra crossing ['zebrə]	passage pour piétons		**lamppost** (GB)	réverbère

Towns, the environment, the country

6.4. People

■ *Noms*

dustman	éboueur	refuse ['refjuːs] collector [-'--]	éboueur
garbage man (US) / garbage collector [-'--]	éboueur	road / street sweeper	balayeur
meter maid (US)	contractuelle	traffic warden ['wɔːdn]	contractuelle

■ *Adjectifs*

busy	animé (rue, quartier)	jammed	embouteillé
deserted	désert (endroit)	filthy ['fɪlθi]	dégoûtant
clean	propre	squalid ['skwɒlɪd]	misérable, sordide
congested	encombré	underground [,--'-]	souterrain
dirty	sale		

Collocations

bustling	animé	*bustling district - a street may be bustling* (grouiller) *with Christmas shoppers*

■ *Verbes*

cleanse [klenz]	nettoyer (les rues)	rake up	ramasser avec un rateau
foul [faʊl]	salir, souiller (chien)	sweep	balayer
collect	ramasser (ordures)	tip	déposer (ordures)
dump	déposer (ordures)	sweep up	ramasser avec un balai
hose down	nettoyer au jet	break up / rip up	défoncer (chaussée, trottoir)

Collocations

dig up	excaver, défoncer	*to dig up a road to repair electricity cables*

Exercices sur le chapitre 13 A (6.1 à 6.4)

1. Testez vos connaissances en traduisant les mots ci-dessous :
A / dead end - B / thoroughfare - C / kerb - D / refuse collector - E / foul

2. Remplacez chaque mot en italiques des phrases, par un des mots ci-dessous :
BUILD UP - CAUSEWAY - CROSS OVER - DIG UP - HIGH STREET - JAMMED - KNOCK DOWN - MAINS DRAINAGE - RUN OVER - STREET - STREETS - STREETS

A / She was now out on the *crescents* because her husband thought that she was working on the *dead ends* and had turned her out into the *signboard*. B / Traffic was *cleansing* by the minute and the *tip* would soon be *swept*. C / Workers were *hosing down* the *embankment* trying to repair the *cleansing truck*. D / The car lurched and *crossed over* two silly little dogs and *raked up* a wild old cat which failed to look both ways before *sweeping up*.

7. Town transport

7.1. Means of transport

■ *Noms*

double-decker	autobus à impériale	**the underground** (GB) ['---]	le métro
the subway / train (US)	métro	**train**	rame (métro)
station	station (métro); gare	**tube** (GB)	métro (v. exemples)

Collocations

bus	autobus; autocar	*bus driver / stop / conductor* (receveur) */ lane* (couloir, voie réservée) */ pass* (carte d'abonnement) */ shelter / station* (gare d'autobus) */ gangway* (couloir dans un autobus)
bus service	service d'autobus	*there may be a good on-the-hour* (à l'heure ronde) *bus service - to provide / offer / run a regular bus service*
cab (US)	taxi	*to go by cab - to take a cab - cabdriver (also: cabman / cabbie / cabby) - cab rank / stand* (station)
car park (GB)	parking	*parking lot (US) - car park attendant* (préposé, gardien)
coach	autocar	*coach station* (gare routière)
elevated railway	métro aérien	*especially in Chicago, also called the el or L - to ride home on the L every evening*
taxi	taxi	*to take / hire / call / hail a taxi - to get a taxi from the local taxi rank / taxi stand - the hotel may be just a short (taxi) ride from the station - taxi-driver (GB)*
transport (GB) **/ transportation** (US) (U)	transport(s)	*both words are uncountable - to provide transport from one place to another - to have got transport* (être motorisé)
the tube (GB)	métro	*a colloquial word for the underground - to go to work on the tube / by tube / by train (US)*

7.2. People, noise and pollution

■ *Noms*

clatter	bruit de ferraille	**pedestrian** [pə'destri_ən]	piéton
passenger ['---]	passager, voyageur	**roar**	grondement, vrombissement
passers-by	passants	**whir(r)** [wɜː]	vrombissement, ronronnement

Collocations

din	vacarme	*the din of heavy traffic*
fumes	exhalaisons, émanations	*exhaust fumes* (gaz d'échappement) *- gas (US) / petrol fumes* (vapeurs d'essence)
horn / hoot	klaxon, avertisseur	*to blow / sound the horn* (klaxonner)
hubbub	brouhaha, vacarme	*the hubbub of city streets*
noise	bruit	*the deafening / ear-splitting noise of rush-hour traffic*
rattle	bruit sec et saccadé	*the rattle of an old car jolting along*
roar	vrombissement, grondement	*the roar of homeward traffic*
rumble	grondement, roulement	*the rumble of a passing truck*
screech	grincement, crissement	*the screech of tyres / of brakes being slammed on*

Towns, the environment, the country

Adjectifs

crowded	encombré	**full**	plein
crammed	bondé	**foul-smelling** [faʊl]	nauséabond
empty	vide	**noisy**	bruyant

Collocations

clamorous ['---]   bruyant, retentissant, sonore   *the district was clamorous with trucks arriving, backing in and out - the air was filled with clamorous, excited voices*

Verbes

catch	attraper, prendre (bus)	**hoot** [huːt] (**one's horn**)	klaxonner
horn	klaxonner	**miss**	rater (bus)

Collocations

clatter	faire un bruit de ferraille	*tramcars clattering past the once quiet houses*
rattle	se bringueballer; faire un bruit saccadé	*trucks rattling through the streets*
rumble	rouler avec fracas	*heavy carts, buses and lorries rumbling into town / down the street*
screech	grincer, crisser	*brakes and tyres may screech - a car may screech to a halt / to a standstill*

Exercices sur le chapitre 13 A (7.1 et 7.2)

1. Testez vos connaissances en traduisant les mots ci-dessous :

A / tube - B / coach - C / screech (n.) - D / to horn - E / to clatter

2. Remplissez la grille ci-dessous à l'aide des définitions :

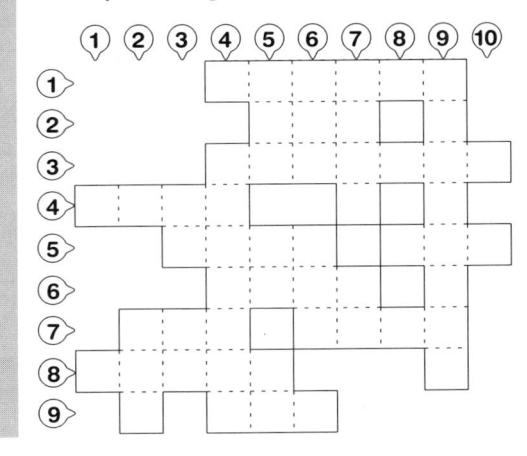

Across:

1. Windows, coins may _____. 2. Bunch of flowers used as a greeting (Hawai). 3. Full. 4. Traffic, lions, lorries _____. 5. Car-drivers sometimes _____ their horns at people crossing over; taxi. 6. Sewing machines _____. 7. Not good; London underground. 8. Issue from gas exhausts. 9. Noise

Down:

2. Passenger - carrying vehicle. 3. Exclamation; I _____. 4. Full. 5. First three letters of a time-adverb; exclamation; if in. 6. A drink; _____ for tat. 7. _____ passes; Rugby Union. 9. Also called the el or the L.

8. Public places and amenities [ə'miːnətiz]

8.1. General

■ *Noms*

baths GB [bɑːðz] / US [bæðz]	bains-douches	restroom (US)	toilettes
bathhouse	bains publics	powder room (US)	toilettes (dames)
checkroom (US)	vestiaire	washroom	toilettes (terme daté)
cloakroom (GB)	vestiaire	comfort station (US)	toilettes publiques
elevator (US) ['----]	ascenseur	the facilities [-'---]	toilettes (euphémisme)
escalator (US) ['----]	escalier roulant	(public) lavatory (GB) ['----]	toilettes
entrance fee	droit d'entrée, d'inscription	toilet(s) (GB)	toilettes
entrance ticket	ticket d'entrée	loo (GB)	toilettes (fam.)
entry	entrée	bathroom GB ['bɑːθruːm] / US ['bæθruːm]	toilettes
'no entry'	'entrée interdite', 'sens interdit'	precinct ['priːsɪŋkt]	enceinte, pourtour
entry fee	droit d'entrée, d'inscription	premises ['premɪsɪz]	lieux, locaux
moving stairs	escalier roulant	revolving [-'--] door	porte à tambour
lift (GB)	ascenseur	swing door	porte battante
exit	sortie	way out	sortie
emergency [-'---] exit	sortie, issue de secours	youth hostel	auberge de jeunesse
ladies / women's room (US)	toilettes (dames)	YMCA	Young Men's Christian Association
gentlemen's / gents / men's room	toilettes (messieurs)	YWCA	Young Women's Christian Association
john (US)	toilettes (hommes) (fam.)	hatcheck girl (US)	dame du vestiaire
public convenience(s)	toilettes publiques		

Collocations

- **entrance** — entrée — *to force an entrance into a place*

8.2. Entertainment and culture

■ *Noms*

amusement arcade [-'-]	galerie de jeux	librarian [laɪ'breərɪ ən]	bibliothécaire
art gallery	galerie d'art	museum [mjuːˈziː əm]	musée
casino [kə'siːnəʊ]	casino	music hall	music-hall
cinema	cinéma	nightclub	boîte de nuit
one-armed bandit	machine à sous	pinball	flipper
club	club	pinball machine [-'-]	billard électronique
concert hall	salle de concert	theatre ['θɪətə]	théâtre
discotheque ['dɪskətek]	discothèque	places of worship	lieux du culte
library	bibliothèque	video arcade (US) [-'-]	galerie de jeux-vidéo
movie house / movie theater (US)	salle de cinéma	foyer ['fɔɪeɪ]	foyer (théâtre)

Towns, the environment, the country 217

8.3. Food and drink

■ *Noms*

bill / check (US)	note, addition	pub crawl	tournée des pubs
diner ['daɪnə]	petit restaurant	restaurant	restaurant
eatery	resto	speakeasy	bar clandestin (pendant la prohibition)
local	café, bistrot du coin		
free house	pub en gérance libre	tip / gratuity	pourboire
happy hours	heure où les boissons sont moins chères	luncheon voucher ['vaʊtʃə]	chèque / ticket-repas
		wine bar	bar à vins
menu	menu	waiter	garçon, serveur
order	commande	waitress ['--]	serveuse
last orders	heure limite des dernières commandes	takeaway / takeout (restaurant)	restaurant de plats à emporter
pub	café, bistrot, pub	off-licence	magasin vendant des boissons alcoolisées; licence (de vente)
public house	pub, bar		
publican	patron de bistrot		

■ *Adjectifs*

table d'hôte [ˌtɑːblˈdəʊt]	(repas) à prix fixe	takeaway / takeout	(plat) à emporter

8.4. Sport and outdoor facilities [-'---]

■ *Noms*

bench	banc (public)	sports facilities [-'---]	équipements sportifs
drinking fountain	jet d'eau potable, fontaine publique	sports ground	terrain de sport
		stadium ['steɪdiəm]	stade
park	parc, jardin public	swimming pool	piscine
public garden	square	tennis courts	courts de tennis

Collocations

amenity [əˈmiːnəti]	aménagement, équipement	*first class hotels with every amenity - to provide amenities for children - a jail may be lacking in basic amenities*
facility [-'---]	équipement, installation, moyen	*to provide catering / eating / educational / medical / play / recreational / research / shopping / transport facilities*

■ *Adjectifs*

free	gratuit	on the house	offert par le patron
licensed ['laɪsənst]	autorisé (à vendre des boissons alcoolisées)		

■ *Verbes*

check (US)	mettre au vestiaire	eat out	manger au restaurant
eat in	manger chez soi	order (from)	commander (à)

Exercices sur le chapitre 13 A (8.1 à 8.4)

1. Testez vos connaissances en traduisant les mots ci-dessous :
A / pinball - B / speakeasy - C / off-licence - D / bathhouse - E / cloakroom - F / to eat out

2. Remplacez chacun des mots en italiques des phrases par un des mots ci-dessous :
BENCH - CHECK (v.) - WAITER - LIBRARIAN - LIBRARY - MENU - MUSEUM - ON THE HOUSE - ORDER (v.) - PUB - PUB CRAWL
A / He asked the *one-armed bandit* for the *diner*. B / He *ate out* his coat and hat and went into the *pinball machine*. C / He sat on the *bill* and *checked* a meal. D / He thought the drinks were *on the bench* and walked out of the *restroom* in a temper. E / He planned to go on a *public house* with a *publican* friend of his who had a good job at the local *swimming pool*.

B. The environment

1. General

■ *Noms*

conservation	défense de l'environnement	environmental law [ɪnˌvaɪrən'mentl]	droit de l'environnement
deforestation [-ˌ--'---]	déboisement	environmental science / studies	science / études de l'environnement
dump site	terrain de décharge		
ecological [ˌ--'---] disaster GB [dɪ'zɑːstə] / US [dɪ'zæstər]	catastrophe écologique	landfill	enfouissement des déchets; déchets enfouis
ecology	écologie	ozone layer	couche d'ozone
ecosystem ['iːkəʊsɪstəm]	écosystème	threshold of tolerance	seuil de tolérance
nuclear waste(s)	déchets nucléaires	landfill site	site d'enfouissement des déchets

Collocations

atmosphere ['---]	atmosphère	*aerosols, sprays, fumes and toxic gases released into the atmosphere may pollute / spoil / damage it badly*
clean-up campaign [-'-]	campagne de nettoyage	*to start / launch a clean-up campaign*
environment [ɪn'vaɪrənmənt]	environnement	*to clean up / protect the environment / man's environment*
fumes	vapeurs, fumées	*to inhale / breathe in gas fumes (US) / petrol fumes (GB) / noxious* (délétères) *exhaust fumes*
nature (U)	nature	*to protect / tame nature - to harness* (exploiter) *the forces of nature - to upset nature's balance*
pollution	pollution	*to combat / fight / prevent pollution*
preservation	conservation, préservation	*sth may be in good preservation / in a good state of preservation*
species (pl. species) ['spiːʃiːz]	espèce	*to try and save an endangered species from extinction - a protected species may survive / become extinct*

Towns, the environment, the country

survival	survie	*to try and assure the survival of a species - the survival of the fittest* (survie des plus forts, des plus aptes)
wastage (U) ['weɪstɪdʒ]	gaspillage déchets, fuites, pertes	*to regret the wastage of natural resources* *to cut down on wastage from containers*
waste (U)	déchets	*to try and dispose of industrial / toxic / radioactive / nuclear waste - (US: wastes)*
water	eau	*to chlorinate* (chlorer) */ fluoridate* (fluorer) */ filter / soften / pollute water - water may flow / evaporate / ooze* (suinter)

2. People

■ *Noms*

ecologist	écologiste		the Greens	les Ecologistes (parti)
conservationist	défenseur de l'environnement		the Green party	le parti des Verts
eco-defender	défenseur de la nature		eco-freak	fana d'écologie
eco-raider	destructeur de la nature		green consumer	consommateur écolo
environmentalist [-,--'---]	écologiste		preservationist [,--'---]	défenseur de la nature

3. Air / atmosphere pollution

■ *Noms*

acid rain (U)	pluie(s) acide(s)		**chlorofluocarbon (CFC)**	chlorofluorocarbone
carbon monoxide [mə'nɒksaɪd]	oxyde de carbone		**crop-spraying**	pulvérisation des cultures
carbon dioxide [daɪ'ɒksaɪd]	gaz carbonique		**factory smoke** (U)	fumées d'usine
emissions	émanations		**greenhouse effect** [-'-]	effet de serre
nitrogen	azote		**nitrogen oxide** ['naɪtrədʒən] - ['ɒksaɪd]	oxyde d'azote
contamination	contamination			

Exercices sur le chapitre 13 B (1 à 3)

1. Testez vos connaissances en traduisant les mots ci-dessous :

A / eco-freak - B / eco-raider - C / carbon dioxide - D / nitrogen oxide - E / dump site - F / landfill

2. Remplacez chacun des mots manquants par l'un des mots ci-dessus :

DAMAGE (v.) - DISPOSE OF (v.) - EXTINCTION - HARNESS (v.) - INHALE (v.) - PROTECT (v.) - POLLUTION - RESOURCES - SPECIES - UPSET (v.) - WASTAGE - WASTE (n.)

A / Aerosols and sprays badly ____ the atmosphere. B / It is not good for one's health to ____ petrol fumes. C / Ecologists try to save endangered ____ from ____. D / One can only regret the ____ of natural ____. E / It is not easy to ____ nuclear ____. F / We must try to ____ man's environment from air ____. G / One must try to ____ the forces of nature without ____ nature's balance.

4. Land and soil pollution

■ Noms

chemical	produit chimique	**insecticide** [ɪn'sektɪsaɪd]	insecticide
fauna	faune	**pesticide** ['pestɪsaɪd]	pesticide
flora	flore	**litter** (U)	détritus, ordures
fossil fuel	combustible fossile	**wildlife**	faune et flore
nitrogen ['naɪtrədʒən]	azote	**mudslide**	coulée de boue
nitrogenous fertilizers [naɪ'trɒdʒənəs]	engrais azotés	**(waste) dump**	décharge (de déchets)

■ Adjectifs

foul	fétide (odeur); infect (endroit); croupie (eau)	**grimy**	encrassé, crasseux
		sullied	souillée (eau)

■ Verbes

dump	déposer, jeter (ordures)	**tip**	déverser (dans une décharge)

5. Marine and water pollution

■ Noms

ground water	nappe phréatique	**oil slick**	nappe de pétrole, marée noire
expansion of the sea	dilatation des océans	**oil spill**	déversement (accidentel) de pétrole
marine [mə'riːn] life	vie marine		
oil patch	petite nappe de pétrole	**spillage**	déversement accidentel
oiled bird	oiseau mazouté	**floating barrier**	barrage flottant

■ Verbes

gush	jaillir	**pour (out)**	(se) déverser (des fumées)
seep	suinter, filtrer	**spill**	(se) répandre, (se) renverser

Exercices sur le chapitre 13 B (4 et 5)

1. Testez vos connaissances en traduisant les mots ci-dessous :

A / foul (adj.) - B / nitrogen - C / grimy - D / oil slick - E / litter - F / ordures
G / déversement accidentel - H / jaillir (eau) - I / engrais azotés - J / combustible fossile

2. Proposez un verbe :

A / Water may ____, that is flow out quickly or it may ____, that is flow out very slowly and in small amounts; alternatively it may be ____ by dirt. B / People are told not to ____ rubbish just anywhere they fancy but to ____ it in specialised sites. C / Petrol may ____ if a tanker runs aground. D / Factory chimneys may ____ ____ black smoke, day and night.

Towns, the environment, the country

6. Causes, effects and cures

6.1 Causes

■ *Noms*

asbestos [æs'bestəs]	amiante	health hazard	danger pour la santé
exhaust(s) [-'-] (fumes)	gaz d'échappement	lead [led]	plomb
detergent	détergent	mercury	mercure
dioxin [daɪ'ɒksɪn]	dioxine	nitrates ['naɪtreɪts]	nitrates
effluents	écoulements polluants	propellant [-'--]	bombe aérosol
(auto) tailpipe	tuyau d'échappement	spray	aérosol, atomiseur
exhaust [-'-] (pipe)	pot d'échappement	polluter [-'--]	pollueur
health risk	risque pour la santé	pollutant [pə'luːtənt]	polluant

Collocations

leak	fuite, voie d'eau	*a ship / pipe may spring a leak* (se mettre à fuir) - *to detect a gas leak*
leakage	fuite, perte	*to trace leakage to a faulty / leaking pipe - sth may be wasted through leakage*

■ *Verbes*

discharge [-'-]	(se) déverser	*factories may discharge large amounts of dangerous waste - oil may discharge into the sea and harm a lot of birds and animals*
leak	fuir, laisser passer, (se) répandre, (faire) couler	*a roof / a pipe may leak - a car may leak oil all over*
leak out	passer, s'échapper (liquide)	*water may leak out of / from a pipe / on to sth*
release	émettre, relâcher	*to release toxic gases into the atmosphere*

6.2. Effects [-'-]

■ *Noms*

asbestosis [,--'--]	asbestose	poison cloud	nuage toxique
climatic changes [klaɪ'mætɪk]	changements climatiques	radioactivity	radioactivité
		radioactive fallout	retombées radioactives
noise pollution	nuisances phoniques	refuse (U) ['refjuːs]	ordures, détritus
global warming	réchauffement de la planète	rubbish (U)	ordures, immondices
lead [led] poisoning	saturnisme	soot [sʊt]	suie
noxious fumes	fumées, émanations délétères	stench	puanteur

Collocations

decibel ['desɪbel]	décibel	*sth may make 90 decibels of noise - decibel count / level / scale / limit*
noise	bruit	*sth may make / produce / reduce / cut down / a(n) constant / background / loud / deafening / shrill / nerve-racking / unbearable / annoying noise - a noise may abate / die down - to try not to make a noise / a lot of noise / too much noise*

■ Adjectifs

energy-guzzling	gourmand en énergie	**unsafe to drink**	non potable
extinct	disparu	**unbreathable**	irrespirable
inedible [-'---]	immangeable	**harmful (to)**	dangereux (pour), nuisible (à),
unfit for drinking	impropre à la consommation		nocif (pour, à)

■ Verbes

asphyxiate [æsˈfɪksɪeɪt]	asphyxier	**harm**	endommager, faire du mal à
belch out / forth	cracher (fumée)	**impair**	abîmer, détériorer
contaminate [-'---]	contaminer	**poison**	empoisonner
damage	endommager, nuire à	**pollute** [-'-]	polluer
destroy	détruire	**spoil**	abîmer
disfigure [-'--]	défigurer	**waste**	gaspiller
endanger [ɪnˈdeɪndʒə]	mettre en danger, menacer	**stink**	puer, empester
foul	polluer, infecter (air)		

Collocations

alter [ˈɔːltə]	modifier	*pollution may alter weather patterns / climatic conditions*
choke	oppresser, suffoquer	*sb may be choked by the pungent smell of sulphur*
stifle	étouffer, suffoquer	*sb may be stifled by the heat / stifled to death by fumes*

Exercices sur le chapitre 13 B (6.1 et 6.2)

1. Testez vos connaissances en traduisant les mots ci-dessous :

A / asbestos - B / propellant - C / leakage - D / réchauffement de la planète - E / saturnisme F / puanteur

2. Remplacez chacun des mots manquants par un des mots ci-dessous :

ALTER - CHOKE - DISCHARGE - LEAK - LEAK - LEAKAGE - RELEASE (v.) - STIFLE

A / Lots of factories ____ dangerous waste and toxic gases into the atmosphere. B / A roof may ____; so can a pipe. C / A car may ____ oil all over the garage floor. D / Some smells may ____ you just as some fumes may ____ you to death. E / Pollution may ____ weather patterns. F / ____ can sometimes be traced to a faulty pipe.

3. Traduisez en anglais :

A / L'amiante, qui peut causer l'asbestose, constitue un véritable danger pour la santé. B / Les atomiseurs et les bombes aérosol endommagent la couche d'ozone. C / Si on emploie trop de nitrate dans une zone donnée, cela peut contaminer les nappes phréatiques de la région. D / Certaines peintures utilisées sur les jouets peuvent provoquer le saturnisme chez les enfants. E / Certains produits chimiques sont nocifs pour la santé. F / Il faut s'efforcer de réduire les bruits qui sont éprouvants pour les nerfs.

6.3. Cures

■ *Noms*

biofuel	bio-carburant	**filter**	filtre
bottle bank	conteneur de collecte de verre usagé	**car-pooling**	co-voiturage
		catalytic converter	pot catalytique

Towns, the environment, the country

methanol	méthanol	**noise abatement**	réductions des nuisances sonores; insonorisation
bottle redemption centre	centre de récupération du verre	**noise abatement**	lutte contre le bruit
waste disposal	traitement des déchets	**noise level**	niveau de bruit
(waste) water treatment plant GB [plɑːnt] / US [plænt]	station d'épuration	**noise protection embankment / wall**	remblai anti-bruit
waste collection site	déchetterie	**pickaback / piggyback**	ferroutage
cleanup	dépollution, assainissement	**waste treatment plant**	usine de traitement des déchets

Collocations

awareness	prise de conscience	*to heighten people's awareness of environmental problems*	
ban	interdiction	*to impose / lift a ban on polluting chemicals*	

■ *Adjectifs*

alternative [-'---]	alternatif, de rechange	**environmental friendly**	sans danger pour l'environnement, écologique
biodegradable [,---'---]	biodégradable	**natural**	naturel
disposable	jetable, à jeter (après usage)	**ozone safe**	sans danger pour la couche d'ozone
ecological	écologique		
cost-effective	rentable, d'un bon rapport coût-performance	**leak-proof**	étanche
		sound-insulated	insonorisé
lead-free [led] / **unleaded**	sans plomb	**ozone-friendly**	qui préserve la couche d'ozone
noiseless	silencieux	**sound-proof**	insonorisé
fuel efficient	économique, qui consomme peu	**insulating**	isolant
		sound-absorbing [əb'sɔːbɪŋ]	anti-sonique

■ *Verbes*

ban	interdire	**protect**	protéger
conserve	conserver, préserver	**purify**	purifier
cut out	supprimer, éliminer	**recycle**	recycler
dispose of	se débarrasser de, détruire	**stop**	arrêter, empêcher
filter	filtrer	**switch from... to...**	passer de ... à ...
noiseproof	rendre silencieux ou insonore	**clean up**	dépolluer, assainir
preserve	préserver	**prevent**	empêcher

Collocations

run on sth	rouler à qch	*a car may run on methanol or clean fuels*
save	économiser	*to save energy - to save up to 75 per cent of heat loss* (déperdition de chaleur) *by efficient insulation*
	sauver	*to save the earth from pollution*
survive	survivre (à)	*to help people to survive the effects of uncontrolled pollution*

Exercices sur le chapitre 13 B (6.3)

1. Testez vos connaissances en traduisant les mots ci-dessous :

A / car-pooling - B / piggyback - C / bottle bank - D / dépolluer - E / anti-sonique
F / centre de récupération du verre

2. Traduisez en anglais :

A / Avoir une voiture qui roule à l'essence sans plomb. B / Sauver la terre de la pollution. C / Survivre aux effets de la pollution. D / Accroître la conscience qu'ont les gens des problèmes de l'environnement. E / Imposer / lever l'interdiction qui pèse sur certains polluants. F / Avoir recours à des énergies alternatives, rentables et sans danger pour l'environnement. G / Utiliser des produits qui préservent la couche d'ozone. H / Des matières isolantes et des murs insonorisés réduisent en principe le niveau de bruit dans certains appartements.

C. The country, landscape and sights

1. General

■ *Noms*

allotment / plot	parcelle, lopin de terre	**mountain**	montagne
bank	talus; rive, berge	**orchard** ['ɔːtʃəd]	verger
brush (U) [brʌʃ]	broussailles, taillis	**pasture land** (U)	pâturage(s)
bush (C) [bʊʃ]	buisson, taillis, fourré	**outback**	cambrousse (Australie)
bush (U) [bʊʃ]	broussailles	**peak**	pic
the bush (U) [bʊʃ]	la brousse	**pond**	étang
cluster	bouquet (d'arbres)	**pool**	flaque; mare
clump	bouquet (d'arbres), massif (d'arbustes)	**puddle**	flaque
		range [reɪndʒ]	chaîne (de montagnes)
bowling-green	boulingrin	**ridge**	arête
crag	rocher à pic	**scarecrow**	épouvantail
ditch	fossé	**scrub** (U)	broussailles
fence	clôture	**shrub**	arbrisseau, arbuste
foliage (U)	feuillage	**shrubbery**	(massif d')arbustes
forest	forêt	**sight**	spectacle, paysage
gate	barrière	**sign**	enseigne
glacier ['glæsɪə]	glacier	**small town**	ville de province
greenery (U)	verdure	**slate roof**	toit d'ardoise
hamlet	hameau	**spa** [spɑː]	ville d'eau
hedge	haie (jardin)	**stile**	échalier
hedgerow	haies (champ)	**turnstile**	tourniquet
hill	colline	**thach(ed) roof**	toit de chaume
hillock	tertre, mamelon	**thicket**	fourré, hallier
hurdle	claie	**tile(d) roof**	toit de tuiles
inn	auberge	**tree**	arbre
market place	place du marché	**valley**	vallée
lake	lac	**village**	village
market town	bourg	**vine** (C)	vigne
mill	moulin	**vine shoot** (C)	sarment
water mill	moulin à eau	**vineyard** ['vɪnjəd]	vignoble
wind mill	moulin à vent	**wood**	bois

Towns, the environment, the country

Collocations

country ['kʌntri]	campagne	*to live in / go into the country - to live off the country* (vivre des produits de la terre)
	paysage(s), région	*good fishing country - to hike through lovely country*
countryside	campagne (paysage)	*to avoid spoiling the beautiful countryside*
field	champ	*to plough / plow (US) the fields with a plough / plow and dig furrows* (sillons), *then reap the corn / harvest*
grass GB [grɑːs] / US [græs]	herbe (fourrage)	*grass grows - to grow grass for fodder and hay* (foin)
grove	bocage, bosquet	*chestnut / olive / pine grove* (châtaigneraie, oliveraie, pinède)
landscape	paysage	*the landscape may be dotted with* (parsemé) *small bushes / scarred* (déchiré) *by quarrying or coal mining / spoilt by depressing concrete buildings*
meadow ['medəʊ]	pré, prairie	*a meadow with cattle grazing on it*
the wild(s)	région sauvage, brousse	*the call of the wild* (l'appel de la nature) *- to go off into the wilds of Alaska* (fin fond) *- to live out in the wilds* (en pleine brousse)

Exercices sur le chapitre 13 C (1)

1. Testez vos connaissances en traduisant les mots ci-dessous :
A / hamlet - B / hedge - C / outback - D / thicket - E / bank - F / hillock - G / puddle - H / shrub

2. Traduisez en anglais :
A / Je vais à la campagne chaque week-end. B / Je n'y vais pas pour regarder pousser l'herbe. C / Je ne fais pas pousser de l'herbe pour avoir du foin ou du fourrage. D / Je me contente de regarder le paysage parsemé de bosquets, de mares et d'étangs que le béton n'a pas encore gâché. E / La campagne a besoin d'être protégée des pollueurs. F / Là où je vis, je me languis de la campagne anglaise.

3. Des lettres ont été déplacées d'un mot à l'autre dans chaque ensemble; remettez de l'ordre :
A / PUSH - BURDLE - HOOL - B / PATCH - REAK - THANGE - C / PLEE - TRILL - MOT - D / FILE - STIDGE - RENCE - E / CLITCH - LUMP - DAKE

2. People

■ *Noms*

basket maker GB ['bɑːskɪt] / US ['bæskət]	vannier	**clergyman**	ecclésiastique
		farmer	fermier
blacksmith	forgeron	**forester / forest ranger** ['reɪndʒə]	(garde ou agent) forestier
cottager	paysan (GB) (terme daté) / propriétaire de maison de campagne (US)	**gamekeeper**	garde-chasse
		gravedigger	fossoyeur
country dweller	campagnard, habitant de la campagne	**hiker**	marcheur, excursionniste
		landlord	patron (de pub)
country folk / people	gens de la campagne	**innkeeper**	aubergiste

pub owner	propriétaire de pub	saddler	sellier
parson	pasteur	sexton	sacristain
curate ['kjʊərət]	vicaire	shepherd ['ʃepəd]	berger
vicar	pasteur	solicitor [-'---]	notaire, avocat
priest	prêtre	notary	notaire, avoué
peasant ['peznt]	paysan	squire	chatelain
poacher	braconnier	tinker	rétameur
postmaster GB ['pəʊstmɑːstə] / US ['poʊstmæstər]	receveur des postes	verger	bedeau
		villager	villageois
		(village) constable ['---]	gendarme
postman ['pəʊstmən]	facteur	vine-grower	viticulteur ou vigneron
publican	patron de bistrot	wheelwright	charron
roadmender	cantonnier	rural policeman [pə'liːsmən]	garde-champêtre

■ *Verbes*

forge	forger	mend	réparer
irrigate	irriguer	reap	récolter
maintain [-'-]	entretenir (routes)	shoe	ferrer (chevaux)

Exercices sur le chapitre 13 C (2)

1. Testez vos connaissances en traduisant les mots ci-dessous :

A / cottager - B / blacksmith - C / parson - D / poacher - E / squire - F / curate - G / hiker
H / verger

2. Complétez :

A / It is the _____'s job to look after a church and its graveyard. B / It is the _____'s job to look after the building and contents of a church. C / It is the _____'s job to look after the sheep. D / It is the _____'s job to take care of wild animals and birds kept on sb's land for shooting or hunting.
E / It is the _____'s job to make and repair saddles and other equipment for horses. F / It is the _____'s job to make horse-shoes or farm tools. G / It is the _____'s job to make and repair carts, carriages and wooden gates. H / It is the _____'s job to look after the trees in a forest and to plant new ones.

3. Places

3.1. Ways and paths

■ *Noms*

bend	courbe, coude (route)	path GB [pɑːθ] / US [pæθ]	sentier, chemin
bridle ['braɪdl] path	piste cavalière	pothole	nid de poule
cart-track	chemin de terre	rut	ornière
footpath	sentier	signpost	poteau indicateur
lane	chemin, petite route	twist	tournant, virage
milestone	borne kilométrique	walkway (GB)	sentier pédestre

Towns, the environment, the country   227

Collocations

way	chemin, voie	to follow a way across the fields

3.2. Buildings

■ *Noms*

bridge	pont	second home	résidence secondaire
coach / bus station	gare routière	house in the country	maison de campagne
church	église	post-office	poste
churchyard	cimetière	pub	café, pub
common	terrain communal	railway station	gare de chemin de fer
country seat	manoir, gentilhommière	square	place
country house	manoir, petit château	smithy	forge
courtyard	cour (de maison)	towing ['təʊɪŋ] path	chemin de halage
farmhouse	ferme (bâtiment)	vicarage	presbytère
farmyard	cour de ferme	village hall	salle des fêtes
graveyard	cimetière		

3.3. Castles

■ *Noms*

castle	château (fort)	loophole	meutrière
bailey	cour	machicolation	machicoulis
barbican	barbacane	merlon	merlon
bastion	bastion	moat (C)	douves, fossés
bartizan	échauguette	postern	poterne
battlements	remparts, créneaux	pillbox	casemate, blockhaus
blockhouse	blockhaus	stronghold	forteresse
citadel ['---]	citadelle	parapet walk ['---]	chemin de ronde
corbel	corbeau	pinnacle ['---]	clocheton
dome	dôme	portcullis	herse
curtain wall	courtine	rampart ['ræmpɑːt]	rempart
drawbridge	pont-levis	stockade [-'-]	palissade
dungeon	cachot	tower	tour
footbridge	passerelle	corner tower	tour d'angle
fort	fort	turret	tourelle
fortress	forteresse	vault	voûte
guard house	corps de garde	walled city	villle fortifiée
keep	donjon	wing	aile
lists	lice		

Collocations

farm	ferme	to live / work on a farm
green	place du village (gazonnée)	also referred to as: 'village green'
well	puits	to draw / get water from a well by lowering a bucket down it

Adjectifs

barren	aride	muddy	boueux
deserted	désert	rough [rʌf]	inégal (sol); accidenté, rocailleux (route)
corbelled	à encorbellement		
crenelated	à créneaux	scattered	dispersé, éparpillé
dusty	poussiéreux	secluded	à l'écart, isolé
mossy	moussu	straggling	tout en longueur (village)
picturesque [,--'-]	pittoresque	thatched	couvert de chaume
quiet	calme, paisible	uneven	inégal, raboteux (chemin)

Verbes

belch forth / out	vomir, cracher (flammes, fumée)	sprinkle	asperger, arroser légèrement
billow out	se gonfler (voiles); s'élever en volutes, tournoyer (fumée)	straggle	s'étendre en longueur (village); être épars ou disséminé (maisons)
bend	faire un coude, tourner	twist	serpenter
spew out	vomir (de la lave)	wind [waɪnd]	serpenter, faire des zigzags
sweep along	(train) avancer rapidement	sweep round sth	(rivière) contourner en une grande courbe
sweep away to	(baie, mer) s'étendre très loin jusqu'à	sweep through	(incendie, ouragan) se répandre (brutalement), balayer
sweep across / over	(pluie, vent) balayer (une surface); traverser (route)		
sweep down to	(route, colline, montagne) descendre (majestueusement ou en pente douce)		

Collocations

splash	éclabousser	*to get splashed by the waves*
	barboter, patauger dans	*a dog may splash through the mud*

Exercices sur le chapitre 13 C (3.1 à 3.3)

1. Testez vos connaissances en traduisant les mots ci-dessous :

A / to spew - B / secluded - C / towing path - D / smithy - E / pothole - F / rut - G / keep - H / pinnacle - I / battlements - J / portcullis

2. Remplacez les verbes manquants par un des verbes ci-dessous au prétérit (sauf C) :

BELCH - BEND - BILLOW - SPLASH - SPRINKLE - STRAGGLE - SWEEP DOWN - SWEEP THROUGH

A / Factory chimney _____ out smoke. B / The road _____ to the left after the first set of traffic lights. C / They walked up the _____ing mountain roads. D / Houses _____ across the countryside. E / Thunderstorms _____ _____ the whole country. F / The light rain _____ the grass. G / The beating rain _____ the windows. H / Flags _____ in the breeze.

14
Violence, danger, disasters, accidents, humanitarian aid

A. Violence

1. General and individual

Noms

abduction [-'---]	enlèvement, rapt
barbary ['bɑːbər_i]	barbarie
bashing	violences physiques, coups
child abuse (U) [əˈbjuːs]	mauvais traitements à enfant
child battering	maltraitance à enfant
ferocity [-'---]	férocité
fierceness	fureur, violence
fury	fureur, déchaînement
harassment ['---]	harcèlement
kidnap(ping) ['--(-)]	kidnapping
ill-treatment (U)	mauvais traitements
mugging	agression, violences
punch	coup de poing
savagery (U) ['----]	sauvagerie
act of savagery	acte de sauvagerie
savageries	actes de sauvagerie
stab	coup de couteau ou poignard
stabbing	agression (à coups de couteau ou de poignard)
viciouness ['vɪʃəsnəs]	brutalité, violence
flogging (C / U)	flagellation, coups de fouet
bash	coup violent
sexual abuse (U) [əˈbjuːs]	sévices sexuels
drive-by shooting	coups de feu tirés d'une voiture en marche

Collocations

abuse (C / U) [əˈbjuːs]	abus	*an abuse of power - abuse of alcohol is harmful*
abuse (U) [əˈbjuːs]	insultes, injures	*to heap / shower abuse on sb - to hurl / shriek abuse at sb - a hail / shower / stream / torrent / term of abuse*
abuse (U)	maltraitance	*many children are at risk from abuse*
aggression [-'---]	agression	*to be a victim of an act of aggression*
assault	agression, attaque	*to commit aggravated assault* (coups et blessures) / *indecent assault* (attentat à la pudeur) / *assault and battery* (voies de fait) *on sb*
blow	coup	*to give sb / deal sb a blow - to strike a blow on / to sb's stomach - to heap / rain blows on sb - to exchange / come to blows over sth - to take a blow to the chin - to ward off* (parer) */ parry / deflect* (faire dévier) */ dodge* (esquiver) *a hard / powerful / severe blow - to aim a blow at sb*
cruelty (U / C)	cruauté	*to display / show / be accused of deliberate / wanton* (gratuite, injustifiée) *cruelty to sb - to suffer beatings and other cruelties*
fight	bagarre	*to have a fight with sb - to put up a good fight* (bien se défendre)
harm	mal, tort	*to do sb harm - to cause (grievous) bodily harm* (blessures) *- to mean no harm*

rape	viol	to commit rape / several rapes - a rape may be a date (par une connaissance) / gang (en réunion) rape - to be a rape victim
stroke	coup (de fouet, etc)	to be sentenced to / receive fifty strokes of the whip / of the cane
struggle	lutte, résistance; bagarre	to put up a bitter (acharné) / desperate / unrelenting (implacable) struggle against sb / against sth / for sth / to achieve sth - to be hurt in the struggle
torture (C / U)	torture	to resort to torture - to inflict torture on sb - to confess sth under torture - to put sb to (the) torture (faire subir des tortures) - sth may be an act of sheer / sadistic torture - to carry out (se livrer à) tortures
violence (U)	violence	violence may break out / erupt suddenly - to witness an escalation / upsurge / outbreak of acts / threats of violence against sb - to use / resort to excessive / unwarranted / racial violence

Exercices sur le chapitre 14 A (1, noms)

1. Testez vos connaissances en traduisant les mots ci-dessous :

A / mugging - B / stabbing - C / viciousness - D / bash (n.) - E / battery

2. Traduisez en anglais :

A / Elle porta à son agresseur un coup dans l'estomac qu'il ne put esquiver. B / Mais cela ne l'arrêta pas – il se mit à la rouer de coups. C / Il fit montre, à son égard, d'une cruauté toute gratuite. D / Ils se battirent; elle se défendit bien. E / Mais elle avait été blessée dans la bagarre. F / Elle pouvait à peine supporter la torture physique qu'il lui infligeait. G / Par chance, quelqu'un fut témoin de l'agression et présent lorsque se déclenchèrent les menaces de l'agresseur et des actes d'une violence que rien ne justifiait. H / Ce témoin intervint et réussit à détourner les coups puissants que l'agresseur lui destinait. I / Il finit par l'emporter et l'agresseur fut arrêté et reconnu coupable de coups et blessures et de tentative de viol.

■ *Adjectifs*

aggressive [-'--]	agressif	**gory**	sanglant, horrible (détail)
bloody	sanglant, ensanglanté	**perverted** [-'--]	pervers
battered	battu (enfants, femmes)	**unrestrained**	sans frein (violence)
brutal	brutal	**vicious** ['vɪʃəs]	brutal, cruel (coup)
fierce	féroce (air, personne)		

Collocations

berserk [bə'zɜːk]	fou furieux	to go berserk
cruel	cruel	cruel person - to be cruel to sb
ferocious [-'--]	féroce, violent à l'extrême	ferocious animal / attack / person
fierce	féroce, acharné	to have a fierce look on one's face - after fierce fighting
murderous ['---]	meurtrier; cruel	murderous person / expression / tendencies - to feel murderous (avoir des envies de meurtre)
rough [rʌf]	brutal, violent	rough person / game - to be rough on / with sb - to give sb a rough time (en faire baver)
savage ['--]	brutal, cruel	to deal sb a savage blow
sexual	sexuel	sexual abuse (sévices) / harassment / intercourse (rapports) / pervert

Violence, danger, disasters, accidents, humanitarian aid 231

tough [tʌf]	dur		*a tough lot* (durs à cuire) - *to take a tough line / get tough with sb* (employer la manière forte)
violent	violent		*violent person / clashes with the police*

■ Verbes

abduct	enlever, kidnapper	beat sb up	tabasser
assault	agresser; violenter	knock sb unconscious	assommer qqn
attack	agresser, attaquer	maim	estropier, mutiler
batter	frapper, maltraiter	manhandle	maltraiter, traiter sans ménagement
club	matraquer		
cosh sb	cogner sur qqn	maul [mɔːl]	déchiqueter; brutaliser
cudgel ['kʌdʒəl]	frapper à coups de trique	molest [-'-]	rudoyer, molester
gag	bâillonner	mug	agresser
harass ['--]	harceler	rape	violer
ill-treat	maltraiter	savage	(animal) attaquer férocement
hit back (at sb)	riposter, rendre les coups	stab	poignarder
hit out (at sb)	envoyer un coup (à)	strangle	étrangler
kidnap ['--]	kidnapper	"Stand and deliver!"	"La bourse ou la vie!"
kill	tuer	torment [-'-]	torturer, martyriser
knock sb out	assommer qqn	torture ['--]	torturer, soumettre à des tortures
knock sb around	maltraiter, malmener		
lambast(e) (lambast [læm'bæst] - lambaste [læm'beɪst])	rosser	harm sb	faire du mal, du tort à qqn; nuire à qqn

Collocations

abuse sth [ə'bjuːz]	abuser de qch	*to abuse one's authority / sb's trust*
abuse sb	insulter, injurier qqn maltraiter	*to abuse sb in the foulest language* *children may be emotionally / physically abused*
bash	frapper, cogner	*to bash sb on the head*
beat	battre	*to beat sb black and blue* (rouer de coups) - *to be beaten senseless / to death*
blackmail sb	faire chanter qqn	*to blackmail sb into doing sth*
fight	se battre	*to fight (with sb) over sth - to fight a duel*
force	forcer, obliger, contraindre	*to force sb to do sth - to force a secret out of sb* (arracher)
hit	frapper	*to hit sb (a blow) on / over the head / in the stomach - to be hit by a stray* (perdue) *bullet*
hurt	(se) faire mal, (se) blesser faire mal, être douloureux	*to hurt sb / oneself / one's arm - to get hurt* *sb's arm may hurt*
injure ['ɪndʒə]	(se) blesser (accident)	*to get injured in a road accident - to injure one's knee*
knife sb	donner un coup de couteau à qqn	*to knife sb in the back*
punch	donner un / des coup(s) de poing	*to punch sb's nose / sb in the nose / in the face - to punch one's way through*
strike sb	frapper, donner un / des coups à qqn	*to strike sb (a blow) on the chin - to be struck by lightning - a stone may strike sb on the head*
struggle	lutter, se battre, se débattre se démener	*to struggle bravely with sb / to do sth / for sth*
whip	fouetter	*to whip sb into obedience / submission*

Exercices sur le chapitre 14 A (1, adjectifs et verbes)

1. Testez vos connaissances en traduisant les mots ci-dessous :

A / to maul - B / to manhandle - C / to savage - D / vicious - E / harceler - F / bâillonner
G / harcèlement - H / flagellation

2. Joignez une phrase de droite à chaque phrase de gauche :

1. Something she said made him go beserk
2. You don't bash a man on the head
3. He tried to whip her into submission
4. He nearly beat his wife senseless
5. Although he looked fierce and rough
6. I'll spare you the gory details
7. I do feel murderous at times and
8. He beat the girl up savagely and
9. He said he would never harm her
10. When the man mugged her

A. but she managed to hit out at him and knock him unconscious.
B. would like to club and cudgel my next-door neighbours.
C. maimed her for life.
D. he was neither brutal nor cruel to anybody.
E. but she said that she'd got hurt in an accident...
F. just because he abused you repeatedly in public...
G. of that ferocious attack.
H. she hit back and forced him to run away.
I. and he hit his wife over the head several times.
J. yet he stabbed and nearly strangled her.

2. Collective violence

Noms

barbarity [bɑː'bærəti]	barbarie, cruauté	persecution	persécution
brutishness	bestialité, grande cruauté	sadism ['seɪdɪzəm]	sadisme
brutality [-'---]	brutalité; sauvagerie	ruthlessness ['---]	nature ou caractère impitoyable (de qqn / de qch)
bloodshed	effusion de sang		
carnage ['kɑːnɪdʒ]	carnage	inhumanity	cruauté, inhumanité
extermination [-,--'---]	extermination	bomb outrage [bɒm] - ['aʊtreɪdʒ]	attentat au plastic
massacre ['mæsəkə]	massacre		
onslaught ['ɒnslɔːt]	attaque, assaut	paki-bashing ['pækibæʃɪŋ]	chasse aux Pakistanais, 'ratonnade'
oppression [-'---]	oppression		

Collocations

atrocity	atrocité	to commit an act of appalling / unheard-of atrocity - to commit atrocities
outrage ['aʊtreɪdʒ]	acte de violence atrocité crime	to suffer outrages at the hands of torturers several outrages may occur / be committed outrage against humanity
riot	émeute, violentes bagarres	sth may cause / spark (off) / touch off / lead to a riot - to try and put down (réprimer) / control (maîtriser) a riot - a riot may break out / erupt unexpectedly
rioting	émeutes	rioting may take place and have to be quelled (réprimé)
slaughter	massacre, carnage	indiscriminate / mass / wholesale slaughter (systématique) may be carried out - the slaughter (hécatombe) on the roads at week-ends

Violence, danger, disasters, accidents, humanitarian aid

■ *Adjectifs*

aggressive [-'---]	agressif	**evil**	mauvais (action, projet)
barbarous ['---]	barbare, peu civilisé	**hostile (to sb)**	hostile (envers qqn)
barbaric [-'---]	barbare, cruel, de barbare	**Ramboesque**	digne de Rambo
blood-thirsty	assoiffé de sang	**outrageous** [-'---]	scandaleux, monstrueux
brutal	brutal, cruel	**riotous**	séditieux; déchaîné
brutish	de brute, bestial	**sadistic**	sadique
destructive	destructeur	**wicked** ['wɪkɪd]	foncièrement méchant, mauvais
evil ['i:vl]	malfaisant, malveillant (personne)		

Collocations

cruel	cruel	*cruel person / murderer / methods - to be cruel to sb - it is cruel (of sb) to do sth*	
wild	désordonné, déchaîné, incontrôlé fou, dingue	*wild crowd / attacks / youths / rioting - children may run wild (se déchaîner, faire les fous)* *to go wild with excitement*	

■ *Verbes*

let sb loose	lâcher, laisser sans contrôle	**quell (sb)**	réprimer (émeute); calmer (qqn)
execute ['---]	exécuter	**ransack**	saccager, mettre à sac
exploit	exploiter	**sack**	mettre à sac
exterminate	exterminer	**run amok**	se déchaîner (foule)
liquidate	liquider	**run riot**	devenir violent
massacre ['mæsəkə]	massacrer	**slaughter**	tuer sauvagement
loot / pillage ['pɪlɪdʒ]	piller	**slay**	tuer (lit.)
oppress	opprimer	**riot**	manifester avec violence, faire une émeute
persecute	persécuter		
put down / suppress	réprimer, étouffer (révolte)	**bash**	frapper, cogner

Exercices sur le chapitre 14 A (2)

1. Testez vos connaissances en traduisant les mots ci-dessous :

A / bloodshed - B / onslaught - C / bomb outrage - D / riot (n.) - E / slaughter (n.) - F / to loot
G / to put down - H / to quell

2. Complétez les amorces de phrases (A à F) par deux ou trois phrases numérotées de 1 à 13, de façon à constituer des séquences logiques (un point d'exclamation indique qu'il s'agit d'une séquence finale).

A / Several outrages were committed - B / He was known to have committed an act of appalling atrocity - C / When the bomb outrage occurred - D / Rioting broke out and - E / The slaughter of the vanquished was so - F / A riotous crowd may run wild

1. was quelled so mercilessly that - 2. and barbaric brutishness, but no one thought - 3. during the riots - 4. and the rioters' revolt may have to be put down firmly - 5. it sparked off another round of riots ! - 6. no one dared claim responsibility for it, - 7. sadistic and outrageous that - 8. that erupted after the young man was jailed ! - 9. one wondered how anyone could run amok to such an extent ! - 10. that he would one day massacre and exterminate a whole tribe ! - 11. so evil and wild was the terrorists' action ! - 12. but not by such brutish means, - 13. however evil the crowd's designs may have been !

3. People involved

■ *Noms*

abductor [-'--]	ravisseur	hooligan	vandale, hooligan, voyou
abuser [ə'bju:zə]	auteur de sévices	housebreaker	cambrioleur
assailant [-'--]	agresseur, assaillant	kidnapper ['---]	kidnappeur
attacker [-'--]	agresseur	mugger	agresseur
bandit	bandit	oppressor [-'--]	oppresseur
blackmailer	maître-chanteur	(sexual) pervert ['--]	pervers sexuel
brute	brute	rapist	violeur
bully ['bʊli] (boy)	dur, brute	vandal	vandale
burglar	cambrioleur	rioter	émeutier
child-killer	infanticide	ruffian	voyou, brute
child molester [-'--]	violeur d'enfant	sadist	sadique
cutthroat	assassin	torturer	tortionnaire
gangster	gangster	thug	casseur; gangster, voyou
gunman	bandit armé, terroriste	tough [tʌf]	dur
highwayman	voleur de grand chemin	trouble-maker	fauteur de troubles, perturbateur
hired killer	tueur à gages	trouble-shooter	expert, médiateur
hitman	tueur à gages		

4. Terrorism

■ *Noms*

bombing ['bɒmɪŋ]	attentat à la bombe	bomb disposal squad [skwɒd]	équipe de déminage
bomb attack on sb / sth [bɒm]	attentat à la bombe contre qqn / qch	highjacking	détournement
captive	captif, prisonnier	bomb scare	alerte à la bombe
explosion	explosion	terrorist outrage	attentat terroriste
car / letter / parcel bomb	voiture / lettre / paquet piégé(e)	bomb outrage	attentat au plastic, à la bombe
highjacker	pirate de l'air	retaliation (U)	représailles
detonator ['----]	détonateur	pirate	corsaire, pirate
firing mechanism	mécanisme de mise à feu	prisoner	prisonnier
bomb disposal [bɒm]	déminage	terrorist	terroriste
bomber ['bɒmə]	plastiqueur	time bomb	bombe à retardement
		saboteur [ˌsæbə'tɜ:]	saboteur

Collocations

ambush	embuscade	to be / lie in ambush for sb - to lay / set an ambush - to draw sb into / run into an ambush
blast GB [blɑ:st] / US [blæst]	explosion, souffle	sth / sb may set off (déclencher) a blast - to be killed by blast
bomb [bɒm]	bombe	to plant (déposer) / explode / detonate a bomb - a bomb may go off / explode

Violence, danger, disasters, accidents, humanitarian aid

hostage	otage		to take / seize hostages - to take / hold / keep sb hostage / sb as a hostage - to hold children hostage
ransom	rançon		to demand / pay a large / huge ransom - to hold sb to ransom (GB) / for ransom (US) (détenir en otage contre rançon)
sabotage (U) ['sæbətɑːʒ]	sabotage		to commit widespread sabotage / several acts of sabotage
terror	terreur		to engage in / resort to terror - to start a campaign of terror
terrorism (U)	terrorisme		to resort to / combat terrorism - to experience several acts of indiscriminate terrorism

■ *Verbes*

blast	détruire (par explosion)	go off	exploser; partir (coup)
blow up	faire sauter (un pont)	highjack	détourner (un avion)
burst	éclater, faire explosion	free / liberate	libérer
defuse	désamorcer	release [rɪ'liːs]	relâcher (un otage)
detonate ['---]	(faire) exploser	peter out	faire long feu
explode	(faire) exploser	claim responsibility [-,--'---] for a bombing	revendiquer un attentat

Collocations

blackmail	exercer un chantage sur	to blackmail sb / sb into doing sth	
terrorize	terroriser	to terrorize sb into doing sth	

Exercices sur le chapitre 14 A (3 et 4)

1. Testez vos connaissances en traduisant les mots ci-dessous :
A / abductor - B / abuser - C / ruffian - D / trouble-maker - E / trouble-shooter - F / bomb scare
G / retaliation

2. Traduisez en anglais :
A / Ils ont dû lui tendre une embuscade. B / Il a dû s'y précipiter et pourtant il a connu des actes de terrorisme auparavant. C / Il dirige l'équipe de déminage de la région depuis de nombreuses années. D / Les bombes à retardement n'ont pas de secret pour lui. E / Il n'est pas le genre à rester à regarder une bombe et attendre qu'elle explose. F / Il sait faire exploser une bombe ou la désamorcer. G / Mais être détenu en otage contre rançon, c'est nouveau pour lui. H / C'est la première fois qu'il est pris en otage. I / Peut-être vont-ils le relâcher ? J / Si c'est le cas, il se consacrera à la recherche des violeurs d'enfants, des cambrioleurs, des tueurs à gage et des casseurs ordinaires : il a du pain sur la planche !

5. Fire arms

■ *Noms*

ammunition (U) [,--'--]	munitions	stock	fût et crosse
barrel	canon (d'une arme à feu)	cartridge	cartouche; douille
breech	culasse	chamber ['tʃeɪmbə]	chambre
butt	crosse (de fusil)	cylinder ['sɪlɪndə]	barillet

front sight	guidon, mire	rear sight	hausse
firearm	arme à feu	rifle	fusil (rayé); carabine de chasse
weapon with a blade	arme blanche	safety catch	cran de sécurité
handgun	pistolet	machine gun [-'--]	mitrailleuse
handgun / knife	arme de poing	light machine gun	fusil-mitrailleur
hammer	chien (de fusil)	submachine gun	mitraillette
leadshot (U) ['ledʃɒt]	grenaille de plomb	shotgun	fusil de chasse
musket	mousqueton	sight	mire
pellet	(grain de) plomb	small arms	armes portatives, petites armes
pellet gun	fusil à plombs	trigger	détente, gâchette
magazine GB [,--'-] / US ['---]	magasin (d'un fusil); chargeur	trigger guard	sous-garde, pontet
		weapon (C)	arme
revolver [-'--]	révolver	muzzle	bouche, gueule
pistol	pistolet	hands up!	haut les mains!

Collocations

bore	calibre	to possess a 12-bore shotgun
bullet ['bʊlɪt]	balle	to shoot a bullet - a bullet may ricochet / lodge in sb's arm - to fire a volley (salve) of bullets - to be met by a hail (pluie) of bullets
gun	arme à feu (fusil, etc)	to load / unload a gun - to aim / point a gun at sb - to hold / turn / draw a gun on sb (menacer)
at gunpoint	à portée d'arme à feu	to have / hold sb at gunpoint (sous la menace d'une arme)
round	cartouche; salve	to have three rounds left - to fire a round of five shots (salve) - a round of ammunition (cartouche)
shot	coup, décharge	to take / have / fire a shot at sb / sth - to have four shots left (balles) - to hear a rifle shot
trigger	détente, gâchette	to press / pull / squeeze the trigger (appuyer) - to be quick / fast on the trigger (réagir vite) - to be trigger happy (avoir la gâchette facile)

■ Verbes

carry / tote a gun	porter une arme	disarm sb	désarmer qqn

Collocations

aim	viser	to aim a blow at sb - to aim a gun at sb - to aim at sth / sb
arm	armer	to arm sb / oneself with a weapon
discharge	décharger, faire partir (un coup), décocher, tirer	to discharge a gun / an arrow at sb / into sth - fifty rounds (coups) were discharged (tirés)
fire	tirer	to fire a shot (coup de feu) at sb - to fire a gun at sb (tirer un coup de feu) sur qqn)
shoot	tirer	a gun may shoot (off) six bullets - to shoot at sb - to be shot in the arm - sb's foot may be shot off / shot away in battle - to shoot sb (exécuter qqn) - to shoot sb (at) point-blank (range)

Exercices sur le chapitre 14 A (5)

1. Testez vos connaissances en traduisant les mots ci-dessous :
A / bore (n.) - B / shotgun - C / rifle - D / breech - E / pistolet - F / douille
G / canon (d'une arme à feu) - H / cran de sécurité

2. Traduisez en anglais :
A / Charger un fusil. B / Tenir quelqu'un sous la menace d'une arme. C / Une salve de 5 coups.
D / Appuyer sur la gâchette. E / Avoir la gâchette facile. F / Viser qqn avec un revolver.
G / Décocher une flèche. H / Tirer un coup de fusil sur qqn. I / Tirer sur quelqu'un à bout portant.

6. Deception, stealing, damaging people's property

Noms

abstraction	appropriation	fraud	escroquerie; fraude
belongings	affaires, possessions	hold-up	attaque à main armée
break-in	cambriolage, effraction	fake	faux; objet truqué
personal belongings	effets personnels	receiving	recel
burglary	cambriolage	possessions [pə'zeʃnz]	biens (personnels)
con	escroquerie	pickpocketing ['----]	vol à la tire
booty (U)	butin	raid	razzia; hold-up
mob	foule désordonnée	bank raid	braquage d'une banque
confidence ['---] trick	arnaque	swindle	escroquerie
double dealing	double jeu,	theft (U)	vol
embezzlement [-'---]	détournement de fonds	ram raiding	pillage de vitrine (défoncée à l'aide d'une voiture)
fabrication	invention, mensonge		
falsehood (C)	mensonge	raider	braqueur
falsehood (U)	caractère mensonger (de qch)	strife (U)	dissensions, conflits
forgery	faux; contrefaçon		

Collocations

arson (U)	incendie criminel	several cases of arson may be recorded in one and the same area - to be found guilty of arson - to suspect arson
damage (U) ['dæmɪdʒ]	dégâts, dommage	to do / cause great / extensive damage to sb's property - malicious damage (causé avec intention de nuire)
damages	dommages-intérêts	to award sb / claim damages over sth / for sth - the damages awarded were very high
deceit (U / C) [dɪ'siːt]	tromperie, duperie	to acquire the habit of deceit - to sue sb in tort for deceit (au civil, pour tromperie) - to expose sb's deceits
deceitfulness (U)	fausseté, duplicité	to show / display great deceitfulness
deception (U / C)	duperie, tromperie	to practise deliberate deception - credit card deceptions (fraude) - to obtain money by deception (moyens frauduleux) - to take a person away by force and deception (tromperie)
foul play (U) [faʊl]	malveillance, acte criminel	to suspect foul play

joyride (C)	balade en voiture (volée ou non)	*sb's car may be taken for a joyride and dumped* (abandonnée) *in the middle of nowhere - to go for / be out for a joyride*
offence (C) [-'-]	infraction, violation	*it is an offence to do sth - to commit / be charged* (inculpé, mis en examen) *with an offence*
property (U)	propriété, biens	*sth is sb's property / the property of sb - a man / woman of property* (qui du bien)
robbery (U / C)	vol	*to commit (a) robbery with violence* (coups et blessures) *- highway robbery* (brigandage) *- to be arrested on charges of armed robbery* (attaque à main armée) *- the number of robberies with entering and breaking* (vol avec effraction) *may be on the increase*
safe	coffre-fort	*to blow* (faire sauter) */ break into / crack* (forcer) *a safe*

Exercices sur le chapitre 14 A (6)

1. Testez vos connaissances en traduisant les mots ci-dessous :

A / abstraction - B / booty - C / embezzlement - D / ram raiding - E / confidence trick - F / fake
G / deceit - H / fabrication

2. Traduisez en anglais :

A / Être mis en examen pour infraction à la loi. B / Forcer un coffre. C / Commettre un vol avec effraction. D / Soupçonner qu'il s'agit d'un acte criminel. E / Enregistrer plusieurs cas d'incendies criminels. F / Faire preuve d'une grande duplicité. G / Provoquer des dégâts importants. H / Accorder des dommages-intérêts.

7. People involved

■ *Noms*

arsonist	pyromane	**possessor** [-'--]	possesseur (de qch)
con(vict)	taulard	**proprietor**	propriétaire
con artist	arnaqueur	**receiver**	recéleur
con man	escroc	**robber**	bandit, voleur
confidence man / trickster ['---]	escroc	**rogue**	coquin, gredin
		rumrunner	contrebandier (d'alcool)
confidence trick	escroquerie	**smuggler / runner**	contrebandier
crook	filou, escroc	**scoundrel** ['skaʊndrəl]	fripouille; crapule
ex-con	ancien taulard	**sharper**	filou; tricheur (professionnel aux cartes)
forger	faussaire		
fraud / fake	imposteur; simulateur	**swindler**	escroc
impostor [-'--]	imposteur	**thief**	voleur
looter	pillard	**trickster**	filou
owner	propriétaire	**trafficker**	trafiquant
pickpocket ['---]	voleur à la tire	**paperhanger**	passeur de faux billets / de chèques falsifiés
shoplifter	voleur à l'étalage	**villain** ['vɪlən]	vaurien, scélérat
plunderer	pillard	**rascal**	vaurien, fripon

Violence, danger, disasters, accidents, humanitarian aid 239

Collocations

threat	menace	*to issue / utter / make / carry out a(n) covert* (voilée) */ idle* (en l'air) *threat to do sth / that ... - sth may constitute a threat to sth / sb*	

■ *Adjectifs*

bogus	faux, bidon	forged	faux (documents)
counterfeit	faux (monnaie)	fraudulent	frauduleux
crooked ['krʊkɪd]	malhonnête	malicious	malveillant; délictueux
damaging ['---]	préjudiciable	untrue	inexact, faux, erroné
dishonest	malhonnête		

Collocations

deceptive [-'---]	trompeur	*deceptive impression / appearances / attitude*	
fake	faux, falsifié, truqué	*fake pictures / antiques / passport / suntan*	
false	faux	*false coin / report / rumour*	
	perfide, mensonger	*false friend / promise / witness / pretences* (prétextes fallacieux)	

■ *Verbes*

alter ['ɔːltə]	altérer (texte); falsifier (preuve)	plagiarize ['pleɪdʒəraɪz]	plagier
appropriate [ə'prəʊprɪeɪt]	s'approprier	plunder	piller
falsify ['fɔːlsɪfaɪ]	falsifier, truquer	raid	braquer (une banque)
belong to sb	appartenir à qqn	receive (stolen goods)	recéler (des marchandises volées)
burglarize / burgle	cambrioler, dévaliser		
embezzle [-'---]	détourner (des fonds)	rip sb off	arnaquer, escroquer qqn
gut	tout détruire (incendie); mettre à sac	ruin	abîmer considérablement
		scratch	rayer (une portière)
launder	blanchir (argent)	traffic in sth	faire le commerce ou le trafic de qqch
loot	piller, mettre à sac		
misappropriate	détourner (des fonds)	tamper with sth	trafiquer qch, dérégler qch, toucher à qch (sans permission)
make away / off with sth	se barrer avec qch		
own sth	posséder, être propriétaire de qch	thieve	voler
possess [pə'zes]	posséder (biens, qualité)	vandalize ['---]	saccager
hold	détenir	walk off with sth	barboter, faucher qch
fake	falsifier, contrefaire	wreck	détruire (par bombe); casser (meubles); bousiller, abîmer
possess oneself of sth	s'emparer de qch		
pillage ['pɪlɪdʒ]	piller, mettre à sac	break in (to a house)	entrer par effraction (dans une maison)
pinch	piquer, faucher		

Collocations

cheat	tricher, tromper	*to cheat (sb) at cards - to cheat on one's wife* (tromper) *- to cheat sb into doing sth* (persuader qqn, avec de fallacieux arguments, de faire qch)	
	escroquer, extorquer	*to cheat money out of sb / sb out of money / sb into doing sth* (amener qqn à faire qch en le trompant)	

con	escroquer, duper	*to claim to have been conned* - *to con sb into doing sth* (amener qqn à faire qch en l'abusant) - *to con sb out of their money*
damage ['dæmɪdʒ]	endommager, nuire à	*to badly damage sb's property* / *sb's reputation*
deceive	tromper	*to deceive sb (into doing sth)* - *to deceive oneself* (se faire illusion) - *to think that one's eyes are deceiving one* (ne pas croire ses yeux)
defraud	frauder, escroquer	*to defraud sb of sth* (priver indûment)
overcharge [ˌ--'-]	faire trop payer	*to overcharge sb for sth*
poach	braconner (terres)	*to poach for salmon* / *on sb's preserves*
rob	voler, dérober, dévaliser	*to rob sb of sth* - *sb may be robbed* (volé) / *a bank may be robbed* (braquée)
shatter	se fracasser, voler en éclats fracasser	*a cup* / *windscreen may shatter* *a stone may shatter a windscreen*
slash	lacérer, taillader	*to slash sb's face* / *car tires*
smuggle	passer en fraude, en contrebande	*to smuggle goods across a frontier* / *into* / *out of a country* / *past* / *through customs*
sting	estamper, avoir (qqn)	*to sting sb for ten pounds for sth* - *to have been stung* (s'être fait avoir)
steal	voler	*to steal sth from sb*
take sth away	emporter qch	*exhibits on show must not be taken away*
threaten	menacer	*to threaten to do sth* - *to threaten sb (with sth)* / *sb into doing sth*

Exercices sur le chapitre 14 A (7)

1. Testez vos connaissances en traduisant les mots ci-dessous :

A / ex-con - B / confidence man - C / plunderer - D / rogue - E / villain - F / crooked
G / malicious - H / to embezzle - I / to burgle - J / to wreck - K / plagier - L / piquer, faucher
M / blanchir (de l'argent) - N / braconner

2. Complétez chacune des amorces de phrases (A à F) par deux phrases (1 à 12), de façon à constituer des séquences logiques (un point d'exclamation indique qu'il s'agit d'une séquence finale).

A / He set up in business as a receiver - B / He devoted most of his time to dishonest activities - C / He wondered whether he should become an arsonist - D / He had a feeling he'd been stung by the shop owner - E / He cheated money out of ageing people - F / He used deceptive means

1. or a rumrunner, as he enjoyed setting houses on fire - 2. and took his revenge by slashing the man's car tires - 3. and kept forged documents and counterfeit money - 4. such as smuggling goods stolen from the customs warehouses - 5. by overcharging them for what they bought from him - 6. but was also fond of defrauding the Inland Revenue ! - 7. and shattering the shop's windows ! - 8. as all con artists do - 9. as well as goods from looted shops ! - 10. selling fake pictures to unsuspecting buyers ! - 11. back into the country of origin ! - 12. or threatening them into lending him huge sums of money !

Violence, danger, disasters, accidents, humanitarian aid 241

B. Danger

1. Escaping danger

■ *Noms*

guard	dispositif de sécurité, garde (sur une machine)	portent ['pɔːtent]	signe annonciateur
guard rail	rampe; glissière de sécurité	refugee [,--'-]	réfugié
haven ['heɪvn]	havre, abri, refuge	sheath [ʃiːθ]	fourreau, gaine (épée)
helmet	casque	survivor [-'--]	survivant
omen ['əʊmen]	augure, présage	warning	avertissement
		hilt / guard	garde (d'une épée)

Collocations

close call / close shave	situation délicate	*to have a close shave* (l'échapper belle) - *sth may be a close call* (il peut s'en falloir de peu)
escape	évasion, fuite	*to make one's escape* (s'échapper) *from a place - sb's successful escape attempt from danger - it may be narrow escape* (il peut s'en falloir de peu)
flight	fuite	*to take to flight* (s'enfuir) - *to put sb to flight*
guard	garde	*to stand guard over sb / sth - to be on one's guard - to put sb on his guard against sth / sb*
protection	protection	*to wear a helmet for protection against rock falls - to ask for police protection* (rapprochée) - *sth may give little / sufficient / insufficient protection against sth*
refuge (U) ['--]	refuge	*to give / provide refuge - to seek / take / find refuge from sth / from sb / in sth / in doing sth*
rescue (U) ['--]	secours	*rescue may come too late - to go / come to sb's rescue*
rescue (U / C)	sauvetage	*rescue (of sb) may sometimes be difficult - many rescues may be accomplished by one rescue squad* (équipe)
safety	sécurité	*to guarantee / assure / jeopardize* (mettre en danger) *sb's safety - to run / dive* (se jeter à terre) *for safety*
security [-'---]	sécurité, mesures de sécurité	*to assure / strengthen / tighten / compromise (sb's) security against sth - to do sth for security reasons*
shelter	abri, refuge	*to seek shelter from sth / sb - to give sb shelter - to provide shelter for sb*

■ *Adjectifs*

careful	prudent; soigneux	failsafe	à sûreté intégrée (dispositif); infaillible
careless	imprudent; négligent	ominous ['ɒmɪnəs]	de mauvaise augure
gentle	doux (méthode)	portentous [-'--]	de mauvais présage; lourd de conséquences
harmful	nocif, nuisible		
harmless	inoffensif	sure-fire	certain, infaillible (remède)
prudent	prudent	unharmed	indemne; intact
foolproof	infaillible (méthode); indétraquable, inderéglable	undamaged [-'--]	en bon état, intact (chose)
		unscathed [ʌn'skeɪðd]	sans une égratignure, indemne

Exercices sur le chapitre 14 B (1, jusqu'à unscathed)

1. Testez vos connaissances en traduisant les mots ci-dessous :
A / unharmed - B / unscathed - C / warning - D / close shave - E / shelter (n.)

2. Remplissez la grille en vous aidant des définitions proposées :

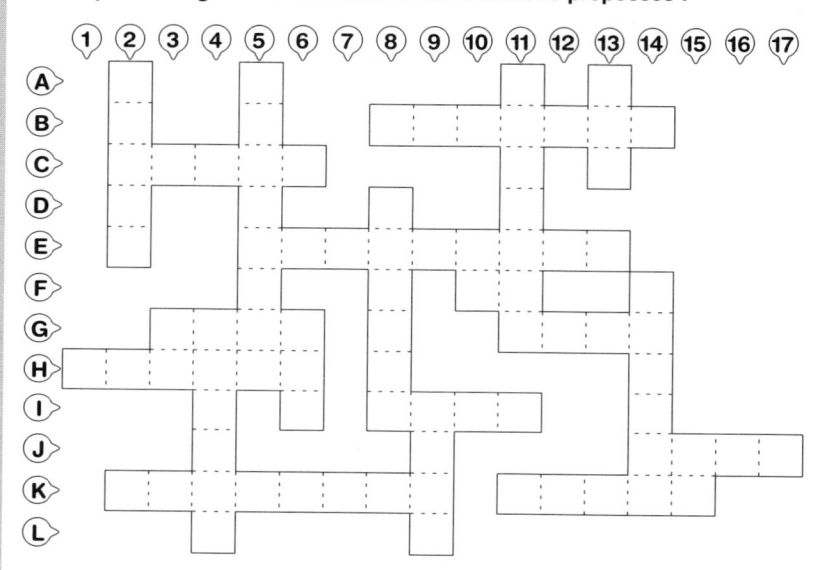

Horizontalement : B. Nocif, nuisible. C. Garde (sur une machine). E. Indétraquable. F. US (en français). G. + 13 = prudent, soigneux; sans danger. H. De mauvais présage (6 premières lettres). I. Dernières lettres de H. J. G + J = imprudent, négligent. K. A sûreté intégrée (dispositif); abri, refuge.

Verticalement : 2. 10 + 2 = réfugié. 3. Abréviation de 'creditor'. 4. Atteindre. 5. Infaillible (remède). 6. Abréviation de 'electronic news gathering'. 8. Fuite. 9. Augure, présage. 10. Voir 2. 11. De mauvais augure. 13. Voir G. 14. Doux. 15. in (en français).

3. Traduisez en anglais :
A / Mettre en danger la sécurité de quelqu'un. B / Chercher refuge contre quelque chose. C / Offrir une protection suffisante. D / L'échapper belle. E / Fournir un abri à quelqu'un.

Collocations

-proof	à l'épreuve de, à l'abri de, qui protège de	*bullet-proof / waterproof / soundproof / inflation-proof*
safe	hors de danger	*everybody may be reported safe after a crash - to arrive / survive sth safe and sound* (sain et sauf)
	sans risque, sans danger en sécurité	*a ladder may not be safe with sb - it is safe to do sth to be / feel safe with sb / on a ladder*
secure [sɪˈkjʊə]	solide, ferme, sûr	*secure place / position in a firm / mechanism - to check that a door is secure* (bien fermée)
	en sûreté, en sécurité tranquille, sans inquiétude	*sth may be secure from / against sth a child may need to feel emotionally secure*
-tight	hermétique, étanche	*airtight / watertight*

Violence, danger, disasters, accidents, humanitarian aid

■ *Adverbe*

safely	sans accident; sans risque, en toute sécurité	*to arrive home safely* (sain et sauf) - *to put sth away safely* (en lieu sûr)

■ *Verbes*

play safe	jouer la prudence	**survive sb / sth**	survivre à qch / à qqn
portend [pɔː'tend]	laisser augurer, annoncer		

Collocations

assure	assurer, promettre	*to assure sb of sth / sb that …*
avoid	éviter	*to avoid sth / doing sth / that …*
escape	échapper	*to escape death / detection / danger / being hurt - to escape from prison / from sb / from sb's hands*
ensure	(s')assurer, garantir	*to ensure sb sth / sb against sth / that …*
fight	combattre	*to fight disease / the enemy*
flee	fuir, s'enfuir se réfugier	*to flee before danger / from temptation* *to flee to another country*
guard	(se) garder, surveiller, mettre en garde	*to guard (sb) against sth / against doing sth / from harm*
protect [-'-]	protéger, empêcher	*to protect sb from / against sth / from being hurt / from doing sth wrong*
rescue ['--]	sauver, secourir	*to rescue sb from danger / from sure death*
save	sauver, empêcher	*to save sb from death / from drowning / from a fire*
shelter	abriter, protéger; recueillir	*to shelter the homeless - to shelter sb / oneself from the sun / from the rain / from the wind*
warn	avertir, prévenir, mettre en garde	*to warn sb not to do sth / sb against doing sth* (dissuader) *- to warn (sb) that …*

Exercices sur le chapitre 14 B (1, de -proof à la fin)

1. Testez vos connaissances en traduisant les mots ci-dessous :

A / to portend - B / secure (adj.) - C / to warn - D / to play safe

2. Traduisez en anglais :

A / Assurer à quelqu'un un traitement équitable. B / Combattre la maladie. C / Fuir devant le danger. D / Sauver quelqu'un d'une mort certaine. E / S'abriter de la pluie. F / Dissuader quelqu'un d'essayer de s'échapper de prison. G / Empêcher quelqu'un de se réfugier à l'étranger. H / Survivre à quelqu'un. I / Éviter de prendre des risques. J / Assurer quelqu'un de son aide. K / Se sentir en sécurité avec quelqu'un.

2. Facing danger

■ *Noms*

body	corps (d'un mort)	**poison**	poison
corpse	cadavre	**venom**	venin

snare	piège, traquenard	**wound** [wu:nd]	blessure, plaie (causée par une arme)
injury ['---]	blessure, lésion		
stampede [stæm'pi:d]	sauve-qui-peut, débandade		

Collocations

casualty (C) ['kæʒu̯əlti]	victime (mort ou blessé)	*there may be no casualties - casualties from / of the fighting may be treated in a nearby hospital*
danger (U / C)	danger	*sb's life may be in danger - sth may involve danger to life and limb* (danger mortel) *- there may be some danger* (risque) *that ... - sb may be a danger to society - to be aware of the dangers of mountain-climbing - to be out of danger*
emergency [-'---]	urgence	*in an emergency* (en cas d'urgence) *- a govenement may declare a state of emergency - to take emergency action* (mesures) *- to be rushed to casualty / emergency (US) / to the casualty / emergency department*
hazard ['hæzəd]	danger, risque	*sth may be a hazard to sb - a health / a fire hazard - sth may present certain hazards for sb*
jeopardy ['dʒepədi]	danger; péril	*sb's life / happiness / business may be in jeopardy - sth may put one's / sb's future in jeopardy*
panic	panique	*to get into a panic - to throw sb into a panic - to do sth in a mad panic - panic may set in / spread / subside - sth / sb may cause / spread panic - to feel panic at sth / at doing sth - to try to prevent / stop panic*
peril	péril, danger	*to do sth at one's peril - sb's life may be in peril - sb may stand in great peril of losing their life - to face / avert a peril*
pitfall	piège, écueil, danger	*to avoid / fall into a pitfall - sth may present many pitfalls for sb*
risk	risque	*to assume / face a risk - to take a calculated risk - to run the risk of impopularity / of being blamed - sth may be a risk to sb - it is a risk to do sth - to do sth at one's own risk / at the risk of being blamed*
toll	bilan, chiffres	*casualty toll* (nombre des victimes: morts et blessés) *- the accident toll on the roads - to try and reduce the death toll / the toll of lives* (pertes en vies humaines)
	conséquences graves	*war may take a heavy toll among the young men - sth may take its toll of sb's health / strength* (entamer)
victim	victime	*to be a victim of sth - to fall victim to sth*

■ *Adjectifs*

chancy	risqué, hasardeux	**ominous** ['ɒmɪnəs]	inquiétant, de mauvais augure
fatal ['feɪtl]	fatal, mortel	**noxious**	nocif; délétère (fumée)
harmful (to sb)	dangereux, nocif (pour qqn)	**perilous**	périlleux
hazardous ['hæzədəs]	risqué, hasardeux	**poisonous**	vénéneux; toxique, venimeux
injurious to sb's health [ɪn'dʒʊəri̯əs]	préjudiciable à la santé de qqn	**risky**	plein de risques, risqué
insecure [,--'-]	peu sûr (endroit); anxieux (personne)	**venomous** ['venəməs]	venimeux (serpent, insecte)

Collocations

dangerous	dangereux	*sth may be dangerous to / for sb - it is dangerous (for sb) to do sth / that ...*
unconscious	sans connaissance, évanoui	*to be / lie / become / be knocked unconscious*

Violence, danger, disasters, accidents, humanitarian aid 245

unsafe	dangereux, peu sûr		*unsafe machine / bridge / method - it is unsafe to do sth - to have unsafe sex* (relations non protégées)

■ *Verbes*

be in for it	risquer des ennuis	**hurt (sb)**	blesser, faire mal (à qqn); faire mal, être douloureux
chance it GB [tʃɑːns] / US [tʃæns]	riquer le coup	**injure** ['--]	blesser (accident)
endanger	compromettre, mettre en danger	**wound** [wuːnd]	blesser avec une arme
		jeopardize ['dʒepədaɪz]	compromettre (ses chances, ses relations)
imperil [ɪm'perəl]	mettre en péril, exposer (vie, fortune)	**poison**	empoisonner

Collocations

panic	paniquer		*to panic (sb) - to panic at sth - to panic sb into doing sth*
risk	risquer		*to risk one's life / one's health - to risk being hurt - to risk doing sth silly*
stampede [stæm'piːd]	(faire) fuir en désordre; amener qqn à faire qch sous l'effet de la panique		*a loud noise may stampede cattle - cattle may stampede for no apparent reason - sb may be stampeded into doing sth*

Exercices sur le chapitre 14 B (2)

1. Testez vos connaissances en traduisant les mots ci-dessous :

A / snare - B / pitfall - C / fatal - D / to stampede - E / risqué - F / toxique
G / peu sûr, dangereux - H / venin

2. Traduisez en anglais :

A / Quand l'homme fut amené aux urgences, il n'y avait aucun signe apparent de blessure par balles. B / Avait-il été blessé dans une bagarre ? C / Était-il victime d'un accident de la route ? D / Le nombre des victimes de la route ne diminue guère. E / Il ne menait pas une vie dangereuse. F / Il n'avait pas d'activité qu'on pouvait considérer comme nuisible à la santé. G / Il n'avait pas reçu de menace de mort inquiétante. H / Peut-être avait-il été empoisonné ou assommé ? I / Rien ne serait fait qui pourrait mettre sa vie en danger ou compromettre ses chances de guérison. J / Sa vie était sans aucun doute en danger. K / Mais rien ne peut affoler les médecins des urgences. L / La panique ne peut, en aucun cas, les amener à faire quelque chose qui soit risqué ou dangereux pour un malade.

C. Disasters

■ *Noms*

act of God	catastrophe naturelle	**freshet**	crue rapide, inondation brutale
fault	faille (géologique)	**spate**	crue (rivière)
fallout (U)	retombées (radioactives); répercussions	**cyclone** ['saɪkləʊn]	cyclone
		tornado [tɔː'neɪdəʊ]	tornade
flood plain [flʌd]	zone inondable	**storm belt**	zone des tempêtes
flood tide	marée haute	**tempest**	tempête

quake	séisme	**lava** (U) ['lɑːvə]	lave
tremor	secousse tellurique	**lava flow**	coulée de lave
amplitude	amplitude	**waterspout** ['wɔːtəspaʊt]	trombe
storm door / window	double porte / fenêtre (contre la tempête)	**twister** (US)	tornade
		whirl	tourbillonnement
thunderstorm	orage	**whirlwind**	tornade, trombe

Collocations

accident	accident	to have / meet with an accident - a bad / nasty / fatal / unforeseeable accident may occur / take place - some people are accident-prone - car / road accidents
disaster GB [dɪˈzɑːstə] / US [dɪˈzæstər]	désastre, catastrophe, sinistre	air / nuclear / natural / rail disaster - disaster may strike suddenly - too much rain may spell (constituer) disaster for plants - to happen to be on the scene of the disaster - a disaster area
catastrophe [kəˈtæstrəfi]	catastrophe	to suffer a major catastrophe - sth may be a catastrophe for sb - sb may be heading for catastrophe
earthquake	tremblement de terre	an earthquake may be light / devastating / may strike suddenly - some countries suffer serious earthquakes regularly - an earthquake of magnitude 7 on the Richter scale
flood [flʌd]	inondation	a bad flood may strike the houses by the river - a flood may rage / subside - a little stream may become a flood / rise to flood level - sb may have a flood in their cellar - a river in flood (en crue)
havoc (U)	ravages, dégâts	floods may create havoc - a storm may cause / wreak havoc on the gardens / make havoc of the gardens - a delay may play havoc with sb's plans (désorganiser)
hurricane GB [ˈhʌrikən] / US [ˈhɜːrəkeɪn]	ouragan	a violent hurricane may strike / hit several cities / may subside (se calmer) / blow itself out after a while
storm	tempête	a storm breaks / hits / strikes / rages / subsides / blows over (passe) - a storm of snow / rain - a hail / dust storm
volcano [vɒlˈkeɪnəʊ]	volcan	an active volcano may erupt at any time / be in a state of eruption / belch forth / spew forth / spout (out) (vomir, cracher) flames and a stream of lava that will cool and harden

■ *Adjectifs*

disastrous GB [dɪˈzɑːstrəs] / US [dɪˈzæstrəs]	désastreux	**hapless**	infortuné (victime); malheureux (amant)
catastrophic [ˌ--ˈ--]	catastrophique	**storm-lashed**	battu par la tempête
		untoward GB [ˌʌntəˈwɔːd] / US [ʌnˈtɔːrd]	fâcheux, malencontreux
direful	sinistre, menaçant		

Collocations

- bound	bloqué	to be snow- / storm-bound
dire	terrible, affreux	dire events / consequences - to be in dire straits (situation désespérée) / in dire need (besoin urgent) of sth
	sinistre	dire warning / predictions

■ *Verbes*

drown [draʊn]	(se) noyer; inonder	**hit**	frapper, toucher, affecter
flood [flʌd]	déborder; inonder	**erupt**	entrer / être en éruption

Violence, danger, disasters, accidents, humanitarian aid 247

howl [haʊl]	hurler (vent)	**submerge**	submerger
strike	frapper, se déclencher	**inundate** ['---]	inonder
roar	gronder (volcan)	**whirl**	(faire) tourbillonner, tournoyer
swamp [swɒmp]	inonder, submerger	**souse** [saʊs]	inonder d'eau

Collocations

beat	battre	*the rain may beat against the windows*
flood out	contraindre à partir	*people may be flooded out (of their houses)*
lash	battre, fouetter, cingler	*the sea may lash against the rocks - the rain / hailstones may lash (at / against) the windows / sb's face*
overflow [,--'-]	déborder, inonder, se répandre	*a river may overflow its banks* (sortir de son lit) / *overflow into the fields*

Exercices sur le chapitre 14 C

1. Testez vos connaissances en traduisant les mots ci-dessous :

A / direful - B / hapless - C / act of God - D / spate - E / waterspout - F / to overflow

2. Remplissez la grille en vous aidant des définitions proposées :

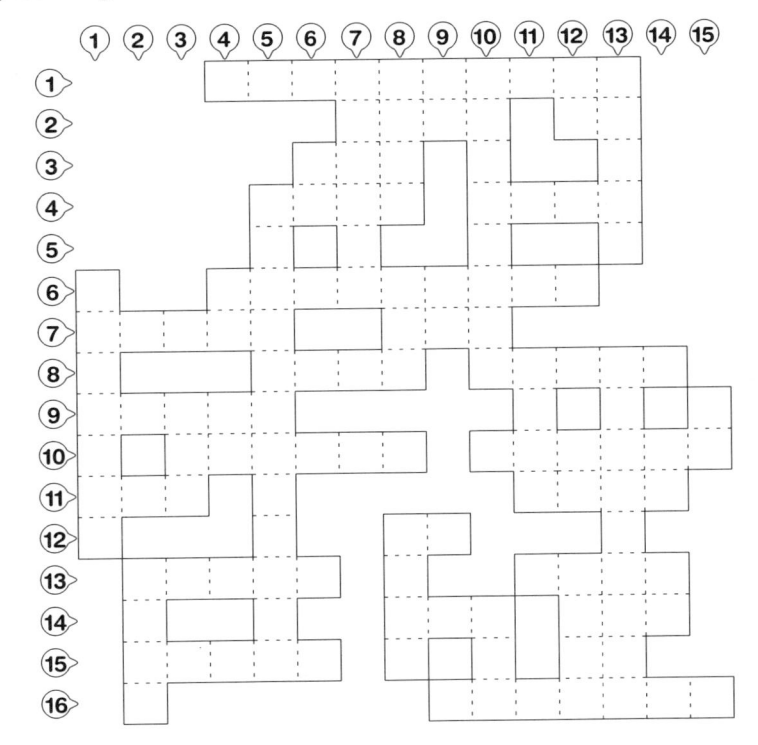

Across : 1. A sudden shaking of the earth's surface. 2. Water falling from the clouds; conjunction. 3. The ___ Office forecasts the weather. 4. Not wild (of an animal); fall in large quantities (rain) (jumbled). 6. Violent wind with a circular movement. 7. From Rome; exclamation. 8. Terrible; die by being under water and unable to breathe. 9. Make completely wet. 10. Hit sharply or forceful-

ly (of a tornade); disappear. 11. Long period of time; not frequent. 12. Hit hard (as if with a whip) (first two letters – see 15 down). 13. Widespread damage; the wind does this. 14. Small lorry; strike forcefully (of a tornado). 15. Make completely wet; not out. 16. Filled or covered with water.
Down : 1. Sudden flood. 2. Direct water onto fires, gardens, etc. 3. United States of America. 4. Exclamation (surprise); short for 'Saint'. 5. Storm of heavy rain and thunder. 6. Master of Arts. 7. Small earthquake. 8. Not love; very cold; comes out of a volcano. 9. Intelligence quotient (jumbled); company. 10. Unexpected and undesirable; nothing. 11. Deep loud continuing sound. 12. Knocked unconscious; not applicable; state in the Midwest of the USA. 13. (of a volcano) explode and pour out fire and lava; also called tornado or twister. 14. South East; low tension. 15. Last two letters of 12 across.

D. Accidents

1. Accidents in the home

■ *Verbes*

break	(se) casser	trickle	tomber, couler goutte à goutte
burst	éclater, sauter (chaudière, tuyau)	rend	déchirer (lit.)
chip	(s') ébrécher	poison oneself	s'empoisonner
bump / knock one's head against sth	se cogner la tête contre qch	nip one's finger	se pincer le doigt
		sharpen one's claws on sth	(chat) se faire les griffes sur qch
knock sth off a table	faire tomber qch d'une table	shatter	fracasser; voler en éclats
knock sth to the ground	faire tomber qch par terre	smash	(se) casser, (se) briser
boil over	déborder (lait)	spill	renverser, se répandre (sel, vin)
crack	fêler	splash	éclabousser
dash sth to pieces	casser qch en mille morceaux	splinter	se fendre en éclats (bois), se briser en éclats (os, verre)
fall	tomber		
cut oneself	se couper	scald [skɔ:ld] one's hand	s'ébouillanter, se brûler la main
cut one's finger	se couper le doigt		
gash sth	entailler; faire un grand accroc à qch, une entaille dans qch	snap	(se) casser avec un bruit sec
		knock over	renverser, faire tomber (tabouret, objet sur une table)
nick oneself / one's face	se couper (en se rasant, légèrement)		
		singe [sɪndʒ]	brûler légèrement (cheveux, chemise au repassage)
drop (sth)	(faire, laisser) tomber (qch)		
drip	goutter, couler (robinet)	scald [skɔ:ld] oneself	s'ébouillanter
dribble	(faire) couler, se répandre (accidentellement)	upset	renverser (table), répandre (tasse)

Collocations

burn	brûler	*to burn one's hand / oneself / a hole in one's coat with a cigarette*
	laisser brûler, attacher	*to burn meat / toast / milk*
	brûler, attacher	*potatoes / milk / toast / paper may burn, if you are not careful*
catch	pincer, (se) coincer, (s')accrocher	*to catch one's fingers / get one's fingers caught in the door - sb's dress may catch in the door*

Violence, danger, disasters, accidents, humanitarian aid 249

choke	s'étrangler	to choke on a fish bone - a baby may choke itself with a plastic bag
fall	tomber	sth / sb may fall (down) / fall flat - to let fall sth / let sth fall - to slip and fall over (par terre) - sth may fall out of a window and hurt sb passing down below - to fall off a chair
prick	piquer; faire un petit trou	to prick oneself / one's finger on a needle - to prick a hole in sth
rip	(se) déchirer, (se) fendre	your trousers may rip when you bend down - you may rip your tights on a nail
run	filer	stockings / tights may run - sb may inadvertently run a ladder in their stockings
	couler	butter / sb's make-up / colours may run
scorch	brûler légèrement, roussir	sb may scorch a shirt ironing it - your clothes may scorch if you stand too near the fire
scratch	griffer	the cat may scratch your arm - you may scratch your face with your fingernails
slip	glisser	to slip on a banana skin - sth may slip out of your hands / off the table and break
stick	enfoncer	to get a bone stuck in one's throat - to stick / run a needle into one's hand
tear [teə]	déchirer, faire un accroc à	to tear one's skirt - to tear a hole in one's trousers - to tear a muscle
	se déchirer	some materials (tissus) tear easily

Exercices sur le chapitre 14 D (1)

1. Testez vos connaissances en traduisant les verbes ci-dessous :

A / crack - B / dribble - C / trickle - D / upset - E / scald one's hand

2. Joignez une phrase de droite à chaque phrase de gauche :

1. The cat tried to scratch my arm
2. As you know, milk may burn
3. Don't knock over the glasses,
4. A bone got stuck in his throat
5. She stood too close to the fire and singed her skirt
6. She dropped the vase inadvertently;
7. She upset the cup
8. He did not just nick his face shaving,

A. she did not deliberately smash it to the ground.
B. and the tea spilled all over the table.
C. and on the very same day ran a ladder in her stockings.
D. he gashed his chin badly.
E. and he very nearly choked to death on it.
F. as they might shatter into pieces.
G. so don't burn it or I'll crack your skull !
H. and caught her tail in the door. Serves her right !

3. Traduisez en anglais :

A / Ébrécher une tasse. B / Se pincer le doigt. C / L'eau coulait goutte à goutte. D / Faire tomber qch par terre. E / S'ébouillanter. F / Brûler légèrement. G / Le lait déborde. H / Se cogner la tête. I / Se piquer le doigt.

2. Fire

■ *Noms*

blaze	incendie	ambulance ['---]	ambulance
conflagration [,--'--]	conflagration	ash	cendre
aerial tanker	Canadair	axe [æks]	hache

blast GB [blɑːst] / US [blæst]	souffle	fire house / hall / station	caserne de pompiers
fire alarm [-'-]	alarme d'incendie	fire warden ['wɔːdn]	responsable de la lutte anti-incendie
bunker suit / bunker clothes	tenue de pompier	fire watcher	guetteur
embers	braises	fire-suppressant foam	mousse ignifugée
fireboat	bateau-pompe	helmet	casque
fire appliance	voiture de pompiers, extincteur	full-face helmet	masque intégral
firebreak	coupe-feu, pare-feu (zone)	hand lamp	lampe portative
firebug / fire-raiser	pyromane	hatchet	hachette
fire door	porte coupe-feu	horn / siren	sirène (ambulance pompiers)
backfire (US)	contre-feu	hook ladder	échelle à crochets
fire trap	immeuble dangereux en cas d'incendie	oxygen mask GB [mɑːsk] / US [mæsk]	masque à oxygène
fire department	(brigade des) sapeurs pompiers	ladder	échelle
fire drill / practice	exercice d'évacuation	nozzle	jet, buse (d'un tuyau)
fire chief (US) / marshall	capitaine des pompiers	turntable ladder	grande échelle
fire hazard / risk	risque d'incendie	breathing apparatus [ˌæpəˈreɪtəs]	appareil respiratoire
fire escape	escalier de secours; échelle d'incendie	resuscitation	réanimation
fire exit	sortie de secours	mouth-to-mouth (resuscitation)	bouche-à-bouche
fire brigade [brɪˈgeɪd]	brigade des pompiers	stretcher	brancard
fire engine / truck	voiture de pompiers	flashing light	gyrophare
firemen / fire fighters	pompiers, soldats du feu	paramedic [ˌ--'--]	auxiliaire médical
fire sprinkler / extinguisher [-'---]	extincteur	plane drop	largage d'eau
fire hose / fire hosepipe	lance (à eau)	turnouts	tenue de pompiers
fire hydrant ['haɪdrənt] / plug (US)	bouche d'incendie	smoke	fumée
fireman's coat	blouson ignifuge	spark	étincelle

Collocations

fire	feu, incendie	a house may catch fire / be on fire / be damaged in a fire / by fire - fire may break out suddenly - to set sth on fire / set fire to sth - to control (maîtriser) / put out a fire	
horn / siren	sirène	fire engines may sound their horns - ambulance sirens scream	
wreckage (U) ['rekɪdʒ]	décombres	sb may have to be cut free from the wreckage (désincarcéré) / hauled clear of the wreckage (extrait)	

■ *Adjectifs*

blazing	en flammes, embrasé	non flamable / non inflamable	ininflammable
burning	en feu	flamable / inflamable	inflammable
charred	carbonisé		
fireproof	ignifuge		

■ *Verbes*

blaze	flamber	burn down	réduire, être réduit en cendres
burn	brûler	control [-'-]	maîtriser

Violence, danger, disasters, accidents, humanitarian aid 251

drop	larguer (de l'eau)	**put out**	éteindre (incendie)
extinguish [-'--]	éteindre	**quench**	éteindre (flammes)
fan	attiser (vent)	**smoke**	fumer
flame up	flamber, reprendre	**spread**	(se) propager
get out of hand	ne plus pouvoir être maîtrisé	**be burnt to death**	mourir dans les flammes
melt	fondre		

Exercices sur le chapitre 14 D (2)

1. Testez vos connaissances en traduisant les mots ci-dessous :

A / fire hydrant - B / turntable ladder - C / paramedic - D / firebug - E / wreckage - F / to put out G / to quench - H / bunker suit

2. Traduisez en anglais :

A / Se déclarer (incendie). B / Prendre feu. C / Désincarcérer quelqu'un. D / Mettre feu à une maison. E / Faire marcher sa sirène (voiture de pompiers).

3. Choisissez le mot qui convient :

A / The firemen tried to *drop / control / melt* the fire. B / The *blazing / charred / fireproof* factory could be seen miles away. C / The wind *smoked / controlled / fanned* the forest fire. D / The *house / two men / blast was / were* burnt to death. E / The church was *got out of hand / put out / burnt down* by the worst *horn / nozzle / blaze* in many years.

3. Rail accidents

■ *Noms*

rail / railway accident	accident de chemin de fer	**signal** ['sɪgnl] **failure**	panne du système de signalisation
derailment	déraillement		
collision	collision	**signal** ['sɪgnl] **box**	poste d'aiguillage
track	voie	**alarm** [-'-] **signal**	signal d'alarme

Collocations

rail	train, chemin de fer	*to be in a rail accident - to travel / send sth by rail - strike action may cause the disruption of rail communications*
rail	rail	*a train may leave / come off the rails*

■ *Verbes*

collide (with) [kə'laɪd]	entrer en collision (avec), se tamponner	**be derailed**	dérailler
		bump into sth	tamponner / rentrer dans qch
bump	heurter, tamponner	**leave the metals**	quitter les rails
derail	fairer dérailler		

Collocations

report	signaler, indiquer	*five people are reported (seriously) injured / dead / killed instantly* (sur le coup) */ missing* (porté disparu)
run / plough [plaʊ] **into sth**	se jeter contre, heurter	*the engine may run into the bumpers (US) / buffers (GB) - it may plough into the platform*

4. Road accidents

■ Noms

road accident	accident de la route	**crumple zones**	zones déformables
bumper bender / fender bender (US)	accrochage, tôle froissée	**speed**	vitesse
black spot	point noir	**speed limit**	limitation de vitesse
blow-out	éclatement (pneu)	**right of way**	priorité
hairpin bend / curve (US)	virage en épingle à cheveux	**emergency blinkers**	feux de détresse
flat	crevaison	**write-off**	épave bonne pour la casse
head-on collision	collision de plein fouet	**toll**	bilan, chiffres (des accidents)
build-up	bouchon	**hydroplaning**	aquaplanage
pileup	carambolage	**hit and run driver**	chauffard (coupable du délit de fuite)
dent	bosse		
jam	embouteillage	**roadhog**	chauffard, mauvais conducteur

Collocation

wreck	épave	*a car may be a wreck after a bad crash*

■ Adjectifs

fogbound	noyé dans le brouillard	**safe**	sûr, sans riques (route)
snowbound	enneigé	**safe and sound**	sain et sauf
twisted	tordu	**thrown out of a car**	éjecté d'une voiture
marooned / stranded [mə'ru:nd]	bloqué	**unsafe**	dangereux
		thrown against sth	projeté
icy	verglacé	**wrecked** [rekt]	gravement accidenté
reckless	imprudent	**damaged**	endommagé
slippery	glissant	**torn off**	arraché
unharmed / unhurt / unscathed [ʌn'skeɪðd]	indemne	**dented**	cabossé, bosselé (carrosserie)

■ Verbes

blow out	éclater (pneu)	**crash**	avoir un accident
bump into sth	heurter qch	**crash one's car**	emboutir sa voiture
burst	crever, éclater	**crash into sth**	percuter qch
claim many lives	faire beaucoup de victimes	**crumple**	se déformer (tôle)
collide (with)	entrer en collision (avec)	**free**	désincarcérer

Violence, danger, disasters, accidents, humanitarian aid

give way (to sb)	céder le passage (à qqn), laisser passer	swerve	faire une embardée
exceed	dépasser (vitesse autorisée)	rescue ['--]	secourir
hit a wall	entrer dans un mur	save sb	sauver qqn
knock sb down	heurter, renverser qqn	run into sth	entrer dans qch
roll over	faire un tonneau	cut in (on sb)	faire une queue de poisson (à qqn)
overturn [,--'-]	se retourner	grit the roads	sabler les routes
run sb down / knock sb over	renverser qqn	spin round	faire un tête-à-queue
		fishtail	chasser, déraper
run over sb / sb over	écraser qqn	drive under the influence	conduire en état d'ivresse
skid	déraper		
somersault ['sʌməsɔːlt]	faire un tonneau	write a car off / total a car	bousiller une voiture, réduire à l'état d'épave
speed along	rouler à vive allure		

Collocations

have	avoir (qch qui vous arrive)	*to have an accident / a crash / a flat (tyre) / a blow-out* (un pneu qui éclate) */ right of way / a puncture* (crevaison)

Exercices sur le chapitre 14 D (3 et 4)

1. Testez vos connaissances en traduisant les mots ci-dessous :

A / to skid - B / crumple zones (of a car) - C / dented - D / to grit the roads - E / fender-bender F / track - G / signal box - H / to leave the metals

2. Choisissez le mot qui convient :

A / The accident *rescued / claimed / rolled over* many lives. B / The car *drove under the influence / blew out / rolled over*. C / The front of the car *crumpled / freed / exceeded* when it *bumped into / saved / ran down* the tree. D / The *twisted / fogbound / reckless* driver was *collided / freed / skidded* from the *wrecked / snowbound / icy* car *unharmed / unsafe / slippery*.

3. Retrouvez les mots en retranchant (–), ajoutant (+) ou changeant (C) une lettre (ou plusieurs) ou en changeant un mot entier (CM) :

A / cattail (v.) (CM) - B / spine (–1) round - C / serve (v.) (+1) - D / rump into (C) - E / cash into (+1) - F / run sb up (CM) - G / give away (–1) to - H / write a car on (CM) - I / hot (v.) a well (CC) - J / jim (C) - K / roadpig (CM) - L / piledown (CM)

5. Accidents in the air

■ *Noms*

air disaster	catastrophe aérienne	near miss	quasi-collision
crash	accident	emergency chute [ʃuːt]	tobogan d'évacuation
crash landing	atterrissage forcé	oxygen mask GB [mɑːsk] / US [mæsk]	masque à oxygène
emergency [-'---] landing	atterrissage forcé		
belly landing	atterrissage sur le ventre	crash team	équipe du service des urgences
mechanical [-'---] failure	panne mécanique		

wreckage ['rekɪdʒ]	épave, restes	*to free sb from the wreckage* (désincarcérer)	

■ Adjectifs / Adverbes

be airborne	avoir décollé	midair	en plein vol, en plein ciel

■ Verbes

catch fire	prendre feu	overturn [,--'-]	capoter
crash land	se poser en catastrophe	spin down / go into a spin	tomber en vrillant
depressurize [diː'preʃəraɪz]	dépressuriser	tailspin	tomber en chute libre
disintegrate [-'---]	se désintégrer	stall [stɔːl]	être en perte de vitesse
evacuate [-'---]	évacuer	stray away from one's route	dévier de l'itinéraire prévu
hedgehog	faire du rase-mottes		
nosedive	descendre en piqué		

Collocations

crash	s'écraser	*a plane may crash - a pilot may crash his plane* (s'écraser au sol)	
fly	voler, se déplacer en avion	*to be fond of flying - to fly from Paris to London / back home / back from New York*	
	piloter	*to be able to fly a plane*	
	transporter par avion	*to fly passengers and goods - to fly in food supplies - to fly out flooded people*	

6. Accidents at sea

■ Noms

buoy GB [bɔɪ] / US ['buː i]	bouée	life preserver	gilet de sauvetage
helicopter ['----]	hélicoptère	life jacket	gilet, ceinture de sauvetage
lifeboat	canot, chaloupe de sauvetage	winch	treuil
lifebelt / lifebuoy	bouée de sauvetage	(ship)wreck	épave

Collocation

shipwreck	naufrage	*to experience (a) shipwreck*	

■ Adjectifs

marooned [mə'ruːnd]	abandonné (sur une île déserte)	stranded	échoué (navire, personnes)
ship-wrecked	naufragé (personne, navire)	wrecked [rekt]	naufragé, échoué (navire)
lost with all hands	perdu corps et biens		

■ Verbes

capsize	(faire) chavirer	overturn [,--'-]	se retourner
keel over	(faire) chavirer	run aground	s'échouer
drown [draʊn]	se noyer	sink	couler
fall overboard	tomber par dessus bord	lower the boats	mettre les canots à la mer

Violence, danger, disasters, accidents, humanitarian aid 255

take to the boats	mettre les canots à la mer, évacuer le navire	**leak**	faire eau
upset	(faire) chavirer	**spring a leak**	commencer à faire eau

Collocations

winch (up or down)	monter ou descendre au treuil	*to winch sb up / out of the water / (down) to safety / (up) into a helicopter* (hélitreuiller)	

Exercices sur le chapitre 14 D (5 et 6)

1. Testez vos connaissances en traduisant les mots ci-dessous :

A / to nosedive - B / to spin down - C / mechanical failure - D / near miss - E / crash team F / winch - G / to sink - H / marooned

2. Traduisez en anglais :

A / Piloter un avion. B / Transporter des voyageurs par avion. C / Faire du rase-mottes. D / Être victime d'un naufrage. E / Désincarcérer quelqu'un. F / Tomber en chute libre. G / Hélitreuiller quelqu'un. H / Faire eau. I / S'échouer. J / Chavirer.

E. Humanitarian aid

1. General

■ *Noms*

airlift	pont aérien	**displaced persons**	personnes déplacées
non-governmental [,---'--] agency	agence, organisation non-gouvernementale	**shipment**	envoi (de vivres)
		subsistence [-'--] **crops**	cultures vivrières de base
assistance [-'--]	assistance	**interference** [,--'--]	ingérence
fund-raising	collecte de fonds	**debtor** ['detə]	débiteur
charitable organisation / charity	organisation caritative	**creditor**	créancier
		recipient [-'---]	bénéficiaire
funding	financement	**misuse of aid**	détournement de fonds
donor ['dəunə]	donateur	**VSO (Voluntary Service Overseas)**	coopération technique à l'étranger
contributor [-'---]	participant (pays)		
calamity [-'---]	calamité	**Peace Corps**	organisation américaine d'aide aux pays en voie de développement
contribution	participation		
plague	fléau; peste		
curse	malédiction	**cooperation**	coopération
scourge [skɜːdʒ]	fléau	**volunteer** [,--'-]	volontaire
refugee [,--'-]	réfugié	**voluntary** ['vɒləntəri] **worker**	bénévole

Collocations

aid [eɪd]	aide, secours	to *allocate* (répartir) / *appeal for* / *channel* (canaliser, diriger) / *dispatch* (expédier) / *grant* / *provide aid* - to run a sale / a show in aid of (au bénéfice de) sth
call for help	appel à l'aide	to respond to / answer calls for help
campaign [-'-]	campagne	to run (mener) / launch a vigorous campaign for / against sth
child labour	travail des enfants main-d'œuvre enfantine	child labour is frequent in poor countries to employ / exploit child labour
debt [det]	dette	to be in debt to sb for sth - to be / get out of debt - to get / run into debt - to contract / run up / collect / recover (recouvrer) / pay off / repay / settle (régler) / write off (passer aux profits et pertes) / cancel a debt
help	aide	to provide / call for help
investment (U / C)	investissement	to have / make large / sound (sain) investments in developing countries - to encourage / expect a return (rentabilité) on investment
project ['--]	projet	to conceive / launch / carry out / fund a public works project
scheme [skiːm]	projet (officiel) projet, plan (douteux)	to devise / think up a scheme to do sth to have a crazy / wild-eyed scheme for getting rich / to defraud the governement
subsistence [-'--]	subsistance, existence	to provide sb with means of subsistence - to live at subsistence level (avoir tout juste de quoi vivre)

■ *Adjectifs*

undeveloped [ˌ--'--]	non exploité (ressources)	**impoverished** [-'---]	appauvri
backward	peu avancé, arriéré	**needy**	nécessiteux
endemic [-'--]	endémique	**disadvantaged** GB [ˌdɪsəd'vɑːntɪdʒd] / US [ˌdɪsəd'væntɪdʒd]	défavorisé
scarce [skeəs]	peu abondant		
developing [-'---]	en voie de développement	**drought-plagued** / **plagued by drought** [draʊt]	victime de la sécheresse
less developed [-'--]	moins avancé		
underdeveloped [ˌ--'--]	sous-développé	**famine** ['fæmɪn] **stricken**	en proie à la famine
emerging	en voie d'émergence	**destitute**	sans ressources
indebted [ɪn'detɪd]	endetté	**uprooted**	déraciné
the Third World	le tiers-monde	**debt-ridden**	criblé de dettes

■ *Verbes*

airlift	évacuer / amener par pont aérien	**ferry**	acheminer (de façon fréquente ou régulière)
assist	assister, aider		
contribute [-'--]	apporter sa contribution	**industrialize** [-'----]	industrialiser
cooperate [-'---]	coopérer	**intervene** [ˌ--'-]	intervenir
distribute [-'--]	distribuer	**invest**	investir
divert GB [daɪ'vɜːt] / US [də'vɜːt]	détourner (l'aide)	**meddle in sth**	s'immiscer dans qch
		interfere in sth	s'ingérer dans qch
donate [-'-]	faire des dons	**supply sth**	fournir qch
drop supplies [-'-]	larguer des vivres	**supply sb with sth**	fournir qch à qqn
evacuate [-'---]	évacuer	**rescue** ['--] **sb**	secourir qqn
feed sb	nourrir qqn, donner à manger à qqn	**provide for sb**	subvenir aux besoins de qqn
		provide sb with sth	fournir qch à qqn

Violence, danger, disasters, accidents, humanitarian aid

relocate [,--'-]	reloger, installer ailleurs	**subsist on sth**	vivre de qch
resettle [-'---]	réinstaller; repeupler	**run out of sth**	être à court de qch, manquer de qch
displace	déplacer		
relieve sb	secourir qqn, venir en aide à qqn, au secours de qqn	**ship sth**	expédier qch
		campaign [-'-] **for sth**	faire campagne pour qch

Collocations

volunteer [,--'-]	être volontaire, proposer ses services	*to volunteer to do sth / for sth - to volunteer money to a fund - to volunteer help* (se porter volontaire)

Exercices sur le chapitre 14 E (1)

1. Testez vos connaissances en traduisant les mots ci-dessous :

A / plague - B / contributor - C / shipment - D / VSO - E / donor - F / fund-raising - G / destitute H / drought-plagued

2. Joignez une phrase de droite à chaque phrase de gauche :

1. They called for help
2. He ran a campaign against famine
3. Some countries have run into debt so heavily that
4. Creditors try to recover money
5. Somebody has devised a scheme to
6. He has thought up some wild-eyed scheme for
7. His job was to appeal for, channel and
8. He contributed to various charities of which he himself was managing director

A. from debtors who, it would appear, just can't get out of debt.
B. with donated money he diverted from the intended recipients.
C. and volunteered money to the famine relief fund.
D. allocate aid to indebted countries.
E. relieve and provide for needy people in impoverished areas.
F. they cannot pay off their creditors.
G. assisting and relocating those in need.
H. but nobody responded to their calls.

2. Desertification, deforestation and drought

■ *Noms*

desert ['dezət]	désert	pesticide ['pestɪsaɪd]	insecticide
desertification [-,---'--]	désertification	logging	abattage
deforestation [-,--'--]	déboisement	development area [-'----]	zone d'exploitation
the rain forest	forêt amazonienne	firewood	bois de chauffage
groundwater	nappe phréatique	warming trend	tendance au réchauffement
quick sands	sables mouvants	sensitive area	zone sensible
pest	insecte nuisible	timber	bois de construction
drinking water	eau potable	water carrier	bidon à eau
well	puits	water cart	voiture de marchand d'eau
tank lorry (GB) / truck (US)	camion-citerne (gas, pétrole)	watertank	réservoir d'eau
		water tower	château d'eau
water tank car / wagon	camion-/wagon-citerne (à eau)	waterworks	système hydraulique
water butt	citerne (à eau de pluie)	water supply [-'-]	approvisionnement en eau

Collocations

drought (U / C) [draʊt]	sécheresse	to endure / suffer (from) / experience (a) severe drought
water	eau	you can draw water from a well - you can boil / sterilize / purify / filter / distill / chlorinate (chlorer) water

■ Adjectifs

dry	sec	barren	aride, sec
dried-up	desséché	desolate ['desələt]	désolé
charred	calciné	parched	desséché (terre, récolte)
scorched	brûlé	waterless	dépourvu d'eau
bald [bɔːld]	dénudé (colline)	water-starved	privé d'eau
infertile [-'--]	stérile		

■ Verbes

axe	couper à la hache	ravage ['rævɪdʒ]	ravager
split	fendre	raze	raser
destroy	détruire	wipe out	anéantir (région, population)
devastate ['---]	dévaster, ravager	wither (away)	se dessécher (plante)
cut down	abattre	lumber	abattre
clear (land)	défricher	saw	scier
dig a well	creuser un puits	drive back	faire reculer (la forêt)
irrigate ['---]	irriguer	exhaust	épuiser (le sol)
erode	éroder	run dry	se tarir, être à sec
preserve	sauvegarder	scorch	dessécher (soleil)
reforest [-'--]	reboiser		

Exercices sur le chapitre 14 E (2)

1. Testez vos connaissances en traduisant les mots ci-dessous :

A / water butt - B / waterworks - C / water wagon - D / barren - E / parched - F / scorched
G / to saw - H / to wipe out

2. Traduisez en anglais :

A / Tirer de l'eau d'un puits. B / Faire bouillir, stériliser de l'eau. C / Chlorer l'eau. D / Subir une sécheresse importante. E / Abattre des arbres. F / Creuser un puits. G / Se tarir

3. Famine

■ Noms

famine ['fæmɪn] relief	secours à ceux qui meurent de faim	cash crops	cultures de rapport
		child labour (U)	travail des enfants
shortage of sth	pénurie de qch	rickets	rachitisme
lack of sth	manque de qch	deficiency	carence

Violence, danger, disasters, accidents, humanitarian aid   259

food (U)	nourriture	staple food	aliments de base
food (C)	aliment	mercy food	aide alimentaire humanitaire
food crops	cultures vivrières	infant mortality	mortalité infantile
food grains	céréales vivrières	malnutrition	malnutrition
foodstuffs	denrées alimentaires	food needs	besoins alimentaires
food supplies [-'-]	vivres	food relief [-'-]	aide alimentaire
food subsidy ['sʌbsədi]	subvention sur les denrées alimentaires	food shortage	pénurie alimentaire
		scarcity of sth	rareté de qch

Collocations

famine (U / C)	famine	*famine may strike a country / be rampant in that country / spread - people may experience / suffer from / die of (a) severe famine*
hunger (U)	faim	*to die of hunger - to satisfy one's hunger*
relief (U) [-'-]	secours	*to mount a relief operation - to send relief / a relief convoy - to start a relief fund - to fly in relief supplies*
starvation	inanition, manque de nourriture	*to face / be threatened by / die of starvation - to live at starvation level (être gravement sous-alimenté)*

■ *Adjectifs*

hungry	affamé	skinny	très maigre
ill-fed / ill-nourished	mal nourri	helpless	impuissant (à agir)
underfed	sous-alimenté	hopeless	désespéré
famine-ridden / -stricken	frappé par la famine	undernourished [ˌʌndəˈnʌrɪʃt]	sous-alimenté
waste	décharné		
with sunken cheeks	aux joues creuses		

■ *Verbes*

be / run short of sth	être / se trouver à court de qch	make do with sth	se contenter de qch
to run out of sth	manquer de qch	ration	rationner
go / do without sth	se passer de qch	be dependent on sth	dépendre de qch
dole out	distribuer (des rations)	ferry / ship sth	expédier, acheminer qch
be rampant	sévir		

Collocations

starve (sb)	être affamé, affamer (qqn)	*to starve for food / to death - to starve sb to death / sb into doing sth*

4. Overpopulation

■ *Noms*

census form	questionnaire (recensement)	family planning	planisme familial
birth rate	taux de natalité	life expectancy	espérance de vie
death rate	taux de mortalité	overpopulation	surpeuplement
fertility rate	taux de fécondité	birth control	contrôle des naissances
demography	démographie	contraceptive device [--]	procédé contraceptif

Collocations

census	recensement	*to conduct / take a census every ten years - to consult the figures at the last census*
population	population	*to survey* (faire une étude de) *the distribution* (répartition) */ figures* (statistiques) */ growth / density / increase of a particular population*

■ *Adjectifs*

demographic [ˌdeməˈgræfɪk]	démographique	**heavily / densely populated**	à forte densité de population
planned	planifié	**sparsely populated**	à faible densité de population
overpopulated [ˌ--ˈ----]	surpeuplé		

Exercices sur le chapitre 14 E (3 et 4)

1. Testez vos connaissances en traduisant les mots ci-dessous :

A / deficiency - B / staple food - C / scarcity - D / rickets - E / denrées alimentaires
F / pénurie de qqch - G / espérance de vie - H / affamer qqn - I / très maigre - J / mal nourri

2. Traduisez en anglais :

A / Envoyer des secours. B / Mourir d'inanition. C / Obliger quelqu'un, en le privant de nourriture, à faire quelque chose. D / Distribuer des denrées alimentaires pour subvenir (meet) aux besoins alimentaires de populations sous-alimentées. E / Région frappée par la famine. F / Faire remplir un questionnaire sur les procédés contraceptifs utilisés. G / Se contenter d'aliments de base. H / S'occuper des gens qui souffrent de la famine et des gens qui en meurent. I / Consulter les statistiques du dernier recensement. J / Se passer de nourriture.

15
Things and objects : shapes, surfaces, aspect and colours

1. Shape, volume, surface

■ *Noms*

highness	hauteur (valeur appréciative)	shortness	insuffisance de longueur (jupe)
height [haɪt]	hauteur (calculable)	sharpness	tranchant, pointe aiguë
length	longueur	steepness	abrupt, raideur (pente)
level	niveau	thickness	épaisseur
narrowness	étroitesse	thinness	minceur
unevenness [-'---]	inégalité, irrégularité	tightness	étroitesse (pantalon, robe)
roughness ['rʌfnəs]	inégalité, rugosité	evenness	caractère uni, égalité (surface)
roundness	rondeur	wideness	largeur (valeur appréciative)
roundedness	caractère arrondi (de qch)	outline	contour
shortness	petite taille, petitesse		
bend	coude; virage	cone	cône
bubble	bulle	point	pointe
bulge [bʌldʒ]	gonflement, renflement	fold [fəʊld]	pli (surface, tissu)
angle	angle	pleat [pliːt]	pli (jupe)
curve	courbe	square	carré
dent	entaille; bosse, bosselure	sphere	sphère
right angle	angle droit	triangle ['traɪæŋgl]	triangle
oblong ['ɒblɒŋ]	rectangle	swelling	gonflement; enflure
rectangle ['---]	rectangle	turn	tour (vis, écrou); virage, tournant
radius ['reɪdɪ‿əs]	rayon (d'un cercle)		
circle	cercle	loop	boucle; méandre
diameter [daɪ'æmɪtə]	diamètre	perpendicular [,--'---]	perpendiculaire
circumference [sə'kʌmᵖfr‿ən ᵗs]	circonférence	volume	volume

Collocations

breadth	largeur, étendue, ampleur	sth may be 10 feet in breadth - the breadth of sb's learning / support - breadth of mind (ouverture d'esprit)
broadness	largeur, étendue (valeur appréciative)	the broadness of sb's humour / point of view / of a road / river
depth	profondeur	depth of a well / river / cupboard - a river thirty feet in depth
form	forme	a church may be built in the form of a cross - an illness may take various forms - to learn the forms of irregular verbs / of plural nouns
shape	forme	sth may be a practical shape - an idea may slowly take shape in sb's mind - houses may come in all shapes and sizes - "What shape is it?"

surface ['sɜːfɪs]	surface	*a surface may be smooth / rough / uneven / plane - to measure / cover a surface - to bring sth to the surface*
width	largeur, étendue	*a garden may be six meters in width - to admire the width and depth of sb's knowledge*
	largeur, lé	*to buy four widths of curtain material*

■ *Adjectifs*

acute [-'-]	aigu (angle)
obtuse [əb'tjuːs]	obtus (angle)
bent	tordu (fil), courbé
broken	brisé (ligne)
	défoncé, raboteux (surface)
bulging	protubérant
circular ['---]	circulaire
crooked ['krʊkɪd]	irrégulier (ligne), tortueux, sinueux (chemin)
	courbé, crochu (nez, canne)
parallel (to) ['pærəlel]	parallèle (à)
concave [-'-]	concave
convex [-'-]	convexe
dotted	en pointillé (ligne)
cylindrical [-'---]	cylindrique
diagonal [daɪ'ægn̩əl]	diagonal
conical ['kɒnɪkl]	conique
dented	cabossé; entaillé
depressed	enfoncée (touche)
cubic	cubique
even	uni, plat, plan
flat	plat
hollow	creux
gentle	doux (pente)
level	d'un seul niveau, plan horizontal; rase (cuillérée)
leaning	penché (mur, tour)
jagged	irrégulier, déchiqueté (bord, déchirure, ligne, rochers)
indented	dentelé, découpé, échancré (bord, littoral)
notched	ébréché (lame); entaillé
pointed	pointu (couteau, nez, toit, crayon)
ragged ['rægɪd]	effiloché (poignet); déchiqueté (bord de page, rocher)
ridged	strié
rough [rʌf]	inégal, rugueux (surface)
uneven [-'--]	inégal, accidenté (terrain)

rugged ['rʌgɪd]	accidenté (paysage); rugueux (écorce); déchiqueté (colline)
smooth	lisse; à la surface égale ou unie
spiked	à pointe (casque)
oblong ['ɒblɒŋ]	oblong, allongé, rectangulaire
loose	ample, lâche, desserré
narrow	étroit
oval	ovale
round	rond
rounded	arrondi
shallow	peu profond
rolling ['rəʊlɪŋ]	onduleux (terrain)
sharp	brusque (tournant)
short / long	court / long
short / tall	petit (de taille) / grand
square	carré
spheric ['sferɪk]	sphérique
steep	à pic, abrupt (pente, falaise); raide, escarpé (escalier, route)
sheer	à pic, abrupt (falaise, rocher)
straight	droit (ligne)
swollen ['swəʊlən]	enflé
thick / thin	épais / mince
tight	étroit, serré, moulant
upright	droit, vertical
triangular [-'---]	triangulaire [-'--]
serrated	en dents de scie
wavy	ondulé (cheveux)
winding ['waɪndɪŋ]	sinueux (chemin)
meandering [mi'ænd̩ərɪŋ]	sinueux (rivière)
oblique [-'-]	oblique
sloping	incliné, en pente, penché (toit, écriture), tombantes (épaules)
slanting	en pente, incliné; bridés (yeux), oblique (pluie)

Things and objects : shapes, surfaces, aspect and colours

Exercices sur le chapitre 15 (1, jusqu'à slanting)

1. Testez vos connaissances en traduisant les mots ci-dessous :

A / pleat - B / outline - C / loop - D / bulging - E / inégal, rugueux - F / peu profond
G / à pic, abrupt - H / bridés (yeux) - I / droit, vertical - J / ébréché (lame)

2. Remplissez la grille, en vous aidant des équivalents en français proposés ci-dessous :

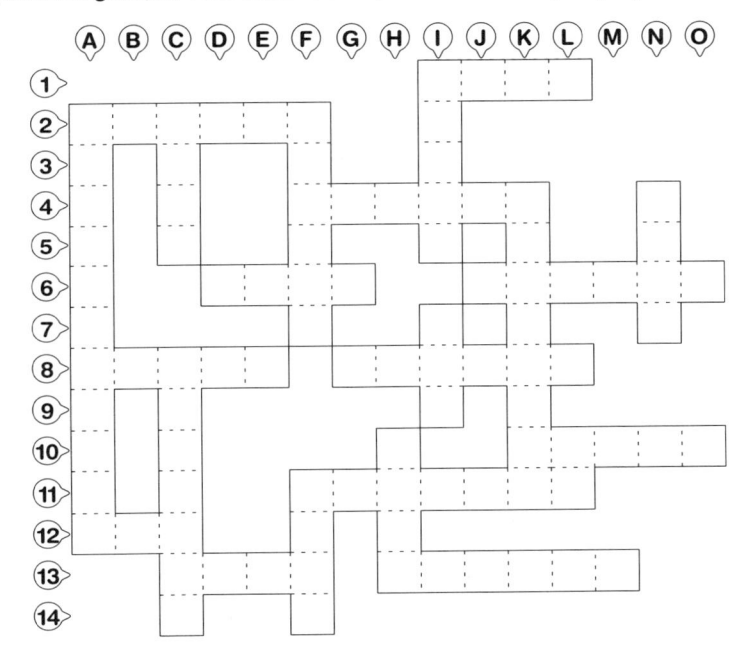

Horizontalement : 1. tordu, courbé - 2. rayon - 4. hauteur - 6. tourner; strié - 8. profondeur; oblong - 10. niveau - 11. crochu (nez) - 12. poser, placer - 13. uni, plat, plan; en pointillé

Verticalement : A. caractère arrondi (de qch) - C. entaille, bosse; pointu - F. sphère; cône - H. pli - I. gonflement, renflement; tout ou tous - K. triangle - L. abréviation de 'edited' - N. comme 13, 1re définition

3. Traduisez en anglais :

A / Avoir 10 pieds de largeur, de profondeur. B / Construit en forme de croix. C / L'étendue et la profondeur des connaissances de quelqu'un. D / Amener à la surface.

Collocations

broad	large, vaste, immense grand, général	broad road / ocean / expanse / smile / grin - to be broad-shouldered the broad outlines of a plan - in the broadest sense
deep	profond	deep hole / water / pond / sea / wound / voice - to be ankle-deep in mud - people may stand ten deep (sur dix rangs)
	large, profond, étendu	deep shelf / cupboard - a plot of ground 15 metres deep
high	haut	a building may be 40 metres high - "How high is that tower?"

tall	grand, de haute taille		*tall person* - *"How tall is he?"* - *"He is 6 feet tall."* - *to stand six feet tall* (faire deux mètres)	
	haut, grand, élancé		*tall chimney / mast / tree*	
wide	large (de bord à bord)		*wide river / table / gap / foot / nose*	
	large, grand, varié		*wide range / selection / experience / support / interests*	

■ *Verbes*

deepen	(s') approfondir	**tighten**	(se) tendre, serrer, resserrer
flatten	aplatir, aplanir (surface)	**straighten**	tendre, étendre (jambe)
lengthen	allonger		remettre droit, ajuster (cravate, vêtements)
sharpen	tailler (en pointe), aiguiser		
shorten	raccourcir	**straighten (out)**	devenir droit (route)
thicken	(s') épaissir	**straighten (up)**	se tenir droit

Collocations

broaden (out)	(s') élargir, (s')étendre, prendre ou donner de l'ampleur à qch		*a road may broaden at one point - travel broadens the mind - sth may broaden sb's horizon / a programme's appeal*
widen	(s') élargir		*to widen a road / discussion - sb's eyes - smile may widen*

bend	faire un coude, tourner	**outline sth**	tracer le contour de qch
bend	(se) courber; plier (genou, jambe)	**pivot** ['pɪvət]	(faire) pivoter
		revolve [rɪ'vɒlv]	tourner (autour d'un axe)
bow [baʊ]	courber (tête)	**ring**	cercler; encercler
bulge	se renfler, former saillie	**protrude** [-'-]	dépasser, faire saillie (rocher, gouttière)
curl	(faire) boucler (cheveux)		
circle	se déplacer en cercle; entourer d'un cercle	**rotate** [-'-]	(faire) tourner, pivoter
coil	(s') enrouler (corde)	**sag**	s'affaisser (toit); pendre (joues), être détendue (corde)
compass ['kʌmpəs]	entourer, faire le tour de qch	**stand out**	ressortir (veine)
curve	(se) courber (ligne, surface), être en courbe (route)	**steep**	(faire) tremper (linge)
	courber, cintrer	**stick out**	avancer (dents); dépasser (clou, mouchoir)
dilate [daɪ'leɪt]	(se) dilater		sortir (le bras)
distend	(se) distendre	**streamline sth**	donner à qch une forme aérodynamique
fold [fəʊld]	plier		
pleat	plisser (jupe)	**surround**	entourer; encercler (hostilité)
hollow (out)	creuser, évider	**swell (out)**	(se) gonfler, enfler
jut out	faire saillie, dépasser (balcon)	**whirl**	(faire) tournoyer (feuilles, danseurs)
loop	passer qch en boucle (corde)		
narrow (sth)	reduire la largeur de qch (route); devenir moins large	**swirl**	tourbillonner (rivière), emporter en tourbillonnant

Collocations

twist	tourner, être sinueux		*a path may twist (and turn)*
	tordre, tourner		*to twist sb's neck - to twist one's neck round - to twist sb's arm / a handle - to twist the lid off (sth) - to twist round to see sth*
	se tordre		*sb's face may twist with pain / in agony*
	entortiller		*to twist sth into sth else / round one's finger*

Things and objects : shapes, surfaces, aspect and colours 265

wind [waɪnd]	tourner		to wind a handle - to wind down (baisser) a car window
	enrouler		to wind wool into a ball / a bandage round sb's arm / a scarf round one's neck
	sinuer, serpenter		a path may wind through the woods
wind (up) [waɪnd]	remonter		to wind (up) a clock - to wind up a car window

■ *Adverbes*

tight / tightly	solidement, bien serré	to screw a nut up tight - to hold sth tight
wide	très, largement	to stand with one's legs wide apart - to open one's mouth wide (grand)

Exercices sur le chapitre 15 (1, de broad à la fin)

1. Testez vos connaissances en traduisant les mots ci-dessous :

A / broad - B / to hollow out - C / to sharpen - D / to streamline - E / to whirl

2. Joignez une phrase de droite à chaque phrase de gauche :

1. His face twisted with pain
2. People stood 10 feet deep to watch him
3. His eyes started swelling
4. He was told not to keep his mouth open
5. The road curved and wound through the woods
6. He liked the balcony that jutted out
7. She had her skirt lenthened last winter
8. She stuck her arm out of the car window as a sign for help

A. and his cheeks began to sag.
B. all the time and to straighten up in order to make a good impression.
C. but he did not like the protruding gutters.
D. then shortened in the spring.
E. while her husband twisted her neck ruthlessly.
F. as he was swirled away by the flooded river.
G. then straightened out in the plain.
H. loop the rope round the wild horse's neck.

2. What the surface may be like

■ *Noms*

blotch	tache, marbrure (peau); bouton	**scar**	cicatrice; balafre
dent	entaille (bois); bosse, bosselure (métal)	**scrape**	égratignure
		scratch	égratignure; éraflure (peinture)
flaw	défaut (marbre, bijou)	**slash**	entaille, taillade, balafre
fleck	moucheture (couleur) petite tache (soleil), particule (poussière)	**smudge**	légère tache, trainée (sur du papier ou du tissu)
		snick	petite entaille; encoche
gash	estafilade, balafre grande déchirure (tissu), accroc	**blot**	tache, pâté (encre)
graze	écorchure, éraflure	**patch**	tache (de couleur); plaque (verglas)
nick	encoche (bois); ébréchure (lame)	**smear** [smɪə]	tache, salissure, trainée (encre)
ray / beam	rayon (lumière, soleil)	**spot**	tache (peinture, sang); pois (robe); taveleure (fruit); bouton (peau)
notch	entaille, encoche; cran (ceinture); entaille, coupure (peau); ébréchure		
		stain	tache (graisse, sang)

splodge	tache, éclaboussure	streak	bande, raie (lumière); trace (sang, couleur dans les cheveux)
stripe	raie, rayure (robe, animal)		
sweep	grande courbe; voussure	dot	point; pois

■ *Adjectifs*

blotchy	marbré (peau, teint); couvert de taches, barbouillé (dessin)	piebald ['paɪbɔːld]	pie (cheval)
		chequered ['tʃekəd] / checkered (US)	à damiers
brindled ['brɪndld]	moucheté, tavelé	checked	à carreaux
dappled	tacheté, moucheté, pommelé	flecked (with)	moucheté, tacheté (de)
dotted (with)	(en) pointillé; parsemé de (points, villages, fleurs)	lined	réglé, à lignes (papier)
		lined (with)	(route) bordée (de)
varicoloured ['veərɪkʌləd]	multicolore; bigarré	unlined / unruled	uni, non réglé (papier)
mottled	tacheté; bigarré; pommelé; marbré (peau)	ruled	réglé, rayé (papier)
		sp(l)attered	éclaboussé
spangled	pailleté	variegated ['veərɪ‿əgeɪtɪd]	bigarré; diapré
specked	tacheté, tavelé	streaky	marbré; zébré; veiné
speckled	tacheté, tavelé	blotched	taché, couvert de taches
spotted (with)	tacheté; à pois; couvert de petites taches (de qch)	strewn with	jonché de
		pointed	pointu, en pointe (barbe)

Collocations

streaked	zébré, strié	*sky streaked with red* (zébré de bandes rouges) - *clothes streaked with mud* (maculés de longues traînées de boue)
striped	rayé, à raies	*striped garment* - *striped with red* (à raies rouges)

■ *Verbes*

blot	tacher, faire des pâtés, barbouiller	stain	tacher (de sang), souiller
		spot	tacher (de fruits, vin)
dab paint on	donner une petite touche de peinture à	gash	entailler, balafrer; déchirer
		slash	entailler (pneus); taillader
stipple	pointiller (à la peinture)	smudge	salir, maculer; laisser une trace
sprinkle	asperger; parsemer, éparpiller	dot (with)	pointiller, parsemer (de)
splodge / splotch	éclabousser, barbouiller, faire des taches (encre)		

Exercices sur le chapitre 15 (2)

1. Testez vos connaissances en traduisant les mots ci-dessous :

A / smudge - B / stain - C / patch - D / scratch - E / stripe - F / bande, raie (vêtements)
G / particule (poussière) - H / marbrure (peau)

2. Choisissez le mot qui convient le mieux :

A / He cut a *flaw / notch / flock* in the stick with a sharp knife. B / He was noticeable for his *variegated / dotted / mottled* skin and the large *gash / smear / smudge* he'd received in a fight long ago. C / He gazed out of the window at the *stippled / dappled / checked* sky above the trees.
D / He picked up an unpainted canvas and *slashed / splodged / gashed* it with ink.

Things and objects : shapes, surfaces, aspect and colours   267

3. Putting / getting together

■ Noms

ball	pelote (laine, ficelle)	tip	décharge (ordures); terril
batch	fournée (pain); groupe (gens); liasse (billets)	huddle	petit groupe (compact); tas, amas (livres)
bunch	grappe; bouquet; trousseau	kit	maquette; kit
bundle	paquet, ballot (vêtements); liasse; fagot	outfit	équipement; tenue
		pair	paire
clump	massif; bouquet (arbres); touffe (herbe)	posse ['pɒsi]	petite troupe (hum.)
		band	bande, troupe
cluster	(petit) groupe (gens, maisons); grappe (fruits)	gang	équipe (travailleurs)
		party	groupe (gens); équipe (travailleurs, secours)
bevy ['bevi]	essaim (jeunes filles); volée		
bank	rangée (avirons, ascenseurs, interrupteurs)	pile	pile, tas
		roll [rəʊl]	rouleau (papier); liasse (billets)
droves of	des foules de (gens)	stacks	rayonnages
flock	troupeau; volée (oiseaux)	pool	fonds commun; équipe (experts)
gaggle	troupeau (oies)		
herd	troupeau (bétail)	team	équipe (sport, recherche)
heap	tas, monceau, amas	string	rang (perles); chapelet (oignons); file (gens)
blend	mélange (calculé)		
mix	mélange (culinaire)	swarm [swɔːm]	essaim, nuée
medley	mélange; pot-pourri	crowd	foule
mixture	mélange; mixture	throng	foule, cohue
clutter	fouillis, encombrement	twist	tortillon, torsade (papier, fil)
muddle	pagaille, confusion	wad [wɒd]	tampon (d'ouate); chique (tabac)
tangle	enchevêtrement		
jumble	mélange, fouillis	stuff	truc(s), machin(s)
stack	tas, pile (papiers); meule; faisceau (armes); carnet (tickets)	row [rəʊ]	rang, rangée (maisons, sièges)
		set	série, jeu ; service (de table)
		tier [tɪə]	gradin (stade); étage (gâteau)

■ Adjectifs

crammed with	bourré de	miscellaneous [ˌmɪsə'leɪniəs]	divers

■ Verbes

blend	mélanger (thés, vins)	tangle	emmêler, entortiller, enchevêtrer
collect	accumuler; rassembler	jumble	mettre ensemble (sans soin)
mingle	(se) mélanger, (se) mêler	bundle up	mettre en paquet, en liasse
mix	(se) mélanger	cluster	se rassembler, se grouper
mix sth in with sth	mélanger qch à qch	crowd	venir en grand nombre
clutter up	mettre en désordre, encombrer	gang up / gang together	se mettre à plusieurs pour faire qch
muddle	mettre le fouillis, tout mélanger		
entangle [-'--]	emmêler; enchevêtrer	heap (up)	entasser, empiler
entwine [ɪn'twaɪn]	(s') entrelacer	pile	s'amonceler; empiler

gather (together)	(se) rassembler, (se) réunir	put together	mettre ensemble; assembler, monter
get together	(se) réunir (gens)	pour in / out	arriver, entrer / sortir en masse; se déverser
pair	appareiller; apparier		
pair off	mettre par paires	swarm in / out [swɔːm]	entrer, sortir en groupes compacts
pool	mettre en commun (ressources)	stack (up)	empiler; mettre en meule

Exercices sur le chapitre 15 (3)

1. Testez vos connaissances en traduisant les mots ci-dessous :

A / bundle - B / gaggle - C / muddle - D / stack - E / swarm - F / foule, cohue
G / équipe (de secours) - H / enchevêtrement

2. Indiquez quels groupes de mots de A à J vont avec les mots ou groupes de mots de 1 à 10; faites la même chose avec K à T et 11 à 20.

A. a clump of	1. stadium or a wedding cake.	K. a roll of	11. onions.
B. a row of	2. rubbish.	L. a pile of	12. toilet paper.
C. a tier in a	3. sightseers.	M. a wad of	13. different nationalities.
D. a twist of	4. Brazilian coffee.	N. a string of	14. beauties.
E. a tip of	5. reeds.	O. a medley of	15. wool.
F. droves of	6. sheep or geese.	P. a bevy of	16. houses.
G. a bunch of	7. seats.	Q. a ball of	17. new books in a shop.
H. a flock of	8. thread.	R. a jumble of	18. cottonwool.
I. a blend of	9. dirty clothes.	S. a cluster of	19. cattle or elephants.
J. a heap of	10. grapes.	T. a herd of	20. confused ideas.

4. Colours and aspect

4.1. General

■ *Noms*

blueness	bleu, aspect bleu	lightness	clarté
duskiness	teint foncé, mat, bistré; manque de lumière (pièce)	darkness	obscurité
		drabness	aspect terne, fadeur
brightness	brillant, éclat	paleness	paleur
hue	teinte, nuance	shabbiness	aspect élimé, rapé
redness	rougeur, rousseur (cheveux)	dinginess	obscurité (pièce); aspect minable, miteux
greenness	vert, couleur verte		
greyness	couleur grise, grisonnement (cheveux)	whiteness	blancheur
		dullness	manque d'éclat, caractère terne
gaudiness	couleurs voyantes, excessives (vêtements)	tan	bronzage, hâle

Things and objects : shapes, surfaces, aspect and colours

Collocations

blackness	couleur noire; noirceur; obscurité, ténèbres	the river's glistening blackness - to walk through deserted streets in the blackness
colour / color	couleur	sth may be a pleasant colour - to want a shirt in a different colour
shade	ombre nuance, ton	to sit in the shade - light and shade (les clairs et les ombres) sth may be several shades darker than sth else
shadow	ombre portée	to be scared of one's own shadow

■ Adjectifs

bright	clair (pièce); vif (couleur)
dark	sombre, noir, obscur foncé (couleur) brun (cheveux, peau)
deep	profond, intense (couleur)
ghastly	blafard; blême
light	clair (couleur)
pale	pale (couleur)
clear	clair, limpide; transparent
opaque [əʊˈpeɪk]	opaque
clearcut	net, précis (forme, contour)
dingy	lugubre, sombre; sale, minable, miteux
gaudy	voyant, criard
garish [ˈgeərɪʃ]	voyant, tape-à-l'œil
pied [paɪd]	bariolé, bigarré; pie (animal)
buff (coloured)	(couleur) chamois
dyed	teint

pitch black	noir comme du charbon noir comme dans un four
off-white	blanc cassé
pastel GB [ˈpæstl] / US [pæˈsteI]	pastel
shabby	élimé, rapé
showy	éclatant, voyant
coloured	coloré, colorié; en couleur (télévision); de couleur (personne)
drab	terne, fade
dull	terne, sans éclat
tan	marron, brun roux (chaussures)
swarthy [ˈswɔːði]	bistré, basané
tanned	hâlé, bronzé
tawny	fauve (pelage du lion)
fawn (brown)	fauve (feuilles d'automne, vêtement)
dun	brun foncé ou brun grisâtre (sol)

Collocations

-coloured	de couleur, aux couleurs	multi- / rose- / straw-coloured

■ Verbes

blacken	noircir, salir; s'assombrir
brighten	aviver (couleur); s'éclaircir
clear	(s') éclaircir (teint)
colour / color	colorer, colorier
darken	foncer, ternir; basaner; s'assombrir
deepen	s'approfondir (obscurité)

light	éclairer (pièce)
lighten	(s') éclaircir (couleur)
redden	rendre rouge, rougir
tan	brunir, bronzer, hâler
tint	teinter
whiten	blanchir

Collocations

dye	teindre	to dye sth black / a different colour

4.2. Specific

(*Remarque:* Les adjectifs suivis d'un astérisque sont aussi des noms, par exemple: grey : sth may be a lovely grey (d'un beau gris) - to want the same model in grey)

■ *Adjectifs*

ashen / ashy	couleur de cendre, plombé	navy-blue*	bleu marine
auburn* ['ɔːbən]	auburn	orange*	orange
black*	noir	pallid	blême, blafard (peau, visage)
blackish	noirâtre	pearl*	nacre
blue*	bleu	mother of pearl*	nacre
bluish	bleuâtre	pink*	rose (joues, papier)
beige* [beɪʒ]	beige	purple*	violet, pourpre
brown*	brun, marron	pinkish	rosâtre
brownish	tirant sur le brun	red*	rouge, vermeil (lèvres)
bronze*	(de) bronze	reddish	rougeâtre; qui tire sur le roux (cheveux)
grey* / gray* (US)	gris		
dusky	brunâtre (couleur), mat (teint), bistré; sombre (pièce)	rose*	couleur de rose
		rosy	rose, vermeil (teint)
ginger* ['dʒɪndʒə]	roux, rouquin	ruby*	couleur de rubis
gold*	or, couleur d'or	russet*	couleur feuille morte
golden	d'or, doré	salmon* ['sæmən]	couleur de saumon
buff*	chamois	sapphire* ['sæfaɪə]	couleur de saphir
flaxen	blond, de lin (cheveux)	scarlet*	rouge, écarlate
green*	vert	turquoise* ['tɜːkwɔɪz]	turquoise
greenish	verdâtre	ultramarine* [ˌ---'-]	outre-mer
jet black	noir comme jais	violet*	violet; couleur de violette
lavender* ['---]	lavande	wan [wɒn]	pâle, blême (teint, sourire)
lilac* ['laɪlək]	lilas	waxen ['wæksn]	cireux
lemon*	citron	white*	blanc
maroon [-'-]	bordeaux	whitish	blanchâtre
mauve* [məʊv]	mauve	yellow*	jaune

Collocations

crimson	cramoisi	*to go / turn crimson with anger / embarrassment*	

Exercices sur le chapitre 15 (4.1 et 4.2)

1. Testez vos connaissances en traduisant les mots ci-dessous :

A / wan - B / maroon - C / buff - D / waxen - E / tan (adj.) - F / teinte, nuance
G / grisonnement (cheveux) - H / manque d'éclat (d'une couleur)

2. Appariez les mots à gauche et les définitions à droite :

A / sth drab   1. is quite distinct from other things.
B / a deep colour   2. is one that is rather dark and depressing and looks dirty and dull.
C / a light colour   3. lacks brightness or colour and is cheerless.
D / sth clear-cut   4. is sth that looks old and in poor condition.

Things and objects : shapes, surfaces, aspect and colours

E / sth garish
F / sth shabby
G / sth dull
H / a dingy place
I / sth dun
J / a swarthy skin

5. lacks brightness.
6. is a pale colour.
7. is rather dark-coloured.
8. is sth bright and harsh, unpleasantly so.
9. is strong and fairly dark.
10. is sth of a dull pale-brown colour.

3. Traduisez en anglais :

A / Avoir peur de son ombre. B / S'asseoir à l'ombre. C / Vouloir quelque chose d'une couleur différente. D / Teindre quelque chose en noir, en une couleur différente. E / Des joues roses. F / Des joues couleur de rose. G / Des cheveux roux. H / Un teint pâle. I / Des boucles de cheveux couleur feuille morte. J / Un teint cireux. K / Des lèvres vermeilles. L / Une jupe bleu-marine. M / Une pièce sombre.

16
Things and objects : properties, state and condition

1. Kinds

■ *Noms*

blend	mélange (thé)	model	modèle
brand / brand name	marque (de fabrique)	sort	sorte, espèce
grade	qualité (marchandise)	species ['spi:ʃi:z] (pl. inv.)	espèce (surtout animale)
kind	genre, espèce	type	type, modèle

Collocations

make	marque (voiture)	*a car of French make* (fabrication)	
variety	variété, diversité	*a variety of noises* (un certain nombre) - *a variety of careers* (un grand choix)	

2. Characteristics - qualities and defects

■ *Noms*

blemish ['blemɪʃ]	imperfection; tache (fruit)	fragility	fragilité
defect ['--]	défaut, imperfection	hardness	dureté
deficiency [-'---]	manque, insuffisance	limpness	mollesse
failing	défaut (notoire)	malleability [,---'----]	malléabilité
fault	anomalie	plasticity	plasticité
flawlessness	perfection	pliability	souplesse, malléabilité
flaw	imperfection, crapaud (bijou, cristal)	rigidity	rigidité
		stiffness	raideur
quality ['kwɒləti]	qualité	suppleness	souplesse
firmness	fermeté	toughness ['tʌfnəs]	dureté
elasticity [,--'---]	élasticité		solidité, résistance
flexibility	flexibilité	delicacy ['----]	délicatesse
flakiness	friabilité	properties	propriétés

■ *Adjectifs*

breakable	cassable, fragile	defective	défectueux
brittle	cassant, fragile	disposable	jetable, à usage unique
crisp	croquant, croustillant	elastic	élastique
cumbersome ['kʌmbəsəm]	encombrant	even	uni, plat, plan
crumbly	friable (biscuits, pâte)	flawless	parfait, sans défaut
flaky	friable (peinture)	flexible	souple, flexible

flimsy	mince (papier); peu solide (maison)	prickly	piquant
floppy	lâche, flottant (vêtement)	rigid	rigide
delicate	délicat	plastic	plastique
firm	ferme	robust [rəʊ'bʌst]	solide, robuste (chaussures, voiture)
faulty	défectueux (appareil)	rough [rʌf]	rugueux, rêche
flawed	imparfait	smooth	lisse
fluffy	duveteux, soyeux (animal) en peluche (jouet)	soft	doux (tissu), moelleux (matelas); gras (crayon)
fragile GB ['frædʒaɪl] / US ['frædʒl]	fragile	solid	solide (corps); massif (or); pleins (pneus)
hard	dur	stiff	raide, rigide (papier); dur (poignée, tiroir)
heavy	lourd	strong	solide (toile, chaussures)
light	léger	supple	souple (cuir)
limp	mou, flasque	tough [tʌf]	solide, résistant (toile, vêtement)
malleable ['mæli‿əbl]	malléable		
pliable ['plaɪ‿əbl] / pliant	malléable, flexible (argile, caoutchouc)	weak	peu solide (structure) faible (café, lunettes)
hefty	lourd (colis); encombrant, gros	friable	friable
powerful	puissant (moteur)	hardwearing	résistant, solide (tissu)

■ *Verbes*

bend	se plier, être souple	rotate [rəʊ'teɪt]	tourner (Terre), pivoter
stiffen	se raidir	roll [rəʊl]	avancer, rouler (voiture); rouler (navire, roulis)
bounce	rebondir (ballon)		
contract [-'-]	(se) contracter (métal)	skid	déraper
dangle	pendiller, laisser pendre	soften	devenir mou (sol); (s') adoucir (couleur); (s') assouplir (cuir)
expand [ɪk'spænd]	(se) dilater (gaz, liquide)		
hang	pendre (rideaux), suspendre, accrocher	spin	tourner, tournoyer (objet suspendu); patiner (voiture)
harden	durcir, (s') affermir (substances)	flake (off)	s'écailler, s'effriter
		tilt	incliner, pencher, basculer (table)
rebound	rebondir (balle)	tip (over)	pencher, se renverser (bouteille)
recoil	se détendre (ressort)	wobble	être branlant (chaise)
revolve	tourner (autour d'un axe) (Terre, porte)	teeter	vaciller (pile)
		totter	chanceler, vaciller (cheminée)
rock	osciller (mât); trembler (sol); se balancer (navire)	toughen ['tʌfn]	(se) renforcer, rendre plus solide
		peel (off)	s'écailler (peinture)

Collocations

run	fonctionner	*a car may run on diesel* (marcher au diesel) - *a radio may run off the mains / off batteries*
	baver, couler	*colours / sb's make-up may run*
	couler, se répandre	*a tap may be left running - milk may run all over the floor*
	filer	*stockings may run*
slide	(faire) glisser, coulisser	*a drawer may slide in and out easily - a door may slide open - to slide a drawer into place*

Things and objects : properties, state and condition   275

Exercices sur le chapitre 16 (1 et 2)

1. Testez vos connaissances en traduisant les mots ci-dessous :

A / flaw - B / properties (of sth) - C / crisp - D / faulty - E / flawless - F / encombrant; lourd (colis)
G / lisse - H / raide, rigide

2. Remplissez la grille, en vous aidant des définitions proposées :

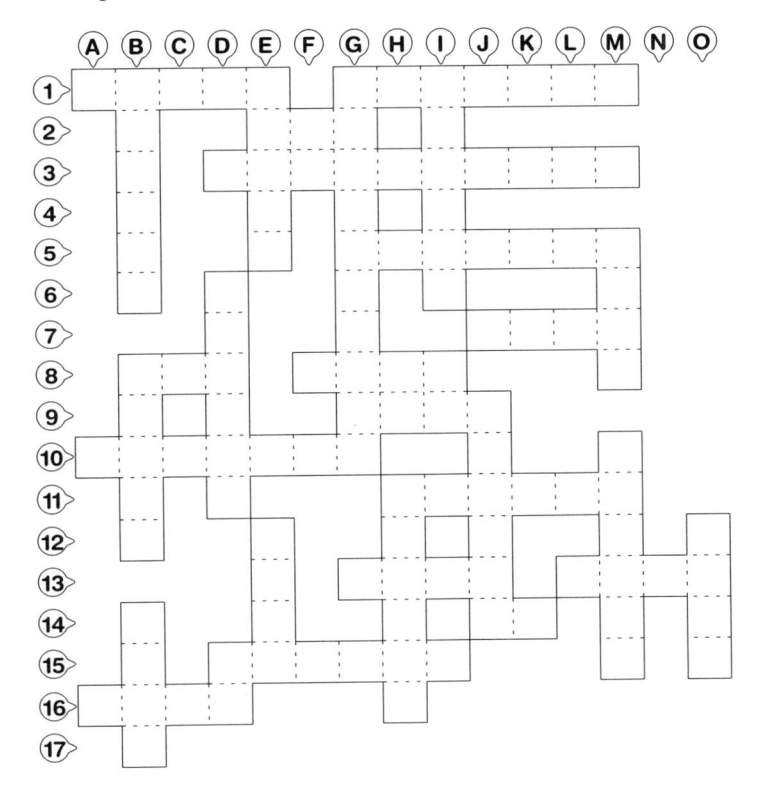

Horizontalement : 1. mélange (thé) (jumbled); piquant - 2. Trois premières lettres de 'rouler' - 3. Manque, insuffisance - 5. Imperfection, tache (fruit) - 7. Uni, plat, plan - 8. Pencher, se renverser; mou, flasque - 9. Incliner, basculer - 10. Qualité - 11. Tourner, pivoter - 13. Suffixe de B et de E; faible - 14. Deux premières lettres du verbe 'se détendre (ressort)' en anglais - 15. mince (papier) - 16. bouée

Verticalement : B / B + 13 : à jeter, usage unique; solide, résistant; B + D : duveteux, soyeux - D / Souple (cuir); voir B (3ᵉ définition) - E / E + 13 : cassable, fragile; voir 14 - F / Préposition - G / Souplesse, malléabilité - H / Note de musique aussi appelée 'E' en anglais; solide, robuste - I / Glaçon (naturel); abréviation de 'Place' - J / Chanceler, vaciller - M / Pendre (rideaux); vaciller (pile) (jumbled) - O / Déraper

3. Traduisez en anglais :

A / Marcher au gas-oil. B / Fonctionner sur le secteur. C / Une couleur peut baver. D / Le lait peut se répandre sur le sol. E / Remettre en place un tiroir. F / Un mât qui oscille. G / Un sol qui devient mou. H / Un ballon qui rebondit. I / Une peinture qui s'effrite.

3. Characteristics connected with air and liquids

■ Noms

bubble	bulle; boursouflure (peinture)	fluid	fluide, liquide
distillation	distillation	grease [gri:s]	graisse
solution	solution	liquid	liquide
evaporation	évaporation	lubricant ['lu:brɪkənt]	lubrifiant
fermentation	fermentation	oiliness	aspect huileux

■ Adjectifs

clammy	suitant (mur); moite (main)	slimy	visqueux, gluant; suitant (murs)
damp	humide		
dank	humide et froid (pièce)	slippery	glissant (sol)
greasy ['gri:si]	graisseux, gras (cheveux, substance)	soggy ['sɒgi]	détrempé (sol)
		sticky	poisseux, gluant
lukewarm	tiède (eau)	tepid ['tepɪd]	tiède (liquide) (péjoratif)
milky	laiteux	viscous	visqueux
soluble ['sɒljʊbl]	soluble	waterproof	étanche (tissu, montre)
oily	huileux (liquide)	watertight	étanche (porte, récipient)

■ Verbes

boil	bouillir	ripple	se rider (eau)
bubble	bouillonner	sail	voguer
distill	distiller	seep	suinter, filtrer
evaporate [-'---]	s'évaporer	shed	perdre (ses feuilles)
drain	s'écouler (liquide)	shoot	bourgeonner
dribble	couler lentement (liquides)	shower	tomber en abondance (grêlons)
drip	tomber goutte à goutte, goutter (robinet)	spill	se répandre (liquide, sel)
		splash	faire des éclaboussures
drift	aller à la dérive; être poussé par le vent	spout	jaillir, sortir en jet
		spray	vaporiser, se répandre (gouttes)
drop	(laisser) tomber goutte à goutte		
ebb	refluer (marée)	spring up	se lever brusquement (vent)
ferment	fermenter	spurt	jaillir (flamme, eau, sang); gicler
grease [gri:s]	graisser, lubrifier		
flap	battre (aile); claquer (volets)	splutter / sputter	cracher (plume); tousser (moteur); crépiter (bougie)
float	flotter (air, eau)		
flood [flʌd]	déborder, être en crue	squirt	jaillir, gicler
flow	couler; monter (marée)	stream	ruisseler, dégouliner (sang)
flutter	flotter (drapeau); voleter (oiseau); battre (ailes)	stream (out)	flotter au vent
		surge	(inondation) déferler; (vagues) s'enfler
gush	jaillir (liquide)		
hover ['hɒvə]	voltiger (papillon); planer (aigle)	sway	osciller (arbre, tour)
		swing	pendiller, se balancer (hamac, objet suspendu)
leak	fuir (robinet)		
ooze	suinter	swirl	tourbillonner (eau, poussière, fumée)
overflow [ˌ--'-]	déborder (rivière, baignoire)		

Things and objects : properties, state and condition

trickle	couler en un filet; tomber ou couler goutte à goutte	**wave**	flotter (au vent); s'agiter (branche); onduler (herbe)
waft [wɑːft]	flotter (odeur, son)	**whirl**	tournoyer, tourbillonner
well (out)	sourdre		

Collocations

blow — souffler (vent) — *a door may blow open* (s'ouvrir sous l'effet d'un coup de vent) - *a hat may blow away* - *the wind may blow a hat* (faire tomber) *off sb's head*

pour [pɔː] — couler à flots, se déverser — *water may pour down the walls* (ruisseler) - *smoke may pour from the chimney* (s'échapper)

Exercices sur le chapitre 16 (3)

1. Testez vos connaissances en traduisant les verbes ci-dessous :

A / seep - B / flow - C / gush - D / ooze - E / suinter, filtrer - F / bourgeonner - G / jaillir, gicler - H / osciller (tour, arbre)

2. Appariez un mot de gauche (A à J) et un verbe de droite (1 à 10) :

A. surface of water   1. boil   F. cork   6. hover
B. smell   2. ferment   G. tide   7. ripple
C. milk   3. ebb   H. wing   8. flood
D. wine / cider   4. float   I. eagle   9. splutter
E. river   5. flap   J. pen or candle   10. waft

3. Appariez les adjectifs (A à H) et les noms (1 à 8) :

A. slippery   1. water or coffee   E. slimy   5. hand
B. lukewarm   2. slug / wall   F. sticky   6. liquid / stain
C. soggy   3. room / clothes   G. damp   7. pavement / soap
D. oily   4. ground / clothes   H. clammy   8. substance / label

4. Traduisez en anglais :

A / Le vent ouvrit la porte. B / Le vent fit s'envoler son chapeau. C / L'eau ruisselait sur les murs. D / De la fumée s'échappait de la cheminée en abondance.

4. The condition things are in

■ *Noms*

devastation	dévastation	**hole**	trou
dirt	saleté, crasse	**tear** [teə]	déchirure
dirtiness	saleté (de qch / de qqn)	**rent**	déchirure, accroc
filth	saleté, crasse (lit.)	**mo(u)ld** [məʊld]	moisissure
filthiness	saleté, caractère dégoûtant (de qch)	**moisture**	humidité (herbe); buée
		muck (U)	saletés, crotte, gadoue
grime	crasse (couche épaisse)	**mustiness**	(goût, odeur de) moisi
litter (U)	détritus, papiers sales, (vieux) papiers	**rot**	pourriture

rubble (U)	décombres; gravats	squalor	conditions de vie misérables, sordides
rust	rouille	tarnish	ternissure; dédorage

Collocations

condition	état	to check the condition things are in - sth may be in good condition (en bon état) / in excellent / perfect / poor (médiocre) condition - to get used to the condition of weightlessness
decay [-'-]	délabrement, décrépitude	a house may fall into decay (tomber en ruines)
destruction (U)	destruction	a flood may cause great / complete destruction
mess	désordre, pagaille; saleté	children sometimes make a mess (mettre le désordre) - to make a mess of a new dress (salir; déchirer) - a house may be (in) a terrible mess (dans un état épouvantable)
repair [-'-]	réparation; état	sth may be under repair / beyond repair / in good / in bad repair
shambles	confusion, pagaille	sb's room may be (in) a shambles (champ de bataille)
squalor	caractère sordide, pauvreté, saleté (lieu, conditions de vie)	to live in conditions of squalor and deprivation in a dirty, damp, smelly flat - to live in squalor in a single room
state	état	to ask about the state of one's bank account - sth may be in a good / bad state of repair (bien / mal entretenu) - the deteriorating state of the country's roads

■ *Adjectifs*

battered ['bætəd]	délabré (maison); cabossé, bosselé (chapeau, voiture)	flat	éventé (bière)
bent	tordu (tuyau, fil)	fresh	frais (nourriture); non congelé, non en conserve
blocked	bouché, obstrué	fusty	qui sent le renfermé, le moisi
blunt	émoussé (lame, couteau)	frowsty (GB) ['frausti] /	qui sent le renfermé; peu
brand-new	tout neuf	frowsy / frowzy	soigné, négligé (vêtements)
broken down	(tombé) en panne (voiture)	foul	vicié, pollué (air); immonde,
chipped	ébréché, écorné (meuble), écaillé (vernis)	grimy	crasseux (endroit); fétide encrassé, noirci (façade)
cracked	fêlé (verre); lézardé (mur)	immaculate [-'---]	immaculé
creased [kri:st]	froissé, chiffonné; qui fait des plis	jammed leaking	bloqué, coincé (porte) qui fuit
damaged ['dæmɪdʒd]	endommagé	locked	bloqué, verrouillé (volant)
dented	cabossé, bosselé (tôle)	marked	marqué, taché (table)
derelict ['---]	(tombé) en ruines; abandonné	messy	sale (pièce); en désordre
dilapidated [-'----]	délabré (maison); dépenaillé (vêtements); déchiré (livre); entaillé (bois)	moist mouldy ['məʊldi]	humide, moite; moelleux (gâteau) moisi
drenched	trempé (vêtement)	melting	fondant (neige)
dusty	poussiéreux	molten ['məʊltən]	en fusion, fondu
clean	propre	mucky	sale, crotté; boueux, bourbeux
dirty	sale	muddy	boueux
empty (of)	vide (de)	musty	qui sent le moisi, le renfermé
faded	fané, passé, décoloré (tissu)	off	desserré (frein); éteint, fermé (appareil)
full (of)	plein (de)		
failed	en panne (machine)	(gone) off	avarié, tourné, rance
filthy	sale, dégoûtant	old	vieux, ancien
flaking (off)	qui s'effrite, s'écaille	new	nouveau

Things and objects : properties, state and condition 279

old-fashioned	démodé, d'autrefois	out of order	dérangé, en panne, détraqué
outdated / out of date	démodé (vêtements)	on	mis (frein), allumé (appareil,
outmoded	qui n'est plus à la mode		lampe), en marche, branché

Exercices sur le chapitre 16 (4, jusqu'à on) :

1. Testez vos connaissances en traduisant les mots ci-dessous :
A / tarnish (n.) - B / rubble - C / rent (n.) - D / filfth - E / crasse - F / crotte, gadoue - G / buée - H / pourriture

2. Traduisez en anglais :
A / Ne laissez pas traîner de papiers sales partout. B / Les chromes des roues ont été rongés par la rouille. C / Inquiétez-vous de l'état de vos pneus. D / Votre voiture est en mauvais état. E / Le moteur est irréparable. F / La tôle est cabossée, le radiateur fuit, le pare-brise est fêlé, les sièges sont gravement endommagés. G / L'inondation a causé de graves destructions. H / Votre chambre est dans un état épouvantable. I / Les enfants ont sali leurs vêtements neufs. J / La dégradation de l'état de votre maison : la peinture qui s'écaille, l'odeur de moisi, les appareils ménagers en panne, les escaliers délabrés, me cause souci.

3. Choisissez celui des deux adjectifs proposé qui convient le mieux :
A / creased / dented dress - B / fresh / brand-new food - C / grimy / fusty house front - D / frowzy / molten clothes - E / musty / muddly river-bed - F / derelict / jammed door - G / drenched / blocked sink - H / blunt / faded colours - I / foul / chipped cup - J / battered / melting hat.

■ *Adjectifs (suite)*

in good order	en bon état	slashed	balafré, entaillé
pristine ['prɪstiːn]	parfait, impeccable (état); d'origine, original (aspect)	smashed	fracassé; brisé, en morceaux
		soaked	détrempé (sol)
badly worn	très usé	soiled	sale, sali (linge); défraîchi
worn-out	complètement usé, usé jusqu'à la corde		(article)
		spick-and-span	impeccable, nickel
upside down	à l'envers	sour ['sau ə]	aigre, acide; tourné
in running / working order	en état de marche	split	fendu
ramshackle	déglingué (appareil); délabré (bâtiment); branlant (table)	spotless	sans tache, impeccable
		squalid ['skwɒlɪd]	misérable, sordide (logement)
rancid	rance	squashed [skwɒʃt]	écrasé (sous le poids)
rent	déchiré (lit.)	squeaky	grinçant, qui grince
rickety	délabré; branlant	stained	taché, sali
ripped	déchiré, arraché, fendu	stale	rassis
rotten	pourri	sticky	collant, gluant, poisseux
ruined ['ruː ɪnd]	en ruine	state-of-the-art	dernier cri
rusty	rouillé	stuck	bloqué, coincé
sagging	détendu (corde); affaissé (sol); fléchi (poutre)	tangled	enchevêtré; emmêlé
		tarnished	terni, dédoré, désargenté
scratched	éraflé (vernis); rayé (verre, disque, tôle)	torn	déchiré, accroché
		twisted	tordu (tige); emmêlé (corde)
second hand	d'occasion	threadbare	élimé, râpé
shaky	peu solide (meuble)	untidy	désordonné (personne)
shattered	fracassé; qui a volé en éclats	untidy	en désordre, sale (pièce)

unsoiled	intact, non souillé	weathered	exposé aux intempéries
used	d'occasion (voiture)	wobbly	qui a du jeu (roue); bancal, branlant
unsteady	instable, branlant (échelle)		
up-to-date	moderne (équipement)	weather-beaten	dégradé, dégradé par les intempéries
watery	délavé (couleur); insipide, fade; aqueux		
		topsy-turvy	sens dessus dessous

■ Verbes

blacken	noircir	muck up	salir; mettre la pagaille
break down	tomber en panne	not be going	ne pas marcher (machine)
burn	(laisser) brûler	not be working	ne pas fonctionner (ascenseur)
blaze	flamber (incendie)	reject	mettre au rebut (pour défaut)
burst	éclater, crever (pneu, tuyau)	rend	déchirer, fendre (lit.)
clear	déblayer; se dissiper (fumée)	rip (up)	déchirer, arracher
collapse	s'effondrer; fléchir (poutre)	flake off	s'effriter, s'écailler
chip	s'ébrécher, s'écorner	run	fonctionner
crack	(se) fêler; se fendiller		faire fonctionner
crease [kriːs]	(se) chiffonner, prendre un faux pli	rot	pourrir
		rust	rouiller
crumble	tomber en ruines; s'effriter (plâtre)	shake	trembler (mur, table)
		shatter	(se) briser (verre); (se) fracasser
crumple	(se) froisser, (se) fripper	mislay	égarer
crash	s'écraser (avion), se percuter (voitures)	smash	(se) briser; (se) fracasser (contre qch)
crush	(se) froisser (vêtement); broyer, écraser	smash up	tout casser (dans une maison); accidenter, bousiller (voiture)
damage ['dæmɪdʒ]	endommager		
decay	s'altérer (pierre); pourrir; se carier	tamper with	toucher à (sans autorisation)
		melt	(faire) fondre
destroy	détruire	dissolve [dɪ'zɒlv]	(se) dissoudre
deteriorate [-'----]	(se) détériorer, s'abîmer	tear [teə]	déchirer, faire un accroc (à)
devastate	dévaster, ravager	tear up	déchirer en morceaux
discard	jeter; se débarrasser de	throw away	jeter
distort	déformer (métal)	twist	(se) tordre (métal); (s') entortiller (corde)
disrupt	perturber (communication)		
dump	jeter (qch d'inutile)	warp [wɔːp]	gauchir (bois); (se) voiler (roue)
explode	(faire) exploser		
fall apart / to pieces	tomber en morceaux	shrivel	se ratatiner
go off	partir (coup de fusil) s'avarier, tourner, rancir	weaken	perdre / enlever de sa solidité (à qch)
		strengthen	(se) consolider, étayer
jam	(se) bloquer, (se) coincer	wear out	(s')user (vêtements, machines)
jerk	cahoter (voiture)	wipe out	anéantir (ville, gens)
go / run to waste	tomber en friche	worsen ['wɜːsn]	empirer, s'aggraver
lay waste	ravager, dévaster	wreck	bousiller, esquinter; mettre hors d'état de fonctionner
mar	gâter, gâcher (l'aspect de qch)		
moisten	(se) mouiller (tissu)	fall (in)	tomber, s'effondrer
moisturize	humidifier (air)	mess (up)	salir; mettre le désordre (dans un lieu)
mo(u)ld [məʊld]	moisir		
move	se vendre (bien ou mal)	spoil	(s') abîmer, s'avarier

Things and objects : properties, state and condition   281

Collocations

break	(se) casser, se rompre; se fracturer (os)	*some things break easily / break in two*
mess (up)	salir; mettre le désordre gâcher, contrarier	*to mess up one's new dress sth / sb may mess up sb's arrangements*
wear	(s') user	*a jacket may wear at the elbows - socks may wear into holes* (se trouer)

Exercices sur le chapitre 16 (4, à partir de in good order)

1. Testez vos connaissances en traduisant les mots ci-dessous :

A / weathered - B / rent (adj.) - C / soaked - D / tangled - E / to rot - F / to crack
G / to decay - H / to dump - I / pourri - J / rouillé - K / rassis - L / tordu - M / trembler
N / déformer (métal) - O / ravager, dévaster - P / flamber (incendie)

2. Joignez une phrase de droite à chaque phrase de gauche :

1. He got stuck in the old ramshackle lift
2. The bodywork had been scratched
3. The toy-train was not working and
4. A toy firm is expected to reject
5. The reason why the toy trains are not moving very fast
6. If you go on crumpling and crushing your clothes the way you do
7. The sewing-machine was not running properly
8. If you tamper with my lap-top

A. fell apart when they tried to repair it.
B. may be because they are tampered with by kids with stickly hands.
C. perhaps because she did not know how to run it.
D. that was supposed to be in working order.
E. and the seats had been stained or ripped.
F. all shaky, wobbly or otherwise not properly functioning toys.
G. you'll wreck it.
H. they'll soon get soiled and stained and look as if they were worn-out.

3. Quel nom (1 à 15) choisissez-vous pour accompagner les adjectifs (A à O) proposés ?

A. split	1. face, skin	I. unsteady	9. colour
B. rickety	2. tyres	J. watery	10. metal
C. tarnished	3. ceiling	K. threadbare	11. lemon
D. slashed	4. room	L. squeaky	12. ladder
E. squalid	5. housing	M. sour	13. door
F. sagging	6. wood	N. state-of-the-art	14. stairs
G. weather-beaten	7. butter	O. rancid	15. clothes
H. topsy-turvy	8. computer		

4. Quel verbe (A à O) choisissez-vous pour accompagner les noms proposés (1 à 15), en position de sujet ou de complément ?

Série 1 :

A. burn	1. smoke
B. jam	2. car on uneven road
C. blacken	3. cup
D. moisten	4. lock
E. jerk	5. tire, pipe
F. chip	6. shot
G. burst	7. sb's eyes; cloth
H. go off	8. fire

Série 2 :

I. collapse	9. one's wallet
J. smash up	10. whole towns in a war
K. moisturize	11. house, structure
L. crumble	12. car in accident
M. mislay	13. wood
N. warp	14. one's hands, skin
O. wipe out	15. plaster

17
Qualitative judgment

1. General

Collocations

■ *Noms*

appreciation [-,--'--]	évaluation, estimation	*to have a correct / thorough / bias(s)ed appreciation of the situation / of sb's worth*
	appréciation, reconnaissance	*to show little / no appreciation of / for sth*
assessment [-'---]	évaluation	*to make a careful assessment of sth - to praise sb's perceptive (perspicace) assessment of sb's work / qualities*
comment ['--]	commentaire	*to make a(n) appropriate / inappropriate / favourable / ironic / nasty / shrewd / sarcastic comment on sth / sb*
judg(e)ment	jugement, opinion	*to pass a(n) fair / unfair value judgment on sb / sth - to come to / form / make a qualitative / value judgment on sth*
opinion	opinion, avis	*sb may have a bad / good / high / low opinion of sb's work / behaviour - sb may form / express an opinion about sb / sth*
masterpiece	chef d'œuvre	*to create / produce a lasting masterpiece - a compliment may be a masterpiece of hypocrisy*
praise	éloge, louanges	*to earn / receive / win praise for sth / for doing sth / from sb - to give sb unstinting (sans réserve) / faint (peu enthousiaste) / fulsome (excessif) / deserved praise - sth may be beyond praise*
prize	prix, récompense	*to award / give / receive / win a booby (consolation) prize*
quality ['kwɒləti]	qualité	*sb may have admirable / endearing / outstanding qualities - sth may be of fine / excellent / low / poor (médiocre) quality*
value	valeur	*to attach value to sth - to make a discovery of great value - sth may be of practical / sentimental value to sb - to place / set little / a high value on sth - to believe in traditional / moral values*
worth	valeur	*to know one's own worth - a book may be of great literary worth - to judge people by their worth*

■ *Adjectifs*

appal(l)ing [ə'pɔːlɪŋ]	épouvantable, abominable	*appalling conditions / murder / cruelty / waste / food - it is appalling to do sth / that ...*
appreciative [ə'priːʃi̯ətɪv]	admiratif	*appreciative comments / look*
	reconnaissant	*to be appreciative of what sb does for you*
awful	affreux, horrible	*awful headache / weather / bore - it is awful to do sth / that ...*
	mal, pas en forme,	*to look / feel awful*
	très gêné	*to feel awful about sth / about doing sth*
	pas sympa, vache	*to be awful to sb*
bad	mauvais	*bad actor / performance / habit / taste - to be bad at sth / about (pour ce qui est de) doing sth - it is bad to do sth - it is too bad (dommage) that ...*
	méchant, vilain	*to be a bad boy / girl*

		coupable	*to feel bad about sth / about sb / about doing sth*
		grave, violent	*bad accident / news / cough / pain*
dreadful		épouvantable	*dreadful weapon / crime / child / weather / bore - it is dreadful to do sth / that ...*
		gêné, embarrassé	*to feel dreadful about sth*
fine		excellent, de bonne qualité	*fine meal / speech / workmanship* (finition) */ lady* (admirable ou élégante)
		fin, délicat	*fine feature / hair / skin / sand / linen*
		beau	*fine weather / day / view*
		subtil, précis	*fine detail / adjustment* (réglage) */ sense of hearing* (fin)
frightful		horrible	*frightful wound / bore - to have a frightful time - it is frightful to think that ...*
good		bon	*good* (braves) *people / husband / habit / news / book / results*
		bon, fort	*to be good at / in maths - to be good* (habile) *with one's hands*
		bon, utile	*sth may be good for sb - sth may be good* (pratique) *for doing sth*
		bon, gentil	*to be good to one's parents - it is good (of sb) to do sth*
		bon, agréable	*it is good to do sth / that ...*
grand		magnifique	*grand house / mountain / idea*
		impressionnant, grand	*grand scheme / style / scale / lady*
		excellent, extraordinaire	*grand job / weather / adventure / plan / friend - to have a grand time doing sth / at a party*
great		grand, important	*great effort / friend / ignorance / willpower / surprise / opinion* (haute opinion)
		magnifique, extraordinaire, formidable	*great voice / guy / news / holiday - it is great to do sth / that... - to have a great time*
		fort, doué	*to be great at sth / at languages*
		bien au courant de	*to be great on sth / on a subject*
imperfect [-'--]		imparfait	*imperfect work / argument / machine / goods / knowledge of English*
invaluable [-'----]		précieux, inestimable	*invaluable data* (données) */ experience / help / information / asset* (atout) *- sth / sb may be invaluable to sb*
marvellous ['--]		merveilleux	*marvellous idea / weather / invention / result - it is marvellous to do sth / that...*
matchless		sans égal, sans pareil	*matchless beauty / vengeance / skill / honesty*
masterly GB ['mɑːstəli] / US ['mæstərli]		magistral	*masterly performance - to do sth in a masterly fashion*
nice		beau	*nice weather / day / house*
		bon	*nice idea / meal / food*
		élégant, bien habillé	*to look nice in a new dress*
		gentil	*to be nice to sb - it is nice (of sb) to do sth / that ...*
		sympathique	*nice person / man*
		bien élevé, convenable, bien	*nice girl / home*
		subtil	*to make nice distinctions*
outstanding		exceptionnel, remarquable	*outstanding ability / performance / writer / quality - to be outstanding in a particular field*
		marquant, mémorable	*outstanding event / feature*
perfect		parfait	*perfect person / health / engine / sight / silence / idiot*
pleasant		agréable	*pleasant person / smile / evening / surroundings - it is pleasant to do sth*
		aimable	*to be pleasant to sb*
remarkable [rɪ'mɑːkəbl]		remarquable	*remarkable person / figure / coincidence / performance / event - sb may be remarkable for his knowledge / for doing sth - it is remarkable to do sth / that ...*

Qualitative judgment

terrible ['---]	atroce, horrible	*terrible accident / pain / heat*
	effroyable, terrible	*terrible storm / damage / blow - it is terrible to do sth / that ...*
	nul	*to be terrible at sth / at English / at doing sth - sb's English may be terrible*
	malade	*to feel terrible*
	coupable, mal à l'aise	*to feel terrible about sth / about sb / about doing sth*
terrific [-'--]	effroyable	*terrific noise / speed / heat / shock / storm*
	considérable	*terrific amount of money*
	formidable, super	*terrific person / singer / dress - to have a terrific time - to be / look terrific*
unheard-of	sans précédent, inouï	*unheard-of cruelty / occurrence - it is unheard-of for sb to do sth*
	inconnu, ignoré	*unheard-of painter / writer*
unparalleled [-'---]	sans pareil	*unparalleled skill / power*
unpleasant	désagréable	*unpleasant experience / surprise / truth - to be unpleasant to sb*
wonderful	merveilleux	*wonderful sight / weather / news / idea - to have a wonderful time*
	superbe	*to wear a wonderful dress - to look wonderful in a new dress*
worse	pire	*sth may be even worse than expected - to make things / matters worse* (pour aggraver les choses)
the worst	le pire, le plus grave	*the worst disaster / winter / error - to come off the worst* (être le grand perdant)

■ *Verbes*

appreciate	apprécier, être reconnaissant	*to sincerely appreciate sth / sb / sb's help / sb doing sth / the fact that ...*
	être conscient de, bien se rendre compte de / que ...	*to appreciate sth / sb's need / that ... / how much ...*
assess [-'-]	évaluer, estimer	*to assess sth / sb / sb's qualities / ability*
comment ['--]	commenter, faire des remarques	*to comment about / on sth / on sb / on sb's attitude / that ...* (faire observer que ...)
judge	juger, estimer	*to judge sth / sb fairly / harshly - to judge sth / sb by sth / by appearances / from sth / from their accent - to judge sb to be about 55*
praise	faire l'éloge de	*to highly praise sb for sth / sb for doing sth - to praise sth / sb's qualities*
stand out	se remarquer, se détacher	*sth / sb may stand out from others / from the crowd / above all the rest / as (being) the best / as a writer*
value	apprécier, faire grand cas	*to greatly value friendship / one's freedom / sb's help / sb's opinion*

Exercices sur le chapitre 17 (1)

1. Testez vos connaissances en traduisant les mots ci-dessous:
A / pleasant - B / praise (n.) - C / invaluable - D / prize (n.) - E / matchless - F / masterly (adj.)

2. Ci-dessous se trouvent deux séries de phrases; les premières (de A à F) constituent les amorces, les secondes (de 1 à 15) sont les phrases qui complètent les amorces. Indiquez pour chaque amorce le numéro des phrases que vous avez choisies pour les compléter. (Les phrases qui sont les dernières à trouver se terminent par le signe !!!)
A / Everybody ... - B / He attaches ... - C / I know he values ... - D / She feels awful - E / I'm making these invaluable data public ...

1 / the love she bears him - 2 / about being appreciated - 3 / praises his unbiased appreciation - 4 / great sentimental - 5 / only for her supposedly marvellous and - 6 / as much as he does the matchless - 7 / and perceptive assessment - 8 / value to the fine workmanship - 9 / of his wife's outstanding qualities !!! - 10 / not just to be nice to a close friend of mine - 11 / paintings she turns out each year !!! - 12 / whose devotion to his wife is unheard-of - 13 / unparalleled painting skill !!! - 14 / of all of her work, not just of the recognised masterpieces !!! - 15 / but also because I am most appreciative of her work !!!

3. Traduisez en anglais :

A / Avoir de la situation une évaluation partielle. B / Prononcer sur quelqu'un un jugement injuste. C / Décerner des éloges sans réserve. D / Quelque chose qui est pour quelqu'un d'une grande valeur sentimentale. E / Attacher peu de valeur à quelque chose. F / Faire des distinctions subtiles. G / Son anglais est effroyable.

2. Positive opinion of people's appearance

Collocations

Adjectifs

alluring [ə'lʊərɪŋ]	séduisant, attrayant	*alluring beauty / dress / prospect*
attractive	séduisant, plein de charme	*attractive young man / girl / manner / idea*
beautiful	beau	*exquisitely beautiful* (d'une grande beauté) / *stunningly beautiful* (d'une beauté incroyable) *woman / song / dress / painting*
bewitching	ensorcelant, séduisant	*bewitching person / beauty / smile*
charming	charmant	*charming young man / manners / style / city / story*
cultured	cultivé	*cultured young lady / mind*
educated	distingué, formé	*educated voice / tastes / ear for music*
exquisite	exquis, raffiné	*exquisite beauty / manners / painting / jewellery / taste*
fabulous	fabuleux, sensationnel	*fabulous dancer / musician / party / beauty / figure*
gifted	doué	*gifted child / musician - to be gifted for sth / for doing sth*
graceful	gracieux, élégant	*graceful person / movement / language*
lovely	joli, charmant	*lovely girl / face / hat / dress*
	très bon	*lovely meal*
	beau, très agréable	*lovely weather / holiday - it is lovely to do sth*
popular	populaire, aimé en vogue	*to be very popular as an actor / with young people* *popular book / movie*
prepossessing [,--'--]	avenant, engageant	*a most prepossessing person - not very prepossessing manners*
refined	raffiné	*refined manners / person / way of speaking / taste*
sparkling	brillant, étincelant	*sparkling beauty / conversationalist*
subtle ['sʌtl]	subtil, ingénieux	*subtle person / argument / choice / approach to a problem*
	mince, léger	*subtle difference / shade* (nuance) *of grey*
talented	talentueux	*talented actor / pianist*
tasteful	raffiné, de bon goût élégant	*tasteful person / choice / work of art* *tasteful clothes / house*
well-dressed	bien habillé	*well-dressed woman*
well-educated	cultivé, instruit	*well-educated person*
well-mannered	qui a de bonnes manières, bien élevé	*well-mannered child*

Exercices sur le chapitre 17 (2)

1. Testez vos connaissances en traduisant les mots ci-dessous:
A / tasteful - B / alluring - C / exquisite - D / graceful

2. Traduisez en anglais :
A / Une personne d'un goût raffiné. B / Une jeune femme d'une beauté ensorcelante. C / De gracieux mouvements. D / Une belle journée d'été. E / Un chanteur très aimé des jeunes. E / Un visage peu avenant. F / Une nuance de sens très légère.

3. Positive opinion of things and people's behaviour

Collocations

Adjectifs

absorbing [əb'sɔːbɪŋ]	prenant, passionnant	*absorbing book / film*
adequate ['---]	suffisant	*adequate supplies / time for sth - sth may be adequate for sb / for sb's needs / to do sth*
	approprié	*to be / prove adequate to a task* (à la hauteur) - *it is adequate to do sth*
becoming	seyant, qui va bien	*becoming dress / clothes / air / style*
	convenable, bienséant	*becoming behaviour / laughter - foul language may not be becoming for sb to use*
breathtaking	stupéfiant, à vous couper le souffle	*breathtaking beauty / stupidity / rudeness*
catchy	entraînant, facile à retenir	*catchy tune / song / lyrics / name / slogan*
choice	de choix, de première qualité	*choice fruit / meat*
	bien choisi, approprié	*choice words / phrase*
colourful	varié, coloré, pittoresque	*colourful village / character / career / period of history / past*
compelling	envoûtant	*compelling book / film - a book may make compelling reading*
	irrésistible	*compelling desire to do sth*
	convaincant	*compelling argument / reason*
convenient [-'---]	commode	*convenient day / time - it is convenient (for sb) to do sth / that ...*
	pratique, bien situé	*sb's house may be convenient for the shops*
delicious	délicieux	*delicious food / feeling / smell / meal*
	adorable	*delicious person*
dazzling	éblouissant, brillant	*a musical may be a dazzling success - to admire sb's dazzling intellect / jewellery*
delightful	charmant, très agréable	*delightful person / evening - it is delightful to do sth*
	merveilleux	*delightful book / film / garden / experience / perfume - to look delightful in a new dress*
enjoyable	agréable, excellent	*a most enjoyable evening / game / film / holiday*
exciting	passionnant, excitant	*exciting events / story / film / experience - to find it exciting to do sth - it is most exciting to do sth / that ...*

exquisite [-'--]	exquis, raffiné	*exquisite painting / politeness / sense of humour / beauty / manners / piece of jewellery*
fascinating	fascinant, captivant	*fascinating book / country / insight* (aperçu) *into sth / glimpse of sth - it is fascinating to do sth / that ...*
first rate	excellent, remarquable	*first-rate student / holiday / food / idea / photograph*
flawless	parfait, sans défaut, sans faille	*flawless argument / beauty / performance / jewel*
gorgeous	splendide, extraordinaire, magnifique	*gorgeous person / day / weather / food / beach / holiday - to have a gorgeous time*
	superbe, très beau	*gorgeous clothes / flat / dancing girls / feeling of enjoyment*
graphic	pittoresque, vivant	*graphic description / account / example* (parlant)
	cru, choquant, qui n'est pas nécessaire, excessif	*to spare sb the graphic details*
gratifying	agréable, flatteur, qui fait plaisir	*gratifying change - sth may be gratifying to sb - it is gratifying to do sth / that ...*
gripping	passionnant, palpitant	*gripping book / film / piece of research*
impressive	impressionnant	*impressive person / sight / building / achievement / result*
luxurious [lʌg'zjʊəri_əs]	luxueux, de luxe, somptueux	*luxurious car / house / clothes / tastes*
	voluptueux	*luxurious feeling / sensation / hot bath*
magnificent [-'---]	magnifique	*magnificent book / performance / building / day / gift*
memorable ['----]	mémorable	*memorable day / occasion / speech / journey*
neat	net, soigné	*neat garden / clothes / work / handwriting - to keep a place neat and tidy* (bien tenue)
	élégant, joli	*neat little house*
	simple, efficace	*neat plan / solution / trick / description / way of doing things*
posh	chic, huppé, élégant	*posh people / accent / place / club / clothes*
precious ['preʃəs]	précieux	*precious object / jewel / time / knowledge - sth may be precious to sb*
	sacré, foutu	*precious liar - sb's precious brother*
satisfactory [,--'---]	satisfaisant	*satisfactory answer / solution - sth may be highly satisfactory to sb - it is satisfactory to do sth / that ...*
sleek	très soigné (sur soi)	*sleek person / dress*
	lisse et brillant	*sleek hair / fur*
	onctueux	*sleek person / tradesman - to be sleek in one's speech*
	aux lignes harmonieuses	*sleek car / limousine / ship*
smashing	super, vachement chouette	*smashing girl / party / time / food*
smooth	qui marche bien, sans à-coups régulier	*smooth solution / plan / running of sth*
		smooth supply / breathing / pulse / flow / strides
	doux, sans heurts	*smooth crossing / flight / takeoff / landing / ride*
	harmonieux	*smooth style*
	calme, paisible	*smooth life / day*
spotless	impeccable	*spotless white shirt*
	sans tache	*spotless character / reputation*
stunning	sensationnel, fantastique	*stunning girl / car / dress*
	stupéfiant	*stunning news / event*
swell	super, chouette	*swell girl / trip / idea - to have a swell time*
thrilling	enthousiasmant	*thrilling play / film / journey / performance*
	passionnant	*thrilling piece of news - it is thrilling to do sth / that ...*
timely	opportun, à propos	*timely remark / warning / arrival of reinforcements*
tuneful	mélodieux	*tuneful voice / music / opera / song*
unforgettable [,--'---]	inoubliable	*unforgettable experience / holiday*
	impossible à oublier	*unforgettable circumstances*

Qualitative judgment

upmarket / upscale (US)	haut de gamme	*upmarket resort* (lieu de villégiature) */ shops*
	cultivé, culturel	*upmarket television programme / audience / newspaper*
valuable	précieux	*valuable time / support / advice / information / experience*
well-thought-out	bien conçu	*well-thought-out plot* (intrigue) */ plan*

Exercices sur le chapitre 17 (3)

1. Testez vos connaissances en traduisant les mots suivants:

A / smashing - B / swell (adj.) - C / satisfactory - D / valuable - E / sleek (hair)

2. Traduisez en anglais :

A / J'ai passé une soirée très agréable à lire un livre envoûtant. B / Il a présenté un certain nombre d'arguments sans faille pour soutenir un projet simple et efficace qui venait à un moment opportun. C / Veillez à n'employer que des expressions bien choisies et à éviter tout langage qu'il ne serait pas convenable qu'emploie une jeune fille bien élevée. D / Vos conseils concernant ce projet, que moi je trouve assez bien conçu et efficace, sont extrêmement précieux. E / Je veux, et vous aussi, un projet qui ne soit pas simplement satisfaisant et qui marche bien. F / Je veux, et vous aussi, quelque chose de sensationnel, d'enthousiasmant, d'inoubliable.

4. Negative opinion of people and their achievements

Collocations

■ *Noms*

disgrace [-'-]	honte, déshonneur	*sth / sb may be a disgrace to sb - to bring disgrace on sb - there may be no disgrace in doing sth*
nonsense (U)	absurdité	*sth may be nonsense / a piece of nonsense / a lot of nonsense - it is sheer nonsense to do sth / that ... - to knock the nonsense out of sb* (ramener à la raison) *- to stand no nonsense from sb* (ne pas se laisser faire)
	absurdités, sottises	*to talk nonsense - to have had enough of sb's nonsense*
point	sens	*there may be no point in sth / in doing sth - "What's the point of sth / of doing sth?"* ("A quoi ça sert... ?")
	question, sujet	*sth may be beside the point / hardly the point / off the point* (hors de propos)
rubbish	nul, mauvais	*a film / book may be rubbish*
	sottises, bêtises	*to talk a load of rubbish*
trash	qch de nul	*a film / television program may be just trash*
	inepties	*to talk a lot of trash*

■ *Adjectifs*

amateurish ['----]	d'amateur, peu sérieux	*amateurish piece of work / efforts / film*
awkward	difficile, peu commode	*awkward person / age - sth / sb may make things awkward for sb*
	peu aimable, peu coopératif	*awkward person - it is awkward of sb to do sth*
	gênant	*awkward situation - it may be awkward to do sth*
	malcommode	*sth may be an awkward shape*

backward	arriéré, peu avancé	*backward country / district / culture*
bland	impassible, neutre, dénué d'émotion	*bland person / language / smile / confession - bland coverage of election results*
	fade, insipide	*bland food / flavour / book*
	terne, falot	*bland person / character / statement*
cheap	de qualité médiocre	*cheap (and nasty) furniture*
	méprisable	*to feel cheap* (honteux)
	de mauvais goût	*cheap attitude / behaviour / joke*
clumsy ['klʌmzi]	peu pratique	*clumsy tool / shape*
	maladroit	*clumsy painting / style / gesture / attempt*
	peu habile, gauche	*to be clumsy at sth / at doing sth / with one's hands - it is clumsy (of sb) to do sth*
common	commun, vulgaire	*common person / clothes / accents*
commonplace	banal, ordinaire	*sth may be / become commonplace - it is commonplace (for sb) to do sth*
confusing	déroutant, source de confusion, embrouillé	*confusing plot / explanation / instructions*
degrading	avilissant, humiliant	*degrading treatment of sb - it is degrading to do sth*
derogatory [-'----]	critique, péjoratif	*derogatory remark / comment*
	désobligeant, peu flatteur	*a remark may be derogatory of sth / to sb / towards sb*
disgraceful	scandaleux, honteux	*disgraceful attitude / action / behaviour - it is disgraceful (of sb) to do sth / that ...*
disreputable [-'----]	peu respectable, louche	*disreputable people / place / club / newspaper*
	déshonorant	*disreputable behaviour*
	miteux, minable	*disreputable clothes / hat*
distasteful	de mauvais goût	*distasteful joke / remark / topic*
	désagréable, déplaisant	*distasteful obligation / task - sth may be distasteful to sb - to find it distasteful to do sth / that ...*
dull	dépourvu d'intérêt, terne	*dull evening / party / book / lecture*
	terne, ennuyeux	*deadly dull person / season*
	terne, sans éclat	*dull colour / eyes / cat's coat* (pelage)
	sombre, maussade	*dull weather / day*
hackneyed ['hæknɪd]	banal, rebattu	*hackneyed phrase* (expression) */ word / scenario*
heavy-handed	dur, qui manque de tact, trop appuyé	*heavy-handed person / treatment of sb / of sth - heavy-handed compliment*
incompetent	incompétent	*incompetent person - to be quite / too incompetent to do sth*
hopeless	nul	*to be hopeless at sth / at doing sth / as a teacher - to be a hopeless teacher*
ignorant	ignorant	*ignorant person / attitude - to be ignorant of / about sth / in languages*
illiterate [-'---]	illettré, analphabète	*illiterate person / hand* (écriture)
indifferent	médiocre	*indifferent work / performance / voice / food / cook - to play an indifferent game*
innumerate	qui ne sait pas compter	*a person may be both illiterate and innumerate*
laughable	ridicule, dérisoire	*laughable attempt / piece of inefficiency - to think an idea laughable - it is laughable that ...*
mean	méchant, mesquin	*mean person - to be mean to sb - it is mean (of sb) to do sth*
	avare, radin	*to be mean with one's money / time*
nasty GB ['nɑːsti] / US ['næsti]	méchant, mauvais, pas sympathique	*nasty person / temper - it is nasty of sb to do sth*
	désobligeant	*nasty remark - to be nasty to sb about sth*

Qualitative judgment

	déplaisant, mauvais, désagréable	*nasty smell / taste / impression / surprise / weather / experience / corner* (dangereux)
	grave, sérieux	*nasty accident / burn / sprain*
nonsensical	absurde, qui n'a pas de sens	*nonsensical person / remark / results - it is nonsensical to do sth*
notorious [nəʊ'tɔːri_əs]	tristement célèbre	*notorious murderer / crook* (escroc) *- to be notorious for sth / for doing sth*
old hat	dépassé, ringard	*trends / methods / music may seem old hat to sb*
outrageous [aʊt'reɪdʒəs]	scandaleux, choquant, révoltant	*outrageous behaviour / manners / joke / prices / language - it is outrageous that...*
	extravagant	*outrageous character / hat*
paltry ['pɔːltri]	dérisoire	*paltry pay increase / sum*
	minable, lamentable	*paltry excuse / TV programme / trick*
petty	tracassier, mesquin	*petty rules and regulations / jealousies / spite - it is petty to do sth*
	petit, sans importance	*petty details / problems*
pointless	qui ne rime à rien	*pointless explanation / reason / joke / story*
	qui ne sert à rien	*it is / seems pointless to do / doing sth*
	vain, futile, dénué de sens	*pointless exercice / task / attempt / violence*
poor	faible	*poor quantity / output / sale figures / chances of success*
	médiocre, piètre	*poor quality / results / taste / weather / performance / violonist / understanding of sth / knowledge*
preposterous [-'---]	grotesque, absurde	*preposterous idea / suggestion / situation - it is preposterous to do sth*
ridiculous	ridicule	*ridiculous person / clothes / attitude - it is ridiculous (of sb) to do sth*
rude	impoli, mal élevé	*rude person - to be rude to sb - it is rude (of sb) to do sth*
	grossier	*rude language / reply / behaviour / noises*
	injurieux	*rude remarks*
	obscène, scabreux	*rude comments*
scruffy	sale et débraillé, miteux	*scruffy-looking person / clothes / building / area*
semiliterate	quasiment illettré	*semiliterate school kids*
senseless	insensé, stupide, dénué de sens	*senseless person / violence / deaths / waste / argument - it is senseless to do sth*
shabby	usé, râpé, minable, miteux	*shabby refugees / area / clothes / house*
	mesquin, méprisable	*shabby compromise / way to treat sb*
shallow	sans profondeur, superficiel, futile	*shallow person / mind / character / conversation / idea / argument*
slick	qui a du bagoût	*slick person / salesman*
	mené rondement	*slick business / performance / scene changes*
	facile, superficiel	*slick explanation / excuse / answer*
	habile, peu sincère	*slick sales talk / packaging*
	doucereux, mielleux	*slick manners*
	excellent (US)	*slick new car / program*
slipshod	mal fait, négligé	*slipshod work / reasoning / piece of research*
	négligent	*to be slipshod in sth / in doing sth*
sloppy	bâclé	*sloppy piece of work / spelling / workmanship* (exécution)
	négligé, débraillé	*sloppy clothes / jeans*
	larmoyant	*sloppy sentimentalism / song / music*
sluggish	peu dynamique, apathique	*sluggish business / engine - to feel sluggish*
	lent	*sluggish traffic / growth / reaction*
superficial	superficiel	*superficial person / education / knowledge of sth*
tasteless	de mauvais goût	*tasteless joke / remark*
	qui manque de goût	*tasteless person / decoration / clothes*
	fade	*tasteless food*

trashy	nul	*trashy idea / book / movie / program*
trite	banal, peu original	*trite remark / idea / speech / alibi*
trivial	banal	*trivial disease / story / dispute*
	peu important	*trivial matter / information / offence / sum*
	sans intérêt	*trivial question / discussion*
unappealing	peu attirant, peu attrayant	*unappealing person / place*
uneven	inégal, irrégulier	*uneven performance / workmanship*
unprepossessing [ˌʌnpriːpəˈzesɪŋ]	peu avenant, peu engageant	*unprepossessing person / place / smile*
unseemly	inconvenant, grossier	*unseemly dress / language*
	déplacé	*unseemly talk / behaviour / haste - it is unseemly (of sb) to do sth*
vulgar	vulgaire	*vulgar person / clothes - it is vulgar to do sth*
	obscène	*vulgar gesture / graffiti / writings / pictures*

■ *Verbes*

disgrace	déshonorer, faire honte à	*to disgrace one's family by doing sth disgraceful - to disgrace oneself at a party* (se tenir mal)
shame	couvrir de honte	*the behaviour of a few children may shame a whole school - it may shame sb that ...*
	faire honte à, faire appel à l'amour-propre de qqn	*to shame sb into apologising / sb out of drinking himself stupid*

Exercices sur le chapitre 17 (4)

1. Testez vos connaissances en traduisant les mots ci-dessous :

A / backward - B / bland - C / disreputable - D / indifferent - E / avare, radin - F / scandaleux G / petit, sans importance

2. Traduisez en anglais :

A / Ce serait une honte et une absurdité totale de ne pas faire savoir que cette émission est nulle. B / Ça n'aurait aucun sens de faire semblant de ne pas voir que la façon dont cette émission traite certains sujets est à la fois dépourvue d'intérêt et maladroite. C / À quoi sert de passer une émission aussi peu sérieuse et superficielle ? D / Il est temps de débarrasser le petit écran de pareilles inepties.

3. Joignez une phrase de droite à chaque phrase de gauche :

1. All his life he was a hopeless teacher
2. I tried to shame him out of his heavy drinking
3. He was a very dull person
4. He was an innumerate person
5. He was a poor violin player
6. It was very mean and rude of you to call
7. He is too sluggish a writer
8. He made statements about his colleagues that were very derogatory

A. who went on and on about commonplace topics with hackneyed phrases.
B. who was notorious for his clumsy handling of the bow.
C. your teacher a scruffy-looking, semiliterate fool.
D. because he was almost illiterate and generally incompetent.
E. to be able to do anything about his sloppy style.
F. and they naturally resented his being nasty to them.
G. but he continued to disgrace himself at parties.
H. who was hopeless at sums but knew how to use pocket calculators.

Qualitative judgment

5. Negative opinion of things and people

Collocations

■ *Noms*

flaw	défaut, imperfection	*there may be a flaw in a(n) design / machine / argument / sb's character*
junk	camelote, saletés, vieux trucs	*to only read junk* (trucs nuls) *- to clear a cupboard of junk - junk food / mail* (pub envoyée par la poste) */ shop* (brocante)

■ *Adjectifs*

characterless	sans caractère, fade	*characterless face / village / city / room*
coarse	gros, grossier	*coarse cloth / linen / sand / salt*
	grossier, vulgaire	*coarse person / language / joke / manners*
colourless	incolore, terne, fade	*colourless person / existence / village*
disgusting	écœurant, dégoûtant	*disgusting person / manners / smell - it is disgusting to do sth / that ...*
filthy	sale, crasseux	*filthy person / room / boots*
	grossier, dégoûtant	*filthy person / habit*
	obscène, ordurier	*filthy book / photographs / mind* (mal tourné) */ joke*
	méchant	*filthy temper / mood* (humeur) *- to give sb a filthy look* (menaçant)
	très mauvais, affreux	*filthy weather*
fishy	louche, pas net	*there may be sth fishy about sth / sb - sth may seem / sound rather fishy to sb*
flashy	voyant	*flashy colour / dress*
	tapageur, tape-à-l'œil	*flashy person / car / clothes / tastes*
gaudy / garish	criard	*gaudy colour / clothes*
	excessif, de mauvais goût	*gaudy display* (étalage) *of sth / of trinkets* (breloques) */ of wealth*
ghastly GB ['gɑːstli] / US ['gæstli]	affreux, épouvantable, horrible	*ghastly dress / interview / news / experience / crime - it is ghastly of sb to do sth*
	blême, livide, blafard	*ghastly face / appearance / pallor / light*
hideous ['hɪdiəs]	hideux	*hideous person / sight / town / appearance*
inadequate [-'---]	insuffisant	*inadequate sum / resources*
	médiocre	*inadequate piece of work*
	inadapté	*inadequate answer / equipment / tool*
	incapable, pas à la hauteur	*inadequate person - to be inadequate for sth*
inconvenient	peu pratique	*inconvenient tool / device / place - it is inconvenient (for sb) to do sth*
	inopportun, gênant	*inconvenient question / time / fact / visitor*
inept	incapable, inapproprié	*inept politician / handling of a crisis / attempt - to be inept at sth / at doing sth*
	inepte, stupide	*inept remark / comment*
lousy ['laʊzi]	dégueulasse, très mauvais, nul	*lousy film / food / holiday - to be lousy at sth / at doing sth*
	misérable, dérisoire	*to be paid a lousy twenty dollars a day*
lurid ['ljʊərɪd]	de feu, flamboyant	*lurid colour / sunset / carpet*
	affreux, horrible	*lurid details / story / report*
	pittoresque, à sensation	*lurid description / account*
mundane [-'-]	banal, terre à terre	*mundane matters / description / occupation / existence*
nondescript	indéfinissable, quelconque, que rien ne distingue	*nondescript colour / person / building / clothes*

showy	qui attire l'attention, un peu voyant, ostentatoire	*showy person / dress / jewel / production of a play / manner*
third rate	de très médiocre qualité	*third-rate politician / hotel*
ugly	laid	*ugly person / appearance / architecture / furniture*
	répugnant	*ugly custom / vice*
	menaçant	*to grow / turn ugly - to give sb an ugly look*
	inquiétant	*ugly situation / wound*
	vilain, déplaisant	*ugly word / rumour / incident / mood / scene / customer* (sale type)
unprepossessing [ˌʌnpriːpəˈzesɪŋ]	peu avenant, peu engageant	*sb / sth may be unprepossessing*
unsightly	disgracieux, laid	*unsightly scar / blotches on sb's face / building*
untimely	inopportun, mal choisi	*untimely time / visitor*
	déplacé	*untimely remark / topic / comment*
	prématuré	*untimely death*
unwieldy	peu maniable, encombrant	*unwieldy piece of furniture / package*
	lourd, pesant	*unwieldy bureaucracy / system*
	maladroit	*unwieldy method / reason / argument*
valueless	sans valeur	*sb's comments may be regarded as valueless*
	inefficace	*an election campaign may be valueless if not backed by an organisation*
worthless	qui ne vaut rien, non valable	*worthless land / goods / passport / treaty*
	inutile, vain	*worthless attempt / advice / suggestion - to feel worthless*
	incapable	*worthless person / wretch* (bon à rien)

■ *Verbes*

discard	jeter (qch d'inutile)	**reject**	mettre au rebut (malfaçon)
	écarter (idée)	**scrap**	envoyer à la casse, à la ferraille
junk	jeter, balancer qch hors d'usage		

Exercices sur le chapitre 17 (5)

1. Testez vos connaissances en traduisant les mots ci-dessous :

A / gaudy - B / fishy - C / lousy - D / ugly - E / peu avenant, peu engageant - F / disgracieux, laid
G / sans valeur - H / indéfinissable

2. Avec lequel des adjectifs (A à H), chacun des noms (1 à 8) se combine-t-il le plus habituellement ?

A / unwieldy   1 / sum of money   E / third-rate   5 / piece of furniture
B / untimely   2 / tool   F / mundane   6 / boots
C / inadequate   3 / matters   G / filthy   7 / hotel
D / inconvenient   4 / city   H / characterless   8 / proposal

18

The five senses

1. Feelings and sensations

■ *Noms*

reaction (to)	réaction (à)	**response (to)**	réaction, réponse (à)
stimulus	stimulus		

Collocations

feeling	sensation
sensation	sensation physique

sb may lose all feeling in their toes after sitting motionless too long - sth may give sb a strange feeling
to feel no sensation in one's arm after an accident

■ *Adjectifs*

distinct	net (sensation)	**sensory**	sensoriel
discernible [dɪˈsɜːnəbl]	perceptible	**sensuous**	sensuel, voluptueux
intense	intense	**sensual**	sensuel, des sens (plaisirs)
sensitive (to)	sensible (à)		

Collocations

numb [nʌm]	engourdi, paralysé

to be numb with fear - sb's hands may be numb with cold - sb's fingers may go numb (s'engourdir)

■ *Verbes*

experience	éprouver (sensation)	**react / respond (to)**	réagir / répondre (à)
perceive	percevoir	**stimulate**	stimuler
sense	sentir (qch de non tangible, la présence de qqn)		

Collocations

feel	(se) sentir
	palper
	donner une sensation de
go	devenir

to feel tired / cold - to feel the cold / the heat (être sensible à)
to feel an object that you can't see
sth may feel cold / silky / hard / soft
sb's fingers may go numb / dead / to sleep (s'engourdir)

Exercices sur le chapitre 18 (1)

Traduisez en anglais :

A / Je ne sens plus rien dans mon bras droit. B / Il ne réagit plus à aucun stimulus. C / Il s'est complètement engourdi après l'accident qui a visiblement causé cette perte de sensation. D / Je suis sensible au froid d'habitude. E / J'éprouve une sensation de brûlure au contact de la glace. F / La glace me donne une sensation bizarre.

2. Seeing

2.1. Sense of sight

■ *Noms*

blindness	cécité	search (for)	recherche (de)
gape	regard ébahi	stare	long regard appuyé
gaze	regard (fixe)	witness (to)	témoin (de)
observer [əb'zɜːvə]	observateur	on-looker	badaud
regard [rɪ'gɑːd]	(long) regard (lit.)	peep	regard furtif
scowl [skaʊl]	mine, air renfrogné(e)		

Collocations

eye	œil	to close / shut / open one's eyes - to roll / drop / lift / raise / strain one's eyes - to feast one's eyes on sth - to see sth with one's own eyes - to notice sb's quick / curious / suspicious eye
eyesight (U)	vue	to have good / poor / bad eyesight
glance GB [glɑːns] / US [glæns]	regard, coup d'œil	to have / take a glance (jeter) at sth - at a glance (d'un coup d'œil) - to steal a glance at sth (furtivement)
glare	regard sans complaisance	to give sb a(n) fierce / angry glare
glimpse	aperçu	to catch a glimpse of sth (entrevoir)
have / take a look	regarder	to have / take a look (at sth / sb) - to have a look round / inside (the house) / for sth (chercher)
look	regard air, aspect	to give sb a black / dirty / enquiring / nasty / furious look to have the look of a police inspector - not to like the look(s) of sb (ne pas trouver sympathique)
peep	coup d'œil, regard furtif	to have / take a peep at sth / sb
recognition	reconnaissance, identification	to improve (sth) / change (sth) out of / beyond all recognition (à en être méconnaissable)
show	démonstration, étalage, semblant étalage, montre, manifestation	to make a great show of one's wealth - to make / put on a show of doing sth (faire semblant) a show of bad temper / of strength - sth may be done just for show
sight (U)	vue	to have good / poor / bad sight - to lose / regain one's sight - to know sb by sight - sth may be in / come into sight - to keep sth in sight - to lose sight of sth / sb - 'I hate / can't bear / stand the sight of him!' - to catch sight of sth (apercevoir) - to shoot on sight (à vue)
sight (C)	spectacle	sth may be a wonderful / sad sight
sighting	apparition, présence	to report sightings of an animal (déclarer avoir vu)
spectacle	spectacle	a military parade may be an interesting specatcle - to survey the spectacle from the top of the stairs
squint	strabisme regard de côté, coup d'œil	to have a squint (loucher) to have / take a squint at sth
view	vue, panorama	to book a room with a sea view - to have a limited / wonderful / breathtaking view of the sea from one's room - one's room may afford a panoramic view across a bay - sth / sb may block the view
vision	vision	sb's vision (= eyesight) may have been impaired by an accident - a car's windows may give the driver an all-round vision
watch	surveillance	to keep (a) close watch on / upon / over sth

The five senses

■ *Adjectifs*

blind	aveugle	observant [əb'zɜːvənt]	observateur
blindfolded	aux yeux bandés	recognizable (by sth)	reconnaissable (à qch)
clear	clair, limpide	see-through	transparent (vêtement)
conspicuous	voyant, qui attire les regards	transparent [træns'pærənt]	transparent
dark	sombre, peu clair	translucent	translucide
dim	sombre (pièce), faible (lumière)	visible	visible
diaphanous [daɪ'æfənəs]	diaphane	visual	visuel
invisible	invisible	optical	optique (illusion)
light	clair (couleur, pièce)	opaque [əʊ'peɪk]	opaque
noticeable ['nəʊtɪsəbl]	perceptible, visible	sightless	privé de vision (yeux)

Collocations

-eyed	qui a l'œil, les yeux de telle ou telle manière	sb may be one- / brown- / dark- / blue- / big- / wild- / cross-eyed	
-sighted	qui possède une vue de telle ou telle nature	sb may be short- / long- / far- / weak-sighted	

Exercices sur le chapitre 18 (2.1, noms et adjectifs)

1. Testez vos connaissances en traduisant les mots ci-dessous :

A / light (adj.) - B / glare (n.) - C / to change sth out of recognition - D / dim (adj.) E / squint (n.) - F / coup d'œil furtif - G / avoir l'air d'un médecin - H / badaud I / transparent (vêtement) - J / cécité

2. Traduisez en anglais :

A / Beaucoup de gens ont rapporté qu'ils avaient vu le monstre du lac. B / Le monstre est étroitement surveillé jour et nuit. C / J'ai loué, il y a peu, une chambre avec vue sur le lac, bien que j'aie une mauvaise vue. D / Je n'ai rien aperçu d'étrange. E / Toutes les dix minutes, je jetais un coup d'œil furtif par la fenêtre ! F / Un témoin d'une apparition récente m'a dit que c'était un spectacle merveilleux. G / Je l'ai vu depuis, la mine renfrognée, manifestant de la mauvaise humeur : on venait de lui dire que les autorités faisaient semblant de s'intéresser aux témoins d'apparitions…

■ *Verbes*

behold	voir, apercevoir (lit.)	glimpse sth	entrevoir qch (un bref instant)
blink	cligner des yeux ; plisser les yeux	gloat upon / over sth	regarder avec une joie malsaine
		make out	distinguer, voir (avec plus ou moins de difficulté)
detect	distinguer, discerner (traces)		
display	montrer, arborer ; exposer	notice	remarquer
espy	apercevoir (lit.)	observe [əb'zɜːv]	observer
frown (at) [fraʊn]	froncer les sourcils	ogle	reluquer, lorgner
gape (at)	ouvrir grande la bouche ; rester bouche bée (devant)	peep (at)	regarder furtivement
		peer (at / into)	regarder avec attention, scruter, examiner de près
gaze (at)	regarder (avec admiration, grand intérêt)	perceive	percevoir
glare (at)	lancer un regard furieux (à qqn)	recognize	reconnaître

eye	regarder, mesurer du regard	witness	être témoin de, assister à
eye sb up and down	toiser du regard	look around	regarder autour de soi
regard [rɪˈgɑːd]	regarder (lit.)	look away	détourner les yeux
scan	scruter, fouiller du regard parcourir des yeux	look down (sth)	regarder vers le bas (de qch)
		look up (sth)	regarder vers le haut (de qch)
scowl (at) [skaʊl]	se renfrogner, regarder d'un air renfrogné	look on	être spectateur (de)
search (for)	chercher des yeux, chercher à découvrir	look for sb / sth	chercher des yeux qqn / qch
		look out for sb / sth	(police) rechercher, guetter
sight	apercevoir (un astre)	look in / into	regarder à l'intérieur (de)
spot	apercevoir, repérer	look out / out of the window	regarder dehors / regarder par la fenêtre
spy	apercevoir, remarquer		
squint	loucher	dim (v.t / v.i.)	baisser (lumière); se ternir, s'estomper
squint at	regarder de biais		
stand out	se voir clairement, se détacher, ressortir	look over	parcourir, feuilleter visiter (maison, ville)
stare (at)	fixer du regard, dévisager, regarder d'un air surpris	look through	examiner (des documents), parcourir, feuilleter
survey	regarder, embrasser du regard	point	(panneau) indiquer (le chemin)
tell sth / sb from sth / sb else	distinguer qch / qqn de qch / qqn d'autre	point (at, to)	montrer, indiquer du doigt
		point (to)	(aiguille) indiquer
watch (sth / sb)	surveiller (qch / qqn de près)	keep a lookout (for)	guetter, être aux aguets, être sur ses gardes
view	voir, visionner; visiter (château)		
wink (to / at)	faire un clin d'œil (à), cligner des yeux	glower (at) [ˈglaʊə]	lancer des regards noirs

Collocations

glance GB [glɑːns] / US [glæns]	jeter un coup d'œil	to glance at sth / over sth (parcourir) / through sth (feuilleter)
look (at)	regarder	'Don't look (at her)'! - to look at sb do / doing sth
look + adj.	avoir l'air	to look happy / tired / pleased
see	voir	to see sth / sb clearly / from a distance - to see sb do / doing sth - to see sb off at the airport (accompagner)
show	montrer accompagner se voir, dépasser	to show sth to sb / sb sth / sb how to do sth / (sb) that … to show sb in / out / to the door sth like fear may show on sb's face - sth like an underskirt may show
watch	regarder (un spectacle, qqn faire qch), observer	to watch television / an operation - to watch sb do / doing sth - to watch what sb does / how sb does sth - to watch for sb / sth (guetter, faire attention à)

Exercices sur le chapitre 18 (2.1, verbes)

1. Testez vos connaissances en traduisant les verbes ci-dessous :

A / glower (at) - B / squint (at) - C / scowl (at) - D / survey - E / rester bouche bée
F / regarder avec une joie malsaine - G / reluquer, lorgner - H / examiner de près

The five senses

2. Indiquez pour chacun des verbes (A à J) le groupe nominal ou l'adverbe qui convient le mieux :

A / to gaze at sth	1 / the sea for survivors.	F / to detect	6 / angrily.
B / to frown at sb	2 / a trace of arsenic.	G / to wink at	7 / a suspect.
C / to make out	3 / a new house.	H / to look over	8 / the small print with difficulty.
D / to display	4 / in great disgust.	I / to look away	9 / admiringly.
E / to look out for	5 / sth in a shop-window.	J / to scan	10 / one's accomplice.

3. Traduisez en anglais :

A / "On voit ta combinaison". B / Il guette l'occasion de parler. C / Il baissa la lumière. D / L'aiguille de la boussole indique le nord. E / Il la montra du doigt. F / Il montra du doigt la porte de la salle de bains. G / Il parcourut la page des sports. H / Il examina les candidatures.

2.2. Lights / Visual effects

2.2.1. General

■ *Noms*

beam	rayon (soleil); faisceau (lumineux)	shadow	ombre projetée
		shaft of light	raie de lumière
burst	jaillissement (flammes)	streak of light	mince bande, filet (couleur)
hue	teinte, nuance (couleur)	streaks of grey	mèches grises (cheveux)
disappearance [,--'--]	disparition	radiation	irradiation
ray	rayon; lueur (d'espoir)	tinge	teinte, nuance (couleur)
reflection	reflet	tinge of sadness	trace, nuance de tristesse
shade	ombre	tint	nuance, trace
	nuance (couleur)	tint of grey	touche de gris
light and shade	les clairs et les ombres (peinture)		

Collocations

apparition	apparition	to see / be a witness to / be visited by an apparition - an apparition may appear / materialize / cease to exist / disappear
appearance	apparition	to make an appearance - to put in an appearance (faire acte de présence)
	apparence, aspect	sth may have a good appearance / all the appearances of sth - not to go by (se fier à) appearances
light	lumière (du jour)	the light may be beginning to fade / may not be good enough to take photographs - to work by the light of the moon

■ *Verbes*

appear	apparaître	light up	bien éclairer
beam	rayonner (soleil); diffuser (par satellite)	radiate ['---]	irradier, rayonner
		reflect	refléter
burst	surgir, apparaître brusquement, percer (soleil)	send out	diffuser, émettre (lumière)
		shade in	ombrer (peinture); hachurer
disappear [,--'-]	disparaître	shade (off) into	se dégrader, s'estomper, se fondre en
emit [-'-]	émettre, lancer (étincelles)		
jar (with)	jurer (avec) (couleurs)	shed	répandre, diffuser (lumière)
light	éclairer	tint	tinter (verre, cheveux)

shade	ombrager, abriter du soleil		to shade one's eyes with one's hands - to shade a light (voiler)

2.2.2. Bright lights

■ *Noms*

blaze	splendeur, flamboiement	flare	éclat, flamboiement
brightness	intensité, luminosité	glare	lumière éblouissante
brilliance	brillant, éclat	splash	tache (de couleur)
dazzle	lumière aveuglante, éclat	radiance	splendeur, rayonnement
flame	flamme		

■ *Verbes*

blaze	flamboyer	dazzle	éblouir, aveugler
brighten	s'éclairer, s'allumer (yeux); s'éclaircir (ciel)	flare	s'enflammer (allumette), briller (bougie)
	rendre brillant, aviver (couleurs)	glare	briller d'un éclat aveuglant

Exercices sur le chapitre 18 (2.2.1 et 2.2.2)

1. Testez vos connaissances en traduisant les mots ci-dessous :

A / hue - B / beam - C / shaft of light - D / burst (n.) - E / streak of light - F / une touche de gris
G / flamboiement - H / répandre, diffuser - I / tinter (verre)

2. Traduisez en anglais :

A / Une apparition peut disparaître. B / On peut voir, être témoin d'une apparition. C / On peut faire acte de présence. D / Ne pas se fier aux apparences. E / Travailler à la lumière d'une bougie. F / La lumière peut commencer à diminuer à 5 heures du soir. G / Le feu flamboie dans la cheminée. H / Ses yeux s'éclairent de joie. I / La lumière m'aveugle. J / Hachurer le ciel dans un tableau. K / Le rouge s'estompe peu à peu en rose. L / Voiler une lumière.

2.2.3. Scintillating / Intermittent lights

■ *Noms*

blink	petit rayon (soleil); lueur vacillante	quivering	frémissement
		sheen	brillant, éclat (cheveux); lustre (soie)
flash	vif éclat; lueur soudaine		
flicker	vacillement (flamme)	shimmer	chatoiement, miroitement
glance GB [glɑːns] / US [glæns]	lueur, rayon, reflet	spark	étincelle
		sparkle	étincellement
glimmer	faible lueur, miroitement	twinkle	scintillement (étoile)
glint	éclair (yeux); reflet (cheveux)	wavering	vacillement
glitter	chatoiement, scintillement (reflet du soleil)	wink	clignement, clignotement

The five senses

■ *Verbes*

blink	vaciller (lumière)	glitter	scintiller (glace, or, bijou, lac)
coruscate ['kɒrəskeɪt]	briller, scintiller (bijou)	quiver	vaciller (flamme), trembler (lumière)
flash	étinceler, briller comme un éclair	shimmer	chatoyer (bijou, satin), miroiter (brume, lac, eau)
flicker	vaciller; danser (flammes)	spangle	pailleter
glance GB [glɑːns] / US [glæns]	étinceler (métal, verre)	spark	jeter des étincelles
glimmer	luire faiblement (feu, lampe), miroiter (eau, mer)	sparkle	étinceler, scintiller, miroiter
		twinkle	scintiller, briller (étoile)
glint	luire, briller (métal, route mouillée, verre, yeux)	waver	vaciller (flamme), osciller
		wink	clignoter (étoile)

2.2.4. (Mostly) soft / steady lights and colours

■ *Noms*

darkness	obscurité (pièce); teinte foncée (couleur); teint brun	gleam	lueur, rayon (lumière); reflet (métal); miroitement (eau)
dye	teinture; couleur (d'un tissu)	glaze	vernis; glaçage, glacé
gloom	obscurité, ténèbres	glisten	miroitement; scintillement
sheen	lustre, brillant (soie); éclat (cheveux)	shine	éclat (soleil, métal)

■ *Verbes*

billow	s'élever en volutes (fumée)	glaze over	devenir terne (yeux)
blanch GB [blɑːntʃ] / US [blæntʃ]	blémir (personne)	gleam	luire (étoile); briller (lame); miroiter (eau)
bleach	(se) décolorer (par le soleil)		
blur	embuer (yeux); (s') estomper	glisten	chatoyer, luire (surface); scintiller (lumière)
darken	foncer (couleur); (s') assombrir	gloss	polir, lustrer
discolour	(se) décolorer, passer	lighten	s'éclaircir (ciel); s'éclairer (visage)
dull	(se) ternir		
fade	s'affaiblir, baisser (lumière); se faner, passer (couleur)	loom	apparaître indistinctement, surgir (à l'horizon)
flush	rougir (honte, colère)	shine	briller (soleil, métal, yeux)
gild	dorer, donner une couleur d'or	wane	baisser, décroître (lumière)
glaze	vernisser; lustrer; glacer (gateau)		

Collocations

dye	teindre	*to dye a dress blue*	

■ *Adjectifs*

bright	brillant,	feeble	faible
crude	cru, vif	fuzzy	flou (photo)
dusky	brunâtre; bistré, foncé; sombre (pièce, soirée)	garish ['geərɪʃ]	cru, éblouissant
		gaudy	voyant, criard (couleur)
faint	pâle, délavé (couleur)	gloomy	sombre, morne (journée)

glossy	luisant, lustré; laqué, poli, brillant (métal); glacé (papier)	sallow	jaunâtre (teint)
		shiny	brillant (surface, nez)
grizzled	grisonnant (cheveux)	streaky	marbré, zébré, veiné (roche)
lackluster	terne, peu brillant	subdued	tamisé, voilé
luminous	lumineux	wan [wɒn]	pâle, blême (teint, lumière)
lurid ['ljʊərɪd]	couleur de sang, empourpré; criard, voyant	spangled	pailleté
		star-spangled	parsemé d'étoiles, étoilé
pale	pale	soft	doux, estompé
pitch-black	noir comme de la suie	steady	stable, régulier

■ *Adjectifs en -ed*

checked	à carreaux (tissu)	speckled	tacheté, moucheté (animal)
chequered / checkered	à damiers	spotted	à pois; tacheté; taché (de)
dappled	tacheté; pommelé (ciel)	streaked with	zébré, maculé (de boue) avec des mèches (de couleur, cheveux)
flecked	moucheté (tissu); éclaboussé		
freckled	couvert de taches de rousseur		
mottled	pommelé; moucheté; bigarré	striped	à raies, à rayures; rayé; zébré
pied	bariolé, bigarré; pie (cheval)	tinged with	teinté, mêlé de gris (cheveux)
spangled	pailleté	unlighted	non éclairé; laissé dans l'ombre
specked	tacheté (de sang); tavelé		

■ *Adjectifs en -ing*

blinding	aveuglant	glaring	éclatant (lumière, couleur)
dazzling	éblouissant	lowering	sombre, menaçant (ciel)

Exercices sur le chapitre 18 (2.2.3 et 2.2.4)

1. Testez vos connaissances en traduisant les mots ci-dessous :

A / flicker (n.) - B / sheen - C / to waver - D / to dye - E / to wane - F / to blur - G / étincelle
H / éclat (soleil, métal) - I / étoilé

2. Les mots ci-dessous ont perdu leurs deux dernières lettres. Rétablissez les choses en choisissant parmi une série de terminaisons proposées plus bas :

1 / BLI__ - 2 / GLITT__ - 3 / SHIMM__ - 4 / FLA__ - 5 / SPARK__ - 6 / WAV__ - 7 / FLICK__
8 / QUIV__ - 9 / TWINK__ - 10 / GLIMM__ - 11 / SPANG__ - 12 / GLI__ - 13 / WI__

Terminaisons :
-NK / -SH / -LE / -ER / -NT

3. Indiquez, pour chacun des adjectifs ci-dessous (A à J, puis K à T) quel(s) est / sont le(s) nom(s) (1 à 10, puis 11 à 20) avec le(s)quel(s) il est habituellement associé :

A / dusky   1 / zebra   K / chequered   11 / nose
B / fuzzy   2 / material   L / faint   12 / light
C / glossy   3 / sky   M / gloomy   13 / sunset
D / checked   4 / face   N / sallow   14 / lighting
E / freckled   5 / banner   O / lurid   15 / colour
F / streaked   6 / photograph   P / shiny   16 / day

The five senses

G / spangled	7 / horse	Q / subdued	17 / leopard
H / striped	8 / magazine, paper	R / spotted	18 / curtain
I / dappled	9 / summer evening	S / blinding	19 / sky
J / pied	10 / hair	T / lowering	20 / complexion

4. Indiquez, pour chacun des verbes ci-dessous (A à H), quel est le nom (1 à 8) avec lequel il se combine le plus habituellement :

A / bleach	1 / snapshot	E / fade	5 / eyes
B / flush	2 / person (with fear)	F / blanch	6 / anger
C / blur	3 / cake	G / glaze	7 / light, colour, flower
D / loom	4 / sun	H / glaze over	8 / iceberg, ship in the fog

3. Hearing

3.1. Sounds in general

■ *Noms*

lilt	rythme, cadence (mélodieuse)
pitch	hauteur (de voix)

singsong voice	voix chantante
singsong	chant en chœur

Collocations

echo	écho	*to shout out sth and listen for the echo - sth may produce / reduce an / the echo - an echo may sound / resound / spread / multiply*
hush	calme, silence	*there may be a sudden / expectant / deathly hush - a hush may fall over / on a room - to drop one's voice to a hush* (murmure) *- to ask to have a bit of hush - in the hush of the night*
noise	bruit	*sb / sth may cut down (on) / reduce the noise - a noise may be continuous / constant / slight* (léger) */ loud / persistent / irregular / sudden / deafening / shrill - a noise may abate / die down* (diminuer) *after a time - sb may make a noise / too much noise - a car engine may make funny noises - high-level noises*
quiet (U)	silence, calme, tranquillité	*to try and have some / complete quiet / peace and quiet - to long for a period of quiet for a few minutes*
silence	silence	*sb's request may meet with silence - (a) complete / utter silence may prevail after sb has finished speaking - a(n) awkward / eerie* (inquiétant) */ ominous / prolonged silence may reign / be broken suddenly - to keep / maintain / observe / impose silence on / about sth*
sound	son, bruit	*sth / sb may emit / produce / transmit a sound - to turn down / turn up the sound - sb may utter / pronounce a sound - a sound may be audible / faint / loud / hollow / clear / distinct / rasping* (grinçant) */ soft / muffled / pleasant / unpleasant - sound travels over long distances - a sound may ring out* (retentir) *- to dance to the sound of recorded music - to hear the sound of a bell / of voices - not to make a sound*

3.1.1. Perceptible

Adjectifs

audible	audible	booming	tonitruant (voix); retentissant (son)
clear	clair		
noisy	bruyant	unmelodious	peu mélodieux
strident ['straɪdənt]	strident	discordant	discordant (son); dissonant
distinct	distinct, clair (voix)	harmonious	harmonieux
ear-piercing	strident (cris)	sharp	perçant, aigu (voix, cri)
ear-splitting	fracassant (explosion)	shrill	criard (voix); perçant (cri); strident (sifflet, rire, musique)
muffled	sourd, voilé (voix); étouffé (bruit)		
resonant ['rezn̩ənt]	sonore (voix)	jarring	discordant (son)
perceptible	perceptible	high	haut (voix); aigu (voix, son)
rasping GB ['rɑːspɪŋ] / US ['ræspɪŋ]	grinçant, crissant (bruit); grinçant, âpre (voix)	acute	fin (ouïe)
		high-pitched	aigu, haut (voix, son, note)
hollow	caverneux (voix); creux (son)	resounding	sonore, retentissant
grating	grinçant (bruit); de crécelle (voix)	low-pitched	bas, grave (voix, note)

Collocations

loud	fort, sonore

to speak in a loud voice - the radio may be too loud (joue trop fort) - *to say sth (out) loud / speak loud* (dire tout haut / parler fort)

3.1.2. Barely perceptible or imperceptible

Adjectifs

noiseless	silencieux (pas, appareil)	muted	sourd, assourdi (voix, son)
imperceptible	imperceptible	silent	silencieux (personne)
hushed	étouffé (voix, conversation)		muet (film)
inaudible	inaudible	soundless	silencieux, qu'on n'entend pas (rire, vol d'un oiseau)
mute	muet (lettre)		

Collocations

quiet	silencieux, tranquille

a quiet person (qui parle peu) - *to keep / stay quiet* (ne pas parler / rester tranquille)

Verbes

hush (up)	(se) taire (une nouvelle), faire taire (qqn); calmer (qqn)
silence	réduire au silence

Collocations

sound	avoir l'air; donner l'impression

sb may sound tired / as though they had a sore throat - sth may sound great on paper / reasonable / a good idea - it may sound to you from (d'après) *sth that ... - sth may sound like a silly idea*

The five senses

Exercices sur le chapitre 18 (3.1 à 3.1.2)

1. Testez vos connaissances en traduisant les mots ci-dessous :
A / shrill - B / rasping - C / high-pitched - D / hollow - E / lift (n.)

2. Traduisez en anglais :
A / Il régnait maintenant un silence inquiétant. B / Le bruit avait diminué peu à peu. C / Plus personne n'osait émettre un son. D / Les jeunes s'étaient arrêtés de danser au son d'une guitare grinçante. E / Dehors retentissait parfois un klaxon. F / On entendait aussi un léger bruit de fond continu, très loin. G / Quelqu'un cria très fort dehors et tout le monde resta à attendre l'écho. H / Mais quelque chose avait dû réduire l'écho, devenu presque inaudible. I / Un homme à la voix sonore dit quelque chose tout fort. J / Le son de sa voix porta jusqu'à la pièce voisine. K / Un enfant poussa un cri aigu. L / À pas silencieux, les gens sortirent de la maison. M / Tout était devenu silencieux. N / Un vieux camion tout déglingué passa sans que personne n'entendît le bruit fracassant qu'il faisait habituellement. O / La vie continuait, mais les sons, les bruits, les échos avaient disparu.

3. Traduisez en anglais :
A / Il avait l'air fatigué au téléphone. B / Ils firent taire les enfants qui faisaient trop de bruit. C / Je vous ai écouté : ce projet paraît intéressant.

3.2. Sounds connected with people

3.2.1. (Rather) loud vocal sounds

■ *Noms*

din	vacarme, tapage	**roars of laughter**	gros éclats de rire
brogue	accent du terroir ou irlandais	squawk	cri rauque
bur(r)	grasseyement	uproar	tumulte, grand bruit
halloo!	taïaut!, ohé!	snort	grognement (dérision ; rire)
hooha / hoopla	brouhaha	yap	jappement
hooray / hurray	hourra	scream	cri aigu, hurlement
hoot	huée	screech	cri strident ; hurlement
howl [haʊl]	hurlement		(douleur, peur, colère)
hullaballoo [ˌhʌləbəˈluː]	boucan, raffut	squeak	petit rire aigu, glapissement
hubbub	vacarme, bruits confus	squeal	cri aigu ou perçant
hue and cry	clameur	guffaw	rire bruyant, gros rire
roars	clameurs (foule)	shriek	hurlement (aigu)

Collocations

call	appel, cri	*to hear a call for help - to be within call* (à portée de voix) - *to ask sb to give you a call* (réveiller)
cry	cri	*to give / utter / hear a cry of anger / pain / delight - a(n) anguished / heart-rending / joyful cry - the cries for help of the victims*
outcry	tollé, protestations	*to raise an outcry about sth* (ameuter l'opinion)
shout	cri	*to give a shout of laughter* (éclater de rire) - *to greet news with shouts of joy*
yell	hurlement	*to let out / give a yell of fright / of laughter* (éclat de rire)

Adjectifs

clamorous	vociférant, bruyant (foule)
stentorian	de stentor (voix)
vociferous [vəʊˈsɪfər_əs]	bruyant (foule)
obstreperous [əbˈstrepərəs]	tapageur, qui proteste bruyamment
ranting	déclamatoire
uproarious	éclatant (rire); hilarant
shrill	perçant, aigu

Collocations

vocal	qui se fait entendre, qui s'exprime bruyamment

sb may be / be getting vocal in claiming their rights

Verbes

bark	crier, vociférer
bawl	brailler (gueuler); brailler (pleurer)
bellow	beugler
bluster (at)	fulminer (contre)
brawl	se bagarrer, se quereller
cheer	acclamer, applaudir
clamour	pousser des cris
clamour for	réclamer à cor et à cri
call	appeler, crier
bur(r)	grasseyer
clatter in / out	entrer / sortir bruyamment
guffaw	rire bruyamment
hail	héler
halloo [-'-]	appeler (à grands cris); crier taïaut
hoot (at sb)	huer qqn, pousser des huées
screech	pousser des cris stridents, hurler (douleur, peur, colère)
shriek (with laughter)	hurler (de rire)
snore	ronfler (personne)
scream	hurler; brailler (bébé)
scream (with laughter)	hurler (de rire)
shriek abuse at sb	hurler des injures à qqn
snort	grogner, ronchonner
shrill	crier d'une voix perçante
squall [skwɔːl]	hurler, brailler (bébé)
squeak	glapir (personne); vagir (poupée)
squeal	pousser un cri, des cris aigus

Exercices sur le chapitre 18 (3.2.1, jusqu'à squeal)

1. Testez vos connaissances en traduisant les mots ci-dessous :

A / to bluster (at) - B / to blur(r) - C / to halloo - D / din (n.) - E / boucan, raffut - F / jappement G / rire bruyant - H / bleugler

2. Traduisez en anglais :

A / Pousser un hurlement de terreur. B / Éclater de rire. C / Se trouver à portée de voix. D / Pousser un cri angoissé. E / Les jeunes aujourd'hui se font beaucoup plus entendre qu'autrefois. F / Hurler de rire. G / Un bébé qui braille. H / Un homme qui aime se bagarrer et brailler. I / Un acteur qui se fait huer. J / Une foule bruyante. K / Avoir une voix de stentor. L / Accueillir une nouvelle avec des cris de joie. M / Parler avec un accent du terroir.

Collocations

call out	pousser un cri, des cris	*to call out for sth* (réclamer) - *to call out to sb* (héler)
cry (out)	crier	*to cry (out) loudly for sth* (réclamer) - *to cry (out) with pain / in fright* - *to cry (out) for mercy* (implorer)
howl [haʊl]	hurler	*to howl with pain / with laughter* - *a baby may howl* (brailler)
roar	hurler, pousser de grands cris	*to roar with pain / with laughter* - *sth may make sb roar* (rigoler) - *to roar with anger* (rugir)
scream	pousser des cris (perçants)	*to scream with pain / laughter / for help / at sb* (crier après qqn) - *to scream oneself hoarse* (s'égosiller)
shout	crier, pousser des cris	*to shout for joy / for help* (appeler à l'aide) / *with laughter* (éclater de rire) - *to shout to / at sb to do sth* (crier à qqn de faire qch) - *to shout for sb to do sth* (demander que qqn fasse qch)
yell	crier très fort, hurler	*to yell (out) with pain / with laughter / at sb* (crier après qqn) - *to yell one's head off* (hurler comme un fou)

3.2.2 Motion

■ *Noms*

bang	claquement (porte)	**pounding**	martèlement (pas)
rap	coup (à une porte)	**racket**	raffut, boucan
smack	bruit sec, claquement (gifle)	**stamp(ing)**	trépignement
thwack / whack	claquement, coup violent	**stumping**	déplacement à pas lourds ou clopin-clopant
clatter	fracas (de voix) cliquetis, bruit (couverts)	**tramp of feet**	bruit de pas
clump	bruit de pas lourds	**thump**	bruit lourd et sourd (de chute)

■ *Verbes*

clump (about)	marcher d'un pas lourd	**rap**	frapper bruyamment des doigts (sur une table)
pound at / on	marteler, donner de grands coups sur	**bang on / at**	frapper bruyamment sur (porte, table)
racket	faire du raffut		
stamp	taper du pied; trépigner	**smack**	frapper sur qch du plat de la main; gifler (qqn)
stump	marcher à pas lourds ou clopin-clopant	**thwack / whack**	donner une claque, un coup sec et bruyant
tramp	se déplacer d'un pas lourd		
bang (v.t. / v.i.)	claquer (porte)	**clatter**	(s') entrechoquer bruyamment

Collocations

thump	taper violemment sur, cogner battre fort	*to thump sb in anger* - *to thump on a piano* - *sb's heart may thump*

Exercices sur le chapitre 18 (3.2.1, fin et 3.2.2)

1. Testez vos connaissances en traduisant les verbes ci-dessous :

A / stamp - B / stump - C / clump - D / pound at / on - E / hoot - F / screech - G / snort
H / squall

2. Choisissez dans chacun des blocs le(s) verbe(s) qui peut / peuvent se combiner avec le groupe nominal indiqué :

1. to call out	5. to yell	9. to stump
2. to roar	6. to shout	10. to bang
3. to shout for joy	7. to rap one's head off	11. to smack across the room
4. to stump	8. to clatter	12. to clatter
13. to roar	17. to smack	21. to clump
14. to bang	18. to whack	22. to smack
15. to pound at a door	19. to thump somebody's bottom	23. to scream over to the window
16. scream	20. to racket	24. to tramp

3.2.3. Not (very) loud vocal sounds

■ *Noms*

buzz	bourdonnement, brouhaha (de conversations)	jar	son discordant
coo	gazouillement	moan	gémissement; plainte
cheep	couinement, piaulement	mumble	marmonnement
cluck	gloussement	murmur	murmure
sniffle / snuffle	reniflement	mutter	marmottement, grommellement
grating voice	voix grinçante	puff	souffle (bouche)
grinding of teeth	grincement de dents	quaver	tremblement, chevrotement
groan	gémissement; grognement (de désapprobation)	rumble	gargouillement (estomac)
		twitter	jacassement (de voix)
		wheeze	souffle court, halètement
jabbering	jacasserie(s), baragouinage	whisper	chuchotement
grumble	grommellement	whistle	sifflement

3.2.4. Motion

■ *Noms*

clap	battement (de mains), applaudissement, petite tape (amicale)	twang	nasillement; bruit de grattement (cordes de guitare)
clatter	entrechoc (objets)	pounding	battement sourd (cœur); martèlement (pas)
clip	taloche, coup sec		
click	claquement (talons); petit bruit sec (serrure)	throb	battement, pulsation (cœur)
		patter of feet	trottinement, petit bruit de pas
clop	bruit de sabots	squelch	flic-flac
drum(ming)	tambourinement	pad of footsteps	(bruit de) pas feutrés
tap	légère tape, petit coup	flop	bruit assourdi de qqn qui s'affale ou tombe
thud	bruit sourd (canonnade, cœur, chute d'objet ou de corps)		

■ *Adjectifs*

dim	indistinct, vague (son)	raucous	rauque
faint	faible (voix); peu clair (son)	jarring	discordant
harsh	criard (voix); discordant, strident (son)	lilting	mélodieux, cadencé
		sharp	perçant, aigu (voix, cri)
husky	rauque ou voilé (voix)	piping	flûté (ton)

The five senses

Exercices sur le chapitre 18 (3.2.3 et 3.2.4)

1. Testez vos connaissances en traduisant les mots ci-dessous :

A / cluck - B / pounding - C / husky (adj.) - D / mumble - E / piping (adj.) - F / lilting (adj.) G / battement (cœur) - H / halètement - I / petite tape amicale - J / bruit sourd

2. Appariez les mots (A à H, puis I à P) et les contextes proposés (1 à 8, puis 10 à 16) :

A / the buzz	1 / of fingers on a window pane.	I / a clap	9 / on the shoulder.
B / the flop	2 / of conversations.	J / the pounding	10 / in sb's stomach.
C / the drumming	3 / of sb dissatisfied.	K / a twitter	11 / of hands.
D / a groan	4 / of a body falling.	L / a tap	12 / of discordant sounds.
E / the grumble	5 / of doves.	M / the rumble	13 / of guitar strings.
F / the cooing	6 / of sb with a bad cold.	N / the quaver	14 / of a heart.
G / the cheep	7 / of pain.	O / the jar	15 / of voices.
H / the sniffle	8 / of a mouse.	P / the twang	16 / of an old man's voice.

3.2.5. Verbs (mostly) connected with vocal sounds

■ *Verbes*

buzz	bourdonner (voix)
coo	gazouiller (enfant)
cackle	caqueter, jacasser ; glousser
cheer	acclamer, pousser des hourras
chortle (over / about sth) ['tʃɔːtl]	rire (sans grande retenue) (de qch), se gausser (de)
chuckle (over)	rire (discrètement) (de), glousser
cluck	marquer tendresse ou désapprobation en claquant la langue
sniffle / snuffle	renifler
grate / grind one's teeth	grincer des dents
groan	gémir (douleur) ; grogner (désapprobation)
grumble	grommeler, se plaindre
grunt	grogner (fatigue, manque d'intérêt)
giggle	pouffer de rire ; rire sottement
hail	saluer, acclamer ; héler
hush	faire 'chut!'
jabber	caqueter ; baragouiner, bafouiller
clack	jacasser, papoter
jar (with)	produire un son discordant ; heurter l'oreille ; détonner
moan	gémir ; maugréer
mumble	marmonner, marmotter
murmur	murmurer
mutter	marmonner, parler entre ses dents
pipe	dire, chanter d'une voix flûtée
pound	battre fort (cœur)
puff	souffler, haleter
quaver	chevroter (voix)
rumble	gargouiller (estomac, pipe)
throb	battre, palpiter (cœur)
wail	gémir, se lamenter
whisper	chuchoter
whine	pleurnicher ; geindre
blubber	pleurer sans pouvoir s'arrêter
sp(l)utter	crachoter, postillonner
pad	matelasser, capitonner (porte)
muffle	assourdir, étouffer (bruit)
stutter (out)	bégayer, dire en bégayant
stammer (out)	bredouiller, bégayer

3.2.6. Motion

■ *Verbes*

clap	applaudir	click	cliqueter (serrure) ; claquer (talons)
clap one's hands	battre des mains		

flop	s'affaler avec un bruit sourd	throb	battre, palpiter (cœur)
squelch along	avancer en pataugeant		

Exercices sur le chapitre 18 (3.2.5 et 3.2.6)

1. Testez vos connaissances en traduisant les verbes ci-dessous :

A / moan - B / groan - C / clap - D / pipe - E / whisper

2. Joignez une phrase de droite à chaque phrase de gauche :

A / His voice began to quaver nervously
B / When the crowd hailed and cheered him
C / Jarring sounds and jarring colours
D / We had the door of his study padded
E / When the kids started whining
F / When he heard the kids jabber and cackle
G / He asked his students to stop spluttering,
H / She told him to stop moaning and wailing

1 / to muffle the sound of his blubbering children.
2 / just because his stomach rumbled.
3 / he grunted and grumbled and slammed the padded door shut.
4 / would set him groaning and grunting with aesthetic displeasure.
5 / his heart throbbed and pounded with joy.
6 / muttering, mumbling and giggling every time he spoke to them.
7 / it made him grind his teeth.
8 / and people could not help chuckling and chortling over the old man's sentimentality.

3.3. Sounds connected with animals

3.3.1. Pets and farm animals

■ *Verbes / Noms*

bark	aboyer; aboiement	growl	grogner, gronder (chien); grognement, grondement
bay (at)	aboyer (après), donner de la voix (chien de meute)	grunt	grogner (porc); grognement
bellow	beugler, meugler; beuglement, meuglement (gros animaux)	low / moo	meugler, mugir; meuglement, mugissement (vache)
bleat	bêler; bêlement	cheep	couiner (souris)
bray	braire; braiment	mew / miaow [mɪ'aʊ]	miauler; miaulement
caterwaul	miauler; miaulement strident	neigh [neɪ]	hennir; hennissement
cackle	caqueter; caquètement	purr	ronronner; ronronnement
clop	(faire un) bruit de sabots	quack [kwæk]	(faire) coin-coin
cluck	glousser; gloussement	snarl	gronder en montrant les dents (chien); grognement agressif, menaçant
croak	coasser (grenouille); croasser (corbeau); coassement; croassement	snort	s'ébrouer (cheval); ébrouement
crow [krəʊ]	chanter (coq); chant	squeak	(pousser de) petits cris aigus (porc)
gaggle / honk	cacarder; cri (oies)	yap	japper (chien); jappement
cry	(pousser un) cri, des cris	squeal	(pousser des) cris perçants
gobble	glousser, glouglouter (dinde); gloussement, glougloutement	whine	geindre, gémir (chien); long gémissement

The five senses 311

squawk [skwɔːk]	pousser des gloussements (poule, perroquet)	**ululate** ['juːljuleɪt]	hurler (chien, sirène, foule)
		ululation	hurlement
yelp	glapir (chien); glapissement	**whinny**	hennir; hennissement

3.3.2. Insects and birds

■ *Verbes / Noms*

buzz	bourdonner, vrombir; bourdonnement	**hum**	bourdonner; bourdonnement
caw	croasser; croassement	**rasp** GB [rɑːsp] / US [ræsp]	crisser (grillon); crissement
call	appeler, crier; cri, appel	**song**	chant (oiseau)
cheep	piauler (oiseau); piaulement	**screech**	crier (hibou); cri
chirp / chirrup	pépier, gazouiller, chanter (insecte); pépiement; chant	**sing**	chanter (oiseau)
		twitter	gazouiller, pépier; gazouillis; pépiement
chuckle	glousser (paons); gloussement		
hoot	hululer; hululement (hibou)	**ululate** ['juːljuleɪt]	hululer (hibou)
coo	roucouler; roucoulement	**whirr**	bruire (ailes d'insecte ou d'oiseau); bruissement
crow	chanter (coq); chant		
hum / drone	bourdonner (abeille); bourdonnement	**ululation**	hululement (hibou)
		whistle	siffler; sifflement (oiseau)

Collocations

flap	battre	*a bird's wings may flap - a bird may flap its wings*

3.3.3. Others

■ *Verbes / Noms*

grunt	grogner; grognement	**roar**	rugir; rugissement
hiss	siffler (serpent); sifflement	**trumpet**	barrir; barrissement
howl [haʊl]	hurler; hurlement		

Exercices sur le chapitre 18 (3.3.1 à 3.3.3)

1. Testez vos connaissances en traduisant les verbes ci-dessous :

A / bellow - B / clop - C / whinny - D / hoot - E / croak - F / hiss - G / bêler - H / glousser
I / hennir - J / pépier, gazouiller - K / ronronner - L / barrir

2. Appariez un nom (A à L) et un verbe (1 à 12) :

A / dogs	1 / coo	G / ducks	7 / drone
B / birds	2 / caw	H / pigs	8 / chuckle
C / peacocks	3 / bark	I / cows	9 / chirp / sing
D / doves	4 / screech / hoot	J / crows	10 / squeak
E / bees	5 / crow	K / cocks	11 / quack
F / owls	6 / purr / mew	L / cats	12 / low

3.4. Connected with things and objects

3.4.1. Daily life

■ *Verbes / Noms*

bang	claquer; claquement (porte)	jangle	cliqueter; cliquetis (bracelets); faire un bruit de métal entrechoqué (cloches, casseroles)
blare	retentir; beugler (radio); bruit strident (klaxon); beuglement		
bleep	biper; bip	jingle	tinter, cliqueter; tintement, cliquetis (clés, clochettes; pièces de monnaie)
blast GB [blɑːst] / US [blæst]	fanfare, sonnerie (trompettes) coup strident (de klaxon, de sifflet)		
		squelch	bruit de fruit mûr qui s'écrase
boom	retentir (trompettes), ronfler (orgue); ronflement	pound	retentir (musique); accords martelés
tinkle	(faire) tinter; tintement	peal	carillonner; carillon
buzz	appeler; appel (par téléphone, interphone)	shrill	retentir (sifflet, sonnerie); son strident
chime	carillonner, sonner; carillon	rattle	trembler (fenêtre); vibration
chink	(faire) tinter; tintement (verres, pièces)		cliqueter, s'entrechoquer; cliquetis (bouteilles, chaînes, assiettes, touches)
chord [kɔːd]	accord (musique)		
click	(faire un) bruit sec, de déclic	rasp GB [rɑːsp] / US [ræsp]	crisser, grincer; grincement, crissement (papier de verre)
click(ing)	claquer (talons); claquement		
crack	claquer; claquement (fouet)	pop	crever (ballon); éclater (maïs à la cuisson), sauter (bouchon), faire un bruit sec, pan
clack	cliqueter; cliquetis (touches)		
clatter	cliqueter; cliquetis; claquer; claquement (clés, touches) résonner (en tombant); bruit de chute d'objet	ring	sonner, retentir, tinter; sonnerie; tintement
		rustle	froisser (papiers); froissement; froufouter (jupe), froufrou
tick	tictaquer; tictac		
clink	(faire) tinter (verres); tintement	scrape	racler, frotter; raclement, frottement
clink glasses with sb	trinquer avec qqn	scream	hurler; hurlement (sirène)
creak	craquer (parquet); grincer (chaussures, gonds); craquement, grincement	screech	crisser; crissement (pneus); grincer (freins); grincement
		swish	claquer (fouet); claquement; bruire, froufouter; bruissement (tissu)
hum	ronfler, ronflement (toupie)		
clang	(faire un) bruit métallique (cloches, barrière métallique)		
		slam	claquer, rabattre avec bruit; claquement (porte, abattant)
crunch	croquer; coup de dents		
grate	grincer (craie); grincement	snap	(se) casser avec un bruit sec; bruit sec, craquement (faire) claquer (doigts, fouet); claquement
crunch	faire craquer, écraser (du pied); craquement, crissement (gravier)		
honk / hoot	klaxonner; coup de klaxon	smash	(se) briser; fracas (chute d'objet cassable)
hoot	mugir, mugissement (sirène); siffler; sifflet, sifflement (train)	squeak	grincer; grincement (roue, craie); craquer; craquement (chaussures); vagir (poupée); vagissement
groan	gémir (parquet); grincer (porte); gémissement, grincement		

The five senses

squeal   grincer (freins); crisser (pneus); grincement; crissement   **(s)crunch**   grincer (gravier, pas); craquer (pâte); grincement,

toll   sonner; carillon (cloche d'enterrement)

twang   vibrer; vibration (corde pincée, raquette)   **whistle**   siffler; sifflement (bouilloire), coup de sifflet

Exercices sur le chapitre 18 (3.4.1)

1. Testez vos connaissances en traduisant les mots ci-dessous :

A / to boom - B / to buzz - C / clack - D / clang - E / to squelch - F / sifflement (train) - G / retentir (musique) - H / son strident - I / fracas (chute) - J / bruire (tissu)

2. Remplissez la grille à l'aide des définitions proposées :

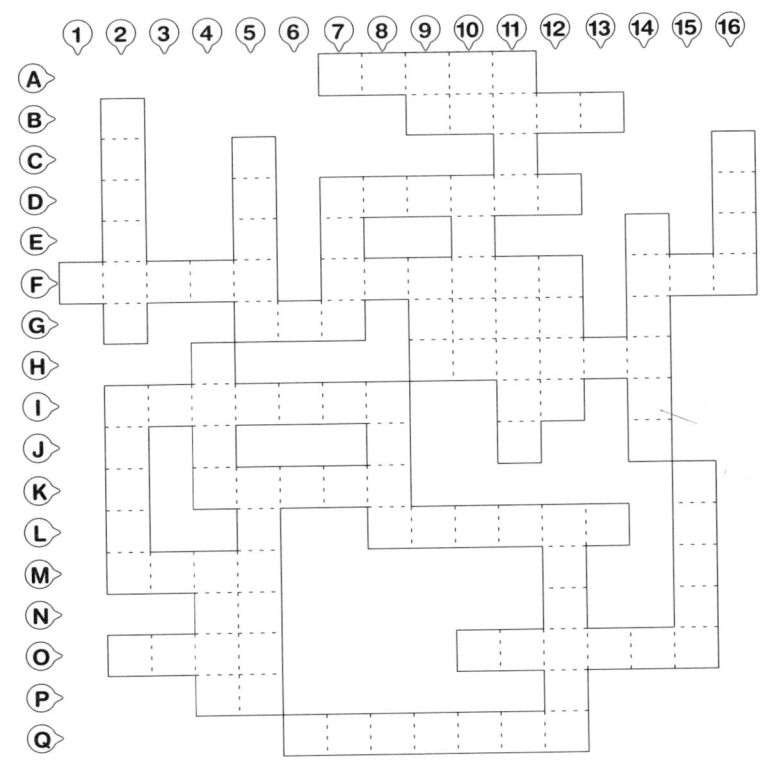

Horizontalement : A. explosion - B. accord (musique) - D. cliquetis, entrechoc - F. beuglement; racler, frotter; encre - G. sauter (bouchon); se casser avec un bruit sec - H. qui vieillit - I. claquement (touches); alternating current - K. gémissement (parquet) - L. Grèce - M. embrasser - N. basse tension - O. carillonner; cliqueter (bracelets) - P. moi - Q. crissement (pneus)

Verticalement : 2. tintement (clochettes); tintement (verres) - 4. claquer (porte); rabattre avec bruit - 5. bip; froisser, froufrouter - 7. crissement (papier de verre) - 8. sonner, retentir - 9. abréviation de 'alternating current'; Royal Society of Arts - 10. chut !; vibration (corde) - 11. sonnerie de cloches; péan - 12. épopée; croquer - 14. tinter (clochettes) - 15. carillonner - 16. tictac

3.4.2. Exceptional occasions

■ *Verbes / Noms*

bang	détoner (canon); forte détonation, fracas, bruit d'explosion	**flap**	claquer (drapeau, voiles); claquement
blast GB [blɑːst] / US [blæst]	faire sauter (roc); explosion (effet de souffle d'une bombe)	**rattle**	agiter (des objets); bringuebaler; cliquetis, entrechoc
		report	détonation
boom	gronder (canon); grondement, rugissement (tempête)	**roar**	tonner (canon); grondement
bray	résonner; éclat sonore (trompette)	**rumble**	gronder; grondement sourd et prolongé (canon)
burst	exploser (obus); éclater (pneu); explosion, éclatement	**shatter**	voler en éclats (vitre); (se) briser avec fracas
clash	s'entrechoquer (épées); résonner (cymbales); fracas métallique	**smash**	(se) fracasser; fracas (collision)
		throb	vibrer; vibration (tambour)
clatter	cliqueter (clés, chaînes); cliquetis; résonner (objets qui tombent avec grand bruit); fracas	**thud**	gronder sourdement (canon); (faire un) bruit sourd (chute, tambour)
		wail	hurler; hurlement (sirène)
crack	claquer; coup (sec), détonation (fusil)	**whine**	gémir, siffler (sirène, obus, balle de fusil); sifflement
crash	s'écraser au sol; (se) percuter; fracas, accident	**whistle**	siffler; sifflement (obus, balles)
		whizz along	se déplacer en faisant siffler l'air, à toute allure
firedamp	coup de grisou		
flak	tirs de DCA	**whizz past**	passer en sifflant (balles)

3.5. Connected with machines

3.5.1. Metallic sounds

■ *Verbes / Noms*

clang	rendre un son métallique (grille qui se ferme, cloche); bruit métallique	**clash**	s'entrechoquer; cliquetis (épées); résonner (cymbales); choc, heurt
clangour	fracas métallique	**clunk**	(faire un) bruit sourd (moteur, porte qui se ferme)
clank	(faire) cliqueter; cliquetis (chaînes); bruit métallique (seaux)	**rattle**	(faire un) bruit de ferraille (tram, voiture)

3.5.2. Other

■ *Verbes / Noms*

blast GB [blɑːst] / US [blæst]	fanfare, sonnerie (trompettes); coup strident (sifflet)	**hum**	vrombir (moteur, moto); vrombissement
	grondement, rugissement (fusée spatiale)	**racket**	(faire du) vacarme (machine)
		sonic boom	détonation supersonique

knock	cogner (moteur); cognement	rumble past	passer avec grand bruit
chug	souffler (machine); haleter; souffle; teuf-teuf	screech	hurler; hurlement (sirène)
		wheeze	souffler, haleter; halètement
throb	vibrer (machine); vibration	whistle	siffler; sifflement
drone [drəʊn]	ronronner (avion); bruit continu (circulation)	whirr	ronronner; vrombir; ronronnement; vrombissement (moteur, ventilateur)
hiss	siffler; sifflement (vapeur)		
roar	(faire) vrombir (moteur); vrombissement	whisper to a halt [hɔːlt]	s'arrêter sans bruit (véhicule)
rumble	roulement, grondement (camion, train)	grind [graɪnd] to a halt [hɔːlt]	s'arrêter dans un crissement de freins
rumble along	rouler avec fracas		

Collocations

din (n.)	fracas, vacarme	*to make / kick up a din* (faire un boucan / chahut insupportable)	
	tapage, chahut	*- to have to put up with the din of traffic / of factories*	
		the din from the classrooms	
din (v.)	résonner bruyamment	*car horns may din unpleasantly when blown in heavy traffic*	
		- sb's criticism may din in your ears long after it was uttered	

Exercices sur le chapitre 18 (3.4.2 à 3.5.2)

1. Testez vos connaissances en traduisant les mots ci-dessous :

A / to blast - B / to whine - C / flak - D / to whirr - E / to clunk

2. Choisissez :

A / They heard the *firedamp / report / screech* of a rifle in the distance - B / The bullet *boomed / blasted / whizzed* past my head - C / The swords *clashed / whistled / chugged* as the men started the fencing contest - D / The flag *clunked / rattled / flapped* in the wind - E / They heard the siren *wheeze / wail / clatter* all of a sudden - F / The trumpet *brayed / hummed / knocked* through the night - G / The door shut with a heavy *clunk / rumble / flak* - H / The old tramcar *rattled / roared / thudded* slowly downhill - I / A stone hit the window and the panes *shattered / twanged / tolled* - J / The tire *burst / droned / throbbed* and the car had to stop.

3.6. Connected with nature

3.6.1. Wind

■ *Verbes / Noms*

blast GB [blɑːst] / US [blæst]	souffler; souffle (d'air)	roar	rugir; rugissement (vent); gronder; grondement (orage)
blast of wind	coup de vent	rustle	bruire; bruissement (feuilles)
bluster	(souffler en) rafale(s)	scream	hurler; hurlement
flap	claquer; claquement (voiles)	whistle	siffler; sifflement aigu (vent, oiseau)
gale	grand vent, coup de vent		
howl [haʊl]	hurler; hurlement	sough [saʊ]	murmurer; murmure (vent)

swish	cingler; sifflement d'un vent cinglant	wail		gémir; plainte, gémissement (vent)
hiss	siffler; sifflement (vent, vapeur)	whisper		murmurer; murmure (feuilles, eau)

3.6.2. Water / rain / liquids

■ *Verbes / Noms*

babble	gazouiller; gazouillement (ruisseau)	gurgle	gargouiller; gargouillement; murmurer, murmure (ruisseau)
burble	murmurer; murmure (ruisseau)		
churn	(faire) bouillonner (eau)	patter	crépiter; crépitement (pluie)
drum(ming)	tambouriner; tambourinement (pluie)	rattle	crépiter (grêle); crépitement
		ripple	clapoter; clapotis
murmur	murmurer; murmure (ruisseau)	splash	(faire) floc, plouf
fizz	pétiller; pétillement (champagne); siffler, sifflement (vapeur)	squirt	(faire) gicler, jaillir; giclée, jet puissant
lap	clapoter; clapotement	tumble	dévaler (eau); dévalement

3.6.3. Fire and other

■ *Verbes / Noms*

crackle	crépiter; grésiller; crépitement; grésillement	roar	ronfler; ronflement
		sizzle	grésiller; grésillement (bacon)
creak	craquer (bois); craquement	clap / crack of thunder	coup de tonnerre
fizzle	pétiller (feu); pétillement	crash of thunder	fracas du tonnerre

Exercices sur le chapitre 18 (3.6.1 à 3.6.3)

1. Testez vos connaissances en traduisant les mots ci-dessous :

A / to swish - B / burble - C / to churn - D / to lap - E / blast

2. Traduisez en anglais :

A / Le tonnerre grondait. B / Un grand vent soufflait en rafales tout autour de la maison. C / La pluie crépitait sur les fenêtres. D / L'eau dévalait la colline. E / Le vent hurlait de plus en plus fort. F / Ce n'était pas simplement le doux murmure d'un vent d'automne qui faisait bruire les feuilles. G / Dans la cheminée, le bois craquait, le feu pétillait joyeusement et, à la cuisine, le bacon grésillait lentement. H / La vapeur de la bouilloire sifflait doucement. I / Qu'importait que, dehors, le vent rugît et que la grêle, après la pluie, crépitât sur les toits ?

4. Smelling

■ *Noms*

aroma [ə'rəʊmə]	arôme (café)	reek	odeur forte, relent
bouquet [bu'keɪ]	bouquet (vin)	scent	parfum, senteur; parfum (en flacon)
odour	odeur (plutôt désagréable)		
perfume	parfum (fleurs, en flacon)	stench	puanteur
redolence ['redələns]	odeur agréable, parfum (évocateur)	tang	odeur forte (et piquante) (de la mer, de la marée)

Collocations

fragrance ['freɪgrəns]	parfum, senteur	*sth may give a fragrance* (embaumer) *of fresh flowers - to sell fragrance-free toiletries* (articles de toilette sans parfum)
smell	odorat	*to have a keen sense* (très développé) *of smell*
	odeur	*sth may have no smell / a(n) acrid / foul / nice / nasty / rank / strong / sweet / musty / pungent smell - there may be a persistent smell of burning / of paint*
sniff	odeur (qu'on perçoit en prêtant attention)	*to get a sniff of gas* (sentir) *- to have / take a sniff at sth* (renifler qch)

■ *Adjectifs*

acrid ['ækrɪd]	âcre (fumée)	odoriferous [ˌəʊdə'rɪfərəs]	odoriférant (lit.)
sickly-sweet	fétide	odorless	inodore (gaz)
aromatic [ˌ--'--]	aromatique	odorous ['əʊdərəs]	odorant (lit.)
balmy ['bɑːmi]	embaumé, parfumé	offensive	agressif; repoussant
evil-smelling	malodorant	pervasive	pénétrant
foul	infect, fétide	pungent	âcre, piquant
fragrant ['freɪgrənt]	parfumé (fleurs; savon)	rank	fort, fétide
heady	capiteux, entêtant	repulsive	repoussant
malodorous [mæl'əʊdərəs]	malodorant (lit.)	spicy	épicé
musty	(de) moisi	stale	confiné, vicié (air)
musky	musqué, de musc	stifling	suffocant
obnoxious	nauséabond	sweet	agréable, suave
nasty	déplaisant, mauvais	sweet-scented	parfumé
nauseating	qui soulève le cœur	sweet-smelling	agréable, doux
noisome	puant, fétide, nauséabond	scented with	parfumé à

Collocations

be redolent of	avoir une / l'odeur de	*a cake of soap may be redolent of lavender*

■ *Verbes*

aromatize [-'---]	aromatiser	waft [wɑːft]	(air) transporter (une odeur)
sniff at sth	renifler		(odeur) flotter
sniff the air	humer l'air	scent with	parfumer de
pervade [-'-]	pénétrer, envahir		

Collocations

reek	puer, empester	*a room may reek of cold cigars*
smell	sentir, avoir une odeur	*sth may smell - sth may smell rotten / musty - sth may smell of onion / like leather / as if it had not been cleaned recently*
	sentir, humer	*to smell flowers - to smell (sth) burning*

Exercices sur le chapitre 18 (4)

1. Testez vos connaissances en traduisant les mots ci-dessous :

A / to sniff - B / reek (n.) - C / stench - D / balmy - E / arôme (café) - F / odeur de moisi
G / nauséabond - H / vicié (air) - I / fétide

2. Traduisez en anglais :

A / Le doux parfum des fleurs de printemps embaumait le jardin. B / Il n'avait pas l'odorat très développé, mais il savait bien si quelque chose avait une odeur âcre, forte, désagréable ou carrément infecte. C / En revanche, il avait beau humer les flacons de parfum les plus capiteux, les plus suaves, il ne sentait rien. D / Un savon à l'odeur de lavande pour lui puait le cigare froid. E / Il ne servait à rien que la brise transportât jusqu'à lui le doux parfum des fleurs du jardin. F / La soupe la plus raffinée pour lui avait une odeur fétide et repoussante.

5. Tasting

Noms

aftertaste	arrière-goût	relish	goût, saveur
flavouring	arôme (mets préparés); parfum (gâteau)	seasoning	assaisonnement
		tang	saveur forte (citron)
foretaste	avant-goût	smack (of sth)	léger goût (de qch)
piquancy	piquant, goût piquant	tastebuds	papilles gustatives

Collocations

flavour	goût	*a nice / strong* (prononcé) *flavour (of sth)*
	parfum	*'what flavour ice-cream do you want?'*
palate	palais	*to have a good palate for wine - spicy food may suit or not suit sb's palate*
savour	goût, saveur	*spices may give a fine savour to casseroles* (ragoût en casserole)
taste	goût	*sth may have a sweet / sour / salt / burnt taste - sth may be sweet to the taste* (sucré au goût) *- to have a taste of the soup* (goûter à) *to make sure that ...*

Adjectifs

acid	acide	bitter-sweet	aigre-doux (fruit)
acrid ['ækrɪd]	âcre	bland	fade (soupe)
appetizing	appétissant	cloying	écœurant, trop sucré
bitter	amer, âpre	delicate	délicat

The five senses

delicious	délicieux	savoury	savoureux, appétissant
flat	éventé, fade (boisson)	**sharp**	âpre, piquant
flavourful	goûteux	**spicy**	épicé, pimenté
flavourless	insipide, sans goût	**sugary**	(goût) de sucre, sucré
floury ['flau̯əri]	farineux	**sweet**	sucré (goût, biscuit); doux (vin)
full-bodied	qui a du corps, corsé (vin)		
hot	relevé; pimenté	**sweet things**	sucreries
insipid [-'--]	insipide	**sour**	aigre
luscious ['lʌʃəs]	succulent	**stringy** ['strɪŋi]	tendineux, filandreux
mouth-watering	appétissant, alléchant	**tangy**	piquant
palatable ['----]	agréable au goût	**tart**	aigrelet, acidulé (fruit)
pasty	farineux, pâteux	**tasteless**	fade, insipide, sans goût
peppery	poivré	**tasty**	savoureux, délicieux relevé, bien assaisonné
pungent	piquant		
salt	salé (goût, eau, beurre, viande)	**unpalatable**	désagréable au goût
salty	(trop) salé (au goût)	**stodgy**	pâteux, lourd
savourless	sans saveur, insipide	**sweet and sour**	aigre-doux (sauce)

■ *Verbes*

sweeten	sucrer (café)	**smack one's lips**	se lécher les babines
season	assaisonner		

Collocations

flavour	donner du goût à, parfumer, assaisonner	*to flavour roast lamb with rosemary*
taste	avoir le / un goût de	*sth may taste sour / bitter / good / bad - sth may taste of / like soap - you can taste* (sentir le goût de) *the ginger in a biscuit*
	goûter à	*to ask to taste the wine*

Exercices sur le chapitre 18 (5)

1. Testez vos connaissances en traduisant les adjectifs ci-dessous :

A / cloying - B / hot - C / salt - D / salty - E / bland - F / pungent - G / tangy

2. Traduisez en anglais :

A / Une nourriture épicée ne convient pas à son palais habitué à des plats sans goût, insipides. B / Il préfère les scones farineux aux succulents gâteaux français. C / Personnellement, je préfère les plats épicés, salés, poivrés, les vins qui ont du corps. D / Lui, se nourrit de viande filandreuse au goût aigre ou sucré. E / Je trouve la façon dont il assaisonne la salade et parfume l'agneau rôti désagréable au goût. F / Lui trouve appétissants les assaisonnements aux fruits aigre-doux ou aigrelets auxquels je ne goûterais pour rien au monde.

6. Touching

■ Noms

graze	éraflure	stroke	caresse (à un animal)
rub	frottement	push	poussée
brush	coup de brosse		

Collocations

caress [kə'res]	caresse	to give sb a loving caress
contact	contact	not to let acid come in(to) contact with one's eyes - one's foot must keep contact with the pedal
feel	sensation (au toucher), contact	sb may like the feel of silk against their skin - to have a feel (palper) to see if sth is silk - a cloth may have a warm woolly feel
pat	petite tape, caresse	to give a child a pat on the head
tap	coup léger	to feel a tap on one's shoulder and turn round
touch	toucher, effleurement	sth may be soft to the touch - to find sth by touch - to feel a touch on one's arm - at the touch (contact) of sb's hand - to rely on one's sense of touch

■ Adjectifs

clammy	moite	slimy	visqueux
coarse	rude (peau); gros (grain)	slippery	glissant
downy	duveteux, velouté	smooth	lisse (surface); lisse, soyeux (tissu)
dripping	mouillé, qui goutte		
even	uni	spongy ['spʌndʒi]	spongieux
flexible	souple, flexible, élastique	hard	dur; durci (neige); ferme (muscle)
flabby	flasque (muscle), mou (poignée de main)	soft	doux, moelleux; mou (neige); doux, satiné (tissu)
flaccid ['flæksɪd]	flasque (muscle, chair)		
fluffy	soyeux (animal); pelucheux (tissu)	supple	souple
		sticky	collant, gluant
gnarled	noueux (bois, main)	stiff	raide; dur (serrure); empesé; ferme (pâte)
greasy	graisseux, gras, huileux		
limp	flasque (corps, peau), mou (poignée de main)	supple	souple
		tactile GB ['tæktaɪl] / US ['tæktl]	tactile; sensible ou agréable au toucher
moist	humide	tangible	tangible
numb [nʌm]	engourdi		
oily	huileux, graisseux	ticklish	qui chatouille, gratte (laine)
oozy	suintant	tough [tʌf]	dur (à mâcher)
palpable	palpable	scratchy	rêche, qui accroche (tissu); qui gratte (laine)
rough [rʌf]	inégal (surface), rêche, rugueux (toile, peau)		
		uneven	inégal, irrégulier (surface)
silky	soyeux (cheveux)	velvety	velouteux, velouté

■ Verbes

brush against	frôler, effleurer	fondle	caresser (amoureusement)
caress [kə'res]	caresser (en général)	graze	frôler, effleurer

The five senses

handle	manier, manipuler	stroke	caresser (animal, menton)
knock (at / on)	frapper, cogner (à / sur)	tap	tapoter (objet)
pat	donner une petite tape, une caresse (à un animal)	tap on sth	taper (doucement) sur qch
		squeeze	presser (tube); serrer (une main)
finger	toucher, manier (des doigts)		
press	presser, appuyer sur (bouton)	squash [skwɒʃ]	écraser (de la main)
paw	tripoter, peloter	sense	sentir (la chaleur à travers un vêtement)
pet	caresser, peloter		
punch	taper (un numéro)	tickle	chatouiller
push	pousser	depress	appuyer sur, enfoncer (touche)

Collocations

feel	sentir, tâter, palper donner l'impression, la sensation de qch; être + adjectif au toucher	*to feel sth - to feel (around) for sth* (chercher à tâtons) *sth may feel soft / clammy / like silk / as if it had not been filed smooth*
rub	frotter	*to rub sth clean - to rub against sb*
touch	toucher	*to touch sth - never to touch alcohol - two things may be touching* (se toucher)

Exercices sur le chapitre 18 (6)

1. Testez vos connaissances en traduisant les mots ci-dessous :

A / graze (n.) - B / stroke (n.) - C / clammy - D / slimy - E / collant - F / glissant
G / pelucheux (tissu) - H / velouté

2. Indiquez (par une lettre suivie d'un ou plusieurs chiffres) quelles sont les combinaisons possibles entre les noms (A à K) et les adjectifs proposés (1 à 11) :

A / silk	1 / gnarled	G / snow	7 / flabby
B / surface	2 / flaccid	H / wool	8 / limp
C / material	3 / spongy	I / muscle	9 / scratchy
D / skin	4 / rough	J / wood	10 / silky
E / hair	5 / smooth	K / soil	11 / soft
F / hand	6 / downy		

3. Traduisez en anglais :

A / Il cherchait sa montre à tâtons dans le noir. B / Quelque chose lui parut, au toucher, être sa montre. C / Cela donnait une sensation de froid. D / Il mania l'objet avec précaution, le tapota, le caressa, le toucha de nouveau, le frotta, le serra dans sa main. E / Brusquement l'objet donna l'impression de quelque chose de collant et d'huileux — ce n'était pas une montre mais quelque chose de flasque et d'humide qu'il avait écrasé de la main.

19
Religion - Faith - Beliefs - Denominations

1. General information

■ *Noms*

afterworld / hereafter	au-delà	fundamentalist [ˌ--'---]	intégriste
tenet	principe, doctrine	god	dieu
agnostic	agnostique	goddess	déesse
atheism ['eɪθiːzəm]	athéisme	heathen ['hiːðn]	païen
atheist ['eɪθiːst]	athéiste	heathenism ['hiːðənɪzəm]	paganisme
bigot ['bɪgət]	fanatique, sectaire	idol	idole
bigotry ['bɪgətri]	fanatisme; bigoterie	mason	Maçon
religious bigot	bigot	monotheism ['mɒnəʊθiːzəm]	monothéisme
Creator	Créateur	monotheist ['mɒnəʊθiːst]	monothéiste
Creation	la Création	non-believer	incroyant
deity ['deɪəti]	divinité, dieu	pagan ['peɪgən]	païen
denomination	confession, religion	paganism ['peɪgənɪzəm]	paganisme
devotion (U)	dévotion, piété	persuasion	confession, religion
divinity (U / C)	divinité (d'un dieu); divinité (dieu)	prophet	prophète
		sect	église, confession; secte
unbeliever	incrédule	seer	prophète; voyant
dogma	dogme	spiritualism ['-----]	spiritisme (science occulte); spiritualisme (philosophie)
fanatic [-'--]	fanatique		
fanaticism [-'----]	fanatisme	Supreme [suˈpriːm] Being	Être Suprême
freethinker	libre penseur	secularism ['-----]	laïcité; laïcisme (doctrine)
freemason	franc-maçon	secularization [ˌ----'--]	laïcisation
freemasonry	franc-maçonnerie	layman	laïque; profane, non initié
fundamentalism [ˌ--'-----]	intégrisme	the laity (v. sg. / pl.) ['leɪəti]	les laïcs

2. Some non-religious festivals and traditions

■ *Noms*

Hogmanay ['hɒgməneɪ]	(réveillon de la) Saint-Sylvestre (Écosse)	V-E Day	jour de la commémoration du 8 mai 1945 (**victory in Europe day**)
New Year's Day	jour de l'an		
New Year gifts	étrennes	V-J Day (US)	jour anniversaire de la victoire des USA sur le Japon (**victory in Japan day**)
New Year's Eve	Saint-Sylvestre		
Poppy Day (GB)	jour anniversaire des deux guerres mondiales		

Collocations

belief	croyance	to express / hold a belief - to give up / lose one's belief (in sb / in sth / that ...) - to do sth in the belief that ... - to entertain the belief that ... (être convaincu que ...)
believer	croyant adepte, partisan	to be a believer (croire) in the Christian religion / in God to be a believer in sth / in doing sth
blasphemy ['---] (C / U)	blasphème	to utter blasphemy - it is (a) blasphemy to do sth - sb's conversation may be full of blasphemies
convert ['--]	converti	to become a convert to a religion (se convertir)
creed	crédo, principes, foi	to adhere to a creed - it is sb's creed that ... - to make no distinction of creed, race or colour
doctrine ['dɒktrɪn]	doctrine	to apply / disprove (réfuter) / establish / preach a doctrine that ...
evil (U) ['i:vl]	le mal	to do evil - to try and root out (extirper) evil
evil (C) ['i:vl]	(un) mal	sth may be a necessary / an unmitigated (absolu) evil - to choose the lesser of two evils
good	le bien	to do good (faire le bien) - sth may do sb good (faire du bien à qqn) - to make good (réussir; compenser) - to return good for evil - to bring out the good in sb - there may be some good in a sinner (de bons côtés)
the good	les gens vertueux, les bons	the good go to heaven / die first
prophecy ['prɒfəsɪ]	prophétie	to make a prophecy - a gloomy / an optimistic prophecy about sth may come true
religion	religion	to abjure / practise a monotheist / polytheist religion / the Christian religion - to enter religion

■ Adjectifs

agnostic	agnostique	**fanatical**	fanatique
bigoted ['bɪgətɪd]	fanatique; bigot	**heathenish** ['hi:ðənɪʃ]	de païen (comportement)
blasphemous ['---]	blasphématoire	**masonic**	maçonnique
denominational	confessionnel; libre (école)	**prophetic**	prophétique
divine [dɪ'vaɪn]	divin	**sectarian**	sectaire
dogmatic	dogmatique	**secular**	séculier (clergé); laïque; profane (musique)
evil ['i:vl]	mauvais		

Collocations

good	bon	to be good to (avec) sb - it is good (bien) (of sb) to do sth / that ...

■ Verbes

create	créer	**fanaticize**	fanatiser
blaspheme (against)	blasphémer (contre)	**prophesy** ['prɒfəsaɪ]	prophétiser
convert (to) [-'-]	convertir (à)	**worship**	adorer
deify	déifier		

Collocations

believe	croire	to believe in sth / that ... - to believe sth to be true

Religion - Faith - Beliefs - Denominations					325

Exercices sur le chapitre 19 (1 et 2)

1. Testez vos connaissances en traduisant les mots ci-dessous :

A / heathenism - B / layman - C / Hogmanay - D / païen - E / prophète - F / confession, religion

2. Remplissez la grille à l'aide des définitions proposées :

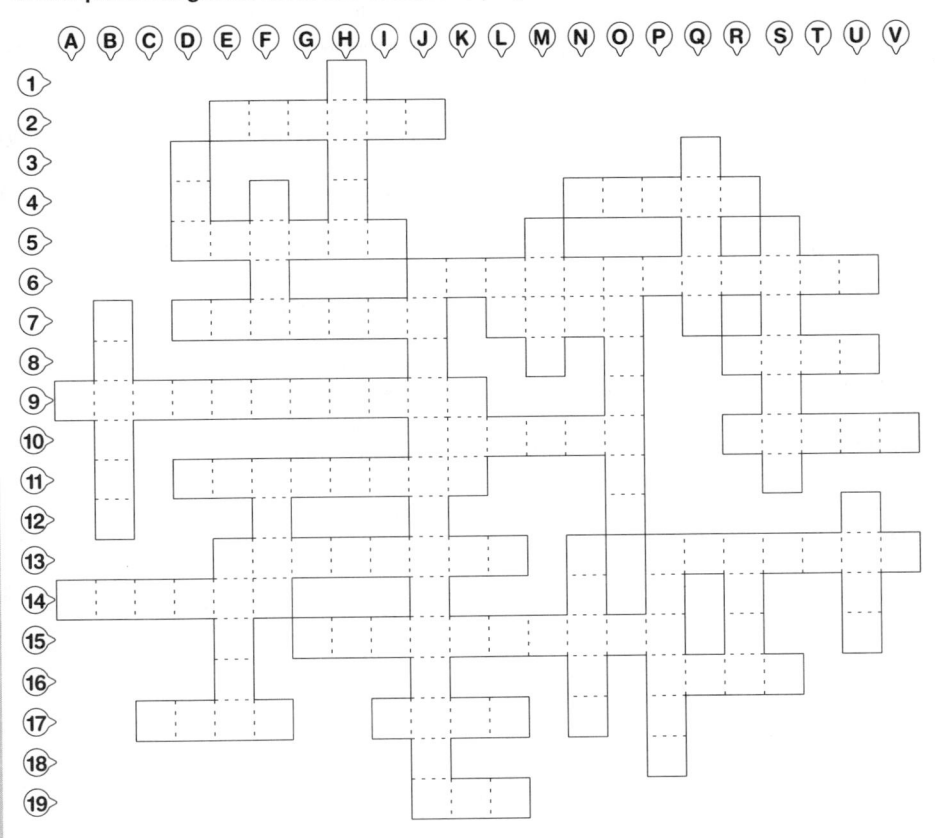

Horizontalement : 2. créer - 4. jour anniversaire de la victoire des USA sur le Japon - 5. divin - 6. spiritualisme - 7. croire; prophète, voyant - 8 + P. monothéiste - 9. blasphématoire - 10. laïque, profane; croyance, crédo - 11. Saint Sylvestre (Écosse) - 13. doctrine; penseur - 14. déesse (lettres mêlées) - 15. fanatiser - 16. oisif - 17. année; cadeau - 19 + 17. étrennes

Verticalement : B. croyance, foi - D. dieu - E. dogme - F. mal (n.); bien (n.) - H. franc-maçon - J. laïcisation - K. dire - L. est (v.) - M + 13. libre penseur - N. c'est-à-dire, divinité - O. convertir (à l'envers) - P. 8 + P : monothéiste - Q. païen - R. idole - S. fanatisme - U. secte

3. Traduisez en anglais :

A / Renoncer à la croyance qu'on a en une religion. B / Se convertir. C / Réfuter une doctrine. D / Être convaincu que.

3. Christian denominations and beliefs

3.1. General

■ *Noms*

alb	aube
Adam ['ædəm]	Adam
adherent of [əd'hɪərənt əv]	adepte de (religion)
the Almighty	le Tout-Puissant
Anabaptist [,--'--]	anabaptiste
angel	ange
Anglican ['---]	anglican
Anglicanism ['-----]	anglicanisme
the Apocalypse [-'---] (Book of Revelations)	l'Apocalypse
apostle [-'--]	apôtre
cassock	soutane
preacher	prédicateur
archangel	archange
Bible	Bible
Bible-basher / thumper	prédicateur plein de feu
Calvinism	calvinisme
Calvinist	calviniste
canon	canon (règle)
canon law	droit canon
Catholic ['---]	catholique
cherub (pl.: cherubim)	chérubin
Christ [kraɪst]	le Christ
Christendom ['krɪsəndəm]	chrétienté (gens et pays)
Christian ['krɪstʃən]	chrétien
Christian ['krɪstʃən] Science	la Science chrétienne
Christianity	chrétienté, caractère chrétien de qch
Crucifixion	Crucifixion
Baptist	baptiste
Creed	crédo (prière)
crusader [kruː'seɪdə]	croisé
d(a)emon ['diːmən]	démon
devil ['devl]	diable
the Devil ['devl]	le Diable, Satan
devotee [ˌdevəʊ'tiː]	adepte (religion)
devoutness	ferveur; dévotion
devotion	dévotion, piété
disciple [dɪ'saɪpl]	disciple
disestablishment	séparation (Église-État)
dissenter	dissident
divine [dɪ'vaɪn]	théologien
divinity	théologie
Doomsday	jour du Jugement dernier
Episcopalian [-,--'---] Church	Église anglicane (ailleurs qu'en Angleterre)
the established Church	l'église établie, la religion d'État, officielle
evangelist [-'---]	évangéliste, propagateur de l'Évangile
Eve	Eve
the Fiend [fiːnd]	le Malin
(the Book of) Genesis ['dʒenəsɪs]	la Genèse
garden of Eden ['iːdn]	jardin d'Éden
the (Good) Book	la Bible
guardian angel	ange gardien
gospel telecaster	évangéliste médiatique
heaven ['hevn]	ciel, paradis
hell	enfer
heresy ['---]	hérésie
heretic ['---]	hérétique
Holy Trinity	Sainte Trinité
Holy Ghost / Spirit	Esprit saint, Saint-Esprit
Jehovah's [dʒɪ'həʊvəz] Witnesses	témoins de Jéhovah
Jesus	Jésus(-Christ)
Kingdom of Heaven ['hevn]	Royaume de Dieu
Church of England	Église d'Angleterre
Last Judgement	Jugement dernier
Last Supper	Cène
lay brother	frère convers
lay reader	prédicateur laïque
Lord	Seigneur
Luther ['luːθə]	Luther
Lutheran ['luːθr‿ən]	luthérien
Lutheranism ['luːθr‿ənɪzəm]	luthéranisme
the Messiah [mə'saɪ‿ə]	le Messie
messiah (C) [mə'saɪ‿ə]	messie
Methodism	méthodisme
Methodist	méthodiste
Mormon	mormon
Mormonism	mormonisme

Religion - Faith - Beliefs - Denominations

Nonconformism [,--'---]	nonconformisme	saint	saint
Nonconformist [,--'--]	nonconformiste; dissident	Satan ['seɪtn]	Satan
orthodox	orthodoxe	Saviour	Sauveur
the Orthodox Church	l'Église orthodoxe	the (Holy) Scripture(s) /	les Saintes Écritures
parable	parabole	(the) Holy Writ (U)	
pilgrim	pélerin	sinner	pécheur
profane [prə'feɪn]	profane	star preacher	prédicateur vedette
profanation	profanation	teachings	enseignements (de l'Église)
puritan	puritain	televangelist [,--'---]	évangéliste médiatique
puritanism	puritanisme	the Ten Commandments	les Dix Commandements
Quaker	quaker	New Testament	Nouveau Testament
Quakerism	quakerisme	Old Testament	ancien Testament
paradise	paradis	theologian	théologien
Presbyterian [,--'---]	presbytérien	theology	théologie
Presbyterianism [,--'-----]	presbytérianisme	Unitarian	unitaire, unitarien
Protestant ['---]	protestant	the Three kings / Wise Men	les Rois mages
Protestantism ['-----]	protestantisme	Unitarianism	unitarisme
purgatory	purgatoire	verse	verset
Reformed Church	Église réformée	the Virgin Mary	la Vierge Marie
religious order	ordre religieux	Wesleyan	disciple de Wesley
Resurrection	Résurrection	surplice ['sɜːpləs]	surplis
Resuscitation	Résurrection	mitre ['maɪtə]	mitre
Roman Catholic ['---]	catholique romain	piety	piété

Collocations

chapel ['tʃæpl]	chapelle; église, temple	to go to chapel (ne pas être anglican) - to be chapel or church (of England)
church	église	to attend / go to church / to the Catholic Church every Sunday - to be at / in church - to enter / join the church (devenir prêtre)
	église anglicane	to go to church, not chapel - to be church (être anglican) / high / low church - to be C of E (Church of England)
	service religieux	to see sb after / before church
crusade [-'-]	croisade	to go on a crusade to the Holy Land
doom	destin, sort	to go to / meet one's doom - sth may seal sb's doom
faith	foi, religion	to adhere to / practise a faith - to abjure / recant / lose / renounce one's faith (in God) - to be a Buddhist by faith - to be raised in the Catholic faith
God	Dieu	to believe in / worship / bless / praise God
the Gospel	l'Évangile	to believe in / preach / spread the Gospel - to take sth for gospel (truth)
grace	grace	divine grace - to fall from grace - to be in a state of grace - by the grace of God
	bénédicité	to say grace before a meal
limbo (U)	limbes	to be in limbo
pilgrimage	pélerinage	to go on / set forth on a pilgrimage to the Holy Land
profanity (U)	caractère profane; impiété	to be outraged at the profanity of a ceremony - to be shocked at acts of profanity
profanity (C)	juron, blasphème	to utter a stream of profanities
redemption	rédemption, rachat	sb may be past redemption (perdu à tout jamais)

sacrilege	sacrilège	to commit (a) sacrilege - it is sacrilege to do sth
salvation	salut	to seek salvation from damnation - to preach / bring the salvation of souls
sin	péché	to commit a deadly / capital / venial sin (against sth) - to expiate / atone for (expier / racheter) one's sins - to forgive sb's sins - it is a sin to do sth
soul [səʊl]	âme	to save sb's immortal soul - to hope that sb's soul is now at rest
spirit	esprit	God is supposed to be pure spirit - the spirit is said to be willing (prompt) but the flesh is weak

Exercices sur le chapitre 19 (3.1)

1. Testez vos connaissances en traduisant les mots ci-dessous :

A / doom - B / the Fiend - C / Last Supper - D / lay reader - E / lay brother - F / the Almighty G / parabole - H / Rois mages - I / Genèse - J / diable

2. Choisissez le mot ou les mots possibles :

A / He's committed a number of *sins / hells / scriptures* and everybody calls him an inveterate *saviour / sinner / messiah*. B / A priest may wear *an alb / a parable / a pilgrim* on certain occasions. C / He's uttered a stream of *limbos / souls / profanities*. D / Jesus was often accompanied by twelve *dissenters / disciples / daemons*. E / Moses received the Ten *Commandments / teachings / surplices* from *God / the Virgin Mary / a Presbyterian*. F / Cherubim are *preachers / angels / crusaders*. G / He was fond of reciting *a verse or two / a divine / a Mormon* from *the Bible-bashers / the Bible / the Holy Trinity*.

3. Traduisez en anglais :

A / Dire le bénédicité. B / Racheter ses péchés. C / Être révolté du caractère profane d'une cérémonie. D / Sauver l'âme de quelqu'un. E / L'esprit est prompt, mais la chair est faible. F / Partir en pélerinage. G / Commettre un sacrilège. H / Être anglican.

3.2. Christian festivals and traditions

■ *Noms*

All Saints' Day	(le jour de) la Toussaint	Easter Monday	lundi de Pâques
All Souls' Day	le jour, la fête des Morts	Epiphany	Épiphanie
Ascension Day	fête de l'Ascension	Good Friday	Vendredi saint
Assumption Day	jour, fête de l'Assomption	Father Christmas	Père Noël
Boxing Day	lendemain de Noël	Holy Week	Semaine Sainte
Candlemas	Chandeleur	Kris Kringle (US)	Père Noël (terme daté)
Advent	l'Avent	Maundy ['mɔːndi] Thursday	jeudi saint
Christmas carol	chant de Noël		
Christmas Day	jour de Noël	midnight mass [mæs]	messe de Minuit
Christmas dinner	réveillon de Noël	Palm [pɑːm] Sunday	dimanche des Rameaux
Christmas tree	arbre de Noël	Pentecost	Pentecôte
(Christmas) crib	crèche	Santa Claus	Père Noël
Easter	Pâques	Shrove [ʃrəʊv] Tuesday	Mardi gras
Easter bunnies	lapins de Pâques (qui apportent les œufs de Pâques)	Twelfth Night	fête des Rois
Easter Day	jour de Pâques	Whit Sunday	dimanche de la Pentecôte
Easter egg	œuf de Pâques	Yule log	bûche de Noël

Religion - Faith - Beliefs - Denominations

Collocations

Christmas	Noël	*to celebrate Christmas - to spend Christmas with friends*
Christmas Eve	veille de Noël	*to celebrate Christmas Eve* (réveilloner)
Lent	le Carême	*to keep Lent* (faire carême) - *in / during Lent*

■ *Adjectifs*

almighty	tout-puissant		hellish	diabolique (intention); infernal (déplaisant)
biblical	biblique			
Catholic ['---]	catholique		heretical [-'---]	hérétique
celestial	céleste (fig. lit.)		holy	saint (personne); bénit (pain); sacré (terre, sol)
Christian ['krɪstʃən]	chrétien			
churchy	bigot, calotin		Lutheran ['luːθr̩ ən]	luthérien
daemonic	démoniaque (rire)		messianic	messianique
demoni(a)c	démoniaque (cruauté)		pious	pieux; bigot
devilish ['devl̩ ɪʃ]	infernal, diabolique		puritan(ical)	puritain
devout	pieux, dévot; fervent (prière)		Roman Catholic	Catholique (Romain)
divine [dɪ'vaɪn]	divin		sacred (to sb)	sacré (pour qqn)
(o)ecumenical [ˌiːkjuˈmenɪkl]	œcuménique		sacrilegious [ˌ--'--]	sacrilège
			satanic	satanique, démoniaque
ever-lasting	éternel (vie)		sectarian	sectaire
eternal	éternel (Dieu)		secular	séculier (clergé); laïque (école); profane (art)
faithful (to)	fidèle (à)			
fiendish ['fiːndɪʃ]	diabolique (sourire, plan)		spiritual ['----]	spirituel; religieux (musique)
godly	dévot, pieux		theological	théologique
heavenly ['hevənli]	céleste, du ciel; merveilleux		Mormon	mormon

Collocations

religious	religieux	*to read religious books* (de piété) - *religious wars - to be very religious* (croyant, pieux) / *a religious person* (pratiquant)
sinful	coupable, inavouable	*to be a sinful person* (pécheur) - *to perform a sinful deed - it is sinful to do sth*

■ *Verbes*

adhere to	devenir adepte de		profane	profaner
canonize	canoniser		reincarnate [ˌ--'--]	réincarner
crucify	crucifier		resurrect [ˌ--'-] / resuscitate	ressusciter
damn	damner			
doom (to)	condamner (à) (destin)		sanctify	sanctifier
incarnate ['---]	incarner		save	sauver

Collocations

redeem [-'-]	racheter, rédimer, sauver	*to redeem sb / mankind from sin / death*

Exercices sur le chapitre 19 (3.2)

1. Testez vos connaissances en traduisant les mots ci-dessous :
A / Boxing Day - B / Candlemas - C / crib - D / Advent - E / Lent - F / Almighty - G / to doom H / to damn

2. Indiquez par deux numéros (par exemple : 1/5) les mots qui vont bien ensemble :
1. Father - 2. Whit - 3. Shrove - 4. Maunday - 5. Christmas - 6. Kris - 7. Easter - 8. Santa - 9. Thursday - 10. Carol - 11. All Saints' - 12. Kringle - 13. Day - 14. Tuesday - 15. Sunday - 16. Good - 17. bunnies - 18. Friday - 19. Twelfth - 20. Claus - 21. Night

3. Traduisez en anglais :
A / Être pratiquant. B / Faire carême. C / Accomplir une action coupable. D / Devenir adepte de la religion des Mormons. E / Sauver l'humanité du péché originel. F / Du pain bénit. G / De la musique religieuse. H / Acte sacrilège. I / Attitude sectaire. J / Terre sacrée. K / Quelque chose qui est sacré pour quelqu'un.

4. Non-Christian denominations

■ *Noms*

Allah	Allah	**Jewry** (U) (article zéro)	Juifs, communauté juive
Ashkenazi [,--'---]	ashkénaze	**Judaism** ['----]	judaïsme
Buddha	Buddha	**Koran** [kɔː'rɑːn] / **Qur'an**	Coran
Buddhism	Bouddhisme	**the laity** (v. pl. / sg.)	les laïcs
Buddhist	Bouddhiste	**Mahomet** [mə'hɒmɪt] /	Mahomet
call to prayer	appel à la prière (musulman)	**Mohammed** [məʊ'hæmɪd]	
chador	tchador	**Moslem** ['mɒzləm] /	musulman
Confucius [-'--]	Confucius	**Muslim** ['mʊzləm]	
Confucianism [-'----]	Confucianisme	**muezzin** [muˈezɪn]	muezzin
crescent ['krezənt]	croissant	**Mahometanism** [-'-----]	mahométisme
Gentile	Gentil, non-Juif	**Mahometan** [-'---]	musulman, mahométan
Dead Sea Scrolls	manuscrits de la mer morte	**Passover**	Pâque (des Juifs)
Druse	Druse	**prayer mat**	tapis de prière
gurdwara ['gɜːdwɑːrə]	temple Sikh	**Rabbi** ['ræbaɪ]	rabbin
head scarf	foulard; pointe	**Ramadan** [,--'-]	ramadan
Hindu	hindu, hindouiste	**reincarnation**	réincarnation
Hinduism	hindouisme	**Sephardic**	séfarade
Infidel	infidèle; incroyant	**Shintoism / Shinto**	shintoïsme / shinto
Islam ['ɪzlɑːm]	Islam	**Shintoist**	shintoïste
Islamism	islamisme	**skull cap**	calotte
Jehovah [dʒɪˈhəʊvə]	Jéhovah	**Talmud** ['tælmʊd]	Talmud
the Islamic religion	la religion islamique	**Torah**	Thora
Jew	Juif	**turban**	turban
Jewess	Juive (terme insultant)	**Veda** ['veɪdə]	Veda
Jewishness	judaïté, judéité	**Ved(a)ism**	védisme

Religion - Faith - Beliefs - Denominations   331

Yom Kippur   Yom Kippour (Grand Pardon)   **Sikh**   Sikh
veil   voile   **bar-mitzva**   bar-mitzva
yarmulke ['jɑːmʊlkə] kippa   **Rosh Hashana(h)**   Rosh Hashana(h) (fête du
yashmak   litham / litsam   nouvel an juif)

Collocations

Sabbath   sabbat   *to keep / observe / desecrate* (profaner) / *violate* (enfreindre) *the Sabbath*

■ *Adjectifs*

Islamic   islamique   **rabbinic(al)**   rabbinique
Jewish   juif   **Sikh**   sikh
Koranic   coranique   **Talmudic** [tæl'mʊdɪk] talmudique
Mahometan [-'---]   mahométan   **Vedic** ['veɪdɪk]   védique
Moslem ['mɒzləm] / musulman
  Muslim ['mʊzləm]

Exercices sur le chapitre 19 (4)

1. Testez vos connaissances en traduisant les mots ci-dessous :

A / Passover - B / Qur'an - C / prayer mat

2. Remplissez la grille à l'aide des définitions proposées :

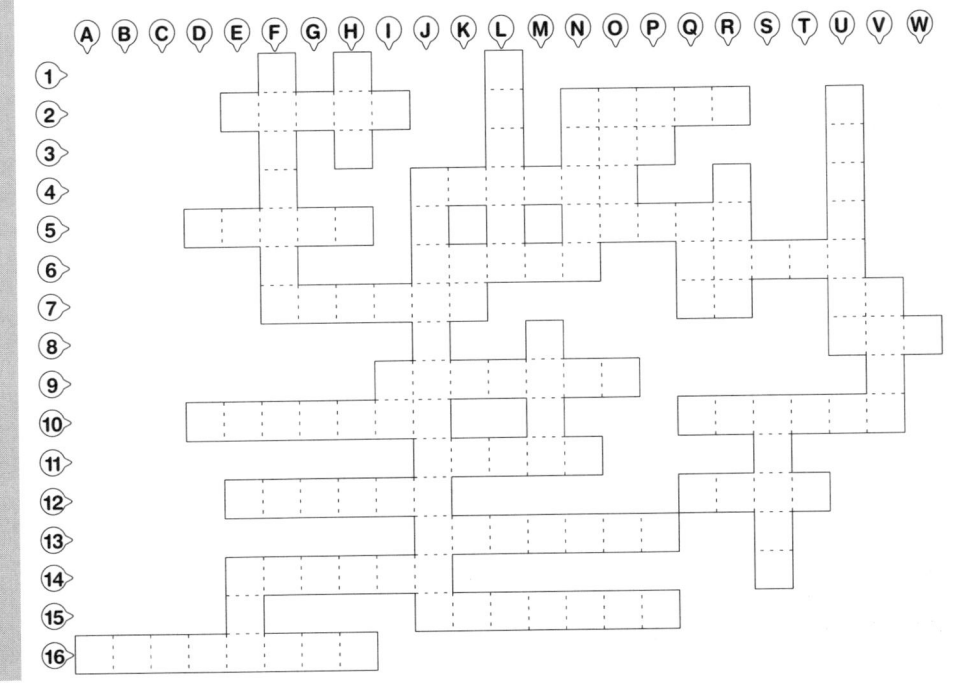

Horizontalement : 2. livre saint; crédo, croyance - 3. voir O. - 4. Musulman - 5. Hindou; chef spirituel juif - 6. début d'hiéroglyphes; crâne : voir H. - 7. voile noir; exclamation; abréviation de Lord - 8. mer : voir V. et U. - 9. Jéhovah - 10. Prophète; ouvrage important du judaïsme - 11. dieu unique des Musulmans - 12. sur la tête; sur le visage - 13. relatif à l'Islam - 14. Jewish girl / woman est le mot préféré à celui proposé ici - 15. appelle à la prière - 16. lieu de culte (Sikhs)

Verticalement : E. Juif - F. relatif au Coran - H. 6 + H : calotte - I. pronom sujet - J. mahométisme - K. abréviation de 'Fisc' en anglais - L. un croissant incomplet - M. (lettres mêlées) Véda - N. croyance - O. O + 3 : jeûne - P. cicéro - Q. abréviation de Boy-Scouts of America - R. adepte d'une des religions de l'Inde - S. les laïcs - U. V + 8 + U : manuscrits célèbres.

5. People, places and communities

5.1. People

■ *Noms*

abbess ['--]	abbesse
abbot	abbé; (Père) supérieur
altar ['ɔːltə] boy	enfant de chœur
archbishop	archevêque
ascetic	ascète
bachelor	célibataire
bishop	évêque
brother	frère
brethren	frères (employé lorsqu'on s'adresse aux fidèles)
canon	chanoine
canoness GB [,--'-] / US ['---]	chanoinesse
cardinal	cardinal
chaplain	aumônier; chapelain
clergyman	ecclésiastique; pasteur, prêtre
cleric	ecclésiastique
celibacy ['----]	célibat
celibate	célibataire
chorister	choriste
bell-ringer	sonneur, carillonneur
choir ['kwaɪə] boy	jeune choriste, petit chanteur
lay reader	prédicateur laïque
congregation	congrégation; (assemblée des) fidèles
churchgoer	pratiquant
curate	vicaire
deacon ['diːkən]	diacre
deaconess GB [,--'-] / US ['---]	diaconesse
dean [diːn]	doyen
ecclesiastic [-,--'--]	ecclésiastique
elder	ancien; membre du conseil de l'église (presbytérienne)
episcopate [-'---] / episcopacy [-'----]	épiscopat
the faithful	les fidèles
father	père
flock	ouailles
friar	frère, Frère; moine, religieux
hermit	hermite
Imam	Imam
messiah [mə'saɪə]	messie
minister	pasteur, ministre
missionary	missionnaire
monk	moine, religieux
Reverend Mother	Révérende Mère
Mother Superior	Mère supérieure
mystic	mystique
novice	novice
padre ['pɑːdri]	aumônier (armée); prêtre, pasteur
pastor	pasteur
patriarch ['peɪtriɑːk]	patriarche
papacy ['peɪpəsi]	papauté
parishioner [-'---]	paroissien
parson	ecclésiastique, pasteur
Pope	pape
popery	papisme
preacher	prédicateur
prelate	prélat
priestess GB [-'-] / US ['--]	prêtresse

Religion - Faith - Beliefs - Denominations

prior	prieur	**vicar**	pasteur (église anglicane)
prioress GB [,--'-] / US ['---]	prieure	**nuncio**	nonce
rabbi ['ræbaɪ]	rabbin	**the Right Reverend**	Monseigneur
prophet	prophète	**Most Reverend**	Révérendissime
prophetess GB [,--'-] / US ['---]	prophétesse	**guru** ['gʊruː]	gourou
		ayatollah [ˌaɪ ə'tɒlə]	ayatollah
reverend	curé; pasteur	**mullah** ['mʌlə]	mollah
seer	prophète	**monsignor**	monsignor
saviour	sauveur	**the Pontiff**	le Pontife
saint	saint	**pontificate** [-'---]	pontificat
sexton	sacristain, bedeau	**His Holiness**	sa Sainteté
sister	religieuse, (bonne) sœur	**ordination**	ordination

Collocations

celibacy ['----]	célibat	*to practise celibacy - to take one's vows of celibacy*
churchman	ecclésiastique	*not to be much of a churchman* (pas très pratiquant)
clergy	clergé	*to be a member of the clergy - to join the clergy* (devenir prêtre)
martyr	martyr(e) (personne)	*to make a martyr of sb - to be / become a Christian martyr - to be (a) martyr to science*
martyrdom	martyre (état)	*to suffer martyrdom*
nun	religieuse, bonne sœur	*to become a nun* (prendre le voile, entrer en religion)
priest	prêtre (catholique); pope (orthodoxe)	*to defrock / ordain / unfrock a high / parish* (de la paroisse) *priest*
ministry	(saint) ministère	*to enter / go into the ministry* (se faire prêtre)
orders	ordres	*to be in / take holy orders* (être / entrer dans les ordres)
priesthood	prêtrise, sacerdoce	*to enter the priesthood*
vow [vaʊ]	vœu	*to take a vow / break one's vows of chastity*

■ *Adjectifs*

ascetic	ascétique	**papal** ['peɪpl]	papal
clerical	clérical; de pasteur, du clergé	**popish**	papiste
ecclesiastical [-,--'---]	ecclésiastique	**practising / religious**	pratiquant
faithful (to)	fidèle (à)	**religious**	religieux
monastic	monastique	**unmarried / single**	non-marié

■ *Verbes*

ordain	ordonner	**take the veil**	prendre le voile
take one's vows [vaʊz]	prononcer ses vœux	**vow** [vaʊ] **obedience**	faire vœu d'obéissance

Collocations

abstain	s'abstenir	*to abstain from sth / from doing sth*
draft GB [drɑːft] / US [dræft]	recruter, désigner	*to be drafted as a bishop*
pledge	(s')engager (à), promettre	*to pledge (oneself) to sth / to do sth / that ... - to be pledged to secrecy* (tenu à garder le secret) *- to pledge a life of poverty / one's support to sb / for a cause - to pledge / swear allegiance to one's country*

333

5.2. Places and communities

■ *Noms*

abbey ['æbi]	abbaye	**bishop's see**	siège épiscopal
archbishopric	archevêché (juridiction)	**chapel** ['tʃæpl]	chapelle
archdiocese	archidiocèse	**friary**	confrérie
archbishop's palace	archevêché (lieu)	**monastery**	monastère
diocese	diocèse	**parsonage**	presbytère
the cloth / the pulpit ['pʊlpɪt]	le clergé	**rectory / vicarage**	presbytère (anglican)
		church hall	salle paroissiale
basilica [-'---]	basilique	**kirk**	église (Écosse)
cathedral [kə'θiːdrəl]	cathédrale	**nunnery**	couvent
church	église	**the Vatican**	le Vatican
temple	temple	**Curia** ['kjʊəri_ə]	curie (gouvernement du Vatican)
synagogue	synagogue		
mosque [mɒsk]	mosquée	**the priesthood**	les prêtres
minster	cathédrale; église abbatiale	**priory**	prieuré
conventicle	conventicule	**the Holy See**	le Saint-Siège
cloister	cloître	**seminary**	séminaire
convent	couvent	**churchyard**	cimetière
bishopric	évêché (juridiction)	**theological college** (GB)	faculté de théologie
bishop's palace	évêché (lieu)	**place of worship**	lieu de culte, de prières
		sanctuary	sanctuaire

Collocations

conclave ['kɒnkleɪv]	conclave	*to hold a conclave / be in secret conclave to elect the Pope*
synod ['sɪnəd]	synode	*to call / summon a synod*

Exercices sur le chapitre 19 (5.1 et 5.2)

1. Testez vos connaissances en traduisant les mots ci-dessous :

A / vow - B / to pledge - C / lay reader - D / curate - E / célibataire - F / chanoine - G / diacre H / moine - I / le Saint-Siège - J / presbytère - K / archevêché

2. Traduisez en anglais :

A / Prononcer ses vœux de célibat. B / Ne pas être très pratiquant. C / Se faire prêtre. D / Souffrir le martyre. E / Prendre le voile. F / Défroquer un prêtre. G / Entrer dans les ordres. H / Faire vœu d'obéissance. I / S'engager à faire quelque chose. J / Apporter son soutien à une cause. K / Réunir un synode. L / Tenir conclave.

3. Trouvez les voyelles manquantes :

_BB_T / _BB_SS / FL_CK / P_DR_ / G_R_ / P_P_ / M_N_ST_R / P_NT_FF / _RD_N_T__N / S_N_D / D__C_S_ / FR__R_ / CL__ST_R / C_NCL_V_ / P_RS_N_G_ / S_N_G_G__ / PR_L_T_ / D__C_N

Religion - Faith - Beliefs - Denominations   335

5.3. Architecture

5.3.1. Outside view

■ *Noms*

apse [æps]	abside	pediment ['---]	fronton
arcade [-'-]	arcade, galerie	pillar	pilier, colonne
arch	arc, cintre, voûte	pinnacle	pinacle
archway	voûte (d'entrée), porche	porch	porche
arching	voussure	portico ['---]	portique
(offertory-) box	tronc	sanctuary	sanctuaire
balustrade GB [,--'-] / US ['---]	balustrade	see	siège (épiscopal)
		spire	flèche, aiguille
belfry ['belfri]	clocher, beffroi; clocheton	square	parvis
bell tower	clocher	steeple	clocher, flèche
capital	chapiteau	tower	tour
buttress	contrefort	transept	transept
churchyard	cimetière	east transept	transept oriental
clerestory ['klɪəstɔːri]	claire-voie, clair-étage	weather cock	girouette
column ['kɒləm]	colonne	west front	parvis ouest
colonnade [,--'-]	colonnade	window	vitrail
dome	dome	joist	doubleau, solive
east door	portail est ou oriental	ambulatory GB [,--'---] / US ['-----]	déambulatoire
flying buttress	arc-boutant		
front	façade	crossing	croisée du transept
gargoyle	gargouille	chevet [ʃə'veɪ]	chevet
gravestone	pierre tombale	Lady chapel ['tʃæpl]	chapelle axiale
graveyard	cimetière	keystone	clé de voûte
minaret [,mɪnə'ret]	minaret	apsidiole	absidiole
lichgate / lychgate	porche de cimetière	side chapel ['tʃæpl]	chapelle latérale
mullion	meneau	archivolt	voussure
pagoda [pə'ɡəʊdə]	pagode		

5.3.2. Inside view

■ *Noms*

aisle [aɪl]	bas-côté; allée centrale	chalice ['tʃælɪs]	calice
altar ['ɔːltə] cloth	nappe d'autel	chancel	chœur
altar ['ɔːltə] piece	retable	chancel screen	jubé, clôture du chœur
altar ['ɔːltə] rail(s)	balustre (de chœur), table de communion	candle	cierge
		candle holder	bougeoir
bell	cloche	candlestick	bougeoir; chandelier
bell rope	corde de cloche	chapel ['tʃæpl]	chapelle
church hall	salle paroissiale	chapel of ease	(église) succursale

chapel of rest	chapelle ardente	reliquary ['----]	reliquaire
choir ['kwaɪ_ə]	chœur	reredos ['rɪədɒs]	retable
choir organ	petit orgue	rose-window / rosace ['rəʊzeɪs]	rosace, rose
choir-stall	stalle (de chœur)		
confessional	confessionnal	sanctuary	sanctuaire
(holy) font / (US) fount	fonds baptismaux	shrine	châsse; tombeau
high altar ['ɔːltə]	maître-autel	stained glass (U)	vitraux; verre coloré
lectern	lutrin	stained-glass window (C)	vitrail
mullion	meneau	stoup [stuːp]	bénitier
nave	nef, vaisseau central	transept	transept
oratory	oratoire	triptych	triptyque
organ	orgue, orgues	vault	voûte; caveau
pew	banc d'église, siège	vestry ['vestri]	sacristie

Collocations

altar ['ɔːltə]	autel	to be at the altar - to take sb to the altar
cross	croix	to make the sign of the cross - to bear one's cross - to die on the cross
holy water	eau bénite	to sprinkle holy water
pulpit ['pʊlpɪt]	chaire	to speak from the pulpit - to ascend / mount the pulpit (monter en chaire)

■ Adjectifs

ancient ['eɪnʃənt]	ancien, antique; historique (monument)	majestic	majestueux
antique [-'-]	antique, de l'antiquité	modern	moderne
Baroque [-'-]	baroque	Norman	roman
classic	classique, de l'époque classique	perpendicular [,--'---] gothic	gothique perpendiculaire anglais
contemporary [-'---]	contemporain	rococo [-'--]	rococo
derelict ['derəlɪkt]	en ruines (tombe)	Roman	romain
dilapidated	délabré	Romanesque [,--'-]	roman
Gothic	gothique	ruined	en ruines
high / lofty	haut / élevé	tall	élevé, élancé (flèche)
in ruins	en ruines	tumbledown	en ruines, délabré
low	bas, peu élevé		

■ Verbes

build	construire, édifier	raise	bâtir, édifier (monument); ériger
construct	construire		
erect	ériger	support	soutenir (pilier)

Religion - Faith - Beliefs - Denominations

Exercices sur le chapitre 19 (5.3.1 et 5.3.2)

1. Testez vos connaissances en traduisant les mots ci-dessous :
A / clerestory - B / pediment - C / joist - D / keystone - E / retable - F / cierge
G / stalle (de chœur) - H / lutin - I / orgue - J / châsse - K / bénitier - L / banc - M / vitrail
N / vitraux - O / girouette

2. Traduisez en anglais :
A / Mener à l'autel. B / Faire le signe de croix. C / Monter en chaire. D / Asperger d'eau bénite.

3. Indiquez si les mots ci-dessous décrivent l'intérieur (I) ou l'extérieur (E) d'une église :
A / altar piece (I/E) - B / chalice (I/E) - C / spire (I/E) - D / belfry (I/E) - E / gravestone (I/E) - F / portico (I/E) - G / stoup (I/E) - H / reredos (I/E) - I / candle holder (I/E) - J / mullion (I/E)

6. Activities

■ *Noms*

adoration	adoration	litany	litanie
act of contrition	acte de contrition	liturgy ['lɪtədʒi]	liturgie
amen	amen	mat(t)ins ['mætɪnz]	matines
anointing of the sick	onction des malades	missal	missel
anointment	onction	morning prayer	prière du matin
anthem	motet	mystic	mystique
apostate	apostat	mysticism ['----]	mysticisme
apostasy	apostasie	proselyte ['prɒsəlaɪt]	prosélyte
Bible class	classe d'instruction religieuse; catéchisme	proselytism ['prɒsələtɪzəm]	prosélytisme
		(prayer) beads / rosary	chapelet
Bible school (US)	cours d'instruction religieuse	prayer book	livre de messe
chant GB [tʃɑːnt] / US [tʃænt]	chant; psalmodie; mélopée	the Prayer Book	le rituel (de l'Église anglicane)
		psalm [sɑːm]	psaume
Blessed / Holy Sacrament	Saint Sacrement	rosary	rosaire
catechism	catéchisme	Sunday school	école du dimanche; catéchisme
confirmation	confirmation	verse (C)	verset
evensong	vêpres; office du soir	vespers	vêpres
goddaughter	filleule	worship(p)er (of)	adorateur (de)
godfather	parrain	the worship(p)ers	les fidèles
godmother	marraine	psalmist ['sɑːmɪst]	psalmiste
godson	filleul	psalmody ['sɑːmədi]	psalmodie
host [həʊst]	hostie	revival	renouveau (religieux)
incense	encens	indoctrination	endoctrinement
incense bearer	thuriféraire	lapsed Catholic	catholique qui a cessé de pratiquer
incense burner	encensoir		
sprinkler	goupillon		

Collocations

ban sth	interdiction, interdit	*to put* (imposer) / *relax* (assouplir) *a ban on sth / on sb's doing*
baptism / christening	baptême	*to accept / administer (to sb) / receive / undergo baptism - to perform a baptism / a christening*
beads	grains (de rosaire)	*to tell / say one's beads* (terme daté : réciter son chapelet)
blessing	bénédiction	*to give / pronounce / say a blessing over sth - to bestow* (accorder) *one's blessing on sb / sth - to say the blessing* (bénédicité) *- to give one's blessing to sth / sb - sth may be a blessing for sb - it is a blessing to do sth / that ...*
ceremony ['----]	cérémonie	*to conduct / hold / perform a wedding ceremony*
circumcision [ˌsɜːkəm'sɪʒn]	circoncision	*to do / perform a circumcision on sb*
collection	quête	*to make / hold / organize / take up a collection*
communion	communion	*to administer / give / take Holy communion*
confession	confession	*to go to confession - to hear sb's confession - to make a public confession about sth / about sb / that ...*
council	concile	*to convoke a council*
curse	malédiction	*to be under a curse - to call down / lay / pronounce / put a curse on sb - to lift* (lever) / *utter* (prononcer) *a curse*
encyclical [ɪn'sɪklɪkl]	encyclique	*to issue an encyclical*
extreme unction / last rites	extrême onction	*to administer / give / receive extreme unction / the last rites*
fast GB [fɑːst] / US [fæst]	jeûne	*to break / observe a fast*
fellowship	communion, solidarité, esprit de camaraderie	*to foster* (encourager) / *promote / urge* (conseiller vivement) *fellowship*
hymn [hɪm]	hymne	*to chant / sing a hymn to sth / sb*
mass [mæs]	messe	*to attend / celebrate / hear / offer / say / go to mass - to say a mass for sb / in sb's memory*
meditation	méditation	*to go in for / practise meditation - to be deep in meditation on sth*
observance	observation, respect	*to urge / practise strict observance of sth*
penance ['penəns]	pénitence	*to do penance*
prayer	prière(s)	*to say a prayer for sb / one's prayers - to be at prayer / at one's prayers - to be kneeling in prayer - to offer / utter a prayer for sth / for sb / that ... (pour que ...) - to go to prayers / Evening Prayer* (office)
procession	procession	*to lead / march in a procession*
repentance	repentir	*to show genuine repentance for sth / for doing sth*
rite	rite	*to perform a pagan / religious rite*
ritual ['rɪtʃuəl]	rituel	*to go through / perform a ritual - to make a ritual of sth / of doing sth*
rosary	chapelet	*to say the rosary*
sacrament	sacrement	*to administer / receive the sacraments* (communier) / *the last sacraments*
service	office, service	*to celebrate / hold a funeral / a memorial / a prayer / religious service - to take services* (assister à) *- to attend the Sunday evening service / a thanksgiving* (d'action de grâces) *service*
temptation	tentation	*to yield to / give in to* (céder) / *resist temptation / the temptation of sth / of doing sth - to lead sb into temptation*
work	travail, œuvres	*to do / perform charitable work - to do missionary work*
worship	adoration, culte, vénération	*to attend worship regularly - to join together in worship - to practise ancestor worship - to find out about forms / places / hours of worship - to blame money worship for all evils*

Religion - Faith - Beliefs - Denominations

Exercices sur le chapitre 19 (6, noms)

1. Testez vos connaissances en traduisant les mots ci-dessous :
A / ban - B / worshipper - C / lapsed Catholic - D / filleule - E / hostie - F / chapelet

2. Remplissez la grille à l'aide des définitions proposées :

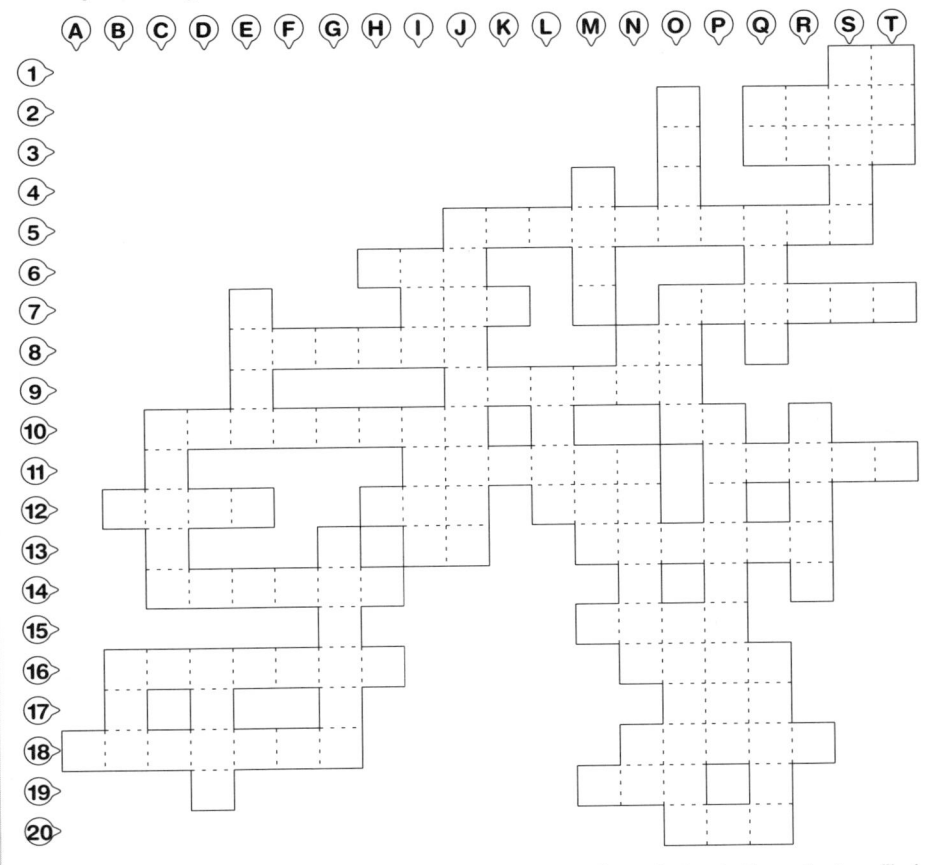

Horizontalement : 1. "bye-bye" (North of England) - 2. fin de prière - 3. chant - 5. application d'huile sainte - 6. Dieu + 7 : filleul - 7. O + 7 : tentation - 8. 6 + père : parrain; c'est-à-dire - 9. motet - 10. auteur de psaumes; post-scriptum - 11. litanie, piété - 12. messe; Tao; abréviation de paragraphe - 13. Tennessee; matines - 14. mystique - 15. travail - 16. encens; rôle - 17. comme les commandements - 18. renouveau; malédiction - 19. interdiction - 20. dû

Verticalement : B. colère (divine) - C. psaume - D. pièce (de monnaie) - E. jeûne (lettres mêlées) - G. missel - I. dare(s) (en français); lamelle (store) - J. adoration - L. piège - M. rite; Vietnam - N. c'est-à-dire; rosaire (à l'envers); circa - O. hostie; + 7 : tentation; rond, arrondi - P. goupillon - Q. exclamation; abréviation de "established"; s'ensuivre - R. mon, ma, mes; verset - S. tenter - T. prénom anglais féminin

3. Traduisez en anglais :

A / Administrer le baptême à un bébé. B / Accorder sa bénédiction à quelqu'un. C / Assister aux offices. D / Céder à la tentation. E / Manifester un repentir sincère. F / Réciter une prière. G / Faire pénitence. H / Dire la messe pour quelqu'un. I / Recevoir l'extrême-onction. J / Observer un jeûne. K / Prononcer une malédiction. L / Aller se confesser.

Adjectifs / Noms

contrite	penaud, contrit	mundane [-'-]	de ce monde, terrestre; quotidien, routinier
the destitute	les indigents, ceux qui sont sans ressources	the oppressed	les opprimés
devotional	de piété (ouvrage); pieux (attitude)	the poor	les pauvres
		repentant	repentant
the downtrodden	les maltraités	sacred (to)	sacré (pour)
earthly	terrestres (biens)	worldly	attaché aux biens de ce monde; mondain, temporel (sens religieux)
irredeemable [,--'---]	incorrigible (personne); irrémédiable		
liturgical [-'---]	liturgique	worldly goods	biens matériels
mystical	mystique	worldly attitude	attitude matérialiste

Collocations

penitent	pénitent	to be penitent for sth / for doing sth (regretter)
tempted	tenté	to be tempted to do sth / into doing sth / by sth / by sb

Verbes

adore	adorer	hallow	sanctifier, consacrer (nom, terre)
canonize	canoniser		
celebrate	célébrer; fêter	observe	observer (une fête)
chant GB [tʃɑːnt] / US [tʃænt]	psalmodier	object to	s'élever contre
		oppose sth	s'opposer à qch
circumcise	circoncire	indoctrinate	endoctriner
collect money	quêter, faire la quête	persecute ['---]	persécuter
communicate	communier	recant	abjurer
condemn [kən'dem]	condamner, désapprouver	profane	profaner (une tradition)
christen	baptiser	prophesy ['prɒfəsaɪ]	prophétiser
consecrate	consacrer (une église); sacrer, consacrer (un évêque)	promulgate	répandre (la foi)
		proselytize ['----]	faire du prosélytisme
desecrate ['---]	profaner (un lieu)	revere [-'-]	révérer, vénérer
perform one's duties as a pastor	remplir ses fonctions de pasteur	sacrifice (to)	sacrifier (à)
		sanctify	sanctifier
curse (sb)	jurer, sacrer; maudire qqn	sin	pécher
denounce sth	dénoncer, condamner qch	solemnize	solenniser (occasion); célébrer (mariage)
explode	démontrer la fausseté de		
expose	révéler au grand jour	venerate	vénérer
evangelise [-'---]	évangéliser	worship	adorer, rendre un culte à; faire ses dévotions
genuflect ['dʒenjuflekt]	faire une génuflexion		

Collocations

anoint	oindre; consacrer par l'onction	to anoint sb king (sacrer qqn roi) - to anoint sb with oil
ban	interdire	to ban sth - to ban sb from doing sth
baptise	baptiser	to baptize sb John / sb into the Catholic Church
bar	exclure; interdire	to bar sb from the church / sb from attending
pray	prier	to pray to God that ... - to pray for sb / sb's soul
preach	prêcher	to preach a sermon / fasting and prayer - to preach (to the congregation) against sth from the pulpit - to preach at sb (sermonner) - to preach that ...

Religion - Faith - Beliefs - Denominations 341

repent	se repentir	*to repent sth / doing sth*
say	dire, réciter	*to say grace / mass / one's prayers / the blessing* (bénédicité)
tempt	tenter	*to tempt sb into sth / to do sth - to be tempted (by sb / sth) into doing sth / to do sth*

Exercices sur le chapitre 19 (6, adjectifs et verbes)

1. Testez vos connaissances en traduisant les mots ci-dessous :

A / to promulgate - B / to worship - C / to expose - D / to recant - E / abjurer
F / s'opposer à qch - G / psalmodier - H / faire une génuflexion

2. Traduisez en anglais :

A / Sacrer quelqu'un roi. B / Prier Dieu que… C / Dire le bénédicité. D / Interdire à quelqu'un de prêcher. E / Se repentir d'avoir péché. F / Sermonner quelqu'un. G / Remplir ses fonctions de pasteur. H / Adorer Dieu. I / Admettre au sein de l'Église par le baptême.

7. Various other beliefs, sects and superstitions

7.1. General

■ *Noms*

allegory ['----]	allégorie		legend	légende
apologue ['---]	apologue		marvel	merveille, prodige, miracle
belief	croyance		mystic	mystique
credibility	crédibilité		mysticism	mysticisme
credulousness / credulity	crédulité		occultism ['----]	occultisme
enigma (to sb)	énigme (pour qqn)		plausibility	plausibilité
evil / malignant spirits	esprits malins		prodigy	prodige, merveille
fable	fable		child prodigy	enfant prodige
gullibility [,--'---]	(grande) crédulité		superstition	superstition
guru ['guru:]	gourou, maître à penser			

Collocations

miracle	miracle	*sth / sb may accomplish / perform / work miracles - it is a miracle that … - by a / some miracle*
mystery	mystère	*to clear up / solve / unravel* (démêler) *a mystery - sb's disappearance may pose a real mystery - it may be a mystery to sb how / when / where / why … - a mystery may deepen as time passes*
puzzle	énigme, mystère	*sth may be a puzzle to sb - to solve a puzzle - sb may be in a puzzle* (perplexe) *about sth / about what to do / how to do it / how sth happened*
riddle	énigme, devinette	*to ask sb a riddle - to solve a riddle - to speak / talk in riddles*

| sect | secte (fraction d'une religion reconnue ou groupement religieux clos sur lui-même) | to belong to / be a member of / join a breakaway sect - a sect may come into being / be formed |
| tale | conte, récit, histoire ; légende | to tell (sb) / act out (mimer) a tale - to tell tales (cafarder) about one's friends |

■ Adjectifs

breakaway	séparatiste, dissident	otherworldly	détaché des choses de ce monde
cabalistic [,--'--]	cabalistique	implausible	peu plausible ; peu vraisemblable
credible	crédible		
credulous	crédule	preternatural	surnaturel
esoteric [,--'--]	ésotérique	supernatural [,--'---]	surnaturel
gullible ['gʌləbl]	crédule, facile à duper	superstitious [,--'--]	superstitieux
misleading	trompeur (information)	paranormal	paranormal
mysterious	mystérieux	transcendental [,--'--]	transcendentale (méditation)
mystical	mystique	trustful / trusting	confiant
naive [naɪ'iːv]	naïf, ingénu	unearthly	mystérieux, pas de ce monde
metaphysical [,--'---]	métaphysique	unnatural	non naturel, anormal
occult	occulte	unsuspecting	qui ne se méfie pas, peu méfiant
overtrusting	trop prêt à faire confiance		
plausible	plausible, vraisemblable		

Collocations

| miraculous | miraculeux | it is miraculous that ... |
| uncritical | dépourvu d'esprit critique | to be uncritical of sth / sb |

Exercices sur le chapitre 19 (7.1, noms et adjectifs)

1. Testez vos connaissances en traduisant les mots ci-dessous :

A / gullibility - B / misleading - C / unearthly - D / riddle (n.) - E / crédule, facile à duper F / détaché des choses de ce monde - G / peu vraisemblable - H / confiant I / gourou, maître à penser - J / esprits malins - K / par miracle - L / surnaturel

2. Traduisez en anglais :

A / C'est un miracle que quelqu'un ait pu résoudre cette énigme. B / Être perplexe sur la façon dont se forment les sectes. C / Mimer un récit. D / Démêler un mystère. E / Accomplir un miracle. F / Rejoindre une secte dissidente. G / Poser à quelqu'un une devinette. H / Un mystère peut s'épaissir à mesure que le temps passe.

■ Verbes

lead sb astray	égarer qqn	swallow ['swɒləʊ]	avaler (ce qu'on vous dit)
manipulate sb	manœuvrer qqn	fall for sb	tomber amoureux de qqn
fall for sth	se laisser prendre à qch		

Collocations

| beguile | tromper, duper | to beguile sb into trusting a self-proclaimed guru - to beguile sb with false promises |

Religion - Faith - Beliefs - Denominations

believe	croire	to believe in sth / sb / that ...
brainwash	faire un lavage de cerveau à	to brainwash sb into thinking that ...
hoodwink	tromper, berner	to hoodwink sb into paying money to sb
deceive	tromper (par de faux semblants)	to deceive sb into doing sth
influence	influencer	to strongly influence sb in sth / sb to do sth
marvel	s'émerveiller	to marvel at sth / at sb / at being accepted into a sect
mislead [mɪsˈliːd]	induire qqn en erreur	to mislead sb into sth / into doing sth (amener, en trompant)
puzzle	se poser des questions, rester perplexe	to puzzle over / about sth / sb / how to do sth
	laisser, rendre perplexe	sth may puzzle sb deeply- sb may be puzzled about sth / not to see why ...
wonder [ˈwʌndə]	se demander	to wonder what sth is / who sb is / whether to do sth / what to do / how to do sth

7.2. Medicine and witchcraft

■ *Noms*

bone-setter	rebouteur, rebouteux		**sorcerer**	sorcier
healer	guérisseur		**sorceress / witch**	sorcière
charm	fétiche		**voodoo** [ˈvuːduː]	vaudou
lucky charm	porte-bonheur		**witchcraft**	sorcellerie
magus [ˈmeɪgəs]	mage		**witch doctor**	sorcier (de tribu)
medicine man	sorcier (Indiens)		**witchery**	sorcellerie; envoûtement (fascination exercée)
marabout [ˈmærəbuː]	marabout; devin, guérisseur		**witch hunt**	chasse aux sorcières
warlock	sorcier (dans les récits)		**wizard** [ˈwɪzəd]	sorcier; magicien, enchanteur
mountebank	charlatan, imposteur		**wizard** [ˈwɪzəd]	génie, qqn de très fort (jeux)
quack [kwæk] **(doctor)**	charlatan		**wizardry** [ˈwɪzədri]	magie, sorcellerie
Satanism [ˈseɪtənɪzəm]	satanisme			génie (dans le comportement)

Collocations

the evil eye	le mauvais œil	to give sb the evil eye
sorcery	sorcellerie	to be accused of practising sorcery
spell	sort; sortilège, charme	to cast / lay / put a spell on / over sb (ensorceler) - to put sb under a spell (envoûter) - to break (rompre) / remove a spell
wand [wɒnd]	baguette	to wave a magic wand

■ *Adjectifs*

fake	faux (médecin)		**satanic**	satanique

■ *Verbes*

charm	enchanter, ensorceler		**voodoo** [ˈvuːduː]	envoûter
heal (of)	guérir (de)			

Exercices sur le chapitre 19 (7.1, verbes et 7.2)

1. Testez vos connaissances en traduisant les mots ci-dessous :

A / to hoodwink - B / to deceive - C / to puzzle - D / mountebank - E / warlock - F / sorcier G / fétiche - H / magie, sorcellerie

2. Traduisez en anglais :

A / Se laisser prendre à une suggestion. B / Tomber amoureux de son maître à penser. C / Amener quelqu'un, en le trompant, à vous faire confiance. D / Amener quelqu'un, en le bernant, à vous donner de l'argent. E / S'émerveiller du pouvoir magique des sorciers. F / Pratiquer la sorcellerie. G / Jeter un sort à quelqu'un. H / Rompre un charme. I / Guérir quelqu'un de quelque chose.

7.3. Astrology

■ *Noms*

astrologer [əˈstrɒlədʒə]	astrologue	**Virgo** [ˈvɜːgəʊ]	Vierge
astrology [əˈstrɒlədʒi]	astrologie	**Libra** [ˈliːbrə]	Balance
Aquarius [əˈkweəriəs]	Verseau	**Scorpio** [ˈskɔːpiəʊ]	Scorpion
Pisces [ˈpaɪsiːz]	Poissons	**Sagittarius** [ˌ--ˈ---]	Sagittaire
Aries [ˈeəriːz]	Bélier	**Capricorn** [ˈ---]	Capricorne
Taurus [ˈtɔːrəs]	Taureau	**signs of the zodiac**	signes du zodiaque
Gemini [ˈdʒemɪnaɪ]	Gémeaux	**sign**	signe
Cancer [ˈkænsə]	Cancer	**the stars**	l'horoscope
Leo [ˈliːəʊ]	Lion		

Collocations

horoscope	horoscope	*to cast* (dresser) *a horoscope - to read one's / sb's horoscope* (consulter)
sign	signe, indication	*sth may be a sign of sth / of sb's doing sth / that ... - 'What sign were you born under?'*
star	étoile	*to have been born under a lucky / unlucky star - to thank one's (lucky) stars* (le ciel) *that ... it may be written in the stars* (être écrit) *that ...*

7.4. Conjuring, palm reading, seers, spiritualism and magic

■ *Noms*

black cloak	cape noire (magicien)	**conjuring** [ˈ---] **trick**	tour de prestidigitation
charm	charme, fétiche, amulette	**cardsharp(er)**	tricheur (professionnel)
chiromancer [ˈkaɪrəʊmænsə]	chiromancien	**card player**	joueur de cartes
chiromancy [ˈkaɪrəʊmænsi] / **palmistry** [ˈpɑːmɪstri]	chiromancie	**card table**	table de jeu
		divining rod	baguette divinatoire
clairvoyant [-ˈ---]	voyante	**enchanter** [-ˈ--]	enchanteur
conjurer [ˈ---]	prestidigitateur, illusionniste	**enchantment** [-ˈ--]	ensorcellement
(crystal) ball	boule de cristal	**enchantress** [-ˈ---]	enchanteresse

Religion - Faith - Beliefs - Denominations 345

fortune-teller	tireuse de cartes; diseuse de bonne aventure	parapsychologist [ˌpærəsaɪˈkɒlədʒɪst]	parapsychologue
fortune-telling	cartomancie	ouija board	oui-ja
illusionist [-'---]	illusionniste	seer	voyant, prophète
legerdemain (U) [ˌledʒədəˈmeɪn]	prestidigitation (terme daté)	sixth sense	sixième sens
		sibyl	sibylle
magic	magie	sleight of hand (U / C) [slaɪt]	tour de passe-passe, dextérité
(magic) wand [wɒnd]	baguette magique		
magician	magicien	soothsayer	devin
medium	médium	spell-binder	orateur de grand talent; qch qui vous tient sous son charme
mind-reader	télépathe		
mind-reading	télépathie	spiritualism ['-----]	spiritisme
necromancer ['----]	nécromancien	spiritualist ['----]	spirite
necromancy ['----]	nécromancie	the tarot (U) [ˈtærəʊ]	le(s) tarot(s)
the occult / the occult sciences [ˈɒkʌlt]	le surnaturel, les sciences occultes	tarot [ˈtærəʊ] card	(carte de) tarot
		telepathy	télépathie
palmist [ˈpɑːmɪst]	chiromancien	thought transfer(ence)	transmision de pensée
palmistry [ˈpɑːmɪstri] / palm reading [pɑːm]	chiromancie	trickery	supercherie, fourberie
		UFO (Unidentified Flying Object)	OVNI
parapsychology [ˌpærəsaɪˈkɒlədʒi]	parapsychologie	seance [ˈseɪɒ̃s] table	table tournante

Collocations

card	carte	*to read the cards / sb's cards* (tirer les cartes)
destiny	destinée	*to achieve / fulfil one's destiny - sth may decide / shape sb's destiny - to control / determine / take charge of one's own destinies - it is sb's destiny to do sth - to try and escape one's destiny*
divination	divination	*to have a sort of gift of second sight or divination*
fate	sort	*to leave sb to his fate - to meet one's fate* (trouver la mort) *- sth may meet with a strange fate / seal sb's fate - fate may have sth in store for sb / decree that ... - sb may decide sb's fate - to tempt fate*
incantation	incantation	*to chant / utter / wail an incantation to the spirits*
magic	magie	*to perform black magic - to show magic tricks*
seance [ˈseɪɒ̃s]	séance de spiritisme	*to attend / hold a spiritualist* (de spiritisme) *seance*
trick	tour	*to do / perform a card / conjuring / hat trick*
vision	vision	*to have / see visions - to have a vision of sth / of doing sth / of being done sth to*

■ *Adjectifs*

demonic	démoniaque, diabolique	doomed to failure	voué à l'échec
destined [ˈdestɪnd] to do sth	destiné à faire qch	doomed to be killed	dont le destin était d'être tué
fated to do sth	destiné, condamné à faire qch		

Collocations

psychic [ˈsaɪkɪk]	psychique, métapsychique	*to be psychic* (télépathe) *- to be in a low psychic state*

Verbes

appear	apparaître	**foretell**	prédire (l'avenir)
disappear [,--'-]	disparaître	**win the charm**	tirer la fève
foresee sth / that ...	prévoir qch / que ...	**do table-turning**	faire tourner les tables
predict (that ...)	prédire (que ...)		

Collocations

read	lire, interpréter	*to read sb's palm / sb's hand / the tea leaves / the teacups / sb's cards* (tirer les cartes)
tell	dire, prédire	*to tell sb's fortune / the future*

Exercices sur le chapitre 19 (7.3 et 7.4)

1. Testez vos connaissances en traduisant les mots ci-dessous :

A / to win the charm - B / legerdemain - C / trickery - D / UFO - E / seance table
F / chiromancien - G / tricheur (aux cartes) - H / prestidigitateur

2. Remplissez la grille à l'aide des définitions proposées :

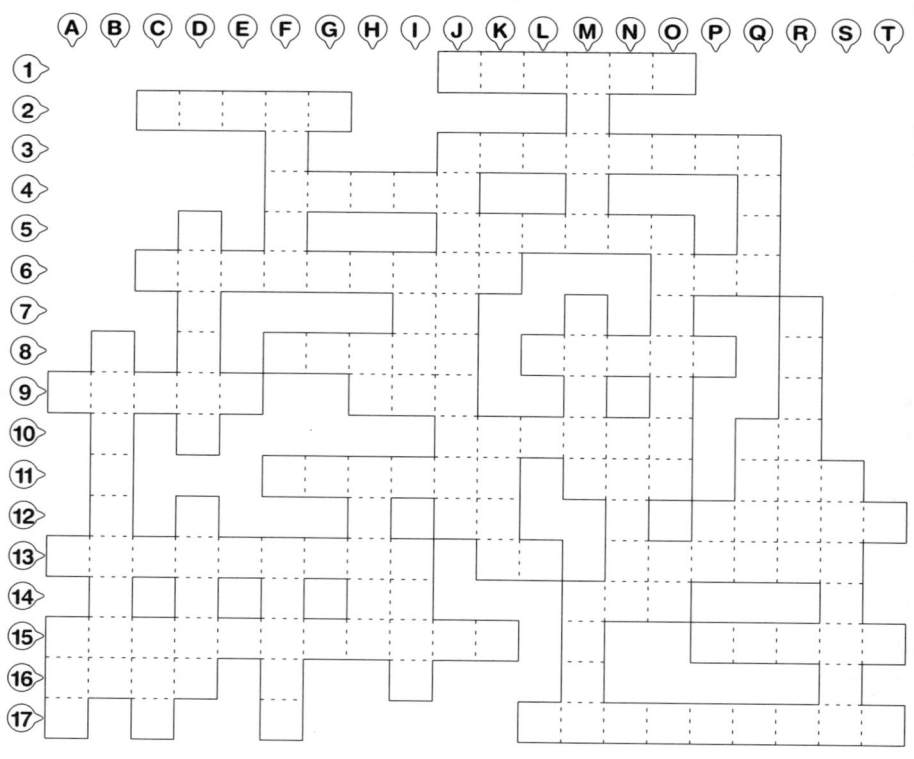

Horizontalement : 1. R + 1 : diseuse de bonne aventure - 2. 2 + 9 : devin - 3. Verseau - 4. Bélier - 5. Taureau - 6. Capricorne; escroquer, duper - 7. les trois premières lettres de D (2) + 7 : Vierge - 8. sort, sortilège; Balance - 9. 2 + 9 : devin; Lion - 10. Gémeaux; Montana - 11. Poissons; Lion; intrauterine device - 12. Royal Academy; intérieur (adj.) - 13. (séparé par un espace) Sagittaire;

Q (2) + 13 (3) : télépathe - 14. Expert system; brouillard - 15. Illusionniste; magie - 16. (inversé) Voyant, prophète - 17. Télépathie

Verticalement : A. colère - B. Table de jeu - C. Lion - D. Cancer; virus - F. (lettres mêlées) Tarot; triade - H. Elevated railroad; Sirene - I. Reluquer, lorgner; Isis - J. Astrologue - K. Article indéfini; Esaü - M. (lettres mêlées) Mois de l'année; sibylle (avec une faute d'orthographe); destin - N. Début de nécromancie - O. Scorpion; par exemple - P. Iowa - Q. Signe; Q + 13 (3) : télépathe - R. R + 1 : diseuse de bonne aventure - S. Derviche

7.5. Various beings and creatures

■ *Noms*

angel ['eɪndʒəl]	ange	guardian angel	ange gardien
archangel	archange	imp	diablotin, lutin
augur ['ɔːgə]	augure (personne)	leprechaun ['leprəkɔːn]	lutin, farfadet
the big bad wolf [wʊlf]	le grand méchant loup	Little Red Riding Hood	le Petit Chaperon Rouge
bogeyman	croquemitaine, père fouettard	mermaid	sirène
brownie	lutin, farfadet	merman	triton
bugbear	croquemitaine, ogre; bête noire	monster	monstre
centaur	centaure	Mother Goose	ma Mère l'Oye
cherub	chérubin	Nessie	monstre du Loch Ness
Cinderella [‚--'--]	Cendrillon	nymph	nymphe
demon ['diːmən]	démon	ogre	ogre
the Demon ['diːmən]	le Démon	Peter Pan	Peter Pan
dryad	dryade	phantom	fantôme; fantasme (vision)
elf	elfe, lutin, farfadet	spook	apparition, revenant (fam.)
exorcist ['---]	exorciste	sprite	lutin, farfadet
fairy	fée	vampire	vampire
extraterrestrial	extra-terrestre	werewolf ['weəwʊlf]	loup-garou
ghost [gəʊst]	fantôme	wraith [reɪθ]	apparition, spectre
ghoul [guːl]	goule, vampire; déterreur de cadavres	spectre	spectre
giant	géant	shade	spectre (terme daté)
gnome [nəʊm]	gnome, lutin	poltergeist ['pɒltəgaɪst]	esprit frappeur
goblin / hob	lutin, farfadet	Titan ['taɪtn]	Titan

Collocations

apparition	apparition	*to see strange apparitions at night*
augury (C / U)	présage, signe; (art de la) prédiction	*sales figures may be a good augury for the future - sb's recovery may defy all medical augury*
exorcism ['----]	exorcisme	*to practise exorcism*
spirit	esprit, revenant	*to conjure up / evoke an evil / a holy spirit - to cast out (chasser) / expel a spirit - the spirit of a dead person may communicate with the living by rapping on the table*

■ *Verbes*

appear	apparaître	suck blood	sucer le sang
haunt	hanter	visit	venir rendre visite à
stomp along	marcher d'un pas lourd	rattle	(faire) cliqueter (des chaînes)

augur [ˈɔːgə]	augurer	*sth may augur well for sth / for sb / for sb's success*	
exorcise	exorciser	*to exorcise sb / a house - to exorcise an evil spirit / a demon from sb's body*	

7.6. Ancient beliefs and mythology

■ *Noms*

alchemist [ˈælkəmɪst]	alchimiste	**Juno**	Junon
alchemy [ˈælkəmi]	alchimie	**Oedipus** [ˈiːdɪpəs]	Oedipe
philosopher's stone	pierre philosophale	**Orpheus**	Orphée
animism	animisme	**Sphinx**	sphinx
animist	animiste	**Ulysses**	Ulysse
Apollo [ˈ---]	Apollon	**the nether world**	les Enfers
Atlas [ˈætləs]	Atlas	**the underworld**	les Enfers; aussi: le milieu, la pègre
Cupid	Cupidon		
Hades [ˈheɪdiːz]	les Enfers	**folklore** [ˈfəʊlkɔː]	folklore
Heaven [ˈhevn]	ciel	**gods**	dieux
Hell	enfer	**goddesses** [ˈ---]	déesses
Hercules [ˈhɜːkjuliːz]	Hercule	**legend**	légende
		mythology	mythologie

Collocations

myth	mythe	*to create / debunk* (démythifier) */ expel* (détruire) */ explode* (dégonfler, démolir) *a myth / the myth that...*	

■ *Adjectifs*

fabulous	fabuleux, de fable	**mythical**	mythique
legendary [ˈ----]	légendaire	**mythological**	mythologie

■ *Verbes*

animate	animer (la matière)	**transmigrate** GB [,--ˈ-] / US [-ˈ--]	(âme) transmigrer
reincarnate [,--ˈ---]	réincarner		

Exercices sur le chapitre 19 (7.5 et 7.6)

1. Testez vos connaissances en traduisant les mots ci-dessous :

A / bugbear - B / brownie - C / wraith - D / croquemitaine - E / loup-garou - F / présage, signe

2. Remplissez la grille en vous aidant des définitions proposées :

Horizontalement : 1. 1 + E (1) : augure - 2. Drogue; big, bad _____ - 3. Pas le paradis - 4. Lutin; fabuleux; 4 (3) + V (1) + 5 + 12 (2) : histoire pour enfants - 5. Voir 4 (3) - 6. Ange; livre saint; Saint - 7. Homme fort; cérémonie d'expulsion du diable - 8. Celui qui pratique 7 (2) - 9. Géant incomplet; ces trois lettres + 10 (1) : ce qu'on voit si on a des visions; antonyme d'immersion - 10. Voir 9 ; fée (à l'envers) - 11. Assoifé de sang - 12. Conte en prose de Perrault; voir 4 (3) - 13. Mythe;

Religion - Faith - Beliefs - Denominations   349

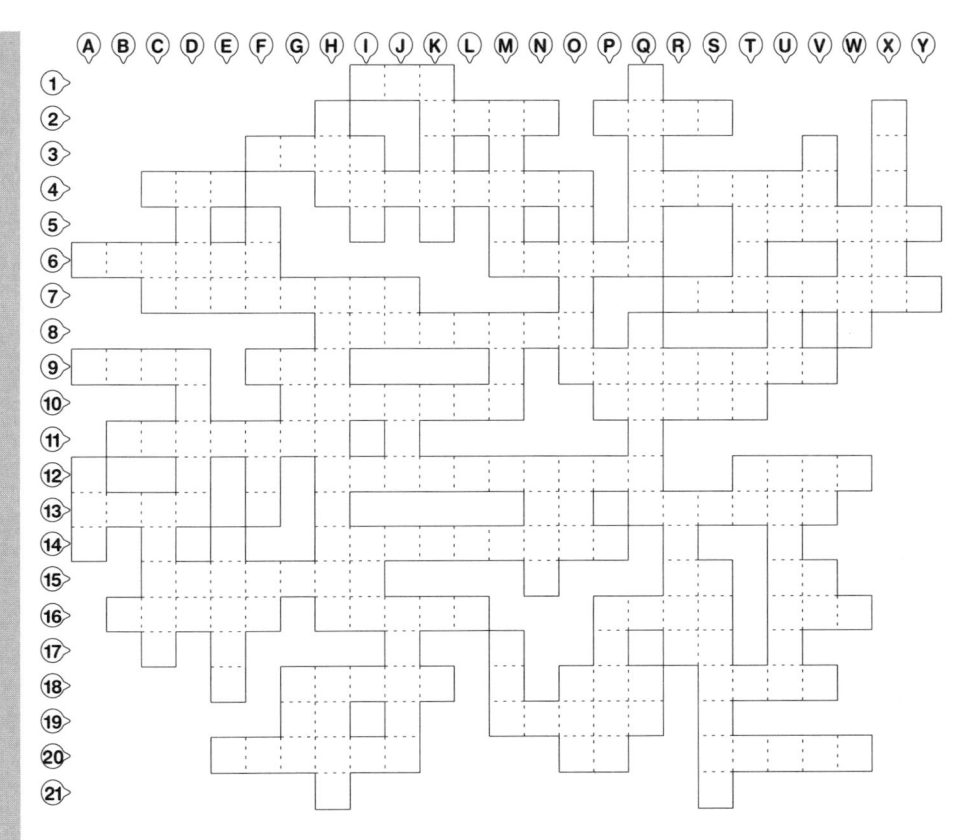

Royal Infantry; ce mot + world : enfers - 14. Plus qu'un ange - 15. En quête d'Euridyce; par exemple; il, elle, cela - 16. Spectre (terme daté); (lettres mêlées) ange; ces quatre lettres (avec un P en trop) + 18 (2) : synonyme de beauté masculin; R2, dans le désordre + ces trois lettres : conte pour enfants - 17. Road - 18. Démon; voir 16 (3); manquer de respect à quelqu'un (argot) - 19. Elisabeth Regina; dryade - 20. Monstre pour touristes; S.E.; marcher d'un pas lourd

Verticalement : A. Diablotin - C. Exclamation; (à l'envers) fantôme - D. Mange les petits enfants; synonyme de grâce féminine; Royal Academy - E. Voir 1; (lettres mêlées) Cupidon - F. Radio et télé (GB); colère; il - G. Paragraphe; Department of Education and Science - H. Elfe; farfadet; gaëlique - I. Laboratoire; ancien; Royal Society of Arts - J. Ainsi, donc, aussi; 1016 kg 05 en GB; petit génie difforme - K. Goule - M. Apparition; ion; dieu - N. Donc (en latin) - O. Lutin, esprit; mensonge; lessive (substance) - P. Mon, ma, mes; Titan aux larges épaules - Q. Lutin; triton; surdose - R. Religious instruction; (lettres mêlées) Pierre (voir 16 (4)) - S. Salutation Army; déesse - T. À trois; si; S.A. - U. Long Island; au Brésil; personne complexée - V. Voir 4; ou; au revoir - W. Visite incomplète - X. Hante

20
Literary terms, appreciation and analysis

Note : Nous avons utilisé, pour ce chapitre, le *Concise Dictionary of Literary Terms* de *Chris Baldick* (Oxford University Press).

0. General

■ *Noms*

literature ['lɪtrətʃə]	littérature	**volume**	volume
booklet	petit livre, brochure, plaquette		

Collocations

book	livre	*to write / publish a book - a book comes out / is out of print / is printing - a book* (collection) *of poems*
text (U / C)	texte	*there may be too much text / 500 pages of text and too few pictures - to annotate / truncate / break* (entrecouper) *a closely-printed text with drawings*

1. Fiction

■ *Noms*

apologue	apologue	**comics / comic strips**	bandes dessinées
beast fable	fable (avec animaux)	**commonplace book**	recueil de citations
bestiary	bestiaire	**detective story**	roman policier
bodice ripper ['bɒdɪs rɪpə]	roman d'amour violent (souvent historique)	**dystopia**	contre-utopie
		epistolary [-'----] **novel**	roman épistolaire
book	livret (opéra)	**extravaganza** [-,--'---]	fantaisie
campus novel	roman qui se passe à l'université	**fable**	fable
		fairy tale / story	conte de fées
chapbook	recueil de ballades, etc. vendu dans la rue	**fantasy**	fantaisie
		funnies (US)	bandes dessinées
chivalric romance	roman de chevalerie	**Gothic novel**	roman noir
chronicle	chronique historique (plus ou moins romancée)	**the grotesque** [-'-]	le grotesque
		historical novel	roman historique
classicism ['----]	classicisme	**historical / 'costume' romance**	roman où l'arrière-plan historique joue un rôle purement décoratif
cloak and dagger story	roman de cape et d'épée		
cock-and-bull story	histoire à dormir debout		

history play	pièce historique	sci-fi [saɪˈfaɪ]	science-fiction (forme abrégée de **'science fiction'**)
legend [ˈledʒənd]	légende	science fiction	science-fiction
lyricism [ˈ----]	lyrisme	screenplay	scénario
miscellanies [-ˈ---]	mélanges littéraires	serial	feuilleton (télévision)
miscellany [-ˈ---]	recueil, sélection, anthologie	serial story	roman-feuilleton
myth	mythe	short story	nouvelle
naturalism [ˈnætʃr̩əlɪzəm]	naturalisme	sketch	portrait ou description rapide
nonsense	non-sens, absurde	spy thriller	roman d'espionnage
novel with a purpose	roman à thèse	strip cartoons [-ˈ-]	bandes dessinées
novelette [,--ˈ-]	petite nouvelle roman de deux sous	symbolism [ˈ----]	symbolisme
		tale	conte, récit
novella [-ˈ---]	longue nouvelle	tall tale / story	histoire, récit peu croyable
parable	parabole	the classics	les classiques
picaresque [,--ˈ-] tale	conte picaresque	the nouveau roman	le nouveau roman
realism	réalisme	three-decker	roman en trois volumes (époque victorienne)
romance [rəʊˈmæns]	idylle, aventure amoureuse le romanesque roman médiéval, chevaleresque roman sentimental	thriller	roman (ou film) à suspense
		Utopia	utopie
		vignette [-ˈ-]	courte description (prose ou vers)
romanticism [-ˈ----]	romantisme		
saga [ˈsɑːgə]	saga; roman-fleuve	whodun(n)it	polar

Collocations

fiction (U)	fiction	*a work of fiction*
novel	roman	*a novel can be a(n) adventure / epic / autobiographical novel*
prose	prose	*to prefer prose to poetry - to write a piece of prose - to write in prose - to do a French prose / prose translation* (thème)
work (U)	travail	*to praise sb's work - to have done fine work / a fine piece of work*
work (C)	œuvre	*sb's latest work - sb's collected works* (œuvres complètes)

■ *Adjectifs*

burlesque [-ˈ-]	burlesque	pathetic	pathétique
classic	classique (auteur, œuvre)	philosophical	philosophique
classical	classique (latin, musique)	psychological	psychologique
dramatic	dramatique (art, critique, artiste, effet) dramatique (événement) spectaculaire (changement)	realistic [-ˈ--]	réaliste
		romantic	romantique
		science fiction	de science-fiction
euphuistic [,juːfjuˈɪstɪk]	précieux (style, genre)	surrealist [səˈrɪəlɪst]	surréaliste (écrivain)
fictional	fictif, imaginaire	surrealistic [sə,rɪəˈlɪstɪk]	surréaliste (décor, comédie)
mock-heroic	burlesque (genre); héroï-comique	symbolic(al) (of)	symbolique (de)
		tragic	tragique
naturalistic [,nætʃr̩əˈlɪstɪk]	naturaliste (écrivain)	Utopian	utopique

Literary terms, appreciation and analysis   353

2. Non-fiction

■ *Noms*

anthology	anthologie	journal ['dʒɜːnl]	journal, revue
article	article (journal)	lampoon [-'-]	libelle
autobiography [,---'---]	autobiographie	magazine GB [,--'-] / US ['---]	revue
bibliography	bibliographie	manual	manuel
biography	biographie	memoir ['memwɑː]	mémoire, étude, notice biographique
codex (pl. codices)	recueil de manuscrits anciens		
collection	collection	proceedings	actes (société savante)
compendium	abrégé, compendium, condensé	memoirs ['memwɑːz]	mémoires
confessions	confessions	pamphlet	pamphlet
diary	journal (intime)	panegyric [,--'--]	panégyrique
dissertation (US)	thèse	piece	article (de circonstance)
epic	épopée; poème ou récit épique	survey	étude (officielle)
encomium	éloge, panégyrique	textbook	livre de classe
eulogy ['---]	panégyrique	the book / directory	l'annuaire (téléphone)
glossary	glossaire	thesis	thèse
hagiography [,--'---]	hagiographie	treatise ['triːtɪz]	traité
handbook	manuel		

Collocations

report [-'-]   rapport   *to write (out) / make out / submit / file* (joindre à un dossier) *a favourable report*

■ *Adjectifs*

biographical	biographique	bibliographical	bibliographique
autobiographical	autobiographique	epic	épique

3. Content of fiction and / or non-fiction

3.1. Structure

■ *Noms*

abstract ['--]	résumé, abrégé	content (U) ['--]	contenu, fond
acknowledgements [ək'nɒlɪdʒmənts]	remerciements	contents ['--]	contenu, éléments
		core	essentiel (problème)
addendum	ajout	crux [krʌks]	cœur, centre
appendix	appendice, annexe	denouement [deɪ'nuːmõ]	dénouement
chapter	chapitre	design	propos, dessein, but
clue / pointer	indice	discrepancy	divergence
commentary	commentaire (journal)	epigraph ['---]	épigraphe
construction	construction; interprétation (d'un texte)	epilogue	épilogue
		episode	épisode

excerpt	passage, extrait	**running commentary**	commentaire détaillé, ligne à ligne; en direct
explanation	explication	**structure**	structure
extract	passage (à commenter)	**subject matter**	sujet, contenu
foreword	avant-propos	**substance**	substance, fond
overall pattern	structure d'ensemble	**subtext**	sujet sous-jacent
passage	morceau, passage	**synopsis**	résumé, précis; synopsis
precis GB ['preɪsiː] / US [preɪ'siː]	résumé, précis	**table of contents**	table des matières
preface / postface (to)	préface /postface (de)	**topic**	sujet (essai, discours)
quote	citation	**topicality** (U)	actualité (d'un sujet)
reference (to)	renvoi (à)		

Collocations

comment (C) ['--]	remarque, observation, commentaire	*to make a comment on / about sth*	
conclusion	conclusion	*to come to the conclusion that ... - to draw / reach a conclusion from sth - sth may lead to the conclusion that ... In conclusion, I would say that ...*	
construction	interprétation	*to put a(n) favourable / unfavourable / wrong construction on sth*	
purpose	objet, propos, but	*sth may be adequate for a specific purpose - sb's purpose in doing sth may not be clear - sth may lack purpose* (ne pas avoir de but précis)	
quotation	citation	*to give / include a quotation from a text / from sb*	
subject	sujet	*to address (oneself to)* (aborder) */ deal with / dwell on / go into / treat a delicate / ticklish subject - to take up / digress from / return to a subject - a subject may come up for discussion - to have little / nothing to say on a subject / on the subject of why / how ... - "while we're on the subject (of style) ..."*	

■ *Adjectifs*

conclusive	concluant, définitif	**topical**	d'actualité (sujet)
debatable	discutable	**touched with**	teinté, rehaussé de, par
summary	sommaire		

■ *Verbes*

extract from	extraire (un passage) de	**round off**	parachever (une phrase)
focus on	se concentrer sur; porter sur (sujet)	**sum up**	résumer (faits, arguments)
keep to the point	rester dans le sujet	**summarize**	résumer (livre, texte)
locate	situer (une scène)	**tackle**	aborder, s'attaquer à (sujet)
quote (from) sb / sth	citer qqn / un texte	**to round off / up** (US)	pour conclure, résumer
quote ..., unquote	ouvrez..., fermez les guillemets	**touch up**	retoucher (texte, œuvre)
recap ['--] **/ recapitulate** [,--'---]	récapituler	**touch upon**	effleurer (sujet)
refer sb to sth	renvoyer qqn à qch	**wander** ['wɒndə] **away from**	s'éloigner de (sujet)
refer to	faire référence à	**wind** [waɪnd] **up**	clôturer, clôre (discours)

Collocations

comment ['--]	faire des remarques, commenter, faire remarquer

to decline to comment (se refuser à tout commentaire) *(on sth) - to comment that...*

Literary terms, appreciation and analysis 355

conclude [-'-]	conclure		*to conclude from sth that... - to conclude by doing sth*
			- to conclude with sth - to conclude (pour conclure)
construe / misconstrue	interpréter / mal interpréter		*sb's silence may be construed as consent - sb may construe sb's*
			words to be a threat - sb's intentions may be wrongly construed

3.2. Description

■ *Noms*

delineation	description détaillée (de qqn ou qch)	**portrayal** [-'--]	portrait (qu'on fait de qqn), peinture (de qch)
depiction	peinture, représentation imagée	**representation**	représentation, façon de représenter (qqn ou qch)
portrait ['--]	portrait (peinture ou roman)		

Collocations

description	description	*to give / provide a fair / bias(s)ed / accurate / clear / detailed / matter-of-fact / vivid / superficial description of sth / of how / why ... - sth may defy / beggar description*

■ *Adjectifs*

accurate ['---]	exact, précis	**lively**	vivant, plein de vie
arresting [-'--]	frappant, saisissant	**long-winded** [ˌlɒŋ'wɪndɪd]	prolixe, interminable
circumstancial [ˌ--'--]	circonstancié (rapport)	**minute** [maɪ'njuːt]	minutieux, détaillé
convincing	convaincant	**objective**	objectif, impartial
descriptive	descriptif	**packed with details**	bourré de détails
detailed	détaillé (récit)	**plain**	simple, direct
drawn from life	puisé dans la vie même, réaliste	**poignant**	poignant
dull	terne, peu intéressant	**sketchy**	sommaire (portrait)
imaginary [-'----]	imaginaire	**subjective**	subjectif
imaginative [-'----]	plein d'imagination	**tedious** ['tiːdiˌəs]	ennuyeux, fastidieux
inaccurate [-'---]	inexact	**thorough** ['θʌrə]	approfondi
irrelevant [-'---]	non pertinent, hors de propos	**tiresome**	ennuyeux, lassant
lengthy	interminable, trop long	**unbelievable**	incroyable
lifelike	vivant, qui semble vrai	**unimaginative** [ˌ--'----]	dépourvu d'imagination

■ *Verbes*

adumbrate ['---]	esquisser, ébaucher	**invent**	inventer
call up	faire penser à, évoquer	**outline**	tracer les grandes lignes de
cheer (up)	égayer	**picture**	représenter, dépeindre
create	créer	**picture to oneself**	se représenter
delineate	décrire, dépeindre (avec précision)	**put sth well / badly**	bien / mal dire, raconter qch
		represent [ˌ--'-]	représenter
depict	dépeindre	**sketch**	esquisser
describe	décrire	**spin out**	allonger, délayer (histoire, scène)
enliven [ɪn'laɪvn]	animer, donner de la vie à	**stress**	faire ressortir (détail), attirer l'attention sur
imagine [-'--]	imaginer		

Collocations

convey	transmettre, communiquer	*sb / sth may convey an impression to sb - a writer may convey to sb that ...* (faire comprendre)
portray	décrire	*to portray sb as* (faire de qqn) *a bitter man*

3.3. Story, plot, theme

■ Noms

essence	essence	**pith**	quintessence, point central (article)
gist [dʒɪst]	fond, essence, point essentiel		
niceties	finesses, raffinements	**purple patch / passage**	morceau de bravoure
pace	pas, allure		

Collocations

account [-'-]	compte rendu, exposé, récit	*to give a first-hand account of sth - by all accounts* (au dire de tous)
impetus ['---]	élan, force	*a story may gain impetus* (prendre de l'ampleur)
momentum [-'--]	force, vitesse	*a story may gain / gather momentum as it nears the end*
plot	intrigue, histoire, action	*to construct / build a contrived* (qui manque de naturel) */ straightforward plot - a plot may thicken* (se corser) */ unfold slowly - a twist* (péripétie) *in the plot*
report [-'-]	rapport	*to write (out) / make out / submit / file* (joindre à un dossier) *a favourable / negative report about / on sth*
story	histoire	*to write / tell sb stories*
	action, intrigue	*not to think much of the story of a film / book - to do the story for a film* (scénario)
theme	thème, sujet	*sb's books may all be variations on the same theme*
	rédaction (US)	*to be set a theme to write on a subject*

- a story / plot / theme may be:

■ Adjectifs

captivating	captivant	**moving**	émouvant
cheering	réconfortant	**plausible**	plausible, vraisemblable
diverting	divertissant	**probable**	vraisemblable
engrossing	prenant, passionnant	**racy**	risqué, osé
entertaining	divertissant, distrayant	**recurrent** [-'--]	fréquent
enthralling	qui vous tient sous le charme	**stirring**	qui remue, émouvant
eventful [-'--]	fertile en événements	**thrilling**	palpitant
exciting	passionnant, excitant	**touching**	touchant, attendrissant
fascinating	fascinant		

- or it may be:

bawdy	paillard	**improbable**	peu vraisemblable
endless	interminable	**improper**	scabreux
forbidding	rébarbatif	**irksome**	ennuyeux
implausible	invraisemblable	**lengthy**	trop long

Literary terms, appreciation and analysis

■ *Verbes*

disclose	révéler (secret)	progress	progresser, avancer
unfold	se dérouler, progresser (histoire)	unravel	débrouiller, éclaircir (mystère / secret)
take place	se dérouler, avoir lieu	illustrate	illustrer

3.4. Atmosphere, setting, action

■ *Noms*

background	arrière-plan	location (U)	lieu, emplacement
backdrop	toile de fond	scenery	paysage, cadre
climax	point culminant, paroxysme	surroundings	alentours, environs
anticlimax	chute, retombée		cadre, décors

Collocations

action	action	*the action may take place in a distant country / in the 17th century - it may drag / pick up* (reprendre) */ move from one place to another - there may be too little / a lot of action - unity of action*
atmosphere	atmosphère	*sth may contribute to create a friendly / hostile atmosphere - an atmosphere of gloom may pervade / permeate a whole scene*
expectancy [-'---]	attente, espoir	*air / look of expectancy*
expectation [,--'---]	attente, espérance	*sth may come up to sb's expectation / may be beyond expectation*
scene	spectacle, vue	*a marvellous scene may spread out before the hero*
	lieu, endroit	*to appear / come on the scene of the accident*
	scène	*a scene may be set in the country*
setting	cadre	*a perfect setting for a horror story*
tension	tension	*tension may build up / develop / gather* (croître) */ mount / ease off / lessen / subside / slacken* (se relâcher)

■ *Adjectifs*

congenial [kən'dʒi:ni‿əl]	sympathique, agréable	strained	tendu
eerie ['ɪəri]	inquiétant (bruit, impression)	successfully rendered	bien rendu
frigid	glacial	uncanny	troublant, mystérieux
genial ['dʒi:ni‿əl]	cordial	unnerving	déconcertant, déstabilisant
heavy	lourd	unreal	irréel
realistic [-'---]	réaliste		

■ *Verbes*

permeate (into / through)	s'infiltrer (dans), filtrer à travers	pervade	se répandre dans, pénétrer dans, infiltrer

3.5. Characters

■ *Noms*

antagonist	antagoniste	archetype ['ɑːkitaɪp]	archétype
antihero	anti-héros	character ['---]	personnage

characterization	peinture des caractères	protagonist [-'---]	protagoniste
characteristic trait / feature	trait caractéristique	round character	personnage complexe
		stereotype	stéréotype
flat character	personnage sans profondeur	trait (of character)	trait de caractère
foil	faire-valoir	type	type
hero ['hɪərəʊ]	héros	villain	traître, méchant
heroine ['herəʊɪn]	héroïne		

Collocations

insight	perspicacité, aperçu, idée de	*to show deep insight - a woman of great insight to provide sb with fascinating / most valuable insights into sth - to gain an insight into sth - sth may give an illuminating insight into a character's psychology*

■ Adjectifs

alive	vivant	improbable	peu vraisemblable
fictitious	fictif, imaginaire	ludicrous ['luːdɪkrəs]	risible
grotesque [-'-]	grotesque	preposterous [-'---]	absurde, grotesque
hollow	creux	ridiculous [-'---]	ridicule
illustrative of sth	qui illustre bien qch		

■ Verbes

bring to life	donner vie à	personify [-'---]	personnifier
characterize ['----]	peindre le caractère de, dépeindre; caractériser	represent [,--'-]	représenter
		ridicule ['---]	tourner en ridicule
come alive / to life	prendre vie	stand for	représenter, vouloir dire
embody [-'--]	donner forme à, exprimer incarner (qualité)	stylize ['staɪlaɪz]	styliser
		symbolize	symboliser
impersonate	se faire passer pour, imiter	visualize	se représenter, s'imaginer

3.6. Ideas

Collocations

■ Noms

idea	idée	*to develop / set out* (exposer) *good / bad ideas about sth - to hate / like the idea of sth / of doing sth / of sb doing sth - it is a good idea to do sth - to have some strange ideas about sth / about how ... - not to have the slightest idea about sth*
issue	problème	*to address (oneself to)* (aborder) */ approach / tackle / evade a hotly-debated issue*

• **ideas may be:**

bright / brilliant	brillant	daring	osé, audacieux
clever	astucieux, habile	ingenious	ingénieux
comical	drôle, cocasse	innovative ['ɪnəʊveɪtɪv]	novateur
consistent	logique, cohérent	lofty	élevé, noble
creative	créatif	new-fangled	dernier cri, trop moderne

Literary terms, appreciation and analysis 359

novel	nouveau, original
profound	profond
realistic [-'--]	réaliste

• **ideas should (perhaps) not be:**

abstruse	obscur, abstrus	**nonsensical**	inepte
base	vil	**obscure**	obscur, abscons
biassed ['baɪ_əst]	partial, peu objectif	**odd**	bizarre
coarse	grossier	**of little worth**	de peu de valeur
confused	confus	**peculiar**	étrange
confusing	déroutant, source de confusion	**quaint**	bizarre, original
devoid of interest	dépourvu d'intérêt	**queer**	curieux, étrange
disconnected	décousu	**recondite** ['rekəndaɪt]	obscur
discrepant [-'--]	divergent	**shallow**	peu profond, superficiel
far-fetched	tiré par les cheveux	**stale**	éculé
flimsy	mince, léger	**strange**	étrange
hackneyed ['hæknɪd]	rebattu	**superficial**	superficiel
hazy	nébuleux	**trite**	banal, commun
hollow	creux	**trivial**	sans intérêt, sans importance
inconsistent	incohérent	**uninteresting**	sans intérêt, inintéressant
irrelevant [-'----]	non pertinent, sans rapport, hors de propos	**vague**	vague
jejune [dʒɪ'dʒuːn]	de peu d'intérêt; simplet	**vile**	infâme

■ *Verbes*

banter	badiner, railler	**hold forth**	disserter, pérorer
dismiss	écarter, abandonner	**put forth**	avancer, émettre
entertain	nourrir, avoir (une idée)	**reject**	rejeter
express	exprimer	**set forth**	faire connaître
favour	soutenir, être partisan de	**set out**	exposer
harp on / upon	revenir sans cesse sur		

3.7. Feelings

■ *Noms*

a tinge of	un soupçon de (regret)	**sentiment** (U)	sentimentalité, sensiblerie
a touch of	une pointe de (émotion)	**intensity**	intensité

Collocations

feeling	sentiment
	sth may arouse / stir up a feeling of awe in sb - to evince (manifester) / show / manifest / hide / repress a deep-seated / subtle feeling

4. Analysis and arguments

■ *Noms*

allusion	allusion
apology	apologie, défense (de qqn)
context	contexte
controversy ['----]	controverse
deconstruction	déconstruction
example	example
interpretation	interprétation
peroration	péroraison
polemic (C)	polémique, controverse
polemics (U)	art de la polémique
subtlety ['sʌtlti]	subtilité
syllogism	syllogisme
tautology	tautologie

Collocations

analysis [ə'næləsɪs]	analyse	*to make a careful / thorough / superficial analysis of sth*
argument	argument	*to put forward / present / refute a groundless / spurious (fallacieux) / well-documented / telling (efficace) / conclusive / sound (solide) argument for / against sth / that ...*
hypothesis [-'---] (pl. **hypotheses**)	hypothèse	*to propose / formulate / confirm a daring hypothesis about sth - sth may confirm / contradict / invalidate a hypothesis*
remark	remarque	*to make a casual / pithy (concis et précis) / relevant / scathing (acerbe, cinglant) / telling (qui porte) / witty / facetious remark - to make the remark that ...*
synthesis ['---] (pl. **syntheses**)	synthèse	*to make a synthesis of various elements*
thesis (pl. **theses**)	thèse	*to propose / advance / challenge / refute a / the thesis about / on sth / that ...*

• **an analysis and / or an argument and / or a remark may be:**

accurate ['---]	exact, précis	**instructive**	instructif
allusive [-'--]	allusif	**keen**	serré, pénétrant
anecdotal [,--'--]	anecdotique	**minute** [maɪ'njuːt]	minutieux, détaillé
apposite	juste, pertinent	**mocking**	moqueur, railleur
appropriate	approprié	**original**	original
apt	pertinent	**outstanding**	exceptionnel (par sa qualité)
biting	mordant, cinglant	**penetrating** ['----]	perspicace, pénétrant
caustic	caustique	**relevant** ['---]	pertinent, approprié, à propos
clever	astucieux, habile	**remarkable**	remarquable
cogent ['kəʊdʒənt]	puissant, efficace, convaincant	**sarcastic** [-'--]	sarcastique
comprehensive	détaillé, complet	**scathing**	acerbe, cinglant
controversial	controversé, discutable	**searching**	fouillé, rigoureux
convincing	convaincant	**short and to the point**	bref et précis
cunning	astucieux	**cutting**	incisif
discerning	judicieux	**striking**	frappant
documented	solide, étayé	**strong**	fort (argument)
exhaustive	poussé, complet	**subtle** ['sʌtl]	subtil
expressive	expressif	**telling**	efficace (argument)
far-reaching	d'une grande portée	**thorough** ['θʌrə]	approfondi
illuminating	éclairant	**to the point**	à propos, pertinent
in-depth	en profondeur	**weighty**	de poids

Literary terms, appreciation and analysis

• **an analysis or an argument and / or a remark (perhaps) should not be:**

beside the point	hors de propos	personal	personnel, indiscret
evasive	évasif	polemic	polémique (œuvre)
facile	creux, superficiel	polemical	polémique (argument)
groundless	mal fondé	shallow	superficiel
imprecise [ˌɪmprɪˈsaɪs]	imprécise	unconvincing	peu convaincant
inaccurate [-'---]	inexact	weak	faible
irrelevant [-'---]	non pertinent, sans rapport, hors de propos		

■ *Verbes*

allude to	faire allusion à	extemporize	improviser
analyse	analyser	gibe [dʒaɪb] at sb	railler, chansonner qqn
approve of	approuver	highlight	mettre en lumière
bespeak	témoigner de, être le signe de	hold forth (on / about)	pérorer, disserter (sur)
betoken	dénoter, être signe de	interpret [-'---]	interpréter
comment ['--] on sth	commenter qch	lampoon [-'-]	tourner en dérision
comment ['--] that ...	faire observer que ...	lay emphasis on / stress ['emᴾfəsɪs]	insister sur, mettre l'accent sur
denote	dénoter	mock at	ridiculiser, railler, se moquer
disapprove of	désapprouver	mock	parodier, singer
draw from	tirer de, puiser dans	render	rendre, interpréter
dwell on	s'attarder sur	signify (that ...)	signifier (que ...)
emphasize ['emᴾfəsaɪz]	souligner, insister sur	stand out	ressortir, se remarquer
enlarge upon	s'étendre sur (sujet)	state that ...	déclarer, affirmer que ...
exemplify	illustrer, être un exemple de	taunt sb [tɔːnt]	persifler, railler qqn
expatiate on [ekˈspeɪʃɪeɪt]	disserter sur	touch on	effleurer (sujet)

Collocations

deal with	traiter de	*a book may deal with a topical subject* (d'actualité)
explain	expliquer	*to explain sth (to sb) - to explain (to sb) that / how / why ..., etc*
imply	impliquer, supposer laisser entendre, insinuer que	*sth may imply a degree of intelligence* *to imply that ...*
observe	observer, faire remarquer observer, scruter	*to observe (to sb) that ...* *to observe sth closely*
point out	signaler, attirer l'attention	*to point sth out (to sb) - to point out (to sb) that ...*
remark	remarquer, observer faire des observations sur	*to remark sb's talent / that ...* *to remark on sth to sb*
treat	traiter	*to treat a story tactlessly / as a joke*
treat (of)	traiter (de), examiner	*a book may treat (of) a hotly-debated issue*

5. Poetry

5.0. General

■ *Noms*

bard	barde; aède	poetic licence	licence poétique
cycle	cycle (de poèmes)	poetics	poétique
minstrel	ménestrel, trouvère, troubadour	poetry (U)	poésie (art)
muse	muse	rhymer / rhymester	rimailleur
piece of poetry	poème, poésie	texture	texture, contexture
poem	poème	verse (U)	vers
poet	poète	verse (C)	strophe; couplet
poetaster [ˌpəʊɪˈtæstə]	mauvais poète, rimailleur	verse (C)	verset (Bible, Coran)
poetess [ˌpəʊɪˈtes]	poétesse	verse (U)	poésie
poetic diction	langage poétique	versification	versification

■ *Adjectifs*

poetic	poétique	poetical	de caractère poétique

■ *Verbes*

declaim	déclamer	say	dire, réciter
recite	réciter (en public)	scan	(se) scander
rhyme (with)	rimer (avec)	versify	versifier

5.1. Rhythm and stress

■ *Noms*

anacrusis [ˌænəˈkruːsɪs]	anacrouse	stress	accent rythmique
beat	temps	stress pattern	schéma accentuel
binary rhythm	rythme binaire	strong beat	temps fort
isochrony / isochronism	isochronie	syllabic verse	vers syllabique(s)
metre / meter	mètre	syllable	syllabe
metrics / prosody [ˈprɒsədi]	prosodie	ternary / triple rhythm	rythme ternaire
rhythm	rythme	weak beat	temps faible
scansion	scansion		

5.2. Metrical feet

■ *Noms / Adjectifs*

anapestic [ˌ--ˈ--]	anapestique	metrical pattern	schéma prosodique
dactyl	dactyle	pyrrhic	pyrrhique
dactylic [-ˈ--]	dactylique	spondaic [spɒnˈdeɪɪk]	spondaïque
iamb [ˈaɪæm] / iambus [aɪˈæmbəs]	iambe	spondee [ˈspɒndiː]	spondée
iambic [aɪˈæmbɪk]	iambique	trochaic [trəʊˈkeɪɪk]	trochaïque
		trochee [ˈtrəʊkiː]	trochée

Literary terms, appreciation and analysis   363

Collocations

foot   pied   *a line of poetry may be divided into feet - a foot consists of a strong beat and one or two weaker ones*

5.3. The line : number of feet, pauses, endings

■ *Noms / Adjectifs*

alexandrine [ˌælɪgˈzændraɪn]	alexandrin	**heroic verse**	(vers en) décasyllabes
blank verse	vers blancs / non rimés	**hexameter** [-ˈ---]	hexamètre
break	coupe	**hexametrical** [ˌ--ˈ---]	hexamétrique
caesura [sɪˈzjʊərə]	césure	**line** (C)	vers
dimeter [ˈdɪmɪtə]	vers composé de deux pieds	**masculine ending**	terminaison masculine
ending	terminaison	**monometer** [-ˈ---]	monomètre
enjamb(e)ment	enjambement	**monometrical** [ˌ--ˈ---]	monométrique
feminine ending	terminaison féminine	**octameter (eight feet)** [-ˈ---]	octamètre
foot	pied, syllabe	**octametrical** [ˌ--ˈ---]	octamétrique
free verse	vers libres	**pause**	pause
hemistich [ˈhemɪstɪk]	hémistiche	**pentameter (five feet)** [-ˈ---]	pentamètre
heptameter (seven feet) [-ˈ---]	heptamètre	**pentametrical** [ˌ--ˈ---]	pentamétrique
heptametrical [ˌ--ˈ---]	heptamétrique	**run(ning)-on line**	enjambement
heroic couplet	distique héroïque	**tetrameter (four feet)** [-ˈ---]	tétramètre
		tetrametrical [ˌ--ˈ---]	tétramétrique
		trimeter [ˈ---] **(three feet)**	vers de trois mètres

5.4. Rhymes and rhyme-schemes

■ *Noms*

a b b a rhyme scheme	rimes embrassées	**refrain** [rɪˈfreɪn]	refrain
alternate [ɔːlˈtɜːnət] **rhymes**	rimes croisées / alternées	**rhyme**	rime
broken rhyme	rime brisée	**rhyme** (U)	poème
burden	refrain	**in rhyme**	en vers (rimés)
crossed rhyme	double rime (interne et externe)	**rhyme pattern / scheme**	agencements des rimes
eye rhyme / sight-rhyme	rime pour l'œil	**rhyme royal (ababbcc)**	rime royale
feminine rhyme	rime féminine	**rhyming couplets**	rimes plates, suivies
free verse	vers libres	**tail rhyme (stanza) (aabccb)**	rime couée
ictus	ictus	**rime riche**	rime riche
leonine rhyme	rime léonine	**rondel / rondeau**	rondeau
linked rhyme	rime enchaînée	**terza rima (aba, bcb, cdc...)** [ˌteətsəˈriːmə]	terza rima, rimes tiercées
masculine rhyme	rime masculine		
narrative rhymes	vers narratifs	**villanelle** [ˌ--ˈ-]	villanelle
ottava rima (ababbcc)	ottava rima		

5.5. Poetic genres and forms

■ *Noms / Adjectifs*

acrostic	acrostiche	**anacreontic poetry**	poème anacréontique

aubade [əʊˈbɑːd]	aubade	keen	mélopée funèbre
ballad	ballade	lament [-ˈ-]	complainte, chant funèbre (Irlande)
blason / blazon [ˈbleɪzn]	blason (poème élogieux ou satirique)	lay	lai
bucolics / bucolic poetry	poésie bucolique, pastorale	limerick	poème humoristique de cinq vers
chanson de geste	chanson de geste	lyric	poème lyrique
clerihew	poème humoristique (pseudo-biographique)	lyric (adj.)	lyrique (poème, poète)
complaint poem	complainte	lyrical (adj.)	lyrique (poésie)
conversation poem	poème sur la nature adressé à des amis	macaronic verse	vers macaroniques
		madrigal	madrigal
couplet	distique	metrical psalm [sɑːm]	psaume versifié
dirge	hymne funèbre	mock-heroic pieces	poèmes héroï-comiques
doggerel [ˈdɒgrəl]	vers de mirliton	monody	monodie
eclogue	églogue	nonsense verse	vers amphigouriques
elegy	élégie	nursery rhyme	comptine
epic (adj.)	épique	occasional verse	vers de circonstance
epic (n.)	épopée	octave / octet	huitain
epigram	épigramme	ode	ode
epistle [-ˈ---]	épître	palinode	palinodie
epitaph	épitaphe	pastoral (adj.)	pastoral, champêtre
epithalamion / epithalamium	épithalame	pastoral (n.)	pastorale
		prose poem	poème en prose
epod(e)	épode	prothalamion [ˌprəʊθəˈleɪmiən]	hyménée
epos	épopée antique		
flyting	échanges d'insultes sous forme de poèmes	psalm [sɑːm]	psaume
		quatrain [ˈkwɒtreɪn]	quatrain
genre	genre	rhyme (U)	poème
georgic poem	poème géorgique, rural	sonnet	sonnet
haiku	haïku	stanza	strophe
hymn	cantique, hymne	tercet / triplet	tercet
idyll	idylle	threnody [ˈθrenədi]	mélopée, chant funèbre
jingle	petit couplet (à assonances)	triolet [ˈtriːəlet]	triolet

6. Drama

6.1. General

■ *Noms*

A-effect / alienation effect	distanciation	braggadocio	bravache
amateur theatricals	théâtre amateur	braggart [ˈbrægət]	matamore
antimasque / antemasque	anti-masque	buffoon [-ˈ-]	bouffon
bardolatry [bɑːˈdɒlətri]	vénération, culte de Shakespeare	cast GB [kɑːst] / US [kæst]	distribution
black comedy	comédie noire (humour noir)	catastrophe [kəˈtæstrəfi]	dénouement tragique

chronicle play	pièce historique, chronique (fin 16ᵉ siècle)	costume drama / piece / play	film / pièce de théâtre en costumes d'époque
climax	point culminant, paroxysme	mime	scène mimée; mimodrame
closet drama	pièce destinée à la lecture	miracle / miracle play	miracle (pièce)
clown	clown	monodrama	pièce ou scène où un seul personnage parle
comedy (C)	comédie		
comedy (U)	comédie, genre comique	morality play	moralité (pièce)
comedy (U)	le comique	musical	comédie musicale
comedy of humours	comédie d'humeurs	mystery / mystery play	mystère (pièce)
comedy of manners	comédie de mœurs	pantomime	pantomine
comic	le comique (genre, acteur)	Passion play	mystère de la Passion
commedia dell'arte	commedia dell'arte	playlet	saynette
confidant(e)	confident(e)	plot	intrigue
coup de théâtre	coup de théâtre	plot line	histoire
crisis	crise	protest theatre	théâtre contestataire, militant
curtain-raiser	lever de rideau	puppet theatre	théâtre de marionnettes
domestic tragedy	drame domestique	radio play	pièce radiophonique
dramatic work (C)	œuvre théâtrale	revue [rɪ'vjuː]	revue
dramatis personae [ˌdræmətɪspɜː'səʊnaɪ]	liste des personnages	situation comedy / sitcom	comédie de situation
		slapstick (comedy)	grosse farce, comédie bouffonne
farce	farce	subplot	intrigue secondaire
fool	fou	tetralogy	tétralogie
interlude	intermède	theater in the round	théâtre en rond
kitchen-sink drama	théâtre réaliste (de gens ordinaires) (années 50-60)	tragedy	tragédie
		tragi-comedy	tragi-comédie
light comedy	comédie de boulevard	trilogy	trilogie
liturgical [lɪ'tɜːdʒɪkl] drama	théâtre liturgique	TV play	dramatique
low comedy	farce	unities	unités (de temps, etc)
masque GB [mɑːsk] / US [mæsk]	comédie-ballet, masque	vaudeville	vaudeville
melodrama	mélodrame	villain	traître, méchant

Collocations

drama (U)	théâtre	*a play typical of the drama of the period - to take drama lessons at a drama school*
drama (C)	(pièce) dramatique	*to appear in a television costume drama*
theatre (U) / theater (US)	théâtre	*to be interested in theater / in Greek theatre - a musical may be wonderful theatre - the Theatre of the absurd*
theatre / theater (C)	théâtre (lieu)	*to go to the theatre - a movie theater* (salle)
part	rôle	*to play a part / the part of Hamlet*
play	pièce	*to direct / perform* (jouer) */ produce / put on / stage* (monter) *a play*
stage	scène	*to be on the stage* (être acteur) */ go on the stage* (devenir acteur) *- to go on stage* (entrer en scène) */ be left alone on stage - to write for the stage*

6.2. Content

■ *Noms*

act	acte	monolog(ue) / speech	tirade
aside	aparté	nemesis ['neməsɪs]	némésis, instrument de vengeance
catharsis [kə'θɑːsɪs]	catharsis		
choral character	personnage du chœur	poetic justice	justice distributive
chorus	chœur	problem play	pièce à thèse
comic relief	intervalle comique	prologue	prologue
coup de théâtre	coup de théâtre	rejoinder	réplique, repartie
denouement [deɪ'nuːmɒ̃]	dénouement	repartee [ˌrepɑː'tiː]	réplique, répartie
dialogue	dialogue	reversal of situation	renversement de situation
dramatic irony	ironie dramatique	scene	scène
dramatic monologue	monologue de théâtre	soliloquy [-'---]	soliloque
dramaturgy ['----]	dramaturgie	stage directions	indications scéniques
dumb [dʌm] show	mime, pantomime	stage whisper	aparté
epic theatre	théâtre épique	stichomythia	stichomythie
exposition	présentation, exposition	stock character	personnage stéréotypé
hubris / hybris	orgueil (démesuré)	unknotting / unraveling [ʌn'rævlɪŋ]	dénouement

Collocations

cue	réplique	*to give sb his cue - to come on (stage) on cue*
line	réplique, rôle	*to learn / know / remember one's lines*

■ *Adjectifs*

comical	comique, drôle	tragic	tragique (genre, acteur)
spectacular	à grand spectacle	tragical	tragique (événement)

■ *Verbes*

act	jouer, être acteur	interpret [-'--]	interpréter (pièce, rôle)
ad lib	improviser (sur scène)	perform	jouer, représenter (rôle, pièce)
declaim	déclamer	play	jouer, interpréter (rôle)
ham it up	cabotiner	prompt	souffler
improvise	improviser (musique, jazz)	rant	dire avec emphase, déclamer

7. Techniques [tek'niːks]

7.1. Literary devices

■ *Noms*

analepsis [ˌ--'--]	analepse	caricature ['----]	caricature
analogy [-'---]	analogie	conceits [kən'siːts]	traits d'esprit, concetti
bathos ['beɪθɒs]	chute du sublime au ridicule	digression / excursus	digression

Literary terms, appreciation and analysis

ellipsis [-'--]	ellipse	parataxis	parataxe
euphemism ['----]	euphémisme	pathos ['peɪθɒs]	pathétique
focalization	focalisation	prolepsis	prolepse
irony	ironie	rhetorical [-'---] question	question rhétorique
leitmotiv ['laɪtməʊtiːf]	leitmotiv	sarcasm	sarcasme
litotes (pl.inv) ['laɪtəʊtiːz]	litote	satire ['sætaɪ̯ə]	satire
malapropism ['mæləprɒpɪzəm]	impropriété de langage	skit (on)	parodie (de), sketch satirique
onomatop(o)eia [ˌɒnəʊmætə'piː̯ə]	onomatopée	spoonerism	contrepèterie
		symbol	symbole
parable	parabole	synaesthesia	synesthésie
paradox	paradoxe	zeugma ['zjugmə]	zeugme

■ *Adjectifs*

allegorical	allégorique	ironic	ironique (genre, langue)
autotelic	autotélique	ironical	ironique (situation)
bathetic	qui passe du sublime au ridicule	onomatop(o)eic [ˌɒnəʊmætə'piːɪk]	onomatopéique
elliptical	elliptique	parataxical	parataxique
eponymous [ɪ'pɒnɪməs]	éponyme	satirical	satirique

■ *Verbes*

caricature ['----]	caricaturer	satirize	faire la satire de

7.2. Narrative techniques [tek'niːks]

■ *Noms*

account [-'-]	récit, narration	epistolary [-'----] novel	roman épistolaire
aloofness	réserve, distanciation	eschatology [ˌ--'---]	eschatologie
ambiguity	ambiguïté	exaggeration	exagération
anachronism [-'----]	anachronisme	euphemism	euphémisme
anachrony	rupture temporelle	framework	trame, charpente (du récit)
anagog(y)	recherche du sens spirituel caché	humour	humour
		imagination	imagination
anti-novel	anti-roman	imitation	imitation
anticlimax	chute, retombée	incidents	péripéties
architectonics [ˌ---'--]	architectonique	index	signe, indice, indication
black humour	humour noir	indirect speech / discourse [ˌ--'-]	discours indirect
consciousness	conscience		
dialectic	dialectique	indirect [ˌ--'-] style	style indirect
dialogism	dialogisme	induction	prologue, introduction
didactics [-'---]	didactique	instalment [ɪn'stɔːlmənt]	épisode (feuilleton)
diegesis [-'--]	diégèse	interior monologue	monologue intérieur
direct speech / discourse	discours direct	interrogation	interrogation
direct style	style direct	intertextuality	intertextualité
embedded narrative ['---]	récit en abyme	literariness ['-----]	littérarité
enumeration	énumération	litany	litanie

mimesis [mɪ'miːsɪs]	mimesis, imitation	proem	préface, introduction
mise en abyme	mise en abyme	quip	raillerie, quolibet
motto	devise	quirk	bizarrerie, excentricité
narratologist	narratologue	repetition	répétition
narratology	narratologie	reported speech	style / discours indirect
obiter dicta [ˌɒbɪtə'dɪktə]	remarques faites en passant	riddle	énigme, devinette
opposition	opposition	statement	affirmation, déclaration
overstatement	exagération (dans les termes)	stream of consciousness	courant sous-jacent de conscience, 'stream of consciousness'
parody	parodie		
pastiche [pæ'stiːʃ]	pastiche		
pathetic fallacy	attribution de sentiments humains à des objets inanimés	stylistic device	procédé stylistique
		sudden development [-'---]	rebondissement
peripeteia [ˌperɪpə'tiːə]	retournement de situation	symmetry	symétrie
persona [pə'səʊnə]	personnage; narrateur implicite	transition	transition
play on words / pun	jeu de mots	understatement	litote, affirmation euphémique
preamble	préambule	verisimilitude [ˌ---'---]	vraisemblance

Collocations

approach	façon d'aborder	a writer's approach to a subject - sb may take a judicious / rational / scholarly approach to a problem
climax	point culminant, paroxysme	the action may come to / reach / work to a dramatic climax - to bring sth to a thrilling climax
comparison	comparaison	to make / draw a far-fetched / overworked (usée, rebattue) / overwrought (surchargée) comparison
contrast ['--]	contraste	sth may be in contrast with sth - sth may form a contrast to sth
function	fonction du récit	the function may be emotive / referential / phatic / conative / metalinguistic / poetic
hint	allusion	to give / drop a hint (to sb / about sth) that... - to take a hint (comprendre à demi-mots)
humour	humour, comique	to use a touch of humour - to understand the humour of the situation - to see no humour in sth / in doing sth
interest ['--]	intérêt	a writer / a writer's works may arouse / keep up / sustain the reader's interest - to know how to revive the reader's interest in the plot - the interest may flag / pick up / intensify - a writer's work may be praised for / blamed for not holding / sustaining the reader's interest or attention
issue	problème	to address (oneself to) / approach / evade a hotly debated issue
narration [-'--]	narration, façon de raconter	the narration may be graphic (vivant) / gripping / dull
narrative (C) ['---]	récit, histoire	one of many exciting narratives of the hero's adventures - first person narrative - frame narrative / story (récit dans le récit)
narrative (U) ['---]	narration, art de la narration	to have a gift for / great skill in narrative - there may be too little argument and too much narrative
narrator GB [-'--] / US ['---]	narrateur	omniscient / 1st or 3rd person / intrusive / unreliable narrator
pattern	schéma, modèle	a play may follow an unusual pattern - a strange pattern of events / of family life / of behaviour may emerge
point of view	point de vue	also referred to as 'standpoint' - events may be viewed from the writer's / a character's point of view
scope	portée	a study may be narrow / broad in scope
	limites	a subject may be within / beyond the scope of a book

Literary terms, appreciation and analysis

■ Adjectifs

asymmetrical	asymétrique	humorous	plein d'humour, comique, humoristique
consummate	consommé (art)	in medias res	au milieu des choses
dialogical	dialogique	[ɪnˌmiːdiæsˈreɪz]	
diegetic [-'---]	diégétique	interrogative [ˌ--'---]	interrogatif
emotive	à forte teneur émotionnelle	interrogatory [ˌ--'----]	interrogateur
exclamatory	exclamatif	mimetic	mimétique
extra- / hypodiegetic [ˌ---'---]	extra- / hypo diégétique	narrative ['---]	narratif
		phatic	phatique
far-fetched	bizarre, tiré par les cheveux, forcé	referential	référentiel
		symmetrical	symétrique

Collocations

implied	implicite	*implied author / reader theory*

■ Verbes

address (oneself to)	aborder (une question); traiter (un sujet)	handle	manier (l'ironie); conduire (une histoire)
compare to	comparer à (qch / qqn de supérieur)	imitate	imiter
		interrogate	interroger
compare with	comparer à, avec (de façon neutre)	narrate GB [-'-] / US ['--]	narrer, raconter
		oppose	s'opposer à, combattre
conjure ['--] away	faire disparaître (comme par magie)	oppose sth to sth	opposer qch à qch
		overstate	exagérer (dans les termes)
conjure ['--] up	faire apparaître (fantôme); évoquer (souvenirs)	parody	parodier
		pun	faire un / des jeu(x) de mots
contrast [-'-] with	constituer un contraste avec mettre en contraste avec	relate	relater, rapporter, raconter
		relate sth to sth	relier qch à qch
digress [daɪˈgres]	faire une digression	relate to	(ch.) se rapporter, toucher à
enhance GB [ɪnˈhɑːns] / US [ɪnˈhæns]	mettre en valeur, rehausser		(p.) entretenir des rapports avec
enumerate	énumérer		
evoke	évoquer (des esprits) susciter (admiration)	repeat	répéter
		rephrase	reformuler
exaggerate	exagérer	rewrite	récrire
exclaim	s'exclamer	set about to do	se donner pour propos de faire
exclaim at	se récrier contre, s'opposer à; se récrier d'admiration devant	take up	aborder, discuter de
		throw into relief	mettre en relief

Collocations

hint	faire (une) allusion à, laisser entendre	*to hint at sth / at sb / at sb doing sth - to hint that ...*
understand	sous-entendre	*a word may be understood - it may be understood that ...*

7.3. Language

■ Noms

anagram	anagramme	antonym	antonyme

aphorism	aphorisme	maxim	maxime
apophthegm ['æpəθem]	apophthègme	metalanguage ['metəlæŋgwɪdʒ]	métalangue
apostrophe [-'---]	apostrophe	neologism [-'----]	néologisme
brackets / parentheses (US) [-'---]	parenthèses	nonce word	mot de circonstance; mot créé pour l'occasion
circumlocution [,---'--]	circonlocution	paraphrase	paraphrase
clause	proposition	periphrasis [-'----]	périphrase
cliché GB ['kli:ʃeɪ] / US [kli:'ʃeɪ]	cliché	phrasal conjunction	locution conjonctive
collocation	collocation	phrase	expression
colloquialism [-'-----]	expression familière	pleonasm	pléonasme
compound	mot composé	polysemy [-'----]	polysémie
connotation	connotation	portmanteau word	mot-valise
correctness [-'--]	exactitude (mot)	proverb	proverbe
dash	tiret	quotes / quotation marks	guillemets (doubles)
dots	points de suspension	register ['---]	registre
denotation	dénotation; sens	saw	dicton
dialect	dialecte	saying	proverbe, adage
double entendre [,du:bl ɒn'tɒnd rə]	mot / expression à double sens	sentence	phrase
homonym	homonyme	single quotation marks	guillemets simples (citation à l'intérieur d'une citation)
homophone	homophone	solecism ['sɒlɪsɪzəm]	solécisme
hyperbaton [haɪ'pɜ:bətɒn]	hyperbate	stylistics (U) [staɪ'lɪstɪks]	stylistique
hypotaxis	hypotaxe	subordinate [-'---] / dependent clause	(proposition) indépendante / subordonnée
idiom	expression idiomatique; langue, idiome, parler	syllepsis [sɪ'lepsɪs]	syllepse
incantation	incantation	synonym	synonyme
inverted commas	guillemets (doubles)	vernacular	langue vernaculaire
main / independent clause	(proposition) principale / indépendante	vocabulary	vocabulaire

Collocations

language	langage, langue	*to use foul* (ordurier) / *improper* / *indecorous* (inconvenant) / *formal* (soigné) / *informal* (familier) / *colloquial* / *conversational* / *bawdy* (obscène) / *popular* / *natural* / *realistic* / *rude* (grossier) / *vulgar* / *witty* / *archaic* / *earthy* (truculent) *language*
word	mot	*to invent / make up / coin a new word - to distort a commonplace / hackneyed word - to revive an old word - to put one's thoughts / feelings into words*

■ *Adjectifs*

badly-expressed / put	mal exprimé	inappropriate [,--'---]	inapproprié
correct [-'-]	exact (mot)	proper	qui convient
demotic [dɪ'mɒtɪk]	populaire, du peuple	sloppy	bâclé, peu soigné
felicitous [-'----]	bien trouvé	textual	textuel
fustian ['fʌsti ən]	grandiloquent, creux	unfortunate	malheureux, malvenu
hypotaxical	hypotaxique	well-phrased / put	bien exprimé

Literary terms, appreciation and analysis 371

■ *Verbes*

quote	ouvrez les guillemets	**unquote**	fermez les guillemets

8. Appreciation of style, tone and language

8.1. Favourable comment

■ *Noms*

accuracy ['----]	exactitude, précision	**overtone**	sous-entendu, implication
clarity	clarté	**propriety**	propriété, justesse
conciseness	concision	**terseness**	laconisme
naturalness	naturel		

Collocations

style	style	*to tune one's style to the style of the newspaper one writes for - sth may lack style / be written in a formal style*
tone	ton	*the optimistic tone of a report - a friendly opening speech may set the tone for the rest of a conference - to speak in an authoritative tone / in cold sarcastic tones*

■ *Adjectifs*

• **general appreciation**

literary	littéraire	**realistic** [-'--]	réaliste
metaphorical [,--'---]	métaphorique		

• **accurate, clear**

abstract ['--]	abstrait	**lapidary** ['læpɪd‿əri]	lapidaire
accurate	exact, précis	**matter-of-fact**	prosaïque
analytical [,--'---]	analytique	**natural**	naturel
chastened ['tʃeɪsənd]	châtié	**neat**	élégant, net
clear	clair	**pedagogical** [,--'---]	pédagogique
compact	ramassé	**plain**	simple, direct
concise	concis	**proper**	approprié, qui convient
concrete	concret	**terse**	laconique
controlled	maîtrisé	**well-balanced**	équilibré
crisp	vif	**well-expressed / phrased**	bien formulé
didactic [daɪ'dæktɪk]	didactique	**well-put**	bien exprimé
down-to-earth	réaliste, terre-à-terre	**well-written**	bien écrit
homely	sans recherche		

• **personal, emotive**

amusing	amusant	**emotive**	chargé de connotations, d'émotion
direct [-'-]	direct		
emotional	qui fait appel à l'émotion	**impassioned**	passionné, exalté
		lucid	lucide

moving	émouvant	**sincere**	sincère
passionate	véhément	**straightforward**	franc, direct

• elaborate

colourful	coloré, éclatant	**graphic**	pittoresque, vivant
dashing	plein de panache	**lively**	vivant
elaborate [-'---]	recherché, travaillé	**oratorical** [,--'---]	oratoire
elegant	élégant	**ornate** [ɔːˈneɪt]	très orné, fleuri
finely honed	ciselé avec soin	**polished**	poli, châtié
flowing	coulant	**refined**	raffiné
fluent	aisé	**skilful**	habilement ciselé
fluid	fluide	**sparkling**	chatoyant
gorgeous	somptueux		

• effective

cogent [ˈkəʊdʒənt]	puissant, efficace, convaincant	**pungent**	mordant, acerbe
effective	qui porte, efficace	**racy**	plein de verve
efficient	économe de ses moyens	**rhythmical**	rythmé
facile GB [ˈfæsaɪl] / US [ˈfæsl]	aisé, coulant	**slashing**	cinglant
		spirited	fougueux
forcible	vigoureux	**unadorned**	dépouillé
impressive	impressionnant	**varied** [ˈveərid]	varié
incisive [ɪnˈsaɪsɪv]	incisif	**vigorous** [ˈvɪɡər əs]	vigoureux
pithy [ˈpɪθi]	concis; qui porte	**vivid**	vivant, coloré
powerful	puissant	**dry (humour)**	pince-sans-rire

• restrained

detached	détaché	**subdued**	contenu
elevated	élevé	**sublime**	sublime
impassive	sans émotion	**subtle** [ˈsʌtl]	subtil
passionless	sans passion	**unobtrusive** [ˌʌnəbˈtruːsɪv]	discret, qui ne se fait pas remarquer
restrained	retenu		

8.2. Unfavourable comment

■ *Noms*

affectation	manque de naturel	**mawkishness**	sentimentalité excessive
archaism [ˈɑːkeɪɪzəm]	archaïsme	**preciousness**	affectation, recherche de l'effet
euphuism [ˈjuːfjuːɪzəm]	euphuisme, préciosité	**sentimentality** [,---'---]	sentimentalité
mannerism	maniérisme		

■ *Adjectifs*

• unclear, clumsy

abstruse	obscur, abstrus	**complex**	complexe
barren	aride, sec	**contrived**	artificiel, forcé
clumsy	gauche, lourd, inélégant	**crabbed** [ˈkræbɪd]	touffu

cramped	sans liberté, contraint	**intricate**	compliqué
diffuse [dɪˈfjuːs]	diffus, prolixe	**involved**	contourné, compliqué
discursive / discursory	discursif; décousu	**pedestrian**	prosaïque, plat, terre-à-terre
entangled	embrouillé	**profuse** [-ˈ-]	débordant
heavy	laborieux, ampoulé	**prolix** [ˈprəʊlɪks]	prolixe
inaccurate	imprécis	**recondite** [ˈrekəndaɪt]	abstrus, obscur

• affected

affected	affecté, maniéré	**mawkish**	mièvre
antiquated	vieillot, suranné	**mincing**	minaudier
archaic	archaïque	**obsolescent** [ˌ--ˈ--]	vieilli
artificial	artificiel	**obsolete** [ˈɒbsəliːt]	obsolète, désuet, dépassé
baroque [-ˈ-]	baroque	**obtrusive**	trop visible, ostentatoire
bombastic [-ˈ--]	ampoulé, grandiloquent	**old-fashioned**	passé de mode
cloyed	surchargé, indigeste	**outmoded**	démodé
confused [-ˈ-]	confus, embrouillé	**pedantic**	pédant
confusing [-ˈ--]	déroutant, source de confusion	**pompous**	pompeux
far-fetched	forcé	**ponderous**	lourd, pesant et solennel
grandiloquent [grænˈdɪləkwənt]	grandiloquent	**quaint**	au charme vieillot, désuet
high-flown	ampoulé	**rambling**	décousu, qui manque de cohérence
highfalutin(g) [ˌhaɪfəˈluːtɪŋ] / [ˌhaɪfəˈluːtɪn]	prétentieux	**ranting**	déclamatoire; vociférant
laboured	laborieux	**sentimental** [ˌ--ˈ--]	sentimental
mannered	maniéré, affecté	**simpering**	minaudier, mignard
maudlin	larmoyant	**stilted**	guindé, emprunté

• dull

banal [bəˈnɑːl]	banal, ordinaire	**prosaic** [prəʊˈzeɪɪk]	prosaïque
colourless	terne, sans couleur	**prosy**	sans relief, insipide
common	commun, ordinaire	**repetitive**	répétitif
commonplace	banal, commun	**stodgy**	lourd, laborieux
drab	morne, fade	**trite**	banal, commun
dry	pince-sans-rire (humour) ennuyeux, aride	**uninspiring**	guère inspirant
		unvaried [ʌnˈveərɪd]	qui manque de variété, uniforme
dull	terne, peu intéressant		
flat	monotone, plat	**vapid**	plat, terne, sans saveur
hollow	creux	**verbose** [vɜːˈbəʊs]	verbeux, redondant
monotonous [məˈnɒtənəs]	monotone	**wordy**	interminable; ronflant
mundane [mʌnˈdeɪn]	banal, à ras de terre		

• slovenly and flashy

feeble	mou, faible	**gaudy**	tapageur
flashy	d'un brillant trompeur	**improper**	impropre
flaunting	qui s'affiche	**indecorous** [ɪnˈdekərəs]	inconvenant, incorrect
flimsy	très léger, pauvre, mince	**inflated**	enflé, boursouflé
florid	plein de fioritures	**jerky**	haché, heurté
flowery	fleuri, orné	**lax**	relâché

loose [luːs] / **limp**	lâche, relâché	**slovenly** / **sloppy**	négligé, bâclé
meretricious [‚--'--]	clinquant	**trashy**	nul
overdone	usé, rebattu	**turgid**	boursouflé, ampoulé
overwrought	outré, trop recherché	**unbridled**	débridé
precious	précieux, affecté	**uncontrolled**	effréné
slipshod	négligé, peu soigné	**unrestrained**	outrancier
sloppy	d'une sensiblerie excessive	**vulgar**	vulgaire

Collocations

■ *Verbe*

put	dire, exprimer	*as the writer puts it*

9. Stylistics

9.0. General

■ *Noms*

oratory ['ɒrət̬əri]	art oratoire, rhétorique, éloquence	**stylistics** [staɪ'lɪstɪks] (U / sg.)	stylistique
		tropes [trəʊps]	tropes

Collocations

figures	figure	*to use stylistic / rhetorical / figures / figures of speech*
irony	ironie	*verbal / dramatic irony - the irony of sth may be that ...*
		- to handle irony skilfully

9.1. Figures of speech, rhetorical [-'---] figures

■ *Noms*

image ['ɪmɪdʒ]	image (mentale)	**rhetoric** ['---]	rhétorique; éloquence
imagery ['----]	images (littéraires)		

Collocations

antithesis [-'---]	antithèse	*sth may be the direct / very antithesis to / of sth - sth may be in complete antithesis to sth - the antithesis between sth and sth may be less important than thought at first*

allegory ['----]	allégorie	**aposiopesis**	aposiopèse
anacoluthon [‚ænəkə'luːθɒn]	anacoluthe	[‚æpəʊsaɪ ə'piːsɪs]	
anadiplosis [‚ænədɪ'pləʊsɪs]	anadiplose	**apostrophe** [ə'pɒstrəfi]	apostrophe
anaphora [ə'næfərə]	anaphore	**asyndeton** [æ'sɪndɪtən]	asyndète
antiphrasis	antiphrase	**bombast** ['--]	grandiloquence, boursouflure
antistrophe	antistrophe	**catachresis** [‚kætə'kriːsɪs]	catachrèse
antonomasia	antonomase	**chiasmus** [kaɪ'æzməs]	chiasme
[‚æntɒnə'meɪzi ə]		**diaresis**	diarèse
aporia [ə'pɔːri ə]	aporie	**epizeugsis** [‚--'--]	épizeuxis

Literary terms, appreciation and analysis

exordium [ek'sɔːdi̯əm]	exorde	**oxymoron**	oxymoron
hendiadys [hen'dai̯ədɪs]	hendiadys	**paranomasia**	paranomasie
hypallage [haɪ'pælədʒi]	hypallage	**periphrasis**	périphrase
hyperbaton [haɪ'pɜːbətɒn]	hyperbate	**personification**	personnification
hyperbole [haɪ'pɜːbəli]	hyperbole	**polysyndeton**	polysyndète
inversion	inversion	**prosopopoeia**	prosopopée
invocation	invocation	[ˌprɒzəʊpə'piːə]	
litotes (pl. inv.) ['laɪtəʊtiːz]	litote	**rhetorical** [-'---] **question**	question rhétorique
meiosis [maɪ'əʊsɪs]	litote	**simile** ['sɪməli]	comparaison
metalepsis	métalepse	**synecdoche** [sɪ'nekdəki]	synecdoque
metaphor ['metəfə]	métaphore	**tenor**	substance
metonymy [-'---]	métonymie	**trope** [trəʊp]	trope
		vehicle	véhicule

9.2. Figures of sound

■ *Noms*

alliteration [-,--'---]	allitération	**euphony** ['juːfəni]	euphonie
assonance ['---]	assonance	**hiatus** [haɪ'eɪtəs]	hiatus
cacophony [-'---]	cacophonie	**rhythm**	rythme
cadence ['keɪdəns]	cadence, rythme	**sibilance**	allitération, consonnes sifflantes
consonance ['---]	consonance		
dissonance ['---]	dissonance	**syncope**	syncope

10. People

10.1. Writers

■ *Noms*

author	auteur	**observer**	observateur
biographer	biographe	**pamphleteer** [ˌ--'-]	pamphlétaire
commitment	engagement (politique)	**pen-name**	pseudonyme
coterie ['kəʊtəri]	coterie, cénacle	**plagiarism** ['pleɪdʒərɪzəm]	plagiat, démarquage
craftsmanship	art	**plagiarist** ['---]	plagiaire
creativity [ˌ--'---]	créativité	**potboiler**	œuvre alimentaire
essayist ['---]	essayiste	**powers of observation**	facultés d'observation
ghost writer	nègre (d'un écrivain)	**scribbler**	plumitif
hack writer	écrivaillon	**script-writer**	scénariste
invention	invention	**short story writer**	nouvelliste
inventiveness	esprit d'invention	**wordsmith**	orfèvre du langage
juvenilia	œuvres de jeunesse	**last work**	dernière œuvre
lexicologist	lexicologue	**latest work**	dernière œuvre (la plus récente)
lexicographer	lexicographe	**sb's early / earlier works**	premières œuvres, œuvres de jeunesse
narrative ['---] **powers**	talents de narrateur		
novelist	romancier	**sb's late / later works**	œuvres tardives ou plus récentes

Adjectifs

brimming with ideas	débordant d'idées	omniscient [ɒm'nɪsi̯ənt]	omniscient
classic	classique (auteur)	prolix ['prəʊlɪks]	prolixe
committed	engagé	realist ['rɪəlɪst]	réaliste (littérature)
gifted	doué	shrewd	habile, astucieux
imaginative [-'----]	plein d'imagination	talented	doué, talentueux
inventive	inventif	uncommitted [,--'--]	non engagé
observant	observateur		

Verbes

capture sb's attention	capter (l'attention de qqn)	plagiarize ['pleɪdʒəraɪz]	plagier
hold sb's interest	entretenir, conserver l'intérêt de qqn	read well	se lire agréablement
		recount	raconter (comment, etc)
inspire sb with sth	inspirer qch à qqn	relate	faire le récit de, rapporter
observe	observer	write	écrire (histoire)

10.2. Critics

Noms

apparatus GB [,æpə'reɪtəs] / US [,æpə'rætəs]	appareil, apparat critique	gynocritics	étude critique des œuvres féminines par des femmes
assessment of	jugement de, opinion sur	innuendo	insinuation malveillante
book reviewer	responsable de la rubrique des livres	intentional fallacy	interprétation erronée des intentions de l'auteur
comment ['--] on	commentaire de, remarque sur	literati [,lɪtə'rɑːtiː]	gens de lettres, lettrés
criterion [kraɪ'tɪəri̯ən]	critère	partiality (for / towards sb / sth)	partialité, prédilection pour, envers qqn / qch
literary critic (C)	critique littéraire	the critique [-'-]	la critique (ensemble des articles parus)
eulogy	éloge, panégyrique		
exegesis [,eksɪ'dʒiːsɪs]	exégèse	tirade [taɪ'reɪd]	diatribe
gloss	glose, commentaire	view (about sth / that ...)	opinion (sur qch / que...)

Collocations

appreciation (U)	appréciation, estime	to have little / no appreciation of classic plays
appreciation	critique, évaluation	to have a correct / throrough appreciation of sb's worth
criticism (U) ['----]	critique (de qch)	to express criticism of sth - to level criticism at sb - to subject sb to harsh / severe / unsparing criticism
evaluation	évaluation, jugement	to make a(n) critical / fair / honest / unfair / harsh evaluation of sb's work
notice	compte rendu, critique	a book / play / film may get good / bad / mixed notices
opinion [-'--]	opinion	a critic may have a good / high / low opinion of sb's work - he may form / express an opinion about sth
praise	éloge(s), louange(s)	to be loud / warm in one's praise of sth / sb - to lavish praise on sb
reservation	réserve	to have one big reservation about a book
review	critique, compte rendu	to write a(n) favourable / unfavourable review of a book

Literary terms, appreciation and analysis

■ *Adjectifs*

appreciative [ə'priːʃiətɪv]	élogieux	lenient (to)	indulgent (envers)
be appreciative of sth	apprécier qch	one-sided	partial, qui ne voit qu'un aspect des choses
controversial [,-'--]	controversé (livre), discutable (jugement)	opinionated [-'----]	dogmatique
derisive [dɪ'raɪsɪv]	moqueur, railleur	partial (to)	partial, injuste (envers)
derogatory [-'----] (to sb)	désobligeant (envers)	partisan	partisan
derogatory [-'----] (of sth)	qui dénigre qch	pejorative [pɪ'dʒɒrətɪv]	péjoratif
fair (to)	juste, équitable (envers)	prescriptive	normatif, puriste
harsh	dur, sévère	scathing	cinglant, acerbe, caustique
impartial	impartial, objectif	unfair (to)	injuste (envers)
laudatory	élogieux	vexed	controversé (question)

Collocations

critical	critique	*critical work* (travaux critiques) - *to be critical of sth* (trouver à redire)

■ *Verbes*

acclaim sth / sb as a ...	acclamer qch / qqn comme étant ...	evince	manifester (de l'intérêt, une qualité)
analyze	analyser	expurgate ['---]	expurger
appreciate	apprécier, bien aimer	extol [ɪk'stəʊl]	chanter les louanges de
assess	évaluer	impress	impressioner, faire impression sur
blame sb (for sth / for doing sth)	reprocher qch à qqn / à qqn de faire qch	pay tribute to	rendre hommage à
bowdlerize ['baʊdləraɪz]	expurger	qualify ['kwɒlɪfaɪ]	nuancer (jugement)
bring out	faire ressortir (un élément)	reproach sb (for sth / sb for doing sth)	reprocher qch à qqn / à qqn de faire qch
censor	censurer	reveal	révéler
comment ['--] on	commenter, faire des observations sur	review	faire la critique, un compte rendu de
criticize sth / sb (for sth / for doing sth)	critiquer qch / qqn pour qch / de faire qch	run sb / sth down	dénigrer, critiquer
detect	détecter (talent)	savage ['sævɪdʒ]	attaquer sans pitié
eulogize ['juːlədʒaɪz] (over)	faire l'éloge de	slate	éreinter, démolir
evaluate [-'---]	évaluer	synthetize ['sɪnθətaɪz]	faire la synthèse de

Collocations

praise	faire l'éloge de	*to praise sth - to praise sb (unreservedly / to the skies) for sth / for doing sth*

10.3. Readers

■ *Noms*

egghead	intello	reader	lecteur
highbrow ['haɪbraʊ]	intellectuel	the reading public	le public des lecteurs
narratee [,--'-]	narrataire, lecteur privilégié		

Collocations

readership	lectorat, lecteurs, public	*a book may have a readership of several thousand*
reading	lecture	*a book may be / make light / heavy / interesting / excellent reading*
		- to finish a book at a reading (d'un seul trait) */ in one reading*
		- sb may prefer light reading (qch de facile à lire)

■ *Noms / Adjectifs / Verbes*

• **the reader may be:**

a regular reader	un lecteur régulier	**engrossed in**	plongé dans
an occasional reader	un lecteur occasionnel	**enthralled** [ɪn'θrɔːld]	captivé, passionné
bewitched	ensorcelé	**fascinated**	fasciné
captivated	captivé	**spellbound**	envoûté
carried away	transporté, emballé	**under a spell**	sous le charme

• **or he may be:**

bored stiff	s'ennuyer à mourir	**frustrated**	frustré
disappointed (at / by)	déçu (de / par)	**snowed under with books**	submergé de livres
disgusted (at)	dégoûté (de / par)	**undecided**	indécis

• **a book may be:**

amusing	amusant	**unputdownable** [,--'---]	captivant, qu'on ne peut plus lâcher
bewitching	ensorcelant		
funny	drôle	**page turner**	livre qui se dévore

• **or it may be:**

| boring | ennuyeux | **unexciting** | peu passionnant |
| disappointing | décevant | **wearisome** ['wɪərɪsəm] | fastidieux |

• **the reader may:**

| be entertained | trouver le livre agréable | **enjoy reading the book** | prendre du plaisir à lire le livre |
| drop the book halfway through | abandonner le livre en cours de route | **respond to** | réagir favorablement à |

Corrigés

Corrigés du chapitre 1

Corrigés du chapitre 1 (1)

1. A / committed   B / consistency   C / freewill   D / workaholic   E / to tap

2. A / to cater for (to cater to, to meet the needs of)   B / to make a point of doing something   C / to opt out   D / to target   E / to venture

3. A / drive   B / target   C / pick   D / purposely   E / to be engrossed in one's work

4. A / She's an up-and-coming young woman. B / He's clever but he won't succeed because he lacks drive. C / Ladies and gentlemen! Take your choice! D / He felt an irresistible impulse to opt out but resolved to stay on a bit longer. E / She was chosen because she was conscientious, dedicated to her work and always willing to learn. F / "Don't waste your energy, don't act on a sudden impulse, always do more than you need to do, don't go back on your commitment to cater for the needs of the have-nots / the dispossessed, don't hesitate over your choices." G / "I know you don't lack ambition and I also know that you are a committed man, and that when you propose to do something, you do it, but... H / " Who is this advice intended for? Do you think I am unwilling to participate in the ambitious projects of your organisation? Surely you know that when I intend to do something, I become dedicated to it body and soul."

Corrigés du chapitre 1 (2)

2. A / ability - caution   B / try - go   C / worked out - drew up   D / enabled   E / check   F / tried - attempted   G / far-seeing - far-sighted

3. A / In spite of strenuous efforts, he couldn't make out the instructions for use of the remote control. B / Who the hell contrived / cooked up such a wild-eyed device? C / Nobody had prepared him to read this kind of texts, when he was at school. D / Now that he is at college, he is dead set on reading all the set books with great care in the set order, however strenuous the task may be, which he hopes will enable him to understand instruction manuals.

Corrigés du chapitre 1 (3)

2. A / 1 - 9   B / 3 - 14   C / 7 - 13   D / 4   E / 8   F / 2 - 10   G / 12 - 16   H / 5 - 6 - 11 - 15

3. A / All available means and legal devices must be used / resorted to in order to help these people out of their predicament / sad plight. B / You must be equal to the task. C / These poor people are no longer self-sufficient economically. D / They can't make do, all their life long, with makeshift shelters or accommodation. E / Emergency steps must be taken and supervision of / over the way they are carried out must be exercised. F / The funds allocated must be geared to the needs of the homeless. G / I do not doubt the propriety of the government's scheme, but... H / If you don't know how to proceed, ask me.

Corrigé du chapitre 1 (4)

2. A / It's time to act / take action and take part in the activities of your friends. B / Helping them in their undertaking, however risky and expensive it may seem at first sight, won't be too heavy a burden for you to bear. C / Are you ready to put into it a lot of work and time? D / If you are, you will be able to set out on a new career. E / Don't tell me you don't know how to set about it / handle the work! F / If you wish, I can supply / provide you with the necessary documents, so you can tackle the task. G / You may have to go without sleep for some time and give up a number of habits. H / You will have to attend to the minutest detail of the schemes under way. I / You are used to remaining idle for hours on end, never doing a stroke (of work) around the house and thus avoiding the daily grind and drudgery..., well, you're going to be very busy now, attending to other people. J / It should be quite a change for you!

Corrigés du chapitre 1 (5)

2. A / 2. 4. 8. 11. 13. 20.   B / 1.5. 9. 17. 21.   C / 3. 6. 10. 14. 18. 22.   D / 7. 12. 16. 19.

3. A / What has thwarted your plans for promoting literacy? B / What prevented them from materialising? C / What formidable obstacles hindered you in your work? D / Was lack of money the only hindrance to your projects? E / Perhaps I shoud not raise so serious an issue here and now ? F / Perhaps this will place / put you in an awkward position? G / But I think that your scheme would have proved effective in fighting illiteracy. H / I think you've made it plain to the public that competition is stiff and that people who can't read and write are at a disadvantage over those who can. I / I wonder what hampered your efforts?

Corrigés du chapitre 1 (6)

2. A / managed - get over / overcome - for B / has had it - has gone wrong C / flying - feat

3. A / To escape deserved punishment. B / To claim a reward for doing one's daily good deed regularly from one's cub mistress. C / To perform / do a heroic deed. D / A woman with many accomplishments. E / To end in failure. F / To cause minor inconvenience. G / To make steady progress. H / To be overcome with grief. I / To be overcome with joy. J / To suffer an unexpected setback. K / To do / work wonders. L / To work out a plan. M / To work out / settle a difference. N / His progress is still very slow.

Corrigés du chapitre 2

Corrigés du chapitre 2 (1.1)

1. I / witty   J / shrewd   K / dope   L / egghead

2. A / What he has done may have looked foolish, but in fact he showed great cunning. B / You seem not to approve of my actions and think that all my ideas, which I for one think are bright, are dumb. C / Do you think I am a nitwit or just a simpleton?

3. A / dull   B / clever   C / shrewd

4. A / genius   B / freakish   C / highbrow   D / witty   E / dumb

Corrigés du chapitre 2 (1.2)

2. A4 - B1 - C5 - D3 - E6 - F2

3. A / OBSESSED   B / IRKSOME   C / TEDIOUS   D / EXAMINE   E / HEED

Corrigés du chapitre 2 (1.3)

1. F / to rack one's brains   G / to realise   H / to search

2. A / Why not try and guess where the mistake comes from? B / It is quite understandable that you should need time to pore over a text which is unknown to you. C / He has no thought of changing his mind. D / Has it never occurred to you that you speak so fast that people can't make head or tail of what you say?

3. A / It dawned on me at last / that I had better think twice / before prying into his private life. B / You ought to know better / than to muse all day long / upon unforeseeable events. C / There is no point in your seeking my advice / since you always disregard my instructions.

Corrigés du chapitre 2 (1.4)

2. A / He doesn't have the slightest inkling of what the grammar of English is, although he claims to have working knowledge of that language. B / Few people are better acquainted than she is with the subtleties of English. C / I am not much of a scholar in German, but I am not what people call a layman either. D / Learn how to use each word in this lesson.

3. A / SWOT   B / SHALLOW   C / LAYMAN   D / LEARNED

Corrigés du chapitre 2 (1.5)

1. D / to quote from memory

2. A / I can't remember saying that. B / Remind him to call me. C / I shall never forget speaking with him in his dressing-room. D / That name rings a bell. E / Oblivious to / of what was happening around him, he recalled the unforgettable memories that the journey had reminded him of. F / Did you remember to turn off the gas?

Corrigés du chapitre 2 (1.6)

2. A4 - B5 - C6 - D1 - E3 - F2

3. A / FORESEE B / TELL C / HUNCH D / FANCY E / INSIGHT

Corrigés du chapitre 2 (1.7)

2. 1C - 2J - 3G - 4A - 5B - 6I - 7F - 8D - 9E - 10H

3. A / SURE B / CERTAIN C / OPINION D / VIEW E / CONCLUDE F / HYPOTHESIS

Corrigés du chapitre 2 (2.1)

1. A / trendy B / original C / effect D / cause E / random

2. A / Is he still likely to find the answer? B / Such hit-or-miss methods are likely to entail serious consequences. C / Some verdicts tend to trigger off riots. D / Overwork is beginning to tell. E / When it comes to making an important choice, he tries to guess what feelings of anger or approval his decisions will arouse.

3. A / He claimed he could bring about miracles. B / I came across this fascinating book at the library. C / The country's current difficulties all stem from political mismanagement.

Corrigés du chapitre 2 (2.2)

2. A / It occurred to me to envisage a possibility that I had ruled out so far. B / He misled her into faking a genuine document which she thought had been made up and therefore fake. C / He / she has a finger missing from his / her left hand. D / Reliable information is always lacking. E / What you are most lacking in, it seems, is tactfulness. F / Whatever the real, deep reasons for his lack of courage may be, it appears clearly that as soon as an unexpected difficulty crops up, he vanishes into thin air. G / I was mistaken about the dummy plastic gun : it may prove (to be) useful in an emergency. H / The murderer faked surprise when he was shown the telltale bloodstains.

3. A / FAKE B / REAL C / HAPPEN D / LACK E / MISTAKEN

Corrigés du chapitre 2 (2.3)

3. A / The police still haven't found any reliable clue as to last night's murder. B / What qualities do you think might make up the ideal man's character? C / I don't go by film reviews in the press. D / It often is a mistake to go on the account given by witnesses. E / At the core of the discussion was the desire of those participating to make a synthesis of the various views expressed. F / The music he plays somewhat partakes of sadness. G / He withdrew from the next election, which made up for greater clarity and offset the unfortunate effects of his earlier speeches. H / They were almost entirely made up of racist talk. I / He severed his relations with the far right and rooted out the corrupt practices of some members in the party. J / He gave a token of his good will by partaking in the evening festivities. K / People got the gist of his latest speech and took note of the particulars he provided on the gaps and loopholes of the present legislation. L / He proposes to remove all social inequalities, which is a feature common to all election speeches.

Corrigés du chapitre 2 (2.4)

2. A / — Must precedence be given to efficiency over working conditions? — It depends on many factors. B / I depend on you to set a good example. C / What a weird idea to specialise in sciences which are closely related to the study of those quaint aliens which are said to vaguely resemble human beings. D / Is it not relevant to establish a link between the unaccountable and rather queer behaviour of the people living in the castle and the unusual rumors which circulate about it?

3. A3 - B5 - C8 - D7 - E2 - F4 - G6 - H1

Corrigés du chapitre 3

Corrigés du chapitre 3 (1)

2. A / CONCERN   B / MOOD   C / STIR   D / FRENZY   E / PANG   F / TOUCH   G / CARE

3. A / The news aroused great excitement. B / He tried to repress his feelings. C / He never seems to feel any pangs of guilt. D / He got into trouble for letting himself be carried away by excessive enthusiasm.

Corrigés du chapitre 3 (2)

1. A / to be fed up   B / hooked   C / craze   D / to have pity on sb

2. A / The project appealed to lots of people. Didn't it to you? B / He's keen on modern music. Aren't you? C / — He's no longer keen on having coffee for breakfast. — Neither am I. D / She can't stand being loved. Too many experiences of unrequited love have completely put her off love. E / The son still cares about his parents very much. So does the daughter, for that matter. F / — He likes helping others. — I don't! G / He is very keen on taking her for a ride every weekend to show her his garden in the country. H / He only relishes gardening. She doesn't, she just loathes it. I / Films of that kind have lost much of their appeal for me. J / His dislike of traditions sometimes leads him to fall for people on the fringes of society.

3. A / LOVE   B / HATE   C / SAKE   D / LIKE   E / LOATHE   F / CARE   G / HATRED

Corrigés du chapitre 3 (3)

2. A4 - B5 - C2 - D7 - E1 - F8 - G6 - H3

3. A / I am looking forward to meeting you. B / Do you mind my smoking? C / I wish he hadn't come. D / I wish he were here. E / I wish he would come as soon as possible.

Corrigés du chapitre 3 (4)

1. A / sad   B / unhappy   C / moan   D / sigh   E / sigh   F / sob

2. A / — Don't you miss me? — Yes, I do very much. B / He leads a drab life, perhaps that's what makes him such a dreary man. C / She heaved a sigh of relief when he left her.

3. A5 - B7 - C6 - D1 - E2 - F4 - G3

Corrigés du chapitre 3 (5)

2. A / cheerful - enjoying themselves   B / enjoyable - thrill   C / delighted   D / relieved   E / raise my spirits - happiness - unfortunate

3. A5 - B1 - C6 - D2 - E3 - F4

Corrigés du chapitre 3 (6)

2. A / ashamed / down   B / bleak / regretted   C / to be   D / Ø

3. A / He felt untold agony at being a liar. B / He killed himself out of despair. C / He shamed the Board of Directors into giving the employees a rise. D / Nothing would raise his spirits more than helping others out of their misery. E / He was badly cut up about other people's unhappiness. F / He lived in dire misery for most of his life.

Corrigés du chapitre 3 (7)

2. 1B - 2D - 3A - 4E - 5G - 6H - 7F - 8C

Corrigés du chapitre 3 (8)

2. A / frightened   B / dread   C / awesome / formidable   D / recoiled

3. A / The fear of the future gives me the creeps. B / I take fright at the slightest ominous sign that unemployment is increasing. C / He recoils from his obligations. He isn't the only one. D / If he goes on like this, I'll have to frighten him out of his appalling plan. E / Civil wars have become a scourge to many countries in Europe and Africa. F / This formidable monarch inspires awe in his subjects.

Corrigés du chapitre 4

Corrigés du chapitre 4 (1)

2. A / Answer the questions I have asked you. B / Try to express yourself clearly and convey your message in a few words. C / No gibberish! Give us accurate information, use simple words. D / Describe the scene to us, describe what happened. E / We get the drift of your previous written statements, the wording of which can still be changed if you wish. F / I thank you for the puns you make in some places. G / But what we expect of you are specific details on the subject concerned without any understatement or humor - we don't much go in for that. H / Stress what you suppose to be the deep meaning of the events. I / Don't forget that this is an inquiry. J / If you have to quote the words used by a witness, what we want are precise accurate quotations, not just vague references. K / It is important for us to be able to keep a record of what people have said. L / You will therefore have to specify certain points. M / Be outspoken. No quizzical smiles. No noncommittal answers. N / We'd like to know what the letters X and Y in your address book stand for. O / Somebody paid $100,000 into your account on July 17, 1996.

Corrigés du chapitre 4 (2)

2. A11 - B5 - C1 - D6 - E3 - F12 - G8 - H2 - I10 - J9 - K4 - L7

Corrigés du chapitre 4 (3)

2. A / is rumoured - voiced - hearsay - grapevine - spoken - out - loud - loudspeaker - hush - up
B / speaking - low - halting - voice - colloquial - grumbling - inarticulate - lisping - articulate
C / drawls - mumbles - soapbox - orator - slow - delivery - lisp - comment

3. A / I've heard about him but I've never heard *from* him. B / Let's talk it over. C / Do not mispronounce my name, please. D / Cackle and chuckle, that's all you can do. E / I didn't tell him anything and he didn't say anything either. F / You can chat away / chatter with each other but don't shout. G / It is not polite to whisper things in your neighbour's ear.

Corrigés du chapitre 4 (4)

2. A / Send a note on notepaper, unlined or lined, rather than the draft of a long letter that nobody can decipher and which is illegible because it is written in shorthand. B / Fill out the form about the notice to quit. Tick off the relevant boxes - consult the handbook. C / Underline or highlight, whichever you like, the main points that you have jotted down in your pocket book. D / Look up the words to translate in a dictionary. E / Give your correspondent my regards. F / Do not scribble your signature. G / And write out a cheque to my order.

3. A / KNOW   B / SIGN   C / PEN   D / PENCIL   E / QUILL

Corrigés du chapitre 4 (5)

2. A4 - B8 - C3 / C7 - D1 - E2 - F3 - G5 / G7 - H6

384   *Words and their collocations*

3.

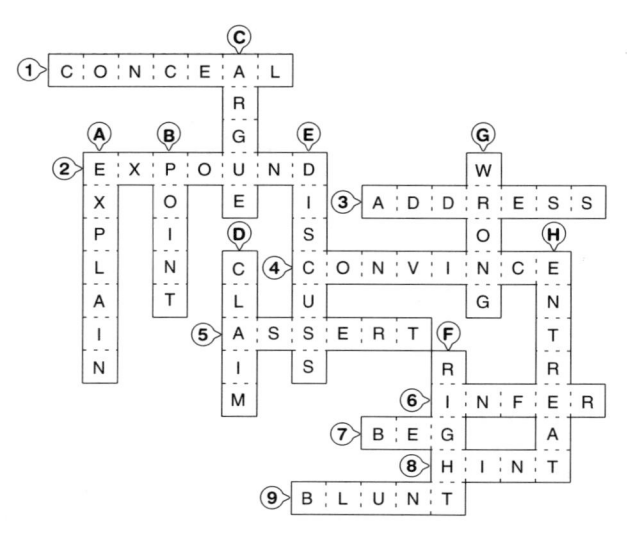

[Crossword grid with answers:
1. CONCEAL
2. EXPOUND
3. ADDRESS
4. CONVINCE
5. ASSERT
6. INFER
7. BEG
8. HINT
9. BLUNT
Down clues: A. EXPLAIN, B. POINT, C. CRG (CRAG?), D. CLUES, E. GUESS, F. FRR (FERRET?), G. WRONG, H. ENTRANT, with intersecting letters COMPLAIN, DISCUSS, etc.]

Corrigés du chapitre 4 (6)

1. A / — Thanks a lot. — Not at all. B / to meet with sb's approval C / to acknowledge receipt of a letter D / to see sb's point

2. A / He acknowledged stealing the money. B / He apologised to his parents who, anyway, did not approve of the way he lived, for giving in to temptation. C / He came to an agreement with the police that if he gave back the money plus interests, he would not go to jail. D / Admittedly, not everybody agreed with that solution which *he* thought was great. E / He undoubtedly had got a point and if he was allowed to make his point clearly, he would talk people round to his point of view.

Corrigés du chapitre 4 (7)

2.

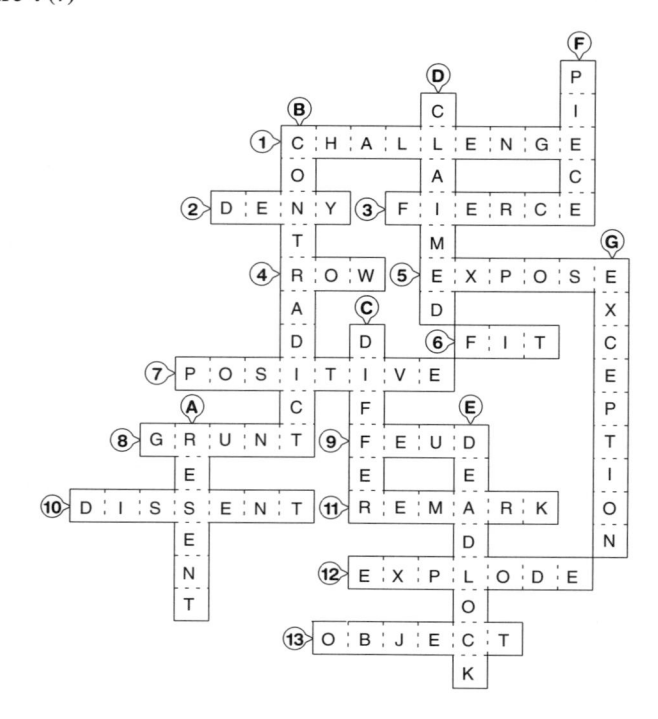

[Crossword grid with answers:
1. CHALLENGE
2. DENY
3. FIERCE
4. ROW
5. EXPOSE
6. FIT
7. POSITIVE
8. GRUNT
9. FEUD
10. DISSENT
11. REMARK
12. EXPLODE
13. OBJECT
Down: A. GRUMBLE, B. COT, C. CD, D. CLAIM, E. DEFEND, F. PICCEPTION (PERCEPTION?), G. EXCEPT, etc.]

Corrigés 385

3. A / The very favourable criticism written by this critic contradicts all the qualifications, the malevolent innuendos and the objections he had emphasised shortly before in another paper. B / He must have harboured deep, bitter resentment and then decided to say what he was resentful about. C / Then he had probably thought about it and qualified his judgement. D / He felt no longer as furious and indignant as he had felt before. E / What had seemed to him to be disputable and objectionable was much less so now. F / Had he got into a terrible row with the writer before the first review? G / Had the writer's arguments seemed to him to be off the point? H / Perhaps the critic could not at the time brook any dissent from anybody. I / Had anybody succeeded in settling their difference? J / Had there been a misunderstanding? K / What had the critic taken exception to? L / What had infuriated him? M / Had the writer brought down upon himself the critic's anger by cutting in on him in the course of a conversation? N / Had the critic then hit the roof? O / Had the writer threatened the critic that he would expose a thing or two about his private life? Nobody will ever know.

4. A / anger - disapproved of   B / explode   C / remarked on - squabbled

Corrigés du chapitre 4 (8)

2. — What may have caused such an uproar? — A quarrel breaking out between two hot-tempered men who suddenly flew into a temper and hurled abuse and rude oaths at each other, abused each other, and called each other bloody bastard and fucking son of a bitch.

Corrigés du chapitre 5

Corrigés du chapitre 5 (1)

2. A / with a vengeance   B / slightly   C / merely   D / flat

3. A / It does not matter what he said last night. It's immaterial to me in any case. B / It would be sheer nonsense to give this incident extensive media coverage at all costs. C / It would only escalate a problem which is serious enough as it is, if one takes into account the prevalent atmosphere in the gallery at the moment. D / There is undoubtedly a misunderstanding between this painter and yourself that it would be wrong to consider trifling. E / This artist is undoubtedly a thorough bore, a big eater whose chief interest in life is grub. F / But he is the foremost painter of our time. He has painted a fair amount of paintings / pictures which are outstanding achievements. G / The overall impression he gives of scruffiness is probably the main reason for the dislike that people feel for him. H / His mere presence, the very mention of his name causes acute embarrassment to some people. I / Other people hold it against him that he earns too much money, as if an artist must necessarily make a bare living and earn a mere 500 dollars a month. J / Others again would like to see him lying full length on his studio floor, a victim to a full-blown heart-attack. K / Setting up a comprehensive list of his failures / defects, going into a thorough search of all his actions, trying to dig up definite evidence as to his private life and make out whether he has or has not a slight foreign accent, would be a trivial task. L / The general hostility towards / against him will / is bound to subside one day … when he dies.

Corrigés du chapitre 5 (2)

2. A / Virtually nothing happened in the first five minutes. B / Nothing short of a miracle could save him. C / It is a fairly good film. D / He was fairly mad with rage. E / He was roughly the same age as she was. F / To blow up a problem. G / To play down a danger. H / A significant discovery. I / A sketchy memory of sth. J / Moderate prices. K / A moderate performance. L / Faint protests. M / A gentle knock on the door. N / Average intelligence. O / To reach a high standard. P / To work out an average. Q / Every other day on an average. R / A mild punishment. S / It was a near miss.

3. A / He was a light sleeper and every evening, even when the traffic was light, he would take precautions that he regarded as elementary, but which I thought were a trifle annoying. B / But what's the good of quarrelling over trifles?

Corrigés du chapitre 6

Corrigés du chapitre 6 (1)

2.

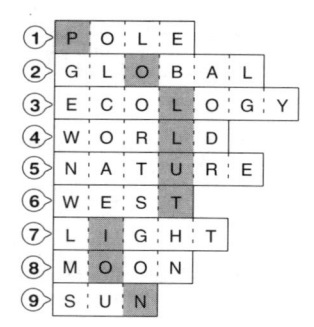

```
1> P O L E
2> G L O B A L
3> E C O L O G Y
4> W O R L D
5> N A T U R E
6> W E S T
7> L I G H T
8> M O O N
9> S U N
```

3. A / to breathe in petrol / gas fumes. B / shooting star. C / inhabitant. D / the sun was beating down. E / a dull, overcast sky. F / the sky is clouding over / clearing up. G / the inhabited parts of the universe

Corrigés du chapitre 6 (2)

2. A / mainland. B / ground - earth. C / land. D / clearing - glade. E / slope - hill. F / ditch - tunnel - moat. G / holy land

Corrigés du chapitre 6 (3)

2. A / to ford a river. B / to have a very rough crossing. C / to be ankle-deep in water. D / to climb (up) a steep mountain / a sheer cliff. E / to go to the seaside to stay on a sandy or shingle beach and watch the sea ebb and flow. F / to go out to sea at (the age of) sixteen. G / to call at a port. H / the river overflowed, flooded the countryside, then it receded.

Corrigés du chapitre 7

Corrigés du chapitre 7 (1)

2. A / We were a bit cramped for space for a game of hide-and-seek. B / We played it all the same when we were cooped up all day. C / We used to lurk motionless in dark corners or in cupboards (when there was only room for two small kids) crawling with black bugs. D / On other occasions we would go out into the garden which was level with the first floor — the sun was shining, the leaves were motionless. E / At the back of the garden, to the left of the flight of steps (or to the right — I can't remember), there was a two-metre tree which seemed very tall to us. F / We would sit underneath it — it was our favourite spot on sunny days.

3. A / right. B / left. C / opposite. D / front. E / location

Corrigés du chapitre 7 (2)

2. A6 - B4 - C7 - D2 - E1 - F5 - G3

3. 1 / balance - setting. 2 / hastened - return - showed. 3 / squashed. 4 / squeeze. 5 / swift - hasty - rushed. 6 / Take - stop. 7 / set. 8 / shadowed - unloading. 9 / sharp

Corrigés du chapitre 7 (3)

2. A / wriggle. B / fidget. C / stoop. D / shiver. E / sneaked. F / sweep. G / shudder. H / saunter. I / tumble - dash. J / jolt. K / plod. L / jostle. M / reel - brisk. N / crawl. O / dart. P / curtsy. Q / wrestle.

3. A / I twitched her sleeve to catch her attention. B / He used to swagger a lot. C / He wandered the streets aimlessly every night. D / Do not wallow in the mud. E / I edged my way towards the window.

4. A / prowl. B / cuddled. C / bent down

Corrigés du chapitre 7 (4.1)

2. A / nudged. B / waved. C / sign - wave. D / clasped. E / a hug and a kiss. F / lean

Corrigés du chapitre 7 (4.2)

2. A / He cast the line delicately and in next to no time pulled a huge fish out of the river. B / He thrust (stuck) his still wet hands into his raincoat pockets. C / He was trundling along a wheelbarrow full of bricks. D / Who would play first ? We tossed for it (to find out). E / She wheeled him around the garden. F / She flung herself on the couch and burst into tears. G / She thrust the book at the student. H / She tossed her head back. I / I fumbled with the keys so clumsily that I dropped them. J / She hurled the books across the room in a fit of temper.

3. 1G - 2H - 3A - 4I - 5B - 6J - 7C - 8D - 9F - 10E

Corrigés du chapitre 7 (4.3)

2. A / He was groping for the exit. B / She handed out free meals to the homeless. C / He held her tight. D / She jerked her hand up and knocked on the door. E / She pointed a gun at the burglar. F / She became interested and lifted her eyes; she saw him and then lowered her eyes again. G / She picked up the telephone, held it in her right hand for a few moments before answering it. H / She reached (lifted) the bag down from the upper shelf. I / Stop rummaging through my drawers. J / She shook the coins out of the piggy bank (money box). K / Rub the stain out.

3. 1G - 2I - 3D (ou 2D et 3I) - 4J - 5B - 6H - 7C - 8E - 9F - 10A

Corrigés du chapitre 7 (5)

2. A / To do a jump of two metres. B / To make a parachute jump. C / To leap (up) for sth. D / To break into a run. E / To crouch (down) out of fear. F / To tiptoe across a room. G / To spring to one's feet. H / to stalk the streets. I / To steal in.

3. A / stalk. B / sail. C / tiptoe. D / limp. E / storm. F / shuffle.

Corrigés du chapitre 7 (6)

2. A / The coach had huddled with the club's president and then had gathered the players for a friendly talk. B / For the last couple of hours, the crowd had been swarming into the stadium, which was now packed full. C / It had been difficult to squeeze in the supporters from the visiting team. D / When the game started, the players clustered around their captain again.

Corrigés du chapitre 8

Corrigés du chapitre 8 (1)

2. A / As a child, he could impersonate all his teachers on demand. B / — Come on, guys ! let's go ! C / He was a good guy and this guy Smith sometimes said to him : "Well, old chap, everything all right ?". D / Some teenagers are said to be a danger for private property. E / Perhaps this is due to many of these youngsters being rootless and having nowhere to go. F / Be tolerant towards them as not all of them come from as privileged a background as yours.

Corrigés du chapitre 8 (1.2 à 1.5 et 2)

2. A / She survived the fire, didn't she ? B / She is mourning her father's death. So are we. C / He's aged a lot recently, but she hasn't. D / — He had a hard time in his youth, poor man ! — So did I ! E / — She was left an orphan at the age of 6. — Correct F / — Didn't they carry out a post-mortem ? — Of course they did ! G / He didn't commit suicide in the end and neither did she, for that matter. H / — He didn't attend the funeral at the village churchyard. — She did. I / She is still in mourning. He isn't.

3. 1D - 2C - 3F - 4G - 5H - 6E - 7A - 8B

4. A / to meet one's death in an accident. B / to be of age. C / to live to a ripe old age. D / an uneventful life. E / to be sb's senior by 15 years. F / to take one's own life. G / to cast / throw in one's lot with sb. H / to be middle-aged. I / to devote one's life to sb. J / to pay a tribute to the deceased. K / to pay the death duties.

5. A / This brought about the break-up of their marriage. B / He saved her life on two occasions. C / It fell to my lot to write the deceased's obituary. D / The firm's junior manager is an expectant mother.

6.

```
         A
    1> D  E  A  T  H
  2> J  U  N  I  O  R
       3> E  L  D  E  R  L  Y
          4> W  I  D  O  W
             5> W  I  L  L
       6> B  E  R  E  A  V  E  D
             7> S  U  R  V  I  V  E
```

Corrigés du chapitre 8 (3)

2. A / — He has a womanish voice. — You think so, do you ? B / — You identify with your father too much. — I don't ! C / — He is quite an honourable father. — So he is. D / — Were you named Leonard after de Vinci ? — I was. E / — I must register for work with the National Employment Agency. — So must I. F / — Jane has had a happy girlhood. — Not all girls do. G / — She is seeking fame. — Aren't you ? H / — He remained a bachelor throughout his life. — He didn't ! — Oh yes, he did ! I / — Patricia is thought to be a changeling. — And isn't she ? — No one knows for sure. — In any case, she is a foundling.

3. A / renowned. B / nickname. C / foster. D / honourable - reputable. E / identity. F / achieved - Ø status - drop - surname

Corrigés du chapitre 8 (4.1)

2. A / She failed but it was through no fault of hers. B / The doctor is at fault for not sending his patient to the hospital earlier. C / The moral of this story is that you cannot raise sb's morale when it has been undermined by repeated failures. D / He flew into a temper and yet he is an even-tempered person whose character has been formed by the trials and tribulations of life. E / A man with very strict morals, he means / wants to wipe out crime, vice and violence — surely a noble task ! F / His works deserve to be widely recognised / acknowledged. G / She acted as my interpreter in the USA. H / Stop acting like the capricious kid that you are. I / He was a well-behaved young man whose innate talent for music would one day make him worthy to perform in the major orchestras.

3. A2 - B11 - C4 - D9 - E6/7 - F10 - G3 - H12 - I13 - J14 - K5 - L8/1 - M15

Corrigés du chapitre 8 (4.2)

2. A / on. B / in. C / nerve. D / self-conscious

3. A / His incredible conceit caused this virtuous man to be disliked by everyone. B / On the promenade, his latest fashion clothes cut quite a dash. C / It takes a lot of spirit / courage to get over / overcome such a blow to one's pride. D / What can an insecure woman do when faced with such a self-assured man ? E / Terrorists' bombings are intended / meant to break the spirit of the populations targeted. F / What does he brag / boast about so (much) ? G / What does she pride herself on ?

Corrigés du chapitre 8 (4.3)

2. A / sensible. B / straightforward. C / subdued. D / consistent

3. A / Stop showing off your knowledge. B / Is he fool enough to believe that ? C / I like the sensible way he tackles problems. D / He made his point in his usual straightforward manner. E / He is a bit too curious / inquisitive about what happens to his neighbours. F / I doubt his / her consistency and wisdom.

4.

	1	2	3	4	5	6	7	8	9	10	11	12	13	14	15
1						L	E		G			O		W	
2						I		U	A	E	Q	K		S	N
3			D	R	I	V	E	S				U		N	O
4		T	O			E	X	H	I	B	I	T	I	O	N
5	I	E	W	S		L		I				E			S
6	G		N	O	S	Y		N			T	O	P	E	E
7	N			A			E	G	A	C		I			N
8	O		L	V	U	T	A		R		L	E	S	S	
9	R	P	A		C	U	R	I	O	U	S				E
10	E		C	O	Y		T			D					
11		H	E	R		S	H	F	R	E					

Corrigés du chapitre 8 (4.4)

1. A / to feel uneasy. B / obstinate refusal. C / easy-going. D / edgy. E / fastidious person. F / fastidious work. G / desperate case. H / highly-strung. I / whimsical. J / uncompromising

2. A3/4 - B6 - C1 - D7 - E2 - F8 - G5 - H4/3

Corrigés du chapitre 8 (4.5)

2. A / How did he dare challenge such a gallant man ? B / Don't hide the truth from me by dodging my questions. C / It takes guts to court an almost certain arrest. D / There is in this character a streak of cowardice not to be found in some manly heroes in the penny dreadfuls. E / He won a puny 15% of the vote - a very poor showing. F / Don't call this daredevil stuntman a coward - just when for once he is wondering if he will be able to stick it out. G / He was bold / daring enough to contradict her. / He made so bold as to contradict her.

Corrigés du chapitre 8 (4.6 et 4.7)

2. A / It is very thoughtful of you to devote all your free time to helping others. B / How nice of you to lend me (some) money. C / I give your generous plan my wholehearted support. D / He is lavish in his praise of my novels. E / It's very decent to show such selflessness. F / I'm doing this out of sheer kindness. G / My patience is wearing thin. H / A conscientious and thoughtful man - these are two words well fitted for the description of this eminently humane man who is also known to be a faithful husband.

3. A / even-handed. B / lavish. C / thoughtless. D / devoted. E / decent. F / devoted. G / dutiful. H / looked up to

Corrigés du chapitre 8 (4.8)

2. She always eyed him with suspicion. B / Experience had taught her to be cautious / prudent in choosing her partners. C / She thought it would be imprudent, rash, even reckless to accept his proposal straight off. D / Oh, she did hesitate ! (How she hesitated !). She had so often been blamed for lacking discretion / common sense. E / She was wary of men who were punctual, discreet, too perfect.

Corrigés du chapitre 8 (4.9)

2.
1.		SMUG
2.		DEPEND
3.		HONESTLY
4.		CONSCIENCE
5.		UNSCRUPULOUS
6.		EXAGGERATE
7.		STRAIGHT
8.		SQUARE
9.		PRIM
10.		CRAFTY
11.		RELIABLE
12.		DEPENDABLE
13.		PLAIN-SPOKEN
14.		SCRUPULOUS
15.		GULLIBLE
16.		DECEIT
17.		PRIG
18.		CAD
19.		CRAFT
20.		DECEIVE
21.		DECEITFUL
22.		SPONTANEOUS
23.		INGENUOUS
24.		UPRIGHT
25.		NAIVE
26.		SLY

Corrigés du chapitre 9

Corrigés du chapitre 9 (1)

2. A / To lull a baby to sleep. B / To provide for one's nephews and nieces. C / To be homesick for somebody. D / To be given a strict or easy-going upbringing. E / All I have left, in the way of a family, are a few remote relatives. F / They are permissive parents who don't take much care of their offspring. G / He lulled him into doing the most horrible things. H / A latchkey child.

Corrigés du chapitre 9 (2)

2. A / a broken home. B / to foster a child out to a foster home. C / to inherit from sb. D / to get pregnant by a stranger. E / to be three months pregnant. F / to be pregnant with a little girl. G / to sue for divorce. H / to celebrate a wedding anniversary. J / a confirmed bachelor. K / to be engaged / married to sb.

Corrigés du chapitre 10

Corrigés du chapitre 10 (1.1)

2. A / Does your doctor make house calls ? B / It is bad form not to call on neighbours who are newcomers to the district — one must give them a warm welcome. C / To attend functions, wear evening dress fitted for each occasion, speak a formal language, mind one's manners (be careful to be on one's best behaviour), mix with people one

hardly knows at all in order not to feel the odd man out, introduce the guests to one another (with the exception of those who are well-known to everybody and need no introduction), join in the games, if any — this is more than an unsociable person (a bad mixer) like me can put up with / stand. D / To play host, welcome the guests with open arms, act as a go-between between people, have M. Brown and Mrs Small meet (up), submit to the game of name-dropping, see to it that the ladies get on well together and will wish to socialize with one another afterwards — you are expected to do all this in high society. E / Running the parties oneself, clearing the rooms that are crowded with furniture (or having them cleared) so that the guests can dance, being careful who has been invited, dropping in on one's parents' friends when abroad, sending one's family (without forgetting / leaving out anybody) a card of greeting(s), keeping in touch with people one has lost sight of since school by asking them to dinner — such are the duties of young ladies from good homes.

Corrigés du chapitre 10 (1.2)

2. A / Don't light a bonfire in your garden on Good Friday, on All Souls' Day or on All Saints' Day. B / Don't sing carols, don't give Christmas boxes or crackers to the kids on Easter Sunday. C / In May, in some parts of England, people dance around a maypole : don't do it on the wrong day ! D / Passover, Whitsun, the Christian New Year are feasts that are little likely to overlap. E / You stand a better chance of feasting off roasted turkey on Thanksgiving (day) than on Shrove Tuesday which is pancake day ! F / Was the day you dressed up as Santa Claus a red-letter day for you ?

Corrigés du chapitre 10 (1.3)

2. A / scandal - giggle. B / guffaw. C / puns. D / hell

3. A / a scandal bursts out. B / to spread gossip. C / to crack a smile. D / to go through hard times. E / subdued laughter. F / to crack a joke. G / to let out a guffaw. H / to poke fun at sb. I / malicious gossip. J / to have a hell of a good time. K / to jest foolishly about everything. L / to smile one's approval.

Corrigés du chapitre 10 (1.4)

2. A / — What's the matter ? B / — I just can't put up with the monotony / routine of my office job. C / — I understand that it can be a bit of a problem for you. D / — A bit of a problem ? It's becoming a matter of survival ! E / — You are exaggerating. Don't kick / make such a fuss, I mean, you could be out of work ! F / — I get bored, so I smoke too much out of sheer boredom. I feel up to some mischief at times ! G / — At your age ? I grant you that your boss is a nuisance, but … . H / — I feel like playing a trick on him, a dirty trick. I / — Don't do that or he'll think you're revenging yourself on him for unrequited love and that you're trying to make bad blood between people in the office. J / — How annoying / provoking you can get ! I think you are trying to provoke me into flying into a temper. K / — Not at all. Oh, I've got an idea, why don't you fuss over him ? L / — No way ! He makes me cross from morning till evening. M / — Does he harass you ? N / — He intrudes on my good mood. O / — That's a funny way of putting it ! P / — He exasperates me, to put it another way. He makes me feel like tricking money out of him. Q / — I sometimes wonder which of you two makes the more a nuisance of themselves !

Corrigés du chapitre 10 (2.1)

2. A4 - B8 - C9 - D3 - E7 - F2 - G10 - H5 - I1 - J6

Corrigés du chapitre 10 (2.2)

2. A / sulking. B / vying. C / vexes. D / jilt. E / nag

3. A / She must have been wild about him to stick ten years of such a rude man, when she can't stand living with such impolite and tactless people ! B / She can't not have taken offence, from the very start, at his malicious remarks, his offensive language, his unfriendly attitude towards her friends. C / She must have been wild with jealously when he counted her out of the wild parties he went to alone. D / What could her feelings have been when he came home half drunk and went for her both physically and verbally ? E / How could she not have felt like doing him in when he threatened to strangle her or when he cut her dead on the streets (which he did out of sheer malice) or grudged her a puny five pounds a week pocket-money ?

Corrigés du chapitre 10 (2.3)

2. A / blow. B / kiss. C / lust. D / take to. E / date. F / pick up. G / rude. H / honey. I / chick

3. A / She just won't date men she suspects of being inveterate lechers. B / Her boyfriend has a crush on me. C / He keeps making eyes at me. D / But I don't let myself be picked up for a short-lived affair. E / He's trying to seduce me into being intimate with him. F / Anyway, a friend in need (not in bed) is a friend indeed.

Corrigés du chapitre 10 (3.1 / 3.2)

2. A / Don't let children lay down the law. B / It is a good thing for children to become gradually independent of their parents but they mustn't be allowed to smoke just because you also smoke. C / You must make them obey your orders; they must learn to be obedient from an early age. D / Children often try to challenge their parents to punish them. E / They hope to get you to consent to satisfy their desires, and accept all their whims without arguing; in short, they want you to give in to them / to yield to them. F / Foil their plans before it's too late. If you do not, they'll have a showdown with you. G / Hold your own against their attacks. H / Put your foot down. I / Why can't you accept the obvious fact that children, not their parents, must obey. J / No father in their right mind will let his children forbid him to go into their room.

Corrigés du chapitre 10 (4.1)

2. A / force - intervene. B / stop. C / suppress. D / insist - meddling. E / high-handed. F / refused - bullied. G / forbid - patronising. H / demand - brought to bear - order - issued.

2. A / My mother flatters herself about being an exceptional mother. B / She's flattered into believing that she has a talented son. C / People admire her for devoting her life to that only son of hers. D / Of course I'm quite thankful to have been born. E / My mother's love for me greatly impresses people. F / Does that mean I have to be grateful to her all my life for bringing me into the world ? G / "I shall never stop congratulating myself on bringing this little genius into the world", she says. H / Everybody looks up to her and pays tribute to <u>her.</u> What about poor little me ?

Corrigés du chapitre 10 (4.2)

2. A / Why does she keep sneering and sniggering at everything I say ? B / She feels nothing but contempt for him and never fails to disparage his efforts in public. C / She is contemptuous of his suggestions, though they don't appear to be despicable or even ludicrous.

3. A / ironic. B / scornful. C / ungrateful. D / contemptible. E / ludicrous. F / despicable. G / spurn. H / scorn.

Corrigés du chapitre 10 (4.4)

2. A / a pretence. B / fibs. C / fool. D / falsehood. E / cheated on. F / taken in

Corrigés du chapitre 10 (4.5)

2. A3 - B5 - C1 - D2 - E4

3. A / to forgive sb sth / sb for sth. B / to excuse sb for sth / sb from sth. C / to reward sb with sth

Corrigés du chapitre 10 (4.6)

2. A / scolding. B / railing at. C / tell off. D / chiding. E / blame on

3. A / What awful grievance does she nurse deep in her heart ? B / Whose death is she trying to avenge ? C / Who is she complaining to, and what about ? Which gods is she filing her complaint with ? D / Who is she trying to revenge herself on ? E / Who does she have it in for ? F / Who does she wish divine retribution to be visited on ?

Corrigés du chapitre 11

Corrigé du chapitre 11 A (1 et 2)

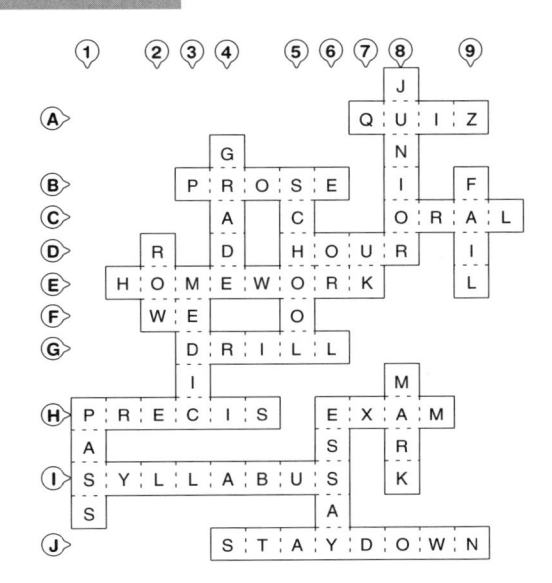

```
              1     2 3 4      5 6 7 8      9
                                     J
    A                           Q  U  I  Z
                       G        N
    B           P  R  O  S  E   I         F
    C              A      C     O  R  A  L
    D        R     D      H  O  U  R      I
    E     H  O  M  E  W  O  R  K         L
    F        W     E      O
    G              D  R  I  L  L
                   I              M
    H     P  R  E  C  I  S     E  X  A  M
          A                    S     R
    I     S  Y  L  L  A  B  U  S     K
          S                    A
    J                 S  T  A  Y  D  O  W  N
```

Corrigé du chapitre 11 A (3, 4, 5)

2. 1C - 2G - 3F - 4B - 5H - 6D - 7E - 8A

Corrigé du chapitre 11 A (6, 7, 8)

2. 1D - 2E - 3A - 4G - 5B - 6H - 7C - 8F

Corrigés du chapitre 11 B (1 à 5)

2. A / RESIT - B / STUDY - C / DON - D / ART - E / DEAN - F / TUTOR - G / PAPER - H / RAG

3. A / He has been researching a very scholarly subject for twenty five years. B / He took up a course in arts and then transferred to art. C / He went in for linguistics and registered for a one-year course in computing as well. D / He sat for his BA degree in June, failed the exam and had to resit it in September.

Corrigés du chapitre 12

Corrigé du chapitre 12 A (0 à 2.4)

2. A / — They mentioned you on the one o'clock news. B / — Did they? C / — They showed some footage of your visit to the Queen. D / — Did they? E / — It was a phone-in programme. All viewers in England must have turned their sets on and called! And the viewing figures must have soared! F / — Well, no. It would appear that people switched channels and tuned in to another channel. G / — They can't have done that. In any case, they'll certainly rerun the programme. H / — I should be very much surprised if they did so!

3. 1D - 2H - 3A - 4G - 5B - 6E - 7C - 8F

Corrigé du chapitre 12 A (3.1 à 3.3)

2. A / to do the crossword (puzzle). B / to make news. C / to run an advert. D / This is a major item of news that is going to arouse scathing comment in some papers. E / The article came in for a lot of (adverse) criticism. F / Not all news hits the headlines. G / The news of his death has just been broken and is likely to raise the circulation of newspapers. H / to go into print journalism. I / to break a minor piece of news as if it deserved editorial treatment.

3. A / syndicated. B / censor. C / issue. D / stop-press news

4. A / managing director. B / ran / published. C / came out / leaked out. D / theatre critic - reviewed / reported on.

Corrigé du chapitre 12 B (1.1)

2. 1G - 2H - 3E - 4F - 5A - 6B - 7C - 8D

Corrigé du chapitre 12 B (1.2)

2. A / I'd prefer you to read the sonnet out to me rather than quote two or three hackneyed or definitely poor lines. B / The chances of coming across far-fetched similes, drab, commonplace descriptions, long uninteresting / dull passages are much less in a short story than in a novel. C / There are novels which I only flip or thumb through — yours, for instance.

3. 1 / DIARY. 2 / STORY. 3 / IMAGE. 4 / HERO. 5 / PLOT. 6 / LINE. 7 / NOVEL

Corrigé du chapitre 12 B (2.1 à 2.5)

2. A / FAUX. B / VRAI. C / FAUX. D / FAUX → best boy - FAUX → gaffer - FAUX → headgrip - propman VRAI - FAUX → stage hand. E / FAUX → before... F / FAUX. G / FAUX. H / FAUX

Corrigé du chapitre 12 B (3.1 à 3.6)

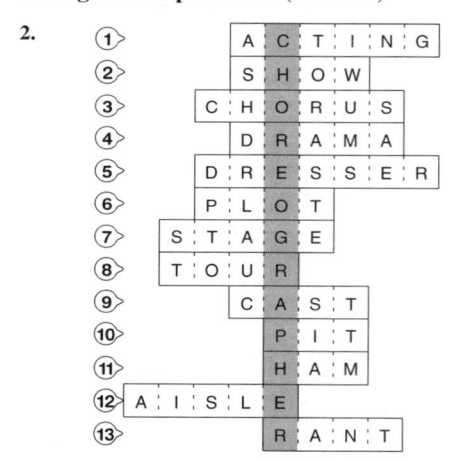

2.

① ACTING
② SHOW
③ CHORUS
④ DRAMA
⑤ DRESSER
⑥ PLOT
⑦ STAGE
⑧ TOUR
⑨ CAST
⑩ PIT
⑪ HAM
⑫ AISLE
⑬ RANT

3. A / 5. B / 10. C / 1+8. D / 12. E / 7. F / 2+6. G / 3 + 9. H / 4 + 11

Corrigé du chapitre 12 B (4.1 à 4.4)

2. A / to dance to jazz music. B / to practise scales. C / to accompany a cellist. D / to strike up the national anthem. E / to have perfect pitch. F / to sing a catchy tune out of tune. G / This violin isn't in tune with the grand. H / to play the cello with a poor quality bow.

Corrigé du chapitre 12 C (4.1 à 4.3)

2. A / Who could have predicted / forecast such an event? B / How did they win a war of attrition? C / What touched off the riots? D / How were they put down? E / Who won a resounding victory? F / The war raged for ten years. G / It broke out ten years ago. H / It spread to the neighbouring countries. I / It came to an end last month. J / Who had devised the plot which was to overthrow the king and bring about the collapse of the government? K / The defeated country has suffered a humiliating defeat and now seeks to inflict a crushing defeat on its enemy. L / Is that what the history of men is all about?

Corrigés du chapitre 13

Corrigé du chapitre 13 A (2)

2. 1E - 2F - 3B - 4A - 5C - 6D

Corrigé du chapitre 13 A (4.1 et 4.2)

2. A2 - B5 - C7 - D6 - E8 - F1 - G10 - H9 - I4 - J3

Corrigé du chapitre 13 A (4.3 et 4.4)

2. A / architect - design - building - B / roof - tiles - C / paper hanger - plastered - papered - D / locksmith - fitted - E / builder's labourer - digging - foundations.

Corrigé du chapitre 13 A (5.2.3)

2. A / building land - building permit - public garden - B / green areas - sandlot - C / premises - D / contractor - sites - E / architecture - F / property - G / waste ground - prefabs.

Corrigé du chapitre 13 A (6.1 à 6.4)

2. A / streets - street - street - B / building up - high street - jammed - C / digging up - causeway - mains drainage - D / knocked down - ran over - crossing over

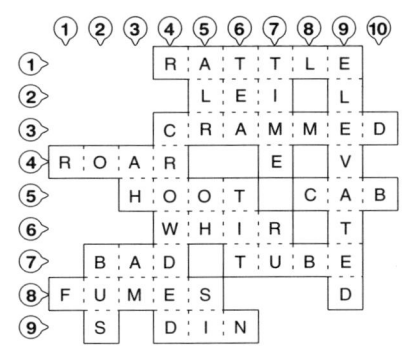

Corrigé du chapitre 13 A (7.1 et 7.2)

2.

	1	2	3	4	5	6	7	8	9	10
1				R	A	T	T	L	E	
2					L	E		L		
3				C	R	A	M	M	E	D
4	R	O	A	R			E		V	
5				H	O	O	T		C	A	B
6				W	H	I	R		T	
7		B	A	D		T	U	B	E	
8	F	U	M	E	S			D		
9				S		D	I	N		

Corrigé du chapitre 13 A (8.1 à 8.4)

2. A / waiter - menu - B / checked - museum - C / bench - ordered - D / on the house - pub - E / pub crawl - librarian - library

Corrigé du chapitre 13 B (1 à 3)

2. A / DAMAGE - B / INHALE - C / SPECIES - EXTINCTION - D / WASTAGE - RESOURCES - E / DISPOSE OF - WASTE - F / PROTECT - POLLUTION - G / HARNESS - UPSETTING

Corrigé du chapitre 13 B (4, 5)

2. A / GUSH - SEEP - SULLIED - B / DUMP - TIP - C / SPILL - D / POUR OUT

Corrigé du chapitre 13 B (6.1 et 6.2)

2. A / DISCHARGE - B / LEAK - C / LEAK - D / CHOKE - STIFLE - E / ALTER - F / LEAKAGE

3. A / Asbestos, which can cause asbestosis, is a real health hazard. B / Sprays and propellants damage the ozone layer. C / If you use too much nitrate over an area, it can contaminate the local groundwater. D / Some types of paint on toys may cause lead poisoning in children. E / Some chemicals are harmful to people('s health). F / We must endeavour to cut down nerve-racking noises.

Corrigé du chapitre 13 C (1)

2. A / I go out into the country every week-end. B / I do not go there to watch the grass grow. C / I do not grow grass for hay or fodder. D / I just gaze upon the landscape dotted with groves, pools and ponds yet unspoiled by concrete. E / The countryside needs to be protected from polluters. F / Where I live, I long for the English countryside.

3. A / BUSH - HURDLE - POOL - B / PEAK - RANGE - THATCH - C / PLOT - TREE - MILL - D / STILE - RIDGE - FENCE - E / CLUMP - DITCH - LAKE

Corrigé du chapitre 13 C (2)

2. A / SEXTON - B / VERGER - C / SHEPHERD - D / GAME-KEEPER - E / SADDLER - F / BLACKSMITH - G / WHEELWRIGHT - H / FOREST-RANGER

Corrigé du chapitre 13 C (3.1 à 3.3)

2. A / BELCHED - B / BENT - C / TWISTING - D / STRAGGLED - E / SWEPT THROUGH - F / SPRINKLED - G / SPLASHED - H / BILLOWED

Corrigés du chapitre 14

Corrigé du chapitre 14 A (1, noms)

2. A / She struck her attacker a blow to the stomach that he was unable to dodge. B / But this did not stop him – he started to rain blows on her. C / He displayed wanton cruelty to her. D / They had a fight; she put up a good fight. E / But she got hurt in the struggle. F / She could hardly put up any more with the physical torture he was inflicting on her. G / Fortunately, somebody witnessed the assault and was present when the assailer's threats and acts of totally unwarranted violence broke out. H / The witness stepped in and managed to ward off the powerful blows the assailer aimed at him. I / He eventually got the better of the assailer who was arrested and convicted of aggravated assault and attempted rape.

Corrigé du chapitre 14 A (1, adjectifs et verbes)

2. 1I - 2F - 3A - 4E - 5D - 6G - 7B - 8C - 9J - 10H

Corrigé du chapitre 14 A (2)

2. A 3/8 - B 2/10 - C 6/11 - D 1/5 - E 7/9 - F 4/12/13

Corrigé du chapitre 14 A (3 et 4)

2. A / They must have set an ambush for him. B / He must have run into it and yet he has experienced acts of terrorism before. C / He has been at the head of the local bomb-disposal squad for many years. D / Time bombs hold no secrets for him. E / He is not the type to stare at a bomb, waiting for it to go off/explode. F / He knows how to detonate or defuse a bomb. G / But he had never been held for ransom before. This is new to him. H / It is the first time that he has been taken (as a) hostage. I / He will perhaps be released. J / If he is, he will devote his energy to trying to trace child molesters, burglars, hired killers, the common run of thugs – he's got his work cut out for him !

Corrigés

Corrigé du chapitre 14 A (7)

2. A 3/9 - B 4/11 - C 1/6 - D 2/7 - E 5/12 - F 8/10

Corrigé du chapitre 14 B (1, jusqu'à <u>unscathed</u>)

2.

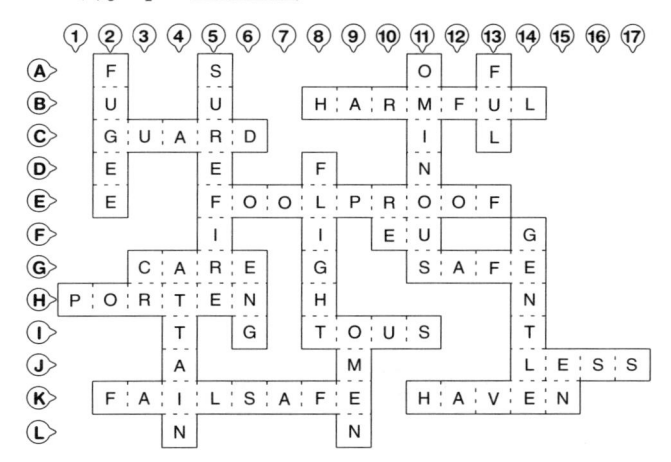

	1	2	3	4	5	6	7	8	9	10	11	12	13	14	15	16	17
A		F			S							O		F			
B		U			U		H	A	R	M	F	U	L				
C	G	U	A	R	D				I			L					
D		E		E		F			N								
E		E		F	O	O	L	P	R	O	O	F					
F				I		I		E	U				G				
G			C	A	R	E		G		S	A	F	E				
H	P	O	R	T	E	N		H					N				
I				T		G		T	O	U	S		T				
J				A				M					L	E	S	S	
K	F	A	I	L	S	A	F	E		H	A	V	E	N			
L				N				N									

Corrigé du chapitre 14 B (2)

2. A / When the man was brought in to the casualty department, there were no apparent signs of bullet wounds. B / Had he got hurt in a fight ? C / Was he a victim of a road accident ? D / The accident toll on the roads shows no sign of diminishing. E / He did not have / lead a dangerous / hazardous life. F / He had no activity that could be regarded as injurious to one's health. G / He had not received any ominous death threats. H / Perhaps he had been poisoned or knocked unconscious. I / Nothing would be done that might endanger his life or jeopardize his chances of recovery. J / The man's life was definitely in jeopardy. K / But nothing can throw the casualty doctors into a panic. L / Whatever happens, they can't be panicked into doing sth that is risky or harmful to a patient.

Corrigé du chapitre 14 C

2.

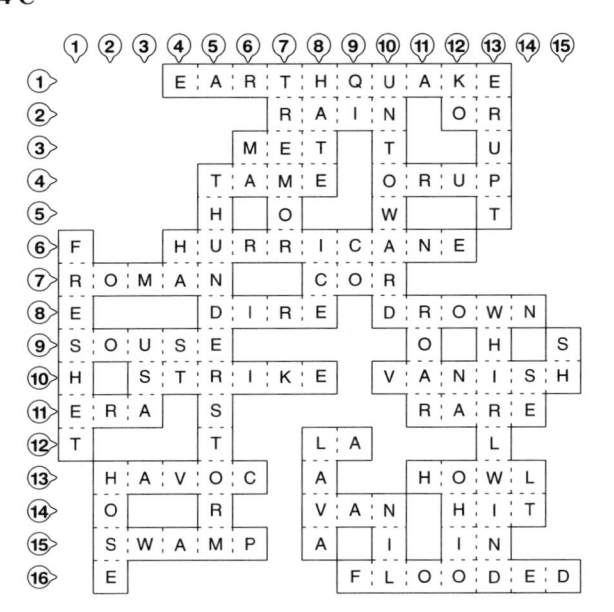

	1	2	3	4	5	6	7	8	9	10	11	12	13	14	15
1				E	A	R	T	H	Q	U	A	K	E		
2						R	A	I	N		O	R			
3					M	E	T		T			U			
4				T	A	M	E		O	R	U	P			
5				H		O			W			T			
6	F			H	U	R	R	I	C	A	N	E			
7	R	O	M	A	N			C	O	R					
8	E			D	I	R	E		D	R	O	W	N		
9	S	O	U	S	E				O		H		S		
10	H		S	T	R	I	K	E		V	A	N	I	S	H
11	E	R	A		S					R	A	R	E		
12	T				T		L	A			L				
13		H	A	V	O	C		A		H	O	W	L		
14		O		R				V	A	N		H	I	T	
15		S	W	A	M	P		A			I		N		
16		E						F	L	O	O	D	E	D	

397

Corrigé du chapitre 14 D (1)

2. 1H - 2G - 3F - 4E - 5C - 6A - 7B - 8D

Corrigé du chapitre 14 D (2)

2. A / control - B / blazing - C / fanned - D / two men; were - E / burnt down; blaze

Corrigé du chapitre 14 D (3 et 4)

2. A / claimed - B / rolled over - C / crumpled; bumped into - D / reckless; freed; wrecked; unharmed

3. A / fishtail - B / spin round - C / swerve - D / bump into - E / crash into - F / run sb down - G / give way to - H / write a car off - I / hit a wall - J / jam - K / roadhog - L / pileup

Corrigé du chapitre 14 E (1)

2. 1H - 2C - 3F - 4A - 5E - 6G - 7D - 8B

Corrigés du chapitre 15

Corrigé du chapitre 15 (1, jusqu'à slanting)

2.

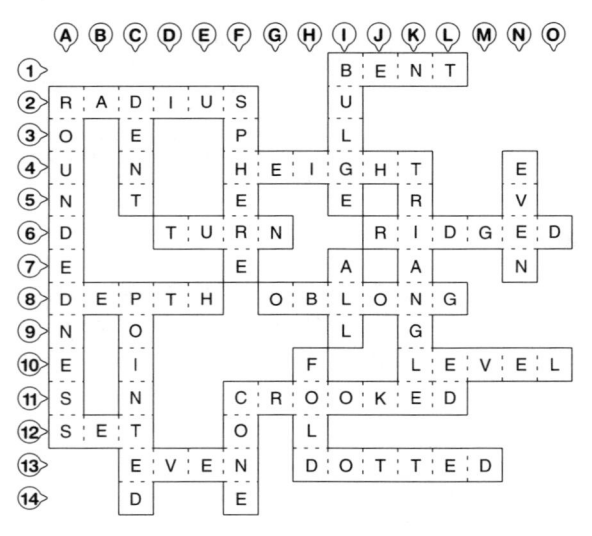

	A	B	C	D	E	F	G	H	I	J	K	L	M	N	O
1								B	E	N	T				
2	R	A	D	I	U	S		U							
3	O		E			P		L							
4	U		N		H	E	I	G	H	T			E		
5	N		T			E		E		R			V		
6	D			T	U	R	N		R	I	D	G	E	D	
7	E					E		A		A			N		
8	D	E	P	T	H		O	B	L	O	N	G			
9	N		O					L		G					
10	E		I			F		L	E	V	E	L			
11	S		N		C	R	O	O	K	E	D				
12	S	E	T			O		L							
13			E	V	E	N		D	O	T	T	E	D		
14			D			E									

Corrigé du chapitre 15 (1, de broad à la fin)

2. 1F - 2H - 3A - 4B - 5G - 6C - 7D - 8E

Corrigé du chapitre 15 (2)

2. A / notch - B / mottled; gash - C / dappled - D / splodged

Corrigé du chapitre 15 (3)

2. A5 - B7 - C1 - D8 - E2 - F3 - G10 - H6 - I4 - J9 - K12 - L17 - M18 - N11 - O13 - P14 - Q15 - R20 - S16 - T19

Corrigé du chapitre 15 (4.1 et 4.2)

2. A3 - B9 - C6 - D1 - E8 - F4 - G5 - H2 - I10 - J7

Corrigés du chapitre 16

Corrigé du chapitre 16 (1 et 2)

2.

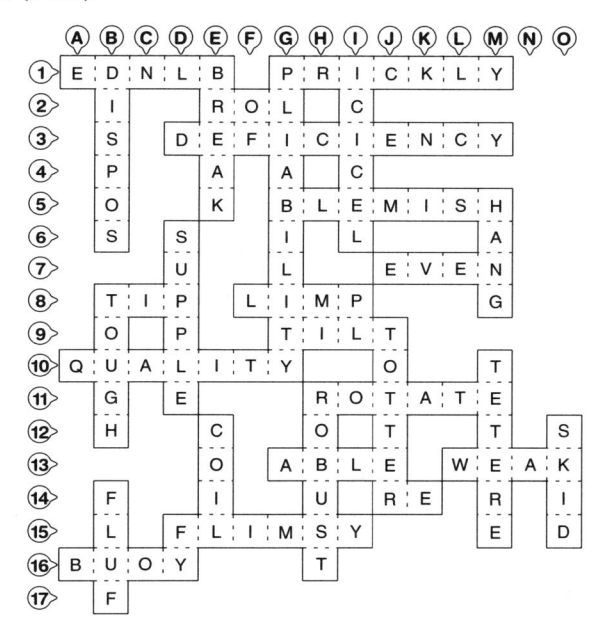

	A	B	C	D	E	F	G	H	I	J	K	L	M	N	O
1	E	D	N	L	B		P	R	I	C	K	L	Y		
2		I			R	O	L		C						
3		S		D	E	F	I	C	I	E	N	C	Y		
4		P			A		A		C						
5		O			K		B	L	E	M	I	S	H		
6		S	S				I		L				A		
7			U				L		E	V	E	N			
8		T	I	P		L	I	M	P				G		
9		O		P			T	I	L	T					
10	Q	U	A	L	I	T	Y		O				T		
11		G		E			R	O	T	A	T	E			
12		H		C			O		T		T		S		
13				O		A	B	L	E		W	E	A	K	
14		F		I			U		R	E			R		I
15		L		F	L	I	M	S	Y				E		D
16	B	U	O	Y			T								
17		F													

Corrigé du chapitre 16 (3)

2. A7 - B10 - C1 - D2 - E8 - F4 - G3 - H5 - I6 - J9

3. A7 - B1 - C4 - D6 - E2 - F8 - G3 - H5

Corrigé du chapitre 16 (4, jusqu'à on)

2. A / Don't leave litter all over the place. B / The chrome on the wheels has been eaten away by rust. C / You should start worrying about the condition your tyres are in. D / Your car is in bad repair. E / The engine is beyond repair. F / The bodywork is dented or battered, the radiator leaks, the windscreen is cracked, the seats are badly damaged. G / The flood has caused great destruction. H / Your room is a mess. I / The children have made a mess of their brand-new clothes. J / The deteriorating state of your house – the flaking paint, the musty smell, the failed household equipment / appliances, the rickety stairs – has me worried.

3. A / creased - B / fresh - C / grimy - D / frowzy - E / muddy - F / jammed - G / blocked - H / faded - I / chipped - J / battered.

Corrigé du chapitre 16 (4, à partir de in good order)

2. 1D - 2E - 3A - 4F - 5B - 6H - 7C - 8G

3. A6 - B14 - C10 - D2 - E5 - F3 - G1 - H4 - I12 - J9 - K15 - L13 - M11 - N8 - O7

4. 1) A8 - B4 - C1 - D7 - E2 - F3 - G5 - H6 - 2) I11 - J12 - K14 - L15 - M9 - N13 - O10

Corrigés du chapitre 17

Corrigé du chapitre 17 (1)

2. A3/7/9 - B4/8/14 - C1/6/11 - D2/5/13 - E10/12/15

Corrigé du chapitre 17 (3)

2. A / I spent a delightful evening reading a most compelling book. B / He put forward a number of flawless arguments to support a simple, effective plan which came at a timely moment. C / Make sure you only use choice expressions / phrases and keep away from any language that would not be becoming for a good-mannered young lady to use. D / Your advice about this plan which I, for one, think is rather well-thought-out and neat, is most valuable. E / I want — and so do you — a plan which is not just satisfactory and smooth-running. F / I want — and so do you — something really stunning, thrilling and unforgettable.

Corrigé du chapitre 17 (4)

2. A / It would be a shame and sheer nonsense not to let it be known that this programme is rubbish. B / There would be no point in pretending not to see that the treatment of certain topics in this programme is both dull and clumsy. C / What's the point of showing a programme that is so amateurish and shallow ? D / It is high time to clear the small screen of such trash / nonsense.

3. 1D - 2G - 3A - 4H - 5B - 6C - 7E - 8F

Corrigés du chapitre 18

Corrigé du chapitre 18 (1)

1. A / I feel no sensation any more in my right arm. B / It does not respond to any stimulus any longer. C / It went dead after the accident which clearly caused this loss of sensation. D / I usually feel the cold. E / I experience a burning sensation when I touch ice. E / Ice gives me a strange feeling.

Corrigé du chapitre 18 (2.1, noms et adjectifs)

2. A / Many people report sightings of the Lake monster. B / This monster is kept (a) close watch upon, day and night. C / A short while ago, I rented a room with a view over the Lake, although I have bad eyesight. D / I did not catch sight of anything strange. E / I would steal a glance out of the window every ten minutes. F / A witness to a recent apparition told me that it was a wonderful sight. G / I've seen him since with a scowl on his face and a show of bad temper — he'd just been told that the local authorities put on a show of being interested in witnesses of apparitions...

Corrigé du chapitre 18 (2.1, verbes)

2. A9 - B6 - C8 - D5 - E7 - F2 - G10 - H3 - I4 - J1

3. A / "Your slip's showing". B / He is watching for a chance to speak. C / He dimmed the light. D / The needle on the compass points to the north. E / He pointed at her. F / He pointed to the bathroom door. G / He glanced over the sports page. H / He looked through the applications.

Corrigé du chapitre 18 (2.2.3 et 2.2.4)

2. 1 / blink - 2 / glitter - 3 / shimmer - 4 / flash - 5 / sparkle - 6 / waver - 7 / flicker - 8 / quiver - 9 / twinkle - 10 / glimmer - 11 / spangle - 12 / glint - 13 / wink

3. Première série : A9 - B6 - C8 - D2 - E4 - F10 - G5 - H1 - I3 - J7. Deuxième série : K18 - L15 - M16 - N20 - O13 - P11 - Q14 - R17 - S12 - T19

4. A4 - B6 - C1 - D8 - E7 - F2 - G3 - H5

Corrigé du chapitre 18 (3.1 à 3.1.2)

3. A / There prevailed / reigned now an eerie silence. B / The noise had gradually abated. C / Nobody dared utter a sound any more. D / The youths had stopped dancing to the sound of a grating guitar. E / Now and again a horn rang out in the street. F / A slight continuous background noise could also be heard in the distance. G / Somebody gave a loud shout outside and everybody listened for the echo. H / Something must have reduced the echo, which had become almost inaudible. I / A man with a resonant voice said something out loud. J / The sound of his voice travelled over into the next room. K / A child gave a sharp cry. L / With noiseless steps, the people walked out of the house. M / Everything was silent. N / An old ramshackle truck passed by but nobody heard the ear-splitting noise it usually made. O / Life was going on — gone were the noises, the sounds and the echoes.

Corrigé du chapitre 18 (3.2.1 fin et 3.2.2)

2. 3 / for joy - 5 / 6 / one's head off - 9 / 12 / across the room - 14 / 15 / a door - 17 / 18 / sb's bottom - 21 / 24 / over to the window.

Corrigé du chapitre 18 (3.2.3 et 3.2.4)

2. A2 - B4 - C1 - D7 - E3 - F5 - G8 - H6 - I11 - J14 - K15 - L9 - M10 - N16 - O12 - P13

Corrigé du chapitre 18 (3.2.5 et 3.2.6)

2. A8 - B5 - C4 - D1 - E7 - F3 - G6 - H2

Corrigé du chapitre 18 (3.3.1 à 3.3.3)

2. A3 - B9 - C8 - D1 - E7 - F4 - G11 - H10 - I12 - J2 - K5 - L6

Corrigé du chapitre 18 (3.4.1)

2.

	1	2	3	4	5	6	7	8	9	10	11	12	13	14	15	16
A							B	L	A	S	T					
B	T						C	H	O	R	D				T	
C	I		B						L						T	
D	N		L	R	A	T	T	L	E						I	
E	K		E	A			W				J				C	
F	B	L	A	R	E	S	C	R	A	P	E			I	N	K
G	E			P	O	P	S	N	A	P		N				
H			B				A	G	E	I	N	G				
I		C	L	A	T	T	E	R		A	C		L			
J		L		N			I			N			E			
K		I		G	R	O	A	N							C	
L		N		U		G	R	E	E	C	E				H	
M		K	I	S	S			R			I					
N			L	T				U			M					
O	P	E	A	L			J	A	N	G	L	E				
P			M	E				C								
Q				S	C	R	E	E	C	H						

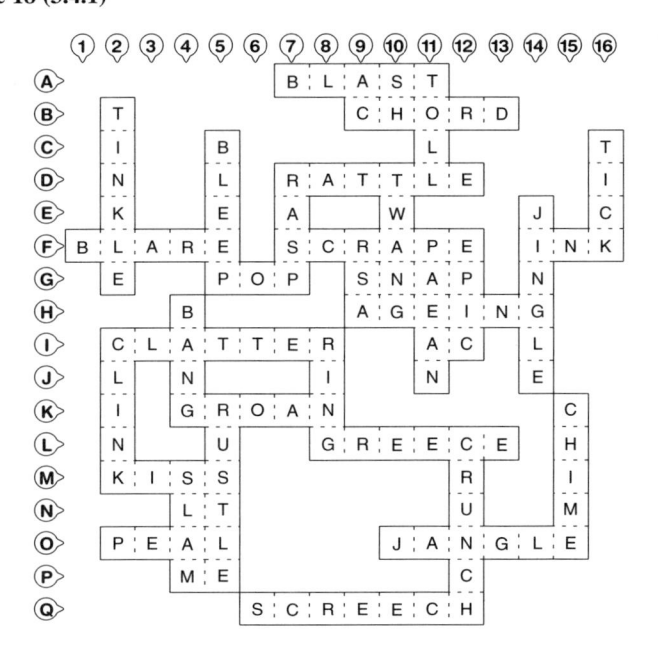

Corrigé du chapitre 18 (3.4.2 à 3.5.2)

2. A / report - B / whizzed - C / clashed - D / flapped - E / wail - F / brayed - G / clunk - H / rattled - I / shattered - J / burst

Corrigé du chapitre 18 (3.6.1 à 3.6.3)

2. A / The thunderstorm roared. B / A gale blustered round the house. C / The rain pattered on the windows. D / The rain-water tumbled down the hill. E / The wind howled / screamed louder and louder. F / It wasn't just the sough of an autumn breeze rustling the leaves. G / In the fireplace the wood creaked and fizzled joyously and in the kitchen the bacon sizzled slowly. H / The steam from the kettle fizzed gently. I / What did it matter if, outdoors, the wind roared and the hail, after the rain, rattled on the roofs ?

Corrigé du chapitre 18 (4)

2. A / The garden was fragrant with the sweet scent of spring flowers. B / He did not have a very keen sense of smell but he could tell if something had a pungent / an acrid or a rank smell, a nasty or a decidedly foul smell. C / But, hum as he might the bottles of the most heady or sweet scents, he could smell nothing. D / A cake of soap, redolent of lavender, to him reeked of cold cigars ! E / There was no point in the breeze wafting in to him the sweet-smelling scent of the garden flowers. F / The most refined soup to him had a sickly-sweet / foul, offensive smell.

Corrigé du chapitre 18 (5)

2. A / Spicy food does not suit his palate which is used to flavourless, tasteless dishes. B / He prefers pasty / floury scones to luscious French pastries. C / I personally prefer spicy, peppery or salty dishes and full-bodied wines. D / He feeds on stringy meat with a sour or sugary flavour / taste. E / I find the way he seasons salad or flavours roast lamb unpalatable. F / He finds some sweet and sour or tart fruit seasonings mouthwatering, that I wouldn't taste for anything in the world.

Corrigé du chapitre 18 (6)

2. A5/10/11 - B4/5/11 - C4/5 - D4/5/6 - E4/5/10 - F1/8 - G11 - H9 - I2/7 - J1/4/5/11 - K3

3. A / He felt for his watch in the dark. B / Something, he thought, felt like his own watch. C / It felt cold. D / He handled the object cautiously, tapped it, stroked it, touched it again, rubbed it, squeezed it in his hand. E / The thing suddenly felt sticky and oily — it was not a watch but something moist and limp that he had squashed with his hand.

Corrigés du chapitre 19

Corrigé du chapitre 19 (1 et 2)

2.

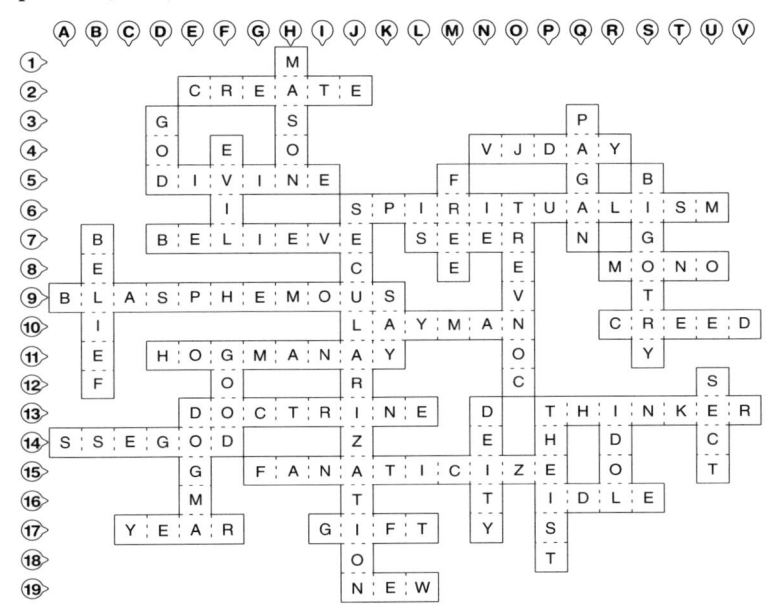

(grille de mots croisés avec les mots : CREATE, MOSO, GOE, VJDAY, PGB, DIVINE, FG, I, SPIRITUALISM, BELIEVE, SEER, NG, BE, C, E, MONO, BLASPHEMOUS, V, I, LAYMAN, CREED, E, O, O, CY, HOGMANAY, F, R, C, S, DOCTRINE, D, THINKER, SSEGOD, Z, E, H, D, C, G, FANATICIZE, O, T, M, T, T, IDLE, YEAR, GIFT, Y, S, O, T, NEW)

Corrigé du chapitre 19 (3.1)

2. A / sins; sinner - B / alb - C / profanities - D / disciples - E / Commandments; God - F / angels - G / verse; Bible

Corrigé du chapitre 19 (3.2)

2. 1/5 - 2/15 - 3/14 - 4/9 - 5/10 - 6/12 - 7/17 - 8/20 - 11/13 - 16/18 - 19-21

Corrigé du chapitre 19 (4)

2.

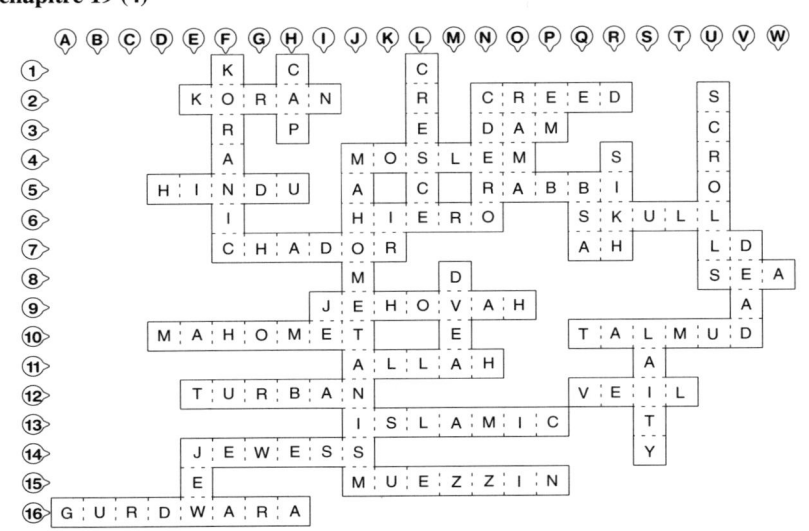

(grille de mots croisés avec les mots : K, C, C, KORAN, CREED, S, R, P, CRE, DAM, SC, A, MOSLEM, S, SR, HINDU, A, C, RABBI, I, O, I, HIERO, SKULL, L, CHADOR, A, H, L, D, M, D, SEA, JEHOVAH, A, MAHOMET, E, TALMUD, ALLAH, A, TURBAN, VEIL, ISLAMIC, T, JEWESS, Y, E, MUEZZIN, GURDWARA)

404 — Words and their collocations

Corrigé du chapitre 19 (5.1 et 5.2)

3. A / ABBOT - ABBESS - FLOCK - PADRE - GURU - POPE - MINISTER - PONTIFF - ORDINATION - SYNOD - DIOCESE - FRIARY - CLOISTER - CONCLAVE - PARSONAGE - SYNAGOGUE - PRELATE - DEACON

Corrigé du chapitre 19 (6, noms)

2.

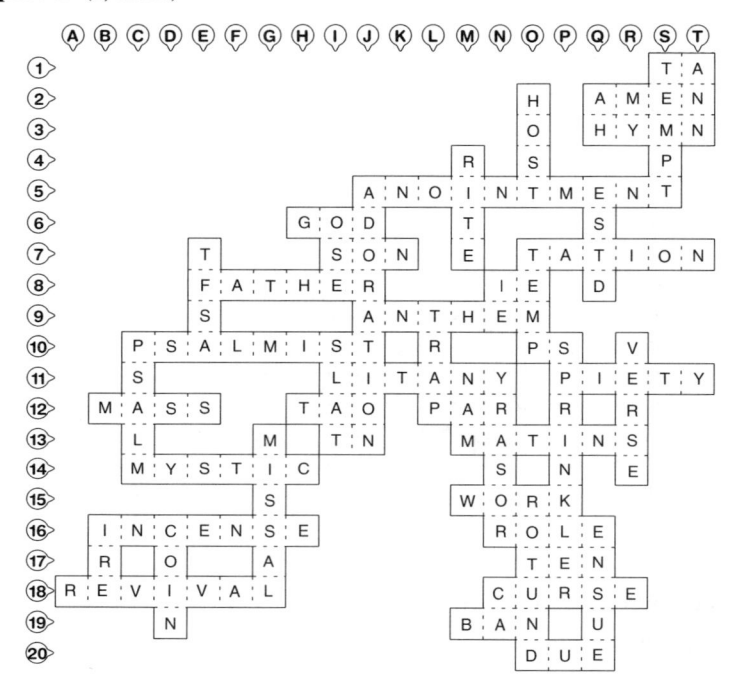

Corrigé du chapitre 19 (7.3 et 7.4)

2.

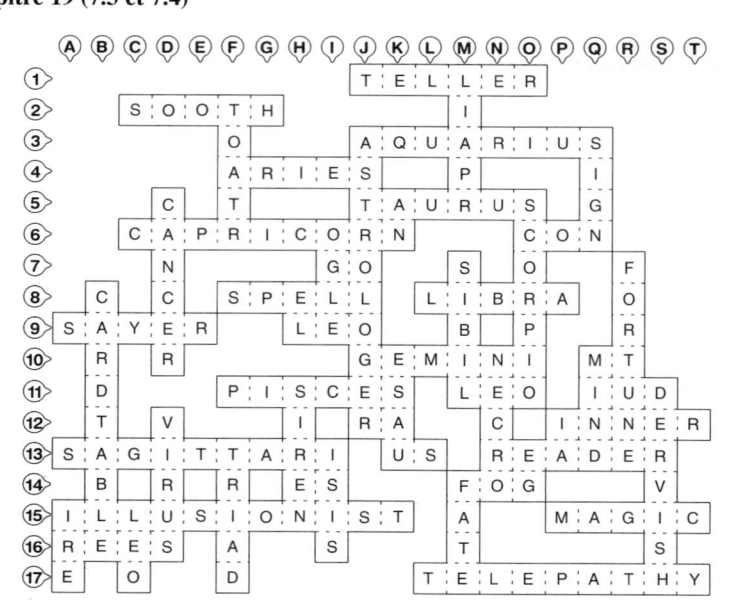

Corrigés   405

Corrigé du chapitre 19 (7.5 et 7.6)

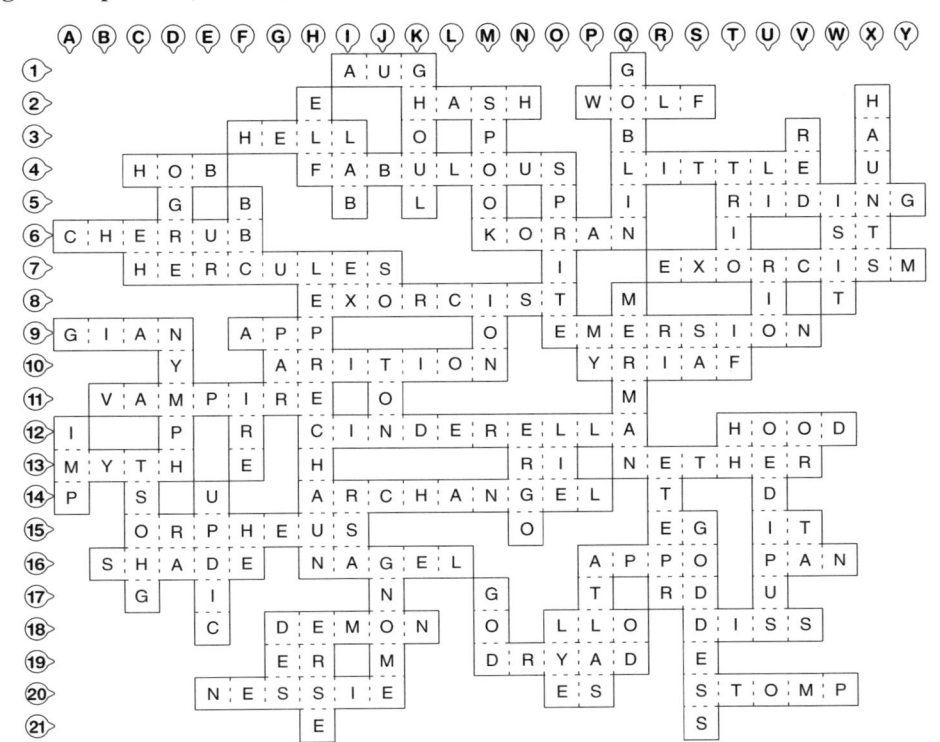

2.

Index français des thèmes traités et des mots les plus importants

Les numéros indiquent à quelle(s) page(s) se reporter.
Note: l'abréviation: ff. signifie: 'following', c'est-à-dire: et pages suivantes; p. signifie: personne.

A

abandonner 12
(s') abîmer 280
abonnement 175
aborder (un sujet) 369
abri 209, 241
abriter 210, 243
absence 34
s'abstenir (ne pas faire) 333
abstraites (relations -) 31
absurde 23
absurdités 289, 291
abus, abuser 145, 146, 229
accent (poésie) 362
accepter 144
accès (crise) 39
accident 246, 248, 252, 253, 254
acclamer 309
accompagner 85
accord 65
accouchement 101
accueil 130
accueillir 130
acte 1,
- **(pièce de théâtre)** 366
acteur 185
action 1, 10,
- **(d'un roman)** 355, 357
activité 10
activités scolaires 156
actualité (presse) 174
admiration, admirer 147, 148
adolescent 99
adopter 128
adorer qch 41
s'adresser à 63
adroit 14
adulte 102
affamer 259
affectueux 41
affirmer 54, 62, 63, 67
affreux 51, 283
agacement 134
âge 100
âgé 102
agir 3, 11, 108
agréable (odeur) 317

agression 229, 231, 234
aide 136, 137, 256,
- (alimentaire) 258,
- (humanitaire) 255
aider 122
aigü 304
air (d'une personne) 296,
(avoir l') - 298
alchimie 348
aller (et venir) 87
s'allonger 85
allusion 41, 55, 63, 368, 369
amateur 289
ambition 1
âme 328
amélioration 13, 15
aménagement 210
amitié 140, 141
amour 40, 140, 141
amusement 132
s'amuser 46
analphabète 56
analyse 360,
- **(littéraire)** 351
analyser 35, 361
ange 347
angoisse 47
animée (rue) 213
année (études) 156
anniversaire 126
annonces 173
annuler 15
anthologie 353
antithèse 374
anxieux 48
apercevoir 298
aperçu 358
apparaître 34, 347
apparence 32, 299
apparition 299, 347
appel 305
appeler 306
appétissant 319
applaudir 309
appréciation (générale) 283, 285,
- **(littéraire)** 351, 375
apprendre 26
approbation 65

approfondi 71
approuver 65, 361
s'appuyer 90
arbres 224
arc (à flèches) 702
architecte 206
architecture 210,
- (église) 335, ff.
archives 54
argument 62, 65, 66, 360
armes 235, 236
arôme 318
arriver (se produire) 33
art, artisanat, artistes 191,
- (outils et matériaux) 192,
- (production) 192
article (journal) 353
aspect 32, 268,
- (des gens) 286, 296, 299
assainir 223
assaisonner 319
s'asseoir 84
assister à 159
astrologie 344
astronomie 197
astrophysique 198
atmosphère 218,
- **(d'un roman)** 357
atrocités 232
attacher 93
atteindre (un lieu) 85
attendre 84
s'attendre à 28
attentat 234
attente 356
attention 22
attentions 147
attirer 63
attitude 107, 147
attrait 40
auberge 224, 225
auditeurs (radio) 171
autel 336
auteur 375,
(droits d') - 177
authentique 33
autobiographie 353
autobus, autocar 214

autorisation, autoriser 144, 145
avantage 13
aversion 40
avertir 55, 243
aveugle 296, 297
avis 61

B

baccalauréat 156
bâclé 291
badaud 296
bagarre 229
baiser (argot) 143
(se) balancer 276
balle (fusil) 236
ballet 184
banal 37, 292
bande (gens) 267,
- (enregistrement) 188
banlieue 202
baptême 338
bas (voix) 304
bâtiment 227
bâtir 207
battement (bruit) 308
battre 91,
- (qqn) 231
bavard 58
beau 284, 286
bébé 100
bénédiction 338
bénévole 255
besoin 1, 3
Bible 326
bibliographie 353
bien (le -) 324
bilan (victimes) 244, 252
biographie 353
biologie 194
bizarre 37, 359
blasphème 324
blesser (physiquement) 231
bloqué 278
bois (forêt) 224
boiter 95
bombe 234

bon 284, 324,
- (qui convient) 9
bondé 97
bonheur 45
bon sens 23
bonté 116
bord 541
bornes 266
Bouddhisme 330
bouée 254
bouillir 276
braconner 240
brevet 156
brillant (lumière) 300, 301,
- (intelligence) 21
briller 301
bruits (décibels) 221
bruits / sons (en général) 303,
- (sourds) 308,
- (faibles) 308,
- (forts) 305 à 307,
- (perceptibles) 304,
- (imperceptibles) 304,
- (liés aux personnes, à la voix) 305 à 310,
- (liés aux choses et objets) 312 à 315
- (de machines) 314,
- (de la nature) 315,
- (de pas) 307,
- (de chute) 307,
- (liés aux mouvements) 307, 308,
- (liés aux animaux) 310, 311,
- (de la vie quotidienne) 312,
- (des occasions exceptionnelles) 314
se brûler 248
brun 270
brute 234
brutal, brutalités 229, 230, 232
bruyant 304
bureau (élève) 159
but (à atteindre) 1, 2, 4, 354
butin 237

C

cabossé 262
(se) cacher 84, 115
cadeau 136
cadre (d'une histoire) 357
calamités 255
calme 104
cambriolage 234, 237, 239
campagne 224,
(gens de la) - 225
capable 5
capacité 5
capitale (ville) 201

caprice 113, 114
caractère 107
caractéristiques 273
carême 329
caresse, caresser 320, 321
cartouche 236
(se) casser 248
cassettes 188
catastrophe 246,
- (aérienne) 253
catholique 329
cause 31, causer 32
cécité 296
céder 145
célèbre 30, 104
célébrité 105
célibat 333
célibataire 127, 332
cercle 261
cérémonie 338
certain 30
chagrin 43
chaire (église) 336
champ 225
chance 240
chanceler 88
chances 29, 32
changer d'avis 25
chant 188, 189,
- (religieux) 337
chapelet 338
chapelle 327, 334
charitable 116
charme 40
château fort 227
chaume 228
chavirer 254, 255
chemin 226
chercher 25
chercheurs 194, 199
chimie 194
chiromancie 345
chœur (église) 336,
- (tragédie) 366
choisir 3, 4
choix 1
choquer 50
Christ 326
chuchotements 308, 309
chuchoter 59
ciel 77, 348
cimetière 102, 227, 335
cinéma 180,
(gens du) - 180
circoncision 338
circulation 212
circuler (personnes) 87
citadin 204
citation 54, 55, 354
cité (HLM) 201

clair (luminosité) 269
claquer (bruit) 307, 312
classe (école) 155, 156, 159
classification (de films) 181
clergé 333, 334
cliqueter 312, 314
clocher 335
cogner 91
colère 66, 69
collant (adj.) 320
collège 155
colline 224
combustible 287
comédie 365
commentaire 354, 371, 372, 376
commenter 354
commérages 132, 133
communication 53,
- (écrite) 60,
- (orale) 53 à 59
communion 338
comparaison 37, 368
comparer 37, 369
compassion 136, 137
compatissant 117
complet (adj.) 71
comportement, se comporter 107, 108, 287
comprendre 25
compte-rendu 355, 376
concerts 188, 189, 216
conclure 30, 355
conclusion 354
se conduire mal 131
conférence 58, 164
confession (religion) 338
confiance 109, 149, 150,
(manque de) - 109, 110
conflit 66
confirmer 63
confondre 67
confort 203
connaissance(s) 26
connaître 26, 61
conscience (de qch) 24
conscience (morale) 119
consciencieux 116
conscient 24
conseil(s) 62, 63
conseil municipal 201
conséquence 31
consister à 35
constater 25
construction (immeubles) 205
construire 207
contact 129, 314
conte 342
content 46

contenu (journaux) 173, 353
contester 67
contractuelle 213
contradictoire 67
contrarié 39, 67
contrariété 134
contraste 368
contribuer à 36
convaincre 63
convenir 9
conversation 57, 62
convoiter 42
copain 136, 140
correspondance 60
corriger (des devoirs) 157
côte (paysage) 80
couler (fard) 249,
- (liquide) 276,
- (navire) 254
couleur(s) 268 ff.
(se) couper 248
coups 229, 230,
- (de feu) 236,
- (de couteau) 231,
- (de poing) 231,
- (de pied) 94, 95
courage 114, 115
courant (adj.) 37, 74
courbe 261
courbé 262
courber 87
courir 95
courrier 70
cours particuliers 161
court (adj.) 262
co-voiturage 222
craindre 50
crédule 120
creux 262
cri (p.) 305 à 307
crier 59, 306, 307
criminels 238
crise (psychologique) 39
critique 66,
- **(littéraire)** 376, 377
croire 30, 324
croisade 327
croix 336
croyance 30, 324, 341
croyant 324
cruauté 229, 232
crue 245
cruel 117, 230, 232
cueillir 113
culte (religieux) 338
cultivé (p.) 286
culture 176
curieux 24
curiosité 24, 110
cursus 156, 157

Index

D

danger 241, 243, 244
dangereux 244, 245
danse 183
déboisement 257
déborder (rivière) 247
debout 84
déception 47, 48
déchaîné (p.) 139
déchiré 279
(se) déchirer 249, 280
déchirure 277
décider 1
se décider 4, 9
décision 1
déclaration 54, 55
décombres 250
déconcerté 49
décourager 40, 139
découvrir 25
décrire 356
déduire (logique) 63
défauts (p.) 107
- (objets) 273, 293
défi 146
définir 36
dégâts 237, 246
dégoût 50
degré 71
délinquant 238
demander 54
se demander 31, 50, 343
démarche (allure) 87
démenti 66
déminage 234
démon 347
dénouement (théâtre) 366
denrées 259
se déplacer 85
déplaisant (odeur) 317
dépolluer 223
déranger 135
déraper 253
désaccord 66, 67
désapprouver 67
désastre 246
désavantage 13
description 53, 54, 355
désert 95
désertification 257
désespéré 113
désespoir 47, 48
déshonneur 289, 290
désinvolte 122
désobéir 146
désordre 278, 279
destin 104, 327
destinée 345

destruction 278
détail 53
(se) détériorer 280
détester 41
détonation 314
détournement (avion) 234
détritus 220
dette (d'un Etat) 256
détruire 258
devenir 295
(se) déverser 277
devin 345
deviner 24, 25
devoir (n.) 1
dialogue 57, 366
dieu 327
différent 37
difficile 6, 14, 15
difficulté 13
dimension 268
diplôme 166, 167
dire 59
discipline (à l'école) 156
discordant 308
discours 58, 62
discussion, discuter 59, 62, 63
disparaître 34
disponible 8, 35
dispute 66, 69
se disputer 67
disques 188
distance 268
divers 35
divination 345
divorce 127
doctrine 324
dommage 237
dortoir 160
doué 21, 286,
 peu - 21
douleur 43
doute 28, 29
douter 30
douteux 30
doux 109, 111,
- (lumière) 301, 302
droite (espace) 83, 262
duperie 237
dur (difficile) 14,
- (au toucher) 320
dureté (matière) 273

E

eau 81, 219, 257, 258
éblouissant (lumière) 302
éboueur 213
s'ébouillanter 248
ecclésiastique 332
échapper 242

échec 16, 17
écho 303
échouer 18
éclat (lumière) 300
écoles 155
écologie 77, 218
s'écraser (avion) 254
écrire 62
l'écrit 177
écrivain 177
édition 177
éducation 155,
- (primaire et secondaire) 155 à 163,
- (universités) 163 à 167
- (d'un enfant) 125
effacer 276
effet 31
efficace 14
efficacité 13
effort 5
effrayer 50
église 327,
- (**architecture**) 335 ff.
égouts 208
électricité 195
électronique 195
élégant 286
élément(s) (d'information) 35,
- (substances) 277
élève 160
éliminer (une possibilité) 34, 36
éloge 283, 285, 376, 377
embarrassé 113
embouteillage 252
embrasser 141
émeute 232
émigrer 276
émotion, émouvoir 39, 40
émouvant 356
empêcher 15, 147
empiler 268
emploi du temps 159
encoche 53
encourager 137
endommager 252
endroit 83
enfance, enfant 100, 101, 125
enfer 348
s'enfuir 242
engagement 1
s'engager (promettre) 333
engourdi 295, 320
énigme 30, 341
enlever 36
ennui (qu'on éprouve) 22, 74, 134

ennuis (problèmes) 39
ennuyeux 23, 356
enquête 53
enrouler 94
enseignant 161, 164
enseignement 155,
- alterné 157,
- supérieur 163
enseigner 162
ensemble (mettre -) 268
entendre 303,
s' - 130
- **dire**,
- **parler de** 59
enterrement 103
enthousiasme 41, 42
entrée 218
entrepreneur 206
envie 42
environnement 93, 218
épais 262
épaisseur 261
épargner qch à qqn 153
épave 252, 254,
- de navire 254
épreuve 14
épreuve de force 144
éprouver (une sensation) 295
épuration 223
équilibre 84
équipe 267
équipements (artistes) 192,
- (cinéma) 180, 181,
- (écoles) 159
errer 88
erreur 33, 66
escroc, escroquer, escroquerie 237 à 240
espérer, **espoir** 46
essai 5
essayer 5
essentiel 35, 71
espace 77
espèce (sorte) 273
espiègle(rie) 134, 135
esprit 21, 27,
- (religion) 328,
- (apparition) 347
état (des choses) 277 ff.
éteindre (incendie) 251
étendue 261
étincelle 300, 301
étoile 344
étonnement 49
étouffer 222
étrange 37, 359
s'étrangler 249
étudiants 165
études 155, 156, 164, ff.

évacuer 254, 256
évaluation 283, 376
évaluer 377
évasion 241
eventualité 33
Evêque 332
évident 30
éviter 11, 153, 242
exactitude 23
exagérer 120
examens (à l'école, à l'université) 156 ff, 165, 166
examiner 23
example 37
excellent 284, 288
exclure (une possibilité) 34
excuses 152
(s') excuser 65
exigeant 113
exigence (requise) 5
exiger 146
exorcisme 347
exorciser 348
expériences (sciences) 195
expliquer 63
exploit 16, 17
exploiter (qqn) 233
exploser 235
explosion 234
exposer (une idée) 359
exposition (art) 192, 193
expression (verbale) 53, 55
exprimer 358
extorquer 239

F

facile 14
facilité 13
façon (de faire) 8
facteur 226
faculté (université) 164
fade 319
faiblesse 107
faim 259
fait (n.) 53
falsifier 34
famille 125
famine 256, 259
fanatisme 323
se faner 115
fantaisie 28
fantôme 347
farce (pièce) 365
fascinant 356
fasciner 42, 46
faune 220
fausseté (de qqn) 119, 120
faux 33, 237, 239
fée 347

feindre 34, 38
félicitations 148
féliciter 148
femme 105
ferme (n.) 227
ferroutage 223
fêtes (et festivités) 131,
- non-religieuses 323,
- chrétiennes 328
feu (incendie) 249, 250
fiable 120
fiançailles 127
fiction 351, 352
fier, fierté 109
figures de style 374
fille 104
films (types de) - 180,
- (classement) 181,
- (industrie) 181,
- (équipement, technique) 181, 182
finances, financement 255
flatter 148
flore 220
flotter (au vent) 276
fluide 276
foi 327
folie 110
(faire) fonctionner 274, 280
fondamental 35
force 145 à 147
forcer 146
forêt 78, 224
forme (aspect) 261
former qqn 162
fort (bruit) 304
foule 129, 267
fournir 12
fournitures scolaires 159, 160
foyer (maison) 125
fragilité 273
frapper 91, 231, 233, 307, 321
fréquenter 131
fuir (s'enfuir) 243,
- (liquide) 221
fuite (d'eau) 221,
- (p.) 241
fumer (feu) 251

G

garçon 99
gare 227
gauche (n.) 83
gauche (adj.) 290
gémir 45
gémissement 308, 309
gendarme 226
gêné 54
gêner 15

généreux 116
génétique 194
génie 21
les gens 99
géographie 77
glissant 276, 320
glisser 95, 249, 274
goût 318,
(de mauvais) - 291
goûter 318, 319
graisse 276
grammaire 56
grande personne 102
grandir 102
gratitude 147, 148
grave / peu grave 74
griffer 249
grimper 81, 87
grinçant 304
grincer 312, 313
grognement 306, 309
gronder (qqn) 153, 154
grosseur 268
grossesse 101, 127
grossier 139
groupe (de gens) 267
grue 267
gué 81
guérisseur 343
guillemets 370
gymnase 160

H

habile 6, 21
habileté 21
habitant 204
habitation 208
habitude 107
habituel 38
haine 40
hameau 224
hanter 347
harcèlement 229
hardiesse 115
hasard 31
hâte 84
haut (voix) 306
hauteur 261
hébergement 208
héritage 127, 128
hésitant 42
hideux 293
hiérarchie religieuse 332
histoire (discipline) 199,
- (intrigue) 356,
-s (faire des -) 134
hommage 147
homme 105
homosexualité 142

honnête 120
honte 47, 107, 289, 292
honteux 48, 107
horaire (scolaire) 159
horoscope 344
horrible 285
hostie 337
hostilité 138
hôtel de ville 201
huer 306
humain (qualité) 116
humanité (espèce humaine) 99
humeur 39, 46, 47,
(mauvaise) - 134
humide 276, 320
humour 133, 367, 368
hurlement 305 à 307
hymne 338
hypocrisie 151
hypothèse 29, 54, 360

I

idée 24, 358
identique 37
identité 105
idiot 21
idylle 141
ignorant 26, 290
île 80
imagination, imaginer 28, 29
imiter 38
immeuble 202
imparfait 284
impeccable 279
imperceptible (son) 304
impitoyable 118
impoli 139
important 71,
(peu) - 71, 72
impossible 33
imprévisible 28
imprévu 26
improbable 33
improviser 366
imprudence 119, 252
impuissant 113
inattendu 49
incapable 294
incendie 249, 250,
- (criminel) 237
incident 33
inclure 35, 36
incompétence 113
inconnu 25
inconscient 24
inconvenant 292
inconvénient 13
incroyable 30
indice 34

Index 411

indifférent 23
indigné 67
indiquer 55
industrie (cinématographique) 181
infecte (odeur) 317
influence 145
influencer 343
informations 53, 54, 174
informatique 196
infraction 238
inhabituel 38
injures 69, 229
inondation 246
inoubliable 27, 288
inquiet 48
inquiéter, inquiétude 39, 48
inscription 166
insipide 319
insolence 110, 111
installations (sport) 217
instruction 156
instruments (de musique) 189
insuffisant 293
insultes 69, 229, 231
intellectuel 21
intelligent 21,
(peu) - 21
intention 1, 3
interdiction 223
interdire 145, 146, 340
intéressé 22, 23
intérêt (de qch) 22,
- (de qqn) 22, 23, 368
interprète (musique) 188
interpréter 346, 355
interprétation 354
interrompre qqn 67
intervenir 146
intrigue (d'un roman) 355, 365
inventer 6, 9, 29
invention 28
investissement(s) 256
invitation, inviter 129, 130
ironie 148, 367, 374
irriter 67
islamisme 330
IUFM 155, 164

J

jaillir (liquide) 276
jeter 90, 91, 564
jeune, jeunesse 101
jeûne 338
jeu(x) (de pouvoir) 144 ff,
- (sur les sonorités) 375
joie 46,
se faire une - de 42

joli 286
jouer (au théâtre) 187, 366,
- (de la musique) 190
journaux 173,
- (contenu) 173,
- (gestion et vente) 174
jugement d'ordre qualitatif 283, 285
jugement (en littérature) 376
juger 36
judaïsme 330
juif 330, 331
jurer (jurons) 58, 59
juste 116

K

kidnapper 231
klaxon 214

L

lac 80, 224
lacérer 240
lâcheté 114
lacune 35
laid 294
laïque 323
laisser (autoriser) 145
se lamenter 45
lancer 90, 91
langage, langue 56, 58, 370
larme 43
las 42
lecteur 375, 377, 378
lecture 378
légende (conte) 341
léger 274
lent (d'esprit) 21, 22
lettre (correspondence) 60
se lever 88
librairie 176
libre arbitre 1
lien 37
lieu 83
limite 541
liquides 276
lisse 262, 274
littérature 176 à 180, 351 ff.
livres 176 à 178, 351,
- (éditeurs) 176 à 178,
- (production) 178,
- (de classe) 353
locataire 204
locaux 211,
- (scolaires) 160,
- (universitaires) 163
logement(s) 208, 209
loger 210
loi 145
long 262

longueur 261
lourd 274
lueur 300
lumière (du jour) 299, 300
lumières (en général) 299,
- (brillantes) 300,
- (scintillantes) 300,
- (stables et / ou douces) 301
luxe (habitation) 203
lycée 155

M

magie 345
mahométan 331
main d'œuvre (enfantine) 379
maison 202, 203,
(parties d'une) - 206
maîtrise (de qch) 13
maîtriser 40
mal (le / un mal) 324,
- (tort causé) 229,
- (faire du) - 231
maladroit 113
mal élevé 139, 291
malentendu 66
malheur 44, 47, 48
malhonnête 151, 239
malin 21, 22
maltraiter 145, 146, 231
malveillance 237
manger (donner à -) 256
manière (de faire) 8
manières (bonnes) 129
manque 33, 258, 259, 273,
- (de confiance) 109
marche, marcher 88
marcher (ne pas -) 280
marée noire 220
marge 266
mari 127
mariage 126 à 128
marraine 337
martyr(e) 333
massacre 232
matériaux de construction 205
matières (école) 162,
- (université) 166
maturité 102
maudire 70
mauvais 283,
- (qui ne convient pas) 9
méchanceté 117, 139
méchant 290
médias 169
médiateur 234
médiocre 115, 290, 291, 293
méfiant 119
se méfier 152
mélancolique 44

mélange 267, 273
mélodieux 308
mélodrame 365
mémoire 29
menaçant 50
menace 239
menacer 140, 240
mensonge, mentir 151, 152
mentionner 64
menu 217
mépris 148, 149
mer 80, 81
mériter 108
merveilleux 285, 287
messe 338
méthode 8
méthodique 9
métro 214
minable 291
mince, minceur 262, 274
minutieux (travail) 6, 72
miracle 341
miraculeux 342
moquerie 148, 149
modéré 74
moisi (goût, odeur, apparence) 277, 278
moisir 280
monde (univers) 77
monotone 44
montagnes 224
montrer 55, 297, 298,
- (du doigt) 93
se moquer 148
morale 107, 108
mort 102, 103
mosquée 334
mot 370
motif 1
motiver 3
mou (objet) 274, 320
moulin 224
mourir 103
mouvements et positions (du corps) 83, 85,
- (statiques) 83,
- (dynamiques) 84 à 86,
- (du corps tout entier) 87,
- (des bras et jambes) 89 à 91,
- (des mains) 92 à 94,
- (des pieds et des jambes) 94 à 96
moyen(s) (n.) 8
moyen (adj.) / moyenne (n.) 74, 157
mur 206
mûr (p.) 102
murmure 308
murmurer 59

musée 216
musique 188
musulman 330
mystère 341
mystérieux 37, 38, 342

N

naissance 101
nature 77, 218
naufrage 254
né 101
nécessaire 2
nécessité 1
nécessiter 7
négligence 122
négliger 6
nervosité 114
net (soigné) 288,
- (forme) 269
nettoyer (rues) 213
neuf 278
nier 67
niveau 156, 261
Noël 131, 329
noir 269, 279
nom 105
notes, noter 156, 157
notes de musique 189
nouer 93
nourrir 256
nouveau 278
Nouvel An 131
nouvelle (roman) 352
nouvelles 59, 170, 174
(se) noyer 246, 254
nul 292
numéro (journal) 175

O

obéir 144, 145
objectif (n.) 1, 2, 4
obligatoire 146
obliger 146
obscène 141, 292
obscurité 301
observer 361
obstacle 13
obstiné 114
occasion 8,
(d') - 279
occultes (sciences -) 345
s'occuper de 11, 12, 126, 128
océan 81
odeur(s) 317
odorat 317
œil 296, 297
œuvre 177, 352
office (religieux) 338
ombre 269, 299

omettre 36
opinion 30, 283, 376
ordinaire 74
ordonné, ordre (qu'on éta-
blit) 9
ordonner, ordre (qu'on donne)
145, 146
ordonner (en religion) 333
ordre religieux 333
ordures 212
origine 31
orphelin 103
orthographe 56, 57
oser 115
otage 235
oubli, oublier 25, 27
outils (de construction) 205
ouvriers (du bâtiment) 206

P

paganisme 323
pâle 269, 302
panique 244
paniquer 245
panne 280
Pâques 131
paquet 267
paraître 33
pardon 152, 153
parenthèse 370
parents 125, 126
paresseux 122
parfait 273, 284
parfum 317
parfumé 317
parking 214
parler 59
parole(s) 58
parrain 337
partager 36, 137
participer 36, 130
partir 87
passer devant qch / qqn 96
passionnant 39, 287, 288
passionné 40, 42
pasteur 226
patience 116
pauvreté 278
paysage 79, 225
péché 328
peine (chagrin) 43
peinture 191
pélerinage 327
se pencher 90
pendre 85
pensionnat 155
en pente 262
pénurie 33, 258
perceptible (son) 304

permission 144, 145
perplexe 49
persécuter 233
persuader 64
personnages (roman) 365
personne 99
personnel (n.) (enseignant)
164,
- (télé) 170,
- (journaux) 173
pétrole 220
peur 50
peureux 115
physique (science) 195
pièce (de théâtre) 184, 365
pied (**en poésie**) 362, 363
piété 326
piller 233, 237
(se) pincer 248
pirate de l'air 234
pire 285
pitié 40, 41
pivoter 264
place (du village) 227
placer 85
plage 81
plainte 153
plaisanterie 63, 133
plaire 41
plaisir 46, 132
plan 5, 25
plancher 206
plat (adj.) 262
pleurer 45
pli 261
plier 92, 264
poésie 362
poids 268
point (**de vue**) 30,
-s (cardinaux) 77
poli 137
pollution 78, 218 à 222
pompiers 250
ponctuation 56
pont aérien 254
population 260
porter 91
poser 85, 93
positions (du corps) 83
possibilité 8
possible 9
postes (services postaux) 227
postures 83
pourboire 217
pourparlers 58
pousser (mouvement) 91
pouvoir (**v.**) 6
pouvoir (n.) (jeux de) - 144

pratiquant (n.) 332,
- (adj.) 333
pratique (n.) 8,
- (adj.) 8, 9, 14, 287,
(peu) - 14, 111, 290
prêcher 340
précis 23
préciser 55
prédire 346
préférence 42, 43
préjugé 30
prendre 86
préparatifs 5
préparation (à l'action) 5
préparer 7
présage 50
se présenter (examen) 158
préservatif 142
presse (**journaux**) 173,
- (écrite) 175
prestidigitation 344
prêt (adj.) 3, 6
prétendre (affirmer) 63
prétexte 151, 152
prêtre 333
prévisible 28
prévu 29
prier 340
prière(s) 338
principal 71
probable 32
problème 358, 368
production (**artistique**) 192,
- (**littéraire**) 178, 179,
- (**cinéma**) 181, 182,
- (**télé**) 170
se produire 33
produits chimiques 221
professeur 161
profond 263
profondeur 261
programme (examen) 157,
-s (télé) 170
progrès 17
projet 2, 5, 256
promesse 136, 137, 140
prononcer 59
(se) propager 251
prophétie 324
prophétiser 340
propre 278
propriétés (d'une chose) 273
prose 352
prostitué(e) 142
protection 241
protéger 243
protester 67
proverbe 370
provoquer (cause) 32

Index

prudence 5
prudent 119
publication (livres) 177
puits 227, 257
punir 18, 153
punition 17

Q

quai 80
qualités (p.) 107, 108,
- (objets) 273,
- (p. ou objets) 283
quartier 201, 202
querelle 66, 67, 69
question(s) 53, 54

R

raconter 369
radio (media) 169
radioactivité 221
raideur 273
raie (lumière) 266, 299
raison 22
raisonnable 111
raisonner 23
ralentir 85
ramper 87
rançon 235
rancune 66, 138
rangée 267
rappeler qch à qqn 27
se rappeler qch 27
rapport (compte-rendu) 353, 356
rassis 279
rattrapage (scolaire) 157
ravages 246
ravi 46
rayé 302
rayon (lumière) 265, 299
rayure 266
réaction 295
réaliser (mener à bien) 18
réalité 33
recensement 260
réchauffement (planète) 257
recherche (université) 164, 165
récit 367, 368
réciter 362
réclamation 153
réclamer 67
récompense 17, 152, 153
récompenser 18
reconnaître 297,
- (admettre) 65
réconforter 46
rédaction 356
rédiger 61
redoubler 157, 158

redouter 51
réfectoire 160
réfléchir 25
reflet 299
refrain 363
refuge 241
réfugié 255
refus 145, 146
regard 296, 298
regarder 296 à 298
région 79
regret 47
regretter 43, 48
régulier (lumière) 301
relations (abstraites) 31, 37,
- **(sociales)** 129 à 135,
- **(humaines)** 136 à 154,
- **(bonnes)** 136 à 138
- **(hostiles)** 138 à 140,
- **(sexuelles)** 142, 143
religieuse (n.) 333
religieux (adj.) 329
religion 323, 324
remarque 66, 354, 360
remarquer 25, 297, 354, 361
remercier 55
remonter (mécanisme) 265
remords 47
(se) rencontrer 130
rendez-vous 140
renoncer 12
rénovation (immeuble) 208
renseignements 53, 54
renverser qqn 253
(se) répandre 276
réparation 278
réponse 54
reportage 61
représentation (théâtre) 186
reproche 153
reprocher 377
répugnant 42, 294
réserves (doutes) 66, 376
résonner 315
résoudre 15, 18
respect 148
responsabilité 122
ressemblant 37
ressemblance 37
ressembler 38
ressortir (se voir) 264
restaurant 217
résultat 13
résulter 15
résumé 54, 55
retentir 312
retirer 36
(se) réunir 97, 126, 130, 267

réussite 16, 17,
- (école) 157
révélation 66
révéler 151
ridicule 291, 358
rime 363
rire(s) 133, 305, 309
risques 244,
(sans) - 242
risquer 245
rite 338
rivage 80
rivalité 139
rivière 81
rôle (au théâtre) 365, 366
roman 352
ronfler (p.) 306,
- (moteur) 312
roulement (bruit) 315
rouille 278
route 226
rue 211, 212
rumeur 58
ruse 119
rythme (en poésie) 362, 363

S

sabotage 235
sacré 340
sacrement 338
sacrilège 328
sagesse 111, 112
saisir 90, 92
saleté 277 à 279
salir 280, 281
salle (de spectacle) 186, 216
salut (religion) 328
satire 367
satisfaisant 288
satisfait 46
saut 94, 95
sauvage (socialement) 130
sauvagerie 229
sauver 243
sauvetage 241
savants 194, 195
saveur 318
savoir (v.) 26, 61
scène (subdivision dans une pièce de théâtre) 365, 366,
- **(lieu où jouent les acteurs)** 183
science(s) 193 à 198,
-s **(exactes)** 193,
- **(de la société)** 198 à 200
scientifique (n.) 194, 199
scier 258
scintillement 300, 301
scolarité 164

scrupuleux 120
SDF 209
sécheresse 258
secourir 253, 256, 257
secours 241, 256, 259
secte 323, 341
sécurité 241
séduire 63
séisme 246
semblant (faire -) 152
sembler 33
sens (signification) 53
sensation(s) 295, 320
sensé 111
sensible 111
sentier 226
sentiments 39 ff.
sentir (odorat) 317, 318,
- (sensations) 295, 321
séparé 35
séparer 36
sérieux (n., adj.) 119, 120, 122, 150
serviable 137
service (religieux) 338
seul 44,
- (unique) 35
sévices sexuels 229
sexualité 142, 143
sifflement 308, 313, 315
signaler 252
signature 61
signe 35, 344,
- (de la main) 89,
- (du zodiaque) 344
signifier 55
silence 303, 304
silencieux 58
simple (facile) 14,
- (clair) 54,
- (sans plus) 74
sinueux 262
soigné 288
soin (soigneux) 10
solide 274,
(peu) - 562
solidité 273
solution 14
sombre (triste) 44
- **(luminosité)** 269
sons: voir bruits
sorcellerie 343
sordide 279
sort 327, 345
sortie (d'un lieu) 216,
- (spectacle) 216
soucis 39, 47
souffler (vent) 277
souhait, souhaiter 42, 43, 128

soulagement 46, 136, 137
soulever 92
soupir, soupirer 44, 45
souplesse (d'utilisation) 273, 274
sourire(s) 133
sournois 120
sous-entendre 369
sous-estimer 31
soutien 136, 137
spécial 35, 37
spécialiste 37
spectacle 183,
- (sur scène) 183,
(gens du) - 185,
- (vue) 296
sphère 261
spiritisme 345
sports (individuels ou collectifs) 217
statut 105
studio 202, 203
stupide 21, 110, 291, 293
stupéfait 50
style (en littérature) 371
substances 277
succéder à 128
succès 16, 17
succulent 319
suffisant 287
suffoquer 222
suggestion 63, 64
suicide 103
suivre 95
sujet (thème) 54, 354, 356,
- **(de discussion)** 289
superstition 341
supplier 63
supporter 41, 137, 139
supposer 30, 361
supposition 24, 29, 54, 55
supprimer 36
sûr 30,
- (affirmatif) 67
surface 262,
(aspects d'une -) 265, 268
surnaturel 342, 345
surpeuplé 260
surprise 49
surveillance 296
surveillant 160
surveiller 243
survie 219
survivant 241
survivre 103, 242
susceptible de 32

syllabe 362, 363
symbole 35, 367
synagogue 334
synonyme 56
synthèse 35, 36, 360

T

tache 265
tâche 11
taché 279
tacher 266
taillader 240
taille 547
talent 122
talentueux 286
tamisé 302
tamponner (accident) 251
taper 93, 96, 307, 321
(se) tarir 258
taquiner 133
tas 267
taudis 209
taxi 214
TD 165
technique (cinéma) 181
technologie 193,
- (de l'espace) 197
teindre 269, 301
téléspectateurs 171
télévision 169,
- (production) 170
témoigner 361
témoin 296, 298
tempête 245, 246
tendre (adj., p.) 41
tendre (v.) 93
tenir 92,
- (bon) 115,
- (le coup) 139
tentation 338
tentative 5
tenté 340
tenter qqn 341
tenter (essayer) 6
terne 269
(se) ternir 301
terre 78
terrorisme 234, 235
testament 103, 127
têtu 113, 114
texte 351
théologie 327
théâtre 183, 185, 365
thème (sujet) 54, 356
thèse 360
tiède 276

timide, **timidité** 110 à 112
tirage (journal) 175
tirer (au fusil) 236,
- (qch) 90, 91
toilettes 216
toit 206
tolérance 116
tomber 87,
(faire) - 248, 249, 254
ton (de voix) 58,
- **(en littérature)** 371
tort (causé à qqn) 229, 231
tortionnaire 234
torture / torturer 230, 231
toucher 320, 321
tourner 88, 264
tournoyer 264, 277
tradition(s) (non-religieuses) 323,
- (chrétiennes) 328
traduction 61, 62
tragédie 365
traitements (mauvais -) 229
traiter de qch 361
transports (en ville) 214
transporter 91
travail 11, 352,
- (des enfants) 256, 258
travailler 12
trébucher 96
trembler 88, 93
triangle 261
tricher 161, 239
trimestre 159
tristesse 44
tromper 34, 151, 152, 342
tromperie 120, 237, 239
trou 561
troubles (psychologiques) 39
se trouver que 32
tuer 231, 233
tueur 234

U

unique 35
université 163 à 167
urbanisme 210
urgence 244
(s') user 280, 281

V

vacances (scolaires) 159
vacarme 305, 315
vaciller (lumière) 300, 301,
- (tas) 274,
- (p.) 88

valeur 283
vallée 65
vanité 109
se vanter 110
variété 553
vaste 263
vengeance 153
vente(s) (média) 174
vérification 5
vérifier 6
véritable 33
vérité 149, 150
vers (poésie) 362, 363
vertu 107
vestiaire 216
veuf 103
vibrer 315
vice 107
victime 244
vie 99, 100, 133,
- (de famille) 125
vieux 102,
vigne 224
village 224
villes 201, 202, 224
viol 230
violence(s) 229 à 232
violer 240
viser 236
vision 296
visite 129
visqueux 320
visuels (effets) 299
vitesse 252
vitrail 336
vivre 102
vœu (en religion) 333
voir 296, 298
voisins 204
voix 58
vol dans l'espace 198
vol (voleur, voler) 240
volcan 246
volontaire (p.) 257
volonté 2
volume 261, 268
voyant (adj.) 269, 293, 301
voyante (n.) 345
vrai 150
vue (yeux) 296, 297,
- (panoramique) 296

Z

zone (industrielle) 201,
- (piétonne) 201

Table of contents

Chapter 1. Action 1
   1. Choice, decision, purpose, necessity 1
   2. Attempt, planning, preparation 5
   3. Ways and means 8
   4. Action and activity 10
   5. Difficulties, obstacles and solutions 13
   6. Success and failure 16

Chapter 2. The mind and abstract relations 21
   1. The mind : intelligence, curiosity, knowledge, memory, imagination, doubt 21
   2. Abstract relations : cause, effect, reality, appearance, elements 31

Chapter 3. Feelings 39
   1. Emotion 39
   2. Love and hate 40
   3. Preference, enthusiasm 42
   4. Sadness 44
   5. Happiness 45
   6. Unhappiness 47
   7. Surprise 49
   8. Fear 50

Chapter 4. Oral and written communication 53
   1. Questions and answers 53
   2. Grammar and punctuation 56
   3. Conversation, talk and talks 57
   4. Written communication 60
   5. Arguing 62
   6. Agreeing 65
   7. Disagreeing 66
   8. Quarrelling 69

Chapter 5. Degree 71
   1. Important, unimportant 71
   2. Average, moderate, mere, standard 74

Chapter 6. The world 77
   1. Space 77
   2. Land 79
   3. Sea 80

Chapter 7. Posture and movement 83
   1. Static 83
   2. Dynamic 84
   3. Body at work 87

4. Arms and hands at work	89
5. Feet and legs at work	94
6. Getting together	97

Chapter 8. People 99
1. Life : early, intermediate and later stages 99
2. Death : dying, burial, mourning 102
3. Identity and status 105
4. Behaviour and morals - qualities and defects : pride and diffidence; shyness and insolence; wisdom and folly; helplessness, obstinacy and whims; courage and cowardice; kindness and unkindness; prudence and imprudence; reliability and deceit; earnestness and negligence 107

Chapter 9. The family and family life 125
1. Parents and relatives 125
2. Married life / Divorce / Inheritance 126

Chapter 10. Social and human relations 129
1. Social relations : festivities, fun, boredom and sociability 129
2. Human relations : good and hostile relations, friendship, love and sex 136
3. Power games : permission, abuse, force 144
4. Attitudes : admiration, contempt, confidence, truth, lies, forgiving, revenge 147

Chapter 11. Education 155
A. Primary and secondary education : schools, activities, discipline, exams; periods; supplies, equipment, premises; pupils, students, staff, subjects 155
B. Higher education : Places and organisation; staff, students, subjects, exams and degrees 163

Chapter 12. The media, culture and science 169
A. The media 169
1. The radio 169
2. Television : equipment, production, viewers 169
3. Newspapers : people; content of a newspaper; management and sale 173

B. Culture 176
1. Literature : books and publishing, literary production (see : chapter 20) 176
2. Cinema : people, types of films, film-rating, the film industry, equipment, technique 180
3. Theatre and stage : various forms of stage entertainment; dancing and ballet dancing; plays, people and their activities, the house 183
4. Music : tapes and records, concerts and singing 188
5. Painting and the arts 191

C. Science 193
1. Science and technology : various sciences and scientists 193
2. Computer science 196
3. Space technology 197
4. The social sciences 198

Chapter 13. Towns, the environment, the country 201
A. Towns, housing and transport 201
1. Towns 201
2. Buildings, houses and flats 202

Table des matières

    3. People 204
    4. Building a house : tools and materials; parts of a house, people 205
    5. Housing : rehabilitation, the housing problem, architecture and town planning 208
    6. Streets : traffic, people, roadway and pavement 211
    7. Town transport : means of transport, people, noise and polution 214
    8. Public places and amenities : culture, food and drink, sport and outdoor facilities 216

B. The environment 218
    1. General 218
    2. People 219
    3. Air / atmosphere pollution 219
    4. Land and soil pollution 220
    5. Marine and water pollution 220
    6. Causes, effects and cures 221

C. The country, landscape and sights 224
    1. General 224
    2. People 225
    3. Places : ways and paths, buildings, castles 226

Chapter 14. Violence, danger, disasters, accidents, humanitarian aid 229

A. Violence : general information; individual, collective violence; people involved; terrorism; fire arms; deception, stealing and damaging people's property, people involved 229

B. Danger : escaping, facing danger 241

C. Disasters : act of God, earthquakes, floods, etc. 245

D. Accidents : accidents in the home, fire, rail and road accidents; accidents in the air and at sea 248

E. Humanitarian aid : general information, desertification, deforestation and drought, famine and overpopulation 255

Chapter 15. Things and objects : shapes, surfaces, aspect and colours 261
    1. Shape, volume, surface 261
    2. What the surface may be like 265
    3. Putting / getting together 267
    4. Colours and aspect 268

Chapter 16. Things and objects : properties, state and condition 273
    1. Kinds 273
    2. Characteristics - qualities and defects 273
    3. Characteristics connected with air and liquids 276
    4. The condition things are in : clean, dirty, old, new, damaged, out of order, state of the art, ramshackle, etc. 277

Chapter 17. Qualitative judgment. 283
    1. General information : assessment, comment, opinion, praise 283
    2. Positive opinion of people's appearance 286
    3. Positive opinion of things and people's behaviour 287
    4. Negative opinion of people's achievements 289
    5. Negative opinion of things and people's appearance 293

Chapter 18. The five senses. 295
    1. Feelings and sensations 295
    2. Seeing : sense of sight, lights and visual effects 296

    3. Hearing : sounds and noises, low, loud; where they come from 303
    4. Smelling : sense of smell, fragrance, stench 317
    5. Tasting : taste, flavour, savour 318
    6. Touching : contact, feel, tactile sensations 320

Chapitre 19. Religion - Faith - Beliefs - Denominations 323
    1. General information 323
    2. Some non-religious festivals and traditions 323
    3. Christian denominations, beliefs, festivals and traditions 326
    4. Non-Christian denominations 330
    5. People, places and communities : architecture (inside and outside of a church) 332
    6. People's activities 337
    7. Various other beliefs, sects and superstitions : general information, medicine and witchcraft, astrology, conjuring, palm-reading, magic; various beings and creatures; ancient beliefs and mythology 341

Chapter 20. Literary terms, appreciation and analysis 351
    0. General information 351
    1. Fiction 351
    2. Non-fiction 353
    3. Content of fiction and / or non-fiction : structure, description, story, plot, theme; atmosphere, setting, action; characters; ideas and feelings 353
    4. Analysis and arguments : what an analysis or an argument may be 360
    5. Poetry : general information; rhythm and stress, metrical feet, lines, rhymes; poetic genres and forms 362
    6. Drama : general information and content 364
    7. Techniques : literary devices, narrative techniques, language 366
    8. Appreciation of style, tone and language : favourable and unfavourable comment 371
    9. Stylistics : general information; figures of speech and sound 374
    10. People : writers, critics, readers 375

Corrigés 379

Index 407

LOUIS-JEAN
avenue d'Embrun, 05003 GAP cedex
Tél. : 04.92.53.17.00
Dépôt légal : 824 — Septembre 1998
Imprimé en France